# The American Civil War

# The American Civil War

### Terry L. Jones
*University of Louisiana at Monroe*

 **Higher Education**

Boston   Burr Ridge, IL   Dubuque, IA   New York   San Francisco   St. Louis
Bangkok   Bogotá   Caracas   Kuala Lumpur   Lisbon   London   Madrid   Mexico City
Milan   Montreal   New Delhi   Santiago   Seoul   Singapore   Sydney   Taipei   Toronto

**Higher Education**

This book is printed on acid-free paper.

1 2 3 4 5 6 7 8 9 0 FGR/FGR 0 9

ISBN: 978-0-07-740294-5
MHID: 0-07-740294-4

Editor in Chief: *Michael Ryan*
Publisher: *Frank Mortimer*
Sponsoring Editor: *Frank Mortimer*
Marketing Manager: *Pamela Cooper*
Developmental Editor: *Nicole Bridge*
Production Editor: *Holly Paulsen*
Manuscript Editor: *Janet Tilden*
Design Manager: *Allister Fein*
Text Designer: *Howie Severson*
Cover Designer: *Allister Fein*
Illustrator: *Mapping Specialists*
Photo Research: *Sonia Brown*
Media Project Manager: *Ron Nelms*
Production Supervisor: *Rich DeVitto*
Composition: *10/12 ITC Caslon 224 Book by Macmillan Publishing Solutions*
Printing: *45# New Era Matte Plus, Quebecor World*

Cover: © Medford Historical Society Collection/Corbis

Credits: The credits section for this book begins on page 697 and is considered an extension of the copyright page.

Library of Congress Cataloging-in-Publication Data has been applied for.

The Internet addresses listed in the text were accurate at the time of publication. The inclusion of a Web site does not indicate an endorsement by the authors or McGraw-Hill, and McGraw-Hill does not guarantee the accuracy of the information presented at these sites.

www.mhhe.com

*Dedicated to the memory of Private Elisha Jones,
Company E, 28th (Gray's) Louisiana Volunteers,
and all the other soldiers who wore the blue and gray.*

# Brief Contents

21.    The Bloody Road to Richmond: From the Wilderness
       to Petersburg   513

22.    From Meridian to Atlanta    542

23.    The Rebellion's Last Gasp    571

24.    From Petersburg to Appomattox: The Final Campaigns    595

25.    Reconstructing the Nation    625

26.    The Long Shadow of War    655

       Bibliography    683

       Credits    697

       Index    700

# Contents

## 19   In the Hands of the Enemy   463

## 20   The Irregular War   487

## 21   The Bloody Road to Richmond: From the Wilderness to Petersburg   513

# Preface

I have been fascinated by the Civil War for as long as I can remember. As a youngster, I spent a great deal of time in northern Virginia and several southeastern states as my father followed his pipeline construction work. My parents appreciated history and took special care to take my brothers and me to various museums and national parks wherever we lived. But it seemed we boys always enjoyed most those places where the blue and gray had slugged it out one hundred years earlier. Perhaps it was because "The Rebel" and "The Gray Ghost" were among our favorite television shows, or perhaps it was because we were well aware of our own Civil War heritage. All of my ancestors wore the gray, and some paid a fearful price for their service. One great-great-grandfather suffered a crippling wound at the Battle of Mansfield, Louisiana, and another was disabled during the Vicksburg Campaign. The latter grandfather and another great-great-grandfather were captured at Vicksburg, and a great-great-uncle was captured on Bayou Teche, Louisiana.

When I embarked on my teaching career, I became aware of a common problem shared by most professors. Teaching the Civil War is a tough assignment because it includes such varied subjects as military strategy and tactics, political and diplomatic maneuvering, economic issues, and social upheaval. Military history, particularly, can be very daunting for students who are unfamiliar with its terminology and tactics. It is difficult to cover such a variety of topics in classroom lectures, and many of the available textbooks are of marginal help because they are almost encyclopedic in nature and written in dull prose. Students using them often have difficulty understanding the complicated political issues and military concepts or deciphering maps that are cluttered with intricate maneuvers. Even students who show some interest in the subject are often less than eager to read the material. The most common complaints I hear are "It's boring!" "There are too many names and dates." "I don't understand all this marching and maneuvering." Such complaints seem to have increased in recent years, perhaps because of the decreasing attention span of today's young people. Having grown up with MTV, Game Boys, and 30-second sound bites, students are used to getting information in short snippets and are often unwilling to take the time necessary to absorb difficult material.

To get today's students to actually use their textbook, it is important to present difficult material in an easy-to-understand manner that does not bog them down in mind-numbing minutiae. I believe the best approach is a well-written, easy-to-read narrative that includes occasional anecdotes, interesting bits of trivia, short biographical sketches, and important primary sources to pique students' interest and spark classroom discussion.

## A FRESH APPROACH

Despite its comprehensive scope, *The American Civil War* does not try to cover every personality, specialty topic, or battle of the conflict. Various historical dictionaries and encyclopedias cover the war in much more detail, but how many students want to read an encyclopedia? Instead, this book reflects my philosophy that a textbook is useful only if students actually read it. Its flowing narrative makes good use of effective quotes and interesting stories, and it includes special features to grab the student's attention. I believe this format is best suited to explain complicated Civil War issues in a clear manner without going into the confusing details that sometimes creep into textbooks.

This book takes special care in presenting military campaigns and battles in an easy-to-understand manner. The text also includes separate chapters that address a variety of topics, such as the role of women, prisons, African Americans, politics, economics, and medicine. These topical chapters show how the Civil War affected all aspects of American life and left a lasting impact on our society. Special care has been taken to incorporate the latest scholarship and interpretations in all the chapters, but the text does not shy away from stating an opinion on sometimes controversial topics. It also carefully examines both the Northern and Southern points of view on major issues in an unbiased manner so students can discuss the pros and cons of each side in informed classroom discussions. Taken as a whole, this blending of intimate story-telling, recent scholarship, and special topics provides a fresh new look at the Civil War that students will appreciate.

## SPECIAL THEMES

Teaching the Civil War is quite a challenge because there is so much material to cover and professors tend to have their own special areas of interest. Some are military historians who do not want to use too much lecture time discussing economics or politics, and some are political historians who are not comfortable explaining battles and campaigns. It is always a delicate balancing act trying to use precious class time to concentrate on the subjects of most importance and interest without ignoring other topics. I believe a textbook that tells a basic chronological story but has stand-alone thematic chapters for special topics fits the needs of most classrooms because it allows professors to use lecture time to cover subjects of their choice while using the textbook to fill in the other areas.

The text begins with an introduction of the divisive issues that split the North and the South and ends with a brief overview of Reconstruction. The chapters that discuss military operations are chronological narratives that allow students to follow the ebb and flow of battle and trace the Union's slow march to victory. But there are also stand-alone chapters that cover important themes that do not always fit neatly into a linear narrative. These include army organization and life in the military; the naval war; African Americans; diplomacy; finance and industry; Union and Confederate politics; the roles of women, children, and Native Americans; medicine; prisons and prisoners; and espionage, guerrilla warfare, and cavalry raids. Of course, these separate thematic chapters cannot be divorced entirely from military events, and it is important to note that these topics are also woven into the narrative throughout the book. For example, African American soldiers are discussed in the military chapters; the effects of slavery and military campaigns on foreign policy are thoroughly explored in the diplomacy chapter; and the political considerations of using black soldiers and their subsequent military record are included in the chapter on African Americans.

## SPECIAL FEATURES

To maintain and hold students' interest, *The American Civil War* includes special features in each chapter. These features provide biographical sketches of various personalities, give first-person accounts of Civil War events, examine the combat record and sacrifice of famous fighting units, and point out little-known facts that help link the war to modern times. A lengthy topical bibliography and an accompanying Web site with links to important primary documents conclude the book.

### Biography

The biographical sketches introduce both well-known Civil War figures and more obscure people who accomplished extraordinary things on the battlefield and the home front. Rather than recounting their wartime accomplishments, however, the sketches concentrate more on their interesting, and sometimes contentious, character traits because their achievements are covered in the narrative. Students will appreciate the humor of Abraham Lincoln; the devotion of America's first black governor, P. B. S. Pinchback; and the sheer ferocity of Rebel cavalryman Nathan Bedford Forrest. More than thirty such biographical sketches are included in the text.

### Eyewitness

Because no one can describe the Civil War as well as its participants, numerous first-person accounts are included in the text to provide an intimate look at what the war was really like. Among these eyewitnesses are an anonymous member of the African American 54th Massachusetts describing the Battle of Olustee, Florida; Georgia native Eliza Frances Andrews recalling the ruin left by Sherman's "March to the Sea"; and Union General Carl Schurz's visit to a field hospital. Such primary sources make the Civil War come alive for students and can also be used to generate classroom discussions.

## Notable Units

The Civil War produced some of America's most famous military units, and their histories are told in these special features. Among the Confederate organizations covered are the rowdy Louisiana Tigers, whose unruly behavior in camp was tolerated only because of their fierce fighting ability, and the Orphan Brigade of Kentuckians who could not return home once they joined the Rebel cause. On the Union side there is the steadfast Irish Brigade, a unit composed of immigrants who served in some of the war's bloodiest battles, and the Mississippi Marine Brigade, an odd army unit that served aboard ships in the Mississippi Valley. Many students have ancestors who served in these units, and they will enjoy learning more about their military heritage. Such units are also an important part of the Civil War story, and some of the units discussed continue to serve in our nation's modern military.

## Did You Know?

This feature examines little-known and fascinating facts about the Civil War. Through them, students will learn how the people of Vicksburg refused to celebrate Independence Day for eighty years because the Yankees captured the city on that day, that the term "shoddy" was first used during the Civil War to describe something of inferior quality, and that the Thanksgiving holiday originated during the Civil War and not with the Massachusetts Pilgrims. In addition to piquing students' interest in the war, this feature also shows how the conflict affected later generations of Americans.

## Topical Bibliography

An in-depth topical bibliography provides a listing of scores of books on various Civil War subjects. These topics include General Studies and Reference Sources; Military Studies; Biographies and Personal Narratives; Political, Economic, and Diplomatic Studies; African American, Women's, and Ethnic Studies; Miscellaneous Topics; Reconstruction; and Journals, Magazines, and the Internet. This detailed bibliography will assist professors in guiding students to further readings and help students prepare research papers. A more detailed bibliography is provided on the book's accompanying Web site.

## Web site

In any Civil War class, student exposure to primary sources is essential. The companion Web site for this text, at www.mhhe.com/jones1e, includes links to dozens of primary source documents like the Confederate Constitution, Alexander Stephens's "Cornerstone Speech," Abraham Lincoln's and Jefferson Davis's inaugural addresses, and the Fourteenth Amendment. Students can use these resources to formulate and defend their arguments and as a study tool to further their understanding of the topics discussed in each chapter. All of these primary materials are discussed in the narrative and can be used to help students understand the mindset of the war's participants so they can participate effectively in classroom discussions. For Further Reading sections at the end of each chapter list the primary sources that will add to or expand on that chapter's topic. In addition to the primary sources, the Web site also includes an additional topical bibliography that provides greater depth than the one included in the book.

## ACKNOWLEDGMENTS

Having been fascinated by the Civil War for so long, I was truly honored to be given the opportunity to write a book such as this. Two people, in particular, deserve my thanks. Donald Willett, an old friend from graduate school and now a history professor at Texas A&M at Galveston, was the one who first informed me that McGraw-Hill was thinking of publishing a new Civil War text. Don was writing a book on Texas history for the press at the time and put me in contact with McGraw-Hill's Steven Drummond. When I discussed my ideas with Steve, he was very supportive and recommended my proposal to his colleagues.

Working with McGraw-Hill has been a very rewarding experience because of its professionalism and outstanding staff. Kristen Mellitt, Jessica Badiner, Suzie Flores, Sonia Brown, Holly Paulsen, Janet Tilden, and Nicole Caddigan Bridge have all been very helpful. Nicole, my managing editor, deserves a special thank you for being so patient and understanding throughout the long process. She shepherded me through the tedious writing phase and gave tirelessly of her time and expertise.

In addition, I would also like to thank the reviewers who made helpful comments that greatly improved the final product:

Paul Anderson, *Clemson University*
John Belohlavek, *University of South Florida*
Judkin Browning, *Appalachian State University*
E. Crowther, *Adams College*
Chris E. Fonvielle, *University of North Carolina-Wilmington*
Brad Lookingbill, *Columbia College*
Kate Masur, *Northwestern University*
James Marten, *Marquette University*

Matthew Mason, *Brigham Young University*
Robert E. May, *Purdue University*
Robert Schelin, *St. Thomas Aquinas College*
Robert Shalhope, *University of Oklahoma*
Scott Stephen, *Ball State University*
Thomas Summerhill, *Michigan State University*
Vernon Volpe, *University of Nebraska at Kearney*
John C. Willis, *Sewanee*

Any professor who has tried to write a book while teaching, advising students, and working on committees knows how difficult it can be. I have been very fortunate to have supportive administrators at the University of Louisiana at Monroe. Were it not for the class load reductions approved by department heads Christopher Blackburn and Marshall Scott Legan, and Deans Carlos Fandal, Mark Arant, and Jeffrey Cass, I would never have been able to finish this project.

Finally, I would like to thank my wife, Carol, and daughters, Laura and Amie, for their usual support. Writing a book is a family affair because of the time and attention it takes from hearth and home. My family has been through this process before, but it never is easy. Thanks for being so understanding.

Terry L. Jones
University of Louisiana at Monroe

# CHAPTER 1

# A House Divided

The Slavery Question

The Antislavery Movement

The States' Rights Debate

The Politics of Expansion

---

Anthony Burns, a nineteen-year-old African American from Virginia, was walking down a Boston street on the night of May 24, 1854, when someone grabbed him by the shoulder and accused him of breaking into a store. Burns barely had time to deny the false allegation before half a dozen men lifted him off his feet and whisked him away to the courthouse. As the confused Burns tried to comprehend what was happening, Charles T. Suttle poked his head into the doorway and politely asked, "How do you do, Mr. Burns?" Instinctively, Burns blurted out, "Master!" As it turned out, Anthony Burns was a runaway slave, and his owner, Charles Suttle, had exercised his rights under the Fugitive Slave Act to have U.S. marshals detain Burns so he could be returned to slavery. Congress had passed the Fugitive Slave Act four years earlier to appease Southerners who demanded stronger measures be taken to apprehend runaways.

Burns admitted that Suttle treated him well and even allowed him to learn to read and write. But Burns, a devout Christian and minister, longed for freedom. He once explained, "I began to hear about a North, and to feel the necessity for freedom of soul and body. I heard of a North where men of my color could live without any man daring to say to them, 'You are my property'; and I determined by the blessing of God, one day to find my way there." Burns eventually escaped to Boston by stowing away on a ship, but he made the mistake of writing a letter to his brother. Suttle intercepted it, discovered where Burns was hiding, and went after him.

After Suttle positively identified Burns, a hearing was scheduled before probate judge Edward G. Loring to decide whether to return him to Virginia. Many Bostonians were determined not to let that happen. The hearing was scheduled for May 27, but a large crowd gathered the night before in Faneuil Hall to hear speakers condemn the marshals' actions. Abolitionists Theodore

Parker and Wendell Phillips gave impassioned speeches encouraging the people to free Burns by force if necessary. Phillips declared, "There is now no law in Massachusetts, and when law ceases, the people may act in their own sovereignty.... See to it, that tomorrow, in the streets of Boston, you ratify the verdict of Faneuil Hall, that Anthony Burns has no master but his God." As Phillips was speaking, a man rushed into the hall and announced that a crowd of African Americans was attacking the courthouse that very minute. Faneuil Hall quickly emptied, and soon 2,000 people were milling in front of the courthouse. When someone fired on them from an upper window, the infuriated mob grabbed a makeshift battering ram and charged the courthouse door to free Burns. The U.S. marshals repelled the mob in a wild melee, but one officer was shot to death and nine people arrested.

The next day, two militia artillery companies and a company each of U.S. soldiers and Marines entered Boston. Five rings of soldiers surrounded the courthouse, and more than one hundred men—described by some as thugs—guarded the courtroom itself. One witness claimed, "The whole building and its environs looked more like a fortress or military camp than anything befitting a court of law." After several days of hearings, Judge Loring declared the law was clear and Burns had to be returned to Virginia. It was May 31—Anthony Burns's twentieth birthday.

On June 2, an estimated 50,000 people lined the streets as a shackled Burns was marched to the wharf. In addition to the U.S. soldiers, Marines, and artillerymen, nearly 2,000 Massachusetts militiamen guarded the streets. Angry citizens draped the buildings in black and displayed a large black coffin labeled "The Funeral of Liberty." Richard Henry Dana, who served as Burns's volunteer attorney, recalled, "Whenever a body of troops passed to or fro, they were hissed & hooted by the people, with some attempts at applause from their favorers." When all was ready, the soldiers formed a hollow square, placed the shackled Burns in the center, and began marching toward a waiting ship. One witness wrote, "I saw the cavalry, artillery, marines, and police, a thousand strong, escorting with shotted guns one trembling colored man to the vessel which was to carry him to slavery. I heard the curses, both loud and deep, poured on these soldiers; I saw the red flush in their cheeks as the crowd yelled at them, 'Kidnappers! Kidnappers!'"

Returning Anthony Burns to slavery cost the government more than $40,000 (approximately $1 million today), but Burns eventually triumphed. In February 1855, members of a black church purchased him for $1,300 and he returned to Boston a free man. Burns's biography was published soon afterward, and the book's profits and a scholarship established by a Boston woman enabled him to attend Oberlin College. He eventually moved to Canada to pastor a small Baptist Church but died during the Civil War on July 17, 1862. Just four days earlier, President Abraham Lincoln had informed two cabinet members that he was preparing a document to free all slaves held in Rebel territory. Although Burns was not aware of it, he had lived long enough to see the beginning of the end of American slavery.

# THE SLAVERY QUESTION

**May 25, 1787: Delegates convene Constitutional Convention in Philadelphia**
**July 13, 1787: Congress enacts the Northwest Ordinance**
**January 1, 1808: Congress abolishes the African slave trade**

Today it is difficult to understand how Americans could slide into the abyss of civil war. Political, economic, and social issues have always been divisive, but we have managed to settle our disputes peacefully for almost 150 years. What was so different in 1861 that caused the United States to split violently along geographical lines? To answer that question, one has to push aside twenty-first-century views on human bondage, politics, and national identity and enter the world of antebellum Americans.

Most of the issues that split the North and South were based on differing economic needs. The two regions developed distinct economies—and labor systems—as they exploited local resources and took advantage of natural features. The South was warm and fertile and perfectly suited for plantation crops such as cotton, tobacco, rice, and sugar cane. Plantations required large amounts of unskilled labor, and planters came to depend on slavery. The North, on the other hand, was too cold and infertile for plantation agriculture, but it was well suited for manufacturing, fishing, and trade. Although Northerners did own some slaves, they relied mostly on free (or wage) labor because their economy was not as labor intensive as that of the South. These basic economic differences fueled virtually every dispute between the North and South that finally led to the Civil War.

## The Peculiar Institution

Of all the differences between the North and South, none was more important than slavery, which euphemistically became known as the "peculiar institution." Although some Northern states initially allowed slavery, that region's soil, climate, and religious makeup led to its being abolished before the outbreak of the Civil War. In the South, however, slavery not only survived, it thrived. By 1860, the South's investment in slaves was about equal to Northerners' investments in railroads and other industries, and Southern plantation owners had invested more capital in slaves than in the land itself. While only about 25 percent of white Southern families owned slaves when the Civil War began, the peculiar institution became the linchpin holding together the Southern economy and social structure.

The importance of slavery to white Southerners cannot be exaggerated. It defined their very identity and sense of self-worth. Slaves performed the most menial labor, thus allowing whites to avoid such tasks. In theory, slavery ensured that all whites were equal because they did not have to engage in the type of hard physical labor slaves performed. It did not matter how poor or illiterate one might be—as long as you were white, you belonged to the superior social

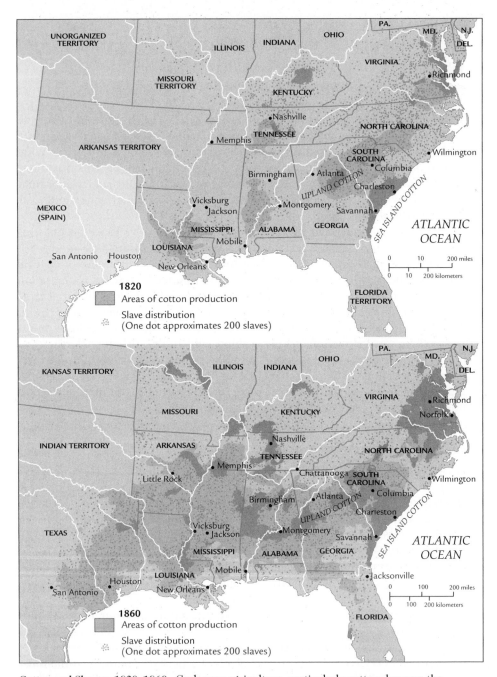

**Cotton and Slavery, 1820–1860.** Cash crop agriculture, particularly cotton, became the backbone of the antebellum South's economy. These two maps illustrate how cotton and slavery came to dominate the region by the time of the Civil War.

class. Conversely, the end of slavery would elevate African Americans to the same social status as poor white farmers, and that was an outcome Southerners would never tolerate.

Southern politics also revolved around slavery because of its importance to the South's economic and social systems. Realizing their argument that slavery enhanced white equality stood on shaky ground, slaveholders strongly discouraged any rational debate about the peculiar institution. Any dialogue about equality might encourage slaves to seek their freedom more vigorously. Also, poor white farmers (who in reality performed many of the same tasks as slaves) might realize slavery only enriched a small number of upper-class whites by allowing them to purchase the best farmland and live a life of luxury. In many ways, slavery actually promoted white *inequality,* but slaveholders were determined not to allow that idea to gain a foothold. Southern politicians, who frequently were slaveholders, equated the smallest criticism of slavery with treason. To avoid unrest among the white masses, they stifled any debate by trying to convince poor whites that they, too, benefited from the slave system. This lack of dialogue led to virtually all Southern whites becoming fierce defenders of slavery while expecting their political leaders, whether Democrat or Whig, to do the same.

## Slavery and the Constitutional Convention

Without question, slavery was a cruel and inhuman system, but it was the politics of slavery rather than its morality that became the central issue. This political debate began at the Constitutional Convention when delegates argued bitterly over whether to count slaves as part of a state's population for taxation and representation purposes. The Southern states wanted to count them for representation but not for taxation. Northerners opposed counting slaves for representation purposes because they had no political rights, but they wanted slaves counted for taxation because they were property. Eventually, the Three-fifths Compromise was reached on the sticky issue, with each slave being counted as three-fifths of a person for both representation and taxation. About the same time, Congress also passed the Northwest Ordinance, which prohibited slavery in the territory that later became Illinois, Indiana, Michigan, Ohio, and Wisconsin. It has been speculated the Southern-dominated Congress passed the measure in return for Northern delegates supporting the Three-fifths Compromise.

Despite slavery emerging as a political issue during the Constitutional Convention, it did not become a critical problem until later. Many people thought slavery was dying a natural death and would disappear in the not-too-distant future. Economic depression in some Southern areas created less demand for slaves, and the Enlightenment caused many Americans, including Benjamin Franklin, to question the morality of human bondage. Southern delegates at the Constitutional Convention even supported the decision to eventually ban the international slave trade, partly because they recognized it was cruel and partly because they were convinced the natural birthrate would fill future slavery needs. Steps were already being taken in a number of Northern states to abolish slavery because it played virtually no role in the economy and had long been under attack by religious groups such as the Quakers. By 1810 about 75 percent of all Northern blacks were free, and that number increased to nearly 100 percent by the time of the Civil War.

Interestingly, the framers of the Constitution never mentioned slavery by name, preferring instead to use euphemisms such as "other persons." Nonetheless, the Constitution did sanction slavery in several ways. The Three-fifths Compromise recognized slaves by counting them as part of the population for representation purposes. This gave the Southern states more representation in Congress than their white populations warranted, and it led Northerners to resent the political clout of the so-called Slave Power. The Constitution also prohibited interference in the domestic slave trade, and it included a fugitive slave clause that required the return of runaway slaves to their owners. Slavery's inclusion in the Constitution became a critical point in the sectional debate as Southerners argued that owning slaves was a constitutional right Congress could not regulate. Only a constitutional amendment approved by three-fourths of the states could change the slave system.

## THE ANTISLAVERY MOVEMENT

**December 21, 1816: Abolitionists help form the American Colonization Society**
**January 1, 1831: William Lloyd Garrison begins publishing *The Liberator***
**August 22, 1831: Nat Turner's Rebellion begins**
**May 26, 1836: Congress adopts the gag rule**

While most Americans viewed the slavery question in economic and political terms, abolitionists saw it as a struggle of good versus evil. Abolitionists were actually rather few in number, and many Northerners viewed them with suspicion and even hatred because the abolitionists wanted to free the slaves *and* grant them political and social rights. Most Northerners had little contact with African Americans and opposed racial equality. In fact, they really did not much care if the South had slaves; they were more concerned about not having to compete with slavery economically or have blacks live in their areas. Many Northerners also were hesitant to support abolition because they had an economic stake in slavery. By 1860, slaves constituted almost $3 billion in property, or about 20 percent of the nation's entire wealth. This nearly equaled the North's entire capital investment in both railroads and manufacturing. Slaves harvested Southern cotton, which fed New England textile mills that employed thousands of people, and Southern planters kept the financial system solvent by borrowing millions of dollars from Northern banks. From laborers to corporate bankers, many Northerners realized their livelihoods might be adversely affected if the abolitionists succeeded in destroying slavery.

## The Abolitionists

The abolitionists were particularly strong in New England and in the Quaker regions of Pennsylvania and the Midwest, but they were a fractious group. Leaders such as William Lloyd Garrison, Cassius Marcellus Clay, Henry Ward Beecher, Theodore D. Weld, and Arthur and Lewis Tappan often disagreed on how to end slavery. Egos, politics, and religion all played a role in keeping them at odds. Some wanted to free the slaves immediately, while others believed gradual emancipation would be less disruptive to the economy and society. Abolitionists also disagreed on what to do with the slaves once they were emancipated. Some wanted to extend complete equality and fully incorporate African Americans into society, while others did not believe blacks and whites could live together in harmony. The latter group even worked with slaveholders to form the American Colonization Society in 1816 to relocate freed slaves in Africa. Abolitionists further disagreed on whether to use direct political action or "moral suasion" to destroy slavery. Supporters of the latter method rejected conventional politics in favor of *convincing* Southerners to free the slaves because it was the right thing to do. A small number of abolitionists rejected both political action and moral suasion and advocated the use of insurrection and violence. Normally, a group as small as the abolitionists would have had little impact on events, but their influence exceeded their numbers because they included some wealthy and influential people.

The abolitionists became much more radical in the 1830s after Great Britain freed its slaves, and pressure mounted on the United States to do the same. A fervent religious movement known as the Second Great Awakening also swept across America, and Northern evangelicals became determined to stamp out slavery and other sins. William Lloyd Garrison, of Massachusetts, was an influential abolitionist who began publishing the newspaper *The Liberator* in 1831. In his first edition, Garrison boldly wrote, "I do not wish to think, or speak, or write, with moderation. . . . I am in earnest—I will not equivocate—I will not excuse—I will not retreat a single inch—AND I WILL BE HEARD." Garrison

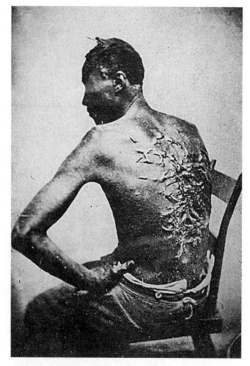

**Whipped Slave.** The Union Army photographed this slave during the Civil War. His scarred back shows how brutal the slave system was.

**Slave Cabin.** This Georgia cabin was fairly typical of the housing in which Southern slaves lived.

also established the American Anti-Slavery Society in Philadelphia, Pennsylvania. Although moderate abolitionists personally disliked Garrison (he once publicly destroyed a copy of the Constitution), they helped him make the Society the most prominent abolitionist organization of the 1830s. The American Anti-Slavery Society boasted hundreds of chapters and more than 250,000 members who spread antislavery propaganda, petitioned Congress to abolish slavery, and pushed for immediate emancipation.

Slaveholders hated Garrison, his newspaper, and the American Anti-Slavery Society. Shortly after Garrison began publishing *The Liberator*, Nat Turner led a slave rebellion in Virginia that killed approximately sixty whites. Southerners saw a direct connection between the two events and accused the abolitionists of encouraging slaves to rise up in rebellion and kill their owners. The Georgia legislature even offered $5,000 for Garrison's arrest and conviction for inciting slave insurrection. Some Northerners also disliked Garrison and his radical cohorts. American Anti-Slavery Society members were often attacked, and a mob once seized Garrison and threatened to hang him, but he continued to publish his paper undeterred.

**Harriet Tubman.** One of many African Americans who served as conductors on the Underground Railroad, Harriet Tubman also guided Union troops into Confederate territory during the Civil War to free more slaves. Here she is seen on the far left with some slaves she helped to escape.

## The Underground Railroad and Black Abolitionists

Historians have long focused on the contributions of white abolitionists, but African Americans were actually the driving force behind the movement. Not only did they serve as a moral compass, but they pressured their white comrades to move away from moral suasion and adopt more direct methods to end slavery. African Americans were also deeply involved in the famous Underground Railroad, a loose organization that helped runaway slaves reach freedom in the North or in Canada. Since it began when railroads were spreading across the nation, railroad terminology was used as code words. Moving mostly at night, runaway slaves known as "passengers" were led by "conductors" who guided them to safe houses called "stations." The escape routes shifted as circumstances dictated, and success depended largely on the conductors' bravery, skill, and knowledge of geography. For the most part, white abolitionists stayed in the background, providing funds and caring for runaways once they reached freedom. The most dangerous work was usually carried out by African Americans themselves.

The Underground Railroad was most active in the Border States because anti-abolition and proslavery sentiment was so prevalent in the Deep South that it was difficult to maintain any type of organized system there. Runaways were pretty much on their own until they reached Missouri, Kentucky, Virginia, Maryland, and Delaware where the Railroad was better established. It is impossible to determine exactly how many slaves reached freedom through the Underground Railroad because no records were kept. Some historians estimate perhaps 1,000 slaves a year moved through the system, while others believe the Railroad's success has been exaggerated.

Three of the most effective African American abolitionists were Harriet Tubman, Sojourner Truth, and Frederick Douglass (see Chapter 9). Harriet

Tubman (1820–1913) was born into slavery in Maryland and lived in brutal conditions, suffering permanent debilitating effects from a blow to the head. Named Araminta at birth, she later took the name Harriet and married a free black named John Tubman. When her husband refused to join her in an escape, Tubman ran away without him and settled in Pennsylvania to work with the Underground Railroad. Nicknamed "Moses," she made eleven trips to the South as a conductor before moving to Canada in 1852. From there, Tubman made nineteen more trips to the South and helped free perhaps 300 slaves. During the Civil War, she continued her work out of Fort Monroe, Virginia, and Beaufort, South Carolina. At Beaufort, Tubman also served as a scout and spy for Major General David Hunter and assisted the Union army in launching raids that freed nearly 1,000 more slaves. The Confederates despised Tubman and offered a reward for her capture. After receiving a mere $300 for her three years' Union service, she moved to New York City after the war and opened the Home for Indigent and Aged Negroes. Tubman died in relative obscurity, and her exploits were not widely known until she became a popular figure during the modern civil rights movement.

Sojourner Truth (1797–1883) was born Isabella Baumfree in a New York Dutch community and spoke only Dutch before being sold from her family at age eleven. She suffered cruel and harsh treatment while being sold several times and eventually was forced to marry another slave. When New York abolished slavery, Baumfree left her husband and settled in New York City, where she worked as a domestic in several religious communes. After having a deep spiritual experience, she changed her name to Sojourner Truth and began traveling through New England preaching the gospel. Truth proved to be an excellent speaker and singer, and she often moved her audiences to tears with stories of slavery. In Massachusetts, she settled in a utopian community and began working with abolitionists such as William Lloyd Garrison and Frederick Douglass. Described by Douglass as "a strange compound of wit and wisdom, of wild enthusiasm and flintlike common sense," Truth became a popular speaker on the abolitionist and woman's suffrage circuit. One of her most famous speeches, entitled "Ain't I a Woman?" was given at a women's convention. After living for a while in Michigan, Truth moved to Washington, D.C., during the Civil War. There she helped former slaves and even met President Lincoln in the White House. After the war, Truth worked with freedmen, lobbied Congress unsuccessfully to grant western land to blacks, and continued preaching and giving public speeches until she retired because of poor health.

## Personal Liberty Laws and the Gag Rule

Personal Liberty Laws were another way in which abolitionists fought slavery. The Constitution and the Fugitive Slave Act required that runaway slaves be returned to their owners. Abolitionists, however, opposed the law, partly because it did not protect the civil rights of the accused. Slave catchers could

# EYEWITNESS
## Harriet Ann Jacobs

*Virginia slave Harriet Jacobs (1813–1897) enjoyed a comfortable childhood and was so well protected that she never thought of herself as property. Her mother's mistress even taught her how to read and sew. When the mistress died, however, twelve-year-old Harriet came under the control of Dr. James Norcom, who began making unwanted sexual advances. Rebuffing Norcom, Harriet became involved with a white lawyer and bore two of his children. "[I]t was," she said, "something to triumph over my tyrant in that small way." Eventually, Harriet decided to escape and made arrangements to be smuggled aboard a boat. Having been bitten by a poisonous snake in a previous escape attempt, she was horrified to discover she first had to hide out in Snaky Swamp. In her memoirs, Harriet describes following her friend Peter into the swamp.*

Peter landed first, and with a large knife cut a path through bamboos and briers of all descriptions. He came back, took me in his arms, and carried me to a seat made among the bamboos. Before we reached it, we were covered with hundreds of mosquitos. In an hour's time they had so poisoned my flesh that I was a pitiful sight to behold. As the light increased, I saw snake after snake crawling round us. I had been accustomed to the sight of snakes all my life, but these were larger than any I had ever seen. To this day I shudder when I remember that morning. As evening approached, the number of snakes increased so much that we were continually obliged to thrash them with sticks to keep them from crawling over us. The bamboos were so high and so thick that it was impossible to see beyond a very short distance. Just before it became dark we procured a seat nearer to the entrance of the swamp, being fearful of losing our way back to the boat. It was not long before we heard the paddle of oars, and the low whistle, which had been agreed upon as a signal. We made haste to enter the boat, and were rowed back to the vessel. I passed a wretched night; for the heat of the swamp, the mosquitos, and the constant terror of snakes, had brought on a burning fever. I had just dropped asleep, when they came and told me it was time to go back to that horrid swamp. I could scarcely summon courage to rise. But even those large, venomous snakes were less dreadful to my imagination than the white men in that community called civilized.

*Harriet was so sick she was unable to follow through with the escape. On the way home, Peter told her, "You must make the most of this walk . . . for you may not have another very soon." "I thought his voice sounded sad," Harriet recalled. "It was kind of him to conceal from me what a dismal hole was to be my home for a long, long time." To protect her from Norcom's wrath, Harriet's family claimed she escaped to New York and for seven years kept her hidden in a small, rat-infested attic crawl space in her grandmother's house. Finally, in 1842, Harriet escaped by boat and settled in New York. Her autobiography,* Incidents in the Life of a Slave Girl, *was published in 1861.*

Source: Harriet Ann Jacobs, *Incidents in the Life of a Slave Girl. Written by Herself.* Edited by L. Maria Child (Boston: n.p., 1861), pp. 171–72.

simply carry away their victims without any kind of court proceeding, which made it easy for free blacks to be seized and taken into slavery. To fight such injustices, a number of Northern states passed Personal Liberty Laws.

Personal Liberty Laws in Ohio, Pennsylvania, and New York required slave catchers to obtain search warrants and stipulated that jury trials had to be provided for runaways before they could be returned. Massachusetts refused to allow state officials to cooperate with slave catchers and prohibited the use of state-owned facilities to hold suspects. By refusing to cooperate with slave catchers, Northern states made the Fugitive Slave Act largely ineffective. If runaway slaves could reach abolitionist areas, they were generally protected, although there was always the chance of being caught by slave catchers who simply bypassed authorities. Abolitionists were confident of the morality of their Personal Liberty Laws, but Southerners condemned them for interfering with a constitutionally sanctioned process.

To maintain public pressure to end slavery, abolitionists also flooded Congress with antislavery petitions. Citizens could send to Congress petitions on any topic and have them read on the floor and entered into the record, but slaveholders flew into a rage whenever abolitionist petitions were introduced. Congress often became bogged down in bitter debates over whether to have the petitions read, but in 1836 Southerners successfully passed the gag rule in the House of Representatives, which automatically tabled, without debate, any abolitionist petition received. Northern congressmen, particularly the eloquent John Quincy Adams, denounced the gag rule as an infringement on the people's right to be heard and were finally able to repeal it in 1844.

## THE STATES' RIGHT DEBATE

**July 14, 1798: Virginia legislature passes the Virginia Resolution**
**December 24, 1798: Kentucky legislature passes the Kentucky Resolution**
**March 2, 1820: Congress passes the Missouri Compromise**
**May 11, 1828: Congress passes the Tariff of 1828**
**July 14, 1832: Congress passes the Tariff of 1832**
**November 24, 1832: South Carolina legislature nullifies the Tariff of 1832**

States' rights was a key issue in the slavery debate. The term *states' rights* referred to the nature of the states' position within the Union and the power they wielded in relation to the federal government. Northerners and Southerners developed different political views on states' rights, with Northerners generally believing the federal government should reign supreme over the states. Southerners, on the other hand, tended to believe the states better protected individual liberty and that states should be able to counter possible federal government tyranny.

Before the Civil War, Americans often identified more closely with their state than with the national government because the thirteen colonies were created, settled, and governed independently of one another. Competition and jealousy were so rampant between them that one visitor predicted "there would be a civil war" if the colonies were left to their own devices. Voters in each colony elected politicians to represent them in the legislature, but prior to the American Revolution the colonies answered to the British Parliament rather than to one another or to any type of American government. This independence continued during the Revolutionary War when the states considered themselves sovereign entities loosely united under the Articles of Confederation to fight in a common cause. The Articles stipulated, "Each state retains its sovereignty, freedom and independence, and every Power, Jurisdiction and right, which is not by this confederation expressly delegated to the United States, in Congress assembled." Except for receiving mail and perhaps seeing a few soldiers, the average American rarely witnessed the national government at work. In the South, particularly, poor communications, a lack of reliable transportation, and regional economies stunted the development of a true national consciousness. It was colonial, and later state and local, governments that built most of the roads, repaired levees, cared for orphans, and defended white settlers against Indian attacks.

Eventually, Independence Day celebrations and pride in winning the Revolutionary War began to create a national consciousness, especially in the North. The Northerners' economy was based more on business, industry, and free labor than that of the South, and Northerners tended to welcome a federal government that could strengthen and unite the economy through national legislation. Southerners also had pride in America, but they were more suspicious of governments in general. Scot-Irish settlers formed the backbone of the white Southern population, and they had a long history of acting independently of governments. The Scot-Irish, in fact, largely moved to America to escape an abusive government. They mostly eked out a living on frontier farms and preferred to be left alone. These Southern whites trusted their state politicians more than federal officials, and if forced to choose between them, most would side with their state rather than with some unseen national government.

## Interpreting the Constitution

The complicated issue of states' rights can be traced to the Constitutional Convention. In drawing up the Constitution, the Founding Fathers created a workable governing system, but they could not address every conceivable problem that might arise. Within a few short years, the framers themselves began disagreeing on the Constitution's intent and the nature of the federal government, and the American people split into factions of strict and loose constructionists.

Strict constructionists feared a strong American government might become as autocratic as Britain's Parliament had been. To prevent this, they relied on the Constitution's giving the federal government only certain *limited* powers necessary to protect the country and run the nation's affairs smoothly. Those powers included maintaining an army and navy, making war and peace, overseeing foreign relations and Indian affairs, regulating interstate and international trade, creating a monetary system, and running the post office. The federal government was not all-powerful; it could only exert its authority in those few areas granted to it by the Constitution. Each state retained its sovereignty, and the Tenth Amendment reserved for them those powers not specifically delegated to the federal government. Strict constructionists believed state governments were closer to the people and more responsive to their will. States protected individual liberty better than the federal government, and each state should control those things that affected people's lives most directly, such as citizenship, voting rights, and slavery within state borders. This belief in a limited federal government and powerful state governments was at the heart of states' rights philosophy.

Loose constructionists believed the states had voluntarily placed themselves in a subservient position to the federal government when they ratified the Constitution because Article VI clearly states that the Constitution and all federal laws are the "supreme law of the land." They also embraced Article I, which gives Congress "implied powers" to "make laws necessary for carrying out the enumerated powers." Loose constructionists argued that Article I authorized Congress to exert authority in areas not specifically mentioned in the Constitution because the federal government had to have the flexibility to adapt to unexpected situations and involve itself in a variety of state matters for the national good. Alexander Hamilton, in particular, believed these implied powers authorized the federal government to take the lead in developing the nation's infrastructure and economy. Only the federal government had the necessary resources (through tax revenue) to construct canals and other expensive internal improvements that could tie the states together economically. If internal improvements were left to the states, poorer states would remain primitive and backward.

Most strict constructionists joined Thomas Jefferson's and James Madison's Republican Party, while most loose constructionists supported Hamilton's and John Adams's Federalist Party. The subsequent political battles were intense because both sides believed they were upholding the Constitution's original intent and defending liberty and freedom.

Eventually, the states' rights debate came to revolve around congressional authority to regulate slavery and, particularly, whether the federal government had the authority to stop the spread of slavery into the territories. At first, however, the debate focused on economics and political power. The Northern economy relied much more on business and industry than the South, and Northerners saw the advantage of a powerful federal government that could stimulate the economy by passing protective tariffs and using tax monies to make internal improvements. Southerners, however, realized the rapidly growing Northern states might eventually dominate the federal government and force their will on the South. Southerners embraced strict construction and states' rights to protect themselves against what could become a tyrannical majority. States' rights philosophy even caused many Southerners to oppose federally funded internal improvements despite the fact that the undeveloped South would benefit most from them. If Congress funded the improvements, Southerners felt, the states would be indebted to the national government and could be pressured to support it whether they believed in its policies or not. Also in the back of Southerners' minds was the fear that Congress might not stop with internal improvements if given such broad power. As one North Carolina senator warned, "If Congress can make banks, roads, and canals under the Constitution, they can free slaves in the United States."

## The Virginia and Kentucky Resolutions

The states' rights debate intensified in 1798 when the Federalist Congress passed the Alien and Sedition Acts in response to increasing tensions with France. Still angry that the United States had signed a separate peace treaty with Great Britain in the Revolutionary War, France was attacking American ships, and it attempted to bribe American diplomats who had been sent to France to negotiate the difficulties in what became known as the X, Y, Z Affair. The Alien and Sedition Acts made it more difficult for immigrants to become citizens and made it illegal for anyone to speak or publish anything against the president or government that was deemed to be "false, scandalous, and malicious." The Federalists argued the measures were necessary to protect the nation against spies, saboteurs, and seditionists, but in reality they were designed to weaken the Republican Party by muzzling its press and cutting off its supply of new voters; most immigrants joined the Republican Party.

Claiming the Alien and Sedition Acts violated the Constitution's guarantees of due process and freedom of speech and the press, Madison and Jefferson wrote the Virginia and Kentucky Resolutions, respectively, in protest. These resolutions, passed by the Virginia and Kentucky legislatures, became cornerstones of states' rights philosophy. While affirming their loyalty to the Union, the resolutions claimed the individual states had a right to oppose such unconstitutional measures. They argued the Union was a compact, or a contractual partnership, created by the thirteen original state governments rather than by the American people as a whole. In other words, the states were the contract's principals, the federal government was their agent, and the Constitution was the contract that bound them together. As the principals, the individual states had the right to judge for themselves if the federal government was violating the compact, and therefore the states had the right to decide for themselves whether a law was constitutional. If a state decided that a federal act was unconstitutional, it could nullify, or void, that law within the state's borders. Jefferson was disappointed when no other states joined Virginia and Kentucky in threatening to nullify the Alien and Sedition Acts; some, in fact, roundly condemned the resolutions.

## Secession

Eventually the crisis with France passed, but the Virginia and Kentucky Resolutions helped popularize states' rights and nullification as constitutional checks against what was perceived as abusive federal power. Privately, Jefferson began considering an even more drastic remedy—secession. Secession was the ultimate states' right: the right of a state to leave the Union altogether and resume its status as an independent, sovereign nation. In a letter to Madison, Jefferson wrote that someday they might have to threaten "to sever ourselves from that union we so much value, rather than give up the rights of self government which we have reserved, and in which alone we see liberty, safety and happiness." Although Jefferson never *publicly* made such a threat, future politicians used the old revolutionary's writings to defend secession.

The legitimacy of secession depended on how one viewed the Union and state sovereignty. Everyone agreed the states were sovereign before ratifying the Constitution, but did a state retain its sovereignty after becoming part of the United States? And if it did, could a state secede if it believed the federal government was a threat to its liberty and welfare? Some strict constructionists said yes. They argued that each state had voluntarily ratified the Constitution and joined the Union, but individual states had never given up their sovereignty. A state's membership in the Union was similar to an individual's membership in a social club. If an individual joins a club and then decides it is a threat, he cannot be forced to remain a member against his will.

To most loose constructionists, secession was dangerous and illogical. Although each state had been sovereign under the Articles of Confederation, they surrendered that sovereignty to the federal government when they ratified the Constitution. The framers would never have created a Union with each state having the right to leap in and out at will because some states would likely secede every time their political party or presidential candidate lost an election. Secession was unconstitutional because it would lead to the destruction of the very nation the Constitution had created.

## The Essex Junto and Hartford Convention

Surprisingly, the Northern states were the first to threaten secession. Many New England politicians supported states' rights because they feared being dominated in a government controlled by other states. This fear caused one group of Federalists, known as the Essex Junto, to take drastic measures after the Louisiana Purchase. The Purchase doubled the size of the United States, and it was obvious new states would be carved from the vast territory. As America's population—and political power—shifted westward, the New England states would diminish in influence. The Essex Junto decided secession was the only way to protect New England, and they secretly plotted to secede from the United States and create a separate confederation.

Their plan, however, was shelved when the Junto was unable to gain New York's support.

New England's dissatisfaction only increased as the Federalist Party rapidly declined in power, largely because of its own miscues with the Alien and Sedition Acts. New England politicians decided to act after the 1807 Embargo Act and the War of 1812 devastated the economy. In December 1814, former members of the Essex Junto and other politicians met in Hartford, Connecticut, and drafted several constitutional amendments to protect New England's position in the Union. Among other things, the amendments would have repealed the Three-fifths Compromise and required a two-thirds vote in Congress to declare war, admit new states, or impose an embargo. Some delegates wanted to threaten secession if Congress refused to pass the amendments, but the majority refused to go along with such a radical idea. In the end, the demands were never presented to Congress because the War of 1812 ended about the time the Hartford delegates reached Washington. Afterward, support for secession largely faded away in New England as the American people took pride in their hard-fought victory and enjoyed the prosperity of westward expansion and economic growth. However, the slavery issue, which had lain dormant for some time, soon exploded on the scene.

## The Missouri Compromise

Slavery was not a major political problem during the first thirty years of the constitutional government because there was a balance of power in the Senate. As long as there was the same number of free states as slave states, the number of senators on both sides was equal and neither faction could impose its will on the other. In 1819, the balance of eleven free and eleven slave states was threatened when Missouri petitioned to be admitted as a slave state. When Northern antislavery congressmen added an amendment to the statehood bill that prohibited bringing more slaves into Missouri and mandated freeing children born of slaves at age twenty-five, Southerners saw it as federal interference in their slavery rights.

The Southern senators were able to defeat the amendment, but the crisis continued for months as the Missouri debate dragged on and on. Finally, in 1820, Speaker of the House Henry Clay secured passage of the Missouri Compromise. This agreement simultaneously admitted Missouri as a slave state and Maine as a free state to maintain the balance of power. To keep Congress from going through a similar crisis every time a Louisiana Purchase territory was considered for statehood, the territory was divided along latitude 36°30′ north. In the future, states admitted north of this Missouri Compromise Line would automatically be free, while those admitted south of it would be slave. The Missouri Compromise worked for the most part and cooled the slavery debate for the next quarter of a century. However, it also demonstrated just how divisive and potentially disastrous the slavery question could be.

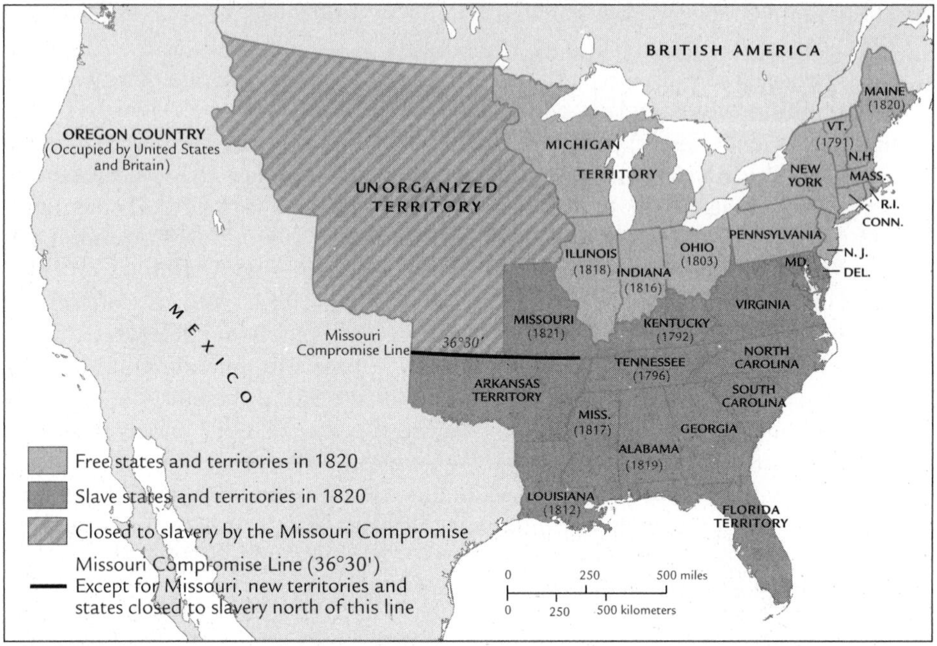
BRITISH AMERICA
MAINE (1820)
VT. (1791)
N.H.
MASS.
R.I.
CONN.
NEW YORK
N.J.
DEL.
MD.
PENNSYLVANIA
OREGON COUNTRY (Occupied by United States and Britain)
UNORGANIZED TERRITORY
MICHIGAN TERRITORY
ILLINOIS (1818)
INDIANA (1816)
OHIO (1803)
MISSOURI (1821)
KENTUCKY (1792)
VIRGINIA
MEXICO
Missouri Compromise Line
36°30′
TENNESSEE (1796)
NORTH CAROLINA
SOUTH CAROLINA
ARKANSAS TERRITORY
MISS. (1817)
GEORGIA
ALABAMA (1819)
LOUISIANA (1812)
FLORIDA TERRITORY
Free states and territories in 1820
Slave states and territories in 1820
Closed to slavery by the Missouri Compromise
Missouri Compromise Line (36°30')
Except for Missouri, new territories and states closed to slavery north of this line
0 250 500 miles
0 250 500 kilometers

**The Missouri Compromise, 1820.** The Missouri Compromise created an uneasy truce between the North and South over the slavery issue. Missouri and Maine were admitted as slave and free states, respectively, and the nation was split at latitude 36°30′ north to separate slave and free territories.

## The Webster-Hayne Debate

The legitimacy of protective tariffs was another contentious issue that ultimately touched off a states' rights crisis. A tariff is a federal tax levied on foreign products either to raise revenue or to protect domestic jobs and industries from foreign competition by making the foreign products cost more. Northerners generally supported protective tariffs because the North had most of the industry and jobs that needed protection. Southerners, however, exported agricultural products and consumed foreign-made manufactured goods. They opposed protective tariffs on both economic and constitutional grounds. Such taxes made imported products more expensive for Southerners and were viewed as unconstitutional because tariffs forced Southerners to pay for the protection of Northern jobs.

The tariff debate exploded in 1828 when Congress passed a high protective tariff. Led by Vice President John C. Calhoun of South Carolina, the Southerners decided to fight this "Tariff of Abominations." Calhoun embraced the theory of nullification when he anonymously wrote a highly charged pamphlet entitled the *South Carolina Exposition and Protest*. Expanding the arguments used in the Virginia and Kentucky Resolutions, he claimed that if a state nullified a law,

# BIOGRAPHY

## Henry Clay: The Great Compromiser

A Virginia native, Henry Clay (1877–1852) received a basic education in local schools, became an attorney, and moved to Kentucky. After becoming a famous criminal lawyer, he entered politics as a Jeffersonian Republican and was elected to the legislature. Clay also served two one-year terms in the U.S. Senate to fill vacated positions before being elected to Congress in 1810. Elected Speaker of the House during his freshman term, he remained in Congress almost continually for the next fifteen years. Clay was the longest-serving Speaker of the nineteenth century and is credited with turning the position into the powerful and influential one it is today. In 1812, he led the so-called War Hawks and secured a declaration of war against Great Britain, partly because he wanted to invade Canada and add it to the United States. Clay also served as a negotiator for the Treaty of Ghent that ended the war.

Clay was an excellent politician, but he was also a bundle of contradictions. He owned as many as sixty slaves, but he condemned the peculiar institution as an evil for both blacks and whites. Clay was one of the few large slaveholders who freed most of his slaves before his death, yet he did not think the two races could live together peacefully and became president of the American Colonization Society to relocate freed slaves in Africa. Although an outstanding orator, Clay was sometimes referred to as the "Dictator" because he was also arrogant, partisan, hot-headed, misleading, and quick to use political tricks. On the other hand, he could be quite charming and tactful, and his persuasive skills were legendary. Once when a freshman congressman was asked if he would like to meet the Speaker, the man replied, "I do not wish to meet Mr. Clay. He is my opponent and I do not want to subject myself to his fascination." Clay also had a penchant for compromise that led President John F. Kennedy to call him the greatest senator in American history. More than once Clay helped end a political crisis with a well-reasoned compromise that both sides could accept. Known as the "Great Compromiser," he was the driving force behind the Missouri Compromise, the compromise tariff of 1833, and the Compromise of 1850.

A loose constructionist who opposed secession, Clay supported territorial expansion, a protective tariff, internal improvements, and a national bank because he believed the federal government should take the lead in developing the nation. As a presidential candidate in 1824, he synthesized these ideas into the "American System," a platform to bind together the North, South, and West economically. Congress eventually decided the close election, and winning candidate John Quincy Adams appointed Clay secretary of state after Clay threw his support to Adams. Losing candidate Andrew Jackson was furious and accused the two of engaging in a "corrupt bargain." Afterward, Clay helped organize the Whig Party to oppose Jackson's Democrats. The Whigs adopted Clay's American System, and he ran unsuccessfully for president three more times.

When the Mexican War began, Clay and many other Whigs opposed it as an unjust war started by Southerners who wanted to spread slavery westward. Tragically, his son was killed in the war. Clay's last great contribution to American politics was the Compromise of 1850 that healed what he called "the five bleeding wounds" then threatening the nation. These problems generally involved slavery and its potential spread westward into the territories the United States had won from Mexico. However, Clay was unable to get the compromise package accepted and soon went home to Kentucky exhausted and dispirited. Final passage of the Compromise was left to others, and Clay died two years later from tuberculosis.

# DID YOU KNOW?

## The Mason-Dixon Line

The Missouri Compromise Line, which only applied to the Louisiana Purchase territory, should not be confused with the Mason-Dixon Line. The Mason-Dixon Line was surveyed between 1763 and 1767 to establish the boundaries of the Delaware, Maryland, and Pennsylvania colonies. Later it was extended 244 miles westward. When Pennsylvania and other states lying north of the line abolished slavery, the Mason-Dixon Line became the de facto boundary between free and slave states. Some people believe the Mason-Dixon Line also was the origin of the word *Dixie,* a nickname for the South. However, the name probably originated in New Orleans, Louisiana, where the word *dix* (French for "ten") was used on some forms of money. New Orleans became known as "Dix's Land," and from that Dixie supposedly was derived.

Congress would either have to abolish the law or secure an amendment to make the law constitutional. If the state still opposed the act even after an amendment was ratified, the state had the right to secede. Calhoun's pamphlet was widely read, and some Southerners, like their New England brethren earlier, began to view secession as a way to protect themselves against growing federal power.

One of the most important moments in the states' rights controversy occurred in January 1830 when Senators Daniel Webster of Massachusetts and Robert Y. Hayne of South Carolina squared off in a historic nine-day debate. Federal land policy was the topic, but the two politicos used the occasion to defend their section's views on the increasingly divisive issues of slavery, tariffs, states' rights, and nullification.

Criticizing federally funded internal improvements as a financial bribe that forced the states to support the national government, Hayne warned, "A moneyed interest in the government is essentially a base interest." He also defended slavery and reminded his fellow senators that Northern slave traders had established the peculiar institution in America. Southerners simply inherited the slave system from their forefathers and had to live with it as best they could. Turning his attention to the tariff, Hayne declared the tax was unconstitutional because it siphoned money out of the South to protect Northern jobs. He also defended states' rights and nullification by emphasizing that the Constitution was a compact made by the state governments, not by the people as a whole. Allowing the Supreme Court to be the final arbiter of federal laws would be "utterly subversive of the sovereignty and independence of the states," he noted. Nullification, Hayne reasoned, was the only way for the South to protect its minority interests against the Northern majority.

Webster mostly ignored the tariff issue but vigorously denounced states' rights and nullification. In Webster's view it was the people, not the state legislatures, who had created the Constitution. If states' rights theory was valid, it meant the federal government not only had been created by the states, it was "the servant of four-and-twenty masters, of different will and different purposes and yet bound to obey all." The Supreme Court, Webster argued, had to be the final arbiter on constitutional matters because the Union would be nothing more than a "rope of sand" if each state was allowed to decide for itself which laws to obey.

The Webster-Hayne Debate helped crystallize opposing views of the Union among Northerners and Southerners. Most Southerners supported Hayne's contention that the Constitution was created by the state governments. Every step in forming the Union had been taken by either state conventions or state legislatures, not individual voters. Such bodies had made the decision to rebel against Great Britain, written the state constitutions, and ratified both the Articles of Confederation and the Constitution. Through the Constitution, the states agreed to give the federal government *certain* powers, but not *unlimited* powers. The Constitution may have granted Congress the right to pass laws for the nation's "general welfare," but it was illogical to believe the states would voluntarily place themselves in a position where they would be powerless to oppose tyrannical legislation. Thus, each state had the right to nullify a law it believed was unconstitutional, and a state had the right to secede if it believed the Union was detrimental to its welfare.

Most Northerners agreed with Webster that the Constitution was a creation of the American people rather than the state governments, and it was the people who had given the federal and state governments their respective powers. The people elected Congress and gave it the right to pass federal laws. Nullification and secession were illegal because the Constitution had made federal law supreme over state law and had created the Supreme Court to settle constitutional disputes. The framers never envisioned creating a nation where the individual parts could simply leave when they disagreed with the majority. If Southerners believed a federal act was unconstitutional, according to this view, they should respect the democratic process and change the Constitution through an amendment, not nullify it or secede.

## The Nullification Crisis

When Congress passed another high tariff in 1832, South Carolina's legislature nullified it over the protests of a vocal minority. Suddenly the Union faced the first real threat of violence over the question of states' rights. If the federal government failed to enforce the tariff in South Carolina, other states almost certainly would embrace nullification in the future. But if the Union tried to collect the tax by force, South Carolina might secede and touch off a civil war. Determined to enforce the law, President Jackson branded nullification as treason and asked Congress to pass the Force Bill to authorize him to use the military to collect the tariff. When a South Carolina congressman attempted to explain why his constituents supported nullification, Jackson cut him off and bluntly warned, "Tell them that they can talk and write resolutions and print threats to their hearts' content. But if one drop of blood be shed there in defiance of the laws of the United States, I will hang the first man of them I can get my hands on to the first tree I can find." Senator Robert Y. Hayne dismissed the threat as a bluff, but not Senator Thomas Hart Benton. Benton knew Jackson well, having once shot him during a street brawl, and he warned Hayne, "[W]hen Jackson begins to talk about hanging, they can begin to look for the ropes."

**The Great Triumvirate.** Henry Clay, Daniel Webster, and John C. Calhoun (left to right). Known as "the Great Triumvirate," Clay, Webster, and Calhoun dominated the Senate and much of politics during the volatile slavery debates of the 1830s and 1840s. Although they represented different sections of the country, they had similar backgrounds. All served as secretaries of state and in both the House and Senate.

Having been recently elected to the Senate, Calhoun resigned as vice-president on December 28 and then vigorously attacked Jackson and the tariff from the Senate floor. Fortunately, no one wanted war, and Senator Henry Clay gained support for a compromise tariff that saved face for everyone. The new tariff started out high to protect Northern industry and then declined over ten years until it approximated the level of the 1816 tariff. South Carolina accepted the compromise tariff, but in a final gesture of defiance it voted to nullify the Force Bill. Civil war was avoided, but Southern radicals known as "fire-eaters" continued to support nullification and to believe that secession was the ultimate solution to protect slavery and defend their states' rights.

## THE POLITICS OF EXPANSION

**May 13, 1846: Mexican War begins**
**August 8, 1846: David Wilmot introduces Wilmot Proviso in Congress**
**February 2, 1848: United States and Mexico sign the Treaty of Guadalupe Hidalgo**
**September 17, 1848: Congress passes the Compromise of 1850**

As long as slavery was confined to the South, Northerners did not see it as an economic threat, and they had little to fear politically because there was not much land south of the Missouri Compromise Line that could become new slave states. But slavery had to expand to survive. Plantation crops such as tobacco leached nutrients out of the soil and eventually left it infertile, and older plantation regions became overcrowded after a few generations. These harsh truths forced planters to move westward continually in search of new land. The peculiar institution quickly spread from east to west, and by the early nineteenth century it stretched from the Atlantic seaboard to Texas and from the Gulf of Mexico to the Ohio River. Southerners knew they had to continue moving west all the way to California if they were to maintain their way of life. This spread of slavery into the western territories became the most divisive issue of the entire slavery debate.

A popular idea known as Manifest Destiny helped fuel this westward expansion. This philosophy was based on the belief that American culture was superior to all others and therefore it was America's destiny to push the nation's boundary across the continent to the Pacific Ocean. Expansionists believed Oregon, which was jointly controlled by the United States and Great Britain, should be annexed, as well as northern Mexico. The Republic of Texas was another possible acquisition, although most Northerners opposed annexing such a huge slave state. Despite the Texas controversy, Manifest Destiny was popular with most voters, and Democratic candidate James K. Polk won the presidency in 1844 by making it a central part of his campaign.

## The Mexican War

Three days before leaving office, President John Tyler stole some of Polk's thunder by signing a joint resolution of Congress annexing Texas as a slave state. Nonetheless, Polk moved quickly to acquire other land. He used the threat of military force to persuade Great Britain to split Oregon and give the United States the modern-day states of Washington, Oregon, and Idaho. Acquiring California and the rest of northern Mexico proved more challenging. Mexico was still angry over losing Texas and refused to recognize the Rio Grande as the Texas-Mexico border. When Mexico rebuffed an American offer to buy California and the desert southwest, the situation deteriorated in 1846 as both sides began massing troops along the Rio Grande. The Mexican army then attacked an American patrol on the north side of the river, and President Polk asked for and received a declaration of war from Congress.

Although bloody, the Mexican War did not last long. After U.S. forces defeated the enemy in northern Mexico and captured California and New Mexico, General Winfield Scott made an amphibious landing at Veracruz and fought his way inland to capture Mexico City. The war ended in 1848 with the signing of the Treaty of Guadalupe Hidalgo, which established the Rio Grande as the boundary of Texas and allowed the United States to buy California and the American southwest for $15 million. The Mexican War was a brilliant victory, and it became known as "the dress rehearsal for the Civil War" because so many future generals gained their first combat experience there. It also set in motion bitter debates over slavery that eventually split the nation apart.

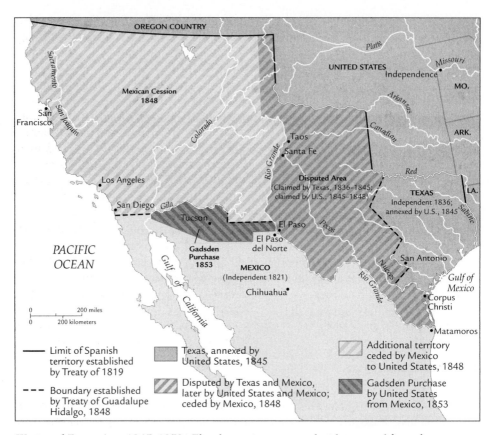

**Westward Expansion, 1845–1853.** The slavery issue erupted with renewed fury after the United States acquired Oregon, Texas, and much of Mexico. Because the Missouri Compromise Line did not extend to the Pacific Ocean, Congress had to address the question of slavery in these new western territories.

## The Free-Soilers

The Mexican War was not popular with many Northerners because they believed it was instigated by Southerners who wanted to spread slavery to California. These critics did not oppose territorial expansion, but they did object to allowing slavery to spread into the new territory. To protect Northern interests, Pennsylvania congressman David Wilmot introduced the Wilmot Proviso, which would have banned slavery in any territory won in the war. Wilmot's motive was not based on abolitionism, however. He actually wanted to reserve the new land for whites by preventing all blacks—free or slave—from entering it. On numerous occasions, the Wilmot Proviso passed the House, but it always failed in the more balanced Senate. Its main impact was to keep the slavery issue alive in Congress and become yet another divisive issue between the sections. Northerners saw the proviso as a way to ensure that slavery would not spread west, while Southerners bitterly opposed it for denying them the spoils of war and interfering with their slavery rights.

The debate over the Wilmot Proviso helped form the Free-Soil movement, a Northern faction made up of Democrats, Whigs, and Liberty Party members who opposed slavery in some fashion. Some Free-Soilers were abolitionists who wanted to free the slaves and grant them equal rights because it was the right thing to do. Most, however, were like David Wilmot. They did not believe in racial equality and only opposed slavery because they considered it a direct threat to the North's free labor system. Free-Soilers generally agreed slavery was morally wrong but did not oppose it so strongly that they supported direct political action against it. They were willing to concede to slavery in the South but were adamant about stopping it from spreading into territories where they might live someday.

Free-Soilers also wanted Congress to pass a homestead act to allow settlers to obtain 160 acres of free federal land if they lived on it for a number of years and made improvements. Most Southerners opposed homesteading because it would attract more small farmers than slaveholders to the west, and the more numerous Northerners would then be able to form a majority in the territorial governments and keep out slavery. In 1848, the Free-Soilers became a political force when they formed the Free-Soil Party under the slogan "Free Soil for Free Men" and nominated Martin Van Buren for president. Although Van Buren was defeated, the Free-Soilers split the Democratic vote and enabled Whig candidate Zachary Taylor to win. When the party lost again in the next election, the Free-Soil Party disappeared as members gravitated back to the Democrats or the new Republican Party.

## The Compromise of 1850

By 1850, a host of problems—most of which involved slavery—began creating tension in Congress. Thousands of Americans streamed west after the Mexican War, and California (thanks to the Gold Rush) quickly qualified for statehood and Utah and New Mexico for territorial status. At issue was whether California and the Southwest should allow slavery. The debate was mostly philosophical because there were virtually no slaves in the West and the vast majority of people there opposed it. Southerners, however, knew they someday would have to abandon their leached-out eastern plantations and did not want the door closed on establishing slavery in the west. They claimed the Constitution gave them the right to expand slavery because it recognized slaves as property, and property was protected by the Fifth Amendment's due process clause. Southerners conceded California had the right to outlaw slavery if it was admitted directly to the Union as a state, but Congress could not forbid slavery in the Utah and New Mexico territories. Only when they became states could the inhabitants decide on slavery's future, and Southerners had to be given an opportunity to establish slavery during the territorial period before the vote was taken. Predictably, Northerners disagreed and argued Congress could forbid slavery in the territories. Utah and New Mexico belonged to all Americans, according to this view, and the Constitution gave Congress the authority to enact rules and regulations for the territories.

Two other highly charged issues of the time were the slave auctions in Washington, D.C., and treatment of runaway slaves. Abolitionists wanted to abolish

# BIOGRAPHY

## Stephen Arnold Douglas: The Little Giant

**Stephen A. Douglas**

Born in Vermont, Stephen A. Douglas (1813–1861) became a life-long Democrat after falling under the spell of Andrew Jackson. As a young man he moved to Illinois, became a lawyer, and helped organize the Democratic Party there. In addition to serving in the legislature, Douglas also was the state's attorney, secretary of state, and Supreme Court justice (which led many people to refer to him as "Judge Davis"). His political acumen was legendary, and his five-feet-four-inch stature and disproportionately large head earned him the nickname the "Little Giant." Douglas married twice, both times to Southern women (his first wife died shortly after giving birth to a daughter), and fathered six children, but only four lived beyond infancy. A shrewd businessman, he became wealthy by speculating in land development around Chicago, and he succeeded in using his political clout to make the city a major railroad hub.

Elected to Congress in 1842, Douglas embraced Manifest Destiny and supported the annexation of Oregon and Texas, but he was a staunch Unionist who once declared, "To me, our country, and all its parts, are one and indivisible." After being elected to the U.S. Senate in 1847, he became an increasingly important political figure as the slavery debate grew more raucous. Douglas supported popular sovereignty, homesteading, a northern transcontinental railroad, and Southerners' right to own slaves, but he opposed slavery in Kansas and the spread of slavery into the western territories. Two of his greatest political victories were the Compromise of 1850 and the Kansas-Nebraska Act. The latter, however, hurt Douglas's popularity among Northerners, and it revealed one of his weaknesses—an inability to see the emotional side of the slavery issue. Instead, he admitted, "I deal with slavery as a political question involving questions of public policy."

While campaigning in the South for president in 1860, Douglas received death threats and was once bombarded with eggs. Despite the election's bitter political fighting, he and Abraham Lincoln never took things personally because they were old acquaintances, and both had courted Mary Todd (who married Lincoln). After losing the election, Douglas quickly became a Lincoln supporter. He held Lincoln's hat during the inaugural speech and escorted Mary to the presidential ball and danced with her. On the Senate floor, Douglas disagreed with Democrats who attacked Lincoln's inaugural speech. It was, he declared, a "peace offering" rather than a "war message," and he appealed unsuccessfully to all parties to compromise and avoid disunion. Continuing to support the Union after fighting broke out, Douglas returned to Illinois and told his fellow citizens, "Every man must be for the United States or against it. There can be no neutrals in this war, *only patriots—or traitors.*" A broken and exhausted man, he died just two months after the Civil War began.

the capital's slave auctions, denouncing them as a disgrace for a nation that claimed to be the world's shining light of liberty. The runaway issue was more emotional than substantial because few slaves ever escaped bondage. However, media coverage and rumors inflated the actual number, and Southerners were livid at the North's Personal Liberty Laws and the abolitionists' involvement in the Underground Railroad. Slaveholders demanded a stronger federal fugitive slave act to put an end to such abolitionist meddling.

Finally, a simmering border dispute between Texas and New Mexico threatened peace in the Southwest. Texas claimed the Rio Grande as its western boundary, while New Mexico argued that the boundary was farther east. The dispute needed to be resolved quickly, because bloodshed had already occurred as the factions fought it out on the high plains.

Work in Congress ground to a halt as members debated these issues, but Henry Clay offered a solution that became known as the Compromise of 1850. The legislation called for California to be admitted as a free state, New Mexico and Utah to be admitted as territories with the right to decide the slavery issue later, the abolishment of slave auctions (but not slavery) in Washington, settling the border dispute in New Mexico's favor in exchange for a $10 million payment to Texas, and passage of a new Fugitive Slave Act. By far the most controversial aspect of the legislation was the Fugitive Slave Act. Much stronger than previous ones, it allowed federal marshals, using nothing more than a slaveholder's sworn affidavit, to track down and capture runaway slaves. Runaways would not be allowed to defend themselves, and citizens and law enforcement officers would be required to assist the marshals or face arrest themselves. The act also attempted to counter Personal Liberty Laws by specifically prohibiting states from interfering with the process. Despite his best efforts, the sick, frail Clay was unable to get the compromise package passed, and he soon returned home to Kentucky, never again to enter the political fray. Illinois senator Stephen A. Douglas carried on the fight and finally got the package passed by breaking it into five separate bills.

Northern opposition to the Fugitive Slave Act was intense, and it reached a fever pitch in 1854 when runaway slave Anthony Burns was captured in Boston, Massachusetts. The Anthony Burns affair marked a dramatic change in Northern attitudes. Prior to 1854, most Northerners opposed the spread of slavery but gave little thought to the plight of African Americans held in bondage. While they may have been aware that slavery was wrong, they were willing to tolerate it in the South as the price to pay for political stability. But Burns's plight touched Northerners' hearts. It forced them to recognize the innate immorality of slavery, and they began to follow a higher law to oppose the Fugitive Slave Act. One Illinois newspaper declared, "Before the repeal of the Missouri Compromise, in all contests between the slaveholders and abolitionists our sympathies were decidedly in favor of the former; but since that act of treachery we have not one word to say.... One year ago there were thousands of men who would have aided you slaveholders in the capture of your slaves, who now say hands off—non-intervention is the policy—let the slaveowners and the abolitionists fight it out."

After the Anthony Burns affair there were several highly publicized cases where Northerners intervened to protect runaway slaves from slave catchers. Northern states passed stronger Personal Liberty Laws despite the federal prohibition against interfering with the marshals. Massachusetts law even required the removal of any state official who cooperated in returning a runaway

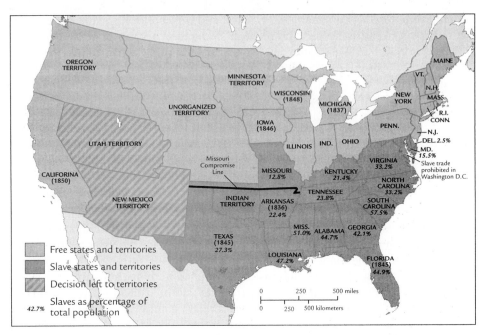

**The Compromise of 1850.** The Compromise of 1850 was the last congressional compromise to address the slavery issue. Although it admitted California as a free state and began organizing territories in the Southwest, the inclusion of the federal Fugitive Slave Act triggered strong antislavery feelings in the North.

slave, and the governor eventually removed Judge Loring because people demanded he be punished for ordering Burns's return to slavery. Ironically, in passing Personal Liberty Laws, Northerners actually embraced the very states' rights philosophy they had condemned Southerners for supporting. By placing state restrictions on the federal Fugitive Slave Act, they essentially nullified the federal law. The Wisconsin Supreme Court even ruled that the 1850 Fugitive Slave Act violated Wisconsin's sovereignty and was, therefore, unconstitutional (the U.S. Supreme Court overturned the ruling in 1859).

The Fugitive Slave Act aside, the Compromise of 1850 for the most part succeeded in calming sectional tensions, and the slavery debate waned in Congress. Unfortunately, this armistice was short-lived, and new battles over the peculiar institution soon ripped the nation apart.

## FOR FURTHER READING

Virginia and Kentucky Resolutions
Webster-Hayne Debate
William Lloyd Garrison's *The Liberator* editorial "I Will Be Heard"
J. D. B. De Bow's essay "Why Non-Slaveholders Should Support Slavery"

# CHAPTER 2

# A Parting of Ways

The Politics of Slavery

The Election of 1860

The Secession Crisis

---

Hundreds of New Yorkers lined up outside the Cooper Union building on the unusually warm night of February 27, 1860, to pay twenty-five cents to attend a political lecture. The speaker was Abraham Lincoln, an Illinois attorney who had emerged as a leading antislavery figure. Lincoln had been invited to Cooper Union by opponents of William H. Seward, a New York senator who was seeking the Republican presidential nomination. They believed Lincoln was a viable western alternative to Seward and hoped his speech would win him eastern support and weaken Seward's candidacy. After accepting the invitation, Lincoln decided to use the occasion to respond to a recent magazine article in which Senator Stephen A. Douglas claimed the framers of the Constitution intended slavery to spread westward. Realizing the importance of his lecture, Lincoln spent weeks researching his topic and preparing for the big night. As he walked onto the stage, however, the audience was largely disappointed. One onlooker wrote, "At first sight there was nothing impressive or imposing about him. His clothes hung awkwardly on his gaunt and giant frame; his face was of a dark pallor, without the slightest tinge of color; his seamed and rugged features bore the furrows of hardship and struggle. His deep set eyes looked sad and anxious."

Despite his unimpressive appearance, Lincoln skillfully disproved Douglas's claim by showing that most of the framers of the Constitution had voting records that supported congressional restriction of slavery. He then declared that the Republican Party was simply staying true to the framers' intentions when it called for federal laws to stop the spread of slavery. Although Lincoln was willing to concede to the peculiar institution in the South, he said Northerners must not let it spread into the western territories or into the free states. The crowd applauded wildly and roared its approval as Lincoln ended his two-hour address with a challenge: "If our sense of duty forbids this, then let us stand by our duty, fearlessly and effectively. . . . Neither let us be slandered from our duty by false accusations against us, nor frightened from it by menaces of destruction to the Government nor of dungeons to ourselves. LET US HAVE FAITH THAT RIGHT MAKES MIGHT, AND IN THAT FAITH, LET US, TO THE END, DARE TO DO OUR DUTY AS WE UNDERSTAND IT."

Two days later, another future president rose in the U.S. Senate to respond to antislavery remarks made by Senator Seward. In his address, Mississippi senator Jefferson Davis supported the spread of slavery into the territories and claimed that the true defenders of liberty were Southerners, not Northerners. The South had never tried to prevent Free-Soilers from taking their labor system and property westward, but the North was attempting to deny Southerners that very right. Southerners simply wanted the same opportunity. As Davis put it, "We have sought not to usurp the Territory to our exclusive possession; we have sought that government should be instituted in order that every person and property might be protected that went into it—the white man coming from the North, and the white man coming from the South, both meeting on an equality in the Territory, and each with whatever property he may hold under the laws of his State and the Constitution of the United States, such is our position."

By 1860 the nation was in crisis over the slavery issue, and everyone knew that the outcome of the presidential election might decide the fate of the Union. The "Cooper Union Speech" was Lincoln's first and only campaign speech, but with it he secured the moral and political high ground in the eyes of Northern voters and received enough national publicity to ensure he would be a presidential contender. Davis had no such aspirations and remained out of the race. Little did he know subsequent events would make him head of a competing American nation.

## THE POLITICS OF SLAVERY

**March 20, 1852: Harriet Beecher Stowe publishes *Uncle Tom's Cabin***
**March 20, 1854: Northerners form the Republican Party**
**May 22, 1854: Congress passes the Kansas-Nebraska Act**
**May 21, 1856: "Border ruffians" sack Lawrence, Kansas**
**May 22, 1856: Brooks-Sumner Affair takes place**
**March 6, 1857: Supreme Court issues the Dred Scott decision**
**August 21, 1857: Lincoln-Douglas Debates begin**
**October 16, 1859: John Brown raids Harpers Ferry, Virginia**

The Compromise of 1850 marked a turning point in North-South relations. Previously, Southern politicians dominated key federal positions and felt fairly secure in their ability to stop the abolitionists, and moderate politicians such as Henry Clay were able to get compromises accepted. Afterward, however, radicalism increased on both sides. Abolitionists rose to important political positions and became more determined to stamp out slavery, and Southerners became increasingly paranoid as the North's growing population gave it more power in Congress. Compromise became increasingly difficult as one crisis after another pummeled the nation during the 1850s.

## Uncle Tom's Cabin

Sectional tension was aggravated by the 1852 publication of *Uncle Tom's Cabin*. Abolitionist Harriet Beecher Stowe wrote the novel to condemn the Fugitive Slave Act and the separation of slave families at auctions. Using strong religious imagery (Stowe once claimed, "God wrote it"), the novel recounted the life of a kind, Christian slave named Uncle Tom who persevered through many hardships and heartbreaks as he was sold from one family to another. In the end, an overseer beat Tom to death when he would not reveal the location of some runaway slaves.

Stowe sold several hundred thousand copies of the book in the first year, and it stirred Northerners' collective conscience. Convinced *Uncle Tom's Cabin* was an accurate portrayal of the slave system, many people who had previously given the peculiar institution little thought now believed it was an evil sin that should be abolished. Southerners, however, were outraged, and one critic, who apparently thought words were inadequate, sent Stowe a slave's severed ear in the mail. Southerners claimed Stowe knew nothing of slavery because she had never witnessed it firsthand, and all of her information was biased because it came from abolitionists or runaway slaves. Most slaveholders, Southerners argued, were decent people who cared for their slaves as best they could. The impact of *Uncle Tom's Cabin* on the nation cannot be exaggerated. During the Civil War, Abraham Lincoln once met Stowe and reportedly commented, "So you're the little woman who wrote the book that made this great war."

## The Kansas-Nebraska Act

While Americans argued over the accuracy of *Uncle Tom's Cabin,* another divisive issue sprang up in the form of proposals for a transcontinental railroad. Actually, the need for such a railroad to California was one of the few things the

*Uncle Tom's Cabin.* Harriet Beecher Stowe's *Uncle Tom's Cabin* had a huge impact on America. Its antislavery message resonated with many Northerners, and it spawned a number of popular plays.

**Harriet Beecher Stowe.** Few writers have affected American history as much as Harriet Beecher Stowe, the author of *Uncle Tom's Cabin.* When she was introduced to Abraham Lincoln during the Civil War, the President supposedly commented, "So you're the little woman who wrote the book that made this great war."

North and South agreed on in the 1850s; what they could not agree on was whether it should take a northern or southern route because both sections wanted the economic growth it would bring. Illinois senator Stephen A. Douglas pushed vigorously for the northern route because Chicago would serve as its eastern terminal, and he believed securing the railroad would win him political support for his 1856 presidential bid. However, a northern railroad would have to cross the empty expanse of the Great Plains, which posed a big problem for Douglas. The federal government sometimes gave large land grants to railroads to help finance the expensive construction, but such land grants could only be made in organized territories. For Douglas to get the northern route, he first had to form into territories the land over which the railroad would cross.

Douglas needed Southern support to get his bill passed, but most Southern congressmen opposed federal funding for a transcontinental railroad that would benefit the North. If Douglas wanted their help in passing his legislation, it was going to cost him. They informed Douglas they would not support his bill unless the Missouri Compromise Line was abolished and replaced with popular sovereignty. Popular sovereignty was the belief that voters of a territory, not Congress, should decide whether to allow slavery. An idea that had been around for some time, it became increasingly popular during the Mexican War when Michigan Democratic senator Lewis Cass proposed it as an alternative to the Wilmot Proviso. Douglas agreed to the Southerners' demands, apparently because he thought slavery would never succeed in the Great Plains anyhow, and because popular sovereignty seemed a fair way to solve the slavery issue. He also knew he needed Southern support to win the presidency.

When Douglas introduced the Kansas-Nebraska Act in 1854 to create the territories of Kansas and Nebraska and replace the Missouri Compromise Line with popular sovereignty, he was surprised at the firestorm of criticism that followed. Most Northerners were quite happy with the Missouri Compromise Line because it prevented slavery from spreading into the northern part of

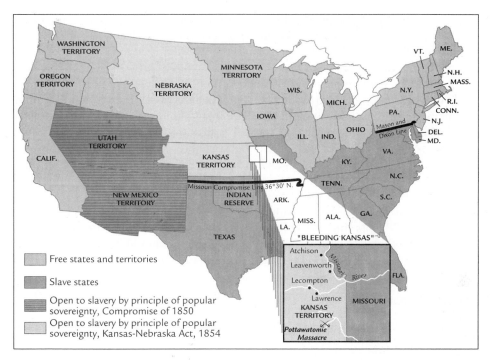

**Kansas-Nebraska Act, 1854.** In an attempt to gain a Northern transcontinental railroad, Senator Stephen A. Douglas succeeded in passing legislation to create the territories of Kansas and Nebraska. However, his inclusion of popular sovereignty to settle the slavery question led to violence along the Kansas-Missouri border.

the Louisiana Purchase. The Kansas-Nebraska Act destroyed that barrier, and Free-Soilers were faced with the nightmarish vision of slavery creeping into areas where they might someday live. With Southerners' help, Douglas was able to get the bill passed, but it changed American politics forever. Not only did the loss of Northern political support dash Douglas's hope of a presidential victory, it also led to the creation of a new political party that dominated national politics for decades.

## The Republican Party

The Kansas-Nebraska Act caused a fundamental realignment of American politics and created our modern two-party system. The nation's first two-party system—the Jeffersonian Republicans and the Federalists—began to collapse at the end of John Adams's administration when Federalists fell out of favor over the Alien and Sedition Acts. In the 1830s, a new two-party system arose with the emergence of the Democratic and Whig Parties. Under Andrew Jackson's leadership, the Democrats became the nation's dominant party, but the Whigs remained an effective minority party for two decades. Eventually, however, the slavery issue split its members when Northern Whigs wanted to contain slavery in the South and Southern Whigs wanted it to spread westward. As a result, the Whig Party was on the verge of collapse by the mid-1850s.

Over the years, issues such as slavery, immigration, and homesteading also led to the creation of several small parties, including the Liberty, Free-Soil, and American (or Know-Nothing) parties. The introduction of the Kansas-Nebraska Act made these small competing parties realize they had to join forces if they wanted to defeat the Democrats and stop the spread of slavery. In 1854, these divergent groups formed the Republican Party, a fractious organization that, nonetheless, became a political powerhouse. Some members were abolitionists who wanted to free the slaves and grant African Americans equal rights; others did not care if the South had slaves but only wanted to stop the spread of slavery. What bound Republicans together was their shared opposition to slavery and their belief that the federal government should promote economic progress by giving land grants to railroads and homesteads to settlers.

## Bleeding Kansas

After the Kansas-Nebraska Act passed, incredible violence quickly erupted in Kansas as both sides marshaled their forces for the upcoming slavery vote. It was obvious Nebraska would vote free since it lay far to the north and was populated by antislavery people, but Kansas was adjacent to Missouri and had both proslavery and antislavery settlers. Proslavery forces, known as "border ruffians," frequently crossed into Kansas and clashed with the abolitionists, and Henry Ward Beecher smuggled rifles, known as "Beecher's Bibles," to the abolitionists in crates labeled "Bibles." In May 1856, proslavery forces sacked the town of Lawrence, which was a station on the Underground Railroad, and abolitionist fanatic John Brown retaliated by raiding proslavery farms on Pottawatomie Creek and murdering five men. As the violence escalated to near civil war, Kansas became known as "Bleeding Kansas." Elections were finally held, but they were marred by violence, corruption, and voter boycotts. When the Southern faction gained control of the legislature and adopted the proslavery Lecompton Constitution, President James Buchanan submitted it to Congress even though it was clear most Kansas voters opposed slavery. The Senate approved the Lecompton Constitution, but the House rejected it, and Kansas remained in turmoil until it finally was admitted as a free state in 1861. It then became a Civil War battleground.

The raw emotions unleashed by the Kansas slavery debate led to a violent encounter in the Senate chamber. The day after the raid on Lawrence, Republican Massachusetts senator Charles Sumner gave a speech entitled "The Crime Against Kansas." In this well-rehearsed diatribe, he claimed the proslavery forces in Kansas were no more than "hirelings picked from the drunken spew and vomit of an uneasy civilization." Although Sumner verbally attacked several senators, he was particularly cruel to Democratic South Carolina senator Andrew P. Butler. Sumner declared Butler had "chosen a mistress to whom he has made his vows, and who, though ugly to others, is always lovely to him; though polluted in the sight of the world, is chaste in his sight—I mean the harlot, Slavery." Congressman Preston Brooks, Senator Butler's cousin, felt compelled to defend his family's honor, and two days after the speech walked into the Senate chamber and clubbed Sumner senseless with his walking cane.

Sumner was seriously injured and remained absent from the Senate for more than three years. An angry Massachusetts legislature refused to replace him and left his seat empty as a silent reminder of the attack. When Sumner eventually did return to the Senate, he became a powerful political figure during the Civil War and Reconstruction and even kept his bloodied coat in a closet to show to curious guests. Northern congressmen could not muster the necessary two-thirds vote to oust Brooks, but he resigned his seat and returned to South Carolina. Hundreds of admirers sent him walking canes to replace the one shattered on Sumner's skull, and voters immediately reelected him and sent him back to Washington. Northerners condemned "Bully" Brooks, and his actions reinforced their opinion that Southerners were out of control and unable to discuss the slavery issue rationally. Southerners, however, were incredulous that Northerners could view the hate-mongering Sumner as a hero and thought he got what he deserved for insulting an elder statesman.

## The Dred Scott Decision

As the fighting raged in Kansas, the nation's attention turned to the Supreme Court, which had announced it would use a case involving the slave Dred Scott to make a sweeping decision on slavery. An army surgeon who owned Dred Scott had taken him to Illinois and the Wisconsin Territory where slavery was illegal. When the surgeon died, abolitionists helped Scott sue for his freedom on the basis that he should have been emancipated when he was taken into the free territory. The case dragged through the court system for ten years before Chief Justice Roger Taney issued a final ruling in March 1857. On a 7–2 vote, the Supreme Court declared African Americans were not U.S. citizens and could not sue in federal court, slaves were property and therefore protected by the Constitution, and the Missouri Compromise Line was in violation of the Fifth Amendment's due process clause. Although not specifically stated, the ruling also meant territories could not use popular sovereignty to outlaw slavery.

Southerners were ecstatic at Taney's ruling because the Supreme Court supported their right to take slavery into the territories. Northerners were stunned at first, then outraged when they learned the Court voted along sectional lines, with all of the majority Southern justices voting for the decision. It appeared to them the case was decided by sectional loyalty, not the law. The decision caused large numbers of Northerners to become disillusioned with the Democratic Party (the party of the Southern justices) and turn to the

**The Political Quadrille, Music by Dred Scott.** This political cartoon illustrates the significance of slavery in the 1860 presidential election. While Dred Scott provides music, the four candidates dance around him. Clockwise from the top left are John C. Breckinridge, Abraham Lincoln, John Bell, and Stephen A. Douglas. Each candidate dances with a member of his perceived constituency. Breckinridge is partnered with a goatlike President James Buchanan (who often supported Southerners on critical issues), and Lincoln dances with a black woman (who represents the Republican abolitionists). Why Bell has a Native American partner is not clear, but it may be a reference to some former nativist Know-Nothing Party members supporting him. Douglas's dance partner is a ragged Irishman, who is wearing a cross. Irish immigrants often joined the Democratic Party, and Protestant Americans viewed their Catholicism with suspicion.

Republicans. Almost forgotten in the turmoil was the fate of Dred Scott. Like Anthony Burns before him, he and his family were purchased by abolitionist friends and quietly freed a few months later.

## The Lincoln-Douglas Debates

In 1858, the increasingly volatile debate on slavery took center stage when the young Republican Party nominated Abraham Lincoln to challenge Stephen A. Douglas for the Illinois senate seat. Lincoln was a popular former state legislator, and he believed Douglas was vulnerable on slavery because of the ill will he created with the Kansas-Nebraska Act. In what became known as the "House Divided Speech," Lincoln accepted his party's nomination and predicted the nation was approaching a showdown. "In my opinion," he declared, "[the slavery debate] will not cease until a crisis shall have been reached and passed. 'A house divided against itself cannot stand.' I believe this government cannot endure permanently half slave and half free. I do not expect the Union to be dissolved; I do not expect the house to fall; but I do expect it will cease to be divided. It will become all one thing, or all the other."

Lincoln and Douglas agreed to hold seven debates in various Illinois towns, but they were more like dialogues since the candidates took turns speaking and rebutting one another rather than fielding questions from the audience or reporters. In his speeches, Lincoln praised the Republican Party for trying to contain slavery so it would die a natural death, and he claimed the Kansas-Nebraska Act proved Douglas was part of the Slave Power trying to spread the peculiar institution into the territories. The campaign, Lincoln declared, involved "the difference between the men who think slavery a wrong and those who do not think it wrong." Douglas, on the other hand, played to the racial prejudices of his Free-Soiler constituents and accused Lincoln of supporting social and political rights for blacks. In addition, he criticized Lincoln's House Divided Speech by pointing out that the nation had endured half free and half slave for decades and could continue to do so.

The most famous debate took place at Freeport, where 15,000 people looked on. Lincoln tried to lure Douglas into a trap by asking if the people of a territory could exclude slavery if they wished. If Douglas answered yes, he would be in violation of the Dred Scott decision and would anger the Southern voters whose support he needed to win the presidency in 1860. If he answered no, he would anger his Illinois constituents and perhaps lose the current senatorial election. Douglas was clever, and his response became known as the Freeport Doctrine. While admitting territories could not outlaw slavery, he argued the people could make it too expensive to bring slaves into a territory by placing high taxes or peace bonds on each slave. The Freeport Doctrine gave Northerners a legal way around the Dred Scott decision and won back some of the support Douglas had lost because of the Kansas-Nebraska Act. But it was a pyrrhic victory. Douglas had adopted popular sovereignty in the first place to win Southern support for his presidential bid. Now he had backtracked with the Freeport Doctrine, and Southerners felt betrayed. Douglas won the senatorial election, but his waffling on the slavery issue cost him Southern support and led to his defeat in the 1860 presidential race.

Douglas's Senate victory was attributable to skillfully playing on his constituents' racial fears and Democratic control of the legislature that actually elected U.S. senators. But most observers believed Lincoln won the debates with his insightful arguments and frequent use of humor. Lincoln appealed to many Free-Soilers because he did not advocate equality for African Americans. Instead, he argued slavery was wrong because it undermined the dignity of free labor by denying slaves the right to eat what they produced with their own hands. Lincoln came to be seen as the most articulate spokesman for the anti-slavery movement, and the debates were the beginning of his potential presidential bid because he gained much-needed national exposure and respect in the senate campaign.

## John Brown's Raid

By 1859, radicals on both sides were predicting the increasingly violent slavery debates might lead to bloodshed and war. Most confined themselves to bold talk; John Brown was an exception. Born in Connecticut, Brown moved frequently and suffered a succession of failed business ventures. He also married twice and fathered twenty children. A deeply religious man, Brown abhorred slavery and viewed himself as God's instrument to end the brutal system and punish the slaveholders. Becoming active in Bleeding Kansas, he and a group of followers retaliated for the attack on Lawrence by murdering five proslavery farmers on Pottawatomie Creek. Among Brown's men were four sons who helped murder the farmers on Brown's orders while he watched. Afterward, Brown received secret financial backing from some prominent abolitionists and devised a scheme to free slaves by attacking the federal arsenal at Harpers Ferry, Virginia, and stealing its weapons. He then would call on slaves to run away from the plantations and join him in the mountains of western Virginia to use the stolen rifles to fight for their freedom. Some came to question Brown's sanity (fifteen family members were treated for mental illness) because it should have been obvious that the federal government would not sit idly by while he attacked an arsenal and incited a violent uprising. Even Frederick Douglass, whom Brown informed of his plan, warned, "You're walking into a perfect steel-trap, and you will never get out alive." But there is no evidence Brown suffered from mental illness. Most likely, he knew the plan would fail but was willing to become a martyr for the abolitionist cause.

Brown and eighteen followers attacked Harpers Ferry, Virginia, in the predawn hours of October 16, 1859. Among his men were two of his sons and five African Americans, one of whom hoped to rescue his wife who was still held as a slave. Without opposition, Brown seized control of the town and took several hostages, including George Washington's great-grandnephew. The raiders also killed one man who tried to escape (ironically, a free black man),

**John Brown's Hanging, 1859.** John Brown was hanged in Virginia after being found guilty of murder for his Harpers Ferry raid. As this illustration depicts, many slaves turned out to witness the execution and honor Brown as a martyr.

but Brown mysteriously released the passengers on a train, and they alerted the militia. Brown was disappointed that none of the area's slaves heeded his call to join him, and by the next day hundreds of militiamen had converged on Harpers Ferry and forced him to seek refuge in the town's brick fire engine house. By then the federal government had sent Lieutenant Colonel Robert E. Lee with ninety Marines to take charge of the situation. When the raiders refused to surrender, Lee had the Marines storm the firehouse, and in a brief gun battle Brown was wounded, two of his men were killed, and all of the hostages were rescued. In all, ten of the raiders were killed (including his two sons), as were four citizens and one Marine. Brown and the eight survivors were quickly convicted of murder and other crimes, and Brown was hanged on December 2.

John Brown's Raid ignited the nation. When it was revealed that a number of wealthy abolitionists had helped finance the raid, Southerners branded Brown and all abolitionists common murderers who intended to end slavery through violent insurrection. While most Northerners condemned Brown's methods, they viewed him as a martyr because of his lofty goal to free the slaves. The song "John Brown's Body" became popular in the North, and during the Civil War its tune was put to Julia Ward Howe's lyrics and became "Battle Hymn of the Republic" (Howe's husband was one of Brown's secret supporters). John Brown's Raid was the last great divisive event before the crucial 1860 presidential election, and it helped destroy any hope the North and South had of finding a peaceful resolution to the slavery problem. Brown seemed to know what lay in store when he wrote one day before he was hanged, "I . . . am now quite *certain* that the crimes of this *guilty land: will* never be purged *away;* but with Blood."

In a strange twist of fate, John Brown brought together many famous Civil War figures. J. E. B. Stuart, Robert E. Lee's future cavalry commander, was a young lieutenant at the time and served as Lee's aide. Thomas J. Jackson, who would become immortalized as "Stonewall," commanded the Virginia Military Institute cadets who guarded Brown's hanging, and among the militiamen who witnessed the hanging was a popular actor named John Wilkes Booth.

## THE ELECTION OF 1860

**April 23, 1860: Democrats begin first convention in Charleston, South Carolina**
**May 9, 1860: Constitutional Union Party convention convenes in Baltimore, Maryland**
**May 18, 1860: Republicans begin convention in Chicago, Illinois**
**June 18, 1860: Democrats open second convention in Baltimore**
**November 6, 1860: Voters elect Lincoln president**

By 1860, the nation was on the verge of splitting over the slavery issue, and everyone knew the presidential election might by the last chance to prevent disunion. The best hope for maintaining the Union lay with the Democratic Party, which was the only true national party at the time. Virtually all Southerners were members, as were millions of Northerners. The Republican Party, however, was purely a Northern party devoted to stopping the spread of slavery. Unfortunately, the Democrats were fragile. Southern Democrats demanded the right to spread slavery to the western territories, while Northern Democrats demanded slavery be restricted to the South. The peculiar institution split the party like a wedge, and it was questionable whether the Democrats could breach the chasm.

## The Democratic Convention

In April 1860, the Democrats held their nominating convention in Charleston, South Carolina. The mood was tense as Northern and Southern delegates huddled together on street corners and in saloons pledging defiantly not to compromise on either the candidate or platform. Alabama delegate William L. Yancey even convinced the Deep South delegates to walk out of the convention en masse if the platform fell short of guaranteeing slavery in the territories. Stephen A. Douglas was the leading contender for nomination, but he, too, refused to compromise. Douglas was convinced the only way to save the nation was to adopt a platform pledging non-interference with slavery in the South while stopping its spread westward. Warning he would not accept the nomination if the platform supported the spread of slavery, Douglas declared, "I do not intend to make peace with my enemies nor to make a concession of one iota of principle." His determination to stand firm on one hand and the Southern commitment to bolt the convention on the other assured a dramatic showdown.

The great confrontation occurred when the Southern-controlled platform committee proposed a plank guaranteeing slavery in the territories. Gaining the floor, Yancey told the delegates, "Ours is the property invaded; ours are the institutions which are at stake; ours is the peace that is to be destroyed; ours is the honor at stake . . . all of which rests upon what your course may ultimately make a great heaving volcano of passion and crime. . . . Bear with us, then, if we stand sternly upon what is yet that dormant volcano, and say we yield no position here until we are convinced we are wrong." Rising to reply, George E. Pugh of Ohio defiantly warned the convention that millions of Northerners would never follow the lead of 300,000 slave drivers. "Gentlemen of the South," he declared, "you mistake us—you mistake us! We will not do it!" The Northerners then voted down the platform. Led by Alabama, the Deep South delegates immediately rose from their seats and dramatically filed out of the building. Cheers erupted when a Mississippian fired a parting shot to predict the Northerners would soon see a united South. With so many delegates departed, the remaining Democrats could not muster the required two-thirds vote to choose a candidate. The convention collapsed, and the remaining delegates soon adjourned and went home.

Realizing their inability to unite behind one candidate would almost certainly throw the election to the Republicans, the Democrats agreed to meet again in Baltimore to salvage the party, but the effort was hopeless. When the delegates arrived in June, neither side was in a mood to compromise. The second Democratic convention ended the same as the first, with the Southern delegates bolting when the Northerners refused to endorse a proslavery platform. Perhaps inevitably, the party then split into the Northern Democratic Party and the Southern Democratic Party. The Northerners nominated Douglas, who pledged not to interfere with slavery in the South but promised to stop its spread into the territories. The Southerners nominated Vice President John C. Breckinridge, a Kentucky slaveholder. His platform rested on the Dred Scott Decision, which recognized slaveholders' right to take their slaves into any territory. The slavery issue had finally destroyed Democratic unity and perhaps the nation's last chance for peace.

## The Republican Convention

A few weeks after the disastrous Charleston convention, the Republican Party met in Chicago. Unlike the somber and tension-filled Democratic gatherings, the Republican convention was filled with optimism and excitement. The 1860 Republican meeting was the largest presidential nominating convention in history at the time, and thousands of delegates and spectators swarmed into Chicago. The wild, raucous meeting was held in the Wigwam, the nation's largest auditorium, which boasted gas lighting and seating for 10,000 people. With the breakup of the Democratic Party, the Republicans knew their time had come, and they were confident of winning the election. It was only a matter of lining up behind the right candidate.

Meeting in Illinois was advantageous to Abraham Lincoln, but he was not the leading contender for the nomination. There were other, more famous, figures, most notably New York senator William H. Seward and Ohio governor Salmon P. Chase. Unfortunately for them, both were haunted by past mistakes. Seward had made many political enemies during his career, and some of his earlier remarks concerned voters. In an 1850 Senate speech, he claimed there was a "higher law than the Constitution" that should guide Americans in the slavery debate. In another speech a few years later at Rochester, New York, Seward predicted slavery had put the North and South on a collision course. There was, he warned, "an irrepressible conflict" on the horizon. Seward's calling on people to follow their religious scruples rather than constitutional law and his declaration that civil war was inevitable made many delegates think twice about nominating him. Salmon P. Chase had equally troubling baggage. He was not very well liked because he had a cold, impersonal nature and surrounded himself with supporters who had questionable ethics. One Republican claimed "every one of his entire political helpers that I know belongs to the class of cheats or nincompoops." Such weaknesses in the front-runners gave Lincoln, a virtual dark horse, a chance to win the nomination. Several influential newspapers backed his candidacy, and the Lincoln-Douglas Debates and Cooper Union Speech had earned him a great deal of respect. People also liked Lincoln's tough, direct western demeanor. "If slavery is right," he once declared, "it ought to be extended; if not, it ought to be restricted—there is no middle ground."

Lincoln and the other candidates did not attend the Chicago convention because it was considered bad taste for a politician to actively pursue the nomination. Instead, his interests were ably represented by campaign manager David Davis. Davis and others proved very effective in Chicago's backroom politicking, and they were not above using tricks to get their man nominated. Lincoln supporters controlled the delegates' seating in the Wigwam and made sure states strongly committed to Seward were isolated at the auditorium's far end and surrounded by other Seward supporters. Lincoln delegates hemmed in wavering states so their enthusiasm would hopefully persuade the uncommitted to vote for him. Davis also printed thousands of counterfeit tickets to pack the Wigwam with yelling Lincoln supporters, and he even brought in a cheerleader who was said to be able to yell across Lake Michigan. Davis ignored Lincoln's orders to the contrary and made secret deals with key politicians to win votes. Later, Lincoln was shocked to learn that Davis had even promised some cabinet positions, but Davis successfully formed an alliance between the western and northeastern states and secured Lincoln's nomination on the third ballot.

## The Panic of 1857 and the Republican Party

In forming their platform, the Republicans were able to take advantage of growing Northern anger toward Democratic politicians. Over the years, the Democrats had lowered the tariff, and many Northerners believed it was a major cause of an economic depression, the Panic of 1857. The nation's economy enjoyed some robust years following the Mexican War, but problems grew in the 1850s. The influx of California gold helped create inflation, and crop prices plummeted when European nations began purchasing less American grain after the Crimean War ended in 1856. A huge surplus in manufactured goods, speculation in land, and several railroad failures further weakened the economy. When a major insurance company closed in an embezzlement scandal, the economy collapsed. A number of interrelated factors caused the Panic of 1857, but many Northerners believed the low tariff was the main culprit because it allowed Great Britain to undersell American manufacturers.

The Panic of 1857 had a significant impact on American politics. Afterward, many Northerners supported the passage of a federal homestead act to help small farmers and others who had been financially ruined. They also wanted to use federal land to finance land grant colleges that would promote education in the mechanical arts and agriculture to strengthen those fields. With the help of President Buchanan's vetoes, however, the Southerners were able to defeat both proposals because they believed the states, not the federal government, should control the land within their borders. Besides the states' rights issue involved, Southerners had little incentive to support the programs. While the Panic of 1857 hit Northern industries hard, the cotton market rebounded quickly, causing Southerners to boast of the superiority of their agricultural system.

The Republican Party took advantage of political fallout from the Panic of 1857 by adopting its own version of Henry Clay's American System. The platform adopted at the Chicago convention promised to use federal power to uplift the nation economically through a higher tariff, homestead rights, internal improvements, and a transcontinental railroad. On the critical slavery issue, the Republicans recognized each state's right to decide for itself whether to allow slavery, but they called for federal legislation to prevent it from spreading to new territories.

## The Constitutional Union Party

One final nominating convention was held that spring. As tensions had increased over the previous decade and the nation had become polarized over slavery, some Democrats and former Whig and Know-Nothing Party members had organized the Union Party on the state level for the purpose of working toward political compromises to prevent the nation from fragmenting. In 1860, the Union Party decided the time was right to create a national Constitutional Union Party and enter the presidential race. Supported largely by the Border States, the party convened in Baltimore in early May. Its leaders promoted days gone by when public servants supposedly served the nation as a whole and not selfish political interests or particular parties. They hoped to offer voters a compromise candidate who represented neither the North nor the South and who could heal the sectional wounds that were ripping apart the nation.

The Constitutional Union Party nominated Senator John Bell, a moderate Tennessee slaveholder who had voted against the Kansas-Nebraska Act and the admission of Kansas as a slave state. Since Bell was running as a compromise candidate, his platform was intentionally vague so as not to offend anyone. Bell asked voters to support the Union, obey the law, and uphold the Constitution. Everyone could support this platform, but it depended on one's interpretation of the Union, the law, and the Constitution.

---

### DID YOU KNOW?

#### "Abe the Rail Splitter"

The mystique of "Abe the Rail Splitter" was born in the spring of 1860 when Illinois Republicans held their state convention. There, Lincoln's supporters wanted to create a catchy name for him much like Andrew "Old Hickory" Jackson and William Henry "Tippecanoe" Harrison. One Republican knew that Lincoln had split rails and performed other manual labor in his youth. Locating an old man who said Lincoln once helped him split rails, the delegate went out and procured two of the actual fence rails. When the state convention began, hundreds of rowdy supporters lifted Lincoln above their heads and carried him to a chair on the platform. Then, as the crowd cheered, the old man entered the room, with more supporters following him carrying the two rails and a banner proclaiming, "Abraham Lincoln. The Rail Candidate For President in 1860." A legend was born, but afterward one man claimed Lincoln's original rails had burned in a fire, and the two used in the convention were actually split by an "old, blind, and helpless" man who was eventually confined to a poorhouse.

# BIOGRAPHY

## Abraham Lincoln: The Great Emancipator

**Abraham Lincoln**

Abraham Lincoln (1809–1865) was born in a Kentucky log cabin to a modest frontier family, but he eventually settled in Springfield, Illinois. A powerful man standing six feet, four inches tall, he served as a militia captain in the Black Hawk War, became a prosperous lawyer, and was elected to the legislature four times as a Whig. In 1844, Lincoln married Mary Todd, a member of a prominent Kentucky slaveholding family who was also courted by Lincoln's political rival Stephen A. Douglas.

Lincoln served one term in Congress during the Mexican War, but he opposed the conflict because he believed it was started by Southerners to add more slave territory to the nation. Choosing not to stand for reelection, he returned to his law practice and joined the newly formed Republican Party. When Lincoln challenged Douglas for his Senate seat in 1858, he made an impressive showing in the campaign's debates through his clear reasoning and good use of frontier wit and humor. When Douglas once accused him of being two-faced, the admittedly unhandsome Lincoln replied, "I leave it to my audience. If I had another face, do you think I would wear this one?"

Elected president in 1860, Lincoln successfully worked with various political and military factions, and his homespun humor and eloquent speeches and writings made him popular with the people. He learned from his mistakes, did not hesitate to relieve generals who failed him, and proved to be both bold and ruthless. Lincoln imposed a blockade of questionable legal standing, suspended the writ of habeas corpus, and jailed hundreds of suspected Confederate sympathizers without charging them with a crime.

Some politicians made the mistake of not taking Lincoln seriously because of his frequent use of humor. Jokes, puns, and stories were a trademark, and he found

## The Threat of Secession

As the campaign heated up, more and more Southerners began to threaten secession if Lincoln was elected because they were convinced he intended to destroy slavery. Whether secession was constitutional may be debatable, but one has to wonder why the Southerners thought it was *necessary*. Southerners held tremendous power and influence in Congress and the Supreme Court because of committee seniority and lifelong appointments. Also, Lincoln could never have convinced Congress to abolish slavery, and he had no authority to do so on his own because slavery was sanctioned by the Constitution. Emancipation would have required three-fourths of the states to ratify a constitutional amendment, and that would have been impossible because well over one-fourth of the states supported slavery.

them to be an effective way to dismiss bothersome people. When a delegation tried to secure a diplomatic post to the Sandwich Islands for a friend who needed to live in a healthier climate, Lincoln sympathetically replied, "Gentlemen, I am sorry to say that there are eight other applicants for that place, and they are all sicker than your man." This humor masked the fact that the war took a great toll on him personally. Lincoln suffered from frequent bouts of depression, and telling jokes was how he lifted his spirits. As he explained to a friend, "I laugh because I must not cry; that is all—that is all."

There was much to depress Lincoln. Two of his four children died at an early age, including his beloved twelve-year-old son, Willie, who died in the White House. Hundreds of thousands of soldiers were killed and wounded, and Lincoln had constant problems with Mary, whose four stepbrothers and two brothers-in-law fought for the Confederates. When one of the latter, a Confederate general, was killed, Mary invited her widowed sister to live in the White House! Mary's emotional outbursts and her compulsive spending also put a strain on the marriage, but Lincoln was always loyal to her.

Despite Lincoln's popularity with many Northerners, his sometimes harsh wartime policies made him the target of relentless hate mail and condemnatory editorials. A New York newspaper called the president "that hideous baboon," and an Illinois paper referred to him as "the craftiest and most dishonest politician that ever disgraced an office in America." It was not until after his assassination that some came to appreciate his greatness. On April 14, 1865, just two days after Robert E. Lee surrendered at Appomattox, Virginia, John Wilkes Booth mortally wounded Lincoln while he attended a play at Ford's Theater in Washington, D.C. He died the next day without ever regaining consciousness. Lincoln's being shot on Good Friday—and after victory was achieved—elevated his stature to that of a martyr and ensured his place among the nation's greatest figures.

The Southerners embraced secession more out of fear of what the future might bring than from any immediate threat. The North's growing population would ultimately give it a majority both at the polls and in Congress, and there would come a time when the Yankees could stop the expansion of slavery into the territories, force protective tariffs on the South, and perhaps even abolish slavery itself. Although Lincoln publicly vowed he had no intentions of interfering with the peculiar institution where it already existed, many Southerners were convinced he was an abolitionist and would support emancipation if elected. It was perception that was important, not reality. In the face of the *perceived* Northern threat, the Southern radical fire-eaters embraced secession as the only way to defend slavery against a Northern majority. Once secession was accepted as a viable option, it was better to do it sooner than to wait until later when the North had grown even more powerful.

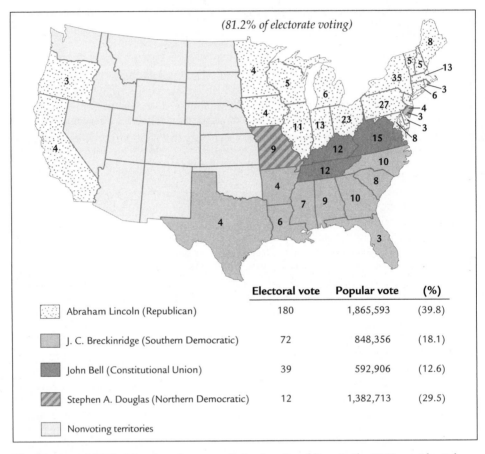

*(81.2% of electorate voting)*

| | Electoral vote | Popular vote | (%) |
|---|---|---|---|
| Abraham Lincoln (Republican) | 180 | 1,865,593 | (39.8) |
| J. C. Breckinridge (Southern Democratic) | 72 | 848,356 | (18.1) |
| John Bell (Constitutional Union) | 39 | 592,906 | (12.6) |
| Stephen A. Douglas (Northern Democratic) | 12 | 1,382,713 | (29.5) |
| Nonvoting territories | | | |

**The Election of 1860.** Most Americans voted along sectional lines in the 1860 presidential election. Lincoln, the antislavery candidate, won a majority of electoral votes by carrying the populous Northern states, while the proslavery candidate, Breckinridge, carried all of the Deep South. Moderate candidates Douglas and Bell split the Border States.

When voters went to the polls in November 1860, it became apparent that the Electoral College would work in the Republicans' favor. Although Lincoln received only 39 percent of the popular vote, he carried the large Northern states and won handily with 180 electoral votes, but he did not receive a single vote in the Deep South because those states refused to put him on the ballot. Breckinridge came in a distant second with 72 electoral votes, while Bell received 39 and Douglas only 12.

## THE SECESSION CRISIS

**December 6, 1860: Congress forms the Committee of Thirty-three**
**December 20, 1860: South Carolina secedes; Senate forms the Committee of Thirteen**

**January 9, 1861: Mississippi secedes**
**January 10, 1861: Florida secedes**
**January 11, 1861: Alabama secedes**
**January 19, 1861: Georgia secedes**
**January 26, 1861: Louisiana secedes**
**February 1, 1861: Texas secedes**
**February 4, 1861: Delegates convene Washington Peace Conference;**
    **Southerners begin Montgomery Convention to form Confederate States**
    **of America**
**February 18, 1861: Confederates inaugurate Jefferson Davis as president**
**March 4, 1861: United States inaugurates Abraham Lincoln as president**

Despite the great publicity given to the fire-eaters, Southern moderates held considerable influence throughout the campaign, and they shied away from secession and advised people to give the political process a chance. But even the moderates suspected Lincoln of having abolitionist tendencies and feared the Republicans might move against slavery if he won the race. This fear caused Southern public opinion to shift dramatically in favor of the secessionists when Lincoln was elected.

## Secession Winter

Always the hotbed of Southern radicalism, South Carolina acted first and convened a secession convention shortly after the election. Despite considerable opposition by moderates, the fire-eaters had their way, and the convention voted to secede on December 20, 1860. Other Deep South states quickly followed suit, and by the end of January 1861 Mississippi, Florida, Alabama, Georgia, and Louisiana also had withdrawn from the Union to protect their slavery rights. Throughout this "secession winter," lame-duck President James Buchanan was paralyzed with indecision. Although he personally did not support secession, he did not think he had the right to interfere and took no steps to prevent the nation's breakup.

The secessionists quickly began seizing all U.S. property within their borders, with some taking action before their states actually seceded. Federal forts, arsenals, mints, and customhouses were occupied by militiamen and declared state property. Although there were brief, tense standoffs between the militia and federal soldiers in some places, these

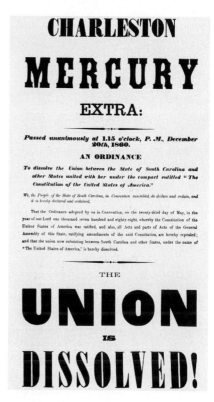

**Secession!** Southerners were convinced the Republican Party intended to destroy slavery and took drastic action after Lincoln won the 1860 election. South Carolina seceded a month later and was soon followed by six other states.

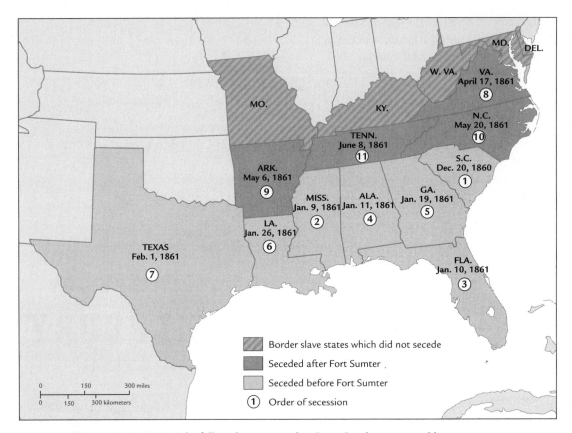

**Secession Winter, 1860–1861.** Like falling dominoes, other Deep South states quickly followed South Carolina into secession. The Upper South, however, was more moderate and those states did not secede until they were forced to take a stand after the firing on Fort Sumter. The Border States never seceded, although the Confederacy recognized Maryland and Kentucky as member states.

occupations were all carried out peacefully. As the secession movement picked up steam, Southern federal officials were forced to take a stand. Most Southern senators and congressmen resigned their positions and left Washington, as did Secretary of War John B. Floyd and Secretary of the Interior Jacob Thompson. Many Southern military officers also resigned their commissions and headed home. In Texas, General David E. Twiggs surrendered to the state all U.S. military positions *before* resigning his commission. Some Southerners, however, remained loyal to the Union. Among the more notable was Texas governor Sam Houston, who later resigned his office rather than swear allegiance to the Confederacy.

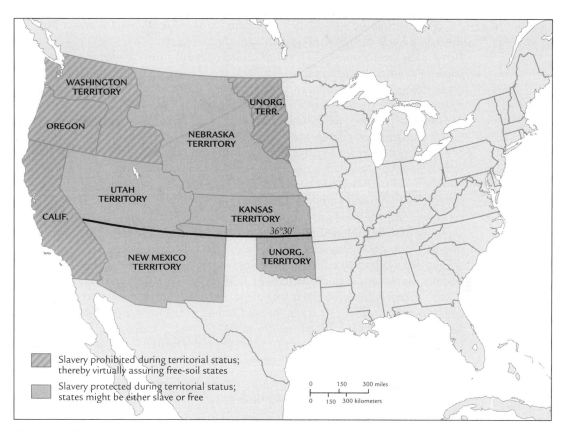

The Crittenden Compromise, 1860. In a desperate attempt to avoid disunion, Senator John J. Crittenden proposed a number of constitutional amendments to address the critical issues. One of them would have extended the old Missouri Compromise Line to California. Unfortunately, sectional passions were too inflamed for compromise, and Crittenden's proposal died in Congress.

## The Crittenden Committee

While President Buchanan did little in the weeks following the election, other politicians worked feverishly to prevent the nation's permanent dissolution. One of these was Kentucky senator John J. Crittenden. Not long after Lincoln's election, Crittenden proposed a series of Senate resolutions to prevent secession. In response, the Senate formed the Committee of Thirteen on the same day South Carolina seceded. Crittenden was appointed chairman, so it was commonly referred to as the Crittenden Committee, and it was charged with working out a compromise that would reunite the country. With eight Democrats and five Republicans, the committee represented different regional and political factions, and the members agreed they would not submit any proposal to the Senate unless it had the support of a majority of both Republican and Democratic committee members.

The committee agreed to use Crittenden's original Senate resolutions as the basis for a compromise, so the resultant proposal became known as the Crittenden Compromise. The compromise called for the passage of several constitutional amendments that would settle the slavery issue permanently. Among other things, these amendments would have reestablished the Missouri Compromise Line and extended it to California, required the federal government to compensate slaveholders for slaves who were aided in escape, and prohibited any future constitutional amendments from interfering with these amendments.

Crittenden's proposed amendments were quickly challenged. Southern committee members wanted even stronger slavery protection laws, while Northern members wanted to better protect Northern interests. After hours of discussion, the five Republicans voted against the proposal, mainly because they opposed reestablishing the Missouri Compromise Line. In the end, no recommendations were made to the Senate because the proposals failed to secure the approval of a majority of both Republican and Democratic committee members. Despite the committee's failure to endorse the compromise, Senator Crittenden decided on his own to present it to the Senate in January 1861. There it failed by a vote of 25 to 23, partly because president-elect Abraham Lincoln ordered Republican senators not to yield. "We have just carried an election on principles fairly presented to the people," he wrote. "Now we are told . . . the government will be broken up, unless we surrender to those we have beaten. . . . [I]f we surrender, it is the end of us, and of the government."

## The Committee of Thirty-three and the Washington Peace Conference

While the Senate tried to find a solution to the political crisis through the Crittenden Committee, the House of Representatives formed the Committee of Thirty-three. One congressman from each state was appointed to the committee to work out a compromise that would reunite the nation. Two proposals were ultimately made, both of which favored the South. One called for admitting the New Mexico Territory as a slave state, and the other called for an inalterable constitutional amendment guaranteeing slavery in the South, the enforcement of the Fugitive Slave Act, and the repeal of Northern Personal Liberty Laws. At first it seemed the Committee of Thirty-three might succeed because both houses of Congress passed the proposals by a two-thirds vote in February and March 1861, and they were submitted to the states in the form of a constitutional amendment. Unfortunately, the secession crisis had gone too far by then, and war erupted before the amendment could be ratified.

Virginia, with the strong support of the Border States, made one final attempt at compromise by sponsoring a peace conference in the nation's capital. The Washington Peace Conference, also derisively called the "Old Gentlemen's Convention," convened on February 4, 1861, with twenty-one states participating (none of the six seceded states attended). The delegates eventually recommended several constitutional amendments to Congress that were similar to those proposed by the Crittenden Committee. Unfortunately, by that time no one was in a mood to make any real concessions, and this last attempt to avoid disunion failed in Congress.

## The Confederate States of America

On February 4, 1861—the same day the Washington Peace Conference convened—the six seceding states met in Montgomery, Alabama, to create a separate nation. Texas seceded just days before and soon joined her sister states at this Montgomery Convention. Working largely in secret, the fifty delegates formed the Confederate States of America and declared themselves the Provisional Confederate Congress. In just five days they created a new government; adopted a constitution; elected Jefferson Davis and Alexander Stephens as provisional president and vice-president, respectively; created a cabinet, post office, and court system; authorized a Confederate army; and issued $15 million in treasury bonds. The new Confederate government made Montgomery its capital, but shortly after war erupted it was moved to Richmond, Virginia.

A month later, the Provisional Congress approved a permanent constitution (see Chapter 13). Because of their reverence for the U.S. Constitution, secessionists had no qualms about basing the new Confederate government on the old republic they loved so much. They believed it was only necessary to make a few constitutional changes to address the most important issues of slavery, limited government, states' rights, and tariffs. The Confederate Constitution removed ambiguities on these subjects to prevent any future interpretive disagreements—most significantly, it prohibited Congress or any state from passing laws that interfered with a person's right to own slaves or to take them into any part of the Confederacy. When the Constitution was ratified by the necessary five states on March 26, President Davis proudly proclaimed, "The Constitution framed by our Fathers is that of these Confederate States."

## The War of Words

On February 18, 1861, under a bright, sunny noonday sky, Jefferson Davis and Alexander Stephens rode in an open carriage from Montgomery's Exchange Hotel to the Alabama State House to be sworn into office. Thousands of spectators lined the street, and the governors of the seceded states walked in procession behind the carriage. The crowd cheered and tossed flowers, and cannons fired in salute as the two rode triumphantly through town. As Davis mounted the porch to give his inaugural address, a band played the "Marseillaise" because there was no Confederate national anthem. In a strong, clear voice he defended the necessity of secession and warned the United States to let the Confederate states go in peace. The creation of the Confederacy, Davis said, was in keeping with "the American idea that governments rest upon the

# BIOGRAPHY

## Jefferson Davis: The Reluctant President

**Jefferson Davis**

Jefferson Davis (1808–1889) was born in Kentucky, but the family moved to Woodville, Mississippi, when he was a child. An 1824 West Point graduate, he resigned his commission in 1835 and married Sarah Knox Taylor, the daughter of Zachary Taylor and the sister of future Confederate general Richard Taylor. Just months after their wedding, "Knoxie" died from fever and a grief-stricken Davis secluded himself on his plantation for years. He eventually married Varina Howell, who was nearly twenty years his junior, and had four sons and two daughters, but three of his children died at a young age. One, Joseph Evan Davis, died during the Civil War when he fell from a balcony at the Confederate White House.

In 1845, Davis was elected to Congress as a Democrat, but he resigned his seat when the Mexican War began and served in his former father-in-law's army as colonel of the 1st Mississippi Rifles. Davis became a hero at the Battle of Buena Vista when he deployed his regiment in an unorthodox manner and annihilated a Mexican lancer charge. One soldier remembered that Davis had stayed on the field even after suffering a serious foot wound and claimed Davis "could infuse courage into the bosom of a coward, and self-respect and pride into the breast of the most abandoned." After the war, Davis was elected to the U.S. Senate and served as President Franklin Pierce's secretary of war. Returning to the Senate in 1857, he staunchly defended Southern rights but did not embrace secession until it became evident no compromise was going to be reached on slavery. He then resigned his seat in January 1861.

Although he preferred a military command, Davis reluctantly accepted the position of Confederate president. Varina remembered how he informed her of his appointment

consent of the governed, and that it is the right of the people to alter or abolish governments whenever they become destructive of the ends for which they were established." The Confederate people hoped to be allowed to depart without violence, but "if this be denied to us, and the integrity of our territory and jurisdiction be assailed, it will but remain for us, with firm resolve, to appeal to arms and invoke the blessings of Providence on a just cause. . . ."

When Davis made his inaugural address, Abraham Lincoln was traveling by train from Springfield, Illinois, to Washington. Thousands of people crowded the tracks and stations to get a glimpse of the first president born west of the Appalachian Mountains. At each stop, Lincoln appeared on the rear platform to say a few words to the crowd. At one stop, future president Rutherford B. Hayes was amused at Lincoln's awkwardness. When he bowed to the crowd, Hayes wrote, "His chin rises—his body breaks in two at the hips—there is bend of the "as a man might speak of a sentence of death." Davis was a devoted nationalist, who, ironically, tried to limit the very states' rights he had championed so long. He supported America's first national military conscription act, the suspension of the writ of habeas corpus, putting state militia under national control, and an impressment act to obtain much-needed supplies. Davis was honest, worked tirelessly, had the tenacity of a bull-dog, felt great empathy for his people, and probably did as well as anyone could have as Confederate president.

Davis's personality proved to be his greatest weakness as president. He immersed himself in unnecessary minutia and insisted on overseeing every administrative detail. Davis also was thin-skinned and took offense at any criticism. Even Varina admitted he "was abnormally sensitive to disapprobation; even a child's disapproval discomposed him." His abrasive personality was aggravated by chronic poor health that often incapacitated Davis and made him ill-tempered. One particularly troublesome ailment was an infection that left him virtually blind in the left eye. Other notable Davis traits were a lack of tact, a pettiness that caused him to hold grudges, and a tendency to stand by incompetent generals whom he liked while banishing to unimportant positions skillful officers whom he disliked. By war's end, Davis's personal flaws had alienated many generals, newspaper editors, and politicians, but he never gave up hope for final victory.

Davis was captured in May 1865 near Irwinville, Georgia, and imprisoned for two years in Fort Monroe, Virginia. He was shackled and hooded much of the time, and his harsh confinement turned him into a martyr for the Lost Cause. After being released in May 1867, Davis failed at several business ventures before he finally accepted an offer to live at Beauvoir, a friend's house in Biloxi, Mississippi. He spent his time corresponding with various war figures and writing his two-volume *Rise and Fall of the Confederate Government,* in which he continued to attack his critics and praise his friends. Davis died in 1889 at age eighty-two, having lived much longer than anyone expected.

knees at a queer angle . . . homely as L. is, if you can get a good view of him by *day light* when he is talking he is by no means ill looking." Later, at a small New York town, Lincoln met and kissed Grace Bedell, a young girl who had written the president-elect earlier advising him to grow a beard to improve his looks.

At Philadelphia, Allan Pinkerton, the nation's most famous private detective, warned Lincoln he would be assassinated when the train passed through Baltimore, Maryland, a known beehive of secessionist activity. Lincoln was persuaded to depart from his published schedule and pass through Baltimore in the dead of night. With Pinkerton and one bodyguard, he boarded a special train disguised in an overcoat and felt hat and reached Washington undetected, but newspapers roundly condemned the midnight ride. While the nation was splitting apart and war loomed on the horizon, the president-elect slipped into the capital like a thief in the night. Journalists greatly exaggerated the incident, and cartoonists

## EYEWITNESS
### Alexander Stephens

*At 7:30 p.m. on March 21, 1861, recently installed Confederate vice president Alexander Stephens addressed a crowd at the Athenaeum in Savannah, Georgia. One reporter claimed it was the largest audience ever assembled in the building. In anticipation of the speech, the huge crowd gave Stephens a thunderous round of applause when he came on stage with the city's mayor and other dignitaries. After being introduced, Stephens spoke to the people about the crisis facing the Confederate States. No official version of the extemporaneous speech was ever printed, but the Savannah* Republican *printed this copy. All italics were in the original.*

. . . .The new Constitution has put at rest *forever* all the agitating questions relating to our peculiar institutions—African slavery as it exists among us—the proper *status* of the negro in our form of civilization. *This was the immediate cause of the late rupture and present revolution.* JEFFERSON, in his forecast, had anticipated this, as the "rock upon which the old Union would split." He was right. What was conjecture with him, is now a realized fact. But whether he fully comprehended the great truth upon which that rock *stood* and *stands*, may be doubted. *The prevailing ideas entertained by him and most of the leading statesmen at the time of the formation of the old Constitution were, that the enslavement of the African was in violation of the laws of nature; that it was wrong in principle, socially, morally and politically.* It was an evil they knew not well how to deal with; but the general opinion of the men of that day was, that, somehow or other, in the order of Providence, the institution would be evanescent and pass away. This idea, though not incorporated in the Constitution, was the prevailing idea at the time. The Constitution it is true, secured every essential guarantee to the institution while it should last, and hence no argument can be justly used against the constitutional guarantees thus secured, because of the common sentiment of the day. *Those ideas, however, were fundamentally wrong.*

even portrayed the disguised Lincoln wearing a Scottish plaid cap and kilt. It was an inauspicious beginning, and he forever regretted the entire incident.

On March 4, 1861, Lincoln and President James Buchanan climbed into an open carriage at Willard's Hotel and rode down Pennsylvania Avenue toward the Capitol Building. Unlike the festive mood in Montgomery for Jefferson Davis's inauguration, Washington was subdued and somber. Soldiers blocked the side streets along the route, sharpshooters dotted the rooftops, and two batteries of artillery were stationed nearby ready for action. After watching Vice President Hannibal Hamlin take his oath of office at the Capitol, Lincoln walked outside onto a platform and was introduced to the crowd. When he seemed unsure what to do with his stovepipe hat, former rival Senator Stephen A. Douglas stepped up, quietly said, "Permit me, sir," and took it from him. Lincoln then pulled out a few sheets of paper and began to read his inaugural address. His

*They rested upon the assumption of the equality of races. This was an error. It was a sandy foundation, and the idea of a Government built upon it—when the "storm came and the wind blew, it fell."*

*Our new Government is founded upon exactly the opposite ideas; its foundations are laid, its cornerstone rests, upon the great truth that the negro is not equal to the white man; that slavery, subordination to the superior race, is his natural and moral condition [Applause]. This, our new Government, is the first, in the history of the world, based upon this great physical, philosophical, and moral truth. . . .*

. . . It is the first Government ever instituted upon principles in strict conformity to nature, and the ordination of Providence, in furnishing the materials of human society. Many Governments have been founded upon the principles of certain classes; but the classes thus enslaved, were of the same race, and in violation of the laws of nature. Our system commits no such violation of nature's laws. The negro by nature, or by the curse against Canaan, is fitted for that condition which he occupies in our system. . . . The substratum of our society is made of the material fitted by nature for it, and by experience we know that it is the best, not only for the superior but for the inferior race, that it should be so.

*When Stephens sat down, the reporter claimed the auditorium exploded "amid a burst of enthusiasm and applause, such as the Athenaeum has never had displayed within its walls." The "Cornerstone Speech" clearly placed slavery at the heart of secession. But not everyone was so enthusiastic. The speech dismayed President Jefferson Davis because he knew it would give antislavery Europe pause in extending diplomatic recognition to the Confederacy.*

Frank Moore, ed., *The Rebellion Record* (New York: G. P. Putnam, 1861), Vol. 1, pp. 44–49.

voice, according to one witness, was "not very strong or full-toned," but it carried to every person in the crowd.

Lincoln again stated he had no intentions of interfering with slavery where it already existed, but he did promise to defend all federal property and collect all tariffs. As for the slavery question, he declared, "One section of our country believes slavery is *right,* and ought to be extended, while the other believes it is *wrong,* and ought not to be extended. This is the only substantial dispute. . . ." Claiming conflict was not inevitable, Lincoln told the Southerners, "In *your* hands, my dissatisfied fellow countrymen, and not in *mine,* is the momentous issue of civil war. The government will not assail *you.* You can have no conflict without being yourselves the aggressors. *You* have no oath registered in Heaven to destroy the government, while *I* shall have the most solemn one to 'preserve, protect, and defend it.'" In closing, Lincoln pleaded, "We are not enemies, but friends. We must not be enemies. Though passion may have strained, it must not break our bonds of affection. The mystic cords of memory, stretching from every battle-field, and patriot grave, to every living heart and hearth-stone, all over this broad land, will yet swell the chorus of the Union, when again touched, as surely they will be, by the better angels of our nature." Lincoln's speech was a mixture of conciliatory words to the South and an unflinching commitment to the Union. However, he left no doubt as to his intentions to defend all federal property, and everyone knew that his commitment would soon be tested.

## FOR FURTHER READING

Charles Sumner's Speech, "The Crime Against Kansas"
Abraham Lincoln's "House Divided" Speech
Seward's "Irrepressible Conflict" Speech
Seward's "Higher Law" Speech
Lincoln's first inaugural address
Davis's inaugural address
South Carolina's secession ordinance
Stephens's "Cornerstone Speech"

# CHAPTER 3

# War!

The Outbreak of War

The Border States

The First Campaigns

In the predawn hours of April 12, 1861, 38-year-old Mary Chesnut tossed in her Charleston, South Carolina, bed unable to sleep. That night her husband James, a Confederate congressman, had joined a handful of other dignitaries in rowing out to Fort Sumter to make one final surrender demand of Major Robert Anderson's Union garrison. They informed Anderson that if he did not surrender by 4:00 a.m., the Confederate batteries would open fire. In her diary, Mary wrote, "I do not pretend to go to sleep. How can I? If Anderson does not accept terms—at four—the orders are—he shall be fired upon. I count four—St. Michael [church bell] chimes. I begin to hope." Thirty minutes later, she heard the deep boom of cannon fire in the distance. "I sprang out of bed. And on my knees—prostrate—I prayed as I never prayed before. . . ." Suddenly, the house was astir with people running to the roof to get a glimpse of the bombardment, and Mary hurried to join them. "I knew my husband was rowing about in a boat somewhere in that dark bay," she scribbled. "And that the shells were roofing it over—bursting toward the fort. . . . The women were wild, there on the housetop. Prayers from the women and imprecations from the men, and then a shell would light up the scene." Faint from worry and excitement, Mary sat down on what she thought was a black stool. "Get up, you foolish woman," a nearby man suddenly yelled, "your dress is on fire." As he quickly patted out the flames, Mary realized she had sat down on a chimney.

Mary and her fellow boarders watched the bombardment continue throughout the day. The noise was so overwhelming regular meals were dispensed with. "None of us go to table," she wrote. "But tea trays pervade the corridors, going everywhere. Some of the anxious hearts lie on their beds and moan in solitary misery." Despite their worry, the women were convinced of victory. Mary noted in her diary, "'God is on our side,' they cry. When we are shut in, we (Mrs. Wigfall and I) ask, 'Why?' We are told: 'Of course He hates the Yankees.'"

As the day wore on, Mary noticed the slaves were the calmest of all the people in the house. "Not by one word or look can we detect any change in the demeanor of these negro servants. . . . You could not tell that they hear even the awful row that is going on in the bay, though it is dinning in their ears night and day. And people talk before them as if they were chairs and tables. And they make no sign. Are they stolidly stupid or wiser than we are, silent and strong, biding their time?" Although they never expressed their innermost thoughts, it is likely the house slaves were thinking the same thing as the whites they served: The Civil War had begun, and nothing would ever be the same again.

## THE OUTBREAK OF WAR

**April 12, 1861: Confederates bombard Fort Sumter**
**April 13, 1861: Fort Sumter surrenders**
**April 15, 1861: Lincoln calls for 75,000 volunteers to put down
    the rebellion**
**April 17, 1861: Virginia secedes**
**April 25, 1861: Tennessee secedes**
**May 6, 1861: Arkansas secedes**
**May 20, 1861: North Carolina secedes; Kentucky declares neutrality**

*Taking control as many south States as possible*

After Lincoln's election, the secessionists quickly began seizing control of the many federal installations in the South. The garrisons of two forts, however, refused surrender demands and prepared to defend themselves. In Pensacola, Florida, U.S. soldiers continued to occupy Fort Pickens on Santa Rosa Island despite being threatened by a large number of secessionists. A similar confrontation took place in the harbor at Charleston, South Carolina. There in late December 1860, Major Robert Anderson evacuated Fort Moultrie on the mainland and moved about 120 soldiers and civilian workers to Fort Sumter, a massive brick fort that sat on a manmade island in the middle of the harbor. With a large complement of cannons and imposing twelve-foot-thick walls, Fort Sumter was much easier to defend than Fort Moultrie. Federal authorities dispatched the *Star of the West* to deliver desperately needed supplies to Anderson, but the South Carolina militia forced it to retire on January 9, 1861, by firing a shot across its bow. President Buchanan made no further attempts to relieve the garrison, but the newly formed Confederate army assembled several thousand troops under Brigadier General P. G. T. Beauregard to take the fort by force if necessary.

### Fort Sumter

No president has ever faced as dangerous a crisis as did Lincoln when he was inaugurated on March 4, 1861. Seven states had left the Union, and the secessionists had seized all federal installations except Forts Sumter and Pickens. Lincoln was willing to consider any reasonable solution to keep the nation united, including a constitutional guarantee of slavery in the South, but he would compromise only within limits. In his inaugural address, Lincoln put the issue of war squarely on the Southerners' shoulders. Having taken an oath to defend all U.S. property, he declared, he would not abandon the two forts. But neither would he take any aggressive action against the South. If war was in the offing, the Confederates would have to initiate it.

The immediate decision facing Lincoln was whether to resupply and reinforce Fort Sumter (Fort Pickens was not as critical because it could be safely supplied by sea out of Confederate cannon range). When asked to summarize the military situation, General-in-Chief Winfield Scott informed the president it would take a large naval force and 25,000 soldiers to secure the fort. Since the entire U.S. Army numbered only 16,000 men, Lincoln did not have enough troops to save the fort, and Major Anderson had only enough supplies to hold out a few more weeks. If the president sent an unarmed supply expedition, the secessionists would undoubtedly fire on the ships and there would be war. It appeared the fort was doomed no matter what course of action Lincoln took.

Every fiber in Lincoln's being told him to support Major Anderson, but on March 15 the majority of his cabinet members advised against trying to resupply Fort Sumter. The cabinet's mood, however, changed suddenly when General Scott informed the president that the only way to ensure the loyalty of Virginia and the other Upper South states was to surrender both Sumter and Pickens. Outraged at what they viewed as blackmail, most of the cabinet members then changed their minds and advised Lincoln to resupply both forts. Many powerful Republicans had been advising Lincoln all along to do just that. This growing support among party members strengthened the president's hand, and he immediately ordered a relief expedition to prepare to sail from New York.

Lincoln was not the only president determined to defend his nation. Jefferson Davis had also taken a sworn oath of office, and the defense of the Confederacy required the United States to abandon all of its installations in the Deep South. If Lincoln refused to do so peacefully, Davis would use force to drive out the Yankees. When the Confederates learned that Lincoln was preparing a relief expedition to Fort Sumter, they made one last surrender demand on April 11, but Anderson refused. Anderson did note, however, that he had only enough supplies to hold out a few more days. Knowing he could not withstand a Confederate attack, he hoped Beauregard would simply wait until the food ran out so he could surrender with honor. The Confederates, however, had to settle the matter before the Union reinforcements arrived, so they opened fire early in the morning of April 12. Anderson realized he was in a hopeless position and kept his men safely holed up deep inside the fort's bunkers and only occasionally returned fire. After enduring a 33-hour bombardment, he finally surrendered the battered fort on April 13. Incredibly, no one on either side was killed.

**Confederate Flag at Fort Sumter.**  The battered walls of Fort Sumter's interior testify to the effectiveness of the Rebels' bombardment. The flag whipping in the breeze is the Confederacy's First National Flag.

Anderson =
Beau = con

which

Unlike many of the battles that followed, the fight for Fort Sumter was conducted with great chivalry, partly because the two commanders were well acquainted. Major Anderson had been Beauregard's artillery instructor years earlier when Beauregard was a cadet at West Point. When the fort caught fire during the bombardment, Beauregard had an aide row out to ask the defenders if they needed help putting out the flames. When he was assured they did not, he allowed Anderson's men time to douse the fire and get back in their bunkers before resuming the cannonade. On another occasion, the Union relief expedition arrived off Charleston during the bombardment, but when the Yankee sailors made no attempt to reinforce Fort Sumter or help put out the fires, the disgusted Confederate gunners loudly booed them for not showing as much grit as Anderson's beleaguered garrison.

To honor the Union soldiers' bravery, Beauregard allowed Anderson to fire a 100-gun salute to the flag he had so doggedly defended. On the 50th shot, the Civil War's first fatality occurred when a cannon accidentally exploded and killed one of the Union artillerymen. Anderson took the fort's flag with him when he returned to the North, and he later retired from the army. In the war's waning days, he was invited back to South Carolina to participate in a victory ceremony. Four years to the day after he took down Sumter's flag in surrender, Brigadier General Robert Anderson had the pleasure of triumphantly hoisting it back over the fort.

## Mobilization

The booming cannons at Fort Sumter drowned out all talk of peace. Lincoln officially declared that the South was in rebellion, ordered a naval blockade of Southern ports, and placed a recruitment quota on each state to raise 75,000 volunteers to put down the insurrection. This last action was little more than an ultimatum to the slaveholding Border States that had not yet seceded. The recruitment quota forced every state to decide whether to stand with the Union and help put down the rebellion or to secede and join the Confederacy. Arkansas, Tennessee, Virginia, and North Carolina refused the call for troops, seceded, and joined their sister Southern states. In Montgomery, Jefferson Davis responded to Lincoln's declarations by issuing his own call for 32,000 volunteers to defend the Confederacy.

War hysteria swept America as volunteers answered their president's call for troops. No one expected the conflict to last long, and one politician naively boasted he could soak up in his handkerchief all the blood that would be spilled. Most people believed the war would be decided by one or two battles, and young men on both sides wanted to enlist and be a part of the adventure before peace was restored. So many recruits signed up that neither government could train or equip them all.

## Union Advantages

The North held all of the obvious military advantages when the Civil War began. There eventually were 25 Union states, with about 22,000,000 people, fighting 11 Confederate states, with about, 9,000,000 people (Table 1.). (Confederate governments were also created in exile for Kentucky and Maryland, which never officially seceded.) The Union's advantage in manpower was even more impressive in light of the fact that both armies initially depended on the white population for their soldiers. Almost the entire Union population was white, while the Confederacy had only 5,500,000 whites. The South's 3,500,000 slaves were an important source of labor to the Confederacy, but they were not considered as potential soldiers when the war began.

Table 1   *Number of Men in Uniform at Date Given*

| Date | Union | Confederate |
|---|---|---|
| July 1861 | 186,751 | 112,040 |
| January 1862 | 575,917 | 351,418 |
| March 1862 | 637,126 | 401,395 |
| January 1863 | 918,121 | 446,622 |
| January 1864 | 860,737 | 481,180 |
| January 1865 | 959,460 | 445,203 |

# BIOGRAPHY

## Pierre Gustave Toutant Beauregard: Creole General

**P. G. T. Beauregard**

Born into a prominent Louisiana Creole family, P. G. T. Beauregard (1818–1893) did not learn to speak English until he attended school in New York City and studied under two brothers who were former officers in Napoleon's army. After graduating second in the 1838 West Point class, he served with distinction with the engineers in the Mexican War under Winfield Scott. Rising to the rank of captain, Beauregard was made West Point's superintendent in January 1861, but the appointment lasted only five days. Like many other Southern officers, he was a secessionist, and his suspicious superiors ordered him to relinquish the superintendent's position after Louisiana seceded.

Beauregard resigned his commission in February 1861 to join the Confederacy, and he eventually became the South's fifth ranking general. Of medium build with dark eyes and olive complexion, he spoke with a slight French accent and was a very dashing, charming man. One subordinate recalled that Beauregard "had more courtesy of manner than any of the other generals with whom I had ever served." Beauregard became the South's first military hero when he captured Fort Sumter, won the First Battle of Bull Run, and designed the Confederate battle flag. He also advised Davis to abandon Southern territory in order to concentrate Confederate strength at strategic points and launch decisive counterattacks against the Union. "The whole science of war," wrote Beauregard, "may be briefly defined as the art of placing in the right position, at the right time, a mass of troops greater than your enemy can there oppose to you." Although Beauregard's plans sometimes had merit, they often were little more than wild fantasies because he tended to overestimate the Confederacy's abilities, and they clashed with Davis's defensive-offensive strategy.

After the First Battle of Bull Run, Beauregard was transferred to the Department of the West. He assumed command of the army when General Albert Sidney Johnston

In virtually all of the major military campaigns, the opposing armies depended on railroads to bring supplies and soldiers to the front and to evacuate the wounded. The Civil War, in fact, was the first war in which railroads were widely used, and the Union again had a huge advantage, producing 451 locomotives in 1861 to the South's 19. The Union also had about 21,000 miles of track (it would lay another 4,000 miles during the war), while the Confederacy had only 9,000 miles. Making matters worse for the Confederates was the fact that trains from one company often could not travel the rails of another because they were of a different gauge. Also, there frequently were long shipping delays in major Confederate cities because the competing companies' tracks did not always connect within a town. Cargo and men often had to be offloaded on one side of town, hauled through the streets, and then reloaded on the other side.

was killed at Shiloh and retreated on the second day of fighting. Unfortunately for Beauregard, he and President Davis had become bitter enemies by that time. Earlier, Beauregard had claimed Davis prevented him from making the victory at First Bull Run more complete by not allowing him to pursue the beaten foe. Davis was furious at Beauregard's official report and told the general it looked like "an attempt to exalt yourself at my expense." Beauregard denied such motives but insultingly replied, "I have always pitied more than I have envied those in high authority." The feud worsened when Beauregard misled Davis by sending a telegram claiming he had won a great victory at Shiloh and then by unexpectedly retreating. When the general took sick leave without permission, Davis removed him from command and shuttled him off to the Department of South Carolina.

Bitter at his demotion, Beauregard complained that the Confederacy had not yet produced a truly great general because "we have a power near the *throne* too egotistical and jealous to allow such a genius to develop itself." Nonetheless, he worked tirelessly to improve Charleston's defenses, and he successfully turned back several Union naval attacks. Eventually transferred to the Department of North Carolina, Beauregard performed one of his greatest wartime services when he cobbled together a small force and stopped a Union attack on Petersburg in the spring of 1864. A few weeks later, he again performed admirably by holding off a much superior Union army and buying precious time that allowed General Lee to arrive to protect the Richmond-Petersburg area. Despite these important victories, Beauregard was never assigned another army command.

After the war, Beauregard was a railroad executive, a representative of the corrupt Louisiana Lottery Company, and Louisiana's adjutant general. One of the Civil War's more controversial generals, he was a talented officer but often an unrealistic one whose pride and pettiness prevented him from enjoying a cordial relationship with most of his superiors.

The North also used its superior railway system much more efficiently than did the South. The Union created the U.S. Military Railroads System and placed the railroads under government control to facilitate their use for the war effort. The Confederate government, however, never took any steps to control what track it did have. The Confederacy's small industrial base also made it difficult to build new tracks (it would lay only another 400 miles during the war), and it could do little to straighten out damaged rails. By war's end, the Confederate railway system was in shambles, suffering from a lack of locomotives and rolling stock and unable to repair damage caused by enemy cavalry raids. The steady decline of its rail system seriously weakened the Confederacy by hampering the government's ability to transport men and supplies to where they were most needed.

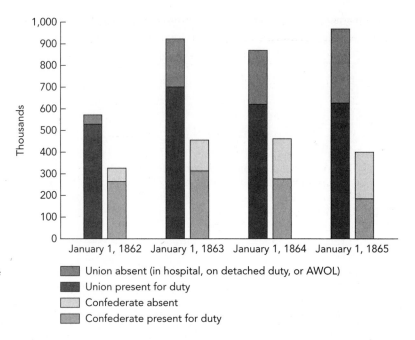

**Comparative Strength of Union and Confederate Armies.** Manpower was just one of many areas in which the North had a huge advantage over the South. However, both armies suffered a high attrition rate. By 1865, more than half of all Confederate soldiers were away from their units in the hospital, on detached duty, or absent without leave.

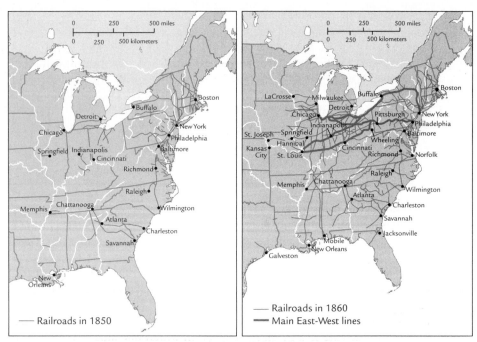

**Railroad Growth, 1850–1860.** The Civil War was the world's first railroad war, with opposing armies depending on railroads for supplies and mobility. These two maps illustrate the tremendous railroad construction that occurred in the decade prior to the war. Note the great advantage held by the North in railroad transportation.

Industrial capacity was another tremendous advantage enjoyed by the Union. The Northern states produced more than 92 percent of the nation's gross domestic product in 1860 and boasted more than 100,000 industrial establishments to the Confederacy's 18,000. All of the major arms manufacturers, such as Springfield, Colt, and Remington, were located in the North. Incredibly, both New York and Pennsylvania *alone* had a larger industrial output than all of the Confederate states *combined*. The North also produced 20 times more pig iron and 17 times more textiles than the Confederacy. And the advantages did not stop there. The Union had a well-trained, albeit small, army and navy; a powerful, experienced national government; a sound financial and monetary system; and an active diplomatic service. The United States was an established nation and had to concentrate only on winning the war, while the Confederacy not only had to defend itself from attack but had to create a new government at the same time.

## Confederate Advantages

It should be realized that the Union's overwhelming advantages did not guarantee victory. History is filled with examples of the weaker side prevailing in wartime, and in some areas the North actually was at a disadvantage. In military strategy, for example, the burden of victory rested with the Union because it had to assume the offensive and actually conquer the Confederacy to win the war. But the Confederacy was huge, about the size of Western Europe, and many observers predicted the Union could never completely conquer it. The Confederacy, on the other hand, could win the war by simply defending its territory and surviving until the North tired of the conflict and quit.

The opposing armies also were more evenly matched than they might have seemed at first glance. While the North enjoyed a tremendous advantage in population, conventional military wisdom in the nineteenth century stated that an attacking force had to be three times larger than the defending force to have a reasonable chance of success. Thus, the four-to-one advantage the Union enjoyed in white population was not as overwhelming as it might have seemed. In addition, the Confederates were convinced they were the superior soldiers and that one Rebel could whip ten Yankees any day. Southerners even had historical precedent to boost their confidence. During the American Revolution, the colonies had won independence against odds that were as great as, if not greater than, those faced by the Confederacy. And it was not lost on the Confederates that some of the Revolution's greatest heroes—George Washington, Thomas Jefferson, Patrick Henry, Francis Marion, Richard Henry Lee, and Dan Morgan—had been Southerners.

The interior line was another advantage the Confederacy had over the Union. The *interior line* is a military concept in which one side can transport men and supplies to any given place more quickly than the other. Generally, the interior line is determined by how transportation systems such as roads, railroads, and rivers are laid out. It usually occurs when one side's position is within a curved boundary so it can shift men and material from one point to another

| Population | North | South |
|---|---|---|
| | 61% | 39% |

| Railroad Mileage | | |
|---|---|---|
| | 66% | 34% |

| Farms | | |
|---|---|---|
| | 67% | 33% |

| Wealth Produced | | |
|---|---|---|
| | 75% | 25% |

| Factories | | |
|---|---|---|
| | 81% | 19% |

**Union and Confederate Resources.** The Union dwarfed the Confederacy in every major war resource. The North even had twice as many farms as the South, even though the South's economy was based almost entirely on agriculture.

along a straight line or radius while the opposing side has to travel around the arc of the circle. On a number of occasions, the Confederacy took advantage of its interior line to mass troops for a particular battle faster than the Union.

Other factors working in the South's favor were geography and the hope of foreign intervention. The Confederates had the advantage of fighting mainly on their own soil, and familiarity with the countryside was vital at a time when accurate maps still did not exist. They had little difficulty acquiring guides who could lead the armies to obscure river crossings or down the labyrinth of back roads. Although the hope never became a reality, many Southerners believed Great Britain and France would eventually help them. A combination of official Confederate policy and the Union naval blockade cut off Southern cotton to those nations, and the Confederates believed the British and French would have to intervene to salvage their economies (see Chapter 10).

## THE BORDER STATES

**April 19, 1861: Baltimore Riot**
**May 10, 1861: Union forces capture Missouri militia at Camp Jackson;**
   **St. Louis Riots**

The fate of the Border States was of particular concern to both Lincoln and Davis after the surrender of Fort Sumter. The Border States contained large populations of potential military recruits; had considerable resources in industry, livestock, and agriculture; and were strategically located between the warring sections. If Kentucky and Maryland seceded, the Confederate border would advance all the way to the Ohio River, and the South's military position would be greatly strengthened.

### Maryland and Secession

Of the three Border States that did not secede, Lincoln worried most about Maryland: If it joined the Confederacy, the Union's capital would be located inside enemy lines! The state's loyalties were divided geographically, with most secessionists living in eastern Maryland and most Unionists in the western part of the state. Baltimore, in particular, had a large pro-Confederate population, and tensions ran high when Union troops began passing through the city on their way to Washington. On April 19, 1861, angry crowds were milling in the streets as the 6th Massachusetts regiment passed by on horse-drawn railroad cars to the connecting railhead. When a mob pelted one car with rocks and obstructed the passage of another, the soldiers disembarked and began marching through the city. The mayor and police chief walked in front of the regiment to calm the situation, but the mob threw more stones, and then shots rang out. The Massachusetts men returned fire, and an ugly riot ensued. The soldiers managed to get through the city, but four Massachusetts soldiers were killed and thirty-nine were injured in the Baltimore Riot. The number of civilian casualties was reported at twelve dead and many more wounded.

The bloodshed sparked a wave of anti-Union sentiment in Baltimore. To prevent additional Northern troops from arriving, city officials burned the bridges north of town to cut railroad service with the North. For a few days, secessionists controlled the city, but passions calmed after a week or so, and the pro-Union majority was able to regain the upper hand. The crisis finally passed when additional Union troops arrived under Major General Benjamin F. Butler.

Lincoln quickly took strong measures to ensure Maryland's loyalty. He used Butler's troops to maintain control of Baltimore, and federal authorities arrested the city's mayor and nineteen Maryland legislators for suspicion of disloyalty. Union troops also occupied Annapolis and began guarding the state's railroads that were being used for troop movements. Lincoln even suspended the writ of habeas corpus along the railroad to Philadelphia to make sure there would be no more interference with reinforcements headed to Washington (see Chapter 12).

The Maryland legislature was dominated by secessionists, but Governor Thomas H. Hicks was a moderate. He helped prevent secession by refusing to convene the legislature until the Union had gained firm control of the state. When Hicks finally did call the legislature into session, it condemned Lincoln's recruiting soldiers to put down the rebellion, but it did not call for a secession convention. Although about one-third of Maryland's Civil War soldiers fought for the Confederacy, there never was a real danger after the spring of 1861 that it would secede.

## Kentucky and Missouri

Kentucky was almost as important as Maryland because it was strategically located on both the Mississippi and Ohio rivers and was rich in manpower, agriculture, and livestock. Appreciating the state's significance, Lincoln once proclaimed, "I think to lose Kentucky is nearly the same as to lose the whole game." Ironically, both Lincoln and Davis were born in Kentucky, as was John C. Breckinridge, the 1860 Southern Democratic presidential candidate. Like Maryland and Missouri, Kentucky was mostly populated by Unionists, but there was a large pro-Confederate minority, including Governor Beriah Magoffin. Magoffin refused Lincoln's call for volunteers, but at the same time he ignored Confederate demands that Kentucky secede. Instead, the pro-Union legislature met in May and took the unique step of declaring the state's neutrality. Although neutrality, in practicality, is virtually impossible during a civil war, both sides at first respected Kentucky's decision to avoid pushing the state into the enemy's camp.

Far to the west in Missouri, the situation was also tense between the Unionist majority and secessionist Governor Claiborne Fox Jackson. He, too, rejected Lincoln's call for volunteers and in May assembled the state's militia at Camp Jackson to seize the federal arsenal in St. Louis. In response, Captain Nathaniel Lyon raised a loyal militia force, attacked Camp Jackson on May 10, and captured nearly 1,000 secessionists. As Lyon marched his prisoners through the streets of St. Louis, an angry mob confronted the column, and a bloody street riot erupted, leaving twenty-eight people dead. Afterward, Governor Jackson called for volunteers to drive out the Union forces before abandoning the state capital and retreating into southwest Missouri to carry on the fight.

## THE FIRST CAMPAIGNS

**May 1, 1861: John Baylor begins his "buffalo hunt"**
**June 3, 1861: Battle of Philippi, Virginia**
**July 11, 1861: Battle of Rich Mountain, Virginia**
**July 21, 1861: First Battle of Bull Run, Virginia**
**August 10, 1861: Battle of Wilson's Creek, Missouri**
**September 13–20, 1861: Battle of Lexington, Missouri**
**October 21, 1861: Battle of Ball's Bluff, Virginia**
**December 9, 1861: Battle of Chusto-Talasah, Indian Territory**
**December 26, 1861: Battle of Chustenahlah, Indian Territory**
**June 20, 1863: U.S. Congress admits West Virginia to the Union**

Realizing Washington's location on the Virginia border made it vulnerable to attack, Lincoln quickly assembled thousands of reinforcements to defend the city. When Union soldiers crossed the Potomac River in early May and occupied Arlington Heights and Alexandria, Virginia, one of Lincoln's close friends became the North's first martyr. Twenty-four-year-old Elmer Ellsworth had studied law under Lincoln before becoming colonel of a New York regiment. On May 24, 1861, Ellsworth's men were securing Alexandria when the colonel noticed a Confederate flag flying defiantly from a hotel rooftop. Rushing upstairs, he tore down the flag but then was confronted by the hotel's owner on the stairway. The Virginian killed Ellsworth with one shotgun blast before being bayoneted and killed by one of the colonel's men. Colonel Ellsworth was the first Union soldier to be killed on Southern soil, and his death led to an outpouring of national mourning. President Lincoln was devastated, and ordered the young colonel's body be laid in state at the White House.

As spring turned to summer, many small skirmishes began to erupt, but it became clear the climactic clash would take place in northern Virginia. In May, the Confederate Congress had transferred the capital from Montgomery to Richmond to reward Virginia's secession. Placing the capital so near enemy territory was a dangerous gamble, but officials deemed it necessary to secure Virginia's riches for the Confederacy. Necessary or not, the fact remained that the Confederate capital was now on the front lines only one hundred miles from Washington, D.C., and it became a fixed target for Union armies. In the years to come, no Confederate general in Virginia could carry out military operations without first making sure Richmond was adequately protected. This sometimes prevented the Confederates from taking advantage of the fluid military situation and maneuvering as freely as they could have if the capital had been left deep in the interior.

## First Battle of Bull Run

In the summer of 1861, the two opposing armies in the Virginia theater camped and trained within a day's march of each other. In Washington, Brigadier General Irvin McDowell commanded the Union forces protecting the capital, and General Beauregard kept a watchful eye over the Confederate army camped twenty-five miles away near Manassas Junction, Virginia. Both armies were composed of untrained, raw recruits, but McDowell was under the most political pressure to act. Since Confederate strategy was simply to defend its borders, Beauregard had no reason to attack Washington. However, Lincoln had to act decisively and crush the rebellion before it grew in strength. The president urged McDowell to advance, but the general argued he needed more time to train his men. As he would do frequently during the war, Lincoln demonstrated an innate grasp of military matters when he told McDowell, "You are green, it is true, but they are green also." In other words, it should be an even fight.

Unable to resist the growing demands for action, McDowell reluctantly advanced toward Manassas in mid-July with 33,000 men, taking two days to cover the twenty-five miles. Certain this battle would break the back of the rebellion, scores of citizens and politicians tagged along to watch the historic clash. Initial probes revealed Beauregard's 22,000-man army was drawn up in a defensive line behind a small creek named Bull Run. McDowell's plan was to fix the Confederates in position along the creek with part of his army, while the rest crossed upstream to sweep down on Beauregard's left flank. As the enemy was pushed downstream, McDowell's entire force would cross over and help finish them off. Based on what McDowell knew, the plan was tactically sound. Unfortunately, what he did not know was that 12,000 additional Confederates under General Joseph E. Johnston had boarded trains in the Shenandoah Valley and were hurrying east to join Beauregard. This was the first time the Confederates used their interior line and the first time in history that large numbers of troops were transferred by rail to make such a strategic move. It would not be the last.

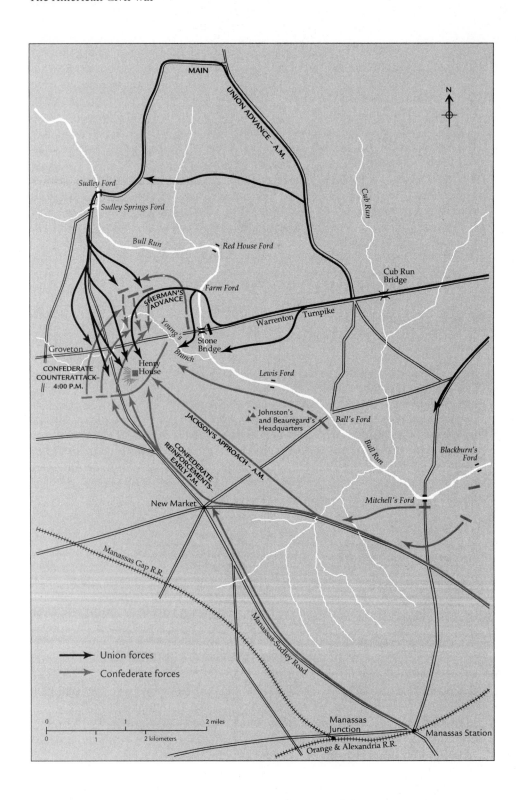

MAIN

UNION ADVANCE – A.M.

N

Sudley Ford

Sudley Springs Ford

Bull Run

Red House Ford

Cub Run

Cub Run Bridge

Farm Ford

SHERMAN'S ADVANCE

Young's Branch

Stone Bridge

Warrenton Turnpike

Cub Run Bridge

Groveton

CONFEDERATE COUNTERATTACK– 4:00 P.M.

Henry House

Lewis Ford

JACKSON'S APPROACH – A.M.

CONFEDERATE REINFORCEMENTS– EARLY P.M.

Johnston's and Beauregard's Headquarters

Ball's Ford

Bull Run

Blackburn's Ford

New Market

Mitchell's Ford

Manassas Gap R.R.

Manassas-Sudley Road

0     1     2 miles

0     1     2 kilometers

→ Union forces

→ Confederate forces

Manassas Junction

Manassas Station

Orange & Alexandria R.R.

McDowell attacked early on the morning of July 21, 1861. At first, the flank attack went well and he slowly pushed Beauregard back. The fighting was intense and bloody with many charges and countercharges, but the Union army began to lose momentum as the day progressed and more and more of Johnston's troops arrived on the field from the Valley. Among them was a brigade of Virginians under Brigadier General Thomas J. Jackson. Jackson realized Henry House Hill was the key to the battlefield, and he occupied it to provide a rallying point for the exhausted Confederates. Under tremendous pressure in the valley below, Confederate Brigadier General Barnard Bee saw Jackson's men on the hill and cried out to his men, "Look! There is Jackson standing like a stone wall! Rally behind the Virginians!" Bee was mortally wounded soon afterward, but Jackson and his brigade had earned their nom de guerre.

With Union strength rapidly weakening in the hot summer sun, the Confederates counterattacked and drove McDowell back. When a Confederate shell wrecked a wagon and blocked a bridge, the Yankees panicked, and the retreat became a rout as soldiers threw away their rifles and equipment and ran back to Washington. Hundreds were captured, as was one congressman who had come out to watch the battle. Jefferson Davis rushed from Richmond when he heard the battle had begun and arrived on the field just as the enemy began to retreat. He and his generals briefly discussed pursuing the foe back to Washington, but they finally decided the men were too exhausted and bloodied in victory to achieve much more, and McDowell's beaten army was allowed to retire unmolested. Some Confederates later criticized Davis for supposedly missing a chance to end the war by capturing Washington, but the decision not to pursue was probably correct.

This first major clash of the war came to be called the First Battle of Bull Run by Union forces and the First Battle of Manassas by the Confederates (the Union tended to name battles after bodies of water and the Confederates after towns). Beauregard had lost about 2,000 men to McDowell's 3,000, and both sides were exhausted and in shock. Apparently a handkerchief would not hold the blood that was going to be spilled, as one politician had predicted, and there was no longer any talk of a six-week war. Everyone now knew it was going to be a long, bloody struggle.

## Western Virginia

In the weeks preceding the First Battle of Bull Run, events unfolded in western Virginia that demonstrated a serious Confederate weakness—not all Southerners supported secession, and many were determined to remain loyal to the

**The First Battle of Bull Run, July 21, 1861.** Early in the battle, Union forces attacked from the north across Bull Run and pushed the Confederates back to the south side of the Warrenton Turnpike. Fighting then raged around Henry House Hill, but Confederate reinforcements steadily arrived, and the Confederates were able to launch a counterattack in the afternoon that forced the Union to retreat.

# NOTABLE UNITS: *The Stonewall Brigade*

The Stonewall Brigade was the most famous unit in the Confederate army. Organized in the spring of 1861, it was composed of men from the Shenandoah Valley in the 2nd, 4th, 5th, 27th, and 33rd Virginia Infantry. Placed under the command of Brigadier General Thomas J. Jackson, the brigade earned its name at First Bull Run when Jackson held the high ground at Henry House Hill. After the battle, one soldier wrote home, "Our Brigade is almost immortalized; but for us the day would have been lost." Jackson was always proud of his men, and he once wrote to his wife, "I am very thankful to our Heavenly Father for having given me such a fine brigade." He declared, "[T]he men of that command will be proud one day to say to their children: 'I was one of the Stonewall Brigade.' I have no right to the name 'Stonewall.' It belongs to the brigade and not at all to me." When Jackson died in May 1863, the War Department honored him by officially naming the brigade the Stonewall Brigade. It was the only brigade in the Confederate army with such a sanctioned nickname.

The Stonewall Brigade was famous for both marching and fighting, and it served in virtually every battle fought by the Army of Northern Virginia. The unit suffered particularly heavy casualties at First and Second Bull Run, Cedar Mountain, Groveton, Chancellorsville, and Gettysburg. When told the brigade was struggling to hold its position at Second Bull Run, Jackson barked, "Go back, give my compliments to them and tell the Stonewall Brigade to maintain her reputation!" The brigade held its ground and continued to fight well in subsequent battles until hundreds of its members were captured during the Union attack on Spotsylvania's Mule Shoe in 1864. Afterward, the Stonewall Brigade was merged with two other brigades and largely lost its separate identity.

Besides Jackson, the brigade's commanders included Richard B. Garnett, Charles S. Winder, William S. H. Baylor, Elisha F. Paxton, James A. Walker, and William Terry. Of these, Winder, Baylor, Paxton, and Garnett were killed (Garnett after leaving the brigade), and Walker was wounded and captured. Approximately 6,000 men served in the Stonewall Brigade, but after fighting in 39 engagements, only 210 men were left when General Lee surrendered at Appomattox.

Constitution. This was particularly true in mountainous areas such as western Virginia, eastern Tennessee, and western North Carolina. The people in these rugged regions had few slaves, and they held a fond memory of General Andrew Jackson and his unwavering opposition to secession. In western Virginia, there also were strong family and trade ties with Ohio and Pennsylvania.

The delegates from the western Virginia counties voted against secession at the state's convention, but they were too few in number to change the outcome. Determined not to be dragged into the Confederacy by the slaveholding elite, representatives from twenty-six western counties met at Wheeling on June 11, 1861, to form a new state and create a separate Virginia government that would be loyal to the Union. Two months later, the Wheeling Convention created the state of Kanawha and elected Francis H. Pierpont to be the Unionist governor of Virginia. In November, a constitutional convention was held to finalize the new state's creation. The name was changed from Kanawha to West Virginia, and the constitution was ratified on April 3, 1862, by voters who had taken an oath of allegiance to the Union. West Virginia then was admitted to the Union in 1863.

The events transpiring in western Virginia were important to both sides. Lincoln was determined to aid and protect the Southern loyalists there and to defend the vital Baltimore & Ohio Railroad and three turnpikes that ran through the region. The Confederates were equally determined to hold on to the area because it would set a dangerous precedent to have part of a state secede from the secessionists. As a result, both sides dispatched troops to western Virginia in the summer of 1861, but Union forces under Major General George B. McClellan routed the Confederates at the small battles of Philippi and Rich Mountain. The Confederates sent General Robert E. Lee to take command of the region, but he, too, was defeated in a minor affair at Cheat Mountain. West Virginia continued to be the scene of cavalry raids and skirmishes throughout the war, but the new state remained firmly in Union hands.

## The Committee on the Conduct of the War

Perhaps unfairly, Lincoln relieved McDowell after the defeat at Bull Run and replaced him with Major General George B. McClellan, the only Union commander who could claim any real victories. McClellan took over the unorganized mob of soldiers defending the capital and turned it into the Army of the Potomac. Before the year was out, McClellan had also replaced the aging Winfield Scott as general-in-chief of all Union forces. Although McClellan was an outstanding organizer, administrator, and disciplinarian, he proved reluctant to advance against the enemy until he had attended to every detail. As a result, the war came to a standstill in Virginia, and Lincoln watched in disappointment as months passed without any further offensive action.

The only serious battle that took place close to Washington in the closing months of 1861 was a disastrous affair at Ball's Bluff, Virginia. By October, Confederate forces were active on the Potomac River upstream from Washington, and Union Brigadier General Charles P. Stone sent one brigade across the river from Maryland to attack the enemy at Ball's Bluff on October 21. The brigade's commander badly mishandled the attack and was trapped on the high bluffs overlooking the river. In the nasty fight that followed, the commander was killed and almost 1,000 of his men became casualties, many of whom drowned while trying to escape back across the river.

By Civil War standards the Battle of Ball's Bluff was not a particularly important event. However, the slain commander happened to be Oregon senator Edward Baker, a close friend of President Lincoln and the namesake of one of Lincoln's sons. Baker's death had far-reaching implications for the Union war effort. Controversy immediately surrounded the battle, and Congress created the Committee on the Conduct of the War to investigate this and other Union

# EYEWITNESS
## Elisha Hunt Rhodes

**Elisha Hunt Rhodes**

*Elisha Hunt Rhodes was one of thousands of young Northerners who flocked to recruiting stations after the firing on Fort Sumter. Nineteen years old at the time, he became a private in the 2nd Rhode Island Volunteers and accompanied the regiment to Washington, D.C. On the morning of July 21, 1861, Rhodes found himself in the forefront of the Union flanking maneuver against the Confederates along Bull Run. His diary describes the sensations of a young soldier's first fight.*

On reaching a clearing, separated from our left flank by a rail fence, we were saluted with a volley of musketry, which, however, was fired so high that all the bullets went over our heads. I remember that my first sensation was one of astonishment at the peculiar whir of the bullets, and that the Regiment immediately laid down without waiting for orders. Colonel Slocum gave the command: 'By the left flank— MARCH!' and we commenced crossing the field. One of our boys by the name of Webb fell off of the fence and broke his bayonet. This caused some amusement, for even at this time we did not realize that we were about to engage in battle.

As we crossed the fence, the Rebels, after firing a few scattering shots, fled down a slope to the woods. We followed to the brow of the hill and opened fire. . . .

Colonel Slocum had crossed a rail fence in our front and had advanced nearer to the brow of the hill than the line occupied by the Regiment. As he returned and was in the act of climbing the fence, he fell on the side next to the Regiment. I, being the nearest man to him at the time, raised him up, but was unable to lift him from the ground. Calling for help, Private Parker dropped his gun and came to my assistance. Together we bore him to a small house on the left of the line. . . .With the sponge, from my cap, I washed the blood from his head and found that the bullet had ploughed a furrow from rear to front through the top of his head, but had not lodged. His ankle was also injured, having two wounds upon it. While unable to speak, he yet appeared conscious, and at my request would move his hand from his wounded

defeats. General Stone was unfairly made the battle's scapegoat, and the committee concluded he was "unsound" on the slavery issue. Branded a traitor, Stone was arrested in early 1862 and was imprisoned for more than six months. Before finally being released in August, he spent fifty days in solitary confinement, yet he was never charged with a crime. The debacle at Ball's Bluff put all Union commanders on notice that this was to be no ordinary war. Military officers who failed on the battlefield also ran the risk of being hauled before the Committee on the Conduct of the War to attest to their loyalty. Military defeat or incompetence carried with it the possibility of being arrested and thrown in jail.

head. When it was decided to place the Colonel in an ambulance, I took the door from its hinges with my gun screw driver, and assisted in carrying him on this door to the ambulance. . . .

The firing, which had gradually receded, now seemed to be nearer, and soon a shell fired into the woods told us that the enemy had returned the combat. I cannot explain the causes of what followed. The woods and roads were soon filled with fleeing men and our Brigade was ordered to the front to cover the retreat, which it was now evident could not be stopped. . . .The Rebels followed us for a short distance, shelling our rear, and then we pursued our march unmolested, until we reached the vicinity of the bridge that crosses Cub Run. Here a Rebel battery opened upon us from a corner of the woods, and the stampede commenced. The bridge was soon rendered impassible by the teams that obstructed it, and we here lost five of the guns belonging to our battery. Many men were killed and wounded at this point, and a panic seemed to seize upon every one. As our Regiment was now broken, I looked for a place to cross the stream, not daring to try the bridge. I jumped into the run and holding my gun above my head struggled across with the water up to my waist. After crossing, the Regiment gradually formed again, and we continued our march. . . .

Of the horrors of that night, I can give you no adequate idea. I suffered untold horrors from thirst and fatigue but struggled on, clinging to my gun and cartridge box. Many times I sat down in the mud determined to go no further, and willing to die to end my misery. But soon a friend would pass and urge me to make another effort, and I would stagger on a mile further. At daylight we could see the spires of Washington, and a welcome sight it was. . . .

*Private Rhodes survived his first battle unscathed, but he was one of the lucky ones. The 2nd Rhode Island lost ninety-three men killed, wounded, or captured at First Bull Run. Among the dead was Colonel John S. Slocum, whom Rhodes had carried from the field.*

From ALL FOR THE UNION by Robert Hunt Rhodes, copyright © 1985 by Robert Hunt Rhodes. Foreword copyright © 1991 by Geoffrey C. Ward. Used by permission of Orion Books, a division of Random House, Inc.

## Violating Kentucky's Neutrality

When Kentucky declared its neutrality early in the war, neither Lincoln nor Davis took any overt action against the state because both hoped to lure it to their side. President Davis appointed General Albert Sidney Johnston to command the Western Department, but unfortunately he had little control over Major General Leonidas Polk, who was stationed along the Mississippi River. Although a West Point graduate, Polk resigned his commission after only a few months' military service, entered a seminary, and eventually became

# DID YOU KNOW?

## Confederate Flags

Today, when people think of the Confederate flag most envision the famous blue St. Andrew's Cross with white stars emblazoned on a red background. But this flag was simply a military banner and not the Confederate national flag adopted by delegates at the 1861 Montgomery Convention. Nicknamed the "Stars and Bars," the original national flag had in its upper corner a blue square with seven white stars in a circle to represent the seven original seceding states and red, white, and blue horizontal bars. Unfortunately, this flag closely resembled the U.S. flag and caused confusion in battle so a second national flag, nicknamed the "Stainless Banner," was adopted in May 1863. It had a white background with the Confederate St. Andrew's Cross in the upper corner. But this flag also caused confusion because it appeared to be a surrender flag with no wind. Thus, in March 1865, a third flag was adopted that had a wide red stripe on the end of the Stainless Banner.

The more famous Confederate battle flag was adopted after the First Battle of Bull Run. During the fight, Beauregard almost ordered a retreat when a Confederate unit appeared unexpectedly on his flank. The general at first thought it was the enemy because their flag resembled the U.S. flag. Afterward, Beauregard (with some input from Joseph E. Johnston) designed a new battle flag so the Confederates would not be mistaken for the enemy. It had a blue St. Andrew's Cross, with a narrow white border, set on a red background. Within the cross were thirteen white stars, representing the eleven seceded states, plus Kentucky and Missouri (which had created secessionist governments in exile). Although this flag was never officially adopted by the Confederate Congress, it became the most famous of all the Southern flags, and its use later spread to the western theater when Beauregard and Johnston were transferred there.

the Episcopal bishop of Louisiana. Polk was uniquely unqualified for high command, but he and Davis had been close friends since their cadet days at West Point, and Davis made him one of the Confederacy's senior generals.

Disagreeing with the government's wait-and-see policy toward Kentucky and disliking his position on the Mississippi River, Polk advanced without orders in September to the more defensible town of Columbus, Kentucky. With the state's neutrality now violated, Union forces were free to counter Polk's move by advancing and occupying Paducah, and General Johnston retaliated by establishing a Confederate defensive line through central Kentucky. Polk's rash, unauthorized move made the Confederates the aggressors and ensured Kentucky would officially remain in the Union. Had he not advanced, Kentucky might have eventually seceded, or at least remained neutral and posed massive logistical problems for the Union's ability to maneuver in the west.

With Confederate troops now occupying much of the state, Kentucky's Confederate sympathizers held a November convention at Russellville and passed a secession ordinance. The new government, led by Governor George W. Johnson, was admitted to the Confederacy in December, but it was merely a symbolic gesture. The Union state government continued to function throughout the war, and the vast majority of citizens did not recognize the secessionists' actions. When later Union victories quickly drove the Confederates from Kentucky, the Rebel government became moot. Nonetheless,

**Flags of the Confederacy.** *Battle Flag:* Designed by General Beauregard after the First Battle of Bull Run, the Confederate battle flag was based on St. Andrew's Cross. *First National Flag ("Stars and Bars"):* Adopted in March 1861, the First National Flag was abandoned because it looked too much like the U.S. flag. *Second National Flag ("Stainless Banner"):* Adopted in May 1863, the Stainless Banner was distinguishable from the U.S. flag, but its white background could be mistaken for a surrender flag with no wind. *Third National Flag:* Approved in March 1865, the Third National Flag had a red stripe to distinguish it from a surrender flag.

ardent Confederates considered Kentucky to be one of their own, and the Confederate battle flag sported a star to represent the Bluegrass State.

## The Battle of Wilson's Creek, Missouri

Following the capture of his militia at Camp Jackson, Missouri, Governor Jackson and his secessionist legislature fled to the southwestern part of the state. Meanwhile, Nathaniel Lyon was promoted to brigadier general for his decisive action in protecting St. Louis from the secessionists, and he formed a Union army to occupy the town of Springfield.

In early August 1861, Confederate Brigadier General Ben McCulloch advanced his 12,000 men against Lyon to secure Missouri for the Confederacy. Learning of the enemy movement, Lyon decided not to wait for the attack and moved forward to engage McCulloch. Dividing his army into two columns,

Lyon surprised McCulloch by attacking him on the morning of August 10 at Wilson's Creek from two directions. The battle was just as confusing as First Bull Run because it was fought in bushes and thickets by inexperienced troops. Once during the heavy fighting, a Union officer allowed a Confederate regiment to approach his position, thinking the soldiers were gray-clad Yankees. It was not until the Rebels suddenly stopped short and opened a devastating fire that the Union soldiers realized they were the enemy and retreated from that part of the field. The Confederates eventually stopped one of Lyon's attacking columns and then repeatedly assaulted the other. Lyon was killed in the bitter fighting, becoming the first Union general killed in battle, but his army managed to hold its position until dark. Exhausted and low on ammunition, it then withdrew during the night, but the Confederates were in no condition to pursue. The Battle of Wilson's Creek was the first large Civil War battle west of the Mississippi River, and the Union army lost 1,300 men to the Confederates' 1,200.

After the battle, Confederate Major General Sterling Price advanced his division to occupy Springfield and then won a small battle at Lexington. This string of Confederate victories seemed to assure Rebel control of Missouri, especially when Governor Jackson convened a legislature in Neosho in October that voted for secession. However, a pro-Union government already had been organized at Jefferson City, so the state remained divided. Both governments were equally determined to control Missouri, but the coming winter put a halt to military activity.

## The Far West

The Civil War in the far west is largely ignored today, but it was an important theater of operation early in the war. In Indian Territory, the Native American population was split in their loyalties, with some volunteering to fight for the Confederacy and some for the Union. Several tribes were literally ripped apart, making the war a true civil war for Indians, but the Confederacy generally had more success than the Union in winning their support. Albert Pike, a well-known Arkansas newspaper publisher, lawyer, and poet, was sent to the Indian Territory as the Confederate Commissioner of Indian Affairs soon after the war began. Pike succeeded in gaining the support of most of the Five Civilized Tribes because of his popularity for earlier representing several tribes in disputes with the federal government. Promoted to brigadier general, Pike then took command of the Department of Indian Territory and defeated the Unionist Indians in two small December battles at Chusto-Talasah and Chustenahlah. The Unionists retreated into Kansas, and for the moment Indian Territory was firmly under Confederate control (see Chapter 17 for more on Native Americans).

An even larger Confederate operation took place in the spring of 1861 when Texan John R. Baylor took it on himself to invade the New Mexico Territory. Under the guise of going on a buffalo hunt, he recruited about 1,000 men and

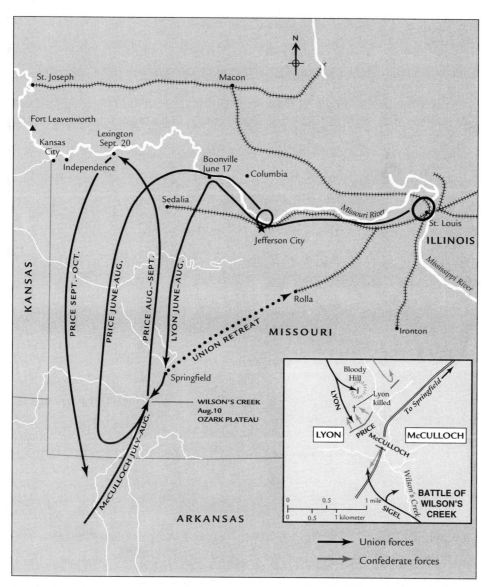

**Missouri, 1861.** After the St. Louis Riots, Sterling Price led the Missouri State Guard to southwest Missouri and joined forces with Confederate General McCulloch. Union General Lyon marched to Springfield and then attacked the Confederates at Wilson's Creek. Lyon was killed in the battle and his men retreated. Price then moved north and defeated the Union garrison at Lexington, but he later retreated to Arkansas after being threatened by growing enemy forces.

departed San Antonio, Texas, in May. Three-fourths of the column dropped out from sickness and exhaustion before reaching El Paso, but the remaining soldiers pushed into New Mexico and reached Fort Fillmore in July. The superior Union garrison there made a half-hearted attempt to drive off Baylor before abandoning the fort and retreating northeast to Fort Stanton. Although outnumbered three-to-one, Baylor set out in pursuit and captured several hundred enemy soldiers. The Yankees then evacuated Fort Stanton and left New Mexico in the hands of the Rebels. On August 1, Baylor unilaterally created the Confederate Territory of Arizona and appointed himself governor. Although Baylor was acting without any official authorization, he had succeeded in stretching the Confederacy's western boundary nearly to California.

As 1861 came to a close, it appeared the South was well on its way to securing independence. Even though the North greatly outmatched the South in every important war-making category, the secessionists made up for it in aggressiveness. In a matter of months the Confederates had created a viable national government, fielded a formidable military force, defeated Union armies in Virginia and Arkansas, gained the upper hand in Indian Territory, and secured a foothold in the Southwest. No one, however, was under any delusion that the war would soon end. While Northerners had experienced serious setbacks, their resolve to preserve the Union was not shaken; and while Southerners rejoiced in their initial accomplishments, they knew independence was not yet secured. Everyone realized victory depended on military strength, and armies had to be organized, equipped, and trained quickly. Politicians, diplomats, businessmen, and civilians would all play important roles in the Civil War; but, in the end, the conflict's outcome would depend on the soldiers.

## FOR FURTHER READING

Lincoln's proclamation calling for 75,000 volunteers
Kentucky's declaration of neutrality

# Soldiering

Thousands of Confederate soldiers had already assembled in formation near their camps at Centreville, Virginia, as a band approached playing the mournful "Death March." Following slowly behind was a covered wagon, escorted by two companies of soldiers with fixed bayonets. Inside the wagon were two men who had been sentenced to death for attacking an officer. Such breakdown in discipline was becoming commonplace in the army, and the generals decided it was time to make an example of these two. Every man in the division but one was forced to watch the execution on this cool, crisp December day in 1861. The exception was the battalion commander, who was excused because one of the condemned men had helped to carry him from the field when he was wounded at First Bull Run. He remained in his tent crying.

Following military tradition, twelve of the condemned men's comrades were chosen by lot to serve as executioners and stood ready with loaded muskets. After the charges and court's sentence were read, the two prisoners' hands were tied and they were led backward, forced to kneel, and fastened to posts. One witness remembered a priest tried to comfort them by holding up a crucifix "which they passionately kiss and over which they pray." After the pair was blindfolded, the order was given, and the firing squad shot them dead. As the gunfire echoed in the cold air, a lone soldier broke ranks, ran up to one of the bodies, and gently held and caressed it. "It was heart-rendering," a newspaper reporter wrote, "to see the poor brother's agony."

The executions were the first carried out in the Army of Northern Virginia, and witnesses never forgot the horrific scene. Soldiers had become accustomed to various forms of military discipline, but this was something entirely new. For many it was the first time they had ever seen a man killed. For everyone it was a harsh reminder that soldiering was not going to be the lark they had expected when they enlisted eight months earlier.

## THE ARMIES

**March 6, 1861: Confederate Congress forms Provisional Army**
**April 15, 1861: Lincoln calls for 75,000 volunteers to put down**
**    the rebellion**
**April 17, 1861: Davis calls for 32,000 volunteers to defend the Confederacy**

Initially, both the North and South prepared to fight a short war with relatively few troops. But they soon realized victory would require hundreds of thousands of soldiers, and they began taking new and controversial steps to raise the necessary men and turn them into effective armies. Because they shared a common history and culture, the opponents organized, trained, and armed their military forces in almost exactly the same manner. Except for the color of their uniforms and the cause for which they fought, there was little difference between the armies.

**The Boys of '61.** These Confederate soldiers are typical of the thousands of young men who volunteered in 1861. Brimming with confidence and filled with youthful enthusiasm, they were blissfully unaware of the horror and suffering that lay ahead.

### The Volunteers

When the war began, a wave of excitement swept America and thousands of young men eagerly volunteered for military service. Civil War soldiers ranged in age from 9 to 80, but most were between 18 and 29. While their backgrounds varied greatly, the typical soldier was a single, native-born Protestant. More than one hundred different occupations were listed on recruitment documents by Confederates and more than three hundred by Union soldiers, but more volunteers were farmers than any other occupation (see Tables 2 and 3). The men ranged in physical size from 3 feet, 4 inches in height to more than 7 feet. On average, they were just over 5 feet, 6 inches and weighed approximately 150 pounds.

**Table 2**  *Previous Occupations of Samples of White Union Soldiers Compared with 1860 Occupations of All Males in Union States from which the Soldiers Came*

| Occupational Categories | Union Soldiers (U.S. Sanitary Commission sample) | Union Soldiers (Bell Wiley* sample) | All Males (from 1860 census) |
|---|---|---|---|
| Farmers and farm laborers | 47.5% | 47.8% | 42.9% |
| Skilled laborers | 25.1 | 25.2 | 24.9 |
| Unskilled laborers | 15.9 | 15.1 | 16.7 |
| White-collar and commercial | 5.1 | 7.8 | 10.0 |
| Professional | 3.2 | 2.9 | 3.5 |
| Miscellaneous and unknown | 3.2 | 1.2 | 2.0 |

*Bell Wiley was a prominent Civil War scholar who specialized in the study of the common soldier.

**Table 3**  *Previous Occupations of Samples of Confederate Soldiers from Alabama, Arkansas, Georgia, Louisiana, Mississippi, North Carolina, and Virginia Compared with 1860 Occupations of White Males in These States*

| Occupational Categories | Confederate Soldiers | White Males (from 1860 census) |
|---|---|---|
| Planters, farmers, and farm laborers | 61.5% | 57.5% |
| Skilled laborers | 14.1 | 15.7 |
| Unskilled laborers | 8.5 | 12.7 |
| White-collar and commercial | 7.0 | 8.3 |
| Professional | 5.2 | 5.0 |
| Miscellaneous and unknown | 3.7 | 0.8 |

What motivated these volunteers to enlist and risk their lives on the battlefield was as varied as the men themselves. Some had grown up listening to their elders tell stories of fighting Indians or fighting in Mexico and wanted to experience their own war. Some were pressured into enlisting by friends, and still others joined the army to obtain a steady paycheck and square meal. Most, however, were truly committed to the cause and enlisted for patriotic reasons.

Northerners were convinced the Union and its democratic experiment were worth fighting for. If secession proved successful, it would mean democracy was a failure because a determined minority would have been able to impose its will on the majority. Southerners were equally convinced their cause was righteous because they were exercising their rights as set forth by the Declaration of Independence. A government derived its authority from the consent of the governed, and the South had withdrawn that consent because the Union was threatening its slavery rights.

As the war dragged on, most men developed a strong bond with their comrades and took pride in their unit. They accepted the risks of battle, not only for patriotic reasons, but out of a sense of honor and a desire not to let their friends or regiment down. For many Northern soldiers who witnessed slavery firsthand, destroying the peculiar institution became a great motivating factor to see the fight through to the bitter end. Southerners often stayed on the firing line to defend their hearth and home from the frequent destruction wrought by Yankee armies.

Religion also played a role in motivating soldiers to fight. Most nineteenth-century Americans believed in God, although not all attended organized religious services. This strong faith had a great impact on Civil War volunteers. Both the North and South were firmly convinced of the righteousness of their cause, and many soldiers enlisted in the army because they thought the war was a struggle of good versus evil. Frequently during the war, the opposing governments called on the people to observe days of fasting and thanksgiving to invoke God's blessings. The belief that God was in control of both the war's outcome and their own fate comforted soldiers and helped them face the horrors of battle with steadfast bravery. Victory was often attributed to God blessing the cause, while setbacks were seen as God's punishment for people who had become weak in their faith or engaged in sinful behavior.

## Volunteer Companies

Civil War volunteers went off to war together as a community, much like today's National Guard. Normally, a community leader took the lead in raising a company—the basic military unit that contained about one hundred men. To stir up interest and invoke local pride, colorful names such as the Raccoon Roughs, Oxford Bears, and Tiger Rifles were usually adopted. Great excitement ensued when residents learned a local company was being formed. One Northern college student wrote his brother, "War! And volunteers are the only topics of conversation or thought. The lessons today have been a mere form. I cannot study. I cannot sleep, I cannot work, and I don't know as I can write."

When the company was formed, members were allowed to elect all of their officers and noncommissioned officers. This democratic process was a tradition among volunteers and was in keeping with the American idea of the citizen-soldier. Such elections were hard-fought as contenders politicked with their comrades, but the man who played the greatest role in organizing the company was usually elected the commanding captain. These elections often weakened military efficiency, however, because they only ensured the most popular men got elected, not necessarily the most qualified. Both governments eventually took steps to eliminate the unqualified by establishing examining boards to quiz the officers on tactics and other responsibilities and weeding out the ones who failed.

Recruiting a company from one neighborhood had mixed results. On the positive side, Civil War soldiers served with their brothers, cousins, and boyhood friends. Five to ten close men formed an informal unit called a mess and shared the same quarters, took turns cooking meals, and generally looked out for each other. This helped keep morale high because soldiers knew if they became sick or were wounded their friends and relatives would look after them. Recruiting companies from a single community also helped thwart cowardice. Today, we marvel at how Civil War soldiers had the courage to stand toe-to-toe with the enemy and exchange volleys of fire at one hundred yards or charge an artillery battery that was blowing holes in their line with canister and solid shot. They did so partly because the soldiers who stood in line with them were neighbors and relatives. If a man showed cowardice, word of it inevitably reached home and ruined his reputation. An Indiana soldier explained this to his wife when he wrote, "If I was to turn back now, many would say I was a coward. I would rather be shot at once than to have such a stigma rest on me." On the other hand, raising companies from the same area caused some communities to lose an entire generation of men. The Pelican Rifles, a company in the 2nd Louisiana Volunteers, is an extreme example of this. Of the 151 men who served in the unit, 119 died in the war. Of the 32 who survived, 31 were wounded.

## Regiments

The company was first sent to a training camp, where it was officially mustered into state service and eventually the national volunteer army. At first, both governments allowed men to enlist for a specific length of time, such as ninety days or one year, but this was soon changed to three years or the war's duration for Union troops and to the war's duration for Confederate troops. The company then was assigned to a regiment, which was the backbone of the army and the unit to which soldiers formed their strongest bond. Infantry regiments usually had ten companies, or about 1,000 men. However, because of casualties, illness, desertion, and detached duty, they never went into combat full strength, and by mid-war most regiments entered battle with perhaps 300 to 400 men. When a company became part of a regiment, it dropped its colorful name and took on a letter designation, such as Company A. The company officers were usually allowed to elect the regiment's field officers of colonel, lieutenant colonel, and major.

Each regiment was numbered according to the order in which it was accepted for service. One sees the Northern advantage in population when looking at regimental numbers. Virginia was the Confederacy's most populous state and its last regiment was the 64th Virginia Infantry. In contrast, Pennsylvania

fielded the 215th Pennsylvania Infantry. The armies' professional soldiers realized creating more regiments out of new recruits was a mistake because the
inexperienced units were rushed into battle and often mauled in their first fight.
At the same time, battle-tested regiments dwindled away and became ineffective
as the men were killed or wounded. A better approach would have been to funnel
new recruits into existing regiments. This would have allowed veteran units to
maintain their strength, and new recruits would have benefited by serving with
veterans who could teach them the skills needed in combat.

## Brigades

When they were assigned to an army, four to six regiments were banded together
to form a brigade. In theory, a brigade numbered from 4,000 to 6,000 men, but
again casualties, sickness, and detached duty greatly reduced the unit's strength.
Few brigades went into combat with more than 1,500 men. A brigadier general
usually commanded a brigade, but it was sometimes led by a colonel—especially
in the Union army. The respective national governments appointed all generals,
but politicians had tremendous influence because these high positions were
spread among the states for political reasons. Frequently, powerful politicians
were appointed generals, even though they had no military experience, because
both Lincoln and Davis needed the support of diverse political factions.

Beginning with brigades, subtle differences began to appear in the opposing
armies. The Confederates referred to their brigades by the commander's name,
such as "Early's brigade," while the Union referred to them by numbers, such
as the "1st Brigade." That was important to know. If a Union soldier became lost
in the dark and blundered into soldiers who identified themselves as members of
Early's brigade, he knew to run. Also, Confederate brigades usually were composed
of regiments from one state, with the commander hailing from the same state,
while the Union more often brigaded together regiments from different states.

## Divisions and Corps

Two to four brigades were grouped together to form a division, which was
usually commanded by a brigadier general in the Union army and a major
general in the Confederate army. Both used the same system for naming divisions as they did for brigades, with the former using a number and the latter
the commander's name.

Early in the war, armies were composed of several divisions, but this
proved unwieldy because it fragmented the army into small groups and made it
difficult for the commander to coordinate them. To simplify organization and
concentrate firepower, both sides soon created corps. A corps was composed
of several divisions and was commanded by a major general in the Union army
and a lieutenant general in the Confederate army. Officially, both sides gave
corps numerical designations, although the Confederates commonly referred
to theirs by the commander's name.

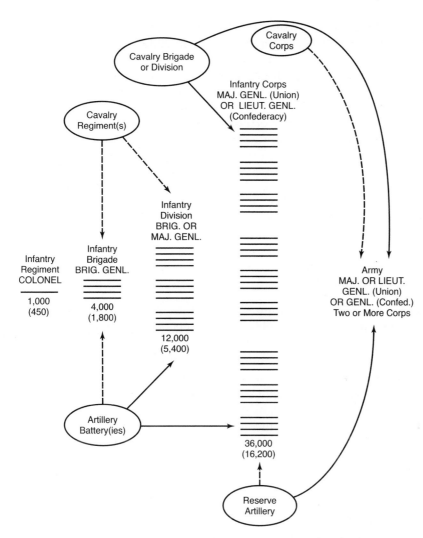

**Organization of Union and Confederate Armies.** Normal commanding officer of each unit appears in capital letters. Numbers below each unit indicate full quota of men; numbers in parentheses indicate typical size of combat units by second year of war. (By the last two years of the war, brigades often contained five or six regiments; divisions sometimes contained four brigades; and corps sometimes contained four divisions.) Arrows indicate attachment of artillery and cavalry to infantry units; broken arrows indicate occasional attachments to these units. Cavalry often operated independently of infantry units.

## Army Organization

Armies were composed of several corps and were usually named for the department or geographical area in which they fought. They were formed and disbanded as necessity warranted, with the Union fielding sixteen armies and the Confederacy twenty-three. The Union generally named its armies after bodies of water, such as the Army *of the* Tennessee, while the Confederates normally used state or regional names, such as the Army *of* Tennessee.

Armies comprised infantry, cavalry, and artillery units. The infantry were the most numerous and important because they were the soldiers who bore the brunt of the fighting. The horse-mounted cavalry, which was organized similarly to the infantry, gathered intelligence on enemy movements, protected against flank attacks, made slashing attacks, and raided behind enemy lines to destroy railroads and lines of communication. The artillery supported both the infantry and cavalry by using its cannons to break up enemy assaults or soften up positions before they were attacked. The basic artillery unit was the battery, which usually contained six cannons and was commanded by a captain.

The opposing sides also had specialized soldiers who served as sharpshooters (snipers), pioneers, and engineers. Sharpshooters were most often placed several yards apart in a skirmish line some distance ahead of the main battle line to give warning of the enemy's proximity, probe the enemy's position, shoot enemy artillerymen and officers, or slow enemy advances. Pioneers were construction soldiers who opened blocked roads, cut new roads, and built bridges and fortifications. Army engineers conducted reconnaissance missions; made maps and detailed drawings of campaign regions and installations; and supervised the construction of fortifications.

## THE NEED FOR MEN

**April 16, 1862: Davis signs into law America's first military conscription act**
**March 3, 1863: Lincoln signs into law first Union conscription act**

There was a tremendous rush of volunteers when the war began, but recruitment quickly slacked off for both armies as casualties mounted and men began to lose their enthusiasm for the fight. This slump in enlistments made it difficult to maintain the armies' strength, and desperate measures had to be taken to bring in more men. Both governments used a combination of enticements and coercion to raise the necessary troops, but none proved popular.

### Bounties and Conscription

The bounty system, or paying men money, was one method the national, state, and local governments used to encourage men to volunteer or veterans to re-enlist. Union bounties usually ran from $25 to as high as $1,500 for a three-year enlistment, while Confederate bounties rarely rose above $50. A drawback to the system was bounty-jumping, a process where unscrupulous men enlisted in one area, claimed their bounty, and then promptly deserted to do it all over again somewhere else.

Bounties encouraged thousands of men to join the army, but it still was not enough. With its smaller population, the Confederacy felt the pinch of declining enlistments more than the Union. By April 1862, the situation was so serious that the Confederate Congress passed America's first national military draft. Except for a few cases of forced service in local militias, conscription had always been shunned in America as an infringement on personal liberty. The Confederates broke all rules of tradition with the conscription act, but Americans had never before faced a conflict like the Civil War in which so many soldiers were needed.

The Confederate conscription law initially made all white males between eighteen and thirty-five eligible for the draft, but it was later changed to include those between seventeen and fifty. In addition, Congress arbitrarily changed all soldiers' enlistments to three years' service or the duration of the war, whichever was shortest. Soldiers howled in protest and some even deserted, but to no avail. Texas Private David Garrett wrote home that his regiment "kicked up a fuss for a while, but since they shot about twenty-five men for mutiny whipped & shaved the heads of as many more for the same offense everything has got quiet & goes on as usual."

After the First Battle of Bull Run, Lincoln called for 500,000 more soldiers and set recruitment quotas for each state. More calls were made later, but by 1863 voluntary enlistments dropped dramatically. This forced Congress to enact its own conscription law to ensure the army could replace its casualties. The Union conscription act went into effect in July 1863, and in its final form made all white men between twenty and forty-six eligible for the draft. Each congressional district was given a draft quota. If it met the quota through voluntary enlistments, there would be no draft; if it did not, a lottery was used to choose those to be conscripted.

Both the North and South actually viewed conscription as a way to encourage voluntary enlistments, not as a draconian measure to drag unwilling men into the military. During the Civil War, there was a great stigma attached to being drafted because it reflected badly on one's loyalty. Overall, the policy worked. Although there is no way of knowing how many soldiers volunteered for service to avoid being labeled a conscript, the number was significant and relatively few men were ever actually drafted.

## "A Rich Man's War and a Poor Man's Fight"

The unpopular conscription acts allowed wealthier men and those whose work was considered vital to the war effort to be exempted from the draft. The Confederates had a provision known as the Twenty Negro Law that exempted plantation owners or overseers who supervised at least twenty slaves, supposedly to ensure slaves would be controlled during the war. Most Southerners, however, believed it was a political ploy to exempt upper-class men from military service. Both governments also provided commutations and substitutions for skilled laborers and religious pacifists. The Confederates allowed a conscript to pay a $500 commutation fee to avoid military service, while the Union charged $300. Draftees could also hire a substitute to serve in their place.

Those men who were conscripted or who enlisted just to get bounties were not equal to the early volunteers in motivation and patriotism. Letters and diaries are filled with condemning remarks about bounty jumpers, substitutes, and conscripts. One soldier noted that 115 of 186 conscripts and substitutes assigned to his Massachusetts regiment deserted. A Confederate spoke for many veteran soldiers when he wrote to his wife, "The conscript Act will do

# BIOGRAPHY

## Edwin McMasters Stanton: Lincoln's Right Hand

**Edwin M. Stanton**

An Ohio native, Edwin Stanton (1814–1869) received little formal education as a boy because he was forced to work in a bookstore after his father died. Nonetheless, he put himself through two years of schooling at Kenyon College and became an attorney. Stanton's practice prospered, and he also served as Pennsylvania's counsel and as a special federal counsel litigating fraudulent California land claims. Although he opposed slavery, Stanton was a political moderate who supported the Dred Scott decision and John C. Breckinridge for president because he believed the Union could only be preserved if the South's slavery rights were protected. He also was a strong supporter of President James Buchanan and briefly served as Buchanan's attorney general.

Stanton became acquainted with Abraham Lincoln before the war, but he was not impressed. Both men served on a team of lawyers involved in a patent infringement case, but the team completely ignored Lincoln. Stanton did not respect Lincoln as a lawyer and asked a colleague, "Why did you bring that damned long armed Ape here; he does not know anything and can do you no good." With such a history, it seemed unlikely Lincoln would ask Stanton to join his cabinet, but Lincoln recognized Stanton's ability and appointed him secretary of war in January 1862 to replace Simon Cameron.

Although scrupulously honest, intelligent, and dedicated to the Union, Stanton also was stubborn, hot-tempered, prickly, and outspoken. Fellow cabinet member Gideon Welles described him as being "arrogant and domineering toward those in subordinate positions [but] a sycophant and intriguer in his conduct and language with those whom he fears." Stanton also made many enemies in the media and industry because he censored the press and clashed with contractors who defrauded the

away with all the patriotism we have. Whenever men are forced to fight they take no personal interest in it. . . ."

Widespread criticism of the exemptions, commutation fees, and substitutions eventually forced both governments to make changes. The Confederacy abolished the substitute system in 1863 and lowered the required number of supervised slaves under the Twenty Negro Law to fifteen and made those exempted pay a $500 fee. The Union abolished commutation the following year. Despite these changes, poor citizens continued to criticize the system for being unfair. In the North, there were bloody draft riots, and Southern men hid out from conscription officers and sometimes even fought them. As the war continued, it became common on both sides to hear the caustic comment that it had become "a rich man's war and a poor man's fight."

government. He proved to be an excellent secretary, however, and eliminated much of the contract fraud that had become widespread under Cameron, organized the Union war machine in a more efficient manner, and strongly supported the Emancipation Proclamation. Next to Lincoln, Stanton was more instrumental to the Union victory than any other Northern politician. He wielded considerable power within the army and attacked generals he thought were uncommitted or incompetent. Stanton bitterly criticized General George B. McClellan for his lack of aggression and frequently urged Lincoln to remove him from command of the Army of the Potomac. Stanton once declared, "If [McClellan] had a million men he would swear the enemy has two millions, and then he would sit down in the mud and yell for three."

Despite entering the cabinet as a Lincoln critic, Stanton came to recognize the president's strengths. For his part, Lincoln trusted Stanton, and the two forged a close bond. On one occasion someone revealed to Lincoln that Stanton had called the president a damned fool. Lincoln replied, "If Stanton said I was a damned fool, then I must be one, for he is nearly always right and generally says what he means." When Lincoln was assassinated, Stanton was the government's rock. He quickly assumed control of the chaotic situation, ordered the roads out of Washington sealed, and began a manhunt for the killers. Lincoln's assassination devastated Stanton, but some people later tried to link him to the murder. Such rumors, however, were utterly false.

Stanton continued to serve under President Andrew Johnson during Reconstruction, but he became a close ally of the Radical Republicans because he believed Johnson was being too lenient toward the defeated South. Johnson's attempt to remove him as secretary of war without Senate approval led to the president's impeachment. When it became apparent Johnson would not be convicted, Stanton resigned his position in May 1868 and returned to private life. In 1869, President Ulysses S. Grant nominated him to the U.S. Supreme Court, but Stanton died just days after his confirmation.

## ARMY LIFE

**December 21, 1861: U.S. Congress authorizes Medal of Honor**
**October 13, 1862: Confederate Congress authorizes Roll of Honor**

For many young American men, the first time they had ever traveled away from home or received any type of medical examination was when they joined the army. By today's standards, these exams were ludicrous. Medical officers asked the recruits some simple questions and looked for any obvious defects by having them walk around or jump. One Union recruit who passed his physical examination claimed the surgeon "requested me to stand up straight, then gave me two or three little sort of 'love taps' on the chest, turned me round, ran

**An Army Encampment.** This wartime photograph shows Union soldiers in Virginia over-looking a typical army camp. Note the tents' linear formation and the wagon train park in the distance.

his hands over my shoulders, back, and limbs . . . then whirled me to the front, and rendered judgment on me. . . ." Not surprisingly, many soldiers were given medical discharges when time in the field showed they could not withstand the physical demands of army life. What is very surprising is that several hundred women disguised as men passed their physicals and entered service.

## Uniforms and Accoutrements

When the war began, there was no standard uniform for either side. The U.S. Army had adopted blue uniforms years earlier, but the hundreds of volunteer companies that entered Union and Confederate service in the spring of 1861 sported a variety of styles and colors. Some Union volunteers actually wore gray, and some Confederate units were outfitted in blue. This caused several cases of mistaken identity and friendly fire incidents at First Bull Run and Wilson's Creek. Therefore, one of the most important tasks facing both armies was to adopt a standard uniform for all their troops.

Blue remained the Union's official color, while the Confederates adopted gray. Both used wool cloth, kepis (hats similar to baseball caps), and uncomfortable ankle-high boots that were made in just a few standard sizes. Because of growing shortages in the Confederacy, however, uniform specifications fell by the wayside as the war dragged on. Soldiers came to prefer slouch hats over kepis and sometimes dressed in captured Union clothing. As material became scarce, Confederate uniforms were often made of homespun fabric dyed a yellowish-brown color made from copperas (ferrous sulphate crystal) and walnut hulls that gave rise to the term *butternut soldiers*.

> ## DID YOU KNOW?
> ### Shoddy
> *Shoddy*, a term referring to anything of poor quality, was a type of woolen cloth used to make Union uniforms early in the war. The material quickly fell apart, and it sometimes actually melted when it became wet. Because of this, Union soldiers began to refer to anything of inferior quality as being "shoddy."

In addition to the official uniforms, some units adopted the style of the French Algerian Zouaves (ZWAHVS), who had gained notoriety in the Crimean War for their colorful uniforms and incredible bravery. The Zouave uniform included striped baggy pants, white gaiters, short jackets, and tasseled red fezzes. Although Zouave uniforms varied from unit to unit, they all were flashy and colorful, with red and blue being the preferred colors for the pants, sashes, jackets, and fezzes. Some Northern units kept the uniforms throughout the war, while Confederate Zouaves were issued standard uniforms when the original clothing wore out.

In addition to his uniform, a Civil War soldier was also issued various accoutrements needed to operate in the field. Most men carried their rations in a large canvas sack, called a haversack, and extra gear in a knapsack, or backpack. The knapsack was hot and heavy, and many soldiers, particularly Confederates, discarded it in favor of putting their goods inside a rolled-up blanket that was worn across the shoulder. Soldiers also had to carry a canteen, rifle, bayonet, and cartridge box. One new Union recruit declared, "[W]e are warriors now in full feathers and trappings: ten pounds of gun; eighty rounds per man of ball cartridge, one pound of powder, five pounds of lead, heavy equipments; knapsack, haversack, three-pint canteen, all full; three days' rations; rubber blanket, woolen blanket, shelter tent, full winter clothing; tin cup, tin plate, knife, fork, spoon, spider, et cetera too numerous to mention, and too many to carry, and a pound of mud on each shoe. We are a baggage train, freight train, ammunition train, commissary train, gravel train, and a train-band, all in one." With such a load, it did not take soldiers long to distinguish between what was important and what was not. Confederate soldiers, especially, refined light marching to an art form. One Rebel noted that in his army "the private soldier, reduced to the minimum, consisted of one man, one hat, one jacket, one pair pants, one pair drawers, one pair socks, one pair shoes, and his baggage was one blanket, one gum-cloth, and one haversack. . . ."

## In Camp and Training

A Civil War soldier's life was not one of constant marching and fighting. The average soldier spent only a few weeks in combat during the entire war; some fought only a few days or none at all. Much more time was spent in camp awaiting orders. Typical of the Civil War soldier's experience was months of mind-numbing boredom interspersed with short periods of sheer terror. While in camp, a soldier's routine rarely changed. Each day he had to assemble in the morning and evening for roll call, engage in tactical combat drills, turn out for inspections and parades, and stand guard duty or man the picket posts (small outposts around the camp to guard against attack).

During the winter, maneuvers were almost impossible because the roads became virtually impassable in wet weather, and armies went into permanent camps consisting of wooden cabins. In warm weather, soldiers lived in large tents so they could move quickly to confront the enemy. When the army was involved in military operations, the large tents were left behind, and soldiers used small tent halves that were the precursors of the modern pup tent. Each soldier carried a tent fly that could be joined together with another to form a small two-man tent. However, many soldiers lacked even these and slept on a blanket in the open air during campaigns.

Training in the Civil War was far different from what American soldiers experience today. Such things as physical exercise, marksmanship, first aid, and field maneuvers were virtually nonexistent. Training consisted almost entirely of learning how to load and fire a rifle and performing tactical drills and maneuvers. These drills were absolutely necessary because it was difficult to maneuver thousands of men without the modern convenience of field radios. Each soldier had to know instantly how to react if ordered to march by the flank, form a hollow square, or throw out a skirmish line. Companies, regiments, and brigades repeated the drills over and over until even the most complex maneuver became second nature.

## Recreation

Boredom was a constant problem in camp, and soldiers relied on many activities to keep themselves occupied. Among the favorites were writing letters; reading; playing baseball, checkers, chess, or cards; snowball fights; putting on plays; holding debates; listening to music; playing with pets; and holding religious services.

Music was particularly popular, and most regiments had a band that provided entertainment during camp and music for special occasions. It is estimated approximately 9,000 new songs were written during the war. Most men preferred songs of a sentimental nature over those with a martial tone, and some universal favorites were "Home, Sweet Home," "When This Cruel War Is Over," "Annie Laurie," "Listen to the Mockingbird," and "Lorena." Another popular song, "Aura Lee," was later used as the tune for Elvis Presley's "Love

# EYEWITNESS
## Edmond Stephens

*Edmond Stephens was a 19-year-old farmer from Minden, Louisiana, who joined the 9th Louisiana Volunteers. He was quickly promoted to sergeant and accompanied the regiment to Virginia. Like thousands of other men, Stephens expected the war to be brief and exciting, but months of monotonous camp life quickly drained him of his enthusiasm. During one quiet moment in November 1861, he sat down to write a letter home describing a typical day in the Confederate army.*

About one hour before the brake of day you are interrupted by a loud beating of a base drum which they call revile. You then at once rise & on double quick time drag on your old dust wallowed coat, & as for your pants it [is] contrary to the rules of camp to take them off during the hours of rest. You then lay an old wool hat on your head which [you] have picked up in the road while traveling up on some wild march & it having been refused to be owned by some layboring Negro. You then lay your feet into a pair of Shoe soles without any uper leather being attached to them. You start with said clothing around you with the speed of some wild flying fowl for the parade ground to answer your name at Roll call. You then proceed to kindle you a fire with a few sticks of wood which was hauld [to] you [a] number of miles, & that [is] nearly imposible with me because there [is] not the first splinter of lightwood here. . . . By chance you get you a little smothered fire to burning, then aply your cooking utensils which are near nothing, iron mashed to geather. . . . You take from the pan some burnt biscuit without either salt, flour or water in them & from said kettle you take a little beefs neck boil[ed] without any water. You then seat your self with four or five of your filthy handed, snot nosed, frisele headed mess mates which would seem to white men not only to be wild but naturally breathed filth & after this is finished about one third are detailed to guard the others & keep them all to wollern in one hole as if they were a parcel of hogs.

*Over the next few years, Stephens experienced some of the war's bloodiest combat before being mortally wounded at the Battle of the Wilderness. In a letter to Stephens's parents, a friend graphically reported how the bullet entered near his anus and exited his lower abdomen, cutting his intestines. Stephens lingered for more than a week before succumbing to the horrific wound. The friend believed Stephens was accidentally shot by his own men.*

Terry L. Jones, *Lee's Tigers: The Louisiana Infantry in the Army of Northern Virginia* (Baton Rouge: Louisiana State University Press, 1987), p. 22.

Me Tender." The Confederates particularly liked "Dixie" (which became the unofficial national anthem) and "The Bonnie Blue Flag," while Union soldiers enjoyed "Hail Columbia!" and "John Brown's Body" (whose tune was later used for the "Battle Hymn of the Republic").

**Sunday Mass.** Many regiments had chaplains who accompanied them in the field to provide religious comfort. This Catholic chaplain is holding Sunday mass for the Irish-dominated 69th New York while it was camped near Washington. The two women with umbrellas at lower left may have been officers' wives.

Bands always accompanied the armies on campaigns, and sometimes the opposing forces were so close soldiers could hear the enemy's music. While they were camped on opposite sides of the Rappahannock River at Fredericksburg, Virginia, the musicians waged their own battle of the bands by taking turns playing such sectional favorites as "Dixie," "John Brown's Body," "The Bonnie Blue Flag," and "The Star-Spangled Banner." As the sun set and the evening grew quiet, a single bugle began playing "Home, Sweet Home." A Union soldier recalled how "all listened intently, and I don't believe there was a dry eye in all those assembled thousands." Just a few weeks later on a bitterly cold night at the Battle of Stones River, opposing bands took turns serenading the armies, separated by fields littered with the dead and wounded.

Religious activities were also important to many soldiers, and most regiments had a chaplain. In addition to holding services, chaplains gathered supplies, wrote letters for soldiers, nursed the sick and wounded, and sometimes even grabbed a rifle and went into battle. To be accepted, however, they not only had to be godly men but also able to tolerate such minor moral infractions as gambling and show genuine concern for their flock. Letters and diaries indicate chaplains had a mixed record in this regard. Some were despised for being lazy and immoral, while others were highly regarded. In the Confederate armies, chaplains were especially valued in the winter of 1863–64 when a fervent religious revival swept through the camps.

## Rations

Food was most important to a soldier, but it generally was of poor quality and in short supply. A mainstay of the diet was hardtack, a large quarter-inch thick cracker made from unleavened flour. Hardtack kept for years, but it was so hard it often had to be soaked in water before eating. For meat, soldiers were issued salt pork (which resembled a thick slab of bacon), salt beef, and sometimes fresh meat and bacon. Bulk quantities of beans, rice, coffee, sugar, vinegar, and salt were also distributed to units to be divided among the soldiers. Hardtack, salt pork, and coffee composed the bulk of the Civil War diet, with coffee being a mainstay (although it became scarce in the Confederacy as the Union blockade became more effective).

The soldiers' rations were bland and monotonous. One Confederate cavalryman recalled, "Sometimes we had a good meal, but generally we . . . had to buckle up our belts to find whether we possessed stomachs." The food often spoiled, and men had to eat meat and hardtack that were moldy, rancid, or filled with worms. A Union soldier claimed his unit sometimes received meat that was covered with flies, but noted, "We do not pay any more attention to that than if it was the wind blowing. We scrape them off and lay the meat in the sun which stops the flies work." For the first time in American history, canned meat also was issued to the armies, but it was so bad soldiers referred to it as "embalmed beef." It is no wonder hunger was a constant theme in Civil War letters and diaries. However, there were ways in which soldiers could supplement their rations. Foraging soldiers regularly targeted nearby farms and either bought necessary goods or simply took them. Private businessmen, called sutlers, were also authorized to set up shop in a tent or shack and sell food and other small consumer goods. The men, however, had little regard for sutlers because they often overcharged them, and outraged soldiers sometimes looted their establishments.

## Maintaining Discipline

Maintaining discipline was a problem for all Civil War armies because the vast majority of men were volunteers who were not used to military ways. Early in the war, discipline also was difficult to enforce because both sides allowed the men to elect their officers, and the officers' positions depended on keeping the soldiers' goodwill. Thanks largely to the professionally trained officers, Civil War soldiers came to accept discipline better as they gained more experience, but it was a constant struggle to keep them under control.

Methods of discipline were the same in both armies and were unusually harsh by today's standards. Officers could hand out summary—and often inventive—forms of punishment for minor infractions. Drunkenness, theft, and unauthorized absence were punished by fines; confinement to the guardhouse; carrying a fence rail on the shoulder; straddling a fence rail for hours; or wearing a barrel shirt, where the ends of a barrel were knocked out so it could be fitted with straps and worn over the body. Often a sign was attached to the barrel to show what offense the soldier had committed. Bucking and gagging was a particularly popular form of punishment that was both humiliating and painful. Forced to sit on the ground, the soldier's hands were tied to his feet, and his knees were slightly bent. A stick was then inserted behind his knees, resting on his arms, and another stick, or even a bayonet, was forced into his mouth as a gag. The "bucked and gagged" offender was left this way for hours, often in full view of his comrades. More serious crimes, such as attacking an officer, murder, spying, desertion, or cowardice, were tried by court-martial, and punishment could range from incarceration to execution. Sometimes when

**"The Rogue's March."** Humiliation was a common part of Civil War military punishment. This soldier was convicted of theft. After having his head shaved, a sign was placed around his neck declaring, "THIEF. This Man, Benj. Ditcher, 55th Mass. Vol's, Stole Money From a Wounded FRIEND." Guards with reversed arms then marched him through camp while musicians played an appropriate tune—"The Rogue's March."

immediate action was needed, such as when a soldier attacked a superior or ran away in battle, officers simply pulled out their pistols and shot the offender on the spot.

Punishment for officers, as a rule, was not as severe as for enlisted men. They were usually confined to quarters, forced to forfeit pay, or cashiered from the service. Officers might also be humiliated by being brought before their men and publicly stripped of their insignia, having their swords broken, and then being drummed out of camp. In most cases, however, authorities believed that publicly punishing officers was bad for morale, and many offending officers were allowed to resign their commissions quietly or were transferred to other areas.

## Decorations

In today's army, soldiers who perform bravely on the battlefield or who are particularly effective in their duties are often honored with medals and other decorations. This has not always been the case. Prior to the Civil War, Americans viewed military service as a patriotic duty and relied on volunteers to fight their

# NOTABLE UNITS: *The Louisiana Tigers*

Few Civil War units needed as much discipline as the rowdy Louisiana Tigers. Louisiana was unique among the Southern states because it had a French Catholic heritage and the most foreign-born residents. Some units drilled entirely in French because the men knew no English, and one Louisiana regiment sent to Virginia counted at least twenty-four nationalities among its members. After watching some Louisianians drill, a Georgia soldier declared in his peculiar accent, "That-thur furriner he calls out er lot er gibberish, an them-thur Dagoes jes maneuver-up like Hell-beatin' tanbark! Jes' like he was talking sense!" Many of the foreign-born soldiers had worked on rough-and-tumble steamboats and wharves where drinking, brawling, and thievery were a way of life. It was even rumored that some units were recruited from New Orleans jails. These men continued their violent lifestyle in the army, and several Louisiana commands became notorious for drunkenness, brawling, and thievery. One of the most feared units was the Tiger Rifles, a New Orleans Zouave company in Major Roberdeau Wheat's 1st Special Battalion. Their criminal behavior became so infamous that all Louisianians in Virginia became nicknamed Louisiana Tigers. Of course, most of the soldiers were decent men, but there were enough criminals to taint them all. Confederate letters and diaries are filled with comments about the notorious Tigers. They were described as being "pirates....from the dregs of all nations" and "adventurers, wharf-rats, cutthroats, and bad characters generally." One Richmond citizen wrote, "From the time of their appearance in Richmond, robberies became frequent." The first two men executed in the Army of Northern Virginia were Tigers.

The Tigers' saving grace was their status as some of the best fighters in the Army of Northern Virginia. At First Bull Run, they were said to have thrown down their rifles after running out of ammunition and charged with Bowie knives, and Stonewall Jackson credited them with winning all of the major battles during his famous Shenandoah Valley Campaign. When one Louisiana brigade ran out of ammunition at Second Bull Run, the men picked up rocks and hurled them at the enemy rather than retreat. At Gettysburg, they attacked Cemetery Hill and captured an enemy artillery battery but were forced to withdraw when no one supported them. General Jubal Early's attitude toward the Tigers was typical. As he stood beside General Lee, Early watched the Tigers overrun two enemy positions at the Battle of Salem Church and then threw his hat to the ground and yelled out, "Those damned Louisiana fellows may steal as much as they please now!"

The Tigers included the 1st, 5th, 6th, 7th, 8th, 9th, 10th, 14th, and 15th Louisiana Volunteers. Several battalions, such as Wheat's, also served but they were soon disbanded. These units made up two brigades in Stonewall Jackson's corps and were commanded by a number of generals, the most famous being Richard Taylor, Harry T. Hays, and Leroy A. Stafford (who was mortally wounded at the Wilderness). There were approximately 12,000 Tigers during the war, but only 373 were on duty at war's end. Today, their name lives on at Louisiana State University. In the early 1900s, the LSU football coach chose "Tigers" as the mascot name because of the Louisiana Tigers' fierce reputation.

wars. Decorations were shunned because recognizing one man over another was contrary to the idea of equality among soldiers, and it might spread jealousy within the army and break down morale. Because the regiment was considered more important than the individual, units were allowed to place the names of battles on their flags as a way of displaying their proud combat record, but the highest honor a soldier could expect was to be commended in his superior's battle report. This policy changed somewhat during the Civil War. Both congresses extended the Thanks of Congress to honor an individual or unit for meritorious service. The Confederates issued the most Thanks and recognized both individuals and units, while the U.S. Congress recognized only individuals.

Union officers could also be honored by receiving a brevet, or honorary promotion to a higher rank. When brevetted, an officer was allowed to use the title of the higher rank, but he did not receive its pay or authority. It could become confusing because an officer might be addressed as "Colonel" when his actual rank was captain. Perhaps the best-known example of the brevet rank was George Armstrong Custer. Although officially a lieutenant colonel at war's end, he had been brevetted major general for his Civil War service. Thus at the time of his death at the Little Big Horn, Custer was referred to as General Custer.

Some individual Northern generals also gave out medals to honor men in their units, but the Medal of Honor was the only official medal adopted by the Union. Authorized by Congress in December 1861, this medal is still the nation's highest decoration for bravery. The Medal of Honor was awarded for combat service above and beyond the call of duty, but during the Civil War its standards were more lax than they are today. Capturing a Confederate battle flag, for example, automatically earned a soldier the medal. This led to abuse because some stragglers who deliberately stayed out of combat picked up flags after the fighting was over and turned them in and received a medal. To correct the record, the War Department reexamined recipients in 1916 and revoked the medals of more than 900 men.

Although authorized by the Confederate Congress, no official medals or decorations were ever awarded to Southern soldiers. Instead, a Roll of Honor was adopted. Any soldier who demonstrated conspicuous bravery or conduct in battle could be nominated to have his name inscribed on the Roll. After battles, this Roll of Honor was read to the troops during dress parades, published in newspapers, and filed in the offices of the adjutant and inspector generals.

## Flags

Flags were very important to all Civil War soldiers. Most regiments carried a regimental and a national flag, and some Irish-dominated units even carried Irish flags. The regimental flag was particularly important as a symbol of pride and identity. It usually was similar to the national flag and bore the regiment's name and the battles in which it had fought. The regiment's flags were carried by color-bearers and were accompanied by the color guard, which was a small squad of men whose duty was to protect the flag from capture during battle. It was considered a great

**Bonnie Blue Flag.** Originally the flag of the Republic of West Florida, the Bonnie Blue Flag became the unofficial flag of secession.

honor to be chosen for these positions, but they were also extremely dangerous because the enemy tended to concentrate his fire on the flags.

The Confederate battle flag, with its St. Andrew's Cross, was the most famous banner carried into battle by Southerners. Almost as well known was the "Bonnie Blue Flag," which is often mentioned in song and film. In the movie *Gone with the Wind,* Rhett Butler named his daughter Bonnie because her eyes were as blue as the Bonnie Blue Flag. This flag had a single star on a blue field and was based on the 1810 Lone Star Flag of the West Florida Republic. When Mississippi seceded, the Bonnie Blue Flag was raised over the capitol, and four other Southern states incorporated it into their flags. It became secession's unofficial banner and was widely used in the South until the Confederates adopted an official flag. A song entitled "The Bonnie Blue Flag," which became almost as popular as "Dixie," was written in 1861 by an Irish actor who witnessed the flag being raised over the Mississippi statehouse.

## CIVIL WAR WEAPONS

From the Revolutionary War through the Mexican War, the standard weapon of the American soldier was a single-shot flintlock smoothbore musket fitted with a triangular bayonet. The musket was a muzzle loader, meaning the powder and ball were loaded into the muzzle of the weapon and seated with a ramrod. The advantage of the smoothbore musket was that it could be loaded quickly because the ball was small enough to fit into the barrel easily. The disadvantage was that it often misfired in wet weather because the pan

**The Tattered Flags.** Union soldiers carried both regimental flags and various designs of the U.S. flag. Here the color guard of the 56th and 36th Massachusetts proudly display their regimental colors. The flags' torn and tattered condition bears testament to the regiments' hard service.

powder got wet, and it was terribly inaccurate. The inside of the barrel was smooth, like a shotgun, and the loose-fitting ball rattled down the barrel with no spin and no accuracy. A good marksman might hit an enemy soldier at fifty yards, but anything beyond that was pure luck. Generals simply lined up as many men as possible in an open field and either overwhelmed the enemy with continuous volleys of fire or fired one volley and then charged with the bayonet.

Some specialized units, such as sharpshooters, used a muzzle-loading flint-lock rifle. These worked the same as the musket, except the inside of the barrel had spiral grooves called rifling. The ball was wrapped in a greased patch of cloth, which made it fit tight in the barrel. When fired, the patched ball gripped the rifling and came out of the barrel spinning, which gave it stability in flight and increased its range and accuracy. While a musket's effective accurate range was about fifty yards, a rifle was accurate out to several hundred yards. The obvious advantage to the rifle was the ability to hit enemy soldiers at a much longer distance. The disadvantage was that it was much slower to load because the ball had to be wrapped in a greased patch and then forcibly rammed down the barrel with the ramrod.

## Evolution of Weapons

In the 1840s, French captain Claude-Etienne Minié developed a new bullet that combined the speed of the musket with the accuracy of the rifle. Known as the "minié ball" (pronounced "minny" in America), it was a hollow-based coni-cal bullet, slightly smaller than the weapon's bore. The powder and minié ball were placed in a paper cartridge, with the powder in one end and the ball in the other. The soldier ripped open the cartridge with his teeth, sprinkled some powder in the pan, and then poured the rest of the powder and bullet down the barrel and seated them with a ramrod. When fired, the powder's explosive gases expanded the hollow base and caused the bullet to grip the barrel's rifling and start to spin. The minié ball could be loaded as quickly as a musket, but it had the range and accuracy of the rifle.

Another major innovation prior to the Civil War was the invention of the percussion cap, which was a small copper cap filled with fulminate of mercury. Rifle muskets using percussion caps had a nipple below the hammer instead of a powder pan. When the hammer struck the cap, the cap exploded and sent fire into the barrel to set off the powder charge. Percussion caps were much superior to the flintlock system because they would fire in wet conditions. The U.S. Army adopted both the minié ball and percussion cap before the Civil War began.

## Infantry and Cavalry Weapons

Union and Confederate authorities used many different types of firearms in their armies, including antiquated flintlock muskets and poorly manufactured weapons purchased in Europe. By mid-war, however, both armies settled on a particular rifle musket as their standard infantry weapon. For the Union, it was the Model 1861 Springfield designed by the Springfield Armory in Massachu-setts. An extremely accurate weapon, the .58 caliber Springfield used a huge 500-grain bullet, had a maximum effective range of 500 yards, and could be fired about six times a minute. The Confederacy did not have an armory capable of turning out enough rifles to arm its soldiers and was forced to import British Enfields. This rifle musket was one of the best in the world and was similar to the Springfield, except it fired a .577 caliber minié ball. Both the Springfield and Enfield rifles were fitted with a long, triangular bayonet, but bayonets were rarely used in combat because the rifle musket allowed soldiers to kill their opponents at long range. Medical records show that less than .004 percent of wounded Union soldiers were injured by bayonets.

Cavalrymen were unable to carry the rifle musket because its length made it difficult to load from horseback. Instead, Union cavalrymen eventually adopted repeating carbines (shortened rifles), while the Confederates often preferred shotguns. Instead of bayonets, cavalrymen were armed with sabers to cut down the enemy. However, modern firearms made the traditional saber largely obso-lete by the time of the Civil War, and cavalrymen on both sides began to rely more on the pistol for close-quartered combat. The preferred pistol was the six-shot Colt revolver in .36 or .44 caliber, with a similar Remington model being a second choice.

Both armies constantly searched for ways to increase their firepower. The Union was more successful in this endeavor and adopted new types of repeating weapons. The Gatling Gun, the forerunner of modern machine guns, was introduced by the North late in the war but it was rarely used. The most effective repeating weapon was the Spencer carbine, which became standard issue for the Union cavalry. A lever-action rifle, it held seven .52-caliber self-contained metallic cartridges that were loaded into a tube magazine in the butt stock. The Spencer was the first repeating weapon to use the metallic cartridge successfully, and its rapid fire proved very effective. The epitome of the Union repeating rifle, however, was the Henry, invented by B. Tyler Henry of Oliver Winchester's New Haven Arms Company. It was a lever-action rifle that fired a .44-caliber rim-fire metallic cartridge fed from a tubular magazine under the barrel. The Confederates referred to this 15-shot weapon as the rifle the "Yankees loaded on Sunday and fired all week." Unfortunately, the Union government only bought about 1,700 Henrys, while individual states purchased a few thousand more.

## Artillery

Civil War soldiers used a wide variety of cannons, including muzzle loaders and breech loaders, smoothbores and rifles. Each had a particular function and could fire a number of different projectiles depending on its mission. Artillery pieces were classified either by the weight of the projectile (a 12-pounder) or the diameter of the bore (a 3-inch rifle). The most common Civil War artillery piece was the smoothbore, muzzle-loading 12-pounder Napoleon, named for France's Napoleon III, who developed it in 1856. The Napoleon had a rather short range of several hundred yards, but it was excellent against advancing infantry. Rifled guns had a longer range and were used against infantry, opposing batteries, ships, and fortifications. One of the most popular rifled guns was the Parrott Rifle, a cast-iron muzzle-loading cannon that came in 3-inch (10-pounder) to 10-inch (250-pounder) models.

Smoothbores and rifles fired a flat trajectory and were used as field artillery against opposing armies and fortified walls. But sometimes artillerymen used mortars, which were short-barreled artillery pieces that fired exploding projectiles at a high trajectory arc so they fell behind walls and fortifications. They, too, were rated according to their bore diameter. Using a massive 20-pound powder charge, the huge 13-inch mortar fired a 220-pound shell approximately 2.5 miles and could be fitted onto ships and railroad cars. Union forces, in particular, made good use of mortars during the numerous sieges they waged against the Confederates.

All artillery pieces were devastating and could be fired two to three times per minute. Depending on their targets, cannons fired such ammunition as solid shot, spherical case, and canister. Solid shot was a solid iron ball that was designed to batter down walls and other obstacles through force rather than explosion. The navies also used hot shot, a solid shot heated red hot in a furnace to set ships or fortifications on fire. Spherical case was invented during the Napoleonic Wars by British General Henry Shrapnel (thus giving us the term *shrapnel*). It was a hollow shell filled with powder and lead or iron balls. When the shell exploded, the balls continued forward in shotgun-fashion, mowing down the enemy's infantry. Canister, a tin can filled with lead or iron balls, was a similar type of ammunition. When the cannon fired, the canister peeled away as it left the muzzle, releasing the balls.

A percussion or time fuse was used to detonate the powder in exploding shells. Percussion fuses were fitted into the shell's nose and exploded on impact, while time fuses were set for a certain number of seconds and were lit by the cannon's blast. Time fuses were tricky because artillerymen had to estimate the distance to the target and the amount of time the shell would take to get there so the fuse exploded the shell on target. If they misjudged or had faulty fuses, the shells exploded over their own troops.

**Union Artillery Park.** This photograph, taken of a Union artillery park during the 1862 Peninsula Campaign, shows some of the heavy weapons that were used in the Civil War. Rifled cannons can be seen in the background, and mortars are lined up along the fence. The massive cannonballs in the foreground are mortar shells.

## CIVIL WAR STRATEGY AND TACTICS

Strategy consists of a nation's political and military plans to achieve a large objective, such as winning a war or a major campaign. Civil War strategy was greatly influenced by Swiss military theorist Baron Antoine Henri Jomini (ZHOE-mee-nee) and the American Dennis Hart Mahan (muh-HAHN). Jomini's writings dominated military thinking in the nineteenth century and greatly influenced West Point officers. A former general in Napoleon's army, Jomini believed war should be limited to the opposing armies and not involve civilians and that wars and campaigns could be won through maneuvers rather than bloody fighting. Jomini stressed such principles as concentrating a superior force against the enemy, using interior lines for greater mobility, surprising the enemy whenever possible, relying on the turning movement to force the enemy to retreat, and maintaining the initiative. Mahan was an American military theorist who graduated first in the West Point class of 1824 and taught at the academy for many years. He had extensive knowledge of military strategy and tactics and taught most of the cadets who became Civil War generals. Mahan's classes stressed the use of strong defensive fortifications to stop an attack and implementation of direct counterattacks and turning movements to defeat the enemy.

## The Anaconda Plan

In preparing for war, Lincoln was fortunate to have General-in-Chief Winfield Scott, a Virginian who remained loyal when his native state seceded. Known as "Old Fuss and Feathers" for his love of pomp and protocol, Scott was seventy-four years old and suffered from dropsy, but the old hero of the War of 1812 and Mexico was still mentally sharp and provided Lincoln with sound military advice. At Lincoln's request, Scott devised a winning strategy for the Union. The heart of his plan was to place a blockade on Confederate ports and to seize control of the Mississippi River. The blockade would prevent the enemy from exporting goods and importing war material, and seizing the river would split the Confederacy in two and prevent the eastern and western sections from supporting one another. Scott believed these two steps would devastate the Confederacy's war-making ability and dampen the people's morale. The Union could then largely halt military operations and give loyal Southerners an opportunity to rise up against the Confederacy and force the secessionists to end the war.

Not everyone was impressed with Scott's strategy, however, particularly when he warned it would take tens of thousands of men many months to subdue the Confederacy. Most people were predicting a short war and ridiculed Scott for proposing a strategy that would slowly constrict and suffocate the Confederacy. Scott's strategy reminded his critics of the South American snake, and they derisively dubbed it the Anaconda Plan. Nonetheless, the Anaconda Plan proved effective, although it took much longer to win the war than even Scott predicted.

## The Confederates' Strategy

The Confederates did not agree on the best strategy to win independence. Jefferson Davis largely followed his own counsel and adopted what he called a defensive-offensive strategy. With it, he hoped to emulate George Washington by defending as much territory as possible while avoiding catastrophic defeats on the battlefield. If an opportunity arose to take the offensive without too great a risk, Davis would do so, but his main objective was to conserve resources and simply survive because he believed time was on the side of the Confederacy. If the South could make the war as bloody as possible and drag it out for years, the Union would exhaust itself, and the Northern people would lose stomach

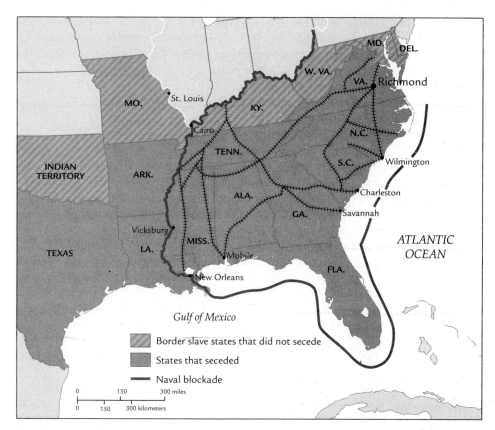

**The Anaconda Plan.**  General Winfield Scott's war strategy called for strangling the Confederacy into submission by blockading its coast and seizing control of the Mississippi River. Such a slow death by constriction led critics to call it the Anaconda Plan.

for the fight. Eventually, Lincoln would have to seek a negotiated settlement just as the British had done in the Revolution.

Some generals, such as Joseph E. Johnston, preferred a purely defensive war in which the South would sacrifice space for time. The Confederacy was huge, nearly the size of western Europe, and it simply did not have the manpower needed to defend every point. Johnston believed the best strategy was to avoid risky offensive operations that might endanger the armies. Again, by staying on the defensive to conserve their strength and retreating when necessary, the Confederates could drag out the war and eventually exhaust the Union resolve.

Robert E. Lee disagreed with both Davis and Johnston. He believed time was on the Union's side and the longer the war lasted the stronger the North would become as it brought its tremendous military advantages to bear. Lee was convinced an offensive strategy was the only way to overcome the overwhelming odds facing the South. The Confederates should force the Union into large decisive battles and defeat it quickly to bring Lincoln to the negotiating table. Although President Davis was not comfortable with Lee's aggressive strategy, Lee usually had his way in planning campaigns. Of all the Confederate generals, he formed the best relationship with Davis through a combination of personal tact and military skill. As a result, Davis came to trust Lee completely and usually approved any plans he made.

## Military Departments

To achieve their respective strategies, both the Union and Confederacy divided their land into military departments, with each being subdivided into several smaller districts. Each department had its own commander and military force, which usually was an army named for the department, such as the Confederate Army of Northern Virginia defending the Department of Northern Virginia.

These departments were very fluid and were created, disbanded, and redrawn according to military and political necessities. Unfortunately, the department system created a provincial attitude that fostered jealousy and hampered cooperation. Since commanders were only responsible for defending their department, they were reluctant to send reinforcements to help one another or to cooperate in military campaigns involving more than one department. Despite these weaknesses, both sides continued to use the department system throughout the war.

## Civil War Tactics

Tactics is the maneuvering of troops in either a defensive or offensive manner on the battlefield. The Union and Confederacy had identical concepts of tactics because they shared a common heritage, had the same military experience, and used officers who were trained in the same military schools. When the war began, the tactical manual used by both armies was known as *Hardee's Tactics* because it was written by former U.S. Army officer (and future Confederate general) William J. Hardee. When rifles came into wider use during the Mexican War, Hardee recognized that traditional Napoleonic tactics were less effective against modern weapons. Because rifles could kill at great distances, speed and flexibility were more important than slow, methodical, massed formations. *Hardee's Tactics* stressed these concepts, but the Union army did not want its soldiers studying a text written by a Rebel so it had General Silas Casey develop a new manual. *Casey's Tactics* became the standard manual for the Union, but it was almost identical to *Hardee's Tactics*.

Although Civil War generals recognized the need to close quickly with the enemy and use maneuvers when possible to avoid the deadly rifled weapons, it was still necessary for armies to mass the infantry together in dense, tightly packed formations or in long battle lines. It was almost impossible to coordinate large formations spread out over huge areas because there were no battlefield communications other than signal flags and mounted couriers. Also, dense smoke quickly enveloped battlefields and cut visibility to near zero. Generals needed to have their men close together so they could see what was happening and make quick decisions. Massing troops was also the only way a commander could maintain control and concentrate volleys of rifle fire to break the enemy's line. Typically, generals formed their men into two parallel lines several yards apart so the second line could relieve the first if necessary and plug gaps produced by casualties. But battles were never the neat affairs so often portrayed in illustrations and films. After the initial volleys were fired, the long lines frequently disintegrated, and the soldiers fought in small groups scattered all over the field. This was particularly true when the fighting occurred in thick woods such as at the Wilderness and Chickamauga.

The frontal attack was the primary tactic used in the war, but it was developed when armies used inaccurate smoothbore muskets. In the Civil War, rifle muskets and entrenchments made frontal attacks nearly suicidal. Nonetheless, generals continued to rely on this tactic because it was easy to control and coordinate, and there was always the possibility that determination and superior numbers could carry the day.

The flank attack, or envelopment, was an alternate way to dislodge the enemy from a strong position. Armies usually fought in long lines roughly parallel to one another, but this left little protection of the flanks or the ends of the line. In other words, if all the soldiers were facing north, only the soldiers on the very end of the line could swing around and face east or west to meet an attack from those directions. In a flank attack, an army maneuvers to get into position perpendicular to the enemy's line and attacks down its narrow length rather than across its broad front. The attacking force could then enfilade (EN-fuh-layd) the enemy, or fire down the length of his battle line, and cause massive casualties. If a flank attack was successful, the enemy soldiers on the flank were driven back and unit after unit became dislodged until the entire line was "rolled up like a blanket." In an ideal situation, Civil War generals tried to hit the enemy with both frontal and flank attacks. Troops were left along the enemy's front to draw his attention away from the flanking maneuver. Once the flank attack was made, the troops facing the enemy would join in with a frontal attack and the enemy would be crushed between the two.

The turning movement was similar to the flank attack, but in a turning movement the attacking force avoided direct contact with the enemy by making a wide sweep completely around the enemy's flank to threaten his supply line in the rear. If successful, the turning movement forced the enemy to abandon his position and retreat to avoid being cut off from his base of supplies.

As the war progressed, tactics changed somewhat as the armies learned how to counter modern weaponry. Attacking forces began to use more flanking and turning maneuvers rather than frontal attacks to dislodge the enemy. Defending forces also began digging elaborate systems of trenches, fortifications, and earthworks to provide protection against rifle and cannon fire. Early in the war, many generals thought fighting behind entrenchments was cowardly, but most came to see the wisdom of digging in. After watching attacking forces being slaughtered at such places as Fredericksburg and Kennesaw Mountain, commanders on both sides realized modern weaponry gave a tactical edge to the army on the defensive. Early Civil War battlefields resembled the wide open fields of Napoleon's Europe, but they eventually took on the appearance of the trench-scarred killing fields of World War I.

## FOR FURTHER READING

Winfield Scott's Anaconda Plan
Excerpt from *Hardee's Tactics*

# Yankee Onslaught: The Western Theater, 1862

When Flag Officer David Farragut's Union fleet dropped anchor at New Orleans on April 25, 1862, the heavens opened and a monsoon-like downpour drenched the riverfront. The city was in complete chaos. Some panicked citizens packed what they could and fled the Yankees while authorities set fire to valuable supplies, ships, and warehouses to keep them out of enemy hands. Clouds of smoke hung heavy over the city, and Canal Street was awash in sticky, ankle-deep molasses that had been dumped in the gutter. Soon a huge mob of defiant civilians gathered on the levee to yell insults and threats at Farragut's sailors, but the Union gunners, still powder smeared from their fight with the Confederates downstream, simply grinned and patted their cannons affectionately.

Suddenly, a gangplank was lowered from one ship, and two unarmed Union officers disembarked on Farragut's orders to wade through the mob to City Hall to demand that the mayor surrender. Lieutenant George H. Perkins was one of those officers, and he later wrote, "Among the crowd were many women and children, and the women were shaking rebel flags, and being rude and noisy. . . . As we advanced, the mob followed us in a very excited state. They gave three cheers for Jeff Davis and Beauregard, and three groans for Lincoln. Then they began to throw things at us, and shout, 'Hang them!' 'Hang them!' We both thought we were in a *bad* fix, but there was nothing for us to do, but just go on." Among the crowd was noted author George Washington Cable. He recalled how the two officers walked side by side, "unguarded and alone, looking not to right or to left, never frowning, never flinching, while the mob screamed in their ears, shook cocked pistols in their faces, cursed and crowded, and gnashed upon them. So through the gates of death those two men walked to the City Hall to demand the town's surrender. It was one of the bravest deeds I ever saw done."

Farragut's capture of New Orleans was just one of several stunning Union victories in early 1862. By then, two theaters of military operation had developed in the Civil War. The eastern theater centered on Virginia and the region surrounding the two opposing capitals, while the western theater included all points west. Most Americans expected the second year of war to begin with a great clash of arms in the eastern theater where George B. McClellan was preparing the Union Army of the Potomac for offensive action. Virginia, however, remained relatively quiet, but the war resumed with all its fury in the west. There, both armies occupied Kentucky, and the fate of Missouri remained uncertain. Within a few months, however, the fortunes of war swung greatly in favor of the Union.

## THE FORTS HENRY AND DONELSON CAMPAIGN

**January 9, 1862: Battle of Mill Springs, Kentucky**
**February 6, 1862: Union forces capture Fort Henry, Tennessee**
**February 12–16, 1862: Battle of Fort Donelson, Tennessee**
**February 23, 1862: Union forces occupy Nashville, Tennessee**

The New Year began with a minor battle in eastern Kentucky that had significant strategic results. Two small armies under Union Major General George H. Thomas and Confederate Major General George B. Crittenden (eldest son of Senator John J. Crittenden) were maneuvering in that part of the state. On the wet, foggy morning of January 9, 1862, they collided at Mill Springs. In a fierce, confused fight, the Confederates at first pushed the Union soldiers back, but Thomas counterattacked and forced Crittenden to retreat across the Cumberland River. In the battle, 529 Confederate soldiers were killed, wounded, or missing, while Thomas counted 262 casualties. The Northern victory at Mill Springs was a relatively small affair by Civil War standards, but it changed the strategic situation in Kentucky by securing the eastern part of the state for the Union.

After the Battle of Mill Springs, General Albert Sidney Johnston, commander of the Confederate western department, established a defensive line running from Bowling Green west to the Mississippi River at Columbus. The center of this line was anchored at Forts Henry and Donelson, located just a few miles south of the Kentucky state line on the Tennessee and Cumberland Rivers, respectively. These forts proved to be a weak link in Johnston's defensive chain because they were vulnerable to attack from both the land and the rivers. If the forts fell, Johnston's line would be cracked along a seam. Union gunboats could then move rapidly up the Cumberland River to capture Nashville and up the Tennessee River into northern Alabama. For the Confederates, losing Forts Henry and Donelson meant losing Kentucky and perhaps even Tennessee.

## Fort Henry

In February 1862, Union Brigadier General Ulysses S. Grant moved against Fort Henry with the support of Commodore Andrew Foote's gunboats. Brigadier General Lloyd Tilghman, the fort's commander, realized his position was untenable when Foote's gunboats arrived in advance of Grant's troops. Tilghman stayed behind with a small detachment to keep the enemy at bay while the rest of the garrison escaped to Fort Donelson, which was only about ten miles to the east. After enduring an intense bombardment, he surrendered on February 6 before Grant's infantry even arrived on the scene.

Five days later, Grant's 15,000 men began the short march to Fort Donelson. Much larger than Fort Henry, it sat atop a high bluff on the Cumberland River's west bank, and heavy cannons dominated the river below. In addition, Brigadier General John B. Floyd's 21,000-man garrison initially outnumbered Grant. As Grant would discover, Fort Donelson was a much tougher nut to crack than Fort Henry.

## Fort Donelson

After arriving at Fort Donelson on February 12, Grant received significant reinforcements that allowed him to encircle the Rebel garrison. Confident of victory, his men enjoyed the unusually mild and balmy weather, and many of them threw away their winter coats while on the march to lighten their load. It was an unfortunate decision because a strong cold front suddenly blew through, dropping the temperature below freezing and pelting the soaked and shivering soldiers with sleet and snow. To make matters worse, the Confederate artillery riddled Foote's gunboats and forced them to retreat when they attacked the fort on February 14. The following day, Grant left his army to consult with Foote on what to do next. While he was gone, the Confederates launched a daring surprise attack to punch a hole through the enemy's line and escape to Nashville. The attack succeeded brilliantly, and the road to Nashville was momentarily opened, but Floyd suddenly lost his nerve and shocked his men by ordering them back into their defensive positions. By that time, Grant had returned to his army and quickly launched a counterattack that closed the hole.

While Grant consolidated his position that night, Floyd convened a war council and decided to surrender. However, he and his second-in-command, Brigadier General Gideon Pillow, had no intention of becoming prisoners of war. Floyd, in particular, wished to escape because he was a former U.S. secretary of war and feared he might be hanged as a traitor if captured. Floyd and Pillow turned the fort over to Brigadier General Simon Buckner, an old friend of Grant's, and then escaped by boat. This disgraceful act was the last of several blunders Floyd had made during the campaign. Although his men initially outnumbered those of Grant, Floyd made no attempt to stop the enemy while they were on the march from Fort Henry. Instead, the timid Floyd surrendered the initiative by staying inside Fort Donelson and allowing Grant to surround him. He then failed to follow through with his breakout attempt and ordered his men back into the fort just as they were on the verge of making a successful escape.

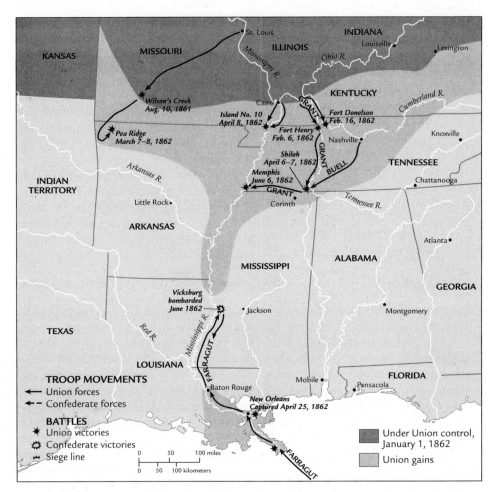

**The War in the West, August 1861–June 1862.** After suffering an initial defeat at Wilson's Creek in August 1861, Union forces in the west went on the offensive in early 1862 and won a string of important victories. The Battle of Pea Ridge secured Missouri and much of Arkansas for the Union, and the capture of Forts Henry and Donelson opened up Tennessee to invasion. Grant then defeated the Confederates at Shiloh, and Pope gained control of the upper Mississippi River by capturing Island No. 10. Downstream, Farragut captured both New Orleans and Baton Rouge and even threatened Vicksburg, Mississippi.

Colonel Nathan Bedford Forrest also made his way out of Fort Donelson but in a more honorable manner than Floyd and Pillow. The talk of surrender at the war council infuriated Forrest, and he boldly told his superiors, "I did not come here for the purpose of surrendering my command." He then stormed out of the meeting and gathered his mounted regiment and some infantrymen who begged to go along. Forrest slipped into flooded woods along the river and made his way around the Union lines. His horsemen broke through the ice that had formed on the backwater, and the infantrymen followed along holding on to the horses' tails. Forrest later claimed most of the garrison could have followed suit and escaped if only Floyd had tried.

When Buckner began negotiating with Grant later that night, he expected his former friend to offer generous surrender terms. Grant, however, informed Buckner he would accept nothing short of unconditional surrender. The harsh terms disappointed Buckner, yet he had no choice but to accept, and on February 16, he gave up the fort, 65 cannons, 20,000 muskets, and nearly 15,000 men. During the campaign, the Confederates had another 2,000 casualties to Grant's 2,800. Union forces quickly followed up their victory by occupying Nashville a week later and sending gunboats on a raid into northern Alabama. The capture of Fort Donelson elevated Grant from a virtual unknown to a popular Northern hero, and newspapers, playing on his initials, gave him the nickname "Unconditional Surrender" Grant.

Having already lost eastern Kentucky in the Battle of Mill Springs, the Confederates reeled from the defeats at Forts Henry and Donelson. The loss of the forts was a devastating, perhaps even fatal, blow because it forced them to abandon the rich agricultural and industrial areas of Kentucky and middle Tennessee. Considering the forts' strategic significance, the Confederates' failure to defend them more aggressively seems almost negligent. The surrenders can largely be attributed to Floyd's poor leadership, but the ultimate blame must fall on Joseph E. Johnston, the departmental commander. When it became obvious that the enemy was moving against the

## DID YOU KNOW?

### My Friend the Enemy

Many opposing officers in the Civil War were old friends who had not only attended West Point together but also fought side by side in the antebellum U.S. Army. For example, Confederate generals Thomas "Stonewall" Jackson, George Pickett, and A. P. Hill were West Point classmates of Union generals George B. McClellan, John Gibbon, and Truman Seymour. Hill and McClellan even roomed together and both courted Ellen Marcy (who ultimately married McClellan). Pickett and Gibbon became good friends at the academy, but at the Battle of Gettysburg it was Gibbon's division that bore the brunt of Pickett's Charge. Another close friendship formed at West Point was that of Ulysses S. Grant and Simon Bolivar Buckner. Grant and Buckner later served together in the Mexican War, and Buckner gave money to the financially strapped Grant on more than one occasion. As fate would have it, Buckner was forced to surrender Fort Donelson to Grant. While discussing details of the surrender, the two friends engaged in good-natured banter. Grant wrote in his memoirs, "In the course of our conversation, which was very friendly, he said to me that if he had been in command I would not have got up to Donelson as easily as I did. I told him that if he had been in command I should not have tried in the way I did." Grant spared Buckner the shame of a formal surrender ceremony and on one occasion discreetly took him aside to offer him money to help ease the discomforts of prison camp. Buckner graciously declined, but he appreciated Grant's attempt to settle his old debts. When Grant died in 1885, Buckner served as a pallbearer.

# BIOGRAPHY

## Ulysses Simpson Grant: The Man Who Won the War

**Ulysses S. Grant**

An Ohio native, Grant (1822–1885) was born Hiram Ulysses, but he became known as Ulysses Simpson after the congressman who appointed him to West Point mistakenly used the maiden name of Grant's mother for his middle name. After graduating in 1839, Grant was awarded two brevets for gallantry in the Mexican War, but he resigned his commission in 1854 to avoid a court martial for drunkenness.

Grant was a loving husband to his wife, Julia, and a caring father to his four children, but he failed in various civilian occupations before the Civil War dramatically changed his fortunes. After being commissioned colonel of the 21st Illinois, he was promoted rapidly as he defeated the enemy at Fort Donelson, Shiloh, Vicksburg, and Chattanooga. Grant partly attributed his success to an obscure incident that changed his entire outlook on strategy. He recalled when the Confederates fled during an early campaign, "It occurred to me at once that [the enemy] had been as much afraid of me as I had been of him. This was a view of the question I had never taken before; but it was one I never forgot afterwards. . . . I never forgot that he had as much reason to fear my forces as I had his."

There was nothing in Grant's personal appearance to suggest he was a great general. One man described him as a "short, round-shouldered man in a very tarnished major general's uniform [with] rough, light-brown whiskers, a blue eye, and rather a scrubby look withal . . . as if he was out of office and on half pay. . . ." Shy, quiet, humble, and unassuming, Grant disdained pomp and ceremony and usually wore a simple private's coat with his general's insignia sewn on the shoulder. Despite his ordinary appearance,

forts, Johnston should have either sent enough troops to defend them or withdrawn the men so they could fight another day. Instead, he did neither and simply left the garrison to fend for itself.

## THE STRUGGLE FOR MISSOURI AND ARKANSAS

**March 3, 1862: Confederates abandon New Madrid, Missouri**
**March 7–8, 1862: Battle of Pea Ridge, Arkansas**
**April 7, 1862: Union forces capture Island No. 10**

Although the Confederates suffered devastating setbacks in Kentucky and Tennessee, they remained strong in other parts of the west. Several thousand Rebels, with heavy cannons and a small flotilla of gunboats, blocked the Mississippi River at New Madrid (MAD-rid), Missouri, and Island No. 10, and Major General Sterling Price's army in southwestern Missouri continued to pose a threat to that state. In however, he had the unmistakable look of determination. One officer claimed Grant looked like he had made his mind up to run his head through a stone wall.

Although Grant enjoyed great battlefield success, he was frequently criticized during the war. There were persistent rumors of drunkenness, but Lincoln came to trust Grant because he rarely complained, did not blame others for his mistakes, and did not constantly call for more reinforcements. When politicians pressured Lincoln to relieve Grant after the Battle of Shiloh, the president told them bluntly, "I cannot spare this man. He fights." Grant was also criticized for appearing to be insensitive to heavy casualties. He sometimes ordered costly frontal attacks (most notably at Vicksburg and Cold Harbor) and became known as the "Butcher." Grant, however, did not deserve the criticism. Robert E. Lee also ordered disastrous frontal attacks on occasion and lost more men proportionately. Grant simply realized victory could be achieved by continually attacking the enemy and bleeding them to death in a war of attrition because the Union could replace its losses, while the Confederacy could not. He accepted the horrendous casualties because they were necessary to win the war as quickly as possible.

Despite the criticism, Grant remained a popular figure after the Civil War and was elected president on the Republican Party ticket in 1868 and 1872. Unfortunately, he proved a disappointing politician because he surrounded himself with unscrupulous men who made his administration one of the most corrupt in American history. After leaving office, Grant fell on hard economic times and was almost penniless when friend Mark Twain persuaded him to write his memoirs as a way of regaining financial stability. While working on the project, Grant was diagnosed with terminal throat cancer (he began smoking up to twenty cigars a day during the war), and he barely finished his *Personal Memoirs* just days before his death. The memoirs, now considered a Civil War classic, sold 300,000 copies and provided financial relief for Grant's widow.

February 1862, Union forces assumed the offensive on both fronts to destroy Price and open the upper Mississippi for an advance on Memphis, Tennessee.

The offensive began when Union Brigadier General Samuel R. Curtis advanced toward Price, but Price withdrew into northwest Arkansas rather than fighting and joined forces with Brigadier General Benjamin McCulloch. Satisfied with forcing the enemy out of Missouri, Curtis then took up a defensive position in northwest Arkansas with about 10,000 men to prevent the Confederates from moving back into the state. Irritated that McCulloch and Price seemed more concerned about feuding with one another over authority than fighting, President Jefferson Davis decided one supreme commander was needed for this vast western region. In March 1862, he sent Major General Earl Van Dorn to Arkansas to take command of all Confederate territory west of the Mississippi River, an area that became known as the Trans-Mississippi Department. Van Dorn combined Price's and McCulloch's forces into one 16,500-man army under his personal command and advanced toward Curtis to recapture Missouri.

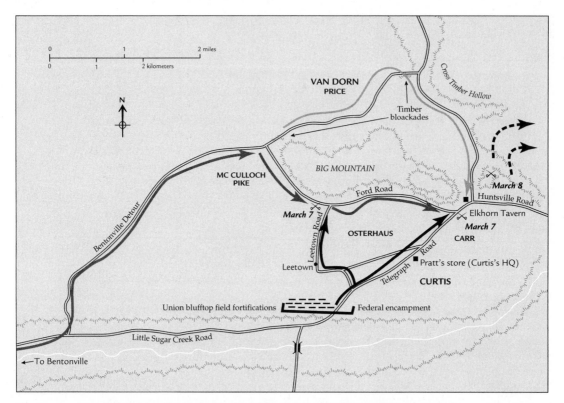

**The Battle of Pea Ridge, March 7–8, 1862.** At the Battle of Pea Ridge (or Elkhorn Tavern),
Arkansas, Curtis's Union army found itself positioned between the separated wings of Van
Dorn's Confederate army. On the morning of March 7, 1862, desperate battles were fought
on the Union's left flank near Big Mountain and on the right at Elkhorn Tavern. That night
both armies concentrated around Elkhorn Tavern, where Curtis attacked the next morning
and drove the Confederates away.

## The Battle of Pea Ridge, Arkansas

When Curtis learned the Confederates were on the move, he positioned his
men along a creek just south of Pea Ridge, Arkansas. After some minor skirmishing, Van Dorn approached the Yankees from the west on the evening of
March 6. To catch the enemy by surprise, he ordered some soldiers to keep
fires burning through the night to make it appear he had camped while he
secretly moved against Curtis. Van Dorn and Price moved around the Union
right flank to attack Curtis from the rear while McCulloch marched toward the
Union left flank. Hopefully, they could trap Curtis between the two converging
columns. Unfortunately for the Confederates, Curtis discovered the maneuver
and split his own army to meet the separate threats, turning the Battle of Pea
Ridge into two distinct clashes nearly two miles apart.

The Confederate attack on Curtis's left wing on the morning of March 7 enjoyed some initial success. Then, as enemy resistance stiffened about mid-morning, McCulloch was killed when he rode ahead to reconnoiter. Brigadier General James McIntosh took command, but he, too, was killed while leading men forward to recover McCulloch's body. A seesaw battle ensued until Union reinforcements arrived and finally repulsed the Confederates. Meanwhile, Van Dorn and Price collided with Curtis's right wing around Elkhorn Tavern. After an intense artillery bombardment to soften up the Union position, Van Dorn sent Price forward and pushed the enemy back almost a mile before darkness finally ended the carnage. The fighting on both fronts had been vicious and close quartered, and Union soldiers later claimed Indians who were fighting with the Confederates scalped many of their dead.

That night both sides concentrated their forces around Elkhorn Tavern. On the morning of March 8, the tactics were reversed when Curtis attacked Van Dorn after a fierce artillery bombardment. When the Confederates discovered they had mistakenly left their ammunition train too far away to bring up munitions quickly, the exhausted men broke and made a disorganized retreat from the battlefield.

The two-day Battle of Pea Ridge was rather small, with Van Dorn losing about 2,000 men while Curtis lost approximately 1,400 men. Yet the clash had great strategic implications for the Civil War in the Trans-Mississippi Department. The Union victory was decisive and, except for guerrillas and cavalry raids, it eliminated the Confederate threat to Missouri for more than two years. The Confederates' hold on Arkansas was also seriously weakened, and Union forces were able to occupy much of that state soon afterward.

## New Madrid, Missouri, and Island No. 10

About the same time that Curtis began his advance into northwest Arkansas, Union Major General John Pope took 18,000 men down the Mississippi River to clear out the enemy at New Madrid and Island No. 10. Unable to resist the onslaught, the Confederates abandoned New Madrid and retreated across the river to a peninsula in Tennessee. In a rather ingenious move, Pope then neutralized the Confederate defenses on Island No. 10 by cutting a canal on the river's west bank so Commodore Andrew Foote's gunboats could avoid running past the island's fortifications and cannons. When the canal was completed in early April, Foote sent two boats through the cut to reenter the river below the island and ferry Pope's troops to the east bank. This maneuver cut off the retreat of the 6,000 Confederates stationed on Island No. 10 and the peninsula and forced their surrender on April 7. Pope had successfully gained control of the upper Mississippi River and opened the way to Memphis at a cost of only 50 men.

# THE BATTLE OF SHILOH, TENNESSEE

**April 6–7, 1862: Battle of Shiloh, Tennessee**
**May 29, 1862: Confederates evacuate Corinth, Mississippi**

On the very day Pope captured Island No. 10, another Union army secured an even greater victory in Tennessee. After the disastrous loss of Forts Henry and Donelson, Confederate General Albert Sidney Johnston retreated to Corinth, an important railroad junction in northeast Mississippi. Ulysses S. Grant's 49,000 men, soon to be named the Army of the Tennessee, followed up and camped on the Tennessee River about twenty-five miles from Corinth at Pittsburg Landing and Shiloh Church. Union Major General Don Carlos Buell's 36,000-man Army of the Ohio had captured Nashville and was preparing to join Grant for an advance on Corinth. Realizing he could not stop the combined forces of Grant and Buell, Johnston decided to launch a surprise attack against Grant to destroy his army before Buell could reach him.

## General Albert Sidney Johnston

Albert Sidney Johnston was widely recognized as the Confederacy's premier general. The 59-year-old Kentucky native had attended West Point with Jefferson Davis, and the two were close friends. Johnston had served in both the U.S. and Texas armies, fought in the Mexican War, and was a former secretary of war for the Republic of Texas. When the Civil War began he was a colonel in the U.S. Army commanding the Department of the Pacific. Johnston did not believe in secession, but he chose to support his adopted state of Texas and made a long, dangerous trek back east through hostile Indian territory. President Davis immediately appointed him the second-highest-ranking Confederate general and put him in command of the large western department. In the following months, Johnston did not quite live up to his reputation. He failed to keep a tight rein on General Leonidas Polk, who violated Kentucky's neutrality, and he doomed Fort Donelson by failing either to reinforce it sufficiently or to withdraw the garrison. Davis, however, retained absolute confidence in Johnston. When some congressmen demanded he remove Johnston because he was "no general," Davis replied that if Johnston was no general "we had better give up the war, for we have no general."

On April 3, 1862, Johnston began moving his 44,000-man army toward Shiloh (which means "place of peace"). Secrecy and surprise were absolutely essential, but the inexperienced soldiers marched slowly along rain-soaked roads, singing and cheering and firing their guns to make sure their powder was dry. What should have been a one-day march took three. Convinced they had lost the element of surprise, General P. G. T. Beauregard, Johnston's second-in-command, advised him to cancel the operation, but Johnston declared defiantly, "I would fight them if they were a million."

## The Battle of Shiloh

When the Confederates approached Shiloh, Grant began receiving reports that a large enemy force was in the woods just outside camp, but he and other officers dismissed the warnings as the imagination of nervous pickets. William T. Sherman, who commanded a division and was Grant's second-in-command, rode out to confer with a colonel who had been sending in alarming reports. When the colonel again claimed large numbers of Rebels were in the woods, Sherman snapped, "Take your damned regiment back to Ohio. . . . Beauregard is not such a fool as to leave his base of operations and attack us in ours. There is no enemy nearer than Corinth." Later that day, Sherman wrote to Grant, "All is quiet along my lines. . . . I do not apprehend anything like an attack on our position."

Convinced they had lost the element of surprise, Beauregard rode to Johnston's headquarters in the predawn hours of Sunday, April 6, to once again ask him to call off the attack. The advance had already begun when he found Johnston drinking coffee about 6:00 a.m. As Beauregard was expressing his concerns, gunfire broke out, and Johnston calmly declared, "The battle has opened, gentlemen. It is too late to change our dispositions." Mounting his horse, Johnston sat silently for a moment and then turned to his aides and confidently predicted, "Tonight we will water our horses in the Tennessee River."

As soon as the Confederates made contact with Grant's army, some Union commanders reacted swiftly and began putting their men into line. Sherman, however, was still slow to grasp the situation. To one colonel who reported he was under attack, Sherman sent a note stating, "You must be badly scared over there." Finally deciding to check on matters himself, Sherman rode to the front and blundered into the advancing Confederates. When the enemy raised their rifles to fire, he cried out, "My God, we're attacked!" and instinctively threw up a hand to shield his face. A Confederate buckshot hit Sherman in the hand and his orderly was killed, but he managed to escape and started rallying his troops.

The Confederates pushed the Yankees back through their camps for a mile, but the forward momentum soon slowed as the Rebels stopped to plunder abandoned tents, commanders lost control of their men in the thick woods, and stubborn Union soldiers formed pockets of resistance. The mass of tangled thickets also made it difficult to tell friend from foe, and there were many friendly fire incidents. When one Confederate unit mistakenly fired on the very men they were coming up to support, the infuriated soldiers immediately shot back. A staff officer rode up to tell the commander he was shooting at fellow Confederates, but the colonel barked, "I know it . . . But dammit, sir, we fire on everybody who fires on us!" Under such confused conditions, the attack soon broke down, and the fight deteriorated into a slugfest.

A small farm was the scene of particularly vicious fighting. There, Union soldiers made a stand in a peach orchard, whose beautiful pink blossoms stood in stark contrast to the torn, bloody bodies strewn under the branches.

After several assaults failed to dislodge the enemy, Johnston realized personal leadership was needed. Riding up to soldiers preparing for another attack, he cried out, "Men! They are stubborn; we must use the bayonet." Johnston then rode among them, clinking their bayonets with a tin cup he had picked up earlier. "These must do the work," he yelled. Taking a position in front of the line, Johnston stood in his stirrups, took off his hat, and dramatically declared, "I will lead you!"

The mid-afternoon attack was successful, and the Confederates finally took control of the Peach Orchard. Johnston rode back from the front lines smiling and apparently unhurt, although bullets had pierced his uniform and a minié ball had clipped his boot heel and left it dangling. In a good mood, the general shook his mangled boot and laughed, "They didn't trip me up that time." Moments later, however, Johnston suddenly slumped down and nearly fell out of his saddle. When the lone aide accompanying him asked if he was hurt, Johnston quietly replied, "Yes, and I fear seriously." The aide helped the general off the horse, but he could find no wound until he discovered Johnston's right boot was full of blood and realized a bullet had cut the artery behind his knee. In the heat of battle, the general apparently never realized he had been hit. The aide knew nothing of tourniquets, and Johnston had sent his personal surgeon to care for some wounded Union prisoners. The Confederates' commanding general bled to death in minutes.

As Johnston lay dying, another bloody fight was unfolding nearby where Union Brigadier General Benjamin Prentiss's division had taken up a strong position along a sunken road in thick woods. For hours, Prentiss held his ground against relentless enemy attacks. When one exhausted Confederate unit fell back and met fresh troops coming up to enter the fray, a soldier warned them, "It's a hornets' nest in there!" The name stuck. The Hornet's Nest was not taken until Beauregard assumed command of the army and massed sixty-two cannons to blast the position. After enduring a devastating two-hour bombardment, Prentiss finally surrendered late in the afternoon. His brave stand had stalled the enemy advance for six hours and helped buy Grant the crucial time needed to organize a last defensive line around Pittsburg Landing. Beauregard made one more attack at sunset, but it was stopped and the battle died down for the day.

Grant had been surprised, pummeled, and pushed back to the river, but he was not yet beaten. In fact, as the rest of the army spent a depressing rain-soaked night, he was surprisingly optimistic. Buell's army had arrived from Nashville, and Grant planned to put it to good use. When one officer asked if things appeared bleak, Grant surprised him by stating, "Not at all. . . . Tomorrow we shall attack them with fresh troops and drive them, of course." A few miles away, General Prentiss was saying the same thing to his captors. One Confederate officer predicted Grant would surrender the next day, but Prentiss defiantly declared, "You gentlemen have had your way today, but it will be very different tomorrow. You'll see. Buell will effect a junction with Grant tonight and we'll turn the tables on you in the morning."

**The Hornet's Nest.** Some of the bloodiest fighting at Shiloh occurred at the Hornet's Nest. There Union soldiers took up a strong position along a sunken road in thick cover and held up the Confederate advance for several hours. Their sacrifice allowed Grant time to prepare a defensive position farther to the rear.

Beauregard, unaware of Buell's arrival, intended to renew the battle the next morning, but Grant moved first with a dawn counterattack. The fighting again was bloody, but the Union soldiers slowly forced back the exhausted Confederates, and Beauregard finally ordered a retreat to Corinth late in the afternoon. The Battle of Shiloh was finally over. The two-day clash was the war's first real bloodbath, with Grant losing about 13,000 men to the Confederates' 11,000. Both sides were shocked at the carnage, for this one battle's losses exceeded all the casualties suffered in all of America's previous wars combined.

Countless officers and men showed incredibly bravery at Shiloh, but many of the ranking generals were criticized for their actions. Despite warning signs of an imminent attack, Grant and Sherman were surprised in their camps, and Grant was even accused—falsely—of being drunk. To their credit, the two quickly recovered from the initial shock and fought very well for the rest of the battle. On the other side, the Confederates lost some advantage when they stopped to plunder enemy camps and eliminate small pockets of Union resistance. Slowing down negated the tactical surprise they enjoyed early in the battle and gave Grant time to organize a defense. Johnston and other generals also wasted men by throwing units into frontal attacks piecemeal rather than massing several brigades for an overwhelming assault.

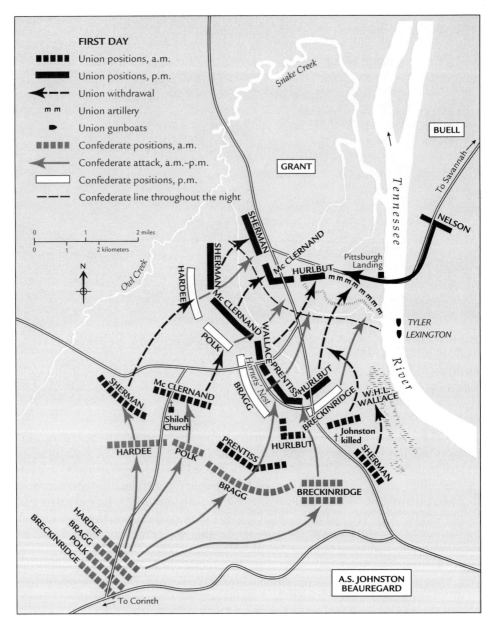

**FIRST DAY**

- ▪▪▪▪▪ Union positions, a.m.
- ▬▬▬ Union positions, p.m.
- ◀--- Union withdrawal
- ⋔ ⋔ Union artillery
- ◗ Union gunboats
- ▪▪▪▪▪ Confederate positions, a.m.
- ◀━━ Confederate attack, a.m.–p.m.
- ▭ Confederate positions, p.m.
- - - - Confederate line throughout the night

**The Battle of Shiloh, April 6–7, 1862.** On the morning of April 6, 1862, Johnston's Confederate army launched a surprise attack against Grant's Union encampment at Shiloh, Tennessee. Although Johnston was killed, his men pushed the enemy back to Pittsburg Landing on the Tennessee River (above). After receiving reinforcements during the night, Grant counterattacked the next morning and forced the Confederates to retreat to Corinth, Mississippi (facing page).

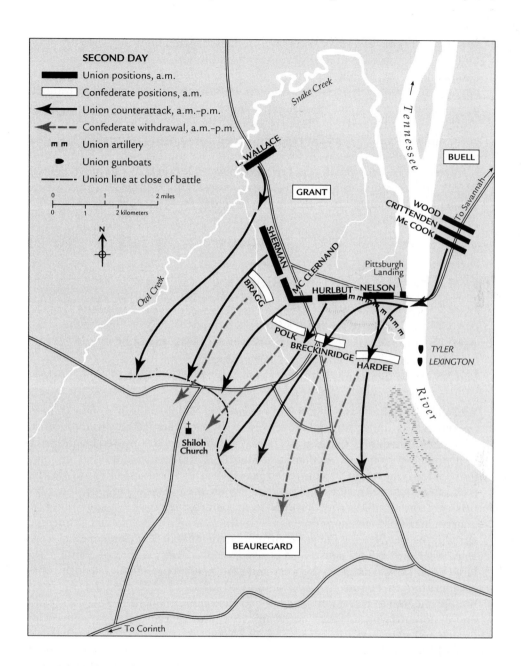

## The Advance on Corinth

After Shiloh, department commander Major General Henry Halleck removed Grant from command of the army. Halleck had served with Grant in California and had always suspected he was an alcoholic. He also had little confidence in Grant's ability and was jealous of his success at Fort

Donelson. Taking charge of the army, Halleck began a painfully slow advance on Corinth to capture that important railroad junction. He was so concerned about an enemy attack, however, that he crawled along about one mile a day and stopped each evening to entrench. Skirmishing increased as Halleck approached Corinth, and it seemed a major battle was imminent. But both armies were wracked by diseases caused by poor living conditions and contaminated water, and Beauregard decided not to fight for Corinth. Without consulting President Davis, he evacuated the city on the night of May 29 and retreated to Tupelo. Davis was furious when he learned of the move. When Beauregard later took an unauthorized leave of absence, the president relieved the Creole and placed Braxton Bragg in command of what now was called the Army of Tennessee.

## THE CAPTURE OF NEW ORLEANS

**April 18–24, 1862: Battle of Forts Jackson and St. Philip, Louisiana**
**April 25, 1862: David Farragut's Union fleet arrives at New Orleans**
**April 28, 1862: Confederates surrender Forts Jackson and St. Philip**
**May 9, 1862: Union fleet captures Baton Rouge**
**May 15, 1862: Benjamin F. Butler issues the "Woman's Order"**

While bloody fighting raged in the woods around Shiloh Church, another Union operation was under way to capture New Orleans, Louisiana. In addition to being the Confederacy's largest city, New Orleans boasted considerable industry that produced ironclads, submarines, munitions, uniforms, and other military items. More important, it controlled access to the Mississippi River from the Gulf of Mexico. Both sides grasped the significance of New Orleans, but, surprisingly, the Confederates did little to prepare its defenses. To state officials' chagrin, most of Louisiana's soldiers were shipped off to Virginia and Tennessee early in the war, leaving the state virtually undefended. The Confederates were also lulled into a false sense of security by Forts Jackson and St. Philip, two large brick forts located on the west and east banks, respectively, near the Mississippi's mouth. Manned by several hundred soldiers and protected by approximately one hundred cannons, the forts seemed more than adequate to stop any enemy force trying to move upstream. In addition, a large boom made from chains and old vessels had been strung across the river to serve as a barrier, and a 12-boat squadron of the River Defense Fleet and numerous fire rafts stood ready to help repel any invaders. As it turned out, however, these defenses were not nearly as strong as they appeared. The forts' cannons were antiquated, and the gunpowder was of poor quality. It also was impossible to coordinate the forts and gunboats because the River Defense Fleet captains refused to take orders from the forts' commander, Brigadier General Johnson K. Duncan.

**Confederate Sharpshooters.** Confederate sharpshooters were deployed along the Mississippi River to harass Farragut's ships as they moved upstream toward Fort Jackson.

## Forts Jackson and St. Philip

In March 1862, U.S. Flag Officer David Farragut assembled a large fleet of warships, mortar boats, and transports at the river's mouth. Onboard the transports were thousands of infantrymen under the command of Major General Benjamin F. Butler to support the navy. After studying the forts, Farragut decided they were too strong to run past or to capture. Instead, he chose to first reduce them with the mortar boats commanded by his foster brother, Lieutenant David Porter, and to then dash past them to New Orleans.

On April 18—Good Friday—Porter's mortar boats began a weeklong bombardment that blasted the forts to rubble. Surprisingly, the defenders suffered relatively few casualties because most of them stayed deep within the forts' protective walls. During the bombardment, Confederate officials in New Orleans dispatched the powerful ironclad *Louisiana* to help protect the forts, but the vessel's engines were inoperative, and it was relegated to serving as a floating battery tied up next to Fort St. Philip. When he believed the forts were sufficiently battered, Farragut prepared to run past them and sent a vessel upriver one night to cut a hole in the chain boom. The Union sailors chosen to make the run were unsure how many enemy guns had been knocked out by their bombardment, but they prepared for the worst. Chain armor was draped alongside each vessel to protect the vital engines, guns and engine rooms were sandbagged, and netting was strung above deck to catch falling debris. Most

# EYEWITNESS
## William J. Seymour

*William J. Seymour was a well-connected New Orleans citizen. His brother-in-law, General Johnson K. Duncan, commanded Forts Jackson and St. Philip; his family owned one of the city's leading newspapers; and his father was colonel of a Louisiana Tiger regiment in Virginia. Seymour had not yet joined the Confederate army in 1862, but he did volunteer to serve as General Duncan's aide at Fort Jackson. After the war, he wrote a detailed account of the mortar bombardment.*

*April 18th* (Good Friday) At 8½ a.m. the distant booming of a heavy gun told us that the long expected bombardment had commenced. . . . Shell succeeded shell in quick succession, falling within the Fort with almost unvariable certainty. When these ponderous missiles fell on the ramparts or parade plein they sunk into the earth to a distance of six or eight feet, and exploding would tear a hole in the earth large enough to admit a barrel. When they struck the brickwork of the Fort, the crashing noise produced was almost stunning, and the bricks and mortar would fly in all directions. I saw a poor fellow, who had narrowly escaped from being crushed by a falling shell, running away from the place laughing in great glee; but before he had run ten yards the shell exploded, throwing fragments of brick in all directions—one of which struck this man in the back, killing him instantly. . . . By actual count the number of mortar shells thrown at Fort Jackson during this day was 2,997, most of which fell within the fort, producing much damage and disabling several of our best guns. . . . The citadel was sadly battered and mutilated. It was set on fire and extinguished several times during the day, but at dusk the flames resisted our utmost efforts to subdue them and [t]his portion of the fort was entirely consumed. . . .

ominously, the decks were covered in white sand to reflect light and to provide traction by soaking up the blood and gore.

In the predawn hours of April 24, Farragut sent seventeen warships upriver, but the Confederates spotted them and opened fire. The Union sailors responded with their own broadsides, and a thick cloud of smoke quickly enveloped the river. General Duncan's aide, William Seymour, recalled, "The roar of the artillery was deafening; the rushing sound of the descending bombs; the sharp, whizzing noise made by the jagged fragments of exploded shells, the whirring of grape shot & hissing of Canister balls—all this was well calculated to disturb the equanimity of the strongest nerved man. . . . A lurid glow of light rested upon the Fort, produced by the almost incessant discharges of our own guns, and the explosion of the enemy's shell[s] above and around us." The small River Defense Fleet also rushed in to engage the enemy, but visibility

*April 22d.* No cessation, or even slacking, of the enemy's fire and their ponderous shells were hurled into the Fort with fatal precision. . . . Those that fell into the water of the moat were unaffected by the water [and] would bury themselves far down into the soft, muddy bottom and explode so violently as to shake the very foundations of the Fort. . . . One shell fell very close to where we were standing. We dodged behind a gun and escaped the flying piece[s] of iron and brick that followed the explosion, but a poor fellow who had just been returned from duty & was standing near us had both legs cut off by a fragment of the shell & died in a few minutes.

Between 12 & 1 o'clock, we were startled by the cry that Magazine No. 2 was on fire. The engine was brought out quickly & the whole garrison went to work to extinguish the flames. The shell that caused all this commotion also struck a member of the St. Mary's Cannoneers . . . crushing him into pieces and burying him out of sight. It was three days afterwards when his remains were exhumed, & so mangled & disfigured were they that they could not have been identified had it not been for the pieces of clothing that adhered to them. A soldier who was standing guard at the Magazine was so terrified that he dropped his gun and fled from the Fort during the confusion caused by the fire.

*After surviving the bombardment, Seymour was captured when the forts surrendered. Returning to New Orleans as a paroled prisoner, he resumed publishing his family's newspaper but quickly ran afoul of General Benjamin F. Butler. The general found Seymour guilty of violating his censorship order and confined him in Fort Jackson for three months. When Seymour was finally released, he made his way to Virginia and became an officer with the Louisiana Tigers.*

Terry L. Jones, ed., *The Civil War Memoirs of Capt. William J. Seymour: Reminiscences of a Louisiana Tiger* (Baton Rouge: Louisiana State University Press, 1991), pp. 16–23.

was so poor the ships sometimes accidentally collided. During the wild melee, at least one fire raft was set loose that singed Farragut's flagship. When dawn broke, all but three of Farragut's ships had successfully passed the forts, and the boats of the River Defense Fleet were either sunk or scattered. Approximately 200 Union sailors were dead or wounded, but 20 were also awarded the Medal of Honor for their heroic action that night, and the fleet now had a clear path to New Orleans.

## The City Surrenders

After anchoring at New Orleans, Farragut sent two officers ashore to demand the city's surrender. The mayor refused, but Confederate Major General Mansfield Lovell did agree to withdraw his men without a fight because

Farragut's cannons could destroy the city. The next day, a Union shore party raised the U.S. flag over the Mint building. When the soldiers at Forts Jackson and St. Philip learned of the city's capture, some of the men in Fort Jackson mutinied, and their officers had no choice but to surrender the two forts on April 28. The captain of the *Louisiana* blew up his ship rather than see it fall into enemy hands. With only light casualties, the U.S. Navy had won another stunning victory that put the Union one step closer to securing the entire Mississippi River.

Sending some of his ships farther upstream, Farragut quickly occupied Baton Rouge and then moved against Vicksburg, Mississippi, with a detachment of Butler's infantry. From late May through June, Farragut periodically bombarded the city without much success, while the infantry began digging a canal across the base of a peninsula on the Louisiana side of the river in hopes of changing the river's course to allow ships to bypass Vicksburg altogether. The Union forces outside Vicksburg suffered terribly from disease and were unable to complete the canal or force the Confederates to surrender. During these operations, the ironclad CSS *Arkansas* briefly spread panic among the Union fleet when it attacked Farragut's ships on the Yazoo River. The *Arkansas* disabled one gunboat, drove off the others, and then steamed completely through the Union fleet before anchoring safely near Vicksburg. The entire operation at Vicksburg was rather humiliating for Farragut, and he finally gave up and returned to New Orleans.

## The Rule of the "Beast"

After Farragut captured New Orleans, the city's civilians immediately began to harass and insult Major General Benjamin F. Butler's occupying soldiers. Only a few days after Butler arrived, a gambler named William Mumford led a group of men in tearing down the U.S. flag from the Mint building and ripping it to shreds. Women, in particular, began cursing the soldiers, spitting on their uniforms, turning their backs as they walked by, and even emptying chamber pots on their heads from bedroom windows. On one occasion, a small group of ladies cheerfully applauded when the coffin of a dead Union officer rolled down the street.

Butler felt compelled to take drastic action to stop the abuse. To the city's horror, he hanged Mumford for his role in the flag desecration, even after Mumford's wife personally met with the general and begged him to spare her husband for the sake of her and the children. Butler also censored the city's newspapers and arrested people and confiscated their property if they engaged in pro-Confederate activity. Fort Jackson veteran and newspaperman William Seymour was one who ran afoul of Butler. He and several other editors met with the general to argue that the censorship order was unconstitutional (conveniently ignoring the fact that the Confederates had rebelled against the Constitution). As the discussion became heated, Seymour finally asked what would happen if he ignored the order. He claimed Butler "roared like a mad bull" and pounded his desk with his fist. "I am the military Governor of this State—the Supreme Power—you cannot disregard my order, Sir. By God, he that sins against me, sins against the Holy Ghost." When Seymour later learned his father had been killed while serving with the Louisiana Tigers, he wrote an obituary in the family newspaper and praised his father's patriotism. Butler declared this a violation of the censorship order, confiscated the newspaper, and sent Seymour back to Fort Jackson to serve a three-month prison term.

Butler's apparent involvement in corruption also did nothing to endear him to the New Orleans people. Rumors of bribery, vice, and other misdeeds were widespread. Butler's brother, Andrew, came to the city and was given almost free rein to engage in illegal trade and other questionable activities, but Butler's role in the matter is not as clear. Many people even falsely accused the general of stealing silverware from abandoned houses and gave him the nickname "Spoons." But it was General Orders No. 28 that earned Butler the most hatred. Better known as the "Woman's Order," it permitted soldiers to treat an insulting woman as a "woman of the town plying her avocation." The order to treat offending women as prostitutes did not have any sexual implications; it simply meant that a soldier was not obliged to treat them as ladies. If a woman cursed a soldier, for example, the soldier could curse her back.

The Woman's Order successfully stopped the insults because few self-respecting women would put themselves in a situation in which they would not be treated as ladies. Afterward, one Union soldier claimed, "[T]he citizens have dropped their surly air, and show a willingness to talk civilly if not cordially." The order also created a storm of controversy. Many Northerners and European diplomats felt it overstepped the bounds of civilized warfare and complained to President Lincoln. Butler became known as the "Beast," and the New Orleans black market sold chamber pots with his picture pasted to the bottom. The Confederate Congress also branded him a war criminal, and Southern soldiers were ordered to hang him if he ever was captured. Butler's actions in New Orleans became so controversial that President Lincoln was compelled to relieve him as commander of the Department of the Gulf in December 1862.

## THE CAPTURE OF MEMPHIS

**May 10, 1862: Battle of Plum Run Bend, Tennessee**
**June 6, 1862: Battle of Memphis**

With the capture of New Madrid, Island No. 10, and New Orleans, Union forces were well on their way to securing the entire Mississippi River in the spring of 1862. By May, U.S. Navy Captain Charles H. Davis was preparing to move downstream with his fleet of gunboats from Island No. 10 to capture Memphis,

# BIOGRAPHY
## Benjamin Franklin Butler: The Beast

**Benjamin F. Butler**

Ben Butler (1818–1893) was born in New Hampshire but grew up in Massachusetts. Small in stature and suffering from crossed eyes, he apparently was not the most trustworthy lad. Known as "a little cockeyed devil," Butler was described by an early biographer as the "dirtiest, sauciest, lyingest child on the road. . . . He was tricky and wanton, serving in youth as a warning to other boys. No boy in the country could lie like Ben Butler." Becoming active in Democratic Party politics, he was elected to the state legislature and senate, and served as a delegate to the 1860 Democratic National Convention. There, Butler voted fifty-seven times to nominate Jefferson Davis because he believed only a Southern moderate could keep the party from splitting. Despite his seemingly pro-Southern sympathies, Butler opposed secession and explained, "I was always a friend of southern rights but an enemy of southern wrongs."

Butler was appointed a general in the Massachusetts militia, but he did not look the part of a dashing officer. One man noticed the general smiled a lot when he talked and declared, "[H]e seemed less like a major general than like a politician who was coaxing for votes." Butler, however, became popular with his men and influential politicians because he worked tirelessly and did not coddle the Rebels. Acting largely on his own, he secured safe passage for Union soldiers through Baltimore after the Baltimore Riots and was appointed the Union's first major general of volunteers. Since military rank was based on seniority, this made Butler the Union army's highest-ranking volunteer general.

While commanding Fort Monroe, Virginia, Butler became the first Civil War general to face the problem of runaway slaves. Refusing to return them to their owners, he declared the slaves were "contraband of war" and kept them within his lines. As a result,

Tennessee. Davis did not believe the surviving Confederates on the river posed much of a threat, but he was in for a rude awakening.

## The River Fleets

Operating on the upper Mississippi River were two rather odd naval forces. The Confederates had a squadron of the River Defense Fleet commanded by Kentucky steamboat captain James E. Montgomery. Earlier in the war, Montgomery had convinced Congress to authorize the fleet, but he only received enough funds to outfit a few small "cottonclads." These warships were so named because cotton was stuffed between the bulkheads for protection instead of iron plating. The lightly protected vessels were much more vulnerable than the heavily armored ironclads, but they still carried a significant offensive punch by being "contraband" became a popular euphemism for runaway slaves. Butler became more famous in August 1861 when he cooperated with the U.S. Navy in capturing Hatteras Inlet, North Carolina, but his career began to falter in April 1862 when he commanded the Department of the Gulf and occupied New Orleans. Butler was implicated in various corrupt activities, and he outraged citizens on both sides with his "Woman's Order." He also was loose with military funds and once admitted, "I never read the . . . regulations, and what is more I sha'n't, and then I shall not know I am doing anything against them." One Englishmen described Butler as a "cunning trickster . . . a sort of compromise between the proud, semi-sanctified autocrat and the depraved sot."

Lincoln removed Butler because of his controversial actions in New Orleans, but the general had too much political clout to be dismissed from the service. In 1864, he was given command of the Army of the James to cooperate with Ulysses S. Grant's Overland Campaign. Grant was so disappointed in Butler's performance at Petersburg that he relieved him of command, but Butler's political connections once again made it impossible to retire him. Only when Butler disobeyed Grant's orders to besiege Fort Fisher, North Carolina, did Grant send him back to Massachusetts. Butler resigned his commission in November 1865 and never forgave Grant for ending his military career.

After the war, Butler returned to politics and was elected to Congress four successive times despite continued accusations of corruption. Switching parties to become a Radical Republican, he became a prominent figure during Reconstruction and originated the tactic known as "waving the bloody shirt," or blaming the Civil War on Democrats. Butler also served as a prosecutor in the impeachment trial of President Andrew Johnson. In 1878, he once again switched his political allegiance by becoming a member of the Greenback Party. After several unsuccessful attempts, Butler was elected Massachusetts' governor in 1882, and he was the unsuccessful Greenback presidential candidate in 1884.

armed with a bow ram and one cannon. When the Confederate navy showed no interest in assuming control of the cottonclads, the River Defense Fleet was put in the hands of Montgomery and other civilian riverboat men who answered directly to the War Department. Much of the fleet was destroyed at Forts Jackson and St. Philip, but Montgomery still commanded eight vessels on the upper river and decided to use them to strike the enemy first.

The Union fleet operating on the upper Mississippi River had an equally unorthodox squadron under the command of Charles Ellet. Ellet was a prominent Pennsylvania engineer who had constructed the world's longest suspension bridges, across the Wheeling and Ohio rivers, before the war. He also had been an observer at the siege of Sevastopol during the Crimean War and was impressed by the use of ironclad rams there. Like Montgomery, Ellet convinced the War Department to create a fleet of ships that was placed under his

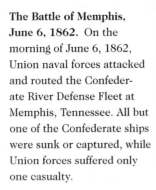

**The Battle of Memphis, June 6, 1862.** On the morning of June 6, 1862, Union naval forces attacked and routed the Confederate River Defense Fleet at Memphis, Tennessee. All but one of the Confederate ships were sunk or captured, while Union forces suffered only one casualty.

personal command and he answered only to Secretary of War Edwin Stanton. Ellet's vessels, however, were unarmed ironclad rams and were officially a part of the army.

## Plum Run Bend and the Battle of Memphis

On May 10, 1862, Montgomery and his eight Confederate cottonclads launched a surprise attack on Captain Davis's twenty-four Union vessels at Plum Run Bend, Tennessee. Montgomery caught Davis completely off guard and rammed and sank the USS *Cincinnati* and *Mound City*. Before the rest of the Union fleet could arrive, Montgomery quickly disengaged and retreated to Memphis. The battle stunned Union officials, but it had no lasting effect on Mississippi River operations because the two sunken ships were soon raised and put back into service.

About a month later, the Union retaliated. At daybreak on the morning of June 6, Ellet's eight rams and five navy ironclads under Captain Davis approached Memphis and Montgomery's waiting River Defense Fleet. Thousands of citizens lined the riverbank to watch the battle that would decide their fate. In a short, decisive clash, the Union fleet sank or captured all but one of the Confederate ships, with Ellet's flagship *Queen of the West* ramming and sinking one enemy vessel. After the battle, Ellet's son, Lieutenant Charles Rivers Ellet, disembarked with two other men and walked into Memphis to raise the U.S. flag over the courthouse. Later that morning, the mayor officially surrendered the city to Davis.

The Confederates lost approximately 180 men in the battle, while the Union forces lost only one; the Union casualty was Charles Ellet, who was mortally wounded in the knee by a pistol shot. The Battle of Memphis was another relatively small battle that had significant strategic implications. Memphis was an important economic center and river port, and Union troops soon began using it as a base for further operations on the Mississippi River. Its capture was one more blow to the Confederacy, which was steadily losing control over its central water artery.

## SIBLEY'S NEW MEXICO CAMPAIGN

**February 21, 1862: Battle of Valverde**
**March 5, 1862: Confederates occupy Albuquerque**
**March 26–28, 1862: Battle of Glorietta Pass**
**May 4, 1862: Sibley reaches Fort Bliss, ending his campaign**

One final, but somewhat obscure, victory in the spring of 1862 secured the vast desert southwest for the Union. When the war began, Jefferson Davis gave Henry Hopkins Sibley permission to raise an army in Texas, march across New Mexico (which included modern-day Arizona), and capture California. The purpose of the operation was to raise recruits from the supposedly pro-Confederate population and to add the mineral- and cattle-rich southwest to the Confederacy.

### The Battle of Valverde

When Sibley reached Fort Bliss (El Paso), Texas, in December 1861, he incorporated Colonel John Baylor's men into his Army of New Mexico. Baylor had invaded New Mexico earlier in the year, on his famous buffalo hunt, and unilaterally declared himself governor of the Territory of Arizona. Now with 2,600 men, Sibley moved up the Rio Grande and entered New Mexico in January 1862. His immediate goal was to capture needed supplies at Fort Craig, a Union outpost manned by Colonel Edward R. S. Canby's 3,800 men. In a surprise move, Canby came out of the fort on February 21 and attacked Sibley at Valverde (val-VURD-ee). When Sibley complained of illness (some accused him of being drunk), Colonel Thomas Green took charge and counterattacked. The Confederates drove Canby back to Fort Craig and captured six cannons in fierce hand-to-hand fighting that cost Green about 260 men and Canby 200. The Confederates had won a tactical victory, but they failed to get the needed supplies and were forced to move on to Albuquerque and Santa Fe.

### The Battle of Glorieta Pass

Sibley soon recovered from whatever ailed him and resumed command of the column. When he reached Albuquerque on March 5, he was disappointed to find the retreating Yankees had removed or destroyed all the supplies. The hungry Confederates found the same thing when they occupied Santa Fe five days later. Sibley then sent part of his command to the northeast to attack Fort Union, an outpost on the Santa Fe Trail, but Colonel John P. Slough moved his garrison out to meet the threat when he learned of the enemy advance. On March 26, Major John M. Chivington's 1st Colorado Volunteers engaged the Confederates at Glorieta Pass and drove them back through Apache Canyon. During the fighting the Rebels were repeatedly flanked and forced to retreat when Chivington's men climbed the steep canyon walls around them.

On March 28, the Confederates advanced again toward Glorieta Pass. This time, they drove Slough back down the Santa Fe Trail, and he retreated during the night. Major Chivington, however, succeeded in slipping a detachment of men to the enemy's rear and destroyed their entire supply train. Left with no food, ammunition, or medicine, the Confederates were forced to retreat to Santa Fe two days later. The fight at Glorieta Pass was small, with the Confederate and Union forces losing approximately 230 and 130 men, respectively, but it forced Sibley on a long march back to Fort Bliss, Texas. Exhaustion and near-starvation created horrific conditions, and he lost more men on the retreat than he had in battle. The entire invasion had been a disaster, and the Confederates never again made a serious attempt to seize the Southwest.

Sibley's New Mexico Campaign was a rather minor event, but it could have had a great impact on the course of the war. If the Confederates had secured New Mexico, they could possibly have moved into Colorado, Nevada, and perhaps even California. The war might have changed dramatically if the tons of silver and gold in those regions had filled Confederate coffers instead of Union. If the Southern financial system had remained strong, inflation checked, and the government paid for supplies with gold and silver coins rather than impressing them, morale might have remained high and thousands of Confederate soldiers might not have deserted to care for their families. It is intriguing to consider what might have happened had Sibley succeeded in capturing the Southwest.

## FOR FURTHER READING

Woman's Order
Grant's surrender demand to Fort Donelson
Johnston's address to his men before the Battle of Shiloh

## CHAPTER 6

# Lee Takes Command: Virginia, 1862

The Peninsula Campaign

Jackson's Shenandoah Valley Campaign

The Seven Days Campaign

The Second Bull Run Campaign

---

The Army of Northern Virginia was facing a crisis in June 1862. The Confederates had acquired a new commander by the name of Robert E. Lee just as George B. McClellan's huge Union army was poised to strike Richmond. Lee's service so far in the war had been mediocre at best. He had been defeated in western Virginia in a poorly executed campaign, which prompted Edward A. Pollard of the Richmond *Examiner* to write, "The most remarkable circumstance of this campaign was, that it was conducted by a general who had never fought a battle, who had a pious horror of guerrillas, and whose extreme tenderness of blood induced him to depend exclusively upon the resources of strategy, to essay the achievement of victories without the cost of life." President Davis next sent Lee to South Carolina, but he angered his troops there by making them dig entrenchments. They referred to him as "Granny Lee," and newspapers bitterly attacked his record and criticized Davis for appointing this seemingly cautious man to such an important post. One prominent Southerner wrote, "Gen. Lee . . . though reputed to be an accomplished & great officer . . . is, I fear, too much of a red-tapist to be an effective commander in the field."

Major Edward Porter Alexander, an officer in the Army of Northern Virginia, was one of many Confederates who wondered what the future held in store when he learned Lee had been given command of the army. While on an inspection ride with presidential aide Joseph C. Ives, he asked the well-informed Ives the question that was on everyone's mind: "Has Gen. Lee the audacity which is going to be required in the command of this army to meet the odds which will be brought against it?" Ives suddenly stopped his horse in the middle of the road, turned to Porter, and emphatically declared, "Alexander, if there is one man in either army, Federal or Confederate, who is, head & shoulders, far above every other one in either army in audacity that man is Gen. Lee, and you will very soon have lived to see it. Lee is audacity personified. His name is audacity, and you need not be afraid of not seeing all of it that you will want to see." Years later, Alexander wrote, "I frequently recalled Ives's words afterward—to the very close of the war—for if ever a prophecy was literally fulfilled this was."

## THE PENINSULA CAMPAIGN

**March 8–9, 1862: Battle of Hampton Roads, Virginia**
**April 1–June 24, 1862: Peninsula Campaign**
**May 5, 1862: Battle of Williamsburg**
**May 31–June 1, 1862: Battle of Seven Pines**
**June 1, 1862: Robert E. Lee takes command of the Army of Northern Virginia**

When McClellan assumed command of the Union forces around Washington after the First Battle of Bull Run, Lincoln expected him to take the field quickly. Instead, McClellan spent months methodically training and building up his Army of the Potomac. No amount of prodding could induce him to advance toward the enemy at Manassas, Virginia, and he refused even to share his plans with the president. Under increasing political pressure to do something, a desperate Lincoln finally forced McClellan's hand. On January 27, 1862, the president issued General War Orders No. 1, which required all Union armies to make a general advance no later than February 22. The arbitrary order was unreasonable, but it did stir McClellan from his malaise and forced him to reveal his plans to Lincoln.

McClellan's rather ingenious strategy was called the Urbanna Plan, and it involved transporting the Army of the Potomac by sea to Urbanna, Virginia, on the Rappahannock River. Such a move would put him in the rear of the Confederate army at Manassas and between it and Richmond. Unfortunately, the Urbanna Plan was ruined when General Joseph E. Johnston suddenly abandoned his Manassas position and fell back behind the Rappahannock River. Adjusting to the new situation, McClellan changed the landing site from Urbanna to Fort Monroe. This Union-held fort was located southeast of Richmond on the tip of the Virginia Peninsula and offered several advantages as a staging area. McClellan's supply line could be maintained by sea and thus secured from marauding cavalry, and his flanks would be protected by the York and James Rivers as he advanced up the Peninsula.

Still uneasy about Washington's safety, Lincoln approved the plan only after McClellan agreed to leave enough troops behind to defend the city from a surprise attack. This disappointed McClellan, but not as much as the president's next decision to remove him as general-in-chief. Although Lincoln claimed it was necessary to allow McClellan to concentrate solely on leading the army to victory, McClellan was not convinced. Unable now to order other armies to support him, the paranoid McClellan believed his removal as general-in-chief was a malicious attempt on Lincoln's part "to secure the failure of the approaching campaign."

## Up the Peninsula

As McClellan prepared to move to Fort Monroe, an historic naval encounter threatened the entire operation. As will be seen in Chapter 8, the Confederate ironclad *Virginia* attacked on March 8 and devastated the Union fleet anchored at Hampton Roads, Virginia. It appeared the campaign was in jeopardy since the *Virginia* could easily destroy the wooden warships and transports. Fortunately for McClellan, the *Monitor,* the Union's first ironclad, arrived in time to drive off the *Virginia* and allow McClellan to continue his landings.

By early April 1862, McClellan had put more than 100,000 men ashore at Fort Monroe. To stop the onslaught, the Confederates had only 17,000 soldiers under Major General John B. Magruder in a line of entrenchments running across the Peninsula from Yorktown to the James River. Magruder was known to old army friends as Prince John for his love of the theater and dramatics. Over the next few weeks, he played the role of a lifetime by using ingenious tactics to mislead McClellan into thinking he was facing a huge Confederate army. Magruder constantly shifted units around to confuse the enemy, and he had empty trains run back and forth behind the lines while bands played and troops cheered for the phantom reinforcements.

McClellan was fooled by Magruder's tricks partly because Allan Pinkerton, head of the Union's secret service, reported large numbers of Rebels on the Peninsula. Pinkerton was the famous detective who had warned president-elect Lincoln of the assassination plot in Baltimore, but now he ran a spy network behind Confederate lines. Relying largely on information gathered from slave informants, he greatly overestimated the Confederates' strength. Pinkerton's errant reports and Magruder's antics caused the naturally cautious McClellan to conclude that the enemy's line was too strong to attack, and he began a lengthy siege of Yorktown. This gave General Johnston time to move down from the Rappahannock River and assemble 60,000 men to defend Richmond.

McClellan's snail-like pace worried Lincoln, and the president wrote the general a not-so-subtle letter on April 9. In an attempt to prod him to action, Lincoln warned McClellan, "The country will not fail to note—is now noting—that the present hesitation to move upon an intrenched enemy, is but the story of Manassas repeated. I beg to assure you that I have never written you, or spoken to you, in greater kindness of feeling than now, nor with a fuller purpose to sustain you. . . . *But you must act.*" Ignoring the president, McClellan continued his siege and informed his wife, Ellen, that if Lincoln wanted to break the Rebels' Yorktown line, "he had better come & do it himself."

# BIOGRAPHY

## George Brinton McClellan: Little Mac

George B. McClellan

Born into a prominent Pennsylvania family, George B. McClellan (1826–1885) graduated second in the West Point class of 1846 and embarked on an impressive military career. He earned two brevets in the Mexican War, taught at West Point, translated into English a French treatise on bayonet exercises, and served as an observer during the Crimean War. McClellan also patented a lightweight cavalry saddle that was still being used in World War II. Despite this excellent record, he resigned his captain's commission in 1857 to seek his fortune in the railroad industry.

Appointed a major general in the regular army when the Civil War began, McClellan took command of the Union army around Washington, D.C., after its defeat at First Bull Run. Brimming with confidence, he wrote his wife, Ellen, "Who would have thought when we were married, that I should so soon be called upon to save my country. . . . I almost think that were I to win some small success now I could become Dictator." McClellan quickly bonded with the Army of the Potomac by restoring discipline and equipping the men for future operations. Known as the "Young Napoleon" and "Little Mac" (he was 5′ 8″), McClellan was the army's most popular commander, and the men usually cheered wildly when he rode down the line tipping his kepi and giving it a characteristic twirl above his head.

Despite McClellan's administrative skills, he began to make enemies among the Radical Republicans because he was a conservative Democrat who believed the purpose of the war was to reunite the Union, not to destroy slavery. A staff officer once overheard the general say if his superiors "expected him to fight with the South to *free the slaves*, they would be mistaken, for he would not do it." McClellan also clashed with General-in-Chief Winfield Scott and complained to Ellen, "How does

In time, McClellan did continue his advance, and bloody, but indecisive, battles were fought at Yorktown and Williamsburg as Johnston slowly retreated up the Peninsula. When Union forces captured Norfolk in early May, the Confederates were forced to destroy the *Virginia* because its deep draft prevented it from retreating up the James River. The U.S. Navy then moved upriver toward Richmond, but Confederate artillery batteries stopped the ships at Drewry's Bluff with intense cannon fire.

## The Battle of Seven Pines

Johnston conducted a skillful retreat, but he began to lose Jefferson Davis's confidence when he took no offensive action to stop the unrelenting enemy advance. Under intense pressure to counterattack, Johnston finally saw the

[Secretary of State William Seward] think I can save this country when stopped by Genl Scott—I do not know whether he is a *dotard* or *traitor*!" McClellan seemed not to like anyone in the administration. He called Secretary of State William Seward a "meddling, officious, incompetent little puppy," Secretary of the Navy Gideon Welles an "old woman," and Attorney General Edward Bates an "old fool." Little Mac was especially critical of Lincoln. Among other things, he called the president "an idiot" and "Nothing more than a well-meaning baboon." Unable to take any more of Little Mac's abuse, General Scott finally resigned his position, and McClellan was made general-in-chief in November 1861.

On the battlefield, McClellan was slow, overly cautious, and constantly overestimating the enemy's numbers. When Robert E. Lee counterattacked in the Seven Days Campaign, McClellan showed little leadership and at times actually abandoned his men on the field. Lincoln was disappointed in McClellan's service, but he recognized the general's administrative skills and reluctantly gave him command of the army again after the Second Battle of Bull Run. McClellan did a superb job whipping the men into shape for the Antietam Campaign, but he continued to overestimate the enemy's strength and moved too slowly, even after Lee's entire campaign plans fortuitously fell into his hands. When McClellan made no effort to pursue Lee after the Battle of Antietam, Lincoln relieved him again in November 1862.

Despite his problems with the Lincoln administration, McClellan remained popular with many people, and the Democratic Party nominated him for president in 1864. The party's platform called for a negotiated peace with the Rebels, however, and this weakened his campaign. McClellan renounced the peace plank and made it clear he would not negotiate with the enemy, but he carried only three states and met a stinging defeat. He resigned his military commission on Election Day and played no further role in the Civil War. After the war, McClellan reentered politics and was elected governor of New Jersey.

opportunity for which he had been waiting. When McClellan reached the outskirts of Richmond, he split his army across the Chickahominy River. Two Union corps were positioned on the south side of the swampy stream around a community known as Seven Pines, while the other three corps remained on the north side. Heavy rains had swelled the Chickahominy, making it difficult for McClellan to cross over and reinforce either wing if attacked.

On May 31, Johnston took advantage of McClellan's tactical error and attacked the isolated Union corps at Seven Pines. Unclear orders and confusion prevented a victory, however, and Johnston was severely wounded in the fighting. The Confederates attacked again the next day, but Union reinforcements successfully crossed a flooded bridge in time to stop the Rebels. The Battle of Seven Pines cost the Confederates approximately 6,000 men to the Union's 5,000, but the most important casualty was Joseph E. Johnston.

He was put out of action for months, and President Davis appointed General Robert E. Lee to assume command.

## JACKSON'S SHENANDOAH VALLEY CAMPAIGN

**May 3–June 9, 1862: Shenandoah Valley Campaign**
**May 8, 1862: Battle of McDowell, Virginia**
**May 23, 1862: Battle of Front Royal**
**May 25, 1862: First Battle of Winchester**
**June 8, 1862: Battle of Cross Keys**
**June 9, 1862: Battle of Port Republic**

The Peninsula Campaign was not the only military operation conducted in Virginia in the spring of 1862. To prevent reinforcements from reaching McClellan, Major General Thomas J. "Stonewall" Jackson began a campaign in the Shenandoah Valley to tie down the Union troops there. In March 1862 his small Valley Army first attacked the enemy at Kernstown. Although Jackson was defeated in this minor clash, his unexpected aggressiveness caused Lincoln to become even more alarmed about Washington's safety and withhold thousands of troops that were scheduled to be sent to McClellan.

Ordered to keep up the pressure, Jackson tried to lure the enemy into a false sense of security by putting his men on trains and moving east over the Blue Ridge Mountains as if he were reinforcing Richmond. Once over the mountains, however, he turned around and secretly returned to the Valley to surprise the Yankees. On May 8, Jackson attacked and defeated Union Major General Robert Milroy at McDowell and drove him completely out of the Valley. Soon afterward, Major General Richard S. Ewell's division arrived to reinforce Jackson. At the head of Ewell's column was Brigadier General Richard Taylor's brigade of Louisiana Tigers. Curious about the infamous Tigers, hundreds of Jackson's Virginians lined the road to watch as they marched in. When the brigade made camp, a regimental band struck up a series of polkas and waltzes and the exhausted men grabbed partners and enthusiastically began to dance. By that time, Taylor had reported to Jackson, whom he found sitting on a rail fence sucking a lemon. Hearing the bands strike up, Jackson stared at the Louisiana camp and muttered, "Thoughtless fellows for serious work." Taylor defended his men by saying he hoped their gaiety did not affect their performance, but Jackson simply kept watching the dancing men and did not respond. The Tigers may not have made much of an impression on Jackson at the time, but he came to appreciate their presence before the campaign was over.

## Clearing the Valley

With the arrival of Ewell's division, Jackson had 17,000 men to continue his campaign. Having already driven one Union force from the Valley, he next turned

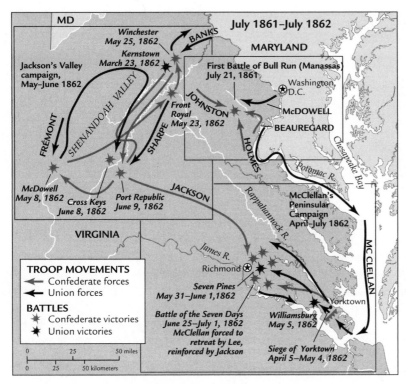

**The Virginia Theater, 1861–1862.** During the first year of war, Confederate forces in Virginia repeatedly defeated the much superior Union army. McClellan took over the Union army around Washington after the defeat at the First Battle of Bull Run and launched the Peninsula Campaign in the spring of 1862 to capture Richmond. To prevent the Union soldiers in the Shenandoah Valley from reinforcing McClellan, Stonewall Jackson conducted his brilliant Valley Campaign that May and defeated several enemy armies. Then in June, Lee's Confederate army defending Richmond counter-attacked McClellan and drove him back down the Peninsula in the Seven Days Campaign.

north to attack Major General Nathaniel Banks's men around Front Royal and Strasburg. Approaching Front Royal on May 23, the Confederates were startled to see a young woman, who one officer wrote was "running like mad down from the hill on our right . . . gesticulating wildly to us." Belle Boyd, a local resident, told Jackson there was only a small number of Yankees in town and "begged him to push on & he could take them all. . . ." Moving quickly, Jackson sent Taylor's brigade to secure a bridge the enemy had set ablaze. The Tigers succeeded in capturing the span although Taylor admitted "it was rather a near thing." The Union garrison then hastily retreated, but Jackson gobbled up 700 prisoners and valuable supplies at the loss of a handful of his own men.

Banks hastily retreated down the Valley from Strasburg to make a stand at Winchester, but Jackson took a detachment of Louisiana Tigers and some cavalry and artillery and cut his column at Middletown on May 24. When Jackson saw the road was crowded with the fleeing enemy, he opened fire with his artillery and completely wrecked a Union wagon train. Afterward he wrote that within minutes "the turnpike, which had just before teemed with life, presented a most appalling spectacle of carnage and destruction. The road was literally obstructed with the mingled and confused mass of struggling and dying

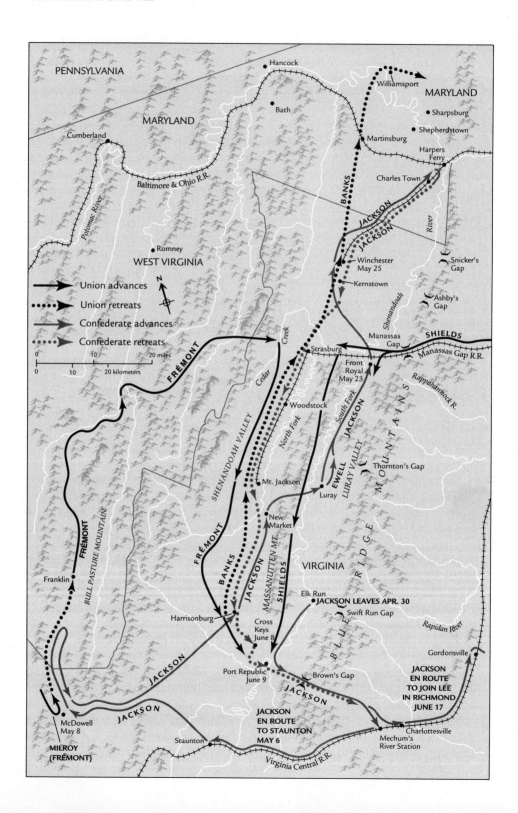

PENNSYLVANIA

Hancock

Williamsport

MARYLAND

MARYLAND

Bath

Sharpsburg
Shepherdstown

Cumberland

Martinsburg

Harpers
Ferry

BANKS

JACKSON

Charles Town

Baltimore & Ohio R.R.

JACKSON

River

Romney

WEST VIRGINIA

Winchester
May 25

Snicker's
Gap

Kernstown

Ashby's
Gap

Union advances

N

Shenandoah

Confederate advances

Manassas
Gap

SHIELDS

Confederate retreats

Creek

Strasburg

Manassas Gap R.R.

FRÉMONT

Front
Royal
May 23

0        10        20 miles

0      10        20 kilometers

Cedar

Woodstock

South Fork

JACKSON

Rappahannock R.

North Fork

Shenandoah Valley

Mt. Jackson

Luray

EWELL

Thornton's Gap

M O U N T A I N S

FRÉMONT

BANKS

New
Market

LURAY VALLEY

JACKSON

Franklin

JACKSON

MASSANUTTEN MT.

SHIELDS

VIRGINIA

Elk Run

JACKSON LEAVES APR. 30

Swift Run Gap

Rapidan River

BULL PASTURE MOUNTAIN

Harrisonburg

Cross
Keys
June 8

B L U E   R I D G E

Gordonsville

Port Republic
June 9

Brown's Gap

JACKSON

JACKSON
EN ROUTE
TO JOIN LEE
IN RICHMOND
JUNE 17

McDowell
May 8

JACKSON

JACKSON
EN ROUTE
TO STAUNTON
MAY 6

Charlottesville

MILROY
(FRÉMONT)

Staunton

Mechum's
River Station

Virginia Central R.R.

Union advances
Union retreats
Confederate advances
Confederate retreats

horses and riders." The Union soldiers at the head of the column continued on to Winchester, while those in the rear moved west out of the Valley. Jackson tried to pursue the enemy, but the Tigers began looting the wagons, instead, and Banks escaped.

Early the next morning, Jackson attacked Winchester in a thick fog. While his main line advanced toward the town, he sent Taylor's brigade around the left flank to attack an enemy fort and silence an artillery battery. Taylor charged up the hill toward the fort just as the fog cleared and the sun came out. It was a picture-book bayonet attack and no one who witnessed it ever forgot the scene. One soldier wrote, "I have rarely seen a more beautiful charge. This full brigade, with a line of glistening bayonets bright in that morning sun, its formation straight and compact, its tread quick and easy as it pushed on through the cloves and up that hill was a sight to delight a veteran." Sustaining moderate losses, Taylor captured the fort, and Banks hastily retreated north to Harpers Ferry and crossed the Potomac River into Maryland. In a little more than two weeks, Stonewall Jackson had driven virtually every Union soldier clear out of the Shenandoah Valley.

## The Escape

While Union commanders in the area reeled from the onslaught, President Lincoln kept his head and saw an opportunity to destroy Jackson's army. He ordered three Union columns to con-

verge on the Valley and trap the Confederates. Jackson, however, realized the danger he was in and quickly retreated. Racing back up the Valley, he managed to stay ahead of Banks pursuing from the rear, but Major Generals John C. Frémont's and James Shields's columns threatened to close the escape route ahead of him. On June 8, General Ewell stopped Frémont at Cross Keys and the next day Jackson tried to cut his way through Shields at Port Republic. Jackson sent

---

## DID YOU KNOW?

### The Rebel Yell

All Civil War soldiers yelled and shouted in the heat of battle, but their styles differed according to which army they served. Union soldiers usually belted out a deep-throated "huzzah!" and shouted in a regular cadence. The Confederates, however, had a "fiendish" high-pitched yelp called the Rebel Yell that reminded many soldiers of an Indian war whoop. Recordings of the Rebel Yell were actually made in the early twentieth century, but by that time the old veterans had no doubt lost much of their zeal. The Rebel Yell's origin is unclear. Some soldiers believed it began at First Bull Run, while others claimed to have first heard it when the Louisiana Tigers attacked a Union fort at Winchester during Jackson's Valley Campaign. Whatever its origin and exact nature, by all accounts the Rebel Yell was a terrifying sound and was unnerving to those on its receiving end. In one battle, Confederate General Jubal Early ordered his men to charge but was told they were out of ammunition. "Damn it," he replied, "holler them across," and they did.

---

**Jackson's Shenandoah Valley Campaign, May–June 1862.** Jackson's Shenandoah Valley Campaign is a classic example of how a smaller force can defeat a larger one by moving swiftly and using the element of surprise. Jackson's foot cavalry tied down 60,000 Union soldiers and prevented them from reinforcing McClellan on the Virginia Peninsula.

part of his army in a frontal attack, but a Union artillery battery positioned on the side of a mountain on his right flank devastated the men. Jackson ordered Taylor to silence the battery. By the time Taylor got into position, Jackson's army was on the verge of defeat, but his men suddenly heard a noise on the mountainside and looked up to see the Tigers storming the battery "like a hawk on a chicken." It took Taylor three tries, but he finally drove the Yankees away from the guns in fierce hand-to-hand fighting and Shields was forced to retreat. After the war, Taylor wrote, "It was a sickening sight, men in gray and blue pile up in front of and around the guns and with the horses dying and the blood of men and beasts flowing almost in a stream." With the battle won, Jackson soon rode up to Taylor and presented his brigade with the six captured cannons as a tribute. Taylor remembered, "I thought the men would go mad with cheering." Crossing over the Shenandoah's South Fork, Jackson then burned the bridge behind him and made his escape.

Through a skillful use of surprise, aggressiveness, and swift marching, Jackson had completely outmaneuvered the superior Union forces. With the Louisiana Tigers often setting the pace, his men earned the famous nickname "foot cavalry" by sometimes marching an incredible 30 miles a day. In the brilliant 30-day campaign, Jackson's Valley Army covered 350 miles, defeated three Union commands in five separate battles, inflicted 5,000 casualties at a cost of 2,000, and captured tons of valuable supplies. More important, Jackson tied down 60,000 Union soldiers that could have been sent to the Peninsula to reinforce McClellan. In his campaign report, Jackson credited the Louisiana Tigers for much of the success, and Taylor was promoted to major general and sent to Louisiana to command the troops there. All of the soldiers in Jackson's command were justifiably proud. One wrote home, "It will be something to boast of hereafter that I was one of Stonewall Jackson's Army. . . . I had rather be a private in such an Army than a Field Officer in any other Army."

## THE SEVEN DAYS CAMPAIGN

June 25–July 1, 1862: Seven Days Campaign
June 25, 1862: Battle of Oak Grove
June 26, 1862: Battle of Mechanicsville
June 27, 1862: Battle of Gaines' Mill
June 29, 1862: Battle of Savage's Station
June 30, 1862: Battle of Frayser's Farm
July 1, 1862: Battle of Malvern Hill

While Jackson was waging his Valley Campaign, Robert E. Lee took command of the army defending Richmond, renamed it the Army of Northern Virginia, and made plans to attack McClellan's Army of the Potomac. The Union forces were still split across the Chickahominy River, with Major General Fitz John Porter's 30,000-man corps isolated on the north side. In a daring cavalry raid,

Confederate Brigadier General James Ewell Brown (Jeb) Stuart discovered Porter's corps was "in the air;" in other words, it was unsupported and not entrenched and completely exposed to attack. With this valuable information in hand, Lee ordered Jackson to bring his men from the Shenandoah Valley to participate in a counterattack. Lee left 25,000 men on the south side of the Chickahominy River to confront McClellan's main force of 70,000 men. The bulk of the Confederate army, some 50,000 men, was massed on the river's north side near Mechanicsville to crush Porter's isolated corps. Jackson was given the operation's key assignment. He was to make a swift march from the Valley and be in position to attack Porter's right flank on June 26. Other Confederate divisions would be facing Porter's line farther west, and they would advance on their front when they heard Jackson begin his attack.

Lee's plan was complicated, involving the coordination of several different commands, and everything depended on Jackson's ability to arrive in time to start the attack. It also was fraught with risks. McClellan might realize his own tactical error and withdraw Porter before the attack could be made. Or he might make a sudden lunge toward Richmond, brush away the few Confederate defenders, and capture the city before Lee could react. Lee, however, took into account McClellan's habitual slowness and timidity and gambled he would not make any sudden attack.

## The Battles of Oak Grove and Mechanicsville

On June 25, one day before Lee planned to attack, McClellan suddenly advanced on the south side of the Chickahominy and engaged the Confederates at Oak Grove. Lee was shocked, thinking perhaps the enemy had discovered his plan and was attacking Richmond. It soon became apparent, however, that the move was simply a reconnaissance in force and not a major offensive. The Battle of Oak Grove began the Seven Days Campaign, but it did not interfere with Lee's plans.

The next day, thousands of Confederate soldiers waited impatiently near the hamlet of Mechanicsville, straining in vain to hear Jackson begin his attack. Frustrated and fearing the enemy might discover their presence, Major General A. P. Hill finally took the initiative and attacked Porter late in the day. Soon, other Confederate divisions launched a series of disjointed attacks, but the outnumbered Porter was posted behind strong defensive works and slaughtered the advancing troops. The Confederates lost almost 1,500 men in the Battle of Mechanicsville, while Porter lost only 350 men. Holding his ground until dark, Porter then skillfully withdrew during the night to a new position across a swampy creek near Gaines' Mill. Once again he placed his men in a formidable defensive line along dominating high ground and positioned his artillery to rake the ground in front.

As the exhausted Confederates settled in for the night among the dead and wounded, they wondered what had happened to Jackson. Historians still debate why the great Stonewall failed to carry out his part of the plan. Jackson's column was unusually slow on the march, and when it did arrive on the field he ordered the men to make camp instead of attacking. It seems unlikely

# BIOGRAPHY

## Robert Edward Lee: Audacity Personified

**Robert E. Lee and his horse, Traveller**

Virginia native Robert E. Lee (1807–1870) was the son of Revolutionary War hero Henry "Light Horse Harry" Lee. Graduating second in the 1829 West Point class, he earned three brevets during the Mexican War and was praised by Winfield Scott as the "very best soldier that I ever saw in the field." After Mexico, Lee served as superintendent of West Point, commanded the U.S. Marines that captured John Brown, and became colonel of the 2nd U.S. Cavalry. He also married Mary Custis, the great-granddaughter of Martha Washington. During the Civil War, federal authorities seized Mary's beloved Arlington House for non-payment of taxes and turned it into a soldiers' cemetery. The Lees never regained their home, and the property was eventually renamed Arlington National Cemetery.

Although he loved the Union and opposed secession, Lee's greatest loyalty was to Virginia and he turned down an offer to command the Union armies when the Civil War began. In a letter to his brother, Lee wrote, "With all my devotion to the Union, and the feeling of loyalty and duty of an American citizen, I have not been able to make up my mind to raise my hand against my relatives, my children, my home." He resigned his commission after Virginia seceded, was appointed a Confederate general, and eventually took command of the Army of Northern Virginia. Lee showed great tactical skill in his campaigns, but he also demonstrated a single-minded obsession for the offensive. He did not believe the Confederacy could survive a long defensive war because the Union would only grow stronger while the Confederacy became weaker.

Jackson misunderstood the role he was to play in the battle, so exhaustion may have been to blame. It was well known that Jackson needed frequent rest, and the long Shenandoah Valley Campaign may have sapped his energy and left him unusually lethargic. Whatever the reason, his men spent the afternoon resting and listening to the battle raging just a few miles away at Mechanicsville.

## Gaines' Mill and McClellan's Retreat

On June 27, Lee pushed on and launched a series of bloody attacks on Porter's position at Gaines' Mill. This time Jackson's divisions joined in the fighting, but the Rebels made no headway against the formidable Union defenses until late afternoon when John Bell Hood's Texas Brigade broke through the enemy's center. Lee then launched a general attack all along the front and forced Porter

As a result, Lee constantly sought to win the war quickly in a decisive battle and sometimes fought when he should have retreated.

Lee believed his responsibility as the army's commander was to make contact with the enemy and develop a general tactical plan. After that, he gave his corps commanders great discretion in fighting the battle, which allowed them to adapt quickly to changing situations. In describing this trait, one officer wrote, "I had frequently noticed . . . that Gen. Lee's instructions to his Corps Comrs are of a very comprehensive & general description & frequently admit of several interpretations—in fact will allow them to do almost anything provide only it be a *success*." Lee's command style worked magnificently when James Longstreet and Stonewall Jackson performed well, but it sometimes led to defeat when his subordinates were not up to the task.

Lee's compassion, skill, and bravery won him the undying loyalty of his men, and he became affectionately known as "Marse Robert." He shared their hardships by usually making his headquarters in a simple tent, eating their meager rations, and exposing himself to danger in combat. One soldier claimed when Lee rode down the battle line, "the men leaned on their muskets and looked at him . . . as tho' a God were passing by." Lee's repeated victories and fierce reputation even affected the enemy. A Union officer wrote home, "He was like a ghost to children . . . something that haunted us so long. . . ."

After his surrender at Appomattox, Lee returned to Richmond and cooperated with federal authorities during Reconstruction. He eventually became president of Washington College (today's Washington and Lee University) and served as an able administrator for five years. Lee died on October 12, 1870, after suffering an apparent stroke. Before he passed away, Lee tried to regain his citizenship rights by taking the required oath of allegiance and writing a letter to President Andrew Johnson requesting a pardon. The oath, however, was apparently misplaced by authorities. After it was discovered in the National Archives, President Gerald Ford granted Lee a posthumous pardon in 1975, and Congress restored his citizenship.

to retreat, but the victory came at a tremendous cost. Lee lost nearly 9,000 men in the daylong fight, and Porter lost approximately 7,000.

McClellan had not expected the bold Confederate offensive, and the two days of heavy fighting seemed to unnerve him completely. Convinced he was greatly outnumbered, he pulled back down the Peninsula. McClellan claimed he was simply shifting his base of supplies from the York River to the James River and not really retreating, but, in reality, the withdrawal was what his soldiers called a "great skedaddle." McClellan abandoned huge quantities of supplies in the process, and he virtually deserted the army. During crucial moments, he left the men on the field with no one in command, and he once boarded a gunboat to scout out suitable camping sites while the army was fighting for its life. To make matters worse, the so-called change of base was a great tactical error. McClellan actually outnumbered the Confederates, and there were many places along the Peninsula that offered good defensible ground to hold his position.

A running battle ensued over the next three days as McClellan successfully reunited his army south of the Chickahominy River, and Lee tried unsuccessfully to deliver a knockout blow. Poor coordination among the Confederate generals and stubborn fighting on the part of the Union soldiers prevented Lee from winning clear-cut victories when he attacked at Savage's Station and Frayser's Farm. Jackson, in particular, continued to move slowly and did not aggressively press the enemy. Such missteps caused Lee to become more and more frustrated at his subordinates, and when General Jubal Early predicted the enemy would get away, Lee angrily snapped, "Yes, because I cannot get my orders carried out!"

## The Battle of Malvern Hill

McClellan finally reached a point of high ground near the James River called Malvern Hill and placed his army in a nearly impregnable position along its slopes. Lines of strong infantry ringed the hill, with batteries of massed artillery positioned to spray deadly canister at any attacking force. Union gunboats in the river also stood by ready to lend support with their heavy guns.

Lee mistakenly believed McClellan's soldiers were completely demoralized and exhausted and that one more attack would finish them. On July 1, he unwisely ordered his infantry to make a frontal assault. Again, there was poor coordination among Lee's officers, and the battle fizzled into a series of disjointed fights rather than one giant attack. The Confederates were mowed down by the Union artillery, and no appreciable gains were made even though some units managed to close with the enemy in vicious hand-to-hand fighting. In the near-suicidal charge, the Confederates lost almost 5,400 men while McClellan lost approximately 3,300. The Seven Days Campaign was over, and the next day McClellan fell back to a strong position at Harrison's Landing on the James River.

## A Costly Victory

The Confederates had successfully driven the enemy from the outskirts of Richmond, but in his official report Lee complained, "Under ordinary circumstances the Federal Army should have been destroyed." Lee's staff had performed poorly in the campaign, and his subordinates (most noticeably Jackson) had been slow and failed to coordinate movements. Lee took immediate steps to prevent such failure again by transferring out of the army a number of generals he felt were weak. Wisely, he kept Jackson.

The Seven Days Campaign demonstrated two important things about Lee. Foremost, it showed his great skill as a battlefield commander. Lee took advantage of McClellan's tactical error and audaciously split his army in the face of a much larger enemy force. He then attacked and maintained the initiative until he decided it was time to stop fighting. But the campaign also showed one of Lee's great weaknesses—his reliance on the attack no matter what the cost. This tactic cost him a staggering 20,000 casualties to McClellan's 16,000. Unfortunately for Lee, the Union could replace its losses indefinitely—the Confederacy could not. Ironically, in such a war of attrition, the Confederates could win every campaign but eventually lose the war by simply running out of men.

For their part, the Union soldiers had fought well. Their retreat may have been a tactical mistake, but it was done in an orderly fashion for the most part. As one Union soldier wrote, "Either we have made an inglorious *skedaddle* or a brilliant retreat." By taking advantage of the terrain and skillfully using artillery, the Yankees held their ground well and made the Rebels pay a terrible price in each battle. However, lower-level officers and the soldiers themselves were more responsible for this success than McClellan's leadership.

## The Soft War Hardens

After the Seven Days Campaign, McClellan felt compelled to write an unsolicited letter to Lincoln with advice on how to fight the war. In his Harrison's Landing Letter, McClellan reiterated his belief that the Constitution and the Union had to be preserved no matter what the cost. However, he wrote, the war "should be conducted upon the highest principles known to Christian civilization. . . . Neither confiscation of property, political executions of persons, territorial organization of States, or forcible abolition of slavery should be contemplated for a moment. In prosecuting the war all private property and unarmed persons should be strictly protected. . . ." In closing, McClellan had the audacity to recommend Lincoln consider appointing a commander-in-chief (i.e., dictator) to prosecute the war, but he added the disclaimer, "I do not ask that place for myself." Needless to say, Lincoln did not act on McClellan's advice.

The Harrison's Landing Letter demonstrated just how out of touch McClellan was with the administration. In the war's early months, many military and political officials supported the soft policy he advocated: McClellan, General Henry Halleck, and others believed victory could be achieved without having to actually conquer the South. They were convinced the war was caused by the slaveholding secessionists and that only a minority of Southerners was truly committed to the Confederacy. The war could be won by destroying the enemy's armies on one hand and protecting civilians' rights on the other. Such a conciliatory policy would show the Southern people that their political and property rights, including slave ownership, would be protected under the Constitution. With no real reason to support the Confederacy, white Southerners would lose interest in the war, and Jefferson Davis's government would collapse as its armies were defeated on the battlefield.

Lincoln himself supported the soft policy at first. When abolitionist generals John C. Frémont and David Hunter arbitrarily abolished slavery in their departments of Missouri and South Carolina, respectively, Lincoln made them rescind the orders. In the latter half of 1861, Radical Republicans passed two Confiscation Acts in Congress that authorized the

# EYEWITNESS

## Campbell Brown

*Twenty-two-year-old Campbell Brown came from a wealthy Tennessee family, and he was the cousin of Jackson's division commander Major General Richard S. Ewell. When the Civil War began, Ewell placed Brown on his staff as a favor to Brown's mother Lizinka, Ewell's first cousin and love interest. This position allowed Captain Brown to circulate among the highest-ranking officers in Lee's army. Well educated in the United States and France, Brown appreciated the war's historical significance and wrote a memoir of his service. One incident he recounted took place at Malvern Hill and demonstrated how dangerous Civil War battles were, even for generals like Stonewall Jackson:*

Gen'l Jackson had two narrow escapes, which I happened to see. About 10 or 11 a.m. he rode out with Gen'l Ewell to our left to meet Gen'l [William H. C.] Whiting, & just as they emerged from the woods into the wheatfield, a piece of artillery passed to the rear, making quite a dust & drawing a heavy fire. One or two shells struck just in front of the party, at the moment of emerging from the woods, just as Gen'l Whiting joined them. They rode on quietly, when one or two more [shells] pitched viciously down just at the head of Gen'l J[ackson]'s horse, which kept on at its shambling gait. Jackson talking earnestly to Gen'l E[well] took no notice, but the latter quickly stooping caught his horse by the bridle & stopped him, a second or two before the shell exploded. They were near enough to it to be covered with dust. . . . About 3 p.m. Gen'l E[well] rode over to the right to become acquainted with the ground, leaving [Thomas] Turner, Maj. [Hugh] Nelson & me near the gate-posts. Jackson was there with Maj. [Robert Lewis] Dabney & two or three couriers. A courier sitting on the fence near the gate-post, had his horse struck in the head by a fragment of a shell which had struck one of the gate-posts & exploded with a tremendous report. The poor creature had part of the head blown away between the brain & the nostrils, making it blind & frantic. Three or four horses much frightened were struggling to get away from their riders—& Gen'l J[ackson]'s old sorrel partaking the general alarm dashed off, pulling him down on his hands & knees. Turner, Maj. Nelson & I ran to him, fearing he was hurt—but he had recovered his feet & his horse kept pulling him along. After 20 or 30 yards of this, he managed to stop it, mounted & at once rode to the rear. I saw him once or twice again, but he very properly established his Hd. Qrs. in a less exposed place, 100 yards back.

*Stonewall Jackson's luck ran out the following year when he was accidentally shot by his own men. As for Brown, he became Ewell's stepson when the general married Lizinka. After the war, Brown tried unsuccessfully to marry General Lee's daughter Mildred and eventually became a nationally known stock breeder in Tennessee.*

Terry L. Jones, ed., *Campbell Brown's Civil War: With Ewell and the Army of Northern Virginia* (Baton Rouge: Louisiana State University Press, 2001), pp. 125–126.

president to confiscate slaves being used to support the rebellion and even to free slaves that came into Union lines. Lincoln signed the laws but never enforced them because he believed they were too harsh (see Chapter 9). By mid-1862, however, attitudes were changing in the North, and Radical Republicans in particular were calling for a hard war: It was obvious to them that most Southern whites did support the Confederacy, and nothing short of all-out war would defeat the rebellion. Southern civilians produced the food and grain that kept their armies in the field, and slaves provided essential labor to build fortifications and maintain the Confederates' infrastructure. An increasingly violent guerrilla war was also being waged in Missouri and Eastern Tennessee, and in those areas Union soldiers had little enthusiasm for coddling civilians they believed harbored bushwhackers. The war was becoming bloodier and more chaotic each passing month, and there was no end in sight. By July 1862, even Lincoln was coming to the conclusion that more drastic measures had to be taken. When McClellan sat down to pen his Harrison's Landing Letter, Lincoln was already preparing the Emancipation Proclamation to free the slaves in rebelling areas as a military measure to weaken the enemy.

## THE SECOND BULL RUN CAMPAIGN

**August 9, 1862: Battle of Cedar Mountain**
**August 25–September 1, 1862: Second Bull Run Campaign**
**August 28, 1862: Battle of Groveton**
**August 29–30, 1862: Second Battle of Bull Run**
**September 1, 1862: Battle of Chantilly**
**September 2, 1862: Lincoln returns McClellan to command**

When McClellan failed to resume the offensive after the Seven Days Campaign, Lincoln decided to give another general a chance. Major General John Pope, the hero of New Madrid, Missouri, and Island No. 10, had been given command of the Army of Virginia to protect Washington and the Shenandoah Valley. In light of McClellan's inactivity, Lincoln changed the army's mission and allowed Pope to take the offensive. The president then essentially demoted McClellan by ordering him to send his men to reinforce Pope.

Pope's pompous nature and tactless manners did not endear him to anyone. Almost immediately, he unintentionally insulted the army by announcing he came from the west where Union soldiers were used to seeing the backsides of Confederates. When a dispatch was published bearing the dramatic heading "Headquarters in the Saddle," the men quipped that Pope's headquarters were where his hindquarters should be. Brigadier General Samuel Sturgis summed up many soldiers' feelings when he reportedly declared, "I don't care for John Pope one pinch of owl dung." For their part, the Confederates hated Pope more

**Manassas Junction, Virginia.** The devastation wrought by Jackson's troops on Pope's Manassas Junction supply depot can be seen in this wartime photograph.

than most Union officers because he gave his men free rein to prey on Southern civilians for supplies, and his advance into Northern Virginia was marked by widespread looting and destroyed homes. It was said that John Pope was the only Union general whom Robert E. Lee disliked personally.

## The Battle of Cedar Mountain

Pope's advance threatened Lee's railroad supply line to the Shenandoah Valley, and Lee realized that if McClellan's army joined Pope there was little chance he could stop the combined enemy force. The Confederates' best strategy was to move north and defeat Pope before he could cut the supply line or McClellan could reinforce him.

In mid-July, Lee sent Stonewall Jackson's 24,000 men north to confront this new threat. On August 9, Jackson encountered the Union advance guard under Major General Nathaniel P. Banks at Cedar Mountain and rashly attacked without first ascertaining the enemy's strength. When Banks unexpectedly counterattacked, Jackson suddenly found himself fighting for his life. Through dogged determination and personal leadership, however, he rallied his troops and finally won the battle at a cost of 1,400 men. Banks had almost twice as many casualties, but Jackson's recklessness somewhat tarnished his reputation, especially coming so soon after his lackluster performance in the Seven Days.

# NOTABLE UNITS: *The Iron Brigade*

In the huge Army of the Potomac, only one brigade was made up entirely of western men. Originally commanded by Brigadier General Rufus King, it included the 2nd, 6th, and 7th Wisconsin, and the 19th Indiana (the 24th Michigan was added later). When Brigadier General John Gibbon took command in May 1862, he adopted a unique black slouch hat for the men, which led to the unit sometimes being called the Black Hat Brigade.

The brigade's first combat experience was at Groveton when King's division was ambushed by Stonewall Jackson. There, in an open field, the inexperienced westerners held their ground and slugged it out with Jackson's veterans for two hours, losing 751 men, or one-third of their strength. Although they did not know it at the time, the westerners' foe was the fabled Stonewall Brigade, which also lost one-third of its men. One Iron Brigade historian claimed after Groveton the men were always ready for battle, but "we were never again eager." A few weeks later, the Iron Brigade attacked the Confederates again at South Mountain during the Antietam Campaign and sustained another 318 casualties. After this second fight, corps commander Major General Joseph Hooker praised the brigade's steely performance in battle and called it his "iron brigade." The name stuck when a war correspondent used the term in a newspaper article about the fight. Days later, the brigade charged into Antietam's infamous cornfield and in short order lost 348 men. One man describing their fight with the Louisiana Tigers wrote, "Men, I cannot say fell—they were knocked out of ranks by the dozen."

The Iron Brigade's bloodiest battle was Gettysburg, where it was rushed into combat early on the first day to help stop the enemy onslaught. At the time, the Confederates thought they were just facing militia. Over the roar of battle, brigade members heard the enemy cry out, "Here are those damned black-hat fellers again . . . 'Tain't no militia—that's the Army of the Potomac!" The brigade lost 1,212 men (over two-thirds of its strength) at Gettysburg, with each regiment suffering more than 70 percent casualties. The Iron Brigade never quite recovered from Gettysburg, although it fought in many more battles. The unit sustained heavy casualties again at Spotsylvania's "Bloody Angle," which one member claimed "was the most terrible twenty-four hours of our service in the war." Before the war ended, the Iron Brigade lost its special identity when several eastern regiments were added, and some of the original regiments either mustered out or were consolidated with others.

## The Turning Movement

When McClellan began evacuating the Peninsula as ordered, Lee realized he no longer posed a threat to Richmond and moved to join Jackson. This concentration of enemy forces made Pope uneasy, so he withdrew to the north side of the Rappahannock River. Unwilling to risk a frontal attack across a wide river, Lee devised a bold turning maneuver to force Pope to retreat. He first divided the army into two wings under Stonewall Jackson and Major General James Longstreet. Lee then remained with Longstreet to keep Pope's attention focused on the river, while Stuart's cavalry led Jackson's wing upstream. Jackson was to make a giant turning movement, crossing over the Rappahannock undetected and sweeping into Pope's rear to threaten his line of communications back to Washington. Pope would be forced to withdraw from the Rappahannock River to avoid being trapped. When he did, Lee and Longstreet would follow Jackson's route and join him to crush the retreating enemy army.

Jackson's foot cavalry quickly covered fifty-four miles in just thirty-six hours, reached Pope's supply base at Manassas Junction undetected, and captured it on August 26. After eating all they wanted and helping themselves to clothing and shoes, the Rebels carted off what they could carry and burned the rest. For the ragged, hungry Southerners, it was a moment to relish. One soldier wrote, "To see a starving man eating lobster salad & drinking rhine wine, barefooted & in tatters was curious; the whole thing is indescribable."

## The Battle of Groteon

After destroying Manassas Junction, Jackson took up a hidden position in some woods near the hamlet of Groveton and waited for the enemy to react. Pope mistakenly believed the attack was nothing more than a Confederate cavalry raid and sent a few units to drive them off. Late in the afternoon of August 28, Brigadier General Rufus King's lone Union division marched down the road past Jackson's hidden position in search of the supposed enemy raiders. King was shocked when Jackson's men came swarming out of the woods and attacked, but his division skillfully swung around to meet the threat, and for several hours the opposing soldiers stood toe-to-toe in an open field and slugged it out. The sun set and darkness enveloped the field, but the two sides continued their brutal fight. Long after dark, the firing finally died out, and Jackson and King mutually withdrew. Some of the heaviest fighting had occurred between the Stonewall Brigade and the Union's Iron Brigade. A Confederate officer who examined their position the next day wrote, "The lines were well marked by the dark rows of bodies stretched out on the broom-sedge field, lying just where they had fallen, with their heels on a well-defined line. The bodies lay in so straight a line that they looked like troops lying down to rest." The Battle of Groveton was indecisive, but Pope now knew there was much more than Rebel cavalry in his rear.

## The Second Battle of Bull Run

Knowing Pope would now be coming at him with a large force, Jackson placed his men along the cuts and embankments of an unfinished railroad on the

**The Second Battle of Bull Run, August 29–30, 1862.** After successfully marching into the Union rear, Jackson destroyed Pope's supply base at Manassas Junction and fought a bloody battle at Groveton. Jackson then took up a strong defensive position on the old Bull Run battlefield and held his ground against repeated attacks on August 29. Lee and Longstreet reached the battlefield later that day and launched a devastating counterattack on August 30 that routed Pope from the field.

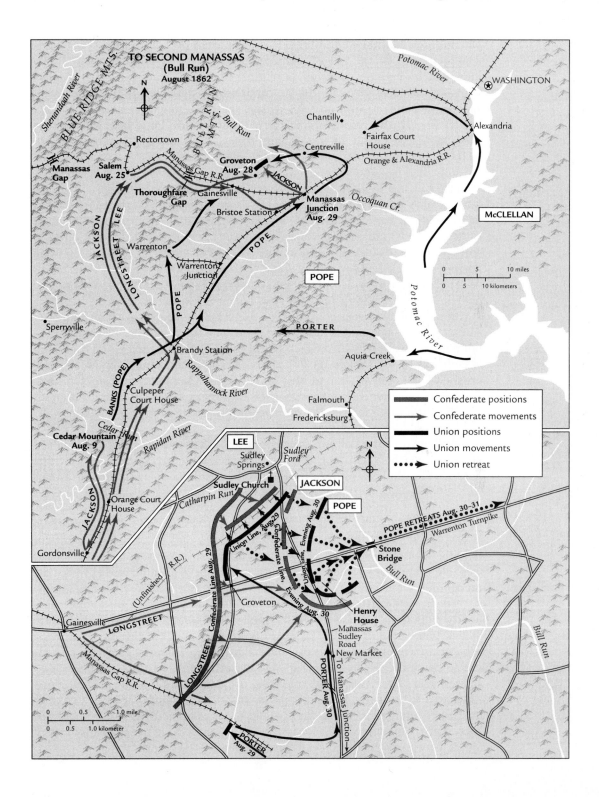

**TO SECOND MANASSAS**
(Bull Run)
August 1862

old Bull Run battlefield and hoped Lee would arrive before the enemy overwhelmed him. On August 29, Pope launched a massive attack with 60,000 men, but he committed a major tactical blunder by not committing all of his troops at once. Instead, the Union divisions were sent in piecemeal, and Jackson was able to shift units to critical spots. Although the attacks actually broke through the Confederate line in some places, Pope failed to support them sufficiently, and all were finally repulsed in vicious, sometimes hand-to-hand, fighting.

Pope had become so preoccupied with Jackson that he neglected to keep informed of Lee's whereabouts across the Rappahannock River. As a result, Lee was able to follow Jackson unmolested and arrived on the battlefield about noon. Without Pope's knowledge, he placed Longstreet at a nearly right angle to Jackson's right flank. The Confederate army now resembled a trap ready to spring shut on the unsuspecting enemy. When Pope ordered General Fitz John Porter to attack Jackson's right flank, Porter ran headlong into Longstreet's veterans. Porter informed his commander that Longstreet had arrived on the field and was threatening *his* flank, but Pope refused to believe him.

Pope's frontal attacks continued on August 30, but Jackson's men held firm. At one critical moment, a brigade of Louisiana Tigers ran out of ammunition but held its position by throwing rocks at the charging enemy. When the Union assault was finally broken up by massed artillery, Longstreet surged forward, crushed Pope's left wing, and sent his army in a headlong retreat. Hoping to annihilate the enemy, Lee sent Jackson in pursuit. On September 1, another bloody battle was fought in the midst of an intense thunderstorm at Chantilly, but Pope escaped.

Walking over the Bull Run battlefield, a Confederate chaplain was shocked at the gory sights. "Oh! May I never again witness such scenes as I saw this day. . . . The Yankees in front of the R[ail] R[oad] occupied by the La. troops were lying in heaps. Those in front of the R.R. had something of the appearance of men, for they were killed with rocks or musket balls and with their face to our men. But those scattered throughout the woods and fields presented a shocking spectacle. Some with their brains oozing out; some with the face shot off; others with their bowels protruding; others with shattered limbs. . . . They were almost as black as negroes, bloated and some so decomposed as to be past recognition."

The Second Battle of Bull Run was another Union disaster, with Pope losing nearly 14,000 men to Lee's 8,000. Pope refused to take responsibility for the defeat, however, and bitterly blamed his subordinates. He particularly singled out Porter, who was court-martialed and dismissed from the army for his failure to make the ordered flank attack. Porter fought to regain his honor and sixteen years later succeeded in getting the conviction overturned and being reinstated in the army. Pope also accused Little Mac of intentionally withholding timely reinforcements so Pope would be defeated and McClellan could win back army command. This accusation actually may have been true, for two of McClellan's corps failed to reach Pope in time for the battle.

## The Return of Little Mac

The Second Bull Run fiasco created a dilemma for Lincoln. Pope obviously could not be kept in command after the rout, but neither was Lincoln very impressed with McClellan's performance. The cabinet, especially Secretary of War Stanton, opposed any attempt to resurrect Little Mac. Stanton, in fact, had the majority of the cabinet sign a petition declaring "our deliberate opinion that, at this time, it is not safe to entrust to Major General McClellan the command of any Army of the United States." Nonetheless, Lincoln knew the soldiers loved McClellan, and he recognized the general's knack for discipline and organization. What was most needed at the time was to protect Washington and rebuild the army. Swallowing his pride, Lincoln ignored the cabinet's wishes and placed McClellan back in command of the Union forces around Washington.

Dressed in his finest uniform, McClellan rode out to meet the defeated army on the afternoon of September 2. Brigadier General John Hatch, no admirer of Pope, was nearby when McClellan informed Pope of the change in command. Hearing the news, Hatch callously ignored Pope's feelings and yelled out, "Boys, McClellan is in command of the army again! Three cheers!" As the news swept down the road, the exhausted soldiers yelled and threw their hats in the air. Little Mac was back!

## *FOR FURTHER READING*

Lincoln's General War Orders No. 1
Lincoln's April 9, 1862, letter to McClellan urging an advance
McClellan's Harrison's Landing Letter to Lincoln

## CHAPTER 7

# Confederate Juggernauts: From Antietam to Stones River

**The Antietam Campaign**

**The Kentucky Campaign**

**The Winter Campaigns**

On September 13, 1862, the exhausted men of the 27th Indiana camped at Frederick, Maryland, on the same ground the Confederates had used a day or so earlier. Robert E. Lee's vaunted Army of Northern Virginia had launched a raid into Maryland, and the Army of the Potomac was moving in to engage it. Scanning the debris left by the enemy, Private Barton W. Mitchell noticed three cigars wrapped in paper lying on the ground. Picking up the prized cigars, he happened to look at the paper and was stunned to discover that it was an official document from Lee's headquarters. General Order No. 191 detailed the entire Confederate strategy and showed in great detail the location of each of Lee's units and their missions. The document was quickly sent up the chain of command to George B. McClellan's headquarters. On reading the document, Little Mac was elated and exclaimed, "Now I know what to do!" Firing off a telegram to Lincoln, he informed the president, "I have all the plans of the Rebels and will catch them in their own trap if my men are equal to the emergency. . . . Will send you trophies." Later, when General John Gibbon paid a visit, a near-giddy McClellan showed him the order and declared, "Here is a paper with which if I cannot whip Bobbie Lee, I will be willing to go home." Few generals have ever enjoyed such good fortune in war. If McClellan moved quickly, his army could catch the widely scattered enemy units and defeat them in detail.

By late summer 1862, the Civil War was settling into a pattern, with the Confederates winning most of the battles in the east and the Union winning most of the clashes in the west. In the eastern theater, Lee had pushed McClellan away from Richmond's doorstep and driven virtually every enemy soldier out of the state. In the west, however, Ulysses S. Grant and other Union officers had won several impressive victories that forced the Confederates out of Kentucky and most of Tennessee and seized control of the upper and lower Mississippi River. The war's outcome was still in doubt, but the North's success in the west gave it reason to be cautiously optimistic. Then in late summer, the Union suddenly found itself on the defensive when the Rebels launched major offensives in both theaters that threatened to change the course of the war.

## THE ANTIETAM CAMPAIGN

September 4–19, 1862: The Antietam Campaign
September 14, 1862: Battle of South Mountain, Maryland
September 15, 1862: Stonewall Jackson captures Harpers Ferry, Virginia
September 17, 1862: Battle of Antietam, Maryland
September 22, 1862: Lincoln issues the Preliminary Emancipation
    Proclamation

Following the successful Second Bull Run Campaign, General Lee had to choose his next course of action. He could take up a strong defensive position in northern Virginia, rest and reinforce his army, and let McClellan make the next move, or he could retain the initiative by assuming the offensive. Going on the defensive would be more in keeping with President Davis's defensive-offensive strategy. Davis believed the South could win its independence by husbanding its strength and dragging the war out so long the Northern people would tire of the conflict. Since McClellan would probably take months to prepare for another offensive, a defensive strategy would give Lee plenty of time to rebuild his army after the terrible losses of the summer campaigns. Lee, however, believed this defensive strategy actually favored the North. He argued time was on the North's side because it had a huge advantage in manpower and industry. The longer the war lasted, the weaker the Confederacy would become and the stronger the Union would grow. Lee felt the North would be forced to negotiate a peace if he destroyed the Union Army of the Potomac in a single great battle. The Confederacy's best chance at victory was to win that battle as quickly as possible.

### The Strategy

In early September 1862, Lee proposed marching north into Maryland and Pennsylvania. Such a move, he argued, would allow the Confederates to maintain the initiative in the east, and it would take the war out of Virginia during the crucial harvest season. Lee also believed thousands of Marylanders would flock to enlist in his army, and the slave state might even secede and join

**The Virginia Theater, August–December 1862.** After the Seven Days Campaign, Lee turned his army northward to confront Pope. Leading the way, Jackson defeated Pope's vanguard at Cedar Mountain in early August and moved into the enemy's rear. The Confederates routed the Union army at the Second Battle of Bull Run and then launched a raid into Maryland. McClellan won a strategic victory at Antietam by forcing Lee to retreat back to Virginia, but McClellan was removed from command because of his slow pursuit. Burnside then took command of the Union army and made another advance toward Richmond, but he was badly defeated at the Battle of Fredericksburg.

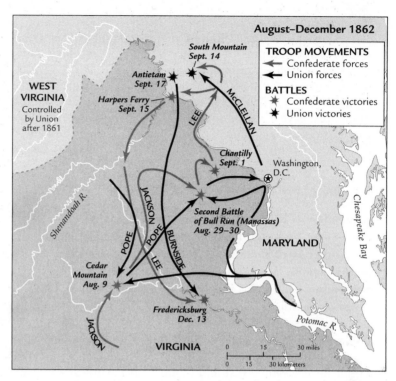

the Confederacy. An offensive would certainly alarm the Northern people and could strengthen the peace movement there, and a victory over the Army of the Potomac on its own soil might convince Europe to extend diplomatic recognition to the Confederacy. As will be seen in Chapter 10, Great Britain and France sympathized with the South and supported Confederate independence as a way of weakening the growing power of the United States. Both recognized the Confederacy as a belligerent and sold it war material, but they had not yet taken the final step of granting diplomatic recognition. Britain and France were now holding back to see if the Confederates really had a chance to win, much as France had withheld recognition from the United States during the Revolutionary War until after the Battle of Saratoga. A great victory on Northern soil might be just the thing to nudge the Europeans into action.

Lee's proposed strategy is often misrepresented as an invasion of the North, when, in fact, it was a large raid. An invasion implies conquering territory and staying there indefinitely, but Lee's objectives were more short-term in nature. The offensive's main goals were to take the pressure off Virginia during harvest time and to force the enemy into a decisive battle on ground of Lee's choosing. The Confederates simply did not have the logistical capability to remain on Northern soil for an extended period of time. Lee knew at some point he would have to return to Virginia.

## The Lost Order

Although Davis had concerns about the proposed campaign, he trusted Lee's judgment, and on September 4, 1862, the battle-hardened Army of Northern Virginia crossed the Potomac River into Maryland. Lee then split the army into two wings under Longstreet and Jackson. Lee remained with Longstreet, whose divisions scattered across the countryside to gather supplies and recruits. Jackson was sent to eliminate the 12,000-man Union garrison at Harpers Ferry, Virginia, so it would not threaten the lines of communication back through the Shenandoah Valley. Afterward, Jackson was to rejoin Lee and Longstreet in Maryland. Splitting the army to achieve two goals was a classic Lee maneuver, but it also was dangerous, and success depended on McClellan being true to his cautious nature. If he moved quickly, McClellan could catch and overwhelm the Confederates' widely separated wings before Lee could concentrate his forces. But McClellan did exactly what Lee expected. He waited three days after the Confederates entered Maryland to start his pursuit and even then moved slowly. McClellan's timidity was based partly on his belief that Lee's men greatly outnumbered his and partly on the fact he did not know Lee's intentions. Was this simply a raid to gather supplies or an ambitious campaign to attack Washington or Baltimore? To be safe, and to calm Lincoln's fears, McClellan was forced to keep the Army of the Potomac between Lee and the two cities.

On September 13 everything changed when Lee's Lost Order fell into McClellan's hands. McClellan now knew the exact disposition and timetable of every enemy unit and was in a position to move quickly and destroy the Confederate army piece by piece before Lee could concentrate it. Speed was of the essence, but incredibly McClellan waited sixteen hours before moving out in pursuit. By that time, Lee realized his scattered army was in danger, although it still is not clear if he knew McClellan had discovered the campaign plans. Lee ordered Jackson to hurry

### DID YOU KNOW?

#### Who Lost the Lost Order?

McClellan's discovery of the Lost Order changed the Antietam Campaign, but which Confederate officer was so careless that he wrapped the order around three cigars and then lost it? The lost order was a copy made for Jackson's division commander and former brother-in-law Major General Daniel H. Hill, but Hill had in his possession a copy of the order throughout the campaign. Historians have sought to explain why there were two copies of the order for Hill and how one of them came to be lost. The best theory is that Hill's copy was one made for him by Jackson. Lee's headquarters staff probably made another copy to send to Hill, not knowing he already had one. The anonymous courier who was to deliver the paper to Hill must have wrapped it around his cigars and then lost it. One can only imagine the courier's anxiety when he realized what he had done and what the consequences would likely be. But nothing happened! Hill already had a copy and never even knew a duplicate was being sent to him. Hearing nothing from Hill, Lee's headquarters assumed he had received the copy sent by the courier. Only the courier knew what had really happened, and he certainly was not going to say anything.

# BIOGRAPHY
## Thomas Jonathan Jackson: Stonewall

Thomas J. "Stonewall" Jackson

Stonewall Jackson (1824–1863) was a native of modern-day West Virginia who graduated from West Point in 1846. He was brevetted twice in the Mexican War but eventually resigned his lieutenant's commission to accept a teaching position at the Virginia Military Institute (VMI). Jackson was a poor teacher who simply memorized the text and recited it to the students. The cadets referred to him as "Tom Fool," and one even tried to bash him with a brick from a third-story window. This poor opinion of Jackson was partly based on his rather eccentric traits. He sometimes dunked his head (with eyes wide open) in a bucket of cold water to strengthen his weak eyes, refused to eat pepper because it made his leg ache, and often raised an arm over his head to even out his body's blood flow. Despite these quirks, Jackson was a friendly man with people he knew well and a loving husband. He particularly enjoyed children and sometimes played with them on the floor.

After Jackson's first wife, Elinor Junkin, died in childbirth along with her baby, Jackson married Mary Anna Morrison, a Presbyterian who converted him to her faith. He became something of a zealot, even refusing to read letters or fight on Sunday if it could be avoided. Jackson attributed everything to God's will, attended church faithfully, and sponsored a Sunday School for African Americans.

Appointed a Confederate brigadier general, Jackson earned his famous nickname at the First Battle of Bull Run. Confederate soldiers, however, rarely called him Stonewall and usually referred to him as "Old Jack." Jackson became one of Robert E. Lee's most trusted subordinates. Lee said of him, "Such an executive officer the sun never

his Harpers Ferry operation and commanded all units to join him at Sharpsburg, Maryland, as soon as possible. Knowing this concentration would take time, Lee sent one infantry division to defend three passes across South Mountain and slow McClellan's progress.

## South Mountain and Harpers Ferry

On September 14, McClellan attacked the South Mountain passes to engage Lee's army and rescue the men at Harpers Ferry. One column fought its way through, but its commander believed he was outnumbered and failed to push on to relieve Harpers Ferry as ordered. At two other passes, the Confederates held on until dark and then retreated to join Lee at Sharpsburg. When McClellan began his advance from South Mountain the next day, Lee knew he was in danger and prepared to retreat back to Virginia. Then Jackson sent word that the capture of Harpers Ferry was imminent, and he would soon be able to shone on. I have but to show him my design, and I know that if it can be done it will be done. No need for me to send or watch him. Straight as the needle to the pole he advances to the execution of my purpose." Jackson, in turn, absolutely trusted Lee, and once remarked, "I am willing to follow him blindfolded."

Despite his many victories, Jackson was not infallible. His performance in the Seven Days Campaign was disappointing, and his line was temporarily broken at Fredericksburg because he failed to place troops at a vulnerable point. Subordinates frequently complained of Jackson's harsh discipline and secrecy, and more than one general was arrested for not living up to his high standards. Division commander Richard S. Ewell once exploded in frustration and proclaimed to an officer that he "was certain of [Jackson's] lunacy, and that he never saw one of Jackson's couriers approach without expecting an order to assault the north pole."

An uninspiring figure, Jackson dressed poorly and was ungainly both walking and riding a horse. One soldier remembered how "the remark was made by one of us after staring at him a long time, that there must be some mistake about him, [for] if he was an able man, he showed it less than any of us had ever seen." Nonetheless, Jackson's men formed a close bond with their chief, and even the enemy was awestruck. One officer recalled an incident when Jackson rode his famous horse, Little Sorrel, down a road past some Union prisoners. "Many of them saluted as he passed and he invariably returned the salute. I heard one of them say as he passed: 'Boys, he's not much for looks, but if we'd had him we wouldn't have been caught in this trap.'"

Tragically, Jackson died when his left arm was amputated after a friendly fire incident at Chancellorsville. When told of the amputation, Lee declared, "He has lost his left arm; but I have lost my right arm." Lapsing in and out of consciousness, Jackson's reported last words were "Let us cross over the river and rest under the shade of the trees."

rejoin Lee in Maryland. With that good news, Lee decided to stay and fight. True to his word, Jackson captured Harpers Ferry on September 16 and left Major General A. P. Hill's division there to parole the Union prisoners while he led the rest of the men to Sharpsburg.

Lee was taking a huge risk when he assumed a defensive position on the west side of Antietam Creek just outside Sharpsburg. He had only a few thousand men, and McClellan would easily crush them if he attacked before Jackson arrived. Also, the Potomac River was just a few miles to the rear. If Lee was defeated at Antietam, his men would be trapped against the river and probably annihilated. There were many reasons why Lee should not have fought at Antietam, but his decision to do so was in keeping with his character. It simply was not in his nature to turn his back on the enemy without a fight, and he had entered Maryland as a liberator. It would have been unthinkable to slink away meekly after entering the state with so much fanfare.

## The Battle of Antietam

McClellan arrived at Antietam Creek on the morning of September 16, but he did not attack the thinly held Rebel line. Instead, he spent his time scouting out the enemy position and devising a tactical plan to attack simultaneously both enemy flanks and the center. The plan was a good one and, if carried out properly, McClellan would probably have won the battle because Lee had only about 40,000 men to face McClellan's 75,000. Unfortunately, McClellan failed to coordinate his army. Instead of moving simultaneously against the Confederates' flanks and center, the Union attacks were made in a disjointed manner.

At daylight on September 17, Major General Joseph Hooker's corps advanced against Lee's left flank, which was held by Stonewall Jackson. As the sun rose over South Mountain, Hooker saw thousands of Rebel bayonets glistening in a 40-acre cornfield and opened fire with his artillery. The effect was devastating. Hooker wrote in his report, "In the time I am writing, every stalk of corn in the northern and greater part of the field was cut as closely as could have been done with a knife, and the soldiers lay in rows precisely as they had stood in their ranks a few minutes before. It was never my fortune to witness a more bloody, dismal battlefield." Hooker then charged into the corn, but his men found there were plenty of enemy survivors. When the Confederates opened fire, hundreds of Union soldiers were cut down. Despite their heavy losses, the Yankees drove Jackson out of the cornfield after fierce fighting and down a road toward the local Dunkard Church, but they were then viciously attacked by Major General John Bell Hood's division. One Union soldier described the Confederates' fire as "a scythe running through our line." Back and forth the two sides fought, launching attacks and counterattacks through the cornfield. When Hooker was wounded in the fierce fighting and his attack stalled, Major General Joseph Mansfield's corps moved into the fray, and another vicious battle broke out in the cornfield and surrounding wood lots. Mansfield soon fell mortally wounded in the stomach, and a third Union corps under Major General Edwin "Bull" Sumner was sent in. At sixty-five, Sumner was the army's oldest corps commander and the father-in-law of Lee's personal secretary. He had the misfortune of advancing into a pocket of woods surrounded on three sides by Confederates. When the Rebels opened fire, Sumner's lead division was cut to pieces and lost 2,200 men in just twenty minutes.

By mid-morning the fighting had sputtered out on Lee's left with little change in the armies' positions. Looking out over the fields covered with dead and wounded, Jackson was pleased he had held his ground and calmly remarked, "God has been very kind to us this day." But the battle was not over. McClellan next launched an attack on Lee's center with Sumner's corps, and the fighting concentrated around a farm road that had eroded several feet below ground level. Daniel H. Hill's Confederate division was placed in this natural trench and held off repeated enemy attacks for three hours. Then, in the confusion of battle, one of his regiments mistakenly withdrew and created a gap in the line. Union soldiers poured through and enfiladed Hill's position, causing massive casualties in what became known as "Bloody Lane." The battle had now reached a critical stage. Lee's center was pierced, and Union officers on the scene appealed to McClellan for fresh reserves to exploit the breakthrough. Uncertain of the battle's final outcome, however, the cautious McClellan decided not to commit his last troops. His decision allowed Hill to retire a short distance and establish a new defensive position.

The fighting then died out in the center, and the battle entered its third phase. A stone bridge spanning Antietam Creek was located on Lee's far right flank. McClellan's plan called for Major General Ambrose Burnside's corps to attack across this bridge when the other units engaged Lee's left and center. Burnside, however, made no progress on his front despite launching repeated frontal attacks against "Burnside Bridge." Incredibly, his entire corps was blocked by just 500 Confederates. The rest of the men on Lee's right flank had been stripped away to reinforce the left and center. In mid-afternoon Burnside finally fought his way across the bridge and pushed the Confederates back. Once again, the battle reached a critical moment as Union troops poured into Lee's right rear—and he had no reserves with which to stop them. From his headquarters atop a hill, Lee then saw a dust cloud approaching his rear, and his heart sank. Lee thought the unexpected column might be Yankees, but another officer studied it through binoculars and suddenly shouted that it was A. P. Hill's division from Harpers Ferry. Hill had paroled the Union prisoners and relentlessly pushed his men all day to reach the battlefield. By chance he arrived at just the right place at just the right moment and saved the day by counterattacking Burnside's men and stopping their advance. The Battle of Antietam ended with the opposing armies in pretty much the same positions they had occupied that morning. Lee remained on the field the following day ready to give battle, but McClellan declined the offer. That night and the next day, the Confederates crossed back over the Potomac River into Virginia, and the Antietam Campaign ended.

## The Aftermath

The Battle of Antietam was the single bloodiest day in American history, with Lee losing approximately 10,300 men to McClellan's 12,400. It was a battle in which Lee showed remarkable tactical skill by taking advantage of the interior line and shifting troops from one threatened area to another. However, it also demonstrated his weakness for accepting battle no matter what the odds. Lee fought with his back to the Potomac River, and in essence risked his entire army for what, in the best case, could only have been a stalemate. For his part, McClellan devised a sound tactical plan, and his men fought bravely, but Little Mac and his officers showed little skill in directing the fight itself. Rather than launching coordinated attacks across the entire front, they committed their units piecemeal, much as the Confederates had done at Shiloh. What was worse, McClellan for the most part stayed far in the rear and kept a large part of his reserve units completely out of the battle. Despite these Union failures and the battle's tactical stalemate, Antietam turned out to be an important

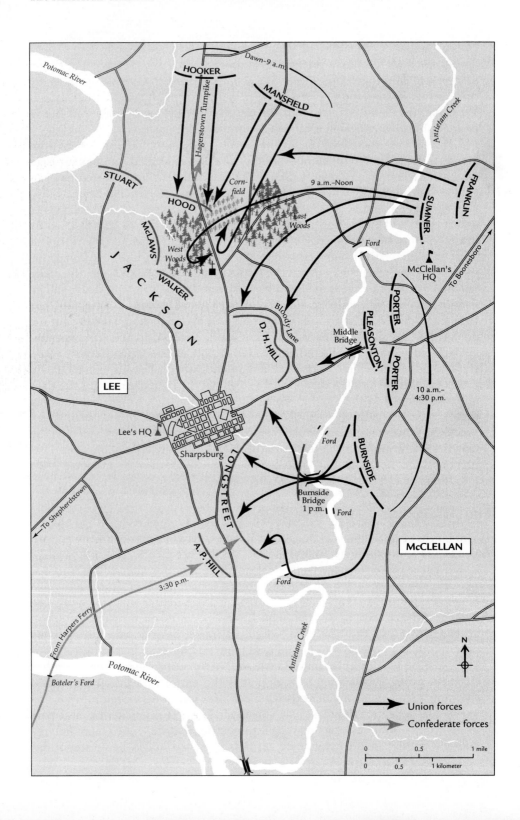

Union forces

Confederate forces

strategic victory for the North. Not only did the battle stop Lee's raid and keep Maryland firmly in the Union, it also made Great Britain and France back away from recognizing the Confederacy. After Antietam, the Europeans lacked confidence in the South's ability to win and never again seriously considered granting recognition or getting involved in the conflict.

Antietam also changed the very nature of the war. The spread of slavery was the issue that led to disunion, but most Northerners were fighting to save the Union, not to destroy slavery. President Lincoln, however, had come to realize slavery was no longer a separate issue. Slaves were an important Rebel asset because they were used as laborers on military projects and toiled in the fields to provide supplies for the Confederate armies. Slavery helped run the enemy's war machine, and its destruction would be a body blow to the rebellion. For military reasons, Lincoln had decided to issue his Emancipation Proclamation some weeks earlier, but the cabinet persuaded him to delay it until the Union won a great victory so

**The Bloody Lane.** Alexander Gardner took this photograph of Confederate dead piled up in Antietam's Bloody Lane two days after the battle. When his employer Matthew Brady put the photographs on public display, it was the first time Americans saw the true horror of the Civil War.

the document could be issued from a position of strength. Although not the decisive victory he wished for, Antietam would do, and Lincoln issued the Preliminary Emancipation Proclamation on September 22 (see Chapter 9). From that moment, the conflict changed from a war to preserve the Union, to a war to preserve the Union without slavery.

**The Battle of Antietam, September 17, 1862.** At Antietam, McClellan planned to attack Lee's left flank, center, and right flank simultaneously, but the attacks were poorly executed. As a result, the battle broke down into three distinct phases. Early in the morning, Union forces launched several attacks against Lee's left wing and suffered heavy casualties in the Cornfield. When the fighting died out there at mid-morning, McClellan next attacked Lee's center at Bloody Lane. Once again the Confederates held their ground, and the battle shifted to the Confederate right wing. There, Burnside fought his way across Antietam Creek but was stopped by Hill's timely arrival from Harper's Ferry.

# BIOGRAPHY

## Braxton Bragg: The Ornery General

**Braxton Bragg**

North Carolina native Braxton Bragg (1817–1876) graduated from West Point in 1833 and soon began showing his famous irascible temper. He was brevetted for gallantry three times during the Mexican War, but his caustic personality made him unpopular, and a soldier once tried to assassinate him by exploding a 12-pound shell under his cot. After the war, Bragg was stationed at an outpost where he served as both the company commander and quartermaster. As commander, he once submitted an invoice to himself as quartermaster requesting supplies. Quartermaster Bragg refused to endorse the request, but commander Bragg resubmitted it with additional information. When quartermaster Bragg still refused to endorse the request, he finally sent all the correspondence to his superior. Looking at the pile of paperwork in disbelief, the officer threw up his hands and cried out, "My God, Mr. Bragg, you have quarreled with every officer in the army, and now you are quarreling with yourself!"

Bragg resigned his captain's commission in 1856 to become a Louisiana sugar planter. After Louisiana seceded, he was put in command of the state militia but was soon made a Confederate general. Bragg skillfully defended Mobile, Alabama, and Pensacola, Florida; commanded a corps at the Battle of Shiloh; and was given command of the Army of Tennessee in June 1862. He quickly demonstrated his talent for discipline and organization by whipping the army into shape. One staff officer claimed, "He was untiring in his labors, methodical and systematic in the discharge of business."

Discipline was one of Bragg's strong points, but many soldiers turned against him because he seemed eager to execute deserters. One Confederate claimed, "None of General Bragg's soldiers ever loved him. . . . He was looked upon as a merciless tyrant. . . ." Unlike Robert E. Lee, there was nothing in Bragg's personal appearance to inspire confidence.

## THE KENTUCKY CAMPAIGN

**August 14–October 26, 1862: The Kentucky Campaign**
**August 30, 1862: Battle of Richmond, Kentucky**
**September 14–17, 1862: Battle of Munfordville, Kentucky**
**September 19, 1862: Battle of Iuka, Mississippi**
**October 3–4, 1862: Battle of Corinth, Mississippi**
**October 7–8, 1862: Battle of Perryville, Kentucky**

As Lee crossed the Potomac River back into Virginia, a second Confederate offensive was reaching its climax in the west. Earlier in the summer, Grant was put back in command of the Army of the Tennessee after General Henry Halleck was called to Washington to replace McClellan as general-in-chief. Camped at Corinth,

A Southern girl wrote he looked "like an old porcupine," and one of Bragg's officers described him as a "tall, slim, rough looking man, with a little round head covered with gray frizzly hair. He has a wild, abstracted look, and pays but little attention to what is passing round him."

Bragg compiled a checkered record with the Army of Tennessee. During the 1862 Kentucky Campaign he won some impressive battles but then retreated. At Stones River, Bragg achieved tactical success on the first day but then retreated again. His only great victory was at Chickamauga, but a few months later he was defeated at Lookout Mountain and Missionary Ridge. Humiliated, Bragg asked to be relieved of command, but Jefferson Davis brought him to Richmond, where he served ably as the president's military adviser and general-in-chief. Late in the war, Bragg was transferred to North Carolina and served under General Joseph E. Johnston until the surrender.

Bragg's talents were simply not suited for army command. While he excelled in preparing an army to fight, he did not have the decisiveness needed to lead it to victory. Bragg's lack of tact and irritable temper also prevented him from getting along with his subordinates. But it would be a mistake to portray him as a complete failure. Bragg had a number of supporters, and he actually was a competent general who simply made some critical mistakes at crucial moments. After Stones River, when many politicians were calling for his removal, General Joseph E. Johnston wrote a Confederate senator, "I think you underestimate Bragg. He has exhibited great energy and discretion in his operations, and has done the enemy more harm than anybody else has done with the same force in the same time. . . . I should regret very much to see him removed."

After the war, Bragg worked as a civil engineer and railroad executive. Today, Fort Bragg, North Carolina, is named for him. It is one of several military bases named for Confederate officers.

Mississippi, Grant was poised to threaten Vicksburg, while in northern Alabama another Union army under Major General Don Carlos Buell was menacing Chattanooga, Tennessee. To face this double threat, the Confederates had Generals Braxton Bragg's and Edmund Kirby Smith's armies at Tupelo, Mississippi, and in Middle Tennessee, respectively. For months, the Confederates had been on the defensive in the west, but Bragg now believed the time was right to go on the offensive.

In late July, Bragg developed a daring plan to turn the tide of war in the west. He proposed to march swiftly from Tupelo to join forces with Kirby Smith and force Grant and Buell to retreat by raiding Middle Tennessee and Kentucky to threaten their supply lines. A small Confederate force left behind at Tupelo could aid in the maneuver by launching a secondary raid into western Tennessee. Bragg believed there was even a possibility the two Union armies could be defeated in detail as they retreated northward. Confident his plan would work, Bragg marched to Chattanooga, Tennessee, to link up with Kirby Smith, but he quickly found the Confederate departmental system had foiled his plan. Bragg wanted Kirby Smith to cooperate with him, but Kirby Smith commanded a separate department and had already launched his offensive. On August 14, Kirby Smith left Knoxville, Tennessee, with 10,000 men and headed toward Kentucky, where he believed large numbers of recruits were eager to join the Confederate army. Deciding to go ahead with his raid, Bragg left Chattanooga on August 28 with 30,000 men and marched north along a path about one hundred miles to the west and parallel to Kirby Smith. Instead of the Confederate armies uniting for one giant offensive as Bragg had hoped, there now were two separate Kentucky operations. When Robert E. Lee entered Maryland soon afterward, it appeared the Confederacy was about to strike a decisive blow against the Union in both theaters of war.

## The Battles of Richmond and Munfordville

In late August, Kirby Smith's advancing cavalry encountered stiff resistance near Richmond, Kentucky. In a running battle on August 30, the Confederates finally broke through the Union lines and pushed the enemy back into Richmond itself. By this time, Major General William "Bull" Nelson had arrived to take command of the Union forces, but he was wounded in the leg while trying to rally the troops and the Confederates broke his line as well. At a cost of about 450 men, the Rebels captured more than 4,000 Union soldiers and opened the way to Lexington and Frankfort, Kentucky.

When Kirby Smith reached Lexington two days later, he could have turned southwest and joined Bragg's column to form a larger army, but instead he dispersed his men across the region to gather supplies and recruits. To the southwest, Bragg entered Munfordville, where he hoped to disrupt the enemy's supply line by destroying a railroad bridge across the Green River. Part of the Union garrison under Colonel John T. Wilder manned a strong blockhouse and proved particularly obstinate when Bragg's cavalry attacked on September 14. The Confederates were repulsed with heavy losses but called on Wilder to surrender to avoid further bloodshed. The gritty colonel refused with the brief message, "If you wish to avoid further bloodshed keep out of the range of my guns."

When Bragg arrived with the rest of the army, the Confederates again informed Wilder of his hopeless situation and demanded his surrender. Wilder was unsure whether duty required him to hold out to the last man or save his men's lives by surrendering. He also was uncertain if the enemy actually outnumbered him as they claimed. In an odd move, Wilder decided to get advice from Major General Simon B. Buckner—the Confederate officer who had earlier surrendered Fort Donelson but had recently been released in a prisoner exchange. Local civilians told Wilder that Buckner was an honorable man, so the colonel walked into the Confederate lines under a flag of truce and requested to see the general. To Buckner's astonishment, Wilder asked him what he should do. Buckner refused to give any advice, but he did allow Wilder to tour the Confederate position to show he really was outnumbered and outgunned. Convinced he had done his duty, Wilder declared, "I believe I'll surrender," and gave up his 4,000 men that morning. Bragg finally burned the vital railroad bridge and moved on.

## The Tide Turns

The Confederates expected to be welcomed with open arms into slave-owning Kentucky and were confident thousands of recruits would flock to their banner. They even believed the state might officially join the Confederacy, and Bragg installed a secessionist state government at Frankfort. The Rebels soon realized it was all a pipe dream, however, for the Kentuckians showed little enthusiasm for the Southern cause, and very few recruits stepped forward. To make matters worse, Union forces were massing for a counterattack against the Confederates' widely dispersed units. Buell's army had advanced through Kentucky on a parallel course west of Bragg. Had Bragg used his cavalry more effectively to scout out the region, he would have been aware of Buell's proximity and could have attacked and broken up his column. Bragg's negligence was a great blunder, and Buell safely reached Louisville. The tide was now turning in favor of the Union as Buell began receiving massive reinforcements, and thousands more troops began assembling at nearby Cincinnati, Ohio.

About two weeks after McClellan turned back Lee's raid into Maryland, Buell advanced several columns out of Louisville. Bragg was confused as to which one posed the greatest threat and kept his forces scattered, but on October 7, Buell engaged the Rebels at Perryville. After some skirmishing, General Leonidas Polk arrived with Confederate reinforcements with orders from Bragg to attack immediately, but he decided to wait and let the enemy make the first move.

## The Battle of Perryville

Early on the morning of October 8, Buell's men advanced and pushed back the Confederates before retiring themselves. Bragg arrived by mid-morning and organized a counterattack that forced the enemy to withdraw in bloody fighting. Because of an unusual natural phenomenon, Buell was not even aware a battle was being fought until about 4:00 p.m. even though his headquarters was only two miles away. Unique atmospheric conditions and topography created an acoustic shadow, where sound carries far in one direction but not in another. As the battle stretched into twilight, General Polk narrowly escaped capture. Seeing what he thought was a Confederate unit shooting at another by mistake, he rode up to the colonel and demanded he stop firing on friendly troops. The colonel responded, "I don't think there can be any mistake about it. I am sure they are the enemy." "Enemy!" cried Polk. "Why, I have only just left them myself. Cease firing, sir! What is your name, sir?" "Colonel Shryock, of the 87th Indiana. And pray, sir, who are you?" Realizing his dark coat appeared blue in the fading light, Polk snapped, "I'll soon show you who I am, sir! Cease firing, sir, at once!" He then turned and rode slowly away.

Tactically, the Confederates won the battle, inflicting some 4,200 casualties on Buell, capturing 11 cannons, and mortally wounding 2 general officers. Bragg, in turn, lost about 3,400 men. This tactical victory was for naught, however, because Bragg decided to withdraw. Several factors convinced him to end the campaign, not the least of which was Buell massing reinforcements to renew the fight the next day. Bragg now was outnumbered, and he knew his exhausted men could not withstand a new attack. He had also learned the troops left in Mississippi to launch a secondary raid into west Tennessee would not be coming to his assistance. Grant had attacked and defeated Major General Sterling Price at Iuka, and Major General William S. Rosecrans had defeated Earl Van Dorn when Van Dorn attacked the important railroad center at Corinth. Other factors that convinced Bragg to retreat were a lack of supplies, a severe drought that made it difficult to water the army, and the Kentuckians' failure to rally to the Confederate cause. Thus, on the night of October 8, Bragg turned the Battle of Perryville into a strategic Union victory by withdrawing from the town, uniting with Kirby Smith, and retreating to Tennessee through the Cumberland Gap. Buell had saved Kentucky for the Union, but, instead of being hailed as a hero, he was relieved of command when he failed to pursue the retreating enemy aggressively.

The Confederates began the Antietam and Kentucky Campaigns with high hopes, for major victories on Northern soil might have presented them with their best chance to bring the Union to the negotiating table. But decisive victory eluded Lee, Bragg, and Kirby Smith, and they were all forced to retreat. What had begun with so much promise in the late summer of 1862 ended with the Confederates being placed back on the defensive in both theaters of war.

## THE WINTER CAMPAIGNS

**December 11, 1862: Union forces begin crossing Rappahannock River at Fredericksburg**
**December 13, 1862: Battle of Fredericksburg**
**December 31, 1862–January 2, 1863: Battle of Stones River**
**January 20–23, 1863: The Mud March**

In the weeks following the Battle of Antietam, McClellan's constant call for more men and equipment and his failure to pursue Lee tried Lincoln's patience. McClellan finally did cross back into Virginia, but no amount of prodding could force him to begin a new campaign. Lincoln's frustration was apparent when he visited the army and stood on a hill overlooking the vast camp. Turning to a companion, he asked if he knew what they were looking at. Rather puzzled, the man replied it was the Army of the Potomac. "So it is called," sighed Lincoln, "but that is a mistake; it is only McClellan's bodyguard." Soon afterward, Stuart's Rebel cavalry again rode entirely around McClellan's army on a raid, and Lincoln's patience snapped when the general blamed his horses' fatigued condition for not chasing after them. "Will you pardon me for asking,"

Lincoln wired, "what the horses of your army have done since the battle of Antietam that fatigue anything?"

## Ambrose E. Burnside

In November, Lincoln relieved McClellan and appointed Major General Ambrose Burnside in his place. Burnside was a West Point graduate, veteran of both the Mexican and Indian wars (he was once wounded while fighting Apaches), and McClellan's close friend. Resigning from the army in the 1850s, he became a firearms manufacturer and designed one of the first breech-loading rifles, the Burnside carbine. Burnside performed well in some early campaigns and rose through the ranks to major general. The troops, who called him "Old Burny," liked the general because he fed them well and looked after their welfare. One of the soldiers claimed they frequently cheered Burnside and noted he had a "manly countenance, bald head, and unmistakable whiskers." Despite being one of the Civil War's most noted generals, Burnside is most often remembered today for those whiskers—which became known as "sideburns." Lincoln believed Burnside was the most suitable corps commander to lead the army because he was popular with the men, but Burnside claimed he was not competent for the important position and turned down the offer twice before finally accepting.

**Ambrose Burnside.** Despite Burnside's reluctance, Lincoln put him in command of the Army of the Potomac after the Battle of Antietam. The president soon relieved Burnside after the disastrous defeat at Fredericksburg, and Burnside led an infantry corps afterward. His performance in the war was lackluster at best, and he is better remembered for his bushy whiskers that became known as "sideburns."

Burnside started out well by formulating an aggressive strategy to march the army rapidly down the Rappahannock River to Falmouth, a small town across the river from Fredericksburg. There he would cross the river by pontoon bridges and be on his way toward Richmond before Lee could bring his scattered units into position to challenge him. At first the plan worked brilliantly. Burnside's 120,000 men arrived at Falmouth in mid-November, and Lee was nowhere in sight. It was one of the few times a Union general surprised Lee, but Burnside's elation was short-lived because the pontoon bridges failed to arrive, apparently as a result of miscommunication. This critical delay gave Lee time to move his 75,000 men to Fredericksburg and occupy the hills behind town. The defensive position was a strong one. When Longstreet, who commanded Lee's left wing, asked his artillery chief if cannon fire could stop an enemy attack, the officer ominously predicted, "A chicken could not live on that field when we open on it."

## The Battle of Fredericksburg

When the pontoon bridges finally arrived, Union engineers began laying them across the river on the morning of December 11. The downstream bridges progressed well, but at Fredericksburg Confederate Brigadier General William Barksdale's Mississippi brigade took up hidden positions in houses along the river and peppered the engineers with rifle fire for hours. Frustrated at the delay, Burnside bombarded the town to drive out the sharpshooters but accomplished little more than destroying much of the city. Finally, Union infantry were put into boats and rowed across the river under heavy fire. They successfully landed on the far shore after suffering many casualties and drove Barksdale out of town in bloody house-to-house fighting. Burnside then sent more of his men across the river into Fredericksburg, and they spent the afternoon and night looting the town.

Burnside divided his army into two wings, with Major General William B. Franklin commanding the left and Major General Edwin V. Sumner the right. On the morning of December 13, the entire Union army surged forward in a massive frontal attack. Stonewall Jackson held Lee's right wing, and he erred by not deploying men in a swampy, wooded area, apparently thinking it was too boggy for troops to advance through. As it turned out, this gap was exactly where Major General George G. Meade's Union division attacked. Meade punched a hole through Jackson's line, and it appeared Burnside's great frontal assault might actually succeed, but Jackson quickly sent in his reserves and forced Meade back in bloody fighting.

The Union right wing attacked Longstreet's men, who were hunkered down in a sunken road that snaked behind a stone wall on Marye's (muh-REE'S) Heights. Wave after wave of Sumner's troops charged the hill, only to be shot down by the hundreds in front of the stone wall. One soldier wrote that the line of men advanced into the storm of lead "half crouching as it ran, and moving *sideways,* as though breasting a 'blizzard' or a wind and hail-storm." Watching from the courthouse cupola, a division commander cried, "Oh, great God! See how our men, our poor fellows, are falling!" The Irish Brigade, in particular, won acclaim for its brave, but futile, charge, losing 545 men out of 1,300 engaged. One regiment, the 69th New York, lost all of its sixteen commissioned officers. Concerned the incessant attacks might eventually overwhelm Longstreet, Lee asked the general if he could hold his position. Longstreet calmly replied, "If you put every man now on the other side . . . on the field to approach me over the same line, and give me plenty of ammunition, I will kill them all before they reach my line."

Fredericksburg was a Union disaster. One survivor summed it up by writing, "The left was a scene of severe fighting, the right one of great slaughter." While watching the carnage, Lee remarked to Longstreet, "It is well that war is so horrible, or else we should grow too fond of it." Burnside lost about 12,500 men in the futile attacks, while Lee lost some 5,300 men, mostly on Jackson's front. In front of the stone wall, thousands of dead and wounded Yankee soldiers

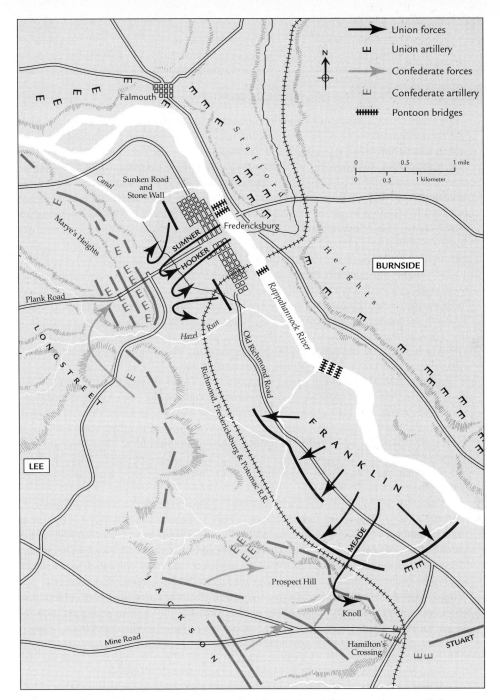

**The Battle of Fredericksburg, December 13, 1862.** Fredericksburg was the worst defeat suffered by the Union army in the Civil War. Although Franklin had some temporary success against Stonewall Jackson on the Union left wing, Sumner and Hooker suffered terrible losses when they attacked Longstreet's Confederates on Marye's Heights.

# NOTABLE UNITS: *The Irish Brigade*

Thousands of Irish immigrants fought on both sides in the Civil War, and they completely dominated some units. The most famous of these was the Union Irish Brigade, which was organized in the fall of 1861 by Brigadier General Thomas F. Meagher (pronounced *MARR*). Meagher was an Irish native whom the British banished to Tasmania after he became involved in Ireland's 1849 uprising. Escaping, he made his way to the United States, where he became a popular lecturer on Irish independence. Meagher believed it was important for the Irish to fight in the Civil War so that afterward an Irish veteran could "take his stand proudly by the side of the native-born, and will not fear to look him straight and sternly in the face, and tell him that he has been equal to him in his allegiance to the Constitution."

A number of regiments served in the Irish Brigade, but at its heart were the 63rd, 69th, and 88th New York, 116th Pennsylvania, and 28th Massachusetts. The soldiers in these units never forgot their native land and became conspicuous on the battlefield by carrying distinctive green Irish flags. Meagher led the brigade until he resigned in late 1863, and afterward a string of subsequent commanders took over, with two being killed in battle. The Irish Brigade became famous for its outstanding service in virtually every major battle fought by the Army of the Potomac. One of its early exploits was a fierce hand-to-hand fight with the Louisiana Tigers at Malvern Hill. Afterward, one regiment's colonel requested new muskets to replace the ones his men had damaged in the clash, but his superior thought the men had simply lost them and refused. The general changed his mind when he was shown a pile of muskets with splintered stocks, bent barrels, and twisted bayonets. One soldier told him, "The boys got in a scrimmage with the Tigers, and when the bloody villains took to their knives, the boys mostly forgot their bayonets, but went to work in the style they were used to, and licked them well, sir."

The Irish Brigade had the third highest casualty rate of the army's brigades. It had particularly heavy losses at Antietam, where it attacked the Bloody Lane, and at Fredericksburg, where it attacked the infamous stone wall on Marye's Heights. At the latter battle, only one regiment still carried an Irish flag because the rest had been sent home for replacement because they had been shot up so badly. Nonetheless, Meagher wanted to make sure his men were recognized as Irish and ordered each soldier to put sprigs of evergreen on his hat. Meagher, himself, was said to be "a picture of unusual grace and majesty" dressed in his tailor-made green suit with a yellow silk scarf around his chest. Charging up Marye's Heights, the men shouted the old Irish cheer "Faugh-a-Bellagh" ("Clear the Way"), and headed straight for a regiment of Confederate Irishmen behind the stone wall. Before opening fire, one of the Rebels looked down the slope and cried, "Oh, God, what a pity! Here comes Meagher's fellows!"

After the Civil War, the 69th New York became part of the state's National Guard and earned the nickname the "Fighting 69th" in World War I. In 2004, the regiment was sent to Fort Hood, Texas, where it was brigaded with the Louisiana National Guard's 256th Infantry Brigade, which traces its origins back to the Louisiana Tigers. The last time the two units had met was on July 1, 1862, when the Tigers and the 69th New York fought on the slopes of Malvern Hill. Almost 150 years later, they were sent to Iraq to fight together.

littered the hillside, and hundreds more were pinned down by rifle and artillery fire, unable to retreat. These unfortunate men experienced untold horrors as the temperature plummeted below freezing, and they were forced to huddle on the ground without fires. The cries of the wounded were too much for 19-year-old Confederate Sergeant Richard Kirkland, who clambered over the wall and began taking water to the wounded. His comrades expected him to be shot at any moment, but Kirkland continued his mission for an hour and a half and was cheered by the watching Union soldiers. Kirkland was dubbed the "Angel of Marye's Heights" for his compassion; he was killed nine months later at Chickamauga.

## The Mud March

Burnside finally withdrew what men he could and retreated across the river on the night of December 15. Unwilling to concede defeat, he soon began an ambitious turning movement to slip around Lee's well-entrenched army. Leaving part of his force at Falmouth to keep Lee's attention focused there, Burnside sent most of his men upstream on January 20, 1863. In a maneuver similar to Lee's Second Bull Run turning movement, Burnside planned to make a rapid march, cross the Rappahannock River far beyond Lee's left flank, and then force the enemy to retreat by threatening their rear. It was a good plan, but speed, secrecy, and luck were required for it to work.

Burnside's luck quickly ran out when the heavens opened up, and it began to rain. Roads turned to bottomless quagmires, and, in some places, mules literally sank out of sight and drowned. Lee quickly discovered the movement and sent troops to shadow the enemy. After two days of continuous rain, Burnside finally canceled what officially became known as the "Mud March." Nothing had been accomplished except to weaken further the Army of the Potomac's morale and the men's confidence in their commander. A satirical prayer that circulated through camp illustrated the soldiers' disgust: "Now I lay me down to sleep, in mud that's many fathoms deep. If I should die before I wake, just hunt me up with an oyster rake." After the embarrassing Mud March, Burnside bitterly blamed his subordinates for the Fredericksburg defeat and demanded that President Lincoln cashier a number of officers from the army. Instead, Lincoln held Burnside responsible for the disaster and replaced him with Major General Joseph Hooker.

## The Battle of Stones River

While Lee and Burnside fought around Fredericksburg, William S. Rosecrans's Army of the Cumberland and Braxton Bragg's Army of Tennessee warily watched each other in Middle Tennessee. On December 26, Rosecrans marched 47,000 men out of Nashville to drive Bragg from his base at Murfreesboro. Bragg positioned his 38,000 men to cover the roads northwest of town but was forced to split them across Stones River, with the right wing being isolated across the river from the main body. Next, Bragg sent Brigadier General Joseph Wheeler's cavalry to disrupt Rosecrans's advance, and Wheeler captured more than 700 prisoners and hundreds of supply wagons. This raid and the rainy weather slowed the Union advance, and Rosecrans did not reach Bragg's position at Murfreesboro until December 30.

Rosecrans's lack of aggressiveness convinced Bragg to seize the initiative and attack with his left wing the next morning. He planned to wheel the attack to the right as the army advanced, crushing the Union right wing and cutting off Rosecrans from Nashville by seizing the railroad and Nashville Pike in his rear. Once he had isolated the enemy, Bragg would drive them into Stones River and annihilate them. The Confederates struck at daylight on December 31 and initially drove the Yankees from their camps, but the advance stalled when dense cedar thickets broke up Bragg's formation. Later in the morning, Brigadier General Philip Sheridan's Union division and other units made a desperate stand along the Wilkinson Pike and slowed up the attack even more. During the fighting Rosecrans rode all over the field rallying his men while covered in blood and brain matter. At first glance it appeared he had been seriously wounded, but the gore came from a nearby aide whose head was taken off by a cannonball. Rosecrans never stayed in one spot for more than thirty minutes, so he did not have a chance to change clothes or wash.

By mid-day, Bragg had pushed Rosecrans back three miles to the Nashville Pike, but there the Union line finally stabilized. Its final position resembled a V with William Hazen's brigade holding the angle at a place that was first called the Round Forest and later Hell's Half Acre. From there the line ran northwest and northeast, with the vital Nashville Pike protected between the two wings. The Confederates made repeated frontal attacks against Hazen's position, only to be annihilated by volleys of rifle fire and massed cannon. The roar of cannons was so great the attacking Rebels picked cotton from an old field and stuck it in their ears. Determined to capture the road, Bragg ordered fresh brigades be brought from across the river on the far right. When these troops arrived at about 2:00 p.m., corps commander General Leonidas Polk wasted them in piecemeal attacks rather than sending them in all at once. The Union line held, and the fighting finally died out about dark.

Both sides were exhausted and New Year's Day of 1863 passed quietly. On January 2, Bragg decided to attack again but this time from a different direction. During the first day's battle, both sides had stripped their lines east of Stones River to reinforce the main battle lines to the west. When Bragg realized Union artillery on this inactive front could enfilade his line, he ordered Major General John C. Breckinridge's division to attack and drive the artillery off the field. Breckinridge vehemently protested the order because the enemy's artillery on the west side of the river would enfilade his troops as they advanced. Bragg insisted, however, and Breckinridge finally obeyed under protest. As Breckinridge prepared his men, he rode up to one brigade commander and told him, "This attack is made against my judgment and by the special orders

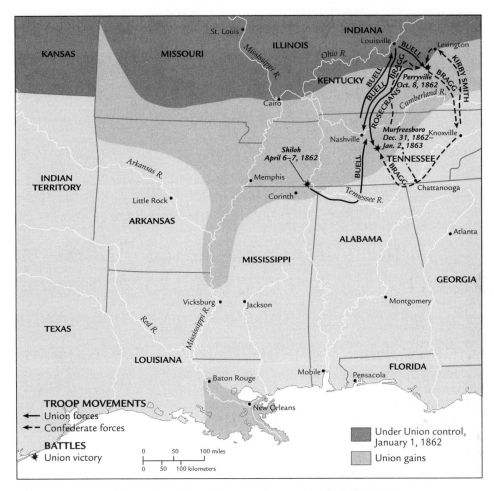

**The Kentucky and Stones River Campaigns, August 1862–January 1863.** In late summer 1862, Confederate forces in the west launched two uncoordinated raids into Kentucky, with Kirby Smith advancing from Knoxville, Tennessee, and Bragg from Chattanooga. The two armies united after winning some initial victories but then withdrew from Kentucky when they encountered Buell's Union forces at Perryville. In late December, Bragg attacked Rosecrans along Stones River at Murfreesboro, Tennessee. Although he pushed the enemy back the first day, Bragg once again retreated when he was unable to drive Rosecrans from the field.

of General Bragg. . . . [I]f it should result in disaster and I be among the slain, I want you to do justice to my memory and tell the people that I believed this attack to be very unwise and tried to prevent it." Breckinridge sent his five brigades forward late in the afternoon and drove the enemy back to the river; but, then, just as he predicted, his men were cut to pieces by fifty-eight massed

# EYEWITNESS
## Sam R. Watkins

*Sam R. Watkins was a 20-year-old college-educated Tennessee native who joined Company H, 1st Tennessee Regiment, in 1861. Few soldiers on either side saw as much combat as he did over the next four years. Twenty years after the war, Watkins wrote a series of newspaper articles about his exploits that later were published as the book Co. Aytch. In it, he gave a sobering account of the bloody Battle at Stones River.*

The crest occupied by the Yankees was belching loud with fire and smoke, and the Rebels were falling like leaves of autumn in a hurricane. The leaden hail storm swept them off the field. They fell back and re-formed. General Cheatham came up and advanced. I did not fall back, but continued to load and shoot, until a fragment of a shell struck me on the arm, and then a minnie ball passed through the same paralyzing my arm, and wounded and disabled me. . . .

The impression that General Frank Cheatham made upon my mind, leading the charge on the Wilkerson turnpike, I will never forget. I saw either victory or death written on his face. When I saw him leading our brigade, although I was wounded at the time, I felt sorry for him, he seemed so earnest and concerned, and as he was passing me I said, "Well, General, if you are determined to die, I'll die with you." . . .

[Our] brigade raised a whoop and yell, and swooped down on those Yankees like a whirl-a-gust of woodpeckers in a hail storm, paying the blue coated rascals back with compound interest. . . . I cannot remember now of ever seeing more dead men and horses and captured cannon, all jumbled together, than that scene of blood and carnage and battle on the Wilkerson turnpike. The ground was literally covered with blue coats dead; and if I remember correctly, there were eighty dead horses. . . .

As I went back to the field hospital, I overtook another man walking along. I do not know to what regiment he belonged, but I remember of first noticing that his left arm was entirely gone. His face was as white as a sheet. The breast and sleeve of his coat had been torn away, and I could see the frazzled end of his shirt sleeve, which appeared to be sucked into the wound. I looked at it pretty close, and I said "Great God!" for I could see his heart throb, and the respiration of his lungs. I was filled with wonder and horror at the sight. He was walking along, when all at once he dropped down and died without a struggle or a groan. I could tell of hundreds of such incidents of the battlefield, but tell only this one, because I remember it so distinctly.

*Before the war was over Sam Watkins participated in many more battles, including Chickamauga, Missionary Ridge, Atlanta, and Franklin. When the Army of Tennessee surrendered in 1865, only he and six other men remained alive out of his 120-man company. Watkins returned to Tennessee, married, and had several children. His memoirs are still one of the most popular wartime reminiscences in print today, although critics sometimes question the credibility of some of his stories.*

# NOTABLE UNITS: *The Orphan Brigade*

This famous Confederate infantry unit was officially known as the 1st Kentucky Brigade. The origin of its nickname is uncertain. Some believe it was a result of the men being homeless after they left Kentucky in February 1862 to enlist in the Confederate army in Tennessee. Afterward, they were unable to return to Kentucky or even get mail delivered to family members. The name may also have come from the Battle of Stones River. When the brigade was shot to pieces while attacking Union artillery on the last day, Lieutenant General John C. Breckinridge cried out in anguish, "My poor Orphans! My poor Orphans!" when he saw the shattered brigade return. Most likely, however, the Orphan Brigade nickname was a post-war creation by the veterans because it does not appear to have been used during the war itself.

For most of the war the Orphan Brigade consisted of the 2nd, 4th, 5th, 6th, and 9th Kentucky regiments. Among its numerous commanders were Simon Bolivar Buckner (who surrendered Fort Donelson), John C. Breckinridge (former U.S. vice president and 1860 presidential candidate), and Joseph Lewis. Two other brigade commanders, Roger W. Hanson and Ben Hardin Helm, were killed in battle at Stones River and Chickamauga, respectively. Helm was married to the sister of Mary Todd Lincoln. After he was killed, Mary invited her widowed sister to live in the White House for a while. As part of the Army of Tennessee, the brigade participated in some of the bloodiest battles of the western theater and compiled an outstanding combat record. Although captured at Fort Donelson, the men were praised for their steadfast service there. One veteran wrote after the war, "Donelson which ought to be remembered as a glorious victory, but, instead, always brings sadness. Such fighting as we did on that field! Such hardships we endured! . . . Ah! it is disheartening to remember." The Orphan Brigade was also highly commended at Shiloh. When Colonel Robert "Old Trib" Trabue brought his men on the field, he approached General William J. Hardee and said, "General, I have a Kentucky brigade here. What shall I do with it?" "Put it where the fight is thickest, sir," instructed the general. The fight was thickest at the Hornets' Nest, and the brigade helped capture the important position after slugging it out with Kentucky Unionists.

After Shiloh, the Orphan Brigade covered the retreat to Corinth; helped defend Vicksburg, Mississippi, in the summer of 1862; and fought at the Battle of Baton Rouge. At Stones River, the brigade sustained heavy losses when it participated in Breckinridge's attack on the third day. The Orphans went on to serve in the Vicksburg, Chickamauga, and Atlanta campaigns. In the latter, they saw especially hard duty. The Orphan Brigade began the Atlanta Campaign with 1,140 men and sustained 1,860 deaths, wounds, and hospitalizations to sickness. The casualty figure was greater than the enrollment because many men had multiple wounds or hospitalizations. On the day after the Battle of Jonesboro, only 240 soldiers were left on duty, but, incredibly, fewer than 10 had deserted during the campaign. After Jonesboro, the Orphan Brigade was a mere shadow of its former self, so many of the survivors were allowed to acquire horses and become mounted infantry. When the brigade surrendered in Georgia in May 1865, only about 600 men were left out of the 4,000 who had served with it during the war.

cannons on the west bank. One Union soldier who witnessed the scene was shocked at the devastation and recalled, "The very forest seemed to fall before our fire." The murderous bombardment quickly drove the Confederates back, and the battle ended.

In a driving rain, Bragg withdrew from Murfreesboro late on the night of January 3. He had enjoyed great tactical success initially, but his retreat allowed Rosecrans to claim a strategic victory. Overall, the three-day Battle of Stones River had no long-term effect on the war except to cost Bragg some 10,000 men and Rosecrans 13,000. The bloody fight ended the campaign season in the west, and both sides went into winter camps to prepare for new operations in the spring.

## *FOR FURTHER READING*

General Order No. 191

## CHAPTER 8

# The War at Sea

**The Navies**

**The Warships**

**The Blockade**

**Privateers and Commerce Raiders**

Sunday, June 19, 1864, broke clear and cool over Cherbourg, France. At mid-morning the famous Rebel cruiser *Alabama* put to sea while hundreds of admiring citizens looked on and cheered, "Vivent les Confederates!" Just outside the harbor, Captain John A. Winslow watched from the deck of the USS *Kearsarge*. Winslow had been hunting the *Alabama* for a year, and now he waited to give battle in the English Channel. The two vessels were well matched, each displacing about one thousand tons. The *Alabama* carried eight guns, the *Kearsarge* seven, but the *Kearsarge* guns were larger. The *Kearsarge* also was in excellent condition, while the *Alabama* was well worn from its long voyage. On the other hand, the Rebel crewmen were battle-hardened veterans, while the Yankee sailors had never fired a shot in anger. *Alabama* Captain Raphael Semmes wrote in his journal the night before, "The combat will no doubt be contested and obstinate, but the two ships are so evenly matched that I do not feel at liberty to decline it. God defend the right, and have mercy upon the souls of those who fall, as many of us must."

Semmes steamed toward the *Kearsarge* and opened fire at one mile. The *Kearsarge* soon replied and the battle was on. Over the next ninety minutes, about 250 shots were exchanged, and the distance closed to a quarter mile. The inexperienced Union gunners proved excellent shots and raked the *Alabama* from stem to stern. One shell wounded Captain Semmes in the hand; another killed or wounded nineteen men. When the *Alabama* eventually began to settle, its deck awash with blood, body parts, and gore, Semmes ordered the flag lowered. To an officer, he explained, "It will never do in this nineteenth century for us to go down, and the decks covered with our gallant wounded." Winslow saw the flag come down but suspected a trick and fired one more broadside into the stricken ship. Just before the *Alabama* slipped beneath the waves, Semmes unbuckled his sword with his good hand, held it above his head for a moment, and then tossed it into the sea. He then abandoned ship and was picked up by a British yacht.

The fight between the *Kearsarge* and *Alabama* was one of the Civil War's few open-water sea battles, and it brought a dramatic end to the Confederate navy's most famous ship. Reflecting on his loss, Semmes wrote, "A noble Roman once stabbed his daughter, rather than she should be polluted by the foul embrace of a tyrant. It was with a similar feeling that [First Officer] Kell and I saw the *Alabama* go down. We had buried her as we had christened her, and she was safe from the polluting touch of the hated Yankee!"

## THE NAVIES

**December 12, 1862: Two torpedoes sink the USS *Cairo* in the Yazoo River**
**February 17, 1864: CSS *H. L. Hunley* sinks the USS *Housatonic* at Charleston, South Carolina, but it sinks as well**
**August 9, 1864: Confederate agents destroy Union munitions ship at City Point, Virginia**

For the most part, the Civil War was a land war, and its outcome was ultimately decided by huge armies maneuvering and fighting over the vast American landscape. However, each side also had navies that fought on both inland waterways and on the high seas. These naval activities consumed a considerable amount of resources and involved foreign nations more than the land war. The navy war also involved several different strategies. Large numbers of Union ships were tied down enforcing the blockade, while many Confederate vessels tried either to slip through the cordon or break its grip on the Southern ports. Dozens of Yankee gunboats also plied inland waters to assist army operations, and a surprising number of Rebel craft frequently engaged them in bloody combat. Out of the hundreds of warships used in the Civil War, however, relatively few ever roamed far out to sea. Those that did were either Confederate commerce raiders in search of unarmed Union merchant ships or U.S. Navy vessels sent to pursue them.

### The U.S. Navy

Naval power was one of many advantages the Union had over the Confederacy. The Northern states (particularly New England) had a large number of trained seamen, a strong industrial base that could quickly turn out new ships, and many excellent ports. The U.S. Navy also was an established and well-trained institution with extensive experience in waging war. Despite these advantages, the Union navy was ill-prepared to fight the type of war it faced in 1861. Large numbers of ships were required to blockade the 3,500 miles of Confederate coastline, and many more vessels were needed for what was called the brown water navy. These

**Union Sailors.** This photograph of Union sailors assembled on the deck of a warship gives a glimpse of how the men spent their off-duty time. Note the African American sailors (segregated on the far right) mending their clothing and the sailors playing a board game and a banjo in the lower left center.

latter ships cooperated with the army in operations along such inland rivers as the Mississippi, Red, and James. Still others were required to patrol the open ocean in search of enemy commerce raiders.

When the war began in April 1861, the U.S. Navy had just 42 warships to carry out these various missions, and most of them were on patrol far out at sea. To increase its numbers, the navy quickly bought private ships to convert into warships and began contracting new vessels. In an amazing feat of productivity, the Union navy increased to more than 260 ships by year's end, with another 100 under construction, and there were 671 warships on duty by 1864. But even these impressive numbers were not enough, and the navy continued to be stretched thin carrying out its myriad duties. When the war ended in 1865, the U.S. Navy was the second-largest in the world, but it quickly disbanded and by 1880 ranked behind even that of Chile.

## The Confederate Navy

Like its army, the Confederacy had to build a navy virtually from scratch—and it did a rather impressive job considering New Orleans, Louisiana, and Norfolk, Virginia, had the only two major naval yards in the South. Even after these two cities fell to the enemy early in the war, the Southerners continued building warships in such inland cities as Shreveport, Louisiana. Much of this success can be attributed to Secretary of the Navy Stephen Mallory, who showed remarkable ingenuity in creating a naval force.

Realizing they were not strong enough to challenge the U.S. Navy in large fleet engagements, the Confederates were forced to become more technologically imaginative and conduct guerrilla warfare on water. The Rebels were the first to put ironclads into action, to sink a warship with a submarine, and to design many new types of explosives to destroy enemy vessels. They also began using single ships to launch audacious surprise attacks and resorted to privateers and commerce raiders to disrupt Northern trade. Although possessing far fewer vessels than the Union, the Confederates were quite successful in harassing the U.S. Navy and forcing it to widely disperse its ships.

## Those Infernal Machines

Because the Confederates could never match the Union's military and industrial might, they became much more inventive in waging war. Southerners proved remarkably ingenious and developed a number of new weapons systems that were referred to as *infernal machines*. The original stealth weapons, these devices were designed to remain hidden from view, and thus were often criticized for being unnecessarily inhumane or treacherous. Land mines, for example, were first invented by the Confederates when they buried artillery shells in roadways, during the Peninsula Campaign, to explode when the pursuing enemy stepped on them. They quickly backed away from the practice, however, after being criticized for using the mines to simply increase casualties without affecting the war's outcome.

Many of the infernal machines involved naval warfare. Among these were torpedoes (modern-day mines) that were used against Union shipping. Large kegs of powder were tied to an anchor and suspended just below the surface. Some torpedoes were contact mines that exploded when a ship ran into them, and some were electrically detonated. The Confederates were the first to successfully use an electric mine when they sank the USS *Cairo* (KAIR-oh) in the Yazoo River in December 1862. The *Cairo* was designed by Samuel M. Pook and belonged to a class of ironclads known as "Pook Turtles." It fought in several battles before joining four other ships in the Yazoo River to support the Union attack on Chickasaw Bayou, Mississippi. Confederates hiding on the river bank detonated two electric mines underneath the ship, and the *Cairo* plunged to the bottom. In the late 1950s, the *Cairo* was raised, and it now is on display at the Vicksburg National Military Park.

Confederate secret agents also developed an explosive device that resembled a piece of coal. Placed in coal piles used by Union ships, these wicked weapons blew the ship to pieces when shoveled into the steam furnace. One such infernal machine destroyed a Union munitions ship at City Point, Virginia, during the 1864 Petersburg Campaign and killed 43 men and wounded 126. When Abraham Lincoln toured Richmond in April 1865 and sat in Jefferson Davis's presidential chair, he found one of the coal bombs sitting on the desk.

Submarines were among the most famous infernal machines. The two-man submarine *Pioneer* was the first one constructed by the Confederates. Built in New Orleans, it was 34 feet long, 6 feet high, 4 feet wide, and powered by a hand-cranked propeller. The *Pioneer* towed a torpedo on a long rope and ran underneath its target to drag the torpedo into the ship. Entering Confederate service in March 1862, the *Pioneer* was never used in battle because the submarine was scuttled a month later to keep it out of Union hands when the U.S. Navy captured New Orleans. Other Confederate submarines were also constructed, but only one proved successful.

The *Pioneer* served as the prototype for the more famous *H. L. Hunley*. Named for its inventor, Horace L. Hunley, this cigar-shaped submarine was constructed in Mobile, Alabama. About 30 feet long and 5 feet in diameter, the *Hunley* was a marvel of engineering with two small conning towers, diving planes, ballast tanks, and a torpedo attached to a bow spar. A crankshaft ran down the center of the boat, and seven crewmen sat on benches running along both sides of the hull to crank the propeller while one man controlled the steering and depth. The *Hunley* was designed to approach its target while submerged, gently surfacing at intervals so the pilot could look out his conning tower to maintain the proper course. When it rammed the target, the torpedo stuck into the enemy's hull. The *Hunley* then backed off to a safe distance and detonated the torpedo with a cord attached to the primer.

Despite its advanced engineering, the *Hunley* became a jinxed vessel when it was taken to Charleston, South Carolina, to undergo testing. In August 1863, it sank during a trial run, and five men of the all-volunteer crew drowned. The *Hunley* was raised, the bodies removed, and another volunteer crew was assembled. Horace L. Hunley was among them, but the boat sank again in October, drowning Hunley and seven more men. The *Hunley* was raised a second time, and Lieutenant George E. Dixon managed to assemble yet another crew of volunteers. Dixon then secured permission from General Beauregard to attack a Union warship in the harbor. On the night of February 17, 1864, Dixon took aim at the USS *Housatonic,* but Union lookouts spotted the *Hunley*'s conning tower just before it rammed the ship and peppered the boat with small arms fire. Seconds later, the torpedo exploded, and the *Housatonic* sank. It was the first successful submarine attack in history, but the *Hunley* never returned to dock. What caused the submarine to sink is unknown, but in 1995 it was discovered several hundred yards from where the *Housatonic* went down. In 2000, the *H. L. Hunley* was raised in remarkably good condition, and the crew members' remains were found still inside.

The Union also experimented with submarines and launched one named the *Alligator.* It was 45 feet long, 5½ feet in diameter, and powered by 16 oars that folded onto the hull. Instead of using a spar torpedo like the *H. L. Hunley,* the *Alligator* carried two divers who were trained to swim out of the submarine and attach electrically detonated mines onto enemy ships. The *Alligator* was sent to Virginia's James River to attack Confederate vessels, but it was unable to operate safely in the shallow tidal waters. In April 1863, the *Alligator* (like the *Monitor* before it) sank in a storm off Cape Hatteras, North Carolina, while being towed to Charleston, South Carolina.

# THE WARSHIPS

**April 20, 1861:** Union forces burn the USS *Merrimac* at Norfolk, Virginia
**March 8–9, 1862:** Battle of Hampton Roads, Virginia
**May 11, 1862:** Confederates destroy the CSS *Virginia*
**July 15, 1862:** CSS *Arkansas* engages Union fleet near Vicksburg, Mississippi
**August 5, 1862:** Crewmen destroy the *Arkansas*
**December 31, 1862:** USS *Monitor* sinks off the North Carolina coast
**August 5, 1864:** Battle of Mobile Bay, Alabama
**October 28, 1864:** Union commandos sink the CSS *Albemarle*

One reason why the Civil War has always interested historians is that it was a transitional war in terms of military technology and tactics. Traditional Napoleonic weapons and maneuvers were combined with modern trench warfare and technically advanced firearms. This blending of old and new was particularly true in the navies. When the war began, the ships were traditional wooden vessels powered by sails, steam engines, or both. While such ships remained in service throughout the war, the opposing navies began to rely more and more on powerful armored vessels that evolved into the modern battleships of the twentieth century.

## Ironclads

The ironclad was one of the most formidable weapons used in the Civil War. These huge steam-powered vessels carried a large number of heavy cannons and were covered above the waterline with sloping iron plating to protect their vital parts (lighter armored vessels were called tinclads). Because their heavy weight greatly reduced speed and maneuverability, ironclads generally performed poorly on the open ocean and mostly served on inland waterways. Great Britain and France built the world's first ironclads and used them in the Crimean War, but they really came of age during the American Civil War. Confederate Secretary of the Navy Stephen Mallory, in particular, relied on them. He knew the Confederacy could never match the U.S. Navy ship for ship and decided to outgun the enemy by constructing fewer, but more invincible, ironclads. As Mallory put it, "Inequality of numbers may be compensated by invulnerability."

The *Virginia* was the first Confederate ironclad. When Union forces evacuated Virginia's Norfolk Navy Yard at the outbreak of war, they burned the USS *Merrimac* to keep it out of Rebel hands. Mallory decided the hulk would be perfect to convert into an ironclad with which to break the Union blockade and had it raised, encased in two feet of wooden siding, and fitted with a cast-iron ram. The wood was then covered with four inches of iron plating slanted at a steep angle to deflect enemy cannonballs. Armed with ten large cannons, the ship was rechristened the *Virginia*. The prototype of future ironclads and

**USS *St. Louis*.** The USS *St. Louis* was typical of Civil War ironclad gunboats. It was the first such ironclad launched by the U.S. Navy.

truly massive in scale, the *Virginia* was 262 feet long, 51 feet wide, and carried a crew of 320. Although it was virtually impregnable to enemy fire, the ship had two major weaknesses: The *Virginia's* enormous size and weight made it slow and difficult to steer, and the deep 22-foot draft prevented it from entering shallow harbors or rivers.

## Monitors

Some Union ironclads, like the *St. Louis* and *Cairo,* were similar to the *Virginia*, but many others were oddly shaped boats designed by Swedish-born engineer John Ericsson. During the antebellum period, Ericsson received thirty patents in Great Britain for inventions such as a hot-air engine, a high-speed locomotive, and a propeller-driven ship. In the 1840s, he co-designed the U.S. Navy's first steam-powered vessel and a new cannon, but the cannon exploded during a demonstration and killed the secretary of state, secretary of the navy, and a host of other dignitaries. Despite his tragic past, Ericsson submitted a plan when Secretary of the Navy Gideon Welles learned the Confederates were building the *Virginia* and called on shipbuilders to offer designs for a Union ironclad. The Navy was not impressed with Ericsson's revolutionary ironclad, but Secretary of State William Seward showed the plans to Lincoln. The president was intrigued and declared, "Well, as the girl said when she put her leg

# DID YOU KNOW?

## The *Monitor*

The USS *Monitor* was a revolutionary vessel that boasted more than forty design patents. Incredibly, it took fewer than 120 days to construct, using parts forged in nine foundries. Among its innovations was the first use of a marine screw (propeller), placing the engines below the waterline, a detachable smokestack, and the first use of mechanical ventilation in a warship (although it worked poorly and the crew suffered from brutally hot and smoky conditions). The *Monitor* also had the world's first flush toilet aboard a ship, and its innovative revolving gun turret is now a standard feature on both warships and tanks. The ship's wreck site was discovered in 1973, and the historic gun turret has been recovered and is being restored at the USS *Monitor* Center, a part of the Mariners' Museum in Newport News, Virginia.

in the stocking, I think there is something in it." With Lincoln's support, Ericsson won the contract and quickly built his ship.

Christened the *Monitor,* the ironclad had a low deck that barely rose above water, and its engines and vital parts were housed below the waterline to reduce the amount of armor required to protect them. The *Monitor* had a 10.5-foot draft, was 172 feet long and 41.5 feet wide, but its most characteristic features were two structures that jutted up from the deck. A small pilothouse was placed at the ship's bow so the captain and pilot could see out to steer the ship, and a revolving steam-driven turret was located amidships. Critics claimed the strange-looking craft resembled a "cheese box on a raft" and laughingly dubbed it "Ericsson's Folly." The ship's peculiar design, however, belied its impressive firepower. Within the turret were two massive 11-inch cannons that could be trained in any direction simply by revolving the turret. This was quite an innovative development because the *Monitor* did not have to engage in intricate maneuvers to deliver a broadside. No matter what position the ship was in, its guns could spin around and take the enemy under fire. Afterward, all Union ironclads having this particular revolving turret became known as *monitors*.

## The Battle of Hampton Roads

The first clash of ironclads took place at Hampton Roads, Virginia, a body of water located at the confluence of the James River and Chesapeake Bay near Fort Monroe. In March 1862, General George B. McClellan was preparing to move the Army of the Potomac by sea to Fort Monroe to begin the Peninsula Campaign. A number of Union warships were anchored at Hampton Roads to protect the landing, and their crews were surprised when the lone *Virginia,* under Captain Franklin Buchanan, attacked on March 8. In short order, the *Virginia* wrecked the woode n sailing vessels. Buchanan rammed and sank the *Cumberland,* set the *Congress* on fire with hot shot, and forced the *Minnesota* to run aground while trying to escape. The *Virginia* then leisurely steamed back to port, leaving in its wake the pride of the Union fleet in shambles and scores of Yankee sailors dead. Casualties onboard the ironclad were light, and the ship itself suffered only a few dents in its armor from enemy cannonballs, but Captain Buchanan was among the wounded.

News of the battle sent Washington into a panic. Secretary of War Edwin M. Stanton and other cabinet members nervously watched the Potomac River, expecting the *Virginia* to move upstream and attack the capital. According to Secretary of the Navy Welles, Stanton was frantic as he "sat down and jumped up . . . swung his arms, scolded and raved." He gloomily predicted the *Virginia* would change the course of the entire war. Looking out across the Potomac, Stanton warned it was likely "we shall have a shell or a cannonball from one of her guns in the White House before we leave this room." Welles remained calm and explained to Stanton the *Virginia* could not negotiate the Potomac's shallow water and then turned and informed the cabinet that Lieutenant John L. Worden's *Monitor* had been ordered to Hampton Roads to neutralize the Rebel threat. "How many guns does she carry?" asked the nervous Stanton. Two, Welles replied. According to Welles, Stanton looked at him with a combination of "amazement, contempt, and distress."

On March 9, the *Virginia* returned to Hampton Roads under the command of Lieutenant Catesby ap Roger Jones to finish off the Union fleet. Jones was taken aback when he saw the strange-looking *Monitor* anchored next to the

VULCAN ARMING NEPTUNE.

**Vulcan Arming Neptune.** The historic clash between the CSS *Virginia* (or *Merrimac*) and the USS *Monitor* sounded the death knell for wooden warships. This cartoon from the British magazine *Punch* was published shortly after the battle to depict how the Battle of Hampton Roads changed naval warfare. Vulcan (the god of fire and smelting) is fitting Neptune (the god of the sea) with his own iron plating.

grounded *Minnesota* but decided to move in for the kill. For the next two hours, the two ironclads slugged it out in an historic battle. The *Virginia* carried much more firepower and protective armor, but the *Monitor* was more maneuverable. The fighting was so close the ships frequently scraped sides, and cannon fire was exchanged at point-blank range. Neither vessel was penetrated by the shells, but the sailors inside were stunned by the tremendous concussions, and some were wounded by rivets popping out of the iron plating. About noon, Worden was temporarily blinded by a shell that exploded against the pilot-house eye slit, and the *Virginia*'s rudder was damaged. Almost simultaneously, both ships disengaged and withdrew. The battle was a tactical stalemate, but the *Monitor* won a strategic victory by protecting the remaining Union vessels.

# EYEWITNESS
## Lieutenant S. Dana Greene

*The Battle of Hampton Roads was the first clash between modern ironclad battleships. Executive Officer Lieutenant S. Dana Greene volunteered to serve on the* Monitor *and manned the gun turret during the historic battle. After the war he wrote a vivid account of what it was like to be in the* Monitor's *turret fighting the huge Rebel ship. In his narrative, Greene refers to the* Virginia *as the* Merrimac.

Our captain . . . made straight for the *Merrimac*, which had already commenced firing; and when he came within short range, gave the order, "Commence firing!" I triced up the port, ran out the gun, and, taking deliberate aim, pulled the lockstring. The *Merrimac* was quick to reply, returning a rattling broadside (for she had ten guns to our two), and the battle fairly began. The turrets and other parts of the ship were heavily struck, but the shots did not penetrate; the tower was intact, and it continued to revolve. A look of confidence passed over the men's faces, and we believed the *Merrimac* would not repeat the work she had accomplished the day before. . . . Our shots ripped the iron of the *Merrimac*, while the reverberation of her shots against the tower caused anything but a pleasant sensation.

The drawbacks to the position of the pilot-house were soon realized. We could not fire ahead nor within several points of the bow, since the blast from our own guns would have injured the people in the pilot-house, only a few yards off. Keeler and Toffey passed the captain's orders and messages to me, and my inquiries and answers to him, the speaking-tube from the pilot-house to the turret having been broken early in the action. . . . The situation was novel: a vessel of war was engaged in desperate combat with a powerful foe; the captain, commanding and guiding, was inclosed in one place, and the executive officer, working and fighting the guns, was shut up in another, and communication between them was difficult and uncertain. . . .

My only view of the world outside of the tower was over the muzzles of the guns, which cleared the ports by only a few inches. . . . The effect upon one shut up in a

Neither ship suffered any serious battle damage, and the value of iron plating was proven. Naval warfare was changed forever. This first clash of ironclads sounded the death knell for wooden sailing vessels and marked the birth of the modern-day battleship.

The Battle of Hampton Roads was the only one in which the two famous ironclads engaged, but neither survived the war. Two months later, the Confederates realized they could not move the deep-drafted *Virginia* up the James River ahead of the advancing Union forces and destroyed it to keep it from falling into enemy hands. At year's end, the *Monitor* was ordered to join the Union fleet off North Carolina. While being towed, it foundered in a storm near Cape Hatteras in the early morning hours of December 31 and sank with sixteen officers and men still onboard.

revolving drum is perplexing, and it is not a simple matter to keep the bearings. White marks had been placed upon the stationary deck immediately below the turret to indicate the direction of the starboard and port sides, and the bow and stern; but these marks were obliterated early in the action. I would continually ask the captain, "How does the *Merrimac* bear?" He replied, "On the starboard-beam," . . . as the case might be. Then the difficulty was to determine the direction of the starboard-beam . . . or any other bearing. It finally resulted, that when a gun was ready for firing, the turret would be started on its revolving journey in search of the target, and when found it was taken "on the fly," because the turret could not be accurately controlled. . . .

Soon after noon a shell from the enemy's gun, the muzzle not ten yards distant, struck the forward side of the pilot-house directly in the sight-hole, or slit, and exploded, cracking the second iron log and partly lifting the top, leaving an opening. [Captain] Worden was standing immediately behind this spot, and received in his face the force of the blow, which partly stunned him, and filling his eyes with powder, utterly blinded him. . . . I went forward at once, and found him standing at the foot of the ladder leading to the pilot-house.

He was a ghastly sight, with his eyes closed and the blood apparently rushing from every pore in the upper part of his face. He told me that he was seriously wounded, and directed me to take command. . . . Blind and suffering as he was, Worden's fortitude never forsook him; he frequently asked from his bed of pain of the progress of affairs, and when told that the *Minnesota* was saved, he said, "Then I can die happy."

*Greene survived the Monitor's sinking off Cape Hatteras and was promoted to lieutenant commander, but he committed suicide after the Civil War. Captain Worden regained his sight, returned to duty, and retired from the navy as a rear admiral.*

Commander S. Dana Greene, "In the Monitor Turret," *Battles and Leaders of the Civil War,* Vol. 1, p. 719.

## Ironclads at War

After the Battle of Hampton Roads, both the Union and Confederate navies began to rely more on ironclads. Over the course of the war, the Confederates started construction on about fifty of the giant vessels but only completed twenty-two. The U.S. Navy commissioned seventy-one, many of which were of the monitor class. Union ironclads saw extensive action while supporting army operations at Forts Henry and Donelson, Island No. 10, Fort Jackson, Vicksburg, Port Hudson, the Red River, and Charleston.

Confederate ironclads usually operated alone and were scattered across the war zone. In the west, crewmen used the *Louisiana* as a floating battery at the Battle of Fort Jackson and then destroyed the ship to prevent its capture.

The *Arkansas* burst on the scene in July 1862 when it surprised Farragut's fleet on the Yazoo River near Vicksburg and disabled one Union vessel and drove off two others. The ironclad's fame was short-lived, however, for in August it steamed down the Mississippi River to participate in the Battle of Baton Rouge. The *Arkansas'* engines stalled just before arriving, and the crew was forced to burn the ship to keep it out of enemy hands.

In the Carolinas, the CSS *Chicora* and *Palmetto State* attacked the Union blockading fleet at Charleston in January 1863 and succeeded in capturing one ship and disabling another, but both ironclads were later destroyed by Confederate forces when they evacuated the city in 1865. One of the most famous and feared Confederate ironclads along the Atlantic coast was the *Albemarle*. In April 1864 it attacked Union forces at Plymouth, North Carolina, and sank one gunboat and forced three others to withdraw. In retaliation, Lieutenant William B. Cushing led a small Union party in a commando-like raid against the behemoth on the night of October 28, 1864. Mounting a spar torpedo on a small boat, Cushing slipped up the Roanoke River, and sank the *Albemarle* by ramming it with the torpedo.

The *Tennessee* was another famous Confederate ironclad that served as Admiral Franklin Buchanan's flagship during the Battle of Mobile Bay in August 1864. When Admiral Farragut's Union fleet entered the bay, Buchanan attacked and damaged six of the Union vessels. After several hours of constant pounding by the enemy guns, however, the *Tennessee* went dead in the water when its smokestacks were perforated, its steering chains shot away, and three of its gun ports jammed. Buchanan was wounded in the fierce fight, many of his crewmen were killed or wounded, and the *Tennessee* was forced to surrender.

## THE BLOCKADE

**April 19, 1861: Abraham Lincoln declares blockade of Southern ports**
**August 29, 1861: Union forces capture Hatteras Inlet, North Carolina**
**September 17, 1861: Union forces capture Port Royal, South Carolina**
**November 7, 1861: Union forces occupy Ship Island, Mississippi**
**February 8, 1862: Union forces capture Roanoke Island, North Carolina**
**March 3, 1862: Union forces capture Fernandina, Florida**
**March 14, 1862: Union forces capture New Bern, North Carolina**
**January 14, 1865: Union forces close Wilmington harbor, North Carolina**

Much of the Civil War at sea involved the blockade of Southern ports that President Lincoln ordered on April 19, 1861. The purpose of the blockade was to hinder the Confederates' ability to export cotton to Europe and import war materials. Bottling up Southern ports also denied home bases to enemy privateers and commerce raiders that threatened Union shipping. At the time, the Union blockade was the largest ever attempted, but at first it existed only on paper because the task facing the U.S. Navy was truly staggering. The navy had to blockade more than 3,500 miles of Southern coastline and nearly 200 points of entry, but it had just 42 warships. Of those, only 12 were available for blockade duty.

Under the leadership of Secretary of the Navy Gideon Welles, the Union quickly rose to the challenge by creating a Blockade Board to formulate a strategy. The Board first recommended creating four blockading squadrons—the North Atlantic, South Atlantic, East Gulf, and West Gulf—both to maintain the blockade and to cooperate with the army in attacking important points along the coast. Welles also began purchasing privately owned vessels to be converted into warships, while the massive Northern industrial machine built scores of new ships. The blockade became more and more effective, and by war's end the navy had hundreds of vessels assigned to blockade duty.

The Blockade Board also recommended capturing Southern ports to serve as coaling stations and safe havens for the ships on blockade duty. In less than a year, the U.S. Navy captured Hatteras Inlet, Roanoke Island, and New Bern, North Carolina; Port Royal, South Carolina; Fernandina, Florida; and Ship Island, Mississippi. These operations were critical to the war effort because they gave the navy secure bases for the Atlantic and Gulf blockading squadrons. From these bases, combined operations also methodically captured the major Confederate ports, and the blockade tightened around those remaining open. This forced the blockade runners to use more remote harbors and rivers that had little transportation facilities to move the supplies inland. In January 1865, the Confederacy's last major port at Wilmington, North Carolina, was closed when Union forces captured Fort Fisher. Only Galveston, Texas, remained open to Confederate blockade runners at war's end, and it was difficult to enter.

## Blockade Runners

The Confederates used fast, sleek ships called blockade runners to carry on their overseas trade with Europe, Bermuda, Cuba, and the Bahamas. Speed was of the essence, and these vessels sometimes had both steam-powered engines and sails. The engines were used when trying to avoid pursuing warships, and the sails were deployed on open water to conserve fuel. Painted a misty grey color, blockade runners were difficult to spot, especially when they slipped in and out of harbors at night or in foul weather. Most blockade runners were owned by private businessmen, and they began to fill their holds with highly profitable luxury goods rather than desperately needed military supplies. One drawback was that the ships were much smaller than those of the antebellum period and carried less cargo because survival depended on speed. Nonetheless, depending on the cargo, blockade runners could net as much as $100,000 on a single voyage. This focus on profit eventually forced the state and Confederate governments to purchase some ships for their own use. When these official ships proved inadequate for the task, in 1863 the Confederates began to force

# BIOGRAPHY

## David Glasgow Farragut: America's First Admiral

**David G. Farragut**

Tennessee native David Farragut (1801–1870) was the greatest Civil War admiral and the foster brother of David D. Porter, the war's second-greatest admiral. Farragut's father was a prominent U.S. Navy officer who once befriended the Porter family, and Commodore Porter (David Porter's father) offered to take the younger Farragut in to reciprocate the good deed.

Farragut entered the U.S. Navy as a midshipman when he was nine years old and served under Commodore Porter during the War of 1812. At the young age of thirteen, he fought alongside Porter aboard the USS *Essex* and was slightly wounded. He went on to fight in many battles during his sixty-year navy career, but that was the only time he was wounded. Although sixty years old when the Civil War began, Captain Farragut performed a handspring on every birthday and often joked he would know he was getting old when it became difficult to do.

Some officials doubted Farragut's loyalty because of his Tennessee birth and the fact that his wife was from Virginia. Secretary of the Navy Gideon Welles, however, did not and wrote, "All who knew him gave him credit of being a good officer, of good sense and good habits." In late 1861, Farragut was placed in command of the West Gulf Blockading Squadron and was given the important mission of capturing New Orleans, Louisiana. Porter, who had recommended him for the position, was given command of the fleet's mortar boats. The two had not seen each other in years, and Porter recalled, "Time had added grey hairs to his head, and a few lines of intelligence, generally called 'crows feet,' round his eyes. Otherwise he seemed unchanged. He had the same genial smile that always characterized him and the same affable manner which he possessed since I first knew him when I was quite a child and he a married man."

blockade runners to reserve part of their cargo space for war material. In 1864, Congress passed a law giving the government authority to reserve up to half of a ship's cargo space for its own use.

Most of the government's cargoes on blockade runners were paid for with cotton bonds, government certificates that owners of blockade runners could use in two ways. They could be used like savings bonds, where the shipowner held on to the certificates for a number of years and then redeemed them for the face value plus interest, or the ship owner could use the certificates to purchase stockpiled Confederate cotton and transport it to Europe to sell at a high profit. Blockade runners frequently chose the latter method because it held the promise of immediate profit. Over the course of the war, they transported approximately 1,250,000 bales of cotton to Europe.

Early in the war, the blockade runners had an advantage over the U.S. Navy because there were few Union warships patrolling the Southern coast, and the

When Farragut's fleet dashed past Forts Jackson and St. Philip, an enemy fire raft struck his flagship *Hartford* and it burst into flames. Seeing some crewmen retreating from the fire, Farragut yelled, "Don't flinch from that fire, boys. There's a hotter fire than that waiting for those who don't do their duty." The flames were extinguished, and at dawn a vessel carrying future naval hero George Dewey pulled alongside the fire-blackened *Hartford.* "Farragut was in her rigging," Dewey recalled, "his face eager with victory in the morning light and his eyes snapping. . . . I shall never forget that glimpse of him." As a reward for capturing New Orleans, Congress voted Farragut the Thanks of Congress, and he was promoted to rear admiral.

Farragut remained on the Mississippi River during the summer of 1862 and made an unsuccessful attack on Vicksburg, Mississippi. After a stint of blockade duty, his fleet next cooperated with the army during Major General Nathaniel P. Banks's Port Hudson Campaign, and in August 1864 he won his greatest victory when he attacked the Confederate fleet at Mobile, Alabama. As Farragut's ships boldly steamed into Mobile Bay, a torpedo sunk the lead monitor and the other captains hesitated. Lashed to the *Hartford's* rigging so he could have a bird's eye view of the battle, Farragut yelled to an officer on deck, "What's the trouble?" and was told, "Torpedoes!" "Damn the torpedoes. . . . Go ahead . . . full speed!" This brief exchange later was edited to become, "Damn the torpedoes! Full speed ahead!" In what he called "the most desperate battle I ever fought," Farragut defeated the Confederate navy, captured the Rebel ironclad *Tennessee,* and won another promotion to vice-admiral. In the war's final months, Farragut commanded gunboats on Virginia's James River. He remained in the navy after the war and in July 1866 became the first American naval officer to be promoted to admiral.

Confederate skippers were much better acquainted with the local waters. This allowed them to use little-known channels and avoid running onto sandbars, and if they were spotted, the blockade runner's faster ship could often simply outrun its pursuer. Speed, stealth, and geographic knowledge were the blockade runners' main weapons. They were rarely armed, and if cornered by a Union warship they had little option but to surrender.

## The Blockade's Effectiveness

It has been estimated that only one in ten blockade runners were captured early in the war. This changed dramatically, however, when the U.S. Navy began increasing the number of ships on patrol, and major ports were captured. As the war progressed, blockade runners became easier targets because they were

## NOTABLE UNITS: *Mississippi Marine Brigade*

The Mississippi Marine Brigade was one of the oddest, and most controversial, Civil War military units. In the western theater, Confederate guerrillas constantly harassed Union shipping in the Mississippi Valley. To counter this threat, Commander David D. Porter and Lieutenant Colonel Alfred W. Ellet came up with an ingenious plan in the summer of 1862. Porter was one of the navy's rising stars, and Ellet was the brother of Charles Ellet, the man who designed and commanded a fleet of army rams on the Mississippi River. Alfred served as his brother's aide during the Battle of Memphis and took command of the rams when Charles was mortally wounded.

Porter and Ellet proposed creating a special unit to fight guerrillas along the Mississippi River. The War Department approved the idea and created the Mississippi Marine Brigade, with Ellet commanding as brigadier general. In November 1862, he organized three units to compose the brigade: the 1st Battalion Mississippi Marine Brigade Infantry, 1st Battalion Mississippi Marine Brigade Cavalry, and Walling's Light Artillery Battery. The first two units were raised in Missouri, while the artillery battery was organized in Ellet's home state of Pennsylvania. Like the Ellet ram fleet, the Mississippi Marine Brigade held a unique position within the Union military, and there was confusion as to which branch of the military it served. The judge-advocate general declared that the brigade was a "special contingent of the Army and not the Navy," but General Grant wrote, "They (the officers and men of the Marine Brigade) are not subject to my orders."

forced into fewer and fewer harbors. Of the approximately 300 Confederate vessels employed as blockade runners, 221 were captured or destroyed. By 1865 a blockade runner had about a fifty-fifty chance of successfully passing through the cordon of Union ships. This statistic is somewhat misleading, however, because over the course of the war blockade runners were successful on about 1,000 out of 1,300 attempted runs.

Blockade runners proved invaluable to the Confederacy. Besides medicine, clothing, food, and luxury items, they provided approximately 60 percent of the Confederacy's weapons, 30 percent of its lead, 75 percent of its saltpeter (used to make gunpowder), and most of the paper used to make cartridges. These impressive statistics call into question just how effective the Union blockade was in preventing the Confederates from receiving foreign aid. Undoubtedly the blockade weakened the Confederacy by making it impossible to conduct normal overseas trade, and shortages ensued because the small blockade runners simply could not carry large cargoes. It is also true that almost half of the blockade runners trying to slip into Southern ports late in the war were captured. Nonetheless, the blockade was never complete, and Confederate armies continued to receive supplies from overseas until war's end. The common belief that the Rebels were forced into submission because they ran out of food, weapons, and ammunition is not true. The Confederates never lost a major battle because

Ellet's brigade was placed on transports and sent down the Mississippi River to Milliken's Bend, Louisiana, in March 1863. For the next seventeen months, it moved through the waterways of the lower Mississippi Valley chasing Confederate guerrillas and sometimes supporting the regular army in various operations. The brigade operated much like the U.S. Army Special Forces that used small navy vessels to conduct quick raids in the watery Mekong Delta during the Vietnam War. The Mississippi Marine Brigade engaged in numerous skirmishes with the Rebels and fought at Port Gibson during the Vicksburg Campaign and with Major General Nathaniel Banks during the Red River Campaign. But it was mostly known for engaging in lawless activity. It burned the towns of Columbia and Austin, Mississippi; looted Lake Village, Arkansas; and destroyed numerous homes and stores. One brigade member wrote, "[T]he Rebels swear vengeance on this Brigade, they hate us more than any other Regt. out, for they know well that we are determined to keep the Mississippi River open." The brigade's effectiveness also was hampered because of personal feuds within the Ellet family (which provided not only the commander but three other officers, as well) and an intense rivalry between the army and navy because both wanted to control the brigade's activities. In the end, the brigade's effectiveness did not warrant its controversial behavior and it was disbanded in August 1864.

of a lack of arms or ammunition, and they still had huge amounts of supplies stockpiled in secure areas when the war ended. The greater problem was a lack of manpower and the demolished Southern railway being unable to deliver the goods where they were most needed.

Galveston, Texas, was a popular port for Confederate blockade runners, but the Union navy captured it in October 1862. In the predawn hours of January 1, 1863, Confederate Major General John B. Magruder slipped into town with a small force of infantry, dismounted cavalry, and two cottonclad gunboats to take it back. Magruder's men quickly pinned down the Union infantry on a beachfront wharf, and the cottonclads closed in on the enemy vessels in the bay. The first shot was fired by a gunnery officer aboard the CSS *Bayou City,* who yelled out, "Well, here goes for a New Year's present!" as he yanked the lanyard. Two rounds later, the huge cannon accidentally exploded, killing the officer and four of his crewmen. Union Commander William B. Renshaw moved quickly to meet the attack, and a wild melee erupted in the bay. Renshaw's USS *Westfield* ran aground while getting under way, but the USS *Harriet Lane* succeeded in ramming the *Bayou City.* In turn, the *Harriet Lane* was rammed by the CSS *Neptune,* but the *Neptune* was heavily damaged in the attack and settled to the bottom in shallow water. The *Bayou City* then rammed the *Harriet Lane,* and both ships became entangled. The Confederates swarmed

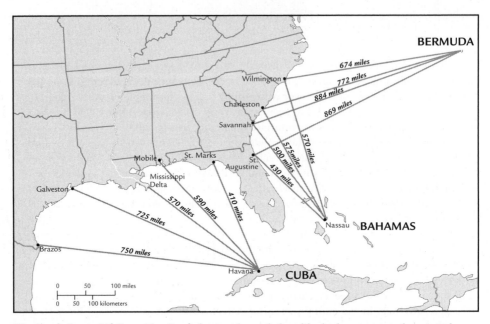

**The Confederate Lifeline.** The Confederates depended on blockade runners to bring vital war material from Spanish Cuba and the British Bahamas and Bermuda. This map shows the distances blockade runners had to sail from some important Southern ports.

aboard, killed the commander and first officer, and forced the Yankee sailors to surrender.

Having the upper hand, Magruder allowed a three-hour truce to give the enemy time to contemplate his surrender demands. Aboard the grounded *Westfield,* Renshaw needed no time to decide. He evacuated most of the crew and then climbed back aboard to blow up the ship rather than allow it fall into Rebel hands. Renshaw lowered an explosive charge into the powder magazine, but the fuse was either defective or set incorrectly. At 10:00 a.m., the charge exploded prematurely, killing Renshaw and thirteen crewmen. By that time, Magruder's infantry had captured most of the Union soldiers on the wharf, and the remaining Yankee gunboats hauled down their truce flags and sailed out to sea.

In the four-hour fight, Magruder inflicted about 400 casualties on the enemy at a cost of only 143 men. Galveston remained in Confederate hands for the remainder of the war and was the only port still open to blockade runners when the South surrendered two and a half years later. Admiral Farragut was disgusted and wrote Secretary of the Navy Welles, "[T]he shameful conduct of our forces at Galveston has been one of the severest blows of the war to the Navy." The Battle of Galveston was a rare bright moment for the western Confederates that year. Elsewhere, the Rebels found it difficult to stop the relentless Yankee advance across that vast region.

# PRIVATEERS AND COMMERCE RAIDERS

April 17, 1861: Jefferson Davis offers letters of marque to Confederate
  privateers
July 29, 1862: CSS *Alabama* leaves Great Britain to raid Union shipping
January 11, 1863: *Alabama* sinks the USS *Hatteras* near Galveston, Texas
June 19, 1864: USS *Kearsarge* sinks the *Alabama*
October 8, 1864: CSS *Shenandoah* leaves Great Britain to raid Union shipping
November 6, 1865: *Shenandoah* surrenders to British authorities

Realizing they could never launch a large fleet to attack Union shipping on the
high seas, the Confederates found privateers and commerce raiders to be a
more economical way to wage their naval war. Privateers were privately owned
ships that received permission, called letters of marque, from one country to
attack the shipping of another, while commerce raiders were commissioned
Confederate warships. Both types of vessels were fast, and often well armed,
and they operated alone to attack Northern merchant ships.

## Privateers

The United States had a long history of privateering and made good use of the
practice in both the Revolutionary War and the War of 1812. In those conflicts, American privateers actually captured or destroyed more British ships
than did the U.S. Navy. Shipowners rarely had difficulty raising a crew because
privateers took their captured vessels and cargoes to port and sold them, and
the crewmen shared in the profit. In 1856, an international agreement known
as the Declaration of Paris outlawed privateering, but the United States refused
to sign because it was an effective way to counter the large British navy. American officials believed there was the possibility a new war might erupt with
Great Britain someday, and they were not about to give up a proven weapon.

When the Civil War began in April 1861, Jefferson Davis began offering letters of marque to Southern shipowners to attack Union vessels. Over the course
of the war, the Confederacy issued such documents to fifty-two privateers, but
perhaps only half of them ever became active, and those that did usually operated close to their home ports. A growing shortage of safe havens was the biggest problem facing Confederate privateers. As the Union blockade increased
in effectiveness, it became more and more difficult for them to bring captured
prizes back to port, so the practice soon fell out of favor.

## The *Enchantress* Affair

Confederate privateers actually were too few in number to pose a serious
threat to Union shipping, but that was not immediately apparent to the Lincoln
administration. Lincoln at first thought the Rebels might inflict serious damage

on the merchant fleet, and he declared that captured Confederate privateers would be executed as pirates to dissuade Southerners from the practice. This announcement, however, soon placed the administration in a quandary.

In July 1861, a Confederate privateer captured the merchant ship *Enchantress* and placed a crew on board to take charge of the prize. About two weeks later, the *Enchantress* was captured again—this time by the U.S. Navy. The ship was taken back to the United States, and the Confederate crewmen were tried for piracy, convicted, and sentenced to death in accordance with Lincoln's policy. The *Enchantress* Affair demonstrated just how legally complicated the Civil War was. For generations, international law explicitly stated privateers were not pirates and should be treated as prisoners of war. Although the 1856 Declaration of Paris had changed that policy by outlawing privateers and allowing them to be treated as pirates, the United States had refused to sign the agreement. Thus, the Confederates and most foreign nations believed the Union was still bound by the traditional custom of treating privateers as prisoners of war, but the Lincoln administration claimed the Rebels did not meet the criteria. Maritime law defined privateers as citizens of one *nation* attacking the shipping of another. The Union did not recognize the Confederacy as a nation; so, in the eyes of the federal government, Confederate privateers were simply American citizens in rebellion. They were guilty of treason, subject to execution, and did not qualify to be treated as prisoners of war.

The Confederates took immediate steps to protect their crewmen. Secretary of War Judah P. Benjamin ordered officials to choose a similar number of Union prisoners to be executed if the Lincoln administration hanged the captured privateers. A lottery was used to select fifteen Union officers to serve as hostages for the crew of the *Enchantress* and the *Savannah,* another privateer that was captured later. Faced with this threat of retribution, Union authorities relented and began treating captured Confederate privateers as prisoners of war. In doing so, the Lincoln administration unintentionally strengthened the Confederates' diplomatic position. Treating Confederate privateers as prisoners of war was de facto recognition of the Confederacy as an independent nation.

## Commerce Raiders

By 1863, the privateers' effectiveness ended when most Southern ports were blockaded, and the Confederates were forced to rely more on commerce raiders to attack Northern merchant ships. These cruisers were official Confederate warships with sails, steam-powered engines, and heavy armament that made them capable of undertaking long ocean voyages and engaging in combat with enemy warships. Like the blockade runners, commerce raiders normally used their sails on the open ocean and only resorted to the engines when navigating a port or engaging in a chase or combat. Like privateers, commerce raiders were allowed to sell captured prizes, but they usually just destroyed their victims because they operated far from friendly ports (many, in fact, never even visited a Confederate harbor). Before the war was over, Confederate commerce raiders had captured or destroyed more than 200 Northern ships.

Great Britain built some of the most successful commerce raiders because early in the war it recognized the Confederacy as a belligerent, or warring, party. Although this was not the same as granting diplomatic recognition, it allowed the Confederates to purchase ships and weapons in Great Britain without giving them the right to hire a crew or arm the ship while it was in British waters. To get around these legal restrictions, the Confederates simply sailed the vessels offshore and fitted them with cannons and crews in international waters. Union diplomats vigorously complained to British officials about this practice and eventually forced the government to seize ships intended for Confederate service, but not before several had made it out to sea.

The first Confederate raider to show the flag in foreign countries was the *Sumter,* a converted packet steamer under the command of Raphael Semmes. It sailed from New Orleans in 1861 and cruised the Gulf of Mexico, the Caribbean Sea, and the Atlantic Ocean, capturing or destroying eighteen vessels in six months. When the U.S. Navy finally blockaded the *Sumter* in Gibraltar, Semmes abandoned his ship. It was later purchased by a British merchant who renamed it the *Gibraltar* and used it as a blockade runner.

The most famous Confederate cruiser was the *Alabama.* Purchased in Great Britain as the *Enrica,* it steamed out of Liverpool in July 1862 and headed to the Azores, where Raphael Semmes assumed command, armed it with four cannons, and christened it the *Alabama.* Over the next two years, the *Alabama* sailed the Atlantic, Caribbean, Gulf of Mexico, and even the Indian Ocean searching for enemy ships. It sailed nearly 75,000 miles and took more than sixty enemy vessels (most of which were burned). Only twice did the *Alabama* ever engage Union warships. One was the USS *Hatteras*, which was on blockade duty off Galveston, Texas, in January 1863. When the *Hatteras* sighted the *Alabama,* it gave chase, but the *Alabama* suddenly turned back and sank it in a thirteen-minute engagement.

The *Alabama*'s second encounter with a Union warship did not go as well. In June 1864, Captain John A. Winslow's USS *Kearsarge* was one of several Union vessels searching for the famous Confederate raider. During a stopover in the Netherlands, he learned the *Alabama* was being refitted at Cherbourg, France, and quickly took up a position outside the Cherbourg harbor and waited for it to come out. Although his ship was in poor condition after months of sailing, Semmes steamed into the English Channel on June 19 to give battle. The *Kearsarge* was better armed than the *Alabama,* and Winslow had the foresight of hanging board-covered chains over the side to protect his ship's engines. The battle was intense, but the *Kearsarge* eventually sank the *Alabama.* Semmes and many of his surviving crewmen were picked up by British boats and taken to safety, but the Confederates lost forty-three men, while the Union under Winslow lost only three. Fifteen of Winslow's crewmen were awarded the Medal of Honor for their heroism.

# BIOGRAPHY
## Raphael Semmes: Rebel Raider

Raphael Semmes (SEMZ) (1809–1877) of Maryland was orphaned at an early age and entered the U.S. Navy as a midshipman at seventeen. He commanded a warship (which sank in a storm) on blockade duty during the Mexican War and was attached to General Winfield Scott's army as a naval observer. After serving thirty-five years in the navy, Semmes resigned in February 1861 when his adopted state of Alabama seceded. He eventually was commissioned a commander in the Confederate navy and was given command of the CSS *Sumter,* the South's first commerce raider. The *Sumter* captured or destroyed eighteen enemy vessels in just six months, but the U.S. Navy finally blockaded it at Gibraltar, and Semmes was forced to abandon his vessel. He later recalled how it saddened him to leave the *Sumter.* "I . . . felt as if I would be parting forever with a valued friend. She had run me safely through two vigilant blockades, had weathered many storms, and rolled me to sleep in many calms."

Semmes was promoted to captain and was sent to the Azores to take command of the *Alabama,* the most feared of all Confederate commerce raiders. From September 1862 to June 1864 he sailed 75,000 miles from the Atlantic Ocean to the China Sea and captured or destroyed sixty-nine Northern ships. Among them was the USS *Hatteras,* a warship Semmes sank off the Texas coast in what he proudly claimed was the "first yardarm engagement between steamers at sea."

Semmes's remarkable career as a raider came to an end when he steamed into Cherbourg, France, in June 1864. The *Alabama,* he wrote, was like "the weary foxhound, limping back after a long chase, footsore and longing for quiet and repose." When Captain John A. Winslow's USS *Kearsarge* arrived offshore, Semmes felt honor bound to leave the port's safety to give battle. Semmes and Winslow were actually friends, having served together in the Mexican War on the USS *Cumberland* (which

Another notable Confederate commerce raider was the *Florida,* a sister ship to the *Alabama* and the first of the cruisers to be constructed in Great Britain. The *Florida* was commanded by Lieutenant John N. Maffitt, another successful skipper. During its career, the *Florida* sank or captured thirty-seven enemy ships, but it, too, fell victim to the U.S. Navy. In October 1864, the *Florida* was docked in Bahia, Brazil, along with the USS *Wachusett.* Bahia was a neutral port, but that did not stop the crew of the *Wachusett* from taking action. When most of the Confederates were ashore on leave in the predawn hours of October 7, the Union sailors rammed the *Florida,* boarded it, and then towed it out to sea. Brazil protested this violation of international law but could not prevent the Yankees from taking the *Florida* to Virginia. Bowing to international pressure, the Lincoln administration finally agreed to return the ship and its captured crewmen to Brazil. While awaiting the move, however, the *Florida* was suspiciously rammed by a transport ship and sank. Although the CSS *Virginia* later sank at Hampton Roads). The *Kearsarge* sank the *Alabama,* but Semmes was plucked from the English Channel by a British yacht and returned to the Confederacy by way of Great Britain and Mexico.

Promoted to rear admiral, Semmes was next placed in command of the James River Squadron, but he was forced to destroy his ships to prevent their capture in April 1865. When Richmond was abandoned, he led his men to North Carolina and joined Joseph E. Johnston's army. President Davis appointed Semmes an army brigadier general, and his sailors were organized into an infantry brigade, but the army commission was not official because the Senate never confirmed the appointment before the war ended.

Semmes was the Confederacy's most famous naval figure and an outstanding officer. He insisted on strict discipline among his multinational crewmen (whom he called "a precious set of rascals"), forced them to keep the ship in tip-top condition, and did not allow them to pillage. The crew viewed Semmes as somewhat aloof and haughty and referred to him as "Old Beeswax" because of the great care he took with his long black moustache. Although Semmes was not always popular with his men, his effectiveness as a raider was unquestioned and he captured or destroyed eighty-seven enemy vessels.

After the surrender, Semmes returned to Alabama, but he was imprisoned and threatened with prosecution by a military court for treason and piracy. The Supreme Court, however, refused to give the military jurisdiction in the case, and Semmes was released after four months. Returning to Alabama, he had a difficult time supporting himself because federal authorities continued to harass him by removing him from an elected judgeship and driving him from positions in education and journalism. Semmes finally established a successful law practice and wrote *Memoirs of Service Afloat: During the War Between the States*.

the United States apologized to Brazil for the incident, it was obvious the sinking was intentional.

The *Tallahassee,* another cruiser built in Great Britain, was originally a blockade runner named the *Atalanta.* Purchased by the Confederate navy in 1864, it was armed with cannons and rechristened the *Tallahassee.* Lieutenant John Taylor Wood took command and raided the New England coast that August and captured or destroyed thirty-three enemy vessels. Eventually, the *Tallahassee* returned to blockade running as the *Chameleon,* but British authorities seized it in April 1865.

One commerce raider actually circumnavigated the world and survived the war. The *Shenandoah* was built in Scotland in 1864 and was purchased by Confederate agent James D. Bulloch. Placed under the command of Lieutenant James I. Waddell, it slipped out of port in October disguised as a British merchant ship and was armed with cannons off the coast of North Africa and christened

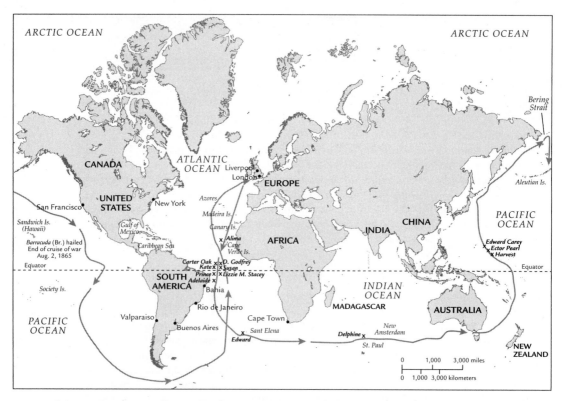

**Cruise of the CSS *Shenandoah*.** The Confederate commerce raider *Shenandoah* made a historic round-the-world voyage late in the war, during which it captured or burned thirty-eight enemy vessels. This map shows the route taken and the places where some of the Northern ships were encountered. Returning to Great Britain five months after the war ended, the crewmen of the *Shenandoah* were the last Confederates to surrender.

the *Shenandoah*. Waddell rounded the Cape of Good Hope, pushed on to Australia, and then headed for the Arctic Ocean, where he devastated the Northern whaling fleet. The Civil War ended while the *Shenandoah* was still in the Arctic, but Waddell ignored reports the war was over until a passing British vessel confirmed the news in August 1865. Fearing he and his men might be treated as pirates for attacking vessels after the close of hostilities, Waddell decided not to surrender to the U.S. Navy. Instead, he disguised the *Shenandoah* as a British merchant vessel, made his way to Great Britain through the Strait of Magellan, and surrendered to authorities in November 1865. The *Shenandoah* captured or sank thirty-eight enemy vessels (two-thirds of which were taken after the war had ended) and completed a 58,000 mile around-the-world cruise. Waddell's was the last Confederate surrender of the war.

The Confederate strategy of using commerce raiders proved highly successful against Northern shipping. Besides the numerous merchant vessels captured or destroyed, the raiders caused havoc in the entire industry by driving up insurance and cargo rates, forcing shipowners to transfer their vessels to foreign flags for protection (more than 700 transferred to the British flag), and making the U.S. Navy scatter its fleet. At the height of the attacks, almost one hundred Union ships were dedicated to hunting down the commerce raiders. They eventually were successful, but it was a significant drain on Union naval resources. Admiral David Porter criticized the government for widely dispersing Union warships to chase the raiders rather than simply having them wait outside known coaling stations to ambush the enemy. "If the *Alabama* knew where to go to catch American merchantmen," he argued, "why did not the Federal Government know where to seek the *Alabama*? . . . It was not the particular smartness of Semmes that enabled him to escape capture. It was the omission or indifference of the Navy Department in not sending proper vessels to the right localities."

The rest of the world took note of the commerce raiders' effectiveness during the Civil War. Germany used the same tactic to devastate Allied shipping in both world wars, although it relied more on submarines than surface vessels. The same shipping lanes prowled by Rebel commerce raiders in the mid-nineteenth century also became the hunting grounds for German wolf packs in the twentieth century.

## The Naval War's Impact

Although not studied to the extent of army operations, naval activity was an important part of the Civil War, but it did not decide the conflict. The most that can be said is that the naval war shortened the land war because the Union fleet was much more effective in accomplishing its goals than was the Confederate fleet. As seen in other chapters of this text, the U.S. Navy played a crucial role in a number of campaigns and was indispensable in capturing the Mississippi River, New Orleans, Memphis, Mobile, and Charleston. Without the navy's help, Union armies would have taken much longer to gain control of these and other critical areas. The Union blockade also helped weaken the Confederacy, although its true effect is usually overstated. The blockade made it more difficult for the Confederates to import needed supplies, but it never completely cut off their overseas trade.

The Confederates committed a large amount of resources to build ironclads in hopes of winning the naval war through advanced technology. Although they did enjoy some limited success in launching raids on the enemy, the Southerners were never a match for the U.S. Navy, and they ultimately failed to stop the advancing Union armies or lift the blockade. Historians have given a good deal of attention to Confederate commerce raiders because of the dramatic exploits of the *Alabama* and *Shenandoah,* but even they did not really affect the war's outcome. The 257 enemy ships taken by the raiders seem impressive, but that was only about 5 percent of the entire Northern merchant fleet, and Union trade was hardly curtailed. Perhaps the commerce raiders' greatest long-term effect was driving privately owned American merchant ships into other nation's fleets. The Confederates destroyed 110,000 tons of Northern shipping, but another 800,000 tons transferred their registry overseas seeking protection under foreign flags. This was more than half of the entire U.S. merchant fleet, and most never came back.

## FOR FURTHER READING

Lincoln's declaration of a blockade on Southern ports

# CHAPTER 9

# The Fight for Freedom

A Cautious Policy

Emancipation

"None Fought More Boldly"

African Americans in the Confederate Army

The 1,200 Union soldiers stationed at Milliken's Bend, Louisiana, waited nervously behind a Mississippi River levee. Intelligence received during the night indicated a large enemy force was approaching their position. Most of the men were local residents, former slaves who had joined the army when General U.S. Grant began his campaign against Vicksburg, Mississippi. Although untrained, they were assigned to guard the supply depot at the small river port just upstream from Vicksburg.

Shortly after sunrise on June 7, 1863, Confederate Major General Richard Taylor sent a brigade of Texans charging across a cotton field toward Milliken's Bend and its untried garrison. Knowing they were about to engage black troops, the Rebels let it be known that there would be no prisoners taken, only death, when they ran toward the levee yelling, "No quarter!" Almost immediately, a regiment of white Union soldiers broke and ran for the river, leaving the black soldiers to fend for themselves. Brigadier General Henry McCulloch, who led the attack, wrote in his report, "[T]his charge was resisted by the negro portion of the enemy's force with considerable obstinacy, while the white or true Yankee portion ran like whipped curs. . . ." In a ferocious hand-to-hand fight, the former slaves held their ground on top of the levee for a few minutes. When overpowered, they fell back to the river, with the Texans following close behind bayoneting many in the back. When the blacks reached another levee along the river bank, they received supporting fire from gunboats and finally forced the Confederates to withdraw.

The Battle of Milliken's Bend was a small affair by Civil War standards, with the Yankees losing 450 men and the Texans losing about 175. The low casualty figures belie the viciousness of the clash, however. The 9th Louisiana Infantry of African Descent had 128 men killed or mortally wounded out of only

285 men engaged. This 45 percent mortality rate is one of the highest for any Union regiment in a single engagement. Union Captain Matthew Miller testified to the ferocity of the fight when he wrote his aunt, "I never more wish to hear the expression, 'the niggers won't fight.' Come with me 100 yards from where I sit, and I can show you the wounds that cover the bodies of 16 as brave, loyal and patriotic soldiers as ever drew bead on a Rebel. The enemy charged us so close that we fought with our bayonets, hand to hand. . . . It was a horrible fight, the worse I was ever engaged in—not excepting Shiloh. The enemy cried 'No quarter!' but some of them were very glad to take it when made prisoners."

Milliken's Bend has received little attention in Civil War military history, but the battle received tremendous coverage during the war. It even made the front cover of *Frank Leslie's Illustrated Newspaper* because it was one of the first fights in which black Union soldiers engaged in combat. For many months, Union troops and politicians had speculated whether blacks would ever make effective soldiers. The Battle of Milliken's Bend answered that question with a resounding, "Yes!"

## A CAUTIOUS POLICY

**August 6, 1861: First Confiscation Act goes into effect**

**August 10, 1861: General John C. Frémont orders slaves freed in his department**

**April 16, 1862: U.S. Congress passes District of Columbia Emancipation Act**

**May 9, 1862: General David Hunter orders slaves freed in his department**

**July 17, 1862: Lincoln signs Second Confiscation Act**

Secession and civil war occurred because the Southerners were determined to protect their slavery rights by establishing a separate nation, and Northerners were equally determined to keep the Southern states within the Union. Lincoln, the Republican Party, and, indeed, most Northerners were dedicated to containing and eventually abolishing slavery, but those goals became secondary once the war began. While Lincoln never faltered in his desire to abolish slavery, suppressing the rebellion took precedence. He also knew he would have to move slowly toward emancipation because of constitutional and practical concerns. The Supreme Court had recognized slaves as property in the Dred Scott decision, and that ruling had to be considered in any action taken against the peculiar institution. Complicating matters was the fact that any interference with slavery might push the critical Border States into the Confederates' camp. Because of these obstacles, Lincoln was very cautious early in the war when it came to the question of emancipation.

### Contraband

To a large extent, slaves themselves forced the Union to address the slavery issue. As soon as Northern armies occupied Southern territory, thousands of runaway

**A Family of Contrabands.**
Soon after war erupted, slaves began to run away to Union lines in a desperate bid for freedom. General Benjamin F. Butler coined the term contrabands for such runaways because their labor had constructed Confederate fortifications. Because slaves had been used to strengthen the Rebel army, Butler argued runaways could be confiscated as contraband of war.

slaves sought refuge inside Union lines. Because there was no federal policy regarding runaways, military commanders acted on their own impulses. Some, like General George B. McClellan, returned them to their owners because they believed protection of secessionist property was necessary to entice moderate Southerners to oppose the Confederacy. Other, more radical, generals took a different tack.

Major General Benjamin F. Butler was a Democrat like McClellan, but he disagreed with Little Mac on how to treat runaway slaves. Butler was convinced runaways should not be returned because slavery strengthened the Rebel army. While in command of Fort Monroe, Virginia, in May 1861, he refused to return slaves who entered his camp. Although they were not technically free, the runaways were paid a small wage and were put to work picking cotton or strengthening Butler's defenses. Butler defended his actions by claiming the runaways had been used to build Confederate fortifications and were, therefore, "contraband of war." Contraband was the term used for illegal goods smuggled into a country and thus subject to confiscation. Applying it to runaway slaves was perhaps stretching the word's meaning and somewhat derogatory, but it became a popular synonym for runaway slaves during the Civil War.

## The First Emancipation Acts

Republican abolitionists applauded Butler's contraband policy and began taking emancipation steps of their own in Congress. Not only was emancipation morally right, the abolitionists believed it would also weaken the Confederates by destroying the Southern planters' single greatest source of wealth and by denying the enemy important military labor. Slaves freed up white men to fight by building fortifications and producing the food and fodder that kept the enemy's armies in the field. The destruction of slavery would force the Confederates to strip their armies of fighting men to perform those tasks.

The Republicans began by passing the First Confiscation Act in August 1861. Introduced by Illinois senator Lyman Trumbull, this bill authorized the president to use legal proceedings to confiscate any property (including slaves) that was being used to support the rebellion. Trumbull introduced a Second Confiscation Act in December that was even stronger. It allowed authorities to fine and imprison anyone supporting the rebellion and forbade Confederate sympathizers to hold political office. The president could also immediately confiscate the property of wealthy Confederates (final adjudication was left to the court system), while poorer Rebels were given sixty days to cease rebellious activity or have their property seized, as well. The bill even freed secessionist-owned slaves who came under Union military control and authorized the president to use them in any manner necessary to defeat the rebellion. Congress debated the measure for seven months because Lincoln and other moderate politicians were uncomfortable with the idea of permanently confiscating non-slave property. While the president did support the acts as necessary wartime measures, he believed confiscating non-slave property was too harsh and doubted its legality because it would punish future generations of Southerners who had nothing to do with secession. To avoid a possible veto, the bill's supporters finally agreed to change the legislation to restrict such property confiscation to the lifetime of the offender. Congress then passed the Second Confiscation Act, and Lincoln signed it into law in July 1862.

The Confiscation Acts established a comprehensive federal policy regarding slavery months before the better-known Emancipation Proclamation. Not only did they free most slaves who came under Union army control, they also allowed the Union army to begin recruiting black troops to fight the Confederates. But the acts had little effect on other Southern property. Lincoln, Attorney General Edward Bates, and most senior military commanders were very conservative, and none was comfortable with the wholesale confiscation of property. As a result, no one vigorously enforced the laws, and little Southern property was ever seized. Most of the Southern property that was confiscated during the Civil War was later restored to the owners during Reconstruction.

In 1862, the Republicans also took steps to abolish slavery in Washington, D.C., when Massachusetts Senator Henry Wilson introduced a bill to emancipate all of the capital's slaves. His legislation appropriated $1 million to compensate loyal Washington slaveholders for their loss, while slaves of pro-Confederate owners would be freed under the First Confiscation Act. Opposition to the measure was fierce. The Border States saw the bill as a first step toward universal emancipation and argued that the money appropriated was far less than the slaves' value. Many city residents also opposed the measure because they did not want a large population of unemployed African Americans living there. Despite the opposition, the District of Columbia Emancipation Act passed in April 1862 and Lincoln signed it into law. Soon afterward, Congress also granted full civil rights to the city's free black population, except for the right to serve on juries.

## Lincoln and Military Emancipation

Lincoln supported the limited emancipation measures passed by Congress because they were in keeping with his own goals and were supported by most Northerners. However, he was determined to move slowly on universal emancipation because he did not want to anger the slaveholding Border States and drive them out of the Union. Twice during the early war years, Lincoln was forced to act decisively when generals took matters into their own hands and tried to free slaves without authorization. The first to do so was John C. Frémont (fruh-MONT), a famous abolitionist, western explorer, and first Republican Party presidential candidate. Lincoln appointed him a major general because of his political influence and sent him to Missouri to command the huge Department of the West. In August 1861, Frémont exceeded his authority by announcing all slaves in his department were freed. Not only did he fail to consult Lincoln beforehand, he failed to inform the president of his declaration until a week later. The recently passed First Confiscation Act allowed Confederate-owned slaves to be freed through court proceedings, but Frémont's proclamation freed *all* slaves by proclamation alone. Lincoln asked him to change the proclamation's wording so it would conform to the Confiscation Act, but the general refused. Lincoln was left with no choice but to repudiate the order to calm the fears of loyal Missouri slaveholders.

The second general who tried to force Lincoln's hand was the president's personal friend, Major General David Hunter. Lincoln had sponsored Hunter's military career and made the inexperienced and rather incompetent officer commander of the Department of the South (South Carolina, Georgia, and Florida). Without consulting the president, Hunter announced in May 1862 that all slaves within his department were free; but, once again, an irritated Lincoln disavowed the proclamation and forced Hunter to recant. Lincoln fiercely opposed slavery, and he had always supported any practical measure to emancipate those held in bondage. But he also was well aware that Frémont's and Hunter's arbitrary emancipation orders could cause tremendous political damage in the Border States, not to mention their encroachment on his executive authority. Lincoln was determined to attack slavery whenever possible, but he would not be pressured into moving too quickly on freeing the slaves.

## EMANCIPATION

**August 20, 1862: Horace Greeley publishes "The Prayer of Twenty Millions"**
**September 22, 1862: Lincoln issues Preliminary Emancipation**
   **Proclamation**

**January 1, 1863: Lincoln signs Emancipation Proclamation**
**January 31, 1865: Congress passes the Thirteenth Amendment**

As Union war losses mounted, more and more Northerners began to agree with the abolitionists on emancipation because something had to be done to break the military stalemate and justify the enormous casualties. Some abolitionists were beginning to lose patience with Lincoln for not being more aggressive in freeing the slaves. One British newspaper criticized him for his lack of action and claimed the president's "great mistake from the first has been not to perceive that revolution could only be met with revolution." The newspaper was mistaken, however, for Lincoln did realize revolutionary measures were needed, and he was about to adopt a radical policy that would change the entire nature of the war.

## "The Prayer of Twenty Millions"

On August 20, 1862, *New York Tribune* editor Horace Greeley put the emancipation issue directly to Lincoln when he published an editorial entitled "The Prayer of Twenty Millions." Claiming he spoke for the Northern people, Greeley urged Lincoln to enforce the Confiscation Acts with vigor, to free the slaves that came into Union lines, and to punish all slaveholders. Greeley published Lincoln's response five days later. The president reminded him that the war's primary objective was to crush the rebellion, not to emancipate the slaves. "My paramount object in this struggle," Lincoln wrote, "*is* to save the Union, and is *not* either to save or to destroy slavery. If I could save the Union without freeing *any* slave I would do it, and if I could save it by freeing *all* the slaves, I would do it; and if I could save it by freeing some and leaving others alone I would also do that. What I do about slavery, and the colored race, I do because I believe it helps to save the Union; and what I forbear, I forbear because I do *not* believe it would help to save the Union."

While Lincoln's reply seemed to indicate he had no intentions of emancipating the slaves, he did note that he personally wished all men were free. An opposition to slavery, in fact, had been a constant throughout his career. As early as 1854, Lincoln declared, "Slavery is founded in the selfishness of man's nature—opposition to it in his love of justice." He had always supported emancipation, but he preferred doing it in a way that would cause the least amount of political, economic, and social turmoil. This included compensating slaveholders for their loss to minimize the economic damage and relocating freed slaves in a foreign land to avoid racial unrest. However, Lincoln could never win enough support from slaveholders or abolitionists for such measures to succeed, and by mid-1862 he realized bolder steps were necessary. When Lincoln wrote his famous reply to Greeley, only a handful of people within the administration knew he had already drawn up an emancipation policy that would change the very fabric of American society.

Lincoln, however, did not think the time was right to announce his intentions publicly.

## The Emancipation Proclamation

Although Lincoln wanted to see slavery eradicated, he avoided taking executive action toward emancipation early in the war because he did not want to anger the Border States. Instead, he supported the Confiscation Acts and the District of Columbia Emancipation Act because they were limited in nature and had wide popular support. But Lincoln finally decided executive emancipation was necessary to break the military stalemate, and in July 1862 he prepared the Preliminary Emancipation Proclamation to free the slaves in Confederate-controlled territory on January 1, 1863, if the Southerners did not stop the war by that date. On the surface, the document seemingly did little because it only freed, with some exceptions, those slaves in territory Union forces did not control. For example, while it did free the slaves living on the Union-occupied Sea Islands of South Carolina and Georgia, it did not apply to the 800,000 slaves being held in the loyal Border States or in other Union-controlled areas because Lincoln did not want to anger slaveholders in those regions.

Despite these exclusions, Lincoln knew the proclamation would have the desired effect. First, it was a dramatic way to show the Confederates how much they stood to lose by continuing to fight. As Lincoln told one Southern loyalist, "This government cannot much longer play a game in which it stakes all, and its enemies stake nothing. Those enemies must understand that they cannot experiment for ten years trying to destroy the government, and if they fail still come back into the Union unhurt." No matter how the Southerners reacted to the proclamation, Lincoln was almost assured a positive result. The Confederates might end the rebellion in order to protect their slaves; but, if they did not, thousands of slaves would undoubtedly run away to reach freedom within the Union lines. Such a mass exodus would weaken the Rebels by denying them much of the labor used to construct fortifications and to raise food, and Confederate fighting strength would diminish because more soldiers would have to remain behind the lines to protect against slave unrest.

There was also an important diplomatic reason to embrace emancipation. Great Britain and France were considering recognizing Confederate independence, and some Europeans even proposed breaking the blockade. Lincoln knew the vast majority of British citizens were against slavery, and an emancipation proclamation would change the war from being a purely internal political struggle to a conflict with moral implications. Such a change in policy would probably force the British and French governments to remain on the sidelines because their citizens would not tolerate becoming involved in a conflict against emancipation.

When Lincoln showed the Preliminary Emancipation Proclamation to the cabinet, Secretary of State William H. Seward convinced him to delay issuing

**The Emancipation Proclamation.** This Southern cartoon of Lincoln writing the Emancipation Proclamation clearly illustrates how the Confederates viewed the document. Lincoln's foot resting on the Constitution is symbolic of his trampling the constitutional right of slave ownership, and the paintings of John Brown and the Santo Domingo slave insurrection reflect Southerners' fear that the Emancipation Proclamation was intended to provoke slave uprisings.

it until the Union won a major battlefield victory so it would be presented from a position of strength rather than appear to be an act of desperation. "If the Proclamation were issued now," Seward told him, "it would be received and considered as a despairing cry—a shriek from and for the Administration, rather than for freedom." Two months later, the Army of the Potomac stopped Lee's Maryland raid at the Battle of Antietam, and Lincoln decided that was victory enough to issue the document. As would be expected, the Confederates rejected the proclamation and continued to fight.

On New Year's Day 1863, Lincoln spent hours shaking hands of well-wishers who filed through the White House before retiring to another room to sign the Emancipation Proclamation. With pen in hand, he looked up at those officials who crowded around and declared, "I never in my life felt more certain that I was doing right than I do in signing this paper. But I have been receiving calls and shaking hands since 9 o'clock this morning, till my arm is stiff and numb. Now this signature is one that will be closely examined, and if they find my hand trembled they will say, 'He had some compunctions.' But anyway it is going to be done." He then carefully signed the document.

Not everyone was impressed with the Emancipation Proclamation. One British newspaper noted suspiciously, "The Government liberates the enemy's slaves as it would the enemy's cattle, simply to weaken them in the coming conflict. . . . The principle asserted is not that a human being cannot justly own another, but that he cannot own him unless he is loyal to the United States." The document was particularly controversial within the Union army because most soldiers were fighting to preserve the Union and not to free the slaves. A large number of these men were outraged at the proclamation and believed

**Lincoln Writing the Emancipation Proclamation.** This David Gilmour Blythe painting depicts Lincoln writing the Emancipation Proclamation in a room cluttered with inspirational and symbolic material. His left hand rests on a Bible, which rests on the Constitution draped across his lap. On the mantle sits a bust of Andrew Jackson, another strong Unionist president, while pro-Southern President James Buchanan's bust hangs by a rope.

they had been betrayed. There were loud protests within the ranks, and some regiments even threatened mutiny. Many Democrats also criticized the measure and threatened not to support a war to free the slaves. Such announcements prompted Lincoln to tell his opponents in August 1863, "You say you will not fight to free negroes. Some of them seem willing to fight for you; but, no matter. Fight you, then, exclusively to save the Union. I issued the proclamation on purpose to aid you in saving the Union."

Eventually, most Northerners came to support the Emancipation Proclamation, even though many did so reluctantly. Some soldiers supported it because they truly felt sorry for the slaves when they saw the pathetic conditions in which they lived. Other Northerners saw the new policy's value in weakening the enemy by causing unrest within the Confederacy's interior. As word of the Emancipation Proclamation spread, slaves became bolder in carrying out acts of defiance, thousands ran away whenever Union armies approached their homes, and Confederate officials were forced to exempt overseers from the draft and form home guard units to keep the slaves working. The Emancipation

Proclamation's impact on the war cannot be exaggerated because it greatly affected both sides and changed the very nature of the war. No longer was it just a conflict over political disputes. Now it was a struggle for the great dual ideas of preserving the Union and bringing freedom to an oppressed people.

## The Thirteenth Amendment

The Emancipation Proclamation was a dramatic change in federal policy, but it did not satisfy abolitionists because slaves in loyal areas were not affected. They wanted to eradicate slavery completely and permanently nationwide and proposed a constitutional amendment to do so. What eventually became the Thirteenth Amendment was a difficult measure to pass because of widespread Democratic opposition to universal emancipation. In April 1864, the Senate passed the proposed amendment by a vote of 38 to 6, but it failed in the House. Lincoln then began personally to lobby many Democrats, and when a second House vote was taken in January 1865, the measure barely passed 119 to 56.

Convincing the required twenty-seven states to ratify the amendment was not easy. Not only did many Northerners oppose the measure, but eleven states had seceded. Ratification of the emancipation amendment depended on a Northern victory to bring the Southern states back into the Union to vote. The amendment would later be a major issue during Reconstruction.

## "NONE FOUGHT MORE BOLDLY"

**September 27, 1862: Louisiana Native Guards enter the Union army**
**May 27, 1863: Battle of Port Hudson, Louisiana**
**June 7, 1863: Battle of Milliken's Bend, Louisiana**
**July 18, 1863: Battle of Fort Wagner, North Carolina**
**April 12, 1864: Battle of Fort Pillow, Tennessee**

For racist reasons, neither side allowed African Americans to enlist in their armies when the Civil War began. Slavery was a cornerstone of Southern culture, and the peculiar institution was based on white supremacy. To enlist blacks as Confederate soldiers was unthinkable because it would recognize them as equal to whites. Rare but well-publicized slave uprisings such as those led by Denmark Vesey (1821) in South Carolina and Nat Turner (1831) in Virginia also made Southerners fearful of future attacks (although this fear seemed at odds with the Southerners' assertion that slaves were contented with their lot). Arming blacks for military service would be an invitation for slave insurrections. Northern reasons for keeping blacks out of the army were more varied. Many Northerners shared the Southern view that whites were superior to blacks and did not believe they had the intelligence necessary to be trained militarily. Some Northerners also suspected blacks had a natural fear of whites that would make them ineffective as soldiers, and there was always the concern that enlisting blacks would anger the slaveholding Border States and perhaps lead to their defection.

Northern attitudes toward using African American soldiers began to change during the war's second year when the Union faced a critical manpower shortage. Casualties in the 1862 campaigns were horrendous, and white enlistments plummeted as the initial war enthusiasm faded. The African American population was the only untapped source of manpower, and the Confiscation Acts and the District of Columbia Emancipation Act authorized black enlistments. African Americans were eager to volunteer because they knew military service was in their best interest. If blacks fought and died to save the Union, they would earn the respect of white Northerners. How could slavery be reinstated or citizenship denied to black veterans who had done their part to win the war? Frederick Douglass realized what was at stake when he wrote, "Once let the black man get upon his person the brass letters, U.S.; let him get an eagle on his button, and a musket on his shoulder, and bullets in his pocket, and there is no power on earth which can deny that he has earned the right to citizenship in the United States."

## U.S. Colored Troops

Despite many officers' misgivings, the Union army began to recruit black soldiers in the summer of 1862. African Americans were allowed to serve as enlisted men and noncommissioned officers, but they served in segregated units that became known as the U.S. Colored Troops (USCT), and, except for the Louisiana Native Guards, all of their commissioned officers had to be white. Most officers who served in USCT units were dedicated soldiers who came to admire their men, but many were racists who volunteered because promotions were more rapid in USCT service.

Racism remained rampant in the army, and the black troops suffered from intense discrimination. White soldiers within their own ranks openly scorned and abused them. One Union soldier wrote home, "The men . . . treat them worse than brutes and when they come into camp, cries of 'kill him' etc. are heard on every hand." Black soldiers were even paid less than white soldiers for no other reason than that they were considered inferior. A white private received $13 per month and was provided free clothing, while a black private received $10 per month and had $3 of that deducted for his clothing. Some black soldiers were so outraged at this blatant discrimination they refused to accept any pay. Congress took a small step to correct the injustice in June 1864 when equal pay was authorized for African American soldiers who were free men when the Civil War began, but equal pay for all blacks was not mandated until March 1865, one month before the surrender at Appomattox.

Despite the discrimination, black soldiers served with honor, and several African American units earned great fame. The 1st Kansas Colored Volunteers, 54th Massachusetts, and the Louisiana Native Guards were among the first black regiments formed. The 1st Kansas Colored Volunteers was officially mustered into service in January 1863. Composed mainly of free blacks, it had the distinction of being the first African American unit to see combat when

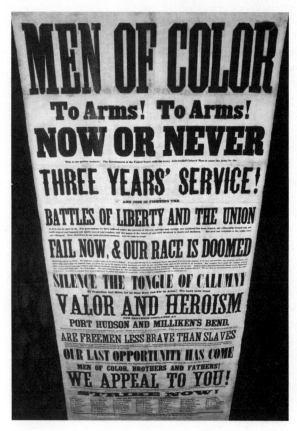

**Philadelphia Recruitment Poster.** The Emancipation Proclamation paved the way for African Americans to join the Union army. This recruitment poster appealed to men's sense of honor and duty and stressed the heroism shown by black soldiers at the battles of Port Hudson and Milliken's Bend, Louisiana.

it engaged in a Missouri skirmish. These black Kansans probably had more battle-field experience than any other African American regiment. The unit fought in twelve battles west of the Mississippi River and is ranked 21st among all Union regiments for the highest percentage of men killed in action.

The 54th Massachusetts was the most famous African American Civil War regiment. Massachusetts traditionally was an abolitionist stronghold, so it was no surprise when Governor John A. Andrew formed a regiment of free blacks in 1863. Robert Gould Shaw (1837–1863), the son of a prominent abolitionist, was chosen as the regiment's colonel. A veteran captain of the 2nd Massachusetts, he left the Army of the Potomac and returned home to begin recruiting. When it became apparent there were not enough interested free blacks in Massachusetts to form the regiment, blacks from other states were allowed to join. The 54th Massachusetts finally filled its ranks and was mustered into service in May 1863. When sent south, the regiment faced the same discrimination as other black units, and the men refused any pay until their pay was made equal to that of white soldiers. After fighting in a number of skirmishes in South Carolina, Georgia, and Florida, however, the men gained the respect of their white comrades. The most famous battle for the 54th Massachusetts was in July 1863 when it led an assault on Fort Wagner, South Carolina (discussed later in this chapter).

## Vindication

One of the most frustrating things for black soldiers was the refusal to use them in combat. African Americans were eager to fight the Rebels because they knew that was the only way to prove their worth as soldiers and to bolster their claim for equal rights. However, even most officers who supported enlisting blacks did not think they would fight well. As a result, USCT soldiers performed menial

**From "Contraband Jackson" to "Drummer Jackson."** These before and after photographs of a young runaway slave named Jackson were used to encourage African Americans to join the Union army. The photo on the left shows Jackson as he appeared when he reached Union lines. The photo on the right shows him after he enlisted in the 79th U.S. Colored Troops.

tasks such as digging ditches, building fortifications, or guarding prisoners and supply depots to free up white soldiers to fight.

It was not until May 1863 that black soldiers were used in a major battle. Needing every man he could muster for an attack on Port Hudson, Louisiana, General Nathaniel P. Banks placed the Louisiana Native Guards in his line and had them charge some of the strongest enemy defenses. In the fight, the black soldiers surprised everyone by advancing as far, if not farther, than the white troops that went in with them. Afterward, one soldier wrote in his diary, "The negroes are fighting bravely, and have triumphantly vindicated themselves from the aspersions cast upon their courage." A Massachusetts soldier at Port Hudson agreed and proclaimed, "All agree that none fought more boldly than the 'native guards.'" The baptism by fire at Port Hudson was soon followed by the bloody clash at Milliken's Bend, Louisiana, which

# NOTABLE UNITS: *Louisiana Native Guards*

When the Civil War began, New Orleans, Louisiana, had a large population of free men of color who were descended from French men and slave women. The 1860 census indicates that a few of them were rather wealthy and educated, but most were clerks, artisans, and craftsmen. These men of color had a long tradition of military service dating back more than one hundred years to the French militia. In 1861, they offered their services to the Confederacy. Governor Thomas Moore accepted them into the state militia, but officials refused to enlist them into the Confederate army. When Union forces occupied the city in the spring of 1862, the black militia disbanded their companies and some men offered their services to General Benjamin F. Butler. Congress had recently authorized the enlistment of black soldiers, so Butler mustered the 1st Regiment of Louisiana Native Guards into Union service in September, making it the first sanctioned regiment of African American troops in the U.S. Army. The black militiamen's change in loyalty led some historians to speculate that their previous offer to serve the Confederacy was made only to protect their economic and social status within the community. However, out of 1,135 men in the original unit, only 108 went on to serve in the Union army. This would seem to indicate that the vast majority of the black militiamen were sincere in their desire to fight for the South.

Some of the regiment's members came from prominent families. During a parade inspection, the Native Guards' colonel told another officer, "Sir, the best blood of Louisiana is in that regiment! Do you see that tall, slim fellow, third file from the right of the second company? One of the ex-governors of the State is his father. That orderly sergeant in the next company is the son of a man who has been six years in the United States Senate. Just beyond him is the grandson of Judge —— . . . ; and all through the ranks you will find the same state of facts. . . . Their fathers are disloyal;

received a great deal of coverage because the untrained black soldiers won. Even General Grant was impressed and wrote, "[T]heir conduct is said . . . to have been most gallant, and I doubt not but with good officers they will make good troops." Assistant Secretary of War Charles Dana went so far as to claim, "[T]he bravery of the blacks at Milliken's Bend completely revolutionized the sentiment of the army with regard to the employment of negro troops. I heard prominent officers who formerly in private had sneered at the idea of the negroes fighting express themselves after that as heartily in favor of it."

Two months later, Colonel Shaw's 54th Massachusetts made more headlines when it led the attack on Fort Wagner. Leading his men in the charge, Shaw reached the top of the Rebel parapet and turned to yell, "Onward, Fifth-fourth," when he was killed by a bullet to the chest. The regiment lost 272 out of 650 men engaged in the unsuccessful attack, and Sergeant William H. Carney was awarded the Medal of Honor for planting the regiment's colors on the enemy works. After the fight, the Confederates collected the Union

[but] these black Ishmaels will more than compensate for their treason by fighting it in the field."

The 2nd and 3rd Regiments, consisting mostly of former slaves, were mustered in later. In July 1863, the three regiments were brigaded together in what became known as the Corps D'Afrique (KOR-dah-FREEK). All three regiments had white colonels, but the line officers in the 1st and 2nd Regiments were black, while the 3rd Regiment had both black and white officers. These Louisianians were the only black officers in the Union army, but their racist superiors eventually purged most of them. By war's end only two black officers remained on duty in the entire U.S. Army, and both were with the Native Guards.

Like all African American soldiers, the Native Guards suffered from blatant discrimination. They received inferior pay, rations, and arms and frequently were harassed by white soldiers. Despite their poor treatment, the men served well and were among the first black units to see combat when they attacked the Confederate defenses at Port Hudson, Louisiana, in May 1863. Their bravery and heavy losses (169 casualties) convinced many Union officers to accept black combat soldiers in the army. After serving in the 1864 Red River Campaign, the Native Guards regiments were designated the 73rd, 74th, and 75th U.S. Colored Infantry. When the Union army attacked Fort Blakely, Alabama, in April 1865, the Native Guards led the charge, and one Union general wrote, "To the Seventy-third U.S. Colored Infantry belongs the honor of first planting their colors on the enemy parapet." The Native Guards were mustered out of service soon after the last Confederate surrender, and many of its members went on to become active in Reconstruction politics, including P. B. S. Pinchback, America's first black governor (see Chapter 25).

dead and buried them in a mass grave. Under a flag of truce, Shaw's men approached the fort to retrieve his body, but the Rebels told them, "We have buried him with his niggers!" Rather than taking this as an insult, Shaw's family saw it as a point of honor. They refused to exhume Shaw after the war and left him buried with his men.

Having proved themselves, black soldiers began to be used more in combat in all theaters of operation. By war's end, some 180,000 had served in the Union army, with more than 80 percent being former slaves in the Confederate states. They fought in approximately 450 battles and skirmishes and sustained 68,178 casualties, and 22 African American soldiers and sailors received the Medal of Honor. Recognizing their contributions, Lincoln predicted late in the war, "Abandon all the posts now garrisoned by black men, take 150,000 [black] men from our side and put them in the battlefield or cornfield against us, and we would be compelled to abandon the war in three weeks."

# EYEWITNESS
## 54th Massachusetts

*After suffering terrible losses at Fort Wagner, South Carolina, the 54th Massachusetts was sent to Florida. There in February 1864 it participated in another bloody battle when a small Union force was defeated at Olustee. Afterward, a black soldier identified only as E. D. W. wrote a letter to the Christian Recorder, a Philadelphia newspaper. In it, he gave a brief account of the Battle of Olustee and then vented his frustration concerning the army's discrimination.*

The battle took place in a grove called Olustee, with the different regiments as follows: First was the 8th U.S.; they were cut up badly, and they were the first colored regiment in the battle. The next were the 54th Mass., which I belong to; the next were the 1st N[orth].C[arolina]. In they went and fired a few rounds, but they soon danced out, things were too warm for them. The firing was very warm, and it continued for about three hours and a half. The 54th was the last off the field. When the 1st N.C. found out it was so warm they soon left, and then there was none left to cover the retreat. But Captain J. Walton, of the 54th, of our company, with shouts and cheers, cried, "give it to them my brave boys! Give it to them!" As I turned around, I observed Col. E. N. Holowell standing with a smile upon his countenance, as though the boys were playing a small game of ball. . . .

When we got there we rushed in double-quick, with a command from the General, "Right into line." We commenced with a severe firing, and the enemy soon gave way for some two hundred yards. Our forces were light, and we were compelled to fall back with much dissatisfaction. Now it seems strange to me that we do not receive the same pay and rations as the white soldiers. Do we not fill the same ranks? Do we not cover the same space of ground? Do we not take up the same length of ground in the grave-yard that others do? The ball does not miss the black man and strike the white, nor the white and strike the black. But, sir, at that time there is no distinction made, they strike one as much as another. The black men have to go through the same hurling of musketry, and the same belching of cannonading as white soldiers do.

It has been nearly a year since we have received any pay; but the white soldiers get their pay every two months; ($13.00 per month,) but when it comes to the poor negro he gets none. The 54th left Boston on the 28th of May, 1863. In time of enlisting members for the regiment, they were promised the same pay, and the same rations as other soldiers. Since that time the government must have charged them more for clothing than any other regiment; for those who died in a month or two after their enlistment, it was actually said that they were in debt to the government. . . . Why is it not so with other soldiers? Because our faces are black. . . .

## African American Sailors

While African American soldiers receive most attention by historians, blacks composed 16 percent of the U.S. Navy by war's end. African Americans actually

**African American Sailors.** Unlike the army, the U.S. Navy had a long tradition of allowing African Americans to serve in its ranks. These black sailors onboard the USS *Vermont* were just a few of the thousands who fought for the Union during the Civil War.

found the navy more racially tolerant than the army. For a number of reasons, the navy had allowed a quota of blacks to serve ever since the Revolutionary War. Most Americans viewed common sailors as lower-class men because they supposedly led a debauched lifestyle of drinking, gambling, and brawling. African Americans were also looked down on, so there was no social conflict in allowing blacks to join the navy and serve with other lower-class men. Also, unlike the volunteer army, the federal government controlled naval recruitment, not the states. This allowed officials to ignore local prejudices and recruit skilled sailors from all races and cultures. While most black soldiers were former slaves from rural areas, black sailors were mostly free men who came from urban areas. Interestingly, one out of eight African American sailors was an immigrant.

The navy abandoned its restrictive quota system and recruited blacks wholesale when it began to sustain high casualties during the Civil War. For the most part, black sailors were treated equally to white sailors aboard Union warships, although there was a great deal of social segregation and occasional racial tensions. Navy regulations required black sailors to be paid the same as whites and to receive the same prize money, discipline, and medical treatment.

However, it is revealing to note that while one out of seven black soldiers died from disease in the war, only one out of forty black sailors died.

## Retribution

Infuriated by the Emancipation Proclamation and the Union policy of recruiting black soldiers, the Confederate Congress passed a retaliatory resolution in May 1863. It stated that white Union officers who trained, led, or armed black soldiers were inciting servile insurrection and could be executed by a military court if captured. Any black soldier who was taken prisoner was to be turned over to the state government and dealt with as officials saw fit. As will be seen in Chapter 19, this refusal to treat black soldiers as prisoners of war led the Union to stop prisoner exchanges and to threaten retaliation for mistreated soldiers.

Many Confederates believed the Union policy of recruiting blacks was intended to incite slave rebellions. For many years, Southerners had suspected some slaves were looking for an opportunity to rise up in a frenzy of murder and rape and that Northern abolitionists encouraged such violence. The recruitment of runaway slaves seemed to confirm such suspicions. The Union's policy of putting former slaves in uniform also outraged the Confederates because it essentially recognized blacks as being equal to whites. With racial feelings running so high, it is no wonder that some of the war's worst atrocities occurred when the Rebels encountered black soldiers on the battlefield.

In October 1863, Confederate guerrillas under William C. Quantrill murdered a large number of black soldiers after surprising them at mealtime at Baxter Springs, Kansas. At Poison Springs, Arkansas, in April 1864, Confederate soldiers killed some members of the 1st Kansas Colored Volunteers who were trying to surrender. Three months later, the Rebels also killed a large number of black soldiers who were trying to surrender in Virginia's bloody Battle of the Crater, and in October 1864, Confederate guerrillas under Champ Ferguson murdered several wounded black soldiers at Saltville, Virginia.

The Battle of Milliken's Bend, Louisiana, which was one of the first battles in which black soldiers participated, also received a great deal of attention because of possible mistreatment of Union prisoners. Confederate correspondence regarding the fight is particularly revealing of the Southern attitude toward black soldiers. In the battle, about fifty blacks and two of their white officers were captured. When Lieutenant General Edmund Kirby Smith learned this, he wrote General Richard Taylor, "I hope this may not be so and that your subordinates who may have been in command of capturing parties may have recognized the propriety of giving no quarter to armed negroes and their officers. In this way we may be relieved from a disagreeable dilemma." That same day, the Confederate assistant secretary of war also wrote Taylor. He emphasized no quarter was to be given to black soldiers, but if any were taken prisoner they were to be turned over to the state government as required by the recently passed congressional measure. The secretary pointed out the advantage of letting the state government handle black prisoners. If the Confederate army executed prisoners, the Union army would retaliate, but such retaliation would be more difficult if Southern courts ordered the executions. For his part, Taylor termed the capture of black prisoners "unfortunate," but he turned them over to Louisiana officials as required by law.

In the following weeks, General Grant received numerous reports that Taylor had summarily executed a number of black prisoners and white officers after the Battle of Milliken's Bend. One newspaper even claimed the Rebels nailed prisoners to boards, leaned them against a house, and set the house on fire. Grant demanded an explanation from Taylor and threatened to retaliate against Confederate prisoners if the stories were true. Taylor vehemently denied the executions and assured Grant, "[M]y orders at all times have been to treat all prisoners with every consideration." Grant believed Taylor and wrote General-in-Chief Henry Halleck the rumors of executions were "entirely sensational." Exactly what happened to the Union prisoners at Milliken's Bend is still uncertain. Modern research into the controversy indicates the Confederates probably did execute two white Union officers shortly after the battle, but there is no evidence of Taylor's involvement. He apparently did follow Congress' instructions and turned his black prisoners over to Louisiana officials. All of them survived the war and returned to their units after the Confederate surrender.

The most famous battle involving the massacre of black soldiers took place at Fort Pillow, Tennessee. Located on the Mississippi River north of Memphis, this Union fort was garrisoned mostly by black soldiers. On April 12, 1864, Confederate Major General Nathan Bedford Forrest surrounded the fort, demanded its surrender, and warned the commander if he refused, "I cannot be responsible for the fate of your command." But the Union commander did refuse because he felt perfectly secure behind his breastworks. Many of the black soldiers even yelled taunts and insults at the enemy during the negotiations. When Forrest attacked and overran the fort, some Union soldiers fled toward the river and the protection of gunboats, while others tried to surrender. Many of the latter were shot dead by the Confederates. Forrest lost 100 men in the fight, while the Union garrison lost more than 500. Of those, 231 were killed outright (an incredibly high proportion of the casualties) and only 58 blacks were taken prisoners.

The Fort Pillow Massacre was one of the most controversial episodes of the war, and it was investigated by the Committee on the Conduct of the War. While there is no doubt Confederate soldiers murdered a large number of black soldiers, Forrest's guilt is disputed. While some Union soldiers testified he calmly watched the slaughter and did nothing to stop it, one officer claimed he saw Forrest trying to rein in his men and even watched him kill one of his own soldiers for disobeying his orders to give the blacks quarter. Union officials accused Forrest of ordering the massacre and branded him a war criminal, but it is more likely the murders were carried out by individual Confederates who hated the black soldiers.

# AFRICAN AMERICANS IN THE CONFEDERATE ARMY

## March 13, 1865: Confederate Congress authorizes enlisting slaves

Much has been written about African Americans serving the Union, but it should not be forgotten that they also played an important role in the Confederate army. While it is true that thousands of Southern slaves escaped captivity and joined the Union, the vast majority remained under Rebel control until war's end. These slaves greatly strengthened the rebellion by providing the South with millions of laborers who toiled on the farms and fortifications and in military factories. A few even donned gray uniforms and fought alongside white Confederates.

## Blacks in Gray

The Confederates depended on slaves to maintain the army by working in the fields and factories, but they did not want to recruit them to fight with the military. Major General Howell Cobb spoke for most white Southerners when he wrote, "If slaves will make good soldiers our whole theory of slavery is wrong." Nonetheless, there is no question that some slaves did make their way into gray uniforms; the more important question is how many.

Most of the evidence of black Confederates is anecdotal or based on second-hand observations. Ex-slave and abolitionist Frederick Douglass once noted, "There are at the present moment many colored men in the Confederate Army doing duty not only as cooks, servants and laborers, but as real soldiers, having muskets on their shoulders and bullets in their pockets, ready to shoot down . . . and do all that soldiers may do to destroy the Federal government." Newspaper editor Horace Greeley agreed and wrote, "For more than two years, Negroes have been extensively employed in belligerent operations by the Confederacy. They have been embodied and drilled as rebel soldiers and had paraded with white troops at a time when this would not have been tolerated in the armies of the Union." Union soldiers sometimes claimed to have seen uniformed black Confederates on the battlefield. One Indiana soldier wrote his father, "I can assure you, of a certainty, that the rebels have negro soldiers in their army. One of their best sharp shooters, and the boldest of them all here is a negro." Quoting a sergeant who was present at the Battle of Missionary Ridge, a Northern newspaper reported, "Ruby says among the rebel dead on the Ridge he saw a number of negroes in the Confederate uniform." The Louisiana Native Guards offered their services to the Confederacy when the war first began, and official records indicate some free blacks served as scouts for Nathan Bedford Forrest's cavalry. Tennessee officials also authorized the enlistment of African Americans into the state's military units, and some of those received state pensions after the war.

Some students of the Civil War have estimated thousands of blacks wore the gray, but there is no evidence to support such an exorbitant claim. Newspapers were notoriously inaccurate and should not be relied on when it comes to verifying African American units, and many of the black Confederates mentioned in letters were probably personal servants who accompanied their masters, even into battle. Some may have even been supplied uniforms when their clothing wore out, further confusing onlookers. The only way to verify the actual number of black Confederates is to examine first-person accounts and enlistment papers. If there were African American military units or large numbers of blacks serving in the Confederate army, white Southerners would have mentioned them in their letters, diaries, and official correspondence. They did not—the silence, in fact, is deafening. Louisiana, with its large population of free blacks and long history of racial mixing, would logically have provided more African American soldiers than any other Southern state (it did supply more black Union soldiers). A survey of state records, however, has revealed only a handful of blacks who served in the Confederate army. A fair assessment of the evidence leads to only one conclusion. Thousands of African Americans may have *accompanied* Confederate armies as cooks, servants, and teamsters, but the number of blacks who actually *served* in those armies was negligible.

## Enlisting Slaves

Few African Americans enlisted in the Confederate army because they had no interest in supporting the government that kept them enslaved, and the vast majority of Southern whites vehemently opposed their service. When some Confederate officers proposed enlisting slaves early in the war, the Confederate government effectively muzzled them. One official claimed after the war that General Richard S. Ewell recommended the enlistment of black troops to Jefferson Davis shortly after the First Battle of Bull Run. Davis rejected the idea on the grounds it would "disgust" the Southern people and that no officer would agree to lead blacks in combat. Undaunted, Ewell boldly replied he would lead them if given the opportunity, but Davis refused the request and asked Ewell not to discuss it further with anyone. In a postwar letter, Davis claimed not to remember such a conversation with Ewell, but he did reveal his feelings on the subject. "In the early period of the war," he wrote, "if the proposition had been made to me, to enroll the Blacks . . . I should have considered the proposition preposterous, but at the same time I desired, with the consent of their masters to have negroes employed and organized as laborers and teamsters and considered that it would be a very good preliminary training for armed service if they should be therefore required. Emancipation, as the the [sic] reward of faithful service in the Army, must have been a a [sic] condition attached to the enrollment of negroes as soldiers. . . ."

The Confederates' resistance to enlisting slaves began to weaken as the war dragged on and they became more desperate. By 1864, the South's white population could no longer replace the tremendous casualties suffered on the battlefield, and it was obvious European powers would never recognize the Confederacy unless slavery was abolished. Both political and military officials began to realize the Confederacy was facing defeat unless something drastic was done. In January 1864, while the Army of Tennessee was camped at Dalton, Georgia, Major General Patrick Cleburne wrote a proposal to enlist slaves with a promise of freedom if they served loyally. Brigadier General Lucius E. Polk claimed Cleburne was motivated by the realization that the Emancipation Proclamation

# BIOGRAPHY
## Frederick Douglass: The Sage of Anacostia

**Frederick Douglass**

Born Frederick Augustus Washington Bailey, Frederick Douglass (1817–1895) was the son of a white Maryland slaveholder and a slave. He was sent to live with a family in Baltimore where the household's mistress educated him even though it was against the law. Bailey was put to work as a ship's caulker and eventually made his escape to Massachusetts by pretending to be a free black sailor. Assuming the name Frederick Douglass to hide from slave catchers, he later married a free black woman named Anna Murray.

Douglass began making antislavery speeches in Massachusetts and was soon hired by the famous abolitionist William Lloyd Garrison to speak for the Massachusetts Anti-Slavery Society. Douglass's stories of slavery made him popular, and in 1845 he wrote the widely read *Narrative of the Life of Frederick Douglass*. Because his work required him to travel extensively (he even toured Great Britain for about two years), Douglass persuaded friends to buy his freedom so he could work without fear of being returned to Maryland as a runaway slave. He and Garrison eventually parted ways, however, because Douglass did not agree with Garrison's policy of moral suasion. Nonetheless, Douglass's fame grew after he began publishing the *North Star,* a New York abolitionist newspaper. In 1859, he was informed of John Brown's plan to raid Harpers Ferry, Virginia, but did not become involved because he thought it would do more harm than good. When Brown was captured, Douglass feared for his own safety because of his prior knowledge of the raid and fled to Canada.

Douglass eventually returned to the United States and continued to speak out for African American rights during the Civil War. "The destiny of the colored American,"

had turned Europe against the Confederates. Polk wrote, "[Cleburne] said the North had more money, & more men & access to the recruiting stations of the world and on account of Lincon's [*sic*] Emancipation proclamation the sympathy of the world and it could only be a question of time, when we would be entirely worn out, hemmed in as we were on every side and that this was a chance and a very good one for us. The Confederacy said to the world, We have the slaves & are willing to free them & this, as it were takes the sails out of Pres. Lincoln's proclamation."

Most of Cleburne's officers supported the proposal, but the army's ranking generals bitterly opposed him when he presented the paper at a meeting known as the Dalton Conference. General William B. Bate later claimed when his men heard rumors of the plan, "Many of my boys were making ready to go home, if it was done." Cleburne's opponents quickly informed Jefferson Davis of the radical proposal, and the president admitted, "The suggestion excited a very indignant feeling among many of the officers of that army. . . ." By that time, he declared, "is the destiny of America." Douglass strongly supported the Union war effort and pressured Lincoln to free the slaves and enlist black troops. The latter cause was a particular goal of his, and soon after the war began, he declared, "The national edifice is on fire. Every man who can carry a bucket of water, or remove a brick, is wanted, but those who have the care of the building, having a profound respect for the feeling of the national burglars who set the building on fire, are determined that the flames shall only be extinguished by Indo-Caucasian hands, and to have the building burnt rather than save it by means of any other. Such is the pride, the stupid prejudice and folly that rules the hour." When officials proved reluctant to use black troops even after the Emancipation Proclamation was issued, Douglass stated, "I hold that the [Emancipation] Proclamation, good as it is, will be worthless—a miserable mockery—unless the nation shall so far conquer its prejudice as to welcome into the army full-grown black men to help fight the battles of the Republic." Eventually, he was successful in helping raise the famous 54th Massachusetts, and two of his sons served in the Union army. Although sometimes frustrated by Lincoln's cautious approach to emancipation and slow acceptance of black troops, Douglass could not help but admire the president. He knew the risk Lincoln took in issuing the Emancipation Proclamation and recalled his anxiety while attending the president's second inauguration. "I felt then that there was murder in the air," Douglass wrote, "and I kept close to his carriage on the way to the Capitol, for I felt that I might see him fall that day."

During Reconstruction, Douglass was an ally of the Radical Republicans, and he served in a number of minor government positions, including marshal for Washington, D.C. (he was the first black to hold the post), and minister to Haiti. At the end of Reconstruction, he bought an estate in Washington's Anacostia district and became known as the "Sage of Anacostia" because of his eloquent speeches.

Davis realized using black soldiers might someday become a necessity, but he was not yet ready to adopt such a policy and ordered the matter dropped to avoid the political firestorm he knew such a proposal would ignite.

Confederate officials said little more about enlisting slaves until early 1865, when Lee's army was facing imminent defeat at Petersburg. Forced to take drastic measures, Lee finally supported a bill that was introduced in Congress in March to enlist slaves into the army. No explicit promise was made to free those who served, but freedom was implied. Lee, who thought the bill's passage was necessary for Confederate survival, wrote, "We must decide whether slavery shall be extinguished by our enemies and the slave be used against us, or use them ourselves at the risk of the effects which may be produced upon our social institutions." When the legislation passed, Lee put General Ewell in charge of raising the black recruits and cautioned him, "It is however of primary importance that the negroes should know that the service is voluntary on their part. . . . Harshness and contemptuous or offensive language or conduct to them must be forbidden and they should be made to forget as soon as possible that they were regarded as inferior."

Ewell and Lee were frustrated when they met stiff opposition from slaveholders who did not want to relinquish their slaves for military duty. And the few slaves who did enlist were sometimes badly treated in violation of Lee's instructions. Ewell wrote, "Some of the bl[ac]k soldiers were whipped—they were hooted at & treated generally in a way to nullify the laws." He became very bitter over the experience and was convinced black Confederate soldiers could have made a difference if Lee's instructions had been followed. Following Virginia's lead, North Carolina and Georgia soon authorized the enlistment of blacks into their state's military units, but by then it was too late to do any good. Apparently, the only black Confederate unit that became fully operational was a small battalion that served in the Richmond defenses and which may have participated in a skirmish during the Appomattox Campaign.

## The Balance Sheet

It is ironic that African Americans probably played a greater role in aiding the Confederacy than runaway slaves did in aiding the Union. While 180,000 blacks served in the Union military, several million continued to toil in the South supplying the Rebels with food and fodder and keeping their war industries operating. Large numbers of slaves also accompanied the Confederate armies serving as laborers, teamsters, and servants. Undeniably, black Union soldiers performed heroic service and their very presence in the army helped boost Northern morale and spread gloom among the Confederates. However, black Union soldiers did not win the Civil War because they made up only about 10 percent of the Union forces. The North still would have won even if no African Americans had volunteered for service, but the Confederacy would have been defeated much sooner if no slaves had been working in the South. Perhaps the most important result of black military service was that it strengthened the hand of African Americans during Reconstruction. Northerners *believed* black soldiers were needed to achieve victory, and African Americans *knew* military service was necessary to bolster their claim for equal rights. It would have been much more difficult for them to have received the right to vote during Reconstruction if they had not done their part to win the war.

## *FOR FURTHER READING*

"The Prayer of Twenty Millions" and Lincoln's reply
Confiscation Acts
John C. Frémont's Proclamation on Slaves
David Hunter's Proclamation on Slaves
The District of Columbia Emancipation Act
Emancipation Proclamation
Thirteenth Amendment

# CHAPTER 10

# The Diplomatic War

The Civil War and Europe

Belligerents and Blockades

Recognition and Intervention

Rams and Raiders

On September 14, 1862, British Prime Minister Lord John Palmerston wrote Foreign Secretary Lord John Russell to inform him of Robert E. Lee's recent victory at Second Bull Run. Union forces "had got a very complete smashing," declared Palmerston, and he predicted the Confederates would likely capture Washington or Baltimore and deal the Union a crippling blow. "If this should happen," he asked, "would it not be time for us to consider whether in such a state of things England and France might not address the contending parties and recommend an arrangement upon the basis of a separation?" Lord Russell agreed and suggested that if the United States refused, "[We] ought ourselves to recognize the Southern States as an independent State." Chancellor of the Exchequer William Gladstone was of the same mind and wrote, "[T]he South cannot be conquered. . . . It is our absolute duty to recognize . . . that Southern independence is established."

Shortly after writing his letter, Palmerston learned Lee was making a raid into Maryland and wrote Russell, "It is evident that a great conflict is taking place to the northwest of Washington, and its issue must have a great effect on the state of affairs. If the Federals sustain a great defeat, they may be at once ready for mediation, and the iron should be struck while it is hot. If, on the other hand, they should have the best of it, we may wait awhile and see what may follow. . . ." Thus, in the end, the British decided to hedge their bets and take no action until it was clear who had won the Antietam Campaign. For nearly a year and a half, the British government had walked a fine line, providing cautious support for the fledging Confederacy without becoming directly involved in the war. It now appeared British foreign policy would be decided on the battlefield.

The Confederates entered the war at a great military disadvantage, having far fewer people, industry, and railroads than the Union. From the outset, Confederate officials realized they would have to acquire much of their war material from Europe, and they were determined to win diplomatic recognition to give the Confederacy legitimacy on the world stage. Some Confederates even believed Great Britain and France would intervene directly in the war and help the South win independence, much as France had aided the United States during the American Revolution. As a result, the Confederates adopted a foreign policy that was the reverse of their military strategy. On the battlefield, they opted to stay largely on the defensive to protect their territory. In diplomacy, however, the Confederates took the offensive, claiming the status of an independent nation, officially declaring war on the United States, and aggressively seeking foreign diplomatic recognition and European military aid and allies.

The Union's foreign policy was also the reverse of its military strategy. Northern armies generally took the offensive to conquer enemy territory, but the government's diplomatic efforts were more defensive in nature. It insisted the conflict was an internal rebellion, not a war between sovereign governments, and tried to prevent foreign nations from recognizing an independent Confederacy or becoming involved in the war militarily. The Union also established a naval blockade of the Southern coast to prevent the Rebels from receiving foreign aid.

In the diplomatic realm, the Confederates had reasons to be optimistic about gaining foreign support. Europeans had become increasingly concerned about the growing power of the United States as the new nation flexed its muscles in the early nineteenth century. The Americans had expanded their border to the Pacific Ocean by using military threats to convince Great Britain to divide the Oregon Territory and by defeating Mexico in war. The Monroe Doctrine also claimed the Western Hemisphere as an American sphere of influence and forbade establishment of any new colonies there. The U.S. Navy had forced Japan to open up to western trade, and Yankee businessmen were competing with the Europeans in the China trade and whaling industry. It seemed obvious to Europeans that the United States would only grow stronger in the future and become more and more a threat to their interests.

## THE CIVIL WAR AND EUROPE

### April 1, 1861: Seward submits to Lincoln "Some Thoughts for the President's Consideration"

With its far-flung empire, Great Britain faced the greatest threats from growing American power. In both the Revolutionary War and War of 1812, the United States had invaded Canada, and its booming economic growth seemed likely to pose a serious threat to British trade. A Confederate nation, on the other hand, would be a natural ally to Great Britain because its economy was almost

entirely dependent on exporting agricultural products and importing manufactured goods. France and Spain also feared the United States might interfere with their plans to extend their influence in the Western Hemisphere.
A friendly and relatively weak Confederate nation would give France a freer
hand in Mexico and Spain in the Caribbean than would a strong, anti-European
United States. In short, even though most Europeans opposed slavery, all three
nations would benefit politically and economically if America split into two
competing countries.

Some European leaders had another reason to support the Confederacy.
Although their views were not shared by all and were often exaggerated, some
members of Europe's aristocracy were concerned that American democracy
might spread across the Atlantic and threaten their status. For the upper class,
it would be better if the United States collapsed into two separate nations to
show Europe's commoners the weakness of democracy. Europe's aristocracy,
however, did not speak for the masses, and many people supported the Union.
Labor leaders knew trade ties with the United States meant jobs, and European abolitionists opposed the Confederacy because it promoted slavery. Many
upper-class European liberals also championed democracy and hoped the
American experiment would survive intact.

## Seward's Thoughts for the President

Many in Britain supported the Confederacy because they intensely disliked and
distrusted U.S. Secretary of State William H. Seward. They believed Seward
was a dangerous man because of anti-British remarks he had made before taking office. On one occasion, he publicly boasted he would intentionally provoke the British, and a German diplomat claimed Seward told him, "If the Lord
would only give the United States an excuse for a war with England, France, or
Spain, that would be the best means of reestablishing internal peace."

The Europeans may have been justified in fearing Seward. On April 1, 1861,
he submitted a rather strange memorandum to President Lincoln entitled,
"Some Thoughts for the President's Consideration." In it, Seward claimed the
administration had no domestic or foreign policy and proceeded to instruct the
president on what action he should take. He urged Lincoln to remain focused
on reuniting the nation and not to become distracted by the emancipation question. Using bold print for emphasis, Seward wrote, "[W]e must CHANGE THE
QUESTION BEFORE THE PUBLIC FROM ONE UPON SLAVERY, OR ABOUT
SLAVERY, for a question upon UNION OR DISUNION." Turning to foreign affairs,
Seward then recommended "explanations" be demanded immediately from
Great Britain, France, Spain, and Russia on their intentions in the Western
Hemisphere, and agents be sent throughout the hemisphere to stir up the
people against the Europeans. If satisfactory explanations were not received,
he advised Lincoln to convene Congress for a declaration of war. Seward ended
his memorandum by recommending that one person be put in charge of this
policy. "Once adopted," he wrote, "debates on it must end, and all agree and

# BIOGRAPHY

## William Henry Seward: "A Dangerous Foreign Minister"

**William H. Seward**

William H. Seward (1801–1872) was a New York native who served as a Whig state senator and two-term governor before becoming a U.S. senator. He was a political reformer who opposed slavery, championed civil rights, and worked to improve education. Although he was a moderate, Seward made two controversial speeches that caused many voters to view him as a dangerous man. In one speech against the Compromise of 1850, he condemned slavery and called for Americans to follow a "higher law than the Constitution, the law of God." In another, Seward warned that an "irrepressible conflict" was brewing between the North and South. After joining the Republican Party, he became a presidential contender in 1856 and 1860, but his earlier inflammatory statements derailed his nomination. Lincoln appointed Seward secretary of state in deference to his party service and political clout, but Seward had difficulty accepting Lincoln as head of state and at first viewed himself as the administration's leader.

In foreign policy, Seward was openly anti-British. Before joining the cabinet, he declared that if he became secretary of state it would "become my duty to insult England, and I mean to do so." Europeans were appalled when they learned Seward advised Lincoln to start a foreign war to diffuse the secession crisis at home. British ambassador Lord Richard Lyons believed he was "a dangerous foreign minister," and even American minister Charles Francis Adams, Sr., claimed the British viewed Seward as "an ogre fully resolved to eat all Englishmen raw."

Despite his sometimes bombastic style, Seward performed well as secretary of state once Lincoln made it clear that he would make foreign policy and lead the administration, rather than relinquish that authority to Seward. It was Seward who skillfully defused the 1861 *Trent* Affair, worked with Adams to convince the British to withhold the Laird Rams from the Rebels, and helped prevent foreign nations from recognizing

abide. It is not in my especial province; but I neither seek to evade nor assume responsibility."

Seward's controversial memorandum has usually been viewed as both a transparent attempt to become the administration's policymaker and a dangerous suggestion to create a foreign war to bring the Southern states back into the Union so Americans could face a common foreign threat together. However, Seward may have simply been acting in good faith as secretary of state. It was well known at the time that France was seeking to turn Mexico into a puppet state to extend its influence in the Western Hemisphere, and Spain had already sent troops to Santo Domingo (modern-day Dominican Republic) to aid rebels there (the following month Spain incorporated Santo Domingo back into the Spanish empire). It would have been entirely appropriate for the United States the Confederacy. Lincoln came to trust him in both diplomatic and domestic affairs and followed his advice to delay issuing the Emancipation Proclamation until after a military victory was achieved so it would not appear, as Seward said, to be "a shriek from and for the Administration, rather than for freedom." By war's end, Seward was one of the most powerful men in government because Lincoln also gave him broad authority to crush internal dissent by detaining political prisoners indefinitely. But he also was often at the center of controversy. Seward particularly clashed with Secretary of the Treasury Salmon P. Chase because they frequently disagreed on issues and both were presidential hopefuls. The pair offered their resignations several times, but Lincoln refused to accept them because he realized it was better to have Seward and Chase working within the administration than to have them on the outside criticizing.

A moderate who disliked all radicals, Seward wanted to build a true national party that would include Republicans, Southern loyalists, and Democrats. He largely succeeded when he helped convince Lincoln to run for reelection on the National Union Party ticket rather than as a Republican. During the 1864 campaign, Seward avoided making emancipation a major issue because many Northerners still opposed fighting to free the slaves. In one speech, he even waffled on the Thirteenth Amendment by stating that the Emancipation Proclamation was a military measure necessary to win the war, and the courts could decide the status of slavery once the Confederates were defeated.

In April 1865, Seward was severely wounded by one of John Wilkes Booth's conspirators on the same night Booth shot Lincoln. The would-be assassin cut up Seward with a knife as the secretary was recuperating in bed from a carriage accident, but Seward recovered from his wounds, resumed his duties, and performed outstanding service for President Andrew Johnson. He supported Johnson's lenient Reconstruction policies, opened negotiations with Great Britain on the *Alabama* Claims, pressured the French to leave Mexico, and supervised the purchase of Alaska ("Seward's Folly") from Russia in 1867.

to seek "explanations" from the French and Spanish to clarify their intentions in the Western Hemisphere. If they were planning to invade Latin America, the United States would also have been justified in going to war to enforce the Monroe Doctrine.

Whatever Seward's true intentions might have been, the memo troubled Lincoln. In particular, he took offense at Seward's contention that the administration had no policy. In a measured response, the president reminded Seward that he had established in his inaugural speech the administration's goals to protect and maintain all federal property and to collect the tariff. Lincoln also pointed out, "This had your distinct approval at the time. . . ." The president did not mention Seward's suggestion that explanations be demanded from foreign powers, but he did declare that while he would seek advice from the cabinet,

IN A POSITION TO BE RECOGNISED.
THE CELEBRATED SEPOY JUGGLER AND ACROBAT, JEFF DAVIS, IN HIS DANGEROUS
GLOBE FEAT

**President Davis, the Acrobat, on Rope of Cotton.** This political cartoon is a clever commentary on the difficulties Jefferson Davis faced when the Confederacy was formed. Waving a flag declaring that the Confederates just want to be left alone, he is trying to maintain his balance on a smoking bomb that represents the Confederacy. Both he and the Confederacy are supported by a cotton rope that is beginning to fray.

he alone would make the administration's policy. "I must do it," Lincoln wrote emphatically.

Fortunately for the Union, the very skillful Charles Francis Adams, Sr., served as minister to Great Britain and helped balance the Anglophobe Seward. The son of former President John Quincy Adams, Charles Francis was a former Massachusetts congressman. Adams's primary mission was to keep the British from recognizing the Confederacy as a legitimate nation and providing it with war materials. Appreciating the difficult task that lay ahead, he wrote in his diary on assuming his post, "My duty here is, so far as I can do it honestly, to prevent the mutual irritation from coming to a downright quarrel. It seems to me like throwing the game into the hands of the enemy. . . . If a conflict with a handful of slaveholding States is to bring us to [grief] what are we to do when we throw down the glove to Europe?" Adams proved to be an effective minister because he had just the right balance of tact and determination. The British appreciated his calm and rational demeanor, and his popularity with officials allowed him to politic behind the scenes during the many dinner parties to which he was invited.

## Cotton Diplomacy

When the Confederates began formulating their foreign policy in 1861, they intended to make good use of their leading export—cotton. For many years, Southerners had referred to it as "King Cotton" because of its importance to the world economy. Southern states supplied 80 percent of Great Britain's cotton, and the secessionists believed they could use it as a persuasive diplomatic weapon. Convinced the Europeans' important textile industry was dependent on their exports, the Confederates believed a cotton embargo would devastate the European economy and throw thousands of laborers out of work. Before the war even began, South Carolina Senator James Hammond predicted if the supply of Southern cotton was disrupted, "Old England would topple headlong and carry the whole civilized world with her."

In an informal policy known as Cotton Diplomacy, the Confederates quickly took steps to put pressure on the Europeans by restricting cotton exports. The Southerners not only relied on the Union blockade cutting off cotton, they also intentionally held back exports to threaten Europe's economy in hopes the Europeans would be forced to extend them diplomatic recognition, offer to mediate a peace with the Union, or even break the blockade to avoid economic disaster. As one Southerner told British war correspondent William Howard Russell, "Why, I expect sir, that if those miserable Yankees try to blockade us, and keep you from our cotton, you'll just send their ships to the bottom and acknowledge us." Unfortunately, the Confederates overestimated Europe's dependence on Southern cotton. Great Britain and France managed to stockpile a cotton surplus from the 1860 bumper crop and were able to weather the initial loss of trade. The embargo did begin to have an adverse effect in Great Britain when the surplus ran out in 1862 and textile mills were forced to cut workers' hours, but the British were eventually able to acquire enough cotton from Egypt, India, and Brazil to make up for the loss.

Besides overestimating the importance of Southern cotton to the European economy, the Confederates also underestimated Europe's need for Northern products. The North actually produced more food crops than the South, and Great Britain was importing tons of wheat after suffering several years of crop failures. Wheat was much more important to the British than cotton, and they simply were not willing to anger the North and risk losing that trade. If forced to choose, they would choose to maintain their food supply.

When the Confederates realized they had made a mistake with Cotton Diplomacy and tried to resume large shipments in 1863, the blockade had become more effective and it became difficult to conduct any foreign trade. In the end, Cotton Diplomacy actually weakened the Confederacy. Desperate for European weapons, medicine, and loans, the Rebels would have been better served if they had adopted a completely different policy. If Davis had shipped as much cotton as possible overseas in the early days of the war when the Union blockade was weak, the Confederates could have stockpiled huge amounts of cotton in Europe to use as collateral for loans and to purchase badly needed war material. This might have kept them financially solvent for a longer period of time and staved off the severe shortages suffered later in the war.

## BELLIGERENTS AND BLOCKADES

**March 16, 1861: Confederates send envoys to Europe to seek diplomatic recognition**

**April 19, 1861: Lincoln declares a blockade of Southern ports**

**May 13, 1861: Great Britain grants belligerent status to the Confederacy**

**May 21, 1861: U.S. threatens to break diplomatic relations with Britain if it continues to meet with Confederate envoys**

**June 12, 1861: Britain agrees to stop meeting with Confederate envoys**

**November 8, 1861: Mason and Slidell are captured in the *Trent* Affair**

**January 1, 1862: Mason and Slidell are released**

# BIOGRAPHY

## Judah Philip Benjamin: Davis's Loyal Friend

**Judah P. Benjamin**

Judah P. Benjamin (1811–1884) was a unique Civil War figure. Born in the Virgin Islands, he was the most prominent Confederate cabinet member (heading three departments), and he was the only Jew to hold a high position in either government. After his British parents moved to the United States in 1816, Benjamin grew up in South Carolina and entered Yale University at age fourteen. Dropping out of college, he moved to New Orleans and became a law partner with influential Louisiana politician John Slidell. While in the Crescent City, Benjamin also married Natalie St. Martin, a member of a prominent Catholic family, but the marriage was not a happy one. After giving birth to a daughter, Natalie moved to Paris and remained there for nearly all of their fifty-plus years of marriage.

After serving in the state legislature, Benjamin was elected to the U.S. Senate in 1852 and there met Jefferson Davis. When Davis became president of the Confederacy, he appointed Benjamin attorney general and trusted his judgment in all matters. In turn, Benjamin was completely devoted to the Confederacy and gave Davis his unwavering loyalty. After seven months, the president made Benjamin secretary of war even though he had no military experience. Davis viewed the War Department as his exclusive domain and simply needed a loyal person to handle the day-to-day administrative details while he formulated policy and ran the military.

Despite having Davis's trust, Benjamin was unpopular in some circles. One Richmond newspaper referred to him as "a foreigner and a Jew," and former Virginia governor Henry A. Wise claimed he "had more brains and less heart than any other civil leader in the South." Benjamin resigned his position in March 1862 after many politicians blamed him for the defeats at Port Royal, South Carolina, and Fort Donelson,

The failure of Cotton Diplomacy was not apparent when Davis and Secretary of State Robert Toombs sent envoys William Lowndes Yancey, Pierre A. Rost, and A. Dudley Mann to Europe. It was a poor selection because two of the three men had absolutely no diplomatic experience. Yancey, an influential Alabama fire-eater, was completely unqualified for his mission, and his volatile personality and uncompromising beliefs were not suited for a diplomat trying to win support from an overwhelmingly antislavery Europe. Rost, a native of France and a Louisiana supreme court justice, was the Confederate representative to France, but he failed to impress his hosts because he did not speak the language well and seemed completely out of touch with reality. When asked how the war was progressing, Rost always replied, "All goes well," even after the enemy had confiscated his Louisiana plantation. Of the three envoys, only Mann had any

Tennessee. Secretary of State Robert M. T. Hunter resigned at the same time, so Davis appointed Benjamin secretary of state. The decision angered many politicians, and some even began referring to Benjamin as Davis's "pet Jew."

Great Britain's refusal to extend diplomatic recognition to the Confederacy frustrated Benjamin. He wrote, "When successful fortune smiles on our arms, the British cabinet is averse to recognition because 'it would be unfair to the South by the action of Great Britain to exasperate the North to renewed efforts.' When reverses occur . . . 'it would be unfair to the North in a moment of success to deprive it of a reasonable opportunity of accomplishing a reunion of the States.'" Benjamin realized slavery was an impediment to gaining foreign recognition and supported enlisting slaves into the army and emancipating them to show the world the war was about Southern independence and not slavery. With Davis's reluctant permission, Benjamin sent an envoy to Europe to seek recognition in return for emancipation, but it was too late to do any good.

Benjamin was a brilliant cabinet member, but many people disliked him because of his Jewish heritage and a perpetual smile that made him appear flippant and unconcerned. He also clashed with professional soldiers such as Stonewall Jackson and P. G. T. Beauregard, who resented taking orders from someone with no military experience. But Benjamin never complained. One observer wrote, "[H]e bore the universal attack with admirable good nature and sang froid. . . . to all appearances, equally secure in his own views and indifferent to public odium, he passed from reverse to reverse with perfectly bland manner and unwearying courtesy." Benjamin took the criticism in stride and claimed it was "wrong and useless to disturb oneself and thus weaken one's energy to bear what was foreordained."

The Lincoln assassination greatly distressed Benjamin because he had prior dealings with some of the conspirators. Fearing arrest, he escaped capture after the Confederate surrender and fled to Great Britain. Becoming a wealthy barrister, Benjamin never returned to the United States.

diplomatic experience. Before the war, the Virginian served as the American consul to a Germanic state and an assistant secretary of state under President Franklin Pierce. Mann, however, also had a contentious and arrogant personality that could make him difficult to work with.

## Belligerent Status

The three Confederate envoys arrived in Great Britain in April 1861 and began lobbying the government for diplomatic recognition. The media gave them a great deal of coverage, and the trio moved easily among London's social elite holding many talks with various officials. In early May, Foreign Secretary Lord Russell even agreed to meet Yancey and Rost informally. Despite failing to secure diplomatic recognition or a treaty of commerce, they did win a significant victory when Great Britain announced its neutrality in the conflict and recognized the Confederacy as a belligerent.

Belligerency was recognized by nineteenth-century international law as one of three wartime categories. A belligerent power was a nation actively involved in the war; a non-belligerent was a nation that perhaps sympathized with a belligerent but was not actually involved in the conflict; and a neutral was a nation that was not involved in the war in any way. Granting belligerent status was not the same as diplomatic recognition, but it did make the Confederacy a legitimate combatant. As belligerents, Rebel ships would enjoy the same rights as Union ships in British ports, and Confederate agents could negotiate for British loans and buy British war supplies. Secretary of State Seward protested Lord Russell's decision and argued that the war was an internal rebellion that did not warrant such foreign action, but his objection was ignored, and France, Spain, and several other nations followed Great Britain's lead.

## Blockade and Privateers

Ironically, two steps taken by President Lincoln helped convince the British to recognize the Confederacy as a belligerent. Most important was the blockade he placed around the Southern coast. International law stated that blockades were only declared in a time of war between two independent *nations*. In declaring the blockade, Lincoln committed something of a diplomatic blunder because he in essence recognized the Confederacy as a belligerent power. Taking advantage of Lincoln's mistake, Britain quickly recognized the blockade and thus stood on firm legal ground in extending belligerent status to the Rebels.

The British decision to recognize the blockade was rather brilliant because they had an ulterior motive. The 1856 Declaration of Paris stipulated a blockade had to be "physically effective" to be legal. In other words, simply declaring a blockade did not make it a fact; the blockading power had to be able physically to prevent ships from passing through the blockade for it to have any legal standing. In the war's early months, Lincoln's blockade was clearly not effective because only a handful of Union ships were patrolling the Confederate coast, but the British recognized it anyhow. By doing so, they ensured American cooperation in future British blockades. Previously, the United States had held strictly to the law that blockades had to be effective to be legal because it wanted to trade with belligerent powers such as France during times of war between France and Great Britain. Great Britain, on the other hand, historically interpreted blockade law rather loosely to stop the United States from trading with France during wartime. During the Civil War, the two nations reversed their policies. The United States interpreted the law loosely because Lincoln wanted Great Britain to respect his ineffective blockade and not trade with the Confederacy, and the British reversed their traditional policy and agreed to respect the blockade but only to further their own diplomatic agenda. By accepting the weak Union blockade as legal and effective, they were forcing the United States to adopt British policy. In the future, the Americans would have to reciprocate and recognize any British blockade, whether or not it was "physically effective."

Lincoln's decision to treat captured Confederate privateers as prisoners of war was the other reason the British recognized the Confederacy as a belligerent. When Lincoln announced Rebel privateers would be treated as pirates, he demanded that other nations adopt a similar policy, but Great Britain refused because it would violate Britain's neutrality by forcing it to favor the North. The British also pointed out that Confederate privateers had to be treated as prisoners of war because the blockade declaration extended belligerent status to the Confederates. When the Lincoln administration backed down from the issue during the *Enchantress* Affair (discussed later in this chapter) and agreed to treat enemy privateers as prisoners of war, the British accepted the decision as de facto Union recognition of the Confederacy as a belligerent power and followed suit.

Gaining belligerent status was a major victory for Confederate envoys Yancey and Rost. Unsure what other concessions the British might give the Southerners, Seward took the drastic step of ordering Minister Adams to break diplomatic relations with Britain if Lord Russell continued to meet with the Confederates. Seward's message was abrupt, and its combative tone surprised and concerned Adams. He wrote in his diary, "[T]he government seems ready to declare war with all the powers of Europe . . . I scarcely know how to understand Mr. Seward." Considering British hostility toward Seward, Adams decided not to show the message to Russell and simply gave him a synopsis of the order. Seward's threat and Adams's diplomatic efforts worked, and Russell refused ever again to meet with the Confederates.

## The *Trent* Affair

Relations between the United States and Great Britain took a dramatic turn for the worse in late 1861 when President Davis appointed James Mason and John Slidell as envoys to Great Britain and France, respectively. Learning of the mission, Captain Charles Wilkes, commander of the USS *San Jacinto,* intercepted the British mail packet *Trent* east of Cuba on November 8 and forcibly removed Mason and Slidell. Described by one man as having "a superabundance of self-esteem and a deficiency of judgment," Wilkes had gained some fame before the war by discovering Antarctica. When Herman Melville learned of the captain's harsh treatment of sailors during the cruise, he based *Moby Dick's* Captain Ahab partly on Wilkes's abusive personality. Initially, Northerners praised Captain Wilkes as a hero, despite the fact that he had acted without orders and violated the long-held American principle of freedom of the seas. Wilkes justified his actions by claiming international law allowed belligerents to stop neutral vessels to search for contraband or enemy dispatches. With rather ingenious logic, he argued Mason and Slidell *were* dispatches by virtue of their knowledge of Rebel plans.

British Prime Minister Lord Palmerston was outraged at the seizure, and he roared at the cabinet, "You may stand for this but damned if I will!" Palmerston rightfully complained that British neutral rights had been violated and demanded an apology and the envoys' release. Even if Mason and Slidell were contraband, he pointed out, the ship should have been taken to a Union port and the seizure carried out properly through a prize court. The *Trent* Affair put Lincoln in a difficult situation. Despite Captain Wilkes's arguments to the contrary, Lincoln and Seward knew the seizures were indefensible and worried that the incident might bring Great Britain into the war on the Confederates' side. Releasing the diplomats, however, would make Lincoln appear weak and could damage the administration politically.

While the Union government pondered what to do, the British prepared for action. In a dangerous display of saber rattling, Palmerston formed a War Committee, alerted the navy for possible action, and shipped 11,000 troops to Canada while bands on the dock played "Dixie." For a few weeks it appeared Secretary of State Seward might get his foreign war after all, but this was not what he had in mind. Conflict with Great Britain and the Confederates at the same time would stretch Union resources to the limit and possibly ensure Southern independence.

Ultimately, it was the Anglophobe Seward who solved the crisis. On Christmas Day, he convinced the cabinet to release the Confederate envoys but without an apology. Seward pointed out Wilkes's action was essentially impressment, the same British policy that started the War of 1812. By releasing the envoys, he argued, the United States was simply staying true to its long-standing commitment to freedom of the seas. Lincoln put it succinctly when he stated, "We must stick to American principles concerning the rights of neutrals. We fought Great Britain [in 1812] for insisting, by theory and practice, on the right to do precisely what Wilkes has done." Interestingly, by condemning the capture of Mason and Slidell, the British were publicly denouncing their own former impressment policy and recognizing America's concept of freedom of the seas. Great Britain reversed its long-standing policy in the *Trent* Affair, just as the United States reversed its policy in the blockade controversy.

Although he claimed it was "the bitterest pill" he'd had to swallow, Lincoln released Mason and Slidell on January 1, 1862, and they continued to Europe to replace Yancey, Rost, and Mann. Neither enjoyed any success in winning diplomatic recognition, but Slidell did arrange the Erlanger Loan (see Chapter 11) to provide some money to the Confederacy. After all the trouble their capture had caused, Mason and Slidell turned out to be almost complete failures.

# RECOGNITION AND INTERVENTION

**September 22, 1862: Lincoln issues Preliminary Emancipation Proclamation**
**July 4, 1863: Battles of Gettysburg and Vicksburg end danger of Europe**
    **recognizing the Confederacy**
**May 5, 1864: Maximilian arrives in Mexico to become emperor**
**June 19, 1867: Mexican forces capture Maximilian**

Two of the Confederacy's most important diplomatic goals were to secure diplomatic recognition from the major European powers and to persuade them to intervene directly in the war on the Confederacy's behalf. As the war dragged on, the British and French gave serious thought to taking such action, and many British citizens supported some sort of intervention simply to halt the slaughter for humanity's sake. Despite their political differences, the Americans and British were cousins, and the British wanted to stop the killing. As one newspaper declared, "Let us do something . . . arbitration, intervention, diplomatic action, recognition . . . let us do something to stop this carnage."

Pragmatic reasons, however, forced Britain to be cautious in its approach to the war. Seward instructed Adams to inform the British that recognition of the Confederacy or involvement in the rebellion could lead to war. Seward warned Britain that if it recognized the Confederacy, "We from that hour shall cease to be friends and become once more, as we have twice before been forced to be, enemies of Great Britain." Such a threat was enough to give Britain reason to pause, for a war with the United States could be devastating. The greatest mistake the British could make would be to poison relations with the United States by moving too quickly to recognize the Confederacy and then see it defeated. Badly needed American trade might be disrupted, Canada might be invaded, and future conflicts created. In Britain's view, any overt action was out of the question unless the Confederates proved they could win the war. Since the war remained a military stalemate for several years, Great Britain adopted a wait-and-see policy, and France, Spain, and Russia followed suit.

Great Britain came closest to intervening in the war in the summer of 1862 when Robert E. Lee won a series of spectacular victories in Virginia. Adams was gravely concerned and warned Seward the British would likely offer to mediate a negotiated peace. Such a move would put the Union in a difficult position. Lincoln, of course, would refuse such an offer, and Britain most likely would then recognize the Confederacy as an independent nation. Such an act would greatly strengthen the Rebels' political position and increase its prestige. To Adams's dismay, Parliament introduced a resolution in July to recognize the Confederacy, but Lord Palmerston succeeded in having it withdrawn without a vote because he opposed Parliament formulating foreign policy.

The diplomatic war reached a climax in September 1862 when Confederate armies took the offensive in both Maryland and Kentucky. In Europe, support for recognition and mediation was growing as the Southerners flexed their

# EYEWITNESS

## D. Macneill Fairfax

*The* Trent *Affair was one of the most important diplomatic events of the Civil War. The crisis created by the capture of Mason and Slidell has been well documented, but little has been written about their actual seizure. Macneill Fairfax was the executive officer of the USS* San Jacinto *and commanded the party of sailors and Marines who boarded the* Trent *to capture the Confederate envoys. In the 1880s, he wrote a detailed account of his mission for a popular magazine.*

As the *Trent* approached she hoisted English colors; whereupon our ensign was hoisted and a shot was fired across her bow. As she maintained her speed and showed no disposition to heave to, a shell was fired across her bow which brought her to. Captain Wilkes hailed that he intended to send a boat on board, and I then left with the second cutter.

The manner of heaving the *Trent* to evidently was galling to Captain Moir. When he did stop his steamer, he showed how provoked he was by impatiently singing out through his trumpet, "What do you mean by heaving my vessel to in this manner?" . . . [B]oarding the vessel, I was escorted by one of her officers to the upper or promenade deck and was introduced to Captain Moir, who, though very gentlemanly in his way of receiving me, was also very dignified and manifested no little indignation as he spoke of the unusual treatment received at our hands. I immediately asked if I might see his passenger-list, saying that I had information that Messrs. Mason and Slidell were on board. The mention of Mr. Slidell's name caused that gentleman to come up and say, "I am Mr. Slidell; do you want to see me?" Mr. Mason, whom I knew very well, also came up at the same time, thus relieving me from Captain Moir's refusal, which was very polite but very positive, that I could not under such circumstances be shown any list of passengers. . . . I informed Captain Moir that I had been sent by my commander to arrest Mr. Mason and Mr. Slidell and their secretaries, and send them prisoners on board the United States war vessel near by.

military muscles, and the British informally approached France about some type of joint action to halt the fighting. When Lord Richard Lyons, the British ambassador to the United States, advised the government to wait and see who won the current military campaigns before taking action, Palmerston and Russell agreed, but neither was very optimistic about the Union's chances of winning the war. Palmerston stated emphatically, "Which ever way Victory now inclines, I cannot think the South can now be conquered." After much discussion, Palmerston and Russell decided that if the Confederates won the Maryland and Kentucky campaigns, they would ask the cabinet for permission to offer to mediate a peace. If the Union stopped the incursions, they would put their plans on hold to await further developments. Union forces did defeat the Confederates, but rather than putting the questions of recognition and intervention

As may readily be understood, when it was known why I had boarded the *Trent*, there was an outburst of rage and indignation from the passengers, who numbered nearly one hundred, many of them Southerners. The captain and the four gentlemen bore themselves with great composure, but the irresponsible lookers-on sang out, "throw the d—— fellow overboard!" I called on Captain Moir to preserve order, but, for the benefit of the excited passengers, I reminded them that our every move was closely observed from the *San Jacinto* by spy-glasses (she was within hailing distance), that a heavy battery was bearing upon them, and that any indignity to any of her officers or crew then on board might lead to dreadful consequences. This, together with Captain Moir's excellent commanding manner, had a quieting effect. . . . Mrs. Slidell having asked me who commanded the *San Jacinto*, I replied, "Your old acquaintance, Captain Wilkes," whereupon she expressed surprise that he should do the very thing the Confederates were hoping for, something to arouse England. . . . "Really," she added, "Captain Wilkes is playing into our hands!". . . .

When all was ready and the boats were in waiting, I notified both Mr. Mason and Mr. Slidell that the time had come to send them to the *San Jacinto*. They came quietly down to the main-deck, and there repeated that they would not go unless force was used, whereupon two officers, previously instructed, escorted each commissioner to the side, and assisted them into the comfortable cutter sent especially for them. . . . [I] informed Captain Moir that Captain Wilkes would no longer detain him, and he might proceed on his voyage. The steamers soon separated, and thus ended one of the most critical events of our civil war.

*Fairfax went on to fight at Fort Jackson, Louisiana, and Charleston, South Carolina. He survived the Civil War and rose to the rank of rear admiral in the peacetime navy.*

D. Macneill Fairfax, "Captain Wilkes's Seizure of Mason and Slidell," *Battles and Leaders of the Civil War*, Vol. 2.

to rest, things became even more complicated when Lincoln issued the Emancipation Proclamation after the Battle of Antietam and the issue of slavery was placed squarely into the diplomatic controversy.

## The Slavery Issue

Slavery complicated both the North's and South's foreign policy. Civil War diplomacy is often simplistically misrepresented as European aristocrats supporting the Confederacy because they identified with the South's hierarchal social system, and the masses supporting the Union because they opposed slavery. Actually, Civil War diplomacy involved economic, moral, diplomatic, and political interests. Slavery was just one of several issues. One British subject summed up the intricacies of diplomacy when he wrote in 1861, "We cannot be very zealous for the North; for we do not like her ambition; we are irritated by her insolence; we are aggrieved by her tariffs; but we still have much feeling of kinship and esteem. We cannot be at all zealous for the South; for though she is friendly and free-trading, she is fanatically slave, and Slavery is the object of our rooted detestation."

The British Empire abolished slavery in 1833, and by the time of the Civil War most of its subjects were committed to abolitionism. Even though slavery continued to exist in the Union's Border States, the British associated it more with the Confederacy because Northern abolitionists had been pushing for emancipation for years. Lord Lyons even predicted, "[T]he taint of slavery will render the cause of the South loathsome to the civilized world." Confederate envoys were unprepared for the strong abolitionism they found in Britain. Henry Hotze, who published a pro-Confederate newspaper in London, wrote that "repugnance to our institutions [is] a part of the [British] national conscience. . . ." Confederate diplomats quickly realized the slavery issue was a serious impediment to winning over the British people.

The slavery issue also plagued Union diplomatic efforts because the North's own policy toward slavery was less than impressive. The proposed compromises of 1860–1861 guaranteed slavery just to keep the Southern states from seceding, and early in the war Lincoln specifically protected slave property rights. Union military officials also frequently returned runaway slaves to maintain the slaveholding Border States' loyalty and to persuade Southern moderates to oppose the Confederacy. The British were hard pressed to see any significant difference between the Union and Confederate policies toward slavery or the plight of Southern slaves and Northern industrial workers. As British conservative Thomas Carlisle observed, it was difficult to admire a people who were "cutting each other's throats, because one half of them prefer hiring their servants for life, and the other by the hour."

Prior to the Emancipation Proclamation, Confederate diplomats quite skillfully downplayed slavery and waged a public relations campaign to convince Europeans the war was about free trade, opposing tyranny, and the constitutional right of secession. Many Europeans believed the South was justified in rebelling and were impressed with the speed with which it established a fully functioning government. Southern diplomats and lobbyists also promoted the fighting ability of Robert E. Lee and Stonewall Jackson to take advantage of the Europeans' admiration for military skill. The British, in particular, respected Confederate soldiers and enjoyed seeing the outnumbered, upstart Rebels give the United States a drubbing on the battlefield.

## The Emancipation Proclamation and Europe

Even after Lee's defeat at Antietam, most British citizens expected the war to drag on in a prolonged stalemate. However, the Emancipation Proclamation did affect public opinion in regard to diplomatic recognition. Besides weakening the

Confederates militarily, Lincoln correctly predicted emancipation "would be so potent to prevent foreign intervention." When the president made emancipation a war goal, Europeans began having second thoughts about supporting the Confederacy. A Southern victory meant slavery would continue indefinitely, while a Northern victory meant slavery would almost certainly be abolished. Before the Emancipation Proclamation, many Europeans cheered the brave Confederate soldiers fighting against tyranny and looked forward to having two relatively weak American nations competing on the world scene. After the Emancipation Proclamation, they realized supporting those brave Confederate soldiers also meant supporting slavery. Once the Civil War became a struggle to end human bondage, European enthusiasm for the Rebels began to wane significantly. On October 2, 1862, Prime Minister Palmerston wrote Foreign Secretary Russell, "I am . . . inclined to change the opinion I wrote you when the Confederates seemed to be carrying all before them, and I am [convinced] . . . that we must continue merely to be lookers-on till the war shall have taken a more decided turn." Henry Adams, son of the American minister to Great Britain, gloated, "The Emancipation Proclamation has done more for us

VERY PROBABLE.

Lord Punch. "THAT WAS JEFF DAVIS, PAM! DON'T YOU RECOGNISE HIM?"
Lord Pam. "HM! WELL, NOT EXACTLY—MAY HAVE TO DO SO SOME OF THESE DAYS."

**Will England Recognize the Confederacy?** The British magazine *Punch* ran this cartoon on August 27, 1864, to address the question of whether or not the British would extend diplomatic recognition to the Confederacy. Lord Pam's (Palmerston) glance at recent headlines from America indicates the extent to which military events affected diplomacy.

here than all our former victories and all our diplomacy. It is creating an almost convulsive reaction in our favor all over this country."

This change in European attitudes did not happen immediately. Some British officials, in fact, initially viewed the Emancipation Proclamation as an act of desperation on Lincoln's part. They suspected he issued it to weaken the Confederacy by inciting slave rebellions. The bloodbath that could follow was unimaginable, and the prospect of such an event led Russell to warn the Lincoln administration that the Emancipation Proclamation "only makes other nations more desirous to see an end to this desolating and destructive conflict." Secretary of State Seward was furious at the veiled threat of foreign intervention. In a burst of anger, he complained Great Britain remained hostile no matter what course of action the Union took. "[Victory on the battlefield] does not satisfy our enemies abroad. Defeats in their eyes prove our national incapacity. . . . At first the government was considered as unfaithful to humanity in not proclaiming the emancipation, and when it appeared that slavery, by being thus forced into the contest, must suffer, and perhaps perish in the conflict, then the war had become an intolerable propagandism of emancipation by the sword." Being as blunt as possible, Seward warned Russell the conflict would turn into "a war of the world" if Britain tried to interfere.

Even after Lincoln issued the Emancipation Proclamation, France's Napoleon III continued to support a mediated ceasefire and suspension of the blockade. The emperor met with Confederate envoy John Slidell in the autumn of 1862 and proposed France, Great Britain, and Russia try to arrange an armistice. He speculated Lincoln would have to accept because a refusal would cause war-weary Northerners to force him from office. Napoleon even hinted at unilaterally recognizing the Confederacy or intervening in the war if Lincoln refused. In the end, however, Britain declined to support him, and he refused to act alone. Palmerston and Russell actually supported Napoleon's plan, but the rest of the cabinet did not, and the Russians refused to cooperate out of fear that such action might lead to war. In October, Foreign Secretary Russell finally did present to the cabinet a memorandum proposing to offer to mediate a peace between the Union and Confederacy, but the cabinet rejected it. Having had more time to reflect on the Confederate defeats in Maryland and Kentucky and the Emancipation Proclamation, European officials believed the war had reached a turning point, and they were not willing to risk conflict with the Union.

Confederate hopes for foreign recognition died completely after the devastating defeats at Vicksburg and Gettysburg in 1863. Jefferson Davis had already come to realize this and told the Southern people in a speech, "Do not put your trust in princes and rest not your hopes on foreign nations. This war is ours; we must fight it out ourselves." That same year, the French ambassador to the United States suggested to Seward that the Union and Confederacy meet to negotiate a settlement to end the conflict. Seward, of course, dismissed the idea, and Congress angrily passed a resolution stating that any nation involving itself in the war would be viewed as unfriendly to the United States. It was the last European attempt to intervene in the Civil War.

## The Mexican Problem

One reason Napoleon III supported the Confederates was his desire to expand the French empire into Mexico and his awareness that a sympathetic Confederate nation on the border would be better for his plans than a hostile United States. In 1862, Napoleon made his move by invading Mexico and eventually overthrowing Benito Juárez's Mexican government and installing Ferdinand Maximilian as emperor. As expected, the United States opposed the venture, and Secretary of State Seward wrote to his minister in France that foreign meddling in American republics could "scatter seeds . . . which might ultimately ripen into collision between France and the United States and other American republics." But the Lincoln administration was too involved in the Civil War to take any direct action against the French, and Maximilian remained in power for several years.

Emperor Maximilian was sympathetic to the South and allowed the Confederates to use Matamoros as a port. In turn, the Confederates supported his regime in hopes of gaining recognition from Napoleon. The Union refused to recognize the new Mexican government and even sent military expeditions to Sabine Pass, Texas, and Louisiana's Red River in an attempt to establish a Union presence in Texas to counter the French in Mexico. Union pressure and European politics finally forced Napoleon to reduce his support of Maximilian, and the emperor's position weakened. When the Civil War ended, the United States sent General Philip Sheridan with 50,000 men to the Rio Grande to threaten Maximilian, while General William T. Sherman held talks with Juarez on restoring him to power. Because of this pressure, Napoleon withdrew his troops from Mexico in May 1866. Without the French army to protect him, Maximilian was overthrown by revolutionaries and executed in 1867.

# RAMS AND RAIDERS

**September 3, 1863: Great Britain detains the Laird Rams**
**May 8, 1871: Treaty of Washington settles the *Alabama* Claims**

Another major diplomatic problem between the United States and Great Britain was the British policy of constructing ships for the Confederacy. The Confederacy contracted British companies to build vessels that were then taken into international waters and converted into warships. This laborious process was required because an 1819 act of Parliament specifically forbade British firms from constructing warships for belligerents when Britain was neutral in the conflict. The United States demanded that the British government stop the ships from sailing because it was common knowledge they were being turned into Rebel warships, but the British refused on the grounds they could not be held responsible for the Confederates arming the ships once they were outside British waters.

## The Laird Rams

Confederate naval agent James D. Bulloch was the man most responsible for securing warships in Great Britain. Bulloch was a former U.S. Navy officer who had a reputation for being scrupulously honest and fair. Entrusted with millions of dollars, he worked secretly with British companies to obtain and outfit the commerce raiders *Florida, Alabama,* and *Shenandoah.* When Charles Francis Adams presented evidence to the British government that the *Florida* was to become a commerce raider, officials took no action to detain the ship. A few months later, Adams notified the British when he learned the *Enrica* was another would-be raider. This time, Lord Russell ordered the ship detained, but it was too late, and the *Enrica* sailed from Liverpool and became the CSS *Alabama.*

Suspecting Great Britain intentionally allowed the *Enrica* to escape, Adams began protesting more vehemently. Union resentment over British shipbuilding policy boiled over when Adams learned Bulloch had contracted the British company John Laird & Sons to build two ironclad rams for the Confederacy. Known as the Laird Rams, these large steam-powered vessels would have been among the most formidable warships afloat. To hide their true purpose, Bulloch had a French firm purchase the ships and claim they were destined for the Egyptian navy. This subterfuge, however, did not fool Adams.

The Laird Rams were constructed between April 1862 and August 1863 at the height of the *Alabama*'s fame. Union officials worried they might be used to break the blockade and put more pressure on the British to stop building such vessels for the Rebels. The British finally seized one of several other ships being constructed for the Confederacy, but Seward had already decided stronger action was warranted. In April 1863, he ordered Adams to inform the British that the rams "complicate the relations between the two countries in such a manner as to render it difficult [to] preserve friendship between them. . . ." Seward's not-so-subtle threat to sever diplomatic relations finally forced the British to act more decisively.

In September, Adams discovered the Laird Rams were preparing to sail and asked that they be detained. By then, the Confederates had been defeated at Vicksburg and Gettysburg, and the British were having doubts whether the Confederates could win the war. Conflict with the United States now would be pointless, so officials decided the rams were not worth risking a diplomatic crisis. When the British threatened to seize the ships in October, the French firm abandoned the project and eventually sold them to the British government. Adams's skill and tenacity won out, and the Union secured a key diplomatic victory in denying the Confederates additional naval firepower.

## The *Alabama* Claims

The diplomatic crisis created by Great Britain building Confederate commerce raiders did not end with the Civil War. During the conflict, Adams began to demand that the British compensate the United States for shipping destroyed by the raiders. Seward pursued the issue after hostilities ended and demanded a payment of $19 million. Since the *Alabama* was the most famous of the raiders, these compensation claims became known as the *Alabama* Claims.

The *Alabama* Claims became the most important diplomatic issue of President Ulysses S. Grant's administration, and they were not settled until Secretary of State Hamilton Fish took up the matter. In the 1871 Treaty of Washington, both sides finally agreed to submit the claims for arbitration. In 1818, an international arbitration board ruled that Great Britain had not lived up to its neutral responsibilities during the Civil War and awarded the United States $15.5 million. In turn, the United States had to pay almost $2 million for losses suffered by British citizens during the war.

## Failure of Confederate Diplomacy

The Confederates largely failed in their diplomatic efforts for a variety of reasons. First, Cotton Diplomacy was a flawed policy because the Confederates overestimated Europe's need for Southern cotton. The Southerners also failed to win strategic battlefield victories that could have strengthened their diplomatic position, and they underestimated how strongly Europeans opposed slavery. Although Confederate envoys succeeded in diverting attention away from the slavery issue in the first year of war, the Emancipation Proclamation changed everything. Once emancipation became a Union war goal, European sympathy for the Confederate cause rapidly weakened.

Another contributing factor to the Confederates' failure was their lack of diplomatic skill and experience. Jefferson Davis showed little interest in foreign affairs, and neither of his secretaries of state had ever traveled abroad or had any previous diplomatic experience. With few exceptions, Confederate envoys were also unskilled in the art of diplomacy and were unprepared for the Europeans' indecisive behavior. James Mason's frustration was evident when he wrote Confederate secretary of state Benjamin from Britain, "I find it very difficult to keep my temper amidst all this double dealing. . . . This is a rascally world, and it is most hard to say who can be trusted." To make matters worse, Mason's frequent crude behavior insulted the British. He once was accused of chewing tobacco in Parliament and spitting on the rug when he missed the spittoon.

The Confederates realized slavery was a major impediment to diplomatic recognition, but they did not try to address the problem until December 1864. At that time, a desperate Davis instructed Secretary of State Benjamin to have Mason and Slidell inquire if the British and French would consider extending diplomatic recognition in return for the Confederacy freeing the slaves. Neither nation embraced the idea, and Napoleon III stated emphatically that slavery had never been a decisive issue to France. Lord Palmerston also claimed emancipation would not have changed Britain's diplomatic position, but other officials disagreed. Privately, one British lord told Mason if the proposal had been made in the summer of 1863 when Lee was moving into Pennsylvania, it would have made a difference. But all of this is a moot point. The Confederacy was committed to slavery and refused to use emancipation to further its foreign policy until it was too late to make any difference. The Civil War was not to be won at European negotiating tables; it would be won or lost on the battlefield.

## *FOR FURTHER READING*

Seward's "Some Thoughts for the President's Consideration"
Lincoln's reply to Seward's "Some Thoughts for the President's Consideration"
Charles Francis Adams's letter to Lord Russell, September 5, 1863

## CHAPTER 11

# Finance and Industry

Union Financing

Union Industry

Confederate Financing

Confederate Industry

The Civil War and the Economy

---

In the predawn hours of May 18, 1864, journalist Joseph Howard anonymously wired a presidential proclamation to seven New York newspapers. The proclamation declared May 26 would be a "day of fasting, humiliation and prayer" and announced Lincoln was calling for an additional 400,000 troops because of "the situation in Virginia, the disaster at Red River, the delay at Charleston, and the general state of the country." Howard was the same reporter who in 1861 had falsely accused Lincoln of donning a disguise to slip into Washington for his inauguration. Now he was setting in motion an ambitious plan to manipulate the gold market by taking advantage of sagging Northern morale. The presidential proclamation, as it turned out, was a complete forgery.

The Northern people were becoming increasingly frustrated that spring. General Ulysses S. Grant had suffered tens of thousands of casualties in the Overland Campaign, and the Army of the Potomac was still bogged down outside Richmond. Nathaniel P. Banks had been defeated in Louisiana's Red River Campaign, and William T. Sherman was slowly fighting his way toward Atlanta, Georgia. It seemed the Union armies were no closer to victory than they had been two years earlier. Howard saw in the dismal war news a way to enrich himself. He first bought a large amount of gold and then sent the false proclamation to the newspapers in the hope that the announcement would send investors into a panic and cause the price of gold to rise so he could sell his hoard for a large profit.

Unfortunately for Howard, most newspapers were suspicious of the bogus story, and only two printed it. That proved enough, however, because gold prices increased 10 percent before people learned that the proclamation was false. Howard did make a nice profit on his scheme, but Lincoln was furious and had the army seize the newspapers that published the story and the telegraph company that wired it. When Howard's role was discovered, he was arrested and imprisoned for three months, but to his credit he exonerated the newspapers from any wrongdoing. Lincoln later was criticized for his heavy-handed response to the hoax, and he worried the incident would hurt his chances for reelection. What's more—something that no one outside Lincoln's inner circle knew at the time—Lincoln had, indeed, planned to call for more soldiers, but the outcry caused by the Gold Hoax forced him to postpone the announcement for two months.

The Gold Hoax reflected another struggle between the Union and Confederacy—a financial struggle. At the start of the war, Union Congressman Roscoe Conkling was quite accurate when he declared, "War is not a question of valor, but a question of money. . . . It is not regulated by the laws of honor, but by the laws of trade. I understand the practical problem to be solved in crushing the rebellion . . . is who can throw the most projectiles? Who can afford the most iron or lead?" No previous event in American history matched the Civil War in spending so much money so quickly with so little oversight. Assistant Secretary of War Charles A. Dana was astonished at the amount of purchases being made by the federal government. After the war, he wrote, "We had to buy every conceivable thing that an army of men could need. We bought fuel, forage, furniture, coffins, medicine, horses, mules, telegraph wire, sugar, coffee, flour, cloth, caps, guns, powder, and thousands of other things. . . . Of course, by the fall of 1863 the army was pretty well supplied; still, that year we bought over 3,000,000 pairs of trousers, nearly 5,000,000 flannel shirts and drawers, some 7,000,000 pairs of stockings, 325,000 mess pans, 207,000 camp kettles, over 13,000 drums, and 14,830 fifes." Such huge expenditures brought out the worst in many people, and both governments faced increasing incidents of fraud, corruption, and, as in Howard's case, unscrupulous profiteers seeking to take advantage of the uncertainty of war. Howard defended his actions by claiming he was "the only spotted child of a large family" and was only guilty of "the hope of making some *money*."

## UNION FINANCING

**August 5, 1861: Congress passes America's first federal income tax**
**February 25, 1862: Lincoln signs the Legal Tender Act**
**July 1, 1862: Lincoln signs into law the Internal Revenue Act**
**May 18, 1864: Gold Hoax occurs**

Although the Union had the advantage of an established financial system, the federal government found it difficult to raise the $4 billion needed to fight the Civil War. For the most part, the North financed its armies by relying on loans, bonds, paper notes, and taxes. The tariff also brought in some revenue from foreign commerce, but it did not amount to much. Loans, bonds, and paper notes accounted for nearly 70 percent of the Union's revenue, while taxes accounted for a little more than 20 percent.

## Loans, Bonds, and Notes

When the war began, the Union quickly borrowed money from various banks and sold bonds to fund the military. These methods raised nearly $2 billion and were the greatest source of income for the federal government. To sell the bonds, officials turned to famous financier Jay Cooke. A native of Ohio, Cooke left home when he was fourteen, eventually became a prominent Philadelphia banker, and helped the government finance loans during the Mexican War. A multimillionaire when the Civil War began, Cooke had considerable experience in selling bonds, so Secretary of the Treasury Salmon P. Chase agreed to Cooke's proposal that he be given a monopoly to sell government bonds on a commission basis. Although frequently accused of improper profiteering, Cooke was very successful, and his agency sold more than $850 million in bonds in the first half of 1865 alone. Much of Cooke's success can be attributed to the fact that he sold the bonds to average people and soldiers. Setting up nighttime agencies he called "workingmen's savings banks," Cooke attracted customers by serving coffee and doughnuts. Despite growing war weariness, most Northerners were dedicated to the cause and wanted to help the government defeat the Rebels. More than 1 million of them bought the bonds in what proved to be the forerunner of the great bond drives of the two world wars. Secretary Chase was quite pleased with Cooke and once boasted, "The history of the world may be searched in vain for a parallel case of popular financial support to a national government." After the war, Chase declared, "The nation owes a debt of gratitude to Jay Cooke that it cannot discharge. . . . Now that we have come out of the struggle successfully no one . . . will hesitate to place the financier of the war along side its great generals."

Equally important in financing the war was the use of notes, or paper money. When the conflict began, the Union government quickly discovered it was severely hampered by the gold standard on which the nation had based its monetary system. The gold standard required there be an equal amount of gold in the treasury's reserves for every dollar of paper money in circulation. This policy gave consumers confidence in the monetary system because they could redeem paper money in gold specie (coins) if they wished. However, it also severely restricted the money supply because the government could not increase the amount of paper money in circulation unless it added the same amount of gold to the treasury. The tremendous costs of the war quickly depleted the Union's gold reserve, and Northern people began hoarding specie fearing an economic collapse. By late 1861, the gold reserve was virtually exhausted, and the Union's money supply was restricted proportionately. In a desperate attempt to maintain their own gold reserves, most major banks suspended paying specie for the redemption of paper money. It appeared the economy was on the verge of collapse, and a worried Lincoln moaned, "[T]he bottom is out of the tub. What shall I do?"

# BIOGRAPHY

## Salmon Portland Chase: The Man Who Would Be President

**Salmon P. Chase**

Salmon P. Chase (1808–1873), a native of New Hampshire, moved to Ohio where he opened a law practice and became active in both politics and the abolitionist movement. He often represented runaway slaves and became known as the "Attorney General for Runaway Negroes." Early in his career, Chase supported the Liberty and Free Soil parties and was elected to the Senate in 1849. Switching to the Republican Party, he was elected Ohio's governor in 1855 and was successfully reelected. Chase also was a contender for the 1860 Republican presidential nomination, but his radical abolitionism and unbridled ambition frightened many Republicans. One fellow Buckeye wrote, "Chase is too supremely selfish to be popular or to have any devoted personal friends among men of sense who know him thoroughly but this is not his worst misfortune. I will not say that he cannot distinguish between a sycophant and a friend but I will say that he ever preferred the former and every one of his entire political helpers that I know belongs to the class of cheats or nincompoops."

After losing the nomination to Abraham Lincoln, Chase returned to the Senate but then resigned his seat in 1861 to become Lincoln's secretary of the treasury. Some of Lincoln's friends believed he was making a mistake appointing a rival to the cabinet. When one told the president-elect, "You don't want to put that man in your cabinet," Lincoln asked why, and the friend replied that Chase "thinks he is a great deal bigger than you are." Lincoln then asked if he knew of any others who thought the same thing because "I want to put them all in my cabinet." Lincoln was a shrewd politician. Not only did he want the most qualified people, he also knew he could better control his rivals by having them serve in the administration.

To prevent an economic calamity, a New York congressman proposed in January 1862 to make paper money legal tender in the Union—but without any specie backing. The only exception was that specie, not paper money, had to be used to pay tariffs and interest on the national debt. Although many politicians questioned the legality of the plan, Attorney General Edward Bates ruled that it was constitutional. The proposal touched off an intense congressional debate, but Secretary Chase, who had previously opposed paper money, backed the legislation because the nation had a $350 million debt and something had to be done to forestall bankruptcy. "Immediate action is of great importance," declared Chase. "The Treasury is nearly empty." This bleak economic assessment finally persuaded Congress to pass the Legal Tender Act, and Lincoln signed it in February 1862.

Chase was not a popular official. He had a cold, aloof personality, was contentious with others, and he held a particularly high opinion of his own abilities. Ohio Senator Benjamin Wade once said of him, "Chase is a good man, but his theology is unsound. He thinks there is a fourth person in the Trinity." Because of various disputes with Lincoln and other cabinet members, Chase offered his resignation three times, but Lincoln declined to accept them. Despite his abrasiveness, Chase served Lincoln well by successfully financing the Union war effort and using his considerable influence and political ability to win passage of important financial bills.

Unfortunately, Chase's political ambition remained unchecked, and he tried to challenge Lincoln for the 1864 presidential nomination by secretly courting Radical Republicans who opposed Lincoln's Reconstruction plan or believed Lincoln was unable to win the war. One of these was Kansas Senator Samuel C. Pomeroy. Pomeroy had a letter secretly distributed among Republicans that criticized Lincoln and praised Chase. Unfortunately for Chase, a newspaper secured a copy of the letter and published it in February 1864. Horrified that his hand had been exposed, Chase denied any knowledge of the so-called Pomeroy Circular and offered to resign. Lincoln refused to accept, and when leading Republicans publicly supported Lincoln's nomination, the chastised Chase abandoned his political intrigue. Chase remained in the cabinet, but when he once again offered his resignation in June 1864, Lincoln accepted it.

Despite their troubles, Lincoln appointed Chase the chief justice of the Supreme Court in December 1864. Chase led the court during Reconstruction and supported efforts to extend civil and political rights to freedmen. But he also angered Radical Republicans by refusing to cater to their whims during President Andrew Johnson's impeachment. Chase's opposition to the Radicals caused him to join the Democratic Party and seek the 1868 presidential nomination. He failed, largely because Democrats were angry at his support of black civil rights. Afterward, Chase continued to serve as chief justice until his death.

---

The Legal Tender Act authorized the government to issue $150 million in non-interest-bearing Treasury notes (later increased to $300 million). Because of the note's green print, the new money was quickly dubbed "greenbacks." Greenbacks greatly improved the Union's ability to finance the war, although some unfortunate side effects included inflation (by August 1862, a one-dollar greenback was worth 91 cents in specie), speculation, and fluctuations in greenback value as battlefield success ebbed and flowed. Overall, the experiment was successful, and approximately $433 million in greenbacks were issued during the war. Greenbacks were so popular, in fact, that the federal government backed away from a plan to retire the notes at war's end. The money remained in circulation after the Civil War, and in 1871 the Supreme Court belatedly ruled that the Legal Tender Acts were constitutional.

## Taxes

Congress was reluctant to rely on taxes early in the Civil War because it believed the conflict would be short and wanted to avoid creating dissent. After the defeat at First Bull Run, however, morale dropped, and Congress realized more taxes were needed when it became increasingly difficult to secure loans or sell bonds. To make sure the government had enough money on hand to pay the interest on bonds, Congress passed America's first federal income tax law in August 1861. Becoming effective in 1862, it placed a flat 3 percent tax on incomes higher than $800 per year; thus, the tax affected only the more affluent citizens because most Northerners earned less than that amount. The income tax did not play a major role in financing the Union war effort, even though it was later increased to 10 percent on incomes above $10,000. The total amount of revenue raised in three years was about $55 million.

Congress also adopted a direct tax requiring each state to pay to the federal government a quota of money based on the state's population. Even the eleven seceded states were technically required to pay their quotas, but this direct tax only brought in about $17 million.

In December 1861, Secretary of the Treasury Chase shocked the Congress by announcing that the government's expenditures were running $40 million more than its revenue. This news prompted Congress not only to pass the Legal Tender Act in early 1862 but also the Internal Revenue Act. Described as a "tax on everything," the Internal Revenue Act was the most comprehensive tax legislation in American history. This complicated law ran thirty pages long and included taxes on such diverse things as tobacco, alcohol, playing cards, pool tables, raw materials, manufactured goods, property, inheritance, professional licenses (except the clergy), and corporations. It also increased the income tax and created the Bureau of Internal Revenue. The Internal Revenue Act touched virtually every Northern citizen and even affected future generations, but people generally accepted it as a military necessity. For the first time, taxes were deducted from federal employees'

---

# DID YOU KNOW?

## "In God We Trust"

When the Civil War began, a number of Northerners wrote Secretary of the Treasury Salmon Chase to suggest that some reference to God be placed on Union currency to invoke the Lord's blessings on the war effort. One minister declared, "This would relieve us from the ignominy of heathenism. This would place us openly under the Divine protection we have personally claimed." Chase liked the idea and instructed James Pollock, director of the U.S. Mint at Philadelphia, to come up with a suitable phrase. "No nation can be strong except in the strength of God," Chase wrote, "or safe except in His defense. The trust of our people in God should be declared on our national coins." Pollock (who also designed the Medal of Honor) worked on the project for two years and submitted plans for several coins that would include one of three proposed phrases: "Our Country," "Our God," or "God, Our Trust." Chase endorsed Pollock's third suggestion but changed it to read, "In God We Trust." Congress approved the phrase on April 22, 1864, and "In God We Trust" was placed on the 2-cent coin. It was not until 1956 that Congress adopted "In God We Trust" as the nation's new motto (replacing *E Pluribus Unum*) and ordered it placed on all U.S. coins.

salaries, and the Bureau of Internal Revenue evolved into today's Internal Revenue Service. Despite the comprehensive nature of the taxes, the federal government did not collect the amount of money for which it had hoped. In fact, all of the Union taxes *combined* amounted to only about $667 million.

## UNION INDUSTRY

### September 17, 1862: Pittsburgh arsenal explodes

In times of war, industrial capacity is one of the greatest assets a nation can have. During World War II, the weapons used by the United States were sometimes inferior to those of the Germans, but America made up for this disadvantage by producing such huge quantities of planes, tanks, and ships that the enemy were overwhelmed. The same was true during the Civil War. The Union's tremendous industrial output far surpassed the Confederates' ability to produce war material. When the war began, the Union's industrial capacity was nearly ten times greater than that of the Confederacy, with more than 110,000 manufacturing establishments. New York and Pennsylvania individually had more industry than all eleven seceding states combined. The Union had approximately 20,000 miles of railroad track and produced 24 times the number of locomotives, 20 times the amount of iron, and 17 times the amount of textiles produced by the South. In addition, the North also had a number of well-established arms manufacturing companies that could turn out tens of thousands of weapons annually.

### The Factories

In 1861, all of America's great gun manufacturers were located in the North. Even after the Confederates seized the federal arsenal at Harpers Ferry, the Union could still outproduce the Rebels. Other federal arsenals and armories were located in Pennsylvania, California, Michigan, Maine, New York, Maryland, Missouri, Massachusetts, and Washington, D.C., and dozens of privately owned factories were scattered across the North. From 1861 to 1866, the Union produced nearly 8,000 cannons, more than 4 million small arms, more than 1 billion rounds of small arms ammunition, nearly 3 million rounds of fixed artillery ammunition, and 26 million pounds of gunpowder. The most important Union arms manufacturer was the federal Springfield Armory in Massachusetts. It could produce only 1,200 rifles per year in 1860, but officials quickly increased production when the Confederates seized the other federal rifle armory at Harpers Ferry. By June 1864, the Springfield Armory was making 300,000 Springfield rifles per year, and it produced nearly 800,000 during the war.

Colt and Remington were the North's two largest private weapons manufacturers. Samuel Colt's factory was located in Hartford, Connecticut. The government paid him $13.50 each for his famous revolvers and bought more than

100,000 during the war. The pistol was so popular, in fact, that soldiers bought many more using their own money. New York's Remington Arms Company produced its own rifle musket and revolver. Next to the Springfield rifle and Colt revolver, Remington made the Union's most popular small arms. During the war, it produced 125,000 revolvers, 39,000 rifle muskets, 15,000 carbines, and 10,000 bayonets.

The Union had several superb foundries to produce heavy weapons. The privately owned West Point Foundry at Cold Springs, New York, was managed by Robert P. Parrott. It produced the powerful Parrott rifle, a rifled cannon that was used extensively during the Civil War. At its peak, the West Point Foundry produced 25 Parrott rifles per week, for a war production total of more than 1,700 cannons. The South Boston and Fort Pitt foundries in Pittsburgh manufactured the heavy Rodman cannon and armor plating for warships. During the war, Fort Pitt produced nearly 1,200 cannons.

A federal arsenal was also located in Pittsburgh, and it was the scene of a terrible industrial accident, one of many that occurred in Civil War factories. On September 17, 1862, a spark, perhaps set off by a horse's hoof striking spilled gunpowder in the street, set off a chain reaction that exploded the gunpowder laboratory. In the war's single worst civilian disaster, 78 of the 156 workers inside (mostly teenage women) were killed. Coincidentally, the war's single bloodiest day occurred that same day a little more than one hundred miles to the southeast at the Battle of Antietam.

## The Railroads

The Civil War was the first war in which railroads played a vital role. Without them it would have been impossible to move and equip the large armies that operated across such vast regions. In addition to its huge industrial advantage, the Union also dwarfed the Confederacy in railroad mileage. The Northern states had approximately 20,000 miles of track, with Ohio and Illinois each boasting about 2,900 miles. Perhaps more important, the Union tracks were more uniform in gauge, which allowed the rolling stock of one company to use the track of another, and Northern officials used their track much more effectively than the Southerners.

In January 1862, Congress passed the Railways and Telegraph Act to create the United States Military Railroads system and essentially place all Northern railroads and telegraphs under government control. The legislation also authorized the president to impress railroad and telegraph systems for the war effort, to regulate their maintenance and security, and to place them under military control. The United States Military Railroads proved invaluable in the efficient transportation of men and material. One of the greatest uses of the federal railroad network occurred in 1863 when Major General Joseph Hooker and two infantry corps were transported from Virginia to Tennessee to reinforce William Rosecrans after the Battle of Chickamauga. During the war, the government gained control of sixteen railroad lines in the east and

**Military Railroads.** One of the Union's advantages during the war was its superior railway system. Not only did the North have more track, it also put the railroads under military control so they could support the army properly. Here, Union soldiers sit atop a train in Virginia to guard it against attack.

nineteen in the west, but all of the lines were returned to their owners when the war ended.

Pennsylvania native Herman Haupt (1817–1905) was the key figure who maintained the critical Union railway system. He graduated from West Point in 1835 but only served three months in the army before resigning his commission to become a railroad engineer and to teach at Gettysburg's Pennsylvania College. Haupt went on to write an authoritative book on bridge construction and become superintendent of the Pennsylvania Railroad. In April 1862, Secretary of War Edwin Stanton appointed Haupt chief of construction and maintenance for the United States Military Railroads. Commissioned a colonel, Haupt proved to be a contentious man, but his work with the railroads was a major factor in the Union victory. He built blockhouses to defend crucial bridges from Confederate raiders, armed and trained workers to defend their trains, and repaired damaged or destroyed lines in seemingly miraculous fashion. Haupt was promoted to brigadier general, but he refused the commission because he did not want military rank to interfere with his ability to conduct private business. Instead, he offered to continue his work without rank or pay. When the government insisted he accept the promotion, Haupt resigned in

September 1863. By that time, however, the United States Military Railroads were well established.

# CONFEDERATE FINANCING

**March 13, 1863: Confederate Laboratory in Richmond explodes**
**March 19, 1863: Emile Erlanger and Company issues the Erlanger Loan**
**March 26, 1863: Congress passes the Impressment Act**
**April 24, 1863: Congress passes comprehensive tax bill**

In financing the Civil War, the Southerners were at a disadvantage because everything had to be created from scratch. When the Confederacy was created in 1861, the new government had only a few million dollars in specie that had been seized from federal mints, and there was neither Confederate currency in place nor a tax structure to raise money for the fight. Impressively, the Rebels quickly rose to the challenge and managed to finance an increasingly difficult war through loans, taxes, and treasury notes. It is estimated that the Confederate government and individual Southern states spent approximately $2.1 billion fighting the Civil War.

## The Monetary System

One of the first things the Confederates had to do was create a national monetary system. The seizure of three U.S. Mints made the new nation $27 million richer, but the Confederacy still remained woefully short of specie. As a result, the government never issued any type of specie coinage. Instead, local and state governments and private entities such as railroads and banks produced a dizzying array of paper notes that could be redeemed in goods or services. By 1865 more than $200 million in such notes had been issued.

For a national currency, the Confederates issued approximately $1.5 billion in treasury notes in denominations from $.50 to $500. This was more than three times the amount of notes issued by the Union, but the Confederacy was forced to do so because of its greater inflation. Similar to paper money, most of these notes were actually interest-bearing bonds that could be redeemed six months after a peace treaty was signed with the Union. Treasury notes accounted for about 60 percent of the Confederacy's wartime spending.

The value of Confederate treasury notes quickly declined because they had no specie backing; they were only valuable because the government said they were legal tender. Since the Southern people could not exchange the notes for gold or silver, they quickly lost confidence in the money, and inflation soared. By war's end, Confederate money was virtually worthless. One Confederate dollar was worth as much as $.80 U.S. in December 1861, but it had fallen to less than $.02 by war's end. This led Southerners to refer derisively to the worthless smaller denominations as "Shinplasters."

**Confederate Money.**  The Confederacy issued paper money without specie backing and quickly found itself drowning in inflation. At top is a $100 Virginia note and at bottom is a $500 Confederate note. On the latter, note the Confederacy's seal on the left with the motto *Deo Vindice* (God Will Vindicate) and Stonewall Jackson's image on the right.

## Loans and Bonds

When Secretary of the Treasury Christopher G. Memminger assumed office in February 1861, his most immediate task was to raise money quickly for governmental operations. Loans were an effective way to do this, and they eventually accounted for about 25 percent of the Confederacy's revenue. As a stopgap measure, Memminger first took out $15 million in loans from banks in Louisiana and Alabama. Three months later, Congress authorized the Produce Loan to raise the tremendous amount of money and supplies needed to sustain the government and fight the war. In this loan, citizens used specie or important produce, raw materials, and finished products to buy twenty-year, interest-bearing bonds. When the bonds matured, the government would pay to the bearer specie in the amount of the face value plus interest accrued. The Produce Loan was fairly successful, and mostly wealthy planters purchased approximately $100 million. Additional money was raised through a different type of loan, known as a "call certificate," through which investors deposited money with the government and were given a certificate that could be redeemed at any time for its face value and interest.

One of Memminger's greatest successes was negotiating approximately $700 million in European loans. The most famous of these was the Erlanger (Er-lahn-JAY) Loan, a French loan secured in March 1863. John Slidell, the Confederate envoy to France, brokered an agreement to allow the French banking house of Emile Erlanger and Company to purchase $14.5 million in Confederate bonds at a discount and sell them at a profit. The twenty-year bonds earned 7 percent interest and were to be redeemed in cotton, below the market price, after the war ended. The Erlanger Loan was a speculative venture because its payment depended on a Confederate victory. Investors were willing to participate, however, because Confederate armies were enjoying great battlefield success when the loan was made. Also, with a cotton shortage in Europe, they stood to make a huge profit at war's end. The bonds at first sold well, but demand quickly declined as the Confederates began losing the war. In two years, the Confederate government realized perhaps $8.5 million from the Erlanger Loan.

Much of the Confederate's European financial activity was carried out by Fraser, Trenholm & Co. Established in Great Britain before the war by George A. Trenholm, it was a subsidiary of a South Carolina company. Fraser, Trenholm & Co. served almost as a Confederate bank and unofficial embassy. It converted currency for the Confederate government, maintained government financial accounts, received government funds, helped arrange the Erlanger Loan, and sold Confederate cotton. The company received little monetary compensation for all of this work, but it did use fifty blockade runners for its own profit.

## The Impressment Act

For the Confederate armies in the field, money was not what was needed most. By 1863, there were chronic supply problems, and soldiers were becoming desperate for the basic necessities of life. Confederate armies and some state governments periodically impressed, or seized, needed supplies from civilians, but there were no standard rules for the process. To provide supplies for the armies under some type of fair guidelines, Congress passed the Impressment Act in March 1863. This act at first only allowed the government to impress supplies needed to feed and sustain the military, but it was later amended to allow authorities to impress virtually anything needed for public use. Even slaves could be impressed to work on fortifications or other military projects, with the owners being paid for each slave impressed and reimbursed the cost of the slave if he died during the work period. Each state was required to establish a board of commissioners that mediated disputes between government impressment agents and civilians and set prices for the goods impressed. Impressment agents scoured the countryside to locate supplies at farms and businesses, and they worked with the owners to set fair prices for the impressed goods. The civilian owners were paid immediately in either Confederate money or with certificates that could be redeemed for money later.

Few Confederate measures were as controversial as the Impressment Act. There were many flaws in the system, and civilians viewed it as a violation of their rights. Because of inflation, government prices rarely matched the actual market value of the supplies impressed, and the law was not applied equally to all people. Those civilians who lived closest to the armies lost more from impressment than those who lived far away. In addition, unscrupulous men pretended to be impressment agents and used counterfeit certificates to obtain goods. Slaveholders also complained that the government did not take care of their slaves, was always late in making payments, and kept slaves longer than the agreed-on time. One Georgian declared, "Unless something is done [to correct the abuses] and that speedily, there will be thousands of the best citizens of the state and heretofore as loyal as any in the Confederacy, that will not care one cent which army is victorious in Georgia."

The actual amount of supplies impressed by the Confederates is unknown, but it may have exceeded $500 million. Unfortunately, much of it was never used. Food often spoiled before it could be delivered to the armies, either because impressment agents did not make the necessary transportation arrangements or because the deteriorating railroad system could not handle the traffic. Overall, the Impressment Act may have actually hurt the Confederates more than it helped because its arbitrary and unfair application only demoralized the people.

## Taxes

Taxes were another way in which the Confederates raised money. At first, Congress was reluctant to pass taxes because it was afraid such a measure would weaken public support for the new government. Also, taxes were seen as an inefficient way to raise money because wealthy cities such as Nashville and New Orleans fell to the enemy early in the war and could not be taxed. Therefore, domestic taxes were not relied on to raise large amounts of money for the Confederacy. One tax passed in August 1861 was a direct tax on real estate, slaves, and other property. This tax, however, was not very effective because it was only .5 percent, and authorities were slow to implement it. Later, a provision was added that allowed individual states to exempt citizens from the tax and gain a 10-percent discount if the state made direct payments to the Confederate treasury in Confederate notes or in specie. This did not help much either, and only about $17.5 million was raised by the direct tax.

When the war began to go against them in 1863, the Southern people actually demanded that Congress pass more taxes. Taxation was seen as necessary to raise money to strengthen the armies so they could turn the tide of war in the South's favor. Responding to the pressure in April 1863, Congress passed a comprehensive tax bill that included taxes on certain products, licenses, and income and a particularly controversial tax-in-kind.

The products tax placed an 8-percent tax on many agricultural products and on liquor, salt, and naval stores, while the license tax ranged from $50 to $500 and was placed on nearly all professions (including theater and circus owners and jugglers). On the recommendation of Secretary of the Treasury Memminger, the Confederate Congress passed the national income tax in April 1863. It exempted annual wages up to $1,000 but placed a 1-percent tax on the next $1,500 and a 2-percent tax on income above $2,500. Unfortunately, these rates proved too low. Memminger later tried to raise the tax rate, but Congress refused to cooperate, and the income tax failed to significantly help the financially strapped government.

The tax-in-kind was adopted in response to the tremendous opposition to the Impressment Act. The tax was designed to raise needed supplies for the army by forcing farmers to give the government such things as wheat, oats, corn, rice, potatoes, sugar, pork, and beef. The law allowed them to keep a certain amount of each product for their own use, but they had to donate 10 percent of the remainder to the government. Government agents were appointed to inventory each farm and inform the farmer the amount of goods he had to surrender. If the farmer believed the amount was excessive, he could appeal to an arbiter.

The tax-in-kind was hated even more than the Impressment Act because it seriously affected the farmers' livelihood, and, despite the government's best efforts, corrupt individuals were sometimes appointed agents and they often seized an excessive amount of goods. Officials also faced the same problem of crops rotting before the broken-down Confederate railroad system could move them to the armies, and such waste only infuriated farmers more. Because of growing opposition, Congress began amending the act in December 1863. Farmers were allowed to pay agents in cash rather than in produce and meat, and some exemptions were allowed for small farms and soldiers' families who were struggling to make ends meet. Despite its flaws, the tax-in-kind did raise perhaps $150 million in cash and supplies that were used to sustain the armies, but it was hardly worth the effort considering the damage it did to morale.

Overall, the Confederate tax system was a failure. The government never passed sufficient taxes to raise the large sums of money needed to fight the war because it feared losing the people's support. The few taxes it did pass angered Southerners anyway because of the tax system's waste, corruption, and inefficiency. Farmers began to hide goods from impressment agents, and more soldiers began to desert to take care of their families when they received letters telling of the abusive conditions back home. This weakening of morale was a high price to pay considering taxes raised only about 7 percent of the government's total wartime revenue.

## CONFEDERATE INDUSTRY

When the Civil War began, the Confederacy had little industry to produce the war material it needed or to transport what material it could make. The eleven seceding states accounted for just 8 percent of the nation's 1860 gross national product, had less than 50 percent of the nation's railroad mileage, less than 5 percent of the locomotives, and produced only 5 percent of the iron and just over 5 percent of the textiles. Considering its lack of industry, it is rather amazing the Confederates managed to wage an effective war for four years.

## Foreign Aid

A significant amount of the Confederacy's war material was manufactured outside the South. Blockade runners imported from Europe at least 400,000 rifles, 3 million pounds of lead, 2.25 million pounds of niter (used to make gun powder), medicine, beef, and myriad other products. Ironically, the Northern states were another source of Confederate war material. In the crucial months after secession, Southern agents spent large sums of money in the North procuring guns and supplies for the fledgling Confederacy. Northern manufacturers had no qualms about selling weapons to the Southerners because the federal government had not yet taken measures to stop secession. Famous gun designer Samuel Colt even sent a complimentary pair of pistols to Georgia politician and future Confederate General Howell Cobb. No doubt, Colt's intentions were to make contacts in Georgia to sell revolvers to the state militia. The Confederates also secured massive amounts of weapons by seizing federal arsenals and armories and by capturing equipment on battlefields.

## Domestic Manufacturing

Despite its small industrial base, the Confederacy managed to produce a respectable amount of military goods at home. Rich areas of raw materials aided the South in this regard. Southeastern Tennessee produced copper to make percussion caps and cannon alloy, and iron, lead, and coal mines were scattered throughout the mountainous areas of Virginia, North Carolina, Tennessee, Georgia, Alabama, Arkansas, and Missouri. The Wytheville, Virginia, lead mines alone produced up to 150,000 pounds per month.

The Confederates also were able to make their own weapons using machinery seized from federal arsenals, and private companies demonstrated remarkable ingenuity and enterprise in setting up factories to turn out a vast array of war goods. The Confederate arms industry peaked in 1863 and then rapidly declined as invading Union armies overran cities and sources of raw material and destroyed the railway system. Another blow came in 1864 when the government cancelled all draft exemptions for skilled laborers, and many workers were conscripted into the army.

Josiah Gorgas (1818–1883) was the man most responsible for developing the Confederates' war industries. Gorgas was a Pennsylvania native and West Point graduate who served in the U.S. Army's Ordnance Department before secession. After service in the Mexican War, he married the daughter of a former Alabama governor and decided to support his adopted state when the Civil War began. Appointed head of the Confederacy's Ordnance Department, Gorgas became one of the South's most important officers, performing an invaluable service keeping the armies supplied with guns and ammunition. He sent purchasing agents to Europe, used captured machinery to establish government arsenals, created new laboratories and armories, urged the government to acquire its own blockade runners, contracted with private firms to make weapons and equipment, and opened mines to gather niter. Late in the war, Gorgas boasted in his diary, "Where three years ago we were not making a gun, a pistol nor a saber, no shot nor shell (except at the Tredegar Works)—a pound of powder— we now make all these in quantities to meet the demands of our large armies. In looking over all this I feel that my three years of labor have not been passed in vain."

## The Factories

The Southern states may have been no match for the North's manufacturing might, but that does not mean they were completely lacking in industry. There were about 18,000 Southern manufacturing establishments in 1860. The Confederacy's largest industrial center was Joseph R. Anderson's Tredegar (TRED-de-gar) Iron Works in Richmond, Virginia. When the Civil War began, Anderson greatly expanded Tredegar to supply the Confederate army with cannons, munitions, and other war material. The giant complex produced almost half of the 2,200 cannons made in the Confederacy, and it was capable of making 5,000 small arms a month. Tredegar was the only Southern facility capable of producing some types of ordnance, and it turned out a wide assortment of other products. These included iron plating for warships (including the *Virginia*), railroad iron, torpedoes, propeller shafts, millions of rounds of ammunition, percussion caps, canteens, leather, shoes, and bricks; Tredegar even helped develop submarines and torpedoes. By 1863, Tredegar employed approximately 2,000 people, about half of whom were slaves and free blacks.

Working closely with Tredegar was the Richmond Armory and Arsenal. Using machinery seized from the federal arsenal at Harpers Ferry, the Richmond Armory produced approximately half of all the ordnance fired by Confederate forces in the Civil War. It turned out an impressive 341 large cannons, 1,306 smaller artillery pieces, nearly 1 million artillery shells, 363,372 small arms, and more than 72 million rounds of small arms ammunition. At peak production, the armory's workers, mostly women and children, also produced 300,000 percussion caps every eight hours.

Georgia was the Confederacy's second most industrialized state. After secession, the state seized the federal arsenal at Augusta and used it to make small arms ammunition and artillery shells. Located in the same city was the Augusta Powder Works, a large facility that was two miles long and consisted of dozens of buildings. It produced 2.75 million pounds of gunpowder, more than 100 cannons, and 10 million rounds of small arms ammunition. Another important Georgia industrial center was Columbus, which had the

**The Tredegar Iron Works.** Richmond's Tredegar Iron Works, shown here, was the South's largest manufacturer of cannons and munitions. It produced almost half of all the cannons made in the Confederacy and employed nearly 2,000 workers. Approximately half of them were slaves and free blacks.

Confederacy's largest shoemaking facility and produced 5,000 pairs a week in 1863. Atlanta also contained significant industry and was home to one of the South's few rolling mills that could produce railroad iron. An arsenal in the city made harnesses, saddles, percussion caps, and ammunition; a quartermaster's depot made shoes and assorted clothing; and another shoe factory provided 40,000 pairs in one month. Thousands of people flocked to Atlanta to work in these industries. The arsenal alone employed 5,500 men and women, and the quartermaster's depot employed 3,000 women.

Selma, Alabama, was that state's most important manufacturing site. The city was ideally situated as an industrial center because it was protected deep in the Confederacy's interior, was close to Alabama's iron and coal fields, and had a good railroad and river transportation system. Private companies in Selma were already making shovels, uniforms, swords, and buttons when the war began, but Josiah Gorgas established more factories there and turned the city into the Confederacy's most important ordnance center. A year later, the government bought out a large private iron foundry and turned it into the Selma Naval Foundry. Placed under Catesby ap Roger Jones, the former commander of the *Virginia*, the foundry concentrated on making large cannons for coastal defenses and warships. So many people came to work in Selma's industries that the town's population mushroomed from 1,800 to 10,000. By 1864, 6,000 people were employed at the foundry, and another 3,000 worked at a nearby army arsenal. These facilities produced cannons and ammunition, and a shipyard on the Alabama River constructed three ironclads (including the famous *Tennessee*).

The Confederate arms industry produced an impressive amount of ordnance, but it could never match the Union's tremendous output, and it was plagued by accidents and other problems. Tredegar burned in 1863 but was rebuilt, and at the Augusta Powder Works an accidental explosion killed nine workers. A similar explosion in a Jackson, Mississippi, factory killed thirty-five. The worst accident occurred at the Confederate Laboratory in Richmond, where as many as fifty women were killed in an explosion on March 13, 1863. In addition to these tragedies, Confederate industry was hampered by constant shortages of raw materials and skilled laborers and an inadequate transportation system. Tredegar was capable of turning out tremendous amounts of goods, but it usually operated at about one-third capacity because of shortages. Selma suffered less from shortages because of the close iron and coal fields, and it continued to produce large quantities of material throughout the war.

Advancing Union armies also steadily destroyed Confederate industries. New Orleans produced submarines, uniforms, munitions, and ironclads, and Nashville made gunpowder and served as the main transportation center for the western armies, but both were captured early in the war. The capture of Atlanta in 1864 further disrupted the railway system, making it difficult to ship the products to places where they were needed. Selma was one of the last Confederate industrial centers in operation, but it was captured by James H. Wilson's cavalry in April 1865.

## The Niter and Mining Bureau

One of the Confederacy's most critical needs was gunpowder, which is made from charcoal, sulfur, and niter (commonly called saltpeter). Niter appears as a whitish crust on the soil and is formed when organic material decays in an alkaline base. Without it, the Confederates could not manufacture gunpowder, and without gunpowder they could not fight the enemy. To collect the critical ingredient, Chief of Ordnance Josiah Gorgas convinced Congress to create a niter corps in April 1862, which became the Niter and Mining Bureau a year later.

The Niter and Mining Bureau was responsible for gathering critical materials such as niter, iron, copper, lead, coal, and zinc to produce ammunition. To carry out its mission, the bureau divided the Confederacy into districts, with each having an official who was responsible for the bureau's activities in that district. Since niter is often found in caves, the first step was to survey caves in East Tennessee and northern Alabama. By mid-1864, the Niter and Mining Bureau had provided about 3 million pounds of niter, and another 2.7 million pounds were brought in by blockade runners. In addition, the bureau collected nearly 5 million pounds of lead, 25,000 tons of iron, and more than 775,000 pounds of copper. The Niter and Mining Bureau was one of the Confederacy's largest employees, providing work for nearly 3,000 white men and 4,500 male slaves.

# The Railroads

The Southern states only had about 9,000 miles of track when the war began, with Arkansas having the least (38 miles) and Virginia the most (1,771 miles). In comparison, the North had about 20,000 miles of track, with Ohio and Illinois each having approximately 2,900 miles of rails. There were no railroads at all connecting Texas with the eastern Confederate states, and because of the difficulty of making railroad iron and the blockade's effectiveness, the Rebels laid fewer than 400 miles of new track during the war.

The Confederate railway system was plagued by a variety of problems. Many of the 170 railroad companies covered short distances and used at least three different gauges of track, so rolling stock from one company often could not use the tracks of another. The tracks frequently did not even connect within a city. Petersburg, Virginia, is a good example of this problem. Much of the supplies going to Richmond and the Army of Northern Virginia traveled through Petersburg, but trains could not roll through the city. The lines stopped on the town's outskirts, and the trains' cargoes had to be off loaded, transported by wagon through town, and then placed aboard a train on the other side. This caused great delays in shipping desperately needed food, ammunition, and reinforcements. Officials made things worse by failing to manage effectively what railroads they did have. Unlike the Union government, which created the United States Military Railroads system, the Confederates never exerted national authority over the railroad companies to make better use of them. With no centralized system of setting priorities or coordinating schedules, the Rebels had great difficulty transporting men and material around the country.

Despite these problems, Southern railroads did provide the Confederates with the military advantage of the interior line. Major Southern railroads linked important cities in a way that allowed the Confederates to move troops to strategic points faster than the Union could. The Confederate army, in fact, was the first in history to take advantage of railroads to win a battle. At the First Battle of Bull Run, thousands of troops were transported from the Shenandoah Valley to Manassas in time to achieve victory. In 1863, most of James Longstreet's corps was moved from Virginia to Georgia in one of the war's largest and most important strategic uses of railroads. Longstreet arrived just in time to help the Confederates win the Battle of Chickamauga.

Unfortunately for the Confederates, the interior line advantage was lost when Union armies captured several important railroad junctions. When cities such as Corinth, Mississippi; Chattanooga, Tennessee; and Atlanta, Georgia, were seized, the Rebels found it difficult to transport men or material any great distance. As the war progressed and Union armies and cavalry raids destroyed more track and rolling stock, the Confederates could not repair the damage because of the shortage of railroad iron and the difficulty of shipping construction material where it was needed. By war's end, the Southern railway system lay in shambles, and the average train's speed had dropped from 25 mph to 10 mph. This collapse of the transportation system had a greater effect on the Confederates' war-making

**Fortified Railroad Bridge.** Railroad bridges were tempting targets for guerrillas and cavalrymen, and the more important ones had to be heavily fortified. This Union railroad bridge across the Cumberland River had gun towers and thick side planking. Note also the heavy doors beneath the towers that could be closed when under attack.

capability than did its lack of men or supplies. Substantial amounts of food, munitions, and soldiers were scattered across the Confederacy in the war's final months, but the government could not move the material from where it was to where it was most needed. In 1864, for example, Selma, Alabama, was still producing great quantities of iron, but it could not be shipped to the Tredegar Iron Works because the deteriorating railroads could not bear the traffic.

## The Resourceful Rebels

It has already been noted how inventive the Confederates were in the use of military technology. The same is true in manufacturing. As the war dragged on, Southerners experienced severe shortages in nearly everything and were forced to find substitutes. When the loss of Tennessee in 1862 created a leather shortage, one Georgia cobbler offered a dollar apiece for dog skins to make boots. Louisianians collected alligator hides to tan, some cobblers made ladies' shoes from squirrel skins, and one even sold wooden shoes. When whale oil became unavailable, Southerners made lubricants from castor beans, peanuts, cottonseed, and fish. Beeswax was turned into candles, and lard was burned in lamps. As metal became scarce, citizens were encouraged to donate bells from churches and plantations and lead pipes and window weights from houses, and copper tubes were scavenged from whiskey stills to make percussion caps. Tall church steeples were converted into shot towers to make ammunition, and nuts were collected to make dye for uniforms. Doctors unsuccessfully experimented with using willow bark as a substitute for quinine, and ground sweet potatoes and dried okra seeds were mixed with coffee beans to make them go further. During the siege of Vicksburg, the city's newspaper even stripped wallpaper and used it as newsprint. The government also encouraged citizens to produce niter locally by preparing niter beds. Pits were dug and filled with organic material such as manure and vegetable matter, and when the material was properly decayed the pit was sprinkled with human urine. Dog carcasses were often thrown into the niter beds, which led to the quip, "Soldiers using this powder are said to make a peculiar *dogged* resistance."

## THE CIVIL WAR AND THE ECONOMY

War has sometimes greatly strengthened the American economy (as during World War II and the Vietnam War) because the federal government purchased tremendous amounts of military equipment and promoted new technologies. Undoubtedly there was a burst of economic activity during the Civil War, but it is questionable whether the war had a positive impact on overall economic development. A close study of productivity during the Civil War does reveal some surprising facts. It is sometimes claimed that the war pushed the nation into an industrial revolution and greatly increased its productivity, but that does not appear to be true. The North had already begun to industrialize before the war started, and the South's agriculture, industry, and overall economy were virtually destroyed by the war. Also, with only a few exceptions, industry continued to use the same production methods that had been used in previous decades, and no great technological leaps were made during the war.

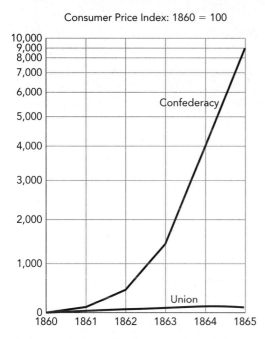

Consumer Price Index: 1860 = 100

**Wartime Inflation.** The Consumer Price Index (CPI) compares the cost of basic goods and services to a fixed base period, in this case 1860. The Union saw comparatively little inflation between 1860 and 1865, but the Confederacy saw prices rise approximately 9,000 percent.

*When the Civil War began, twenty-year-old Kate Stone (1841–1907) lived with her widowed mother and six siblings on a Louisiana plantation known as Brokenburn. She was keenly observant, possessed a sense of humor, and described herself as being "tall, not quite five feet six, a shy, quiet manner, and talk but little." Kate grew up in typical plantation luxury, but within a year her comfortable world crumbled. Her brothers left to join the Confederate army, Union forces moved up the Mississippi River toward her home, and shortages of food and clothing became widespread.*

*In May 1862, Kate wrote in her diary about how the war had changed everyday life. A year earlier, white men had refused to do any type of physical labor because it was viewed as slaves' work, and fine food and clothing were taken for granted. One year of war, however, made everyone adapt to a new reality.*

A year ago we would have considered it impossible to get on for a day without the things that we have been doing without for months. Fortunately we have sugar and molasses, and after all it is not such hard living. Common cornbread admits of many variations in the hands of a good cook—eggbread (we have lots of eggs), muffins, cakes, and so on. Fat meat will be unmitigated fat meat, but one need not eat it. And there are chickens, occasional partridges, and other birds, and often venison, vegetables of all kinds minus potatoes; and last but not least, knowing there is no help for it makes one content. There is hardly a family in the parish using flour constantly. All kept some for awhile for company and for the sick, but it is about exhausted now.

Clothes have become a secondary consideration. Fashion is an obsolete word and just to be decently clad is all we expect. The change in dress, habits, and customs is nowhere more striking than in the towns. A year ago a gentleman never thought of carrying a bundle, even a small one, through the streets. Broadcloth was *de rigueur*. Ceremony and fashion ruled in the land. Presto-change. Now the highest in rank may be seen doing any kind of work that their hands find to do. The men have become

## The Negative Effects

Some Northern industries, such as weapons, wool textiles, shoes, leather, and coal, enjoyed huge increases in production because the federal government purchased large quantities of those goods for the war effort. At the same time, cotton textiles (the North's largest industry) experienced a decline in production because factories were cut off from Southern raw materials and markets and they experienced labor shortages as workers joined the army. Railroads and the production of iron and copper did grow during the war but at a much lower rate than before secession. One revealing statistic is that the nation's total commodity output in the 1860s was only one-third of what it had been in the 1850s and would be again in the 1870s.

"hewers of wood and drawers of water" and pack bundles of all sorts and sizes. It may be a pile of blankets, a stack of buckets, or a dozen bundles. One gentleman I saw walking down the street in Jackson, and a splendid-looking fellow he was, had a piece of fish in one hand, a cavalry saddle on his back, bridle, blankets, newspapers, and a small parcel in the other hand; and over his shoulder swung an immense pair of cavalry boots. And nobody thought he looked odd. Their willingness to fetch and carry is only limited by their strength. All the soldiers one sees when traveling are loaded down with canteen, knapsack, haversack, and blankets. Broadcloth is worn only by the drones and fireside braves. Dyed linsey is now the fashionable material for coats and pants. Vests are done away with, colored flannel, merino, or silk overshirts taking the place. A gentleman thinks nothing of calling on half a dozen young ladies dressed in home-dyed Negro cloth and blue checked shirt. If there is a button or stripe to show that he is one of this country's defenders, he is sure of warmest welcome. Another stops to talk to a bevy of ladies. He is laden down with a package of socks and tin plates that he is carrying out to camp, and he shifts the bundles from side to side as he grows interested and his arms get tired. In proportion as we have been a race of haughty, indolent, and waited-on people, so now are we ready to do away with all forms and work and wait on ourselves.

The Southerners are a noble race, let them be reviled as they may, and I thank God that He has given my birthplace in this fair land among these gallant people and in a time when I can show my devotion to my Country.

*Kate and her family paid a high price for being part of the "noble race." A year later, during the Vicksburg Campaign, most of their slaves ran away, Union forces looted their home, and the family fled to Texas as refugees. Before the war was over, two of Kate's brothers died in Confederate service. After the war, she returned to Louisiana, married, and raised a family.*

John Q. Anderson, ed., *Brokenburn: The Journal of Kate Stone, 1861–1868* (Baton Rouge: Louisiana State University Press, 1972), pp. 109–110.

Without doubt, the Civil War adversely affected most working-class families. Because there was an increase in mechanization and a steady influx of immigrants provided an almost unlimited supply of labor, wages remained low and purchasing power actually declined. Prices in the North rose 70 percent during the war, but wages increased only 40 percent. This decline in purchasing power was one reason labor unions became more popular after the Civil War and labor violence increased during the Gilded Age of the late 1870s and 1880s.

## The Positive Effects

Civil War manufacturers did begin to implement modern techniques such as using standardized parts and relying more heavily on mechanical equipment.

A new, more flexible, financial system was created; more efficient management techniques were developed; and the market system became national rather than regional. The business-friendly Republican Party came to dominate the federal government and used its political power to promote economic expansion in the decades that followed. A devastated South had to be rebuilt, which greatly increased the demand for Northern manufactured goods, and returning veterans eagerly headed west to work in newly established gold and silver mines or to claim homesteads on the Great Plains. Several transcontinental railroads were also completed after the war to accommodate this western expansion. These are the things that made the Civil War so important to the nation's economy—America's bloodiest conflict set the stage for one of the nation's greatest periods of economic growth in the late nineteenth century.

## FOR FURTHER READING

"The Fortunes of War," in *Harper's Monthly* (July 1864)

Excerpt on Confederate money from George Cary Eggleston, *A Rebel's Recollections*

# CHAPTER 12

# The Politics of Union

One week after Robert E. Lee's Army of Northern Virginia began its retreat from the Battle of Gettysburg, Union officials met at the New York City conscription office to conduct the city's first draft lottery. A traditional Democratic stronghold, New York was an emotional powder keg because of intense opposition to the draft and other administration policies. The large number of Irish immigrants, in particular, condemned conscription for unfairly targeting poor men and Democratic districts. They also opposed making emancipation a war goal and were angry because African Americans were being used to replace striking dockworkers that summer.

The conscripts' names were published in newspapers on Sunday, July 12, 1863, and the city exploded when the draft resumed the next day. Mostly Irish mobs roamed the streets sacking the draft office and attacking Republican newspapers and African Americans. One witness reported the mobs chased blacks "as hounds would chase a fox." The police were quickly overwhelmed, and the rioters looted stores and burned down a black orphanage and church. The office of the *New York Tribune* was ransacked, the provost marshal's home was attacked, and many African Americans were murdered. A resident recalled that "three objects—the badge of a defender of the law, the uniform of the Union army, the skin of a helpless and outraged race—acted upon these madmen as water acts upon a rabid dog."

To regain control of the city, officials called in regiments from the Army of the Potomac, fresh from the Gettysburg battlefield. The soldiers efficiently, and sometimes brutally, took back the streets. One New Yorker wrote, "There was some terrific fighting between the regulars and the insurgents; streets

**The New York City Draft Riot, July 13–17, 1863.** In July 1863, a bloody riot erupted in New York City when conscription officials implemented the military draft. The mobs were composed of poor, largely Irish, residents who resented loopholes in the law that allowed wealthier men to avoid military service.

were swept again and again by grape [shot], houses were stormed at the point of the bayonet, rioters were picked off by sharpshooters as they fired on the troops from housetops; men were hurled, dying or dead, into the streets by the thoroughly enraged soldiery; until at last, sullen and cowed and thoroughly whipped and beaten, the miserable wretches gave way at every point and confessed the power of the law." Order was finally restored, and the draft was renewed in August without further incident. The New York City Draft Riot was the worst civil unrest of the Civil War, but the number of people killed is disputed. Newspapers at the time claimed hundreds died, but modern historians put the number at fewer than one hundred. Other smaller bursts of anti-draft violence occurred in Pennsylvania, Massachusetts, Vermont, New Hampshire, Wisconsin, and Ohio. The widespread violence was a clear indication that not all Northerners supported Abraham Lincoln's war policies.

## PARTY POLITICS

### July 4, 1861: Lincoln calls special session of Congress

The New York City Draft Riot was a stark reminder of the complexities of the Civil War. Despite the later nostalgic view that all Northerners were committed to the war, Lincoln actually faced tremendous difficulties in fighting both a military conflict against the Confederates and a political war at home to maintain public support for his policies. Lincoln's problems were compounded by the fact that the North was badly split into various factions. Not only did the Democratic and Republican parties fight one another for political power, there were also many conflicts within each party. This unrest forced the president to use both political persuasion and brute force to win support, suppress internal disloyalty, and keep the people fighting.

## The Republican Party

Shortly after the conflict began, Lincoln called a special session on July 4, 1861, to obtain congressional approval of his wartime actions. The Republicans were fortunate to have a comfortable majority in both houses of Congress because the Southern delegations had resigned during the secession crisis. Congress supported Lincoln by recognizing that a state of insurrection existed and calling for 500,000 volunteer soldiers to put it down. This initial cooperation between the executive and legislative branches eroded somewhat as war weariness set in and the Democrats gained more strength, but the Republicans never lost control of Congress during the Civil War.

The Republicans may have controlled two branches of government, but they did not all agree on policies, and the party soon split between the Radicals and moderates. Both factions' goal was to destroy the Confederacy and reunite the nation, but the mostly abolitionist Radicals also wanted to free the slaves, grant them some equality, and punish the Rebels for starting the war. The moderates, on the other hand, believed issues such as emancipation and extending rights to freedmen were of secondary importance to saving the Union. Although a moderate politically, Lincoln personally agreed with many of the Radicals' beliefs and successfully worked with both factions to hold together a rather fragile alliance throughout the war.

The Radicals played an important role in the Union government, and their influence far outweighed their numbers because they held key positions in Lincoln's cabinet and dominated the Committee on the Conduct of the War. They were able to adopt measures such as the Confiscation Acts and the enlistment of black troops, and they urged Lincoln to issue the Emancipation Proclamation. Among the most influential Radicals were Congressman Thaddeus Stevens (Pennsylvania), Secretary of the Treasury Salmon P. Chase (Ohio), and Senators Charles Sumner (Massachusetts), Henry Wilson (Massachusetts), Zachariah Chandler (Michigan), and Benjamin Wade (Ohio).

## The Democratic Party

The Civil War posed a particularly complicated problem for the Democrats. After secession most Southern Democrats joined the Confederacy, and the Republican Party was able to dominate the Northern Democrats. When the conflict began, Northern Democrats had to decide whether to support Lincoln's war policies against their former political allies. Some, such as Senators Andrew Johnson and

Stephen A. Douglas, did support the use of military force to suppress the rebellion and were referred to as War Democrats. War Democrats often voted with Republicans to pass measures such as the Confiscation Acts, income tax, Conscription Acts, Legal Tender Acts, Homestead Act, Pacific Railroad Act, and the Morrill Acts. However, the War Democrats did not necessarily support all of the administration's policies, particularly the suspension of the writ of habeas corpus.

Other Northern Democrats, especially in Illinois, Indiana, and Ohio, opposed the war altogether and became known as Peace Democrats. Some were conscientious objectors who opposed war for religious reasons, while others did not think it was worth the blood and money required to force the Southern states back into the Union. Many Peace Democrats believed it was in the nation's best interest to stop the war as soon as possible, even if that meant negotiating with the Confederates on the issue of independence, because they thought Lincoln was a dangerous tyrant and were convinced his wartime policies threatened Northern civil rights. A small minority even believed the South had the right to secede, and the Confederates were simply exercising their constitutional rights.

## ADMINISTRATION POLITICS

**January 15, 1862: Lincoln appoints Stanton secretary of war**
**June 29, 1864: Lincoln accepts Secretary of the Treasury Chase's**
**    resignation**
**November 24, 1864: Attorney General Bates resigns**

Much of the Union's political intrigue and turmoil occurred in the highest levels of the administration. Lincoln's cabinet was an eclectic mix of former Democrats, presidential hopefuls, moderates, and Radicals. Campaign managers at the 1860 Republican convention forced some cabinet members on Lincoln, while the president chose others. The guiding principle used in appointing the cabinet was to pick skilled men from different geographical regions and philosophies to bring together the various loyal factions. Lincoln also included presidential contenders such as William H. Seward and Salmon P. Chase because he knew it was better to have them on the inside working with the administration than on the outside criticizing his policies.

### The Cabinet

Lincoln's original cabinet included Secretary of State William H. Seward (New York), Secretary of War Simon Cameron (Pennsylvania), Secretary of the Treasury Salmon P. Chase (Ohio), Attorney General Edward Bates (Missouri), Postmaster General Montgomery Blair (Missouri), Secretary of the Interior Caleb B. Smith (Indiana), and Secretary of the Navy Gideon Welles (Connecticut).

Although most were competent, these men frequently clashed personally, disagreed on policies, and engaged in political skullduggery.

Seward, Chase, and Cameron were the most important cabinet members. Secretary of State Seward was a disappointed presidential candidate who was appointed to the cabinet because of his strong political influence and service to the party. He accepted with the apparent intention of forcing his opinions on Lincoln and making himself the administration's key policymaker. Lincoln, however, skillfully resisted Seward's efforts, and the secretary soon became one of the president's strongest supporters. Both Secretary of the Treasury Chase and Secretary of War Cameron were closely allied with the Radicals. Chase generally served Lincoln well in financing the war, but he was ambitious and contentious. Cameron, who proved to be one of the most controversial cabinet members, was forced on Lincoln by campaign managers in return for his carrying Pennsylvania in the election. So many accusations were made against Cameron concerning corruption, purchasing poor and overpriced equipment, and appointing favorites to government positions that Congress eventually censured him.

Of the remaining cabinet members, Attorney General Bates, Postmaster General Blair, and Secretary of the Navy Welles were moderates. Bates had an abrasive personality that often created conflict with other cabinet members, and he opposed the Emancipation Proclamation. Blair ran an efficient postal department and supported most of Lincoln's policies, but he was less than enthusiastic about emancipation. Both men's moderate views caused them to clash with the Radicals. Welles had no real naval experience, but he performed admirably with the help of his talented Assistant Secretary Gustavus Fox.

Secretary of the Interior Smith simply seemed out of place in the administration. He was another cabinet member who received his post through promises made at the Republican convention without Lincoln's knowledge. Smith's blatant nepotism, self-serving use of patronage, and the fact he seemed to be on the wrong side of every major issue quickly irritated Lincoln.

Personality clashes, political differences, and corruption caused a number of cabinet changes during the war. In fact, only Seward and Welles kept their positions throughout Lincoln's administration. Secretary of the Interior Smith was the first to resign in December 1862 because of poor health. In 1864, Radical criticism finally drove out Attorney General Bates, and Postmaster General Blair stepped down after Radicals made his resignation a condition for supporting Lincoln's reelection. Secretary of the Treasury Chase resigned the same year after unsuccessfully challenging Lincoln for the presidential nomination. John P. Usher (Indiana) took over the Interior Department, James Speed (Kentucky) filled the attorney general's position, William Dennison (Ohio) became Postmaster General, and William P. Fessenden (Maine) and Hugh McCulloch (Indiana) served as treasury secretaries.

The most important change in the cabinet occurred in January 1862 when Lincoln finally rid himself of corrupt Secretary of War Cameron by appointing him minister to Russia. Cameron was replaced by Edwin M. Stanton (Ohio), a Democrat who served briefly as President Buchanan's attorney general. Early in the war, Stanton was a vocal critic of the administration, but Lincoln highly respected his ability and offered him the position. Stanton was stubborn, prickly, and outspoken, but he proved to be successful in rooting out fraud and organizing an efficient Union war machine. He also came to despise General George B. McClellan and sometimes opposed and criticized Lincoln's policies, but the two men forged a close working relationship and came to appreciate each other.

An almost unseen member of the administration was Hannibal Hamlin, a Maine native who had served as a congressman, senator, and governor. Hamlin was chosen as Lincoln's running mate because he was a moderate Easterner, a former Democrat, and the friend of powerful Republican William H. Seward. Lincoln, however, took little note of Vice President Hamlin's counsel, especially when Hamlin urged immediate emancipation and the recruitment of black troops. Offended at the slight, Hamlin enlisted as a private in the Maine Coast Guard and even attended its annual summer encampment in 1864. He wanted to serve a second term, but Lincoln gave him no public support, and he lost out to Andrew Johnson.

## A Clash of Politicos

Most of the administration's political turmoil swirled around Secretary of the Treasury Chase and Secretary of State Seward. Both were headstrong and ambitious presidential hopefuls, and they took opposing views on many issues. Chase was an abolitionist who had the Radicals' support, while Seward was more moderate and had the support of Lincoln. The two men battled each other from the start. When the cabinet was being formed in 1861, the Radicals demanded Lincoln not offer Seward a position, while Seward's supporters told Lincoln he would not serve in a cabinet that included Chase. Shrewdly, Lincoln realized it would be wise to have both rivals in the cabinet so they would counter each other and he could keep an eye on their political activities. Both men finally accepted their appointments, but they never got along.

After the disastrous defeat at Fredericksburg in 1862, Chase and the Radicals made a bold move to take control of the cabinet so they could direct the war effort and increase Chase's influence. Chase began criticizing Seward and blamed him for the cabinet's disharmony and inability to work well together. He once wrote that Seward "exercised a back stair and malign influence upon the President, and thwarted all the measures of the Cabinet." Using this inside information, Radical senators demanded Seward be removed and a new cabinet be formed that could work together on major policies. The blatant power grab created a crisis for Lincoln, but he put his considerable political skill to work and settled the issue decisively by asking the senators to meet with him to discuss the matter. When they arrived for what they thought would be a private meeting, the senators were shocked to find the entire cabinet (except Seward) present. Lincoln then turned to Chase and asked him for his opinion on the cabinet situation. Taken aback by the president's directness and forced to take a public stand, Chase backed down from his private allegations and admitted that the cabinet worked well together. He was temporarily humbled by the experience, and cabinet relations improved. During the controversy, Chase, Seward, and Stanton offered their resignations, but Lincoln refused to accept them.

## SEEDS OF DISSENT

**April 27, 1861: Lincoln suspends the writ of habeas corpus for the first time**

**September 24, 1862: Lincoln suspends the writ of habeas corpus throughout the North**

**March 3, 1863: Congress passes the Habeas Corpus Act**

**July 13–17, 1863: New York City Draft Riot**

**July 5, 1864: Lincoln suspends the writ of habeas corpus in Kentucky**

The vast majority of Northerners were fiercely dedicated to the Union and determined to defeat the secessionists. The Union was the world's shining beacon of liberty and democracy, and they were willing to do their part to ensure that a rebellious minority did not extinguish that light. Hundreds of thousands of men volunteered for military service and risked their lives for the cause, while thousands of women worked as nurses to treat the wounded and labored in factories to supply the soldiers with ammunition. Approximately one million Northerners bought war bonds to keep the armies in the field until the enemy was vanquished. This unwavering devotion was critical to ultimate victory, but Northerners did not always agree on how to win the war. Some people criticized Abraham Lincoln's policies as being unconstitutional, dangerous, and dictatorial. As a result, Lincoln had numerous enemies who sometimes viciously attacked him. Among other names, Northern newspapers called the president an ape, baboon, bigot, bully, clown, demagogue, despot, eunuch, idiot, lunatic, monster, traitor, tyrant, and usurper.

## Conscription

Conscription was one of Lincoln's most unpopular policies. Forced military service was almost unheard of in America, and the conscription act's many provisions for exemption, commutation, and substitution allowed wealthy men to avoid the draft. Conscription officials were often attacked and threatened, and mobs sometimes gathered in towns to prevent the draft lottery from even being held. Anti-draft violence took place in virtually every Northern state, but the opposition was particularly active in the Democratic strongholds of the Midwest and New York City. General-in-Chief Henry Halleck was concerned about how many men it took to implement the draft and once quipped, "It takes more soldiers to enforce it than we get from its enforcement." The New York City

Draft Riot in July 1863 killed scores of people, but Lincoln refused a request to appoint an investigative commissioner to look into the cause of the riot because he feared it might provoke even more violence. Aware of the strong Northern discontent, the president warned his advisers, "One rebellion at a time is about as much as we can conveniently handle."

After the riot, New York's Democratic Governor Horatio Seymour asked Lincoln to suspend conscription in his state because it was unconstitutional and New York's draft quota was unfairly high. Lincoln offered to adjust the quota if Seymour could prove it was unfair, but he refused to cancel the draft. Lincoln told the governor, "We are contending with an enemy who, as I understand, drives every able-bodied man he can reach into his ranks, very much as a butcher drives bullocks into a slaughter-pen. No time is wasted, no argument is used. This produces an army which will soon turn upon our now victorious soldiers already in the field, if they shall not be sustained by recruits." The president was prepared to federalize New York's militia to enforce conscription if necessary, but Seymour finally relented and the draft resumed peacefully in August 1863.

## The Emancipation Proclamation

Millions of Northerners, particularly in the Midwest and Border States, opposed the Emancipation Proclamation either because they had no interest in freeing the slaves or because they believed it was a dangerous and illegal expansion of executive power. When Lincoln issued the proclamation, one newspaper declared he was "adrift on a current of radical fanaticism," and even the Illinois legislature passed a resolution condemning the proclamation as "a gigantic usurpation" that would lead to murderous slave insurrections. In Congress, the Democrats tried unsuccessfully to pass a resolution that branded the Emancipation Proclamation "an assumption of powers dangerous to the rights of citizens and to the perpetuity of a free people."

The Emancipation Proclamation also had a profound effect on many soldiers who felt betrayed because they had only volunteered to fight for the Union. Death on the battlefield was an acceptable risk to obtain that patriotic goal, but they had no intention of dying to free the slaves. Desertions increased, and some regiments threatened mutiny. Six days after he signed the proclamation, Lincoln wrote Vice President Hamlin to lament, "We have fewer troops in the field at the end of the six days than we had at the beginning—the attrition among the old outnumbering the addition by the new." This Northern resentment against the Emancipation Proclamation was made even more evident when the Republicans lost a number of congressional seats in New York, Pennsylvania, Ohio, and Illinois in the 1862 elections.

## Censorship

Censorship was another unpopular administration policy. While Civil War media was not subjected to the strong censorship that became common in later wars, Union officials did sometimes act decisively to control the press. Lincoln usually preferred appealing to the press' sense of patriotism and requesting restraint in printing sensitive information. Individual army commanders, however, did not hesitate to censor the media, control access to the telegraph, or drive offending reporters out of camp. Major Generals William T. Sherman and George G. Meade, in particular, earned reporters' wrath. Sherman once threatened to court-martial a reporter as a spy and wrote his brother, "As to the press of America, it is a shame and a reproach to a civilized people. . . ." When Meade expelled one reporter from the Army of the Potomac in 1864, fellow war correspondents retaliated by conspiring to snub Meade by omitting his name from all of their stories—unless it was in connection with a military defeat.

Sometimes generals accused newspapers of aiding the enemy and shut them down. Ambrose Burnside closed the *Chicago Times* in 1863 when its editor harshly criticized the Emancipation Proclamation, but Lincoln lifted the order a few days later. Major General John Dix closed the *New York World* and the *Journal of Commerce* for two days in 1864 for being involved in the Gold Hoax, and an Ohio editor was indicted by a federal grand jury for printing seditious stories.

## Suspension of the Writ of Habeas Corpus

Lincoln's most unpopular wartime measure was suspending the writ of habeas corpus. A writ of habeas corpus ("you should have the body") is a constitutional protection against illegal arrest and imprisonment. If someone is detained by authorities, they can have a judge issue the writ and force the authorities to go to court and inform the judge of the crime being charged. It is a safeguard to prevent someone from being held in custody without being charged with a crime. The writ of habeas corpus is one of America's greatest constitutional guarantees, but the Constitution does permit the government to suspend it during public emergencies. Suspending habeas corpus was rarely done, however, and such action had not been taken since 1815 when Andrew Jackson declared martial law in New Orleans during the War of 1812.

During the Civil War, Lincoln suspended the writ of habeas corpus a number of times so officials could enforce the draft and arrest and detain suspected Confederate sympathizers without having to prove a case against them. Lincoln saw the suspension as a tool with which to silence critics and prevent citizens from aiding the enemy. The first suspension occurred early in the war on April 27, 1861, to facilitate the shipment of troops to the capital and to prevent Maryland from seceding, but it only applied to the area between Washington, D.C., and Philadelphia, Pennsylvania. Although many people criticized the harsh action, Attorney General Edward Bates wrote a legal opinion supporting Lincoln. As opposition grew,

## EYEWITNESS
### Abraham Lincoln

*In August 1863, James C. Conkling invited Abraham Lincoln to attend a political rally in Lincoln's hometown of Springfield, Illinois. Duties prevented the president from leaving Washington, but he wrote a letter to Conkling to be read to those assembled. Much of the letter to Conkling was a well-argued defense of the Emancipation Proclamation and Lincoln's personal commitment to stand firm on emancipation.*

. . . . There are those who are dissatisfied with me. . . . [T]o be plain, you are dissatisfied with me about the negro. . . . You dislike the emancipation proclamation; and, perhaps, would have it retracted. You say it is unconstitutional—I think differently. I think the constitution invests its commander-in-chief, with the law of war, in time of war. The most that can be said, if so much, is that slaves are property. Is there—has there ever been—any question that by the law of war, property, both of enemies and friends, may be taken when needed? And is it not needed whenever taking it, helps us, or hurts the enemy? Armies, the world over, destroy enemies' property when they can not use it; and even destroy their own to keep it from the enemy. . . .

But the proclamation, as law, either is valid, or is not valid. If it is not valid, it needs no retraction. If it is valid, it can not be retracted, any more than the dead can be brought to life. Some of you profess to think its retraction would operate favorably for the Union. Why better *after* the retraction, than *before* the issue? There was more than a year and a half of trial to suppress the rebellion before the proclamation issued, the last one hundred days of which passed under an explicit notice that it was coming, unless averted by those in revolt, returning to their allegiance. The war has certainly progressed as favorably for us, since the issue of the proclamation as before. I know as fully as one can know the opinions of others, that some of the commanders of our armies in the field who have given us our most important successes, believe the emancipation policy, and the use of colored troops, constitute the heaviest blow yet dealt

Lincoln finally paroled the prisoners who had been denied habeas corpus and granted them amnesty in February 1862, but in September he suspended habeas corpus throughout the North to stop resistance to the draft and to quell the growing criticism of the Emancipation Proclamation. This latter action was largely successful because newspaper editors and private citizens became much more cautious about what they wrote for fear of being thrown in jail.

Criticism of the habeas corpus policy grew because of the large number of people being detained and because it was being suspended in states that remained loyal to the Union. One soldier wrote that Lincoln was "only prevented from exercising a Russian despotism by the fear he may have of shocking too to the rebellion. . . . Among the commanders holding these views are some who have never had any affinity with what is called abolitionism, or with republican party politics; but who hold them purely as military opinions. I submit these opinions as being entitled to some weight against the objections, often urged, that emancipation, and arming the blacks, are unwise as military measures, and were not adopted, as such, in good faith.

You say you will not fight to free negroes. Some of them seem willing to fight for you; but, no matter. Fight you, then, exclusively to save the Union. I issued the proclamation on purpose to aid you in saving the Union. Whenever you shall have conquered all resistance to the Union, if I shall urge you to continue fighting, it will be an apt time, then, for you to declare you will not fight to free negroes. I thought that in your struggle for the Union, to whatever extent the negroes should cease helping the enemy, to that extent it weakened the enemy in his resistance to you. Do you think differently?

I thought that whatever negroes can be got to do as soldiers, leaves just so much less for white soldiers to do, in saving the Union. Does it appear otherwise to you? But negroes, like other people, act upon motives. Why should they do anything for us, if we will do nothing for them? If they stake their lives for us, they must be prompted by the strongest motive—even the promise of freedom. And the promise being made, must be kept.

*More than 50,000 people cheered when Lincoln's letter was read at Springfield, and it was widely published in Northern newspapers. Senator Henry Wilson described it as a "noble, patriotic, and Christian letter," and the* Chicago Tribune *called it "one of those remarkably clear and forcible documents that come only from Mr. Lincoln's pen." Lincoln's letter helped boost Republican morale, and the party swept the state elections that November.*

Roy P. Basler, ed. *The Collected Works of Abraham Lincoln,* 8 Vols. (New Brunswick, N.J.: Rutgers University Press, 1953), Vol. 6, p. 406.

much the sense of decency of the whole world," and a Democratic senator accused the president of "declaring himself a Dictator. . . ." Chief Justice Roger Taney also objected because he believed only Congress could take such action. To address this legal point, Congress passed the Habeas Corpus Act in March 1863 specifically to authorize the suspension and to protect military officers from being prosecuting for carrying out their duties. Having received congressional approval, Lincoln again suspended habeas corpus throughout the North in September 1863. Reliable records were not always kept regarding the arrest of dissidents during these times of suspension, so the exact number of people who were detained is unknown; however, the number was probably at least 13,500.

# THE COPPERHEADS

**May 5, 1863: Officials arrest Clement Vallandigham**
**August 29, 1864: Sons of Liberty intend to start uprising**
**in the Northwest Conspiracy**

Lincoln was not motivated by personal gain in any of his forceful actions. He was simply determined to defeat the Rebels and used specific weapons to accomplish specific war goals. Conscription was intended to encourage men to volunteer for military service; the Emancipation Proclamation was issued to gain the moral high ground for the Union, prevent European intervention, and weaken the Confederacy by denying it slave labor; and censorship and the suspension of habeas corpus were enacted to suppress sedition. However, these policies frequently had an effect opposite to Lincoln's intentions. Many Northerners believed such harsh measures threatened their liberty, and they became critical of the administration. This opposition manifested itself in decreasing numbers of volunteers for military service, increasing occurrence of anti-draft riots, and escalating attacks on the administration by politicians and newspapers. Public criticism and administration reaction proved to be a vicious cycle. When fewer men volunteered for military service, Lincoln was forced to rely on the unpopular draft to fill the ranks. When increasing numbers of politicians and newspapers began criticizing the suspension of civil liberties, Lincoln detained even more people without the benefit of habeas corpus to crack down on what he perceived to be disloyalty. The stronger the measures adopted to silence critics and defeat the Confederates, the shriller the opposition became. Some Peace Democrats came to hate Lincoln so much they moved beyond vocal criticism and began to engage in subversive activities to aid the Confederates. Known as Copperheads, these Confederate sympathizers supposedly earned their nickname because they struck without warning like the poisonous copperhead snake.

## Seditious Organizations

The Copperheads were thought to be pervasive throughout the North, and they were accused of serving in clandestine organizations such as the Knights of the Golden Circle, the Order of American Knights, and the Sons of Liberty. But in reality, the Copperhead movement was rather loose knit, and these secret groups existed mostly in people's minds.

The Knights of the Golden Circle was actually a Southern organization and not even a part of the Copperhead movement. It was created in 1854 to promote the annexation of northern Mexico for the purpose of extending slavery, but during the secession crisis the Knights created new chapters (called "castles") in the South and Border States to promote disunion. After war erupted, they actively supported the Confederates by gathering intelligence and carrying out acts of sabotage. Since the Knights of the Golden Circle was a secret organization, actual membership is unknown, but the number was probably quite low; they just seemed omnipresent because Northerners generally blamed them for all anti-war incidents. The Order of American Knights was also a small and ineffective anti-war organization, but Union officials were greatly concerned about their activities, and they received a lot of publicity. Founded in St. Louis, Missouri, in 1863, the American Knights opposed the Emancipation Proclamation, the suspension of habeas corpus, and other harsh Union war measures. Modern studies, however, indicate the American Knights existed largely on paper. Of all the Copperhead organizations, in fact, only the Sons of Liberty were ever actually implicated in a seditious plot.

## The Northwest Conspiracy

Formed in Indianapolis, Indiana, in early 1864, the Sons of Liberty was a small organization, but Confederate agents working in Canada collaborated with it to start an uprising in the old Northwest. The plan called for an attack on Camp Douglas, Illinois, to free the Confederate prisoners of war being held there. The Confederates would then aid the Sons of Liberty in taking control of several state governments in the Midwest to form a Northwest Confederation and offer their support to the Confederacy. They believed such a move would force Lincoln to end the war quickly rather than see the Confederacy and Northwest Confederation unite against the Union.

In late summer 1864, Confederate agents made contact with Sons of Liberty members in Chicago and planned to launch the uprising in August during the Democratic National Convention. Before they could act, however, the Camp Douglas commandant and a Chicago newspaper editor uncovered the plot. Several arrests were made, but no evidence of a large-scale conspiracy was ever found. Soon after the arrests, Indiana's Governor Oliver P. Morton suspected there was a similar conspiracy in his state after a raid was made on a leading Sons of Liberty member. Union officials manipulated papers discovered in the raid to convince citizens a conspiracy did exist. When authorities seized a shipment of pistols sent to the man's business, the Sons of Liberty member and a Democratic newspaper editor were arrested, and Governor Morton declared that the "Northwest conspiracy" had been foiled.

There were many rumors in both the North and South that a Northwest Conspiracy might bring peace, and the Confederates were greatly disappointed that nothing much happened. The truth is that there never was any real danger of such an uprising because the Copperheads were not strong enough or sufficiently organized to carry out such a plot. While the Midwest was a Peace Democrat stronghold, most people there drew the line at actively aiding the Rebels, and the state governments remained alert to crush any such disloyal activity.

## THE ELECTION OF 1864

**June 8, 1864: National Union Party nominates Lincoln**
**August 31, 1864: Democrats nominate George B. McClellan**
**November 8, 1864: Lincoln wins reelection**
**March 4, 1865: Lincoln's second inauguration**

# BIOGRAPHY

## Clement Laird Vallandigham: Copperhead

Clement L. Vallandigham (center)

A native of Ohio, Vallandigham (vuh-LAN-di-gum) (1820–1871) became the most famous of all the Northern Copperheads. Educated at a local academy, he taught school in Maryland before entering Pennsylvania's Jefferson College in 1840. Returning to Ohio, Vallandigham became a lawyer, legislator, newspaper editor, and state militia general. After being defeated for Congress three times in the early 1850s, he finally won a seat in 1858 as a Democrat. Reelected in 1860, Vallandigham was a moderate who supported states' rights, opposed radical abolitionists, and backed Stephen A. Douglas for president.

As a states' rights advocate, Vallandigham opposed Lincoln's attempt to force the seceding states back into the Union. He also criticized many of the administration's other wartime measures, such as conscription and the suspension of habeas corpus. Vallandigham became a leading Copperhead, and his activities angered influential War Democrats. In retaliation, Democratic leaders redrew the boundaries of Vallandigham's congressional district in 1862 and engineered his defeat for reelection. In a January 1863 speech on the House floor, an outraged Vallandigham accused Lincoln of destroying civil liberties as soon as the war began. "Constitutional limitation was broken down; habeas corpus fell; liberty of the press, of speech, of the person, of the mails, of travel, of one's own house, and of religion; the right to bear arms, due process of law, judicial trial, trial by jury, trial at all; every badge and muniment of freedom in republican government or kingly government—all went down at a blow. . . . Whatever pleases the President, that is law!" Lincoln's policies, Vallandigham declared, had turned the country into "one of the worst despotisms on earth."

By 1864, the Northern people had suffered several hundred thousand casualties, and war weariness was setting in because the end was nowhere in sight. Although the Union had won great military victories in the west and secured the Mississippi River, the Confederate Army of Tennessee remained a formidable threat, and Rebel guerrillas plagued Missouri and Tennessee. In the east, Robert E. Lee's army continued to block the way to Richmond. After three years of fighting, the war was still in a stalemate, and millions of Northern voters were also angry at administration policies such as conscription, the suspension of habeas corpus, and the Emancipation Proclamation. Bloody riots had even erupted in some cities to protest the draft, and that spring the Gold Hoax threw the nation into a brief financial panic.

Undaunted by his failure to win reelection, Vallandigham tried to secure Ohio's Democratic gubernatorial nomination in 1863, but he lost again. That same year, he clashed with Ohio's military commander, Major General Ambrose E. Burnside. Burnside forbid anyone to make anti-war statements, but Vallandigham only increased his attacks in hopes of winning sympathy among Peace Democrats by forcing Burnside to arrest him. Burnside finally did arrest Vallandigham and denied him a writ of habeas corpus. Convicted in a military court, Vallandigham was sentenced to two years in prison, but he remained a popular figure among Copperheads, and his harsh treatment threatened to resurrect his flagging political career. Outraged by the military arrest and trial, Ohio's Democratic Party nominated Vallandigham for governor in June 1863. Torn between the need to muzzle anti-war protestors and his reluctance to make Vallandigham a martyr, Lincoln commuted Vallandigham's sentence and exiled him to Confederate territory.

Vallandigham did not stay in the Confederacy long. Within a few weeks, he traveled to Canada by way of Bermuda and launched his gubernatorial campaign from Ontario. With Lincoln's support, however, the Republican candidate easily won the election. In June 1864, a disguised Vallandigham slipped back into Ohio and once again began participating in Democratic politics, but by that time Lincoln had decided he was not much of a threat and ignored his presence. Ironically, Vallandigham played a role in Lincoln's reelection in 1864 by attending the Democratic National Convention and helping to create the peace platform that contributed to George B. McClellan's defeat. Unable to resurrect his political career, Vallandigham resumed his law practice and died in a bizarre 1871 incident. While demonstrating to other lawyers how a murder victim could have killed himself accidentally, he succeeded in shooting himself. Vallandigham died the next day—but he won the case.

Some Radical Republicans did not believe Lincoln could—or should—be reelected and looked for ways to prevent his nomination. Newspaper editor Horace Greeley wrote, "Mr. Lincoln is already beaten. He cannot be elected. And we must have another ticket to save us from utter overthrow." One of those maneuvering for the nomination was Secretary of the Treasury Salmon P. Chase, who worked behind the scenes to secretly court leading Republicans. To assist the secretary, Kansas senator Samuel C. Pomeroy had a letter prepared for private circulation criticizing Lincoln and praising Chase. Unfortunately for Chase, the Pomeroy Circular was made public when newspapers published it in February 1864. Horrified that the backroom politicking had been exposed, Chase denied any knowledge of the letter and offered to resign, but Lincoln refused. When powerful Republicans began lining up behind Lincoln's nomination, a chastised Chase abandoned his scheme to run for the presidency. A few months later in June 1864, Chase was surprised when Lincoln accepted his fourth offer to resign. Despite their differences, Lincoln recognized Chase's ability and appointed him chief justice of the Supreme Court in December.

## The Parties and Platforms

Republicans worried about Lincoln's chances for reelection and knew they had to have some Democratic backing to win. To gather this critical bipartisan support, the Republican Party referred to itself as the National Union Party in the 1864 election to make it easier for non-Republicans to vote for Lincoln, and Lincoln accepted the party's nomination in June 1864. Democrat Andrew Johnson, the military governor of Tennessee and the only Southern senator to remain loyal to the Union, was nominated for vice president. Lincoln's and Johnson's platform was to prosecute the war vigorously and bring the Southern states back into the Union without slavery. "[W]e pledge ourselves," the platform stated, "as Union men, animated by a common sentiment and aiming at a common object, to do everything in our power to aid the Government in quelling by force of arms the rebellion now raging against its authority, and in bringing to the punishment due to their crimes the rebels and traitors arrayed against it."

The Democrats, who faced their own problems in the crucial election, nominated George B. McClellan, the former commander of the Army of the Potomac. With the war deadlocked, many Democrats were eager to end the bloodshed by any means necessary and, much to McClellan's chagrin, the Copperhead faction secured a platform plank calling for negotiations with the Confederates. The platform declared the war effort had failed, and "the Constitution itself has been disregarded in every part, and public liberty and private right alike trodden down and the material prosperity of the country essentially impaired—justice, humanity, liberty, and the public welfare demand that immediate efforts be made for a cessation of hostilities." The Democrats pledged they would try to negotiate a peace "at the earliest practicable moment" to restore the Union. McClellan, however, vehemently disagreed with this peace platform. The general was still a Union man despite his opposition to both the Emancipation Proclamation and the increasingly brutal war being waged against Southern civilians. When he accepted the nomination, McClellan publicly repudiated the peace platform and promised to prosecute the war more effectively than Lincoln. Despite this pledge to continue fighting, he could not shake the Copperhead image and was not as successful in winning the soldiers' vote as he had hoped.

## The Election

Union armies were bogged down on all fronts during the summer of 1864 (see Chapters 21–23). On the very day Lincoln was nominated, Confederate cavalry under John Hunt Morgan was running amok in Kentucky. Two separate Union armies had already suffered stinging defeats in the Red River and Camden expeditions in Louisiana and Arkansas, respectively. After sustaining 60,000 casualties in just thirty days, General Grant's armies were unable to capture Richmond and were forced to dig in for a long, bloody siege at Petersburg. Confederate General Jubal Early then launched a raid in July that reached the outskirts of Washington and briefly threw the city into a panic. In the west, General William T. Sherman was inching toward Atlanta, Georgia, but no one dared guess how long it would take him to capture that city. In the far west, Sterling Price's Rebel army launched a massive raid into Missouri in August, demonstrating the Confederates' ability to move north almost at will. Adding to Lincoln's woes was the fact that he angered the Radicals and their supporters by pocket vetoing the harsh Wade-Davis reconstruction bill in July (see Chapter 25), and the very next day he antagonized Border State voters by declaring martial law and suspending habeas corpus in Kentucky.

All of these setbacks made Lincoln acutely aware that no American president had been reelected since Andrew Jackson. In August, he wrote a friend, "You think I don't know I am going to be beaten, *but I do* and unless some great change takes place *badly beaten*." Preparing for the worst, the president sat down on the morning of August 23 and wrote out a short memorandum. Later, he pulled the memo out at a cabinet meeting, neatly folded so the text was hidden, and had each cabinet member sign it without reading the contents. Only after the election did he reveal what they signed. The memo declared, "This morning, as for some days past, it seems exceedingly probable that this Administration will not be re-elected. Then it will be my duty to so co-operate with the President elect, as to save the Union between the election and the inauguration; as he will have secured his election on such ground that he can not possibly save it afterwards."

Lincoln did not think the Democrats or McClellan were traitors who would immediately grant Confederate independence if elected. However, he did believe McClellan would be forced to negotiate a ceasefire if he became president. Once an armistice was declared, it would be virtually impossible to renew the war, and Confederate independence would be a reality. Apparently, the purpose of the memorandum was to force the cabinet to support Lincoln's working with McClellan in case McClellan won the election. John Hay, the president's secretary, later claimed Lincoln planned to meet with McClellan after the election to secure his cooperation to win the war before McClellan's inauguration. McClellan could parlay his popularity into raising more troops for the army, while Lincoln would do everything in his power to use the army most effectively. Lincoln apparently did not think the plan would work, but he said, "I should have done my duty and have stood clear before my own conscience."

Millions of Northerners appreciated Lincoln's steadfast devotion to the Union and emancipation, and he may have won the 1864 election entirely on the merits of his character and platform. But he remained doubtful of the election's

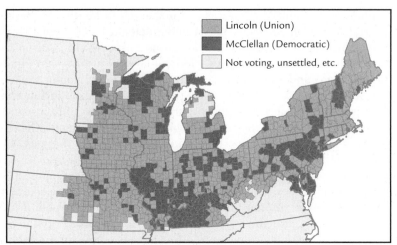

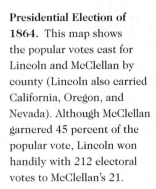

**Presidential Election of 1864.** This map shows the popular votes cast for Lincoln and McClellan by county (Lincoln also carried California, Oregon, and Nevada). Although McClellan garnered 45 percent of the popular vote, Lincoln won handily with 212 electoral votes to McClellan's 21.

outcome until several major battlefield victories helped create a groundswell of support for the administration. In the three months before the election, David Farragut destroyed a Confederate fleet and seized control of Mobile Bay, Alabama, and other Union forces captured Plymouth, North Carolina. Philip Sheridan's army crushed Jubal Early in the Shenandoah Valley, ending the threat from that region, and in the west Rebel cavalryman John Hunt Morgan was killed and Price's raid into Missouri was turned back. Most important, Sherman's armies finally captured Atlanta just two days after McClellan's nomination. Things also began improving for Lincoln on the political front that autumn. Loyal voters in Louisiana ratified a constitution that opened the way for that state's readmission to the Union, and Maryland voters ratified a new constitution abolishing slavery. All of these victories gave Northerners hope the war was nearly won and convinced most of them to stand by Lincoln until final victory was achieved. To encourage voters to stay the course, Lincoln's managers used the catchy slogan, "Don't swap horses in the middle of the stream."

Leaving nothing to chance, Lincoln took special measures to allow soldiers in the field to vote. Although Union soldiers were still fond of McClellan, they did not want their suffering and sacrifice to have been in vain, and most realized Lincoln was more likely to achieve victory than Little Mac. Secretary of War Stanton saw to it that absentee ballots were delivered to the men, and those governors who supported Lincoln made sure their soldiers were allowed to vote in the field when possible. Lincoln also asked Sherman to furlough Indiana soldiers so they could go home to vote the National Union Party ticket, and similar requests were made of Generals Meade, Sheridan, and Rosecrans. The tactic worked, and Lincoln received an estimated 78 percent of the military vote.

Coincidentally, approximately 78 percent of the Union's voters turned out for the election. In the popular vote, Lincoln won 2.2 million (55 percent) to McClellan's 1.8 million (45 percent). Only Andrew Jackson had received a larger majority in any previous presidential election. More important, Lincoln carried all but three states (New Jersey, Delaware, and Kentucky) and won an electoral landslide with 212 votes to McClellan's 21. The National Union Party also had great success in the federal and state elections. When the votes were counted, the party held 149 of the congressional seats (78 percent) to the Democrats' 42, and 42 of the senate seats (81 percent) to the Democrats' 10. Several state legislatures were also won, and the only gubernatorial seat lost was in McClellan's home state of New Jersey. What is particularly interesting about the 1864 election is that Lincoln only increased his popular votes by 1 percent over the 1860 contest. The election, therefore, might more accurately be interpreted as demonstrating how the Northern people were beginning to rally behind the Radicals than behind Lincoln personally.

## Lincoln's Second Inauguration

On March 4, 1865, Lincoln attended the inauguration of Vice President Andrew Johnson in the Senate chamber, at which time Johnson appeared to be drunk. Embarrassed at the spectacle, Lincoln quietly ordered that Johnson not be allowed to speak to the crowd assembled outside, then walked to a platform at the Capitol's east entrance to deliver his second inaugural address. At 703 words (just 25 sentences), it was one of the shortest in presidential history. However, the speech proved to be one of Lincoln's greatest, and the tone of his words and the atmosphere in which he spoke were more optimistic than his first address. The war was coming to a victorious close, and Lincoln used the occasion to set the stage for reunion.

Lincoln carefully avoided mentioning the Confederacy by name and did not place specific blame for who started the conflict. "Both parties deprecated war," he observed, "but one of them would *make* war rather than let the nation survive, and the other would *accept* war rather than let it perish, and the war came." Frequently using biblical references, Lincoln invoked the image of a vengeful Old Testament God who ordained the war to wipe out slavery. "Both read the same Bible and pray to the same God," he pointed out, "and each invokes His aid against the other. . . . The prayers of both could not be answered. That of neither has been answered fully. The Almighty has His own purposes. . . . [I]f God wills that [the war] continue until all the wealth piled by the bondsman's two hundred and fifty years of unrequited toil

Long Abraham Lincoln a Little Longer.

**"Long Abraham Lincoln a Little Longer."** This cartoon, which appeared in *Harper's Weekly* shortly after Lincoln was reelected, is a play on the president's lanky physique.

**Lincoln's Second Inauguration, March 4, 1865.** In this photograph of Lincoln's second inauguration, the president can be seen standing at the white lectern. Hidden among the crowd is future assassin John Wilkes Booth.

shall be sunk, and until every drop of blood drawn with the lash shall be paid by another drawn with the sword, as was said three thousand years ago, so still it must be said, 'the judgments of the Lord are true and righteous altogether.'" But Lincoln also suggested a New Testament forgiveness that offered hope for a peaceful reunion. "With malice toward none," he pledged, "with charity for all, with firmness in the right as God gives us to see the right, let us strive on to finish the work we are in, to bind up the nation's wounds, to care for him who shall have borne the battle and for his widow and his orphan, to do all which may achieve and cherish a just and lasting peace among ourselves and with all nations."

Lincoln was pleased with the speech and claimed it was "better than anything I have produced. . . ." Frederick Douglass agreed and told him it was a "sacred effort." But not everyone shared their feelings. Among the crowd listening was John Wilkes Booth, a noted actor and Confederate sympathizer. Booth had malice toward many people, especially Lincoln, and a month later he would set in motion a plot to kill the president.

# OTHER POLITICAL ISSUES

**March 2, 1861: Senate passes the Morrill Tariff**
**May 20, 1862: Lincoln signs into law the Homestead Act**
**July 1, 1862: Lincoln signs into law the Pacific Railroad Act**
**July 2, 1862: Lincoln signs into law the Morrill College Land Grant Act**
**October 3, 1863: Lincoln proclaims the Thanksgiving holiday**

Civil War politics in the Union were not always about the war. Despite the high casualties and controversies over conscription and the suspension of habeas corpus, the North prospered, and Congress took steps to ensure that prosperity would continue. Civil War congressional measures, in fact, completely transformed America and still affect us today. Many of the wartime legislative acts had been introduced during the Buchanan administration when the Republicans embraced their version of Henry Clay's American System. They pushed a number of bills to improve the economy and uplift the poor, but Southern opposition and Buchanan's veto prevented passage. When the Southern states seceded and their congressional delegations resigned, however, Northern politicians finally had the opportunity to pass their legislative agenda.

## The Homestead Act

Homesteading was one of several issues that divided the North and South before the Civil War. It was a practice allowing settlers to obtain free federal land by living on the property and making improvements over a number of years. Northerners generally supported homesteading, and the Free-Soil Party was created largely to lobby for it in Congress. Northern support increased after the Panic of 1857 because people saw homesteading as a way to uplift those who were left impoverished by the depression. Southerners, however, opposed the policy because they believed the states should control public land within their borders and feared Northerners might populate the western territories and install antislavery governments.

A homestead policy was part of the Republican's 1860 presidential platform, and Congress passed the Homestead Act in May 1862. Effective in January 1863, adult citizens, veterans, and heads of households could pay a $10 fee and claim 160 acres of federal land. If they lived on the property for five years and made improvements during that time, they received the land for free. Homesteading proved immensely popular, and Northern citizens claimed approximately 1.2 million acres of land in just 18 months. After the

Civil War, even more settlers—many of them veterans—took advantage of the liberal land policy and moved west.

## DID YOU KNOW?

### Thanksgiving

Most American students have been taught from kindergarten that the Thanksgiving holiday originated with the Pilgrims in early Massachusetts. Actually, Thanksgiving was created by Abraham Lincoln during the Civil War. Since the colonial days, Americans had celebrated some sort of feast or festival in the autumn to coincide with harvest time, but it was never a formal holiday. Lincoln issued a presidential proclamation on October 3, 1863, setting aside the last Thursday of November as "a day of Thanksgiving and Praise to our beneficent Father" to give thanks to God for the nation's blessings in a terrible time of war.

## The Transcontinental Railroad

Besides passing the Homestead Act, Congress helped settle the west by authorizing a transcontinental railroad. As seen in Chapter 2, the transcontinental railroad was another issue that divided the North and South during the antebellum period because both wanted it located in their region. When the Southern states seceded, however, there no longer was any opposition to a Northern route and Congress was able to pass the Pacific Railroad Act on July 1, 1862. This act authorized two companies to build a railroad linking California with the rest of the states. The Central Pacific started in Sacramento, California, and built east, while the Union Pacific started in Omaha, Nebraska, and built west. To help cover the tremendous construction costs, the federal government agreed to pay up to $48,000 and to give 6,400-acre land grants for each mile of track laid. The land grants were parceled out in checkerboard fashion on alternate sides of the track, and the amount of land was doubled in 1864.

To receive the greatest amount of money and land possible, the two railroads competed to lay the most track. The Central Pacific began work on October 26, 1863, while the Union Pacific laid its first rail on December 2. After tremendous difficulties, the two lines met at Promontory Summit, Utah, after the Civil War, and a ceremony referred to as the "Wedding of the Rails" was held on May 10, 1869, to connect the two lines officially. A large crowd watched as Leland Stanford, president of the Central Pacific Railroad, grabbed a heavy sledgehammer to drive in a golden spike to complete the line. Stanford made a mighty swing—and missed. His vice president tried next, but he missed as well, much to the amusement of the construction workers present. Finally, a construction foreman drove in the golden spike (which was promptly replaced with an iron one) and the transcontinental railroad was officially opened. Over the next few decades, thousands of settlers, many of whom were Civil War veterans, used this railroad and others to stream into the Great Plains to purchase land from the railroads or to claim their homesteads.

## The Morrill Acts

Vermont Congressman Justin Morrill sponsored two of the most important pieces of Civil War legislation. One was the Morrill Tariff in March 1861, which ushered in several decades of high tariffs to protect Northern industries from foreign competition. It eventually reached 47 percent and changed America's tariff from one of the lowest in the world to one of the highest. It is sometimes inaccurately claimed that the Morrill Tariff was intended to raise money to help fight the war. Actually, it passed the House in May 1860, *before* secession occurred. Lincoln supported the bill during the election, and the Senate passed the tariff two days before he was inaugurated. The high tariff had some adverse effect on British trade, and it was one reason many British citizens supported the Confederacy.

Congress passed the Morrill College Land Grant Act in 1862 to improve the higher education system. When the Civil War began, most universities were expensive private institutions that stressed liberal arts, but many Americans believed college should be made available to average students who could study subjects that actually applied to everyday life. For example, fewer than 1 percent of colleges had a department of agriculture, even though agriculture employed more Americans than any other field. During the Buchanan administration, Northerners introduced a bill to use federal land within the states to help finance agricultural and mechanical schools, but the Southerners defeated it because they were not interested in higher education and believed the states should control the federal land within their borders. It was not until the Southern states seceded that Congress was able to take action. In 1862, it created a new federal Department of Agriculture to promote modern agricultural techniques and passed the Morrill College Land Grant Act. This bill gave federal land to the individual states so they could sell it to settlers and use the proceeds to fund public colleges to teach "agriculture and mechanical arts." Approximately 25 million acres were turned over to the states, and at least seventy colleges were designated land grant colleges and benefited from the act. Among them were Iowa State University, Louisiana State University, Michigan State University, and Pennsylvania State University.

## The Supreme Court

While fighting the Civil War, Lincoln was fortunate that the Supreme Court usually supported his actions. This was no accident; Lincoln appointed four of the ten Civil War–era justices, including Salmon P. Chase, who became Chief Justice when Roger B. Taney died in 1864. Had Lincoln faced a more hostile court, many of his policies might have been derailed and the war effort weakened.

The Supreme Court made several decisions that affected how the war was fought. One of the most difficult issues it faced was deciding the legal status

**The U.S. Supreme Court.** President Lincoln appointed four of the ten Supreme Court justices who served during the Civil War. As a result, the court tended to support his wartime policies. This photograph (Chief Justice Salmon Chase is fourth from the right) was taken by Matthew Brady in 1869. It was the first photograph ever taken of the Supreme Court.

of the Confederates. Technically, they were traitors and subject to execution if captured. The Confederates, however, claimed they were citizens of an independent belligerent nation and demanded to be treated as prisoners of war. If the Union began executing captured enemy soldiers, it was certain the Confederates would retaliate in kind. Under Taney, the court straddled this difficult issue by establishing a double-status principle that stated the federal government was not only sovereign over the Confederates but also a belligerent fighting against them. This allowed Lincoln to continue to deny secession's legality while at the same time treat Confederate captives as prisoners of war.

The way in which Lincoln wielded executive power was another issue the Supreme Court had to address. Lincoln believed the Constitution gave him emergency powers to suspend certain constitutional rights during the rebellion without having to receive congressional approval. However, being a good politician, he frequently submitted his actions to Congress for ratification because he also needed its support. Sometimes, Lincoln had to act during congressional recesses, and the executive action was already a fait accompli by the time Congress took up the issue. One such case was when he declared the South was in rebellion on April 15, 1861, and established the blockade soon afterward, but Congress did not recognize the rebellion until July 13. Owners of Confederate blockade runners that were captured between the two dates sued for their ships' return on the grounds that Lincoln had overstepped his constitutional authority when he announced the blockade before Congress recognized a state of insurrection existed. In what became known as the Prize Cases, the Supreme Court narrowly ruled (5-4) that the president had the responsibility to suppress a domestic rebellion as soon as it occurred and did not have to wait for Congress to "baptize it with a name." On July 13, the same day Congress recognized the rebellion, the court also ruled that the conflict was a legal state of war and gave Lincoln the authority to assume wartime powers.

The confiscation acts also troubled Lincoln because it was questionable whether Congress had the constitutional authority to confiscate property before the courts found anyone guilty of a crime. If secession was illegal, as Lincoln claimed, Southerners were still U.S. citizens and protected by the Constitution. In that case, it would seem the confiscation acts were illegal and discriminatory because the Fifth Amendment guaranteed all citizens their property rights—secessionists included. How could it be constitutional to confiscate a Confederate's property in Alabama, and not a Copperhead's property in Ohio? Lincoln eventually supported the confiscation acts as a necessary wartime measure, and once again the Supreme Court upheld the acts by declaring that the wartime emergency justified Congress in taking extreme measures to weaken the Rebels militarily.

Lincoln's most controversial wartime actions were suspending habeas corpus and trying civilians in military courts. In *Ex parte Merryman,* Chief Justice Taney ruled against the suspensions because they were not sanctioned by Congress, and he criticized Lincoln for not showing "a proper respect for the high office he fills. . . . He certainly does not faithfully execute the laws if he takes upon himself the legislative power, by suspending the writ of habeas corpus, and the judicial power also, by arresting and imprisoning a person without due process of law." At first, Lincoln followed the tactic used by Andrew Jackson when Chief Justice George Marshall ruled in favor of the Cherokees during the Indian removal period. Lincoln simply ignored the court and continued to suspend habeas corpus when he thought it was necessary; but, in March 1863, Congress finally passed the Habeas Corpus Act to comply with the court's ruling.

In 1866, a year after the war ended, the Supreme Court again considered the legality of Lincoln's wartime actions in *Ex parte Milligan.* Benjamin F. Butler, the government's chief lawyer, dramatically defended the late president for suspending habeas corpus when he exclaimed, "We do not desire to exalt the martial above the civil law. . . . We demand only that when the law is silent; when justice is overthrown . . . when the judge is deposed; when the juries are dispersed; when the sheriff, the executive officer of the law, is powerless; when the bayonet is called in as the final arbiter; when on its armed forces the government must rely for all it has of power, authority, and dignity . . . then we ask that martial law may prevail, so that the civil law may live again, live, to the end that this may be a 'government of laws and not of men.'" But in this important case, the court ruled against the government by declaring it was unconstitutional for military courts to try civilians in regions where the civilian courts still functioned. Although *Ex parte Milligan* had no effect on the Civil War, it did limit the government's powers in future emergencies.

## FOR FURTHER READING

Lincoln's Thanksgiving Proclamation
Lincoln's letter to James Conkling
1864 Union Party platform
1864 Democratic Party platform
Lincoln's Second Inaugural Address

# CHAPTER 13

# The Politics of Rebellion

**The Confederate Government**

**The Loyal Opposition**

**Southern Unionism**

On the morning of April 2, 1863, hundreds of women and a few boys surged through the streets of Richmond, Virginia. The Civil War had been raging for two years. Shortages were becoming commonplace for Southerners, and the angry crowd demanded that officials provide more food for the people. Some of the women were armed with knives and hatchets, and one boasted she would have either "bread or blood" that morning. The crowd soon abandoned all restraint and began breaking windows and looting stores for jewelry and clothing. Governor John Letcher and Mayor Joseph Mayo confronted the mob with militiamen and tried unsuccessfully to calm the people. A witness reported that Mayo "had the Riot Act read . . . and then threatened to fire on the mob. He gave them five minutes' time to disperse in, threatening to use military force . . . if they did not comply with the demand."

With watch in hand, Mayo was counting down his deadline when President Jefferson Davis suddenly appeared and climbed atop a wagon to address the crowd. If the people were expecting satisfaction, they were quickly disappointed when Davis began scolding them for demanding bread while burglarizing stores for loot. He warned the mob such behavior would only frighten area farmers and prevent any food from being delivered to the city. Then to shame the women, the president pulled out what money he had in his pockets, threw it to the ground, and declared, "You say you are hungry and have no money. Here is all I have. It is not much, but take it." Dramatically, Davis then took out his own watch and repeated Mayo's order to disperse. "We do not desire to injure anyone," he said, "but this lawlessness must stop." When the militiamen readied their weapons, the crowd finally began to melt away. To prevent more disorder and to prop up morale, Davis ordered the city newspapers to avoid any reference to the riot and the telegraph company not to transmit news of the incident over the wires.

The Bread Riot was a stark reminder that popular support for the war effort depended a great deal on how it affected people's daily lives. Like his Northern counterpart, Abraham Lincoln, Davis found it difficult to maintain support for his administration as he was forced to take more draconian measures to fight the enemy. States' rights philosophy was the bedrock of Southern principles, but Confederate leaders were pragmatic and frequently sacrificed those principles for the good of the nation. Such actions, however, led to a vicious cycle. As power was centralized in the national government and stronger measures were taken to maintain the armies and suppress dissent, opposition became increasingly vocal. Most Southern whites continued to fight for independence throughout the war, but many began to question whether the Davis administration was capable of winning that fight.

## THE CONFEDERATE GOVERNMENT

**February 4, 1861: Delegates convene the Provisional Congress in Montgomery, Alabama**
**February 8, 1861: Provisional Congress adopts the Provisional Constitution**
**February 18, 1861: President Davis and Vice President Stephens are sworn in as provisional officers**
**March 11, 1861: Provisional Congress adopts the Permanent Constitution**
**March 21, 1861: Stephens delivers the "Cornerstone Speech"**
**March 26, 1861: States ratify the Constitution**
**November 6, 1861: Elections are held to select permanent officials**
**February 22, 1862: Davis is inaugurated as permanent president**

When the Southerners seceded and formed the Confederacy, they proudly proclaimed it was the Second American Revolution. Secessionists viewed the rebellion as conservative in nature and necessary to safeguard the republican ideals established by the Founding Fathers. During the Montgomery Convention, Vice President Alexander Stephens reflected this conservative mood when he declared, "No body looking on would ever take this Congress to be a lot of Revolutionists." The Confederates had no desire to reshape society as the French had done seventy years earlier because they believed the South had always stayed faithful to the Constitutional framers' intent of creating a federal republic based on state sovereignty. It was the North, they claimed, that had begun usurping power in violation of that intent. The Southern states did not secede because they opposed the Constitution and the Union but because they believed the North had corrupted the Constitution and Union. In 1861, even South Carolina fire-eater Robert Barnwell Rhett declared, "[T]he South was always satisfied with the Constitution of the United States." But Southerners believed their attempts to safeguard constitutional rights by the existing political process had failed, and secession was the only way to protect themselves against perceived Northern tyranny.

# The Confederate Constitution

In some regards, the Confederate Constitution's preamble was strikingly different from that of the United States. The former declared, "We, the people of the Confederate States, each State acting in its sovereign and independent character, in order to form a permanent federal government, establish justice, insure domestic tranquility and secure the blessings of liberty to ourselves and our posterity—invoking the favor and guidance of Almighty God—do ordain and establish this Constitution for the Confederate States of America." Although the differences in the two preambles seem subtle at first, they reveal strong differences in political theory. Not only did the Confederate preamble pointedly declare that each state was sovereign, it also reflected the Southerners' strict constructionist philosophy. The Confederate preamble made no mention of promoting "the general welfare," a phrase that loose constructionists sometimes used to defend federally funded internal improvements and other economic policies. The Confederates also specifically asked the blessings of Almighty God.

Since slavery was the most important states' rights issue that led to secession, it is not surprising the Confederate Constitution addressed it in great detail. While the U.S. Constitution never actually mentioned slavery by name, the Confederate document referred to it ten times. To guarantee the continued existence of the peculiar institution, the Constitution stipulated neither Congress nor any state could pass a law that would interfere with a person's right to own slaves or to take them into any part of the Confederacy. Ironically, this constitutional protection was a direct contradiction of states' rights theory because it took slavery rights out of the states' hands and placed them in the hands of the national government. The Confederates also recognized slaves as three-fifths of a person for representation purposes as did the U.S. Constitution, adopted an almost identical fugitive slave law, and continued to ban the African slave trade. The latter action was taken to keep Europe friendly toward the new nation and to prevent competition with some older states that wanted to sell their excess slave population.

The Confederate Constitution also took steps to limit the national government's power. Many Southerners had long believed the U.S. Congress had overstepped its constitutional authority by creating the Bank of the United States, funding internal improvements, and passing protective tariffs. The Confederate Constitution, besides making no reference to promoting the nation's general welfare, specifically stated that Congress had only those powers "delegated" to it. Protective tariffs were prohibited, although a revenue tariff was permitted to help fund the government, and congressionally funded internal improvements were limited to improving navigation on natural bodies of water. On this latter point, one congressman declared, "This clause alone is worth all the sacrifice we may be called on to encounter in the great revolution in which we are engaged."

The Confederates recognized each state's sovereignty and made sure their Constitution included numerous states' rights safeguards. For example, individual

## DID YOU KNOW?

### Nullification and Secession

Nullification and secession were two rights Confederates held dear, but neither was even mentioned in their Constitution. The framers may have thought it unnecessary since most citizens accepted these rights without question; secession, after all, directly led to the creation of the Confederate States. A more likely explanation of why the framers left them out is because they realized nullification and secession might threaten the new nation. Except for West Virginia (which was occupied by Union troops early in the war), secession never occurred in the Confederacy, but it is interesting to contemplate. Would Jefferson Davis have allowed a state to leave the Confederacy peacefully in the midst of war, or would he have followed Abraham Lincoln's example and used all of his presidential power to keep the Confederacy intact?

state governments were given the power to impeach Confederate judges and officials and have them tried by the Senate (this power was never exercised). Civil suits involving citizens from different states were heard in a state, not Confederate, court, and state courts could issue writs of habeas corpus to protect citizens from being conscripted for military service by national conscription agents. Each state was also allowed to levy its own export and import tariffs on goods traveling between states. Unlike the U.S. Constitution, which required constitutional amendments to originate in Congress, the Confederates allowed the states to initiate amendments. Congress was forced to convene a constitutional convention attended by all states if three or more states called for one. Amendments required ratification by two-thirds of the states, and a two-thirds vote by both houses of Congress was required to admit new states.

## The Branches of Government

When the seceding states' delegates met at the Montgomery Convention, they formed a Provisional Congress and appointed President Jefferson Davis and Vice President Alexander Stephens as provisional officers. It was agreed that Davis, Stephens, and the congressmen would serve in their positions until elections could be held in November 1861 to select permanent officials. At that time, Davis and Stephens were elected without any serious opposition, and they and the newly elected congressmen were sworn into office in February 1862.

The Confederate Constitution created a three-branch government similar to that of the United States. The executive branch included the president, vice president, and the cabinet. Both the president and vice president served a six-year term, but the president was ineligible for reelection. This was seen as an advantage over the U.S. system because it gave a president more time to accomplish his agenda without having to worry about reelection. The president appointed the cabinet members and they served at his discretion. Both the Confederate president and the cabinet members were given political powers not found in the U.S. government. Davis enjoyed the privilege of line item veto, for example, and cabinet members were allowed to attend congressional sessions and enter debates (but not vote) on issues concerning their departments.

While the Provisional Congress was unicameral, the permanent Congress included a house and senate. Eventually, thirteen states were represented in Congress because the Confederates recognized secessionist governments in Kentucky and Missouri, even though those two states never officially seceded. There also were non-voting representatives from the Arizona Territory and several Indian nations.

The Confederate Constitution also provided for district courts and a Supreme Court. The former were created by simply recognizing the existing U.S. federal district courts as Confederate courts. The Supreme Court, however, was never actually established because of congressional disagreements on states' rights issues. Some congressmen wanted the Supreme Court to have the same appellate jurisdiction over state courts as the U.S. Supreme Court, while others wanted state court decisions to be final because they believed the states should have the right to interpret for themselves the constitutionality of national laws. Unable to agree on the matter, Congress never mustered the necessary votes to create a Supreme Court.

## The Cabinet

Although set up in a similar manner, the Confederate cabinet lacked the strong personalities and political influence found in the U.S. cabinet because Davis did not allow his department heads to wield much power or influence. Nonetheless, he did share Lincoln's problems of having to contend with conflicting personalities and personal agendas. One important difference was that Davis did not have to campaigning for reelection because the Constitution limited him to one six-year term.

The Confederate Constitution created six departments within the executive branch and allowed the president to appoint the heads of each. Like Lincoln, Davis tried to gain the support of various political factions by picking capable men who were representative of the entire Confederacy. He told his wife, "I can trust my own methods so far that they are humanitarian, and, I feel sure, honest—but I want the stand-point of other honest eyes, single to the good of our people and of the country." Most of Davis's appointees fulfilled their duties as well as circumstances permitted, and they represented nine of the eleven Confederate states. The original cabinet included Attorney General Judah P. Benjamin (Louisiana), Secretary of the Navy Stephen R. Mallory (Florida), Postmaster General John H. Reagan (Texas), Secretary of State Robert Toombs (Georgia), Secretary of the Treasury Christopher G. Memminger (South Carolina), and Secretary of War Leroy P. Walker (Alabama). Of the fourteen men who eventually served in the cabinet, Benjamin was the most important because he held three different positions and enjoyed considerable influence with Davis.

Over the years, the cabinet underwent frequent changes as some secretaries resigned for political or personal reasons, and others were replaced by Davis. Only Mallory and Reagan kept their positions for the entire war. Secretary of the Navy Mallory performed well, creating a navy from scratch, developing new technologies such as ironclads and submarines, and sending highly successful agents to purchase European vessels. Postmaster General Reagan strongly supported Davis and created a functioning postal system by using captured Union equipment and supplies and hiring former U.S. postal employees. Because he needed every available man for his department, Reagan frequently clashed with the War Department, however, because he wanted to exempt postal employees from being conscripted into the army.

Four men served as attorney general. In September 1861, Davis transferred Benjamin to the more important War Department and appointed Thomas Bragg attorney general. Bragg was from North Carolina and the brother of General Braxton Bragg. His service in the cabinet is somewhat odd because he had strong doubts as to whether the Confederacy could even survive. In February 1862, Bragg wrote in his diary, "I must confess that taking a survey of our whole field of operations it seems to me that our cause is hopeless—God grant that I may be mistaken." Despite his doubts, Bragg served well and generally got along with Davis. He tried to ensure that impressment agents paid a fair price for goods taken and lobbied unsuccessfully to create the Supreme Court. Bragg resigned his position for unknown reasons in March 1862 and was replaced by Thomas H. Watts (Alabama). Because there was no Supreme Court, Watts spent much of his time writing legal opinions to interpret Confederate law, and he usually supported administration policy. Among his more important opinions, Watts ruled conscription was legal and declared some state laws were unconstitutional because they conflicted with Confederate law. Watts resigned in August 1863 after being elected Alabama's governor and was replaced by George Davis (North Carolina), another strong Davis supporter.

Three men served as secretary of state, but none succeeded in winning diplomatic recognition for the Confederacy. Toombs was the original secretary, but he and Davis frequently clashed. The hard-drinking, self-centered Toombs (whom one man described as "the great I am") was jealous of Davis because he, too, had been a presidential contender at the Montgomery Convention. Becoming angry at Davis's constant interference in his department, Toombs resigned in July 1861, became a brigadier general, and went to war. He was replaced by Robert M. T. Hunter (Virginia), whose most important action was to send James Mason and John Slidell on their ill-fated mission to Europe. When Hunter resigned in February 1862 to join the senate, Judah P. Benjamin was appointed secretary of state, and he held the position until war's end. Although unpopular with many Confederates, Benjamin was loyal to Davis and earned the president's trust.

Secretary of the Treasury Memminger was another Davis supporter, but he frequently clashed with Congress because it interfered in his department. Memminger opposed Cotton Diplomacy and issued millions of dollars in treasury notes even though he had always supported specie. Blamed for much of the Confederacy's economic failure, he made many enemies in the government and resigned in July 1864 amid growing criticism. George A. Trenholm

(South Carolina) then took over the Treasury Department, but by then the Confederate economy was in shambles and Trenholm could do little to improve the situation.

It is not surprising that the War Department experienced the most cabinet changes because Davis often angered the secretaries by micromanaging that department more than any other. Davis first appointed Leroy P. Walker as secretary of war even though he had no military experience. Walker, described by one man as "a profuse spitter," was successful in creating an army, but he did not believe the war would last long and failed to order enough weapons from Europe to arm all of the recruits. Walker was reputed to be "one of the giant intellects of the South," but he also was one of the cabinet's weakest members because he was quarrelsome, a poor administrator, and lacked tact. Walker resigned in September 1861 after clashing with Davis on strategy and becoming tired of the president's meddling. He was replaced by Judah P. Benjamin, but Benjamin resigned in March 1862 after many congressmen blamed him for the defeats at Forts Henry and Donelson. George W. Randolph (Virginia) then took over the War Department and served nine months. During that time he greatly improved the department by appointing Josiah Gorgas to head the Bureau of Ordnance, weeding out waste and corruption, and pressuring Davis to allocate more resources to defend the west. However, Randolph did not work well with the president and resigned in November 1862 after becoming increasingly frustrated at Davis's interference. General Gustavus W. Smith (Kentucky) took over as interim secretary for a few days before Davis appointed his good friend James A. Seddon (Virginia).

Seddon served as secretary of war longer than any other because he accepted Davis's interference and deferred to him in nearly all matters concerning strategy and personnel. This loyalty, particularly his acquiescence in the 1864 firing of General Joseph E. Johnston during the Atlanta Campaign, earned Seddon many enemies in Congress. Davis successfully deflected strong political pressure to fire him, but Seddon finally resigned in February 1865. He had given the Confederacy his best, but Seddon's son claimed the former secretary "was completely crushed" when the South surrendered and that he "considered his life to have been a complete failure." The last secretary of war was John C. Breckinridge (Kentucky), the former U.S. presidential candidate and a popular general. He served well with the few resources at hand, supported an honorable surrender when there was no hope for victory, and participated in the surrender negotiations between Generals William T. Sherman and Joseph E. Johnston in North Carolina.

Of all the members of the executive branch, Vice President Stephens proved to be the odd man out. A moderate and Unionist, he actually opposed secession in 1861 but was appointed vice president because of his impeccable character and popularity with Georgia voters. Stephens almost immediately clashed with Davis over matters of policy and bitterly opposed such measures as conscription and the suspension of habeas corpus. He once wrote of the president, "While I do not and never have regarded [Davis] as a great man or

# BIOGRAPHY
## Alexander Hamilton Stephens: Little Aleck

**Alexander Stephens**

Georgia native Alexander Stephens (1812–1883) was unusually intelligent and graduated first in the 1832 Franklin College class. An outstanding public speaker and popular Whig politician, he served as both a state legislator and congressman before the Civil War. Stephens was a lifelong bachelor and a frail and sickly man who became known as "Little Aleck" because he never weighed more than 90 lbs. One acquaintance claimed, "A more pinched up, misshapen, dead-and-alive specimen of humanity" could not be found. Stephens's emaciated pasty face and frizzled gray hair made him look far older than he was, and he even described himself as "a malformed ill-shaped half finished thing."

Stephens joined the Democratic Party and became a leading Southern moderate who supported slavery and states' rights but not at the peril of the Union. In the 1860 election, he supported Stephen A. Douglas but remained a close friend of Abraham Lincoln. Stephens stood virtually alone as a Unionist when he attended the Georgia secession convention and spoke passionately against disunion. When the secession ordinance passed, however, he bowed to the inevitable and signed the document. Despite his well-known Unionism, Stephens was chosen as a delegate to the Montgomery Convention. Although he stood up for his Unionist beliefs, people still trusted him, and even fire-eater Robert Barnwell Rhett admitted, "I like Stephens better than any one of them." The high regard in which other Confederates held Stephens was evident when he was chosen the provisional vice president. Unfortunately, Stephens and Jefferson Davis clashed almost immediately. Davis was particularly angry at Stephens's highly publicized "Cornerstone Speech," in which Stephens declared slavery was "the immediate cause of the late rupture and present revolution." Davis's anger stemmed not from any disagreement

statesman on a large scale, or a man of any marked genius, yet I have regarded him as a man of good intentions, weak and vacillating, timid, petulant, peevish, obstinate, but not firm." In turn, Davis virtually ignored Stephens's advice on all matters. Completely frustrated, Stephens finally returned to Georgia and remained there for most of the war.

## THE LOYAL OPPOSITION

**February 27, 1862: Congress authorizes Davis to suspend habeas corpus**
**April 2, 1863: Richmond Bread Riot**
**October 13, 1863: Second suspension of habeas corpus**
**February 17, 1864: Third suspension of habeas corpus**

with Stephens's assessment of slavery but from his trying to downplay the slavery issue to gain European diplomatic recognition.

In November 1861, Stephens was elected to a permanent six-year term, but his relationship with Davis continued to worsen. Davis viewed the executive department as his personal domain and tended to ignore Stephens's advice on important issues. Stephens also angered Davis by opposing conscription and the suspension of habeas corpus. Rejecting Davis's argument they were necessary to win the war, Stephens declared that such policies threatened personal liberty. "Away with the idea of getting independence first, and looking for liberty afterwards," he proclaimed. "Our liberties, once lost, may be lost forever."

Stephens eventually joined forces with fellow Georgians, Governor Joseph Brown and former Secretary of State Robert Toombs, to oppose nearly all of Davis's policies. Their relationship spiraled downward to the point that Stephens finally left Richmond and returned to Georgia. He remained there for most of the war and became a virtual nonentity within the Confederate government. From his home, Stephens continually called on Davis to negotiate a peace. In his words, "[T]he only peace that the sword alone will bring us in fighting the united North will be the peace of death & subjugation." In early 1865, he returned to Richmond to attend the Hampton Roads Peace Conference because of his friendship with Lincoln and because of his long-time support of a negotiated peace. The conference failed, however, and Stephens was forced to recognize that a negotiated settlement was impossible.

Because he had served as a high-ranking Confederate official, Stephens was imprisoned in Fort Warren, Massachusetts, after the war and remained there until he was paroled in October 1865. Despite being constantly at odds with Davis during the Civil War, he remained popular in Georgia and was elected to the U.S. Senate in January 1866. The Radical Republicans refused to seat him, however, so Stephens practiced law until he won a congressional seat in 1872. He also wrote *A Constitutional View of the Late War Between the States* and was elected governor in 1882.

The Confederate people have often been portrayed as slaveholding farmers who agreed on the main political issues. In reality, few white Southerners owned slaves, and they had long been fragmented into factions that looked after various specific interests. People in the different geographic areas competed with one another economically and fought to secure railroads and other improvements for their regions. Often, these economic goals were more important than political philosophy. It has been seen in earlier chapters that most Southerners opposed federally funded internal improvements and protective tariffs. Louisiana sugar planters, however, actually supported sugar tariffs to protect against foreign competition, and some progressive businessmen pushed for internal improvements to modernize the South's transportation system. Frequently, personality cults played a larger role in Southern politics than they did in the North as voters became divided not so much by issues as by following particular dynamic political personalities.

## The Discontented

What united most Confederates was a firm belief in slavery, personal liberty, and states' rights. As long as the government protected those things, most white Southerners enthusiastically supported the Confederacy and the war effort. However, it became more and more difficult for the people to present a united front when those basic values were attacked, and the war began to hit home in a more personal manner. Eighty percent of the eligible adult white males served in the Confederate army, so virtually every family mourned the deaths of friends and loved ones. Nearly everyone suffered from food shortages and grumbled about unpopular government policies that became more and more intrusive on private lives. People who lived in combat areas also endured untold hardships as Union armies swept through the region confiscating what livestock and food the Confederate impressment agents had left behind. Typical of a disgruntled Confederate was an Arkansan who wrote, "[W]e are now overrun by a brutal and unrelenting foe, our wives, children and every thing dear to us is exposed to the wants and appetites of an unprincipled army who are now in force within our state. . . . [S]tarvation and unparalleled suffering will be the fate of our people unless some relief is speedily afforded." Once the enemy departed, Southern civilians often found their own troops took what was left. North Carolina governor Zebulon Vance may have been contemplating that fact when he wrote, "If God Almighty had yet in store another plague for the Egyptians worse than all others, I am sure it must have been a regiment or so of half-armed, half-disciplined confederate cavalry."

Even deep in the heartland where the armies never ventured, citizens were victimized by bands of Jayhawkers. These heavily armed gangs of criminals and deserters stole what they wanted from helpless families left unprotected when the local men joined the army. One citizen wrote, "As often as that lawless band visits this part of the country, outrages of the deepest dye are daily committed in our midst. . . . They do not as much as respect private rooms, but enter in spite of tears and entreaties, and turn up beds, rip them open, search closets, brake open what happens to be locked, [and] in fact they leave no corner untouched." Louisiana Governor Thomas Moore believed such trouble on the home front stemmed from the fact that the "large proportion of the good material of our State is in the Army, pretty much *all* the bad left. . . ." By mid-war, Jayhawkers had become so active in North Louisiana that Confederate cavalry had to be sent into several parishes to restore order.

Despite growing complaints about food shortages, Jayhawkers, and unpopular government policies such as conscription, impressment, and taxes, most Southern whites continued to support independence. But many did begin to question whether Jefferson Davis was capable of achieving that goal. Their anger tended to focus on administration policies that seemed to violate their civil rights and the government's inability to maintain order. A Mississippian complaining of his state's myriad problems declared that "no power can arrest it unless the Executive can do so." This "loyal opposition," however, should not be confused with the Southern Unionists who actively opposed the Confederacy and supported the Union.

A number of powerful Confederate politicians also began to oppose Davis because they believed he was either incompetent or a threat to civil liberties. Vice President Stephens was an early critic, but instead of fighting Davis within the government, he went home to Georgia and continued to complain from there. James Henry Hammond, a wealthy South Carolina planter, criticized the president for being inefficient and for adopting oppressive policies that threatened individual liberty. Tennessee congressman Henry Foote was a former Mississippi governor who had been a political foe of Davis for years. His main goal was to protect the Mississippi Valley, and he became a bitter opponent when the enemy took control of the river in 1863. Foote claimed Davis was trying to become a dictator, had only "power for mischief," and would serve the Confederacy best by being placed in a mental institution. Several other politicians, such as Senator Louis Wigfall (Texas), agreed with Foote that the western theater was more critical than Virginia. Wigfall started out a Davis supporter and even introduced the conscription bill, but he soon lost confidence in the president, whom he called a "dish of skimmed milk." Wigfall joined Foote and Generals Joseph E. Johnston and P. G. T. Beauregard (two of Davis's most vocal military critics) to pressure Davis to allocate more resources to protect the Mississippi Valley and Georgia.

Influential state governors also frequently clashed with Davis over certain states' rights issues. Georgia's Governor Joseph E. Brown accused the Confederate government of usurping power from the states and opposed policies such as conscription, impressment, and suspending habeas corpus. When the draft bill was passed, Brown wrote a letter to Davis declaring conscription was "subversive of [Georgia's] sovereignty, and at war with all the principles for the support of which Georgia entered into this revolution." The governor fumed, "No acts of the Government of the United States prior to the secession of Georgia struck a blow at constitutional liberty so fell as has been stricken by the conscript acts." Brown fought the conscription act by demanding many exemptions for Georgia citizens and by refusing to turn over control of the state militia to Confederate authorities. Georgians, in turn, supported Brown for exempting men from conscription and providing relief measures such as taking control of the state's salt supply and selling it at discounted prices. Brown also opposed high taxes because of their disproportionate impact on the poor. "[T]he poor," he wrote, "have generally paid their part . . . in military service, exposure, fatigue and blood, the rich, who have been in a much greater degree exempt from these, should meet the money demands of the Government." It is little wonder that Joseph E. Brown was one of the Confederacy's most popular governors. While he put the needs of his people first and was not hesitant to condemn what he thought were unfair Confederate policies, the governor was still devoted to independence. "Georgia," he declared, "has the power to act independently but her faith is pledged by implication to her Southern sisters. . . . [Georgia] will triumph with her Southern sisters or sink with them in common ruin."

North Carolina's Zebulon Vance, a proslavery Unionist before secession, was another governor who was connected to the loyal opposition. North Carolina suffered more deaths in the Confederate army than any other state, and it led the Confederacy in the number of blockade runners. Not surprisingly, Vance believed his people carried more than their fair share of the war burden and was convinced his primary duty was to use the state's resources to take care of its own soldiers and citizens first. He was particularly successful in providing his men with uniforms and blankets throughout the war. Once North Carolinians were properly supplied, however, Vance willingly shared his resources with other states. In his relationship with Davis, Vance walked a fine line between supporting many government policies and opposing others. He backed conscription as a military necessity and saw the need for impressing supplies and passing high taxes, but he opposed the suspension of habeas corpus and quarreled with Davis when corrupt impressment agents abused their authority. Vance also took Davis to task for trying to draft state officials into military service and for not promoting North Carolina officers. "It is mortifying," he wrote, "to find entire brigades of North Carolina soldiers commanded by strangers, and in many cases our own brave and war-torn colonels are made to give place to colonels from distant states."

A number of newspaper editors belonged to the loyal opposition that criticized Davis. Most notable were Robert Barnwell Rhett of the *Charleston Mercury* and John Daniel and Edward Pollard of the *Richmond Examiner*. None held a very high opinion of the president. Early in the war, Rhett opined, "Jeff Davis now treats all men as if they were idiot insects," and Pollard once wrote that Davis brushed off advice from congressmen "with a politeness so studied as to be almost sarcastic, with a manner that so plainly gave the idea that his company talked to a post." Despite the editors' sometimes vicious criticism, the Davis administration never attempted to censor anti-government newspapers. The only strong steps taken to control the press were to make sure sensitive military information was not leaked to the enemy. In the war's first months, the Confederate government appointed agents to monitor and censor military information being transmitted by telegraph, and the postal service was authorized to censor the mail. These measures were never enforced rigorously, however, and officials usually just appealed to the press's sense of patriotism and requested restraint in printing sensitive information. Because little was done to prevent newspapers from criticizing government policies, the loyal opposition had ready access to the media to spread their points of view.

## The No Party System

The lack of political parties through which to challenge Davis's leadership weakened the Confederacy's loyal opposition. A one-party system had been characteristic of the Deep South for some time. When the Whig Party began to collapse in the mid-1850s, Whigs in the upper South and Border States struggled on, but voters in the Deep South united within the Democratic Party to oppose growing Republican power. This one-party system was evident at the Montgomery Convention, where the delegates appeared united on the critical issues of slavery, secession, and independence. In what was seen as a cooperative atmosphere reminiscent of the Revolutionary War, they prided themselves on the ability to work together to form a new government and not pursue divisive party politics. When the permanent Congress convened in early 1862, the president pro tem even boasted to the congressmen that "the spirit of party has never shown itself for an instant in your deliberations."

This apparent sense of unity and cooperation was misleading, however. As seen earlier, Southern whites were actually deeply divided over a number of issues, but it was impossible to debate them effectively without a party system. In contrast, Northern political parties remained in place after the war began, and the Democrats became the loyal opposition. Many Republicans were also critical of Lincoln, but they generally toed the line and supported him out of party loyalty and to gain political patronage. No such party system existed in the Confederacy, however, and Davis's critics had no vehicle through which to channel their opposition. For the most part, administration opponents did not even have the means to hand out the patronage necessary to gain support and win converts. Thus, the loyal opposition was fragmented, unfocused, and unable to challenge seriously the administration and was left to form cliques and factions that often coalesced around particular personalities.

## Suspending the Writ of Habeas Corpus

While the loyal opposition lacked the necessary means to challenge Davis's leadership effectively, Davis had one powerful weapon with which to silence his critics. Like its U.S. counterpart, the Confederate Constitution allowed for the suspension of the writ of habeas corpus in times of emergency. To maintain civil order, and particularly to detain critics and enforce the conscription act, the Confederate Congress approved suspending habeas corpus three times between February 1862 and February 1864. These suspensions demonstrate just how willing Confederate leaders sometimes were to sacrifice states' rights and personal liberty in order to prosecute the war more effectively. Each of the measures, however, expired after an explicit period of time. In hindsight, the suspension of habeas corpus may have actually hurt the Confederacy because it created even more discontent among citizens who saw it as a dangerous expansion of government power and a violation of their civil rights.

The people were tired of war and government intrusion by the time Davis requested a third suspension in his 1864 annual message to Congress. One Southerner noted the suspension request "was read amid profound silence." Negative reaction was immediate and intense. A Virginian claimed approval of the request would be "the last organized act of the Confederacy," and an Arkansas politician warned his colleagues if they passed the measure, "you may bid farewell for a long time to any support from the Trans Mississippi." Despite the intense opposition, a majority of congressmen felt the suspension was necessary to maintain order and approved Davis's request. However, Congress declined to cooperate when the president came back in November to ask for a fourth suspension.

## An Exhausted People

Civilian opposition to the Confederate government was directly linked to battlefield defeats and worsening conditions on the home front. Early in the war, most Southern whites supported the Davis administration. It was not until substantial Confederate territory was lost, casualties mounted among friends and family, and supply shortages increased that a large number of people began speaking out against the government. Food shortages particularly outraged lower-class citizens and led to Richmond's 1863 Bread Riot. When similar disturbances occurred in other Confederate towns, some people were convicted of and imprisoned for rioting.

In addition to an absolute belief in slavery, a strong commitment to personal liberty and states' rights were two reasons why Southerners had supported secession in the first place. When Davis began wielding governmental power to force citizens to support the war effort, many saw it as oppression and were hard-pressed to see any difference between the Davis and Lincoln administrations. Planters opposed a policy that forced them to grow food items rather than cotton, and shipowners resented being required to reserve a percentage of their precious cargo space on blockade runners for government supplies. Conscription, impressment, and taxation were particularly unpopular with the lower classes because they often were not applied equally. The Twenty Negro Law (see Chapter 4) exempted wealthy planters and overseers from military service, and unscrupulous conscription officers sometimes exempted friends and family members. Small farmers complained they were forced to give 10 percent of their crops to the government under the tax-in-kind law while nonagricultural workers only paid a 2 percent income tax. Slave ownership, the Confederacy's greatest financial asset, was not taxed at all. Such inequities led people to criticize the conflict as "a rich man's war and a poor man's fight." Many citizens refused to cooperate with controversial measures and hid draft dodgers and deserters from conscription officers and resources from impressment agents. By 1863, such widespread discontent led many Confederates to seek independence through a negotiated peace rather than battlefield victory. These peace advocates argued that negotiating would strengthen the Northern peace movement and put tremendous political pressure on Lincoln to end the war. But Davis disagreed, claiming it was pointless to negotiate because Lincoln had clearly stated he would accept nothing short of a reunited nation.

## Desertion

Growing civilian discontent and unpopular government policies had a dire effect on the army as family members pressured soldiers to come home to care for them. Because there was virtually no postal censorship, relatives were free to write loved ones about the hardships they suffered from food shortages, impressment abuses, high taxes, and Jayhawker attacks. The vast majority of Confederate soldiers were committed to independence but when forced to choose between serving in the army or providing for their families, thousands of men voted with their feet and went home. Many others deserted to avoid combat or because they believed the army had treated them unfairly.

Desertions only increased as the prospect of victory became more remote. Friends and family willingly hid deserters from the authorities, and many soldiers found it difficult to counter the logic of those who encouraged them to run away. A Georgia soldier on furlough wrote to his brother in the army, "There is no sens of fighting any longer no how for we are done gone up the spout. . . . The confederacy is done whipped it is sensles to deny it any longer. . . . The people here are nearly all unanimously against war holding on any longer. . . . There is no difficulty now in staying at home [and] no opposition from the citizens. . . . I can tell you if you can only get here with out being took up it is all right—for in the place of opposition you will have protection."

Jefferson Davis and his generals were reluctant to punish deserters harshly because they feared it would lower morale. Instead, they often used amnesty proclamations to encourage absent soldiers to return to the army voluntarily. A large number of men deserted in the spring of 1862 after Congress passed the conscription act, which forced soldiers already on duty to remain in the army for the war's duration. On May 9, the War Department ordered all absentee soldiers back to their units and implied they would be granted amnesty. When desertions increased after the military reversals of 1863, Davis issued a second proclamation on August 1. This time he specifically offered amnesty to those soldiers (except multiple offenders) who returned within twenty days. Army and department commanders issued similar proclamations, but generally such offers had little success because deserters usually were not severely punished even if apprehended.

## SOUTHERN UNIONISM

**June 11, 1861: Wheeling Convention convenes**
**April 3, 1862: West Virginia ratifies its state constitution**
**August 10, 1862: Union sympathizers murdered at Nueces River, Texas**
**October 1–20, 1862: Great Hanging at Gainesville, Texas**
**January 18, 1863: Southern Unionists murdered at Shelton Laurel, North Carolina**
**June 20, 1863: Congress admits West Virginia to the Union**

Less visible than the loyal opposition were Southern whites who hated the Confederacy and supported the Union. Fearing retaliation, many of them suffered in silence, but approximately 100,000 actively supported the Union by enlisting in loyal military units. Others served as Union scouts and spies or carried out acts of sabotage. Southern Unionists were strongest in certain geographic regions, such as the mountains of Virginia, North Carolina, Alabama, Arkansas, and Tennessee; large cities like New Orleans, Nashville, and Atlanta; and some parts of Texas. What motivated Southern Unionists to oppose the Confederacy is rather complicated. Many did so because they were poor mountain people who owned few slaves and adhered to Andrew Jackson's style of nationalism. But Unionism cut across both class and geographic lines. Many wealthy New Orleans residents supported the Union because they had economic or family ties to the North. Other lower- and middle-class Southerners were recent Northern transplants who did not share their neighbors' views on slavery and secession. Still others considered Davis's impressment and conscription policies to be the same type of tyranny that had caused the South to secede. Many looked back on the Union with nostalgia and came to believe their rights had been better protected under the old flag and the U.S. Constitution. The South also had a significant number of European immigrants who had come to America to enjoy the benefits of U.S., not Confederate, citizenship. And it should not be forgotten that almost half of the Southern population were slaves, and virtually all of them supported the Union.

## West Virginia

The residents of western Virginia opposed secession so strongly they created a new state. This anti-secession sentiment was clustered in twenty-six mountainous counties that politically opposed the rich plantation tidewater region. Western Virginia had few slaves (about 4 percent of the population), and the region had economic and family ties to Pennsylvania and Ohio. During the secession crisis, the western counties urged their fellow Virginians to give Lincoln a chance. Several large public meetings were held there, and the attendees at one declared it was "unwise, impolitic, and unpatriotic not to give Mr. Lincoln a fair trial before we either secede from the Union or condemn his administration." After the firing on Fort Sumter, these western counties sent forty-seven delegates to the state's secession convention, and thirty-two of them voted against secession (65 percent of the western voters also voted against secession when a statewide referendum was held).

Although outvoted by the secessionist majority, the Unionists refused to endorse rebellion and held the Wheeling Convention on June 11, 1861, to form a loyal government for Virginia. The convention's president declared, "We are determined to live under a State Government in the United States of America and under the Constitution of the United States. It requires stout hearts to execute this purpose; it requires men of courage—of unfaltering determination; and I believe, in the gentlemen who compose this

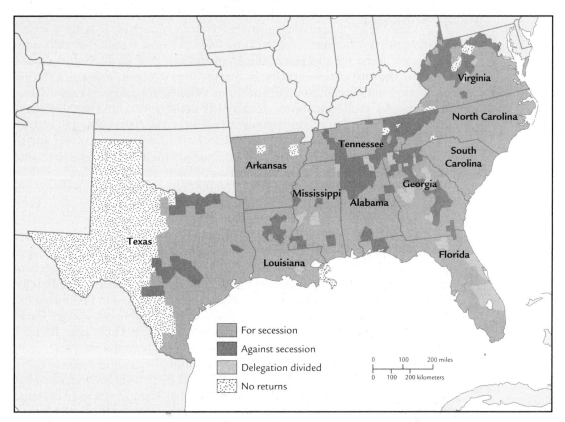

**Opposition to Secession, 1860–1861.** This map shows by county those areas of the South that opposed secession. While there were pockets of resistance scattered throughout the South, most anti-secessionists were concentrated in the mountainous Appalachian regions where there were few slaves.

Convention, we have the stout hearts and the men who are determined in this purpose." Not only did the delegates elect Francis H. Pierpont governor and two new loyal senators, they even decided to create a new state out of the western counties that opposed secession. Originally, the new state was to be called Kanawha, but when a convention was held in November to draft a state constitution the name was changed to West Virginia. The constitution was ratified on April 24, 1862, by a vote of 18,862 to 514. Governor Pierpont's Unionist government in Wheeling then approved the creation of West Virginia to satisfy the constitutional requirement that an existing state has to give its approval before a new state can be created out of its territory. West Virginia was admitted to the Union as the thirty-fifth state on June 20, 1863, and Governor Arthur I. Boreman declared it was "the child of the rebellion."

## Peace Societies

Soon after the war began, Southern Unionists created a number of what were called peace societies to oppose the Confederacy, and these groups gained support as the suspension of habeas corpus, impressment, and conscription became more unpopular. Such organizations clandestinely encouraged desertions, opposed (and sometimes murdered) conscription and impressment agents, aided Union forces, and openly called for a negotiated peace to restore the Union. Confederate authorities tried to hunt down peace society members, but the task was difficult because citizens hid their membership by using secret oaths, handshakes, and passwords.

It is estimated that approximately 100,000 Southerners belonged to such secret organizations as the Peace Society and the Heroes of America. The Peace Society was probably created within Union lines in 1862 and was active in Alabama, East Tennessee, Mississippi, Georgia, and perhaps Florida. Its greatest success occurred in August 1863 when it helped elect to the Confederate Congress six candidates who advocated ending the war and restoring the Union (two-thirds of all the congressmen elected that year had opposed secession). Besides influencing elections, the Peace Society also had some success in infiltrating the Confederate army. In December 1863, at least sixty Society members were found to be serving in James H. Clanton's Alabama brigade on the Gulf Coast. It is not known how many other members were scattered throughout the army.

The Heroes of America was a powerful organization originating in North Carolina that supported William Woods Holden, editor of the North Carolina *Standard* and a vocal Davis critic. Growing in strength after the Confederates were defeated at Gettysburg and Vicksburg, the Heroes held more than one hundred meetings in the summer of 1863. They flew the U.S. flag at some gatherings, and members called for a negotiated peace. "The Constitution as it is, and the Union as it was" became a popular catchphrase. Hundreds of deserters and draft dodgers took advantage of the turmoil and organized insurrections in some counties. Confederate troops were sent in to restore order, and soldiers destroyed Holden's press, but most of the Heroes avoided capture by hiding out in the hills and caves. The use of Confederate military force only strengthened the movement, and peace advocates won a number of congressional seats in the 1863 election.

More Heroes of America meetings were held in 1864, and members began calling on the people simply to bypass the Davis administration. It was suggested that the individual states begin negotiating with Lincoln, even if it meant returning to the Union. "We would prefer our independence, if that were possible," Holden declared, "but let us prefer *reconstruction* infinitely to *subjugation*." Davis responded by suspending habeas corpus, but Holden was undeterred and ran for governor against Zebulon Vance on a peace platform. In retaliation, pro-Vance newspapers portrayed the Heroes of America as traitors and exposed their secret signs and passwords. Some members came forward to admit their membership and to ask for pardons, while others stayed away from the polls for fear of being discovered. Vance won the election, and the Heroes

**The Great Gainesville Hanging, October 1862.** When German Americans around Gainesville, Texas, demonstrated support for the Union, their Confederate neighbors retaliated by hanging approximately forty of them in a week-long period. This 1864 illustration from *Frank Leslie's Illustrated Weekly Newspaper* depicts one day when nineteen Unionists were hanged from an elm tree.

of America faded away in North Carolina, although it did remain active in surrounding states.

## Retaliation

Confederate authorities sometimes took strong measures to crush Unionist activity. In north Texas, a large number of German immigrants and other recent settlers from the Midwest opposed secession in 1861. When eleven north Texas counties voted against secession, neighbors harassed the Unionists and even murdered some. The bitter feelings festered until August 1862, when approximately sixty-five German Unionists left their homes near Fredericksburg for Mexico to secure passage to Louisiana to join the Union army. Approximately one hundred Confederates gave chase and caught up with the party at the Nueces (noo-WAY-sis) River near the Mexican border. On the morning of August 10, 1862, the Confederates attacked the Germans' camp and killed nineteen of the men. Nine wounded Germans were later executed.

Later that year, more anti-Unionist violence occurred at Gainesville, Texas. There German immigrants formed a secret Peace Party and began holding meetings to discuss ways to oppose the Confederacy in general and the conscription act in particular. When local secessionists learned that the Unionists were planning a violent uprising in October 1862, they arrested a large number of the Germans in Cooke County. Two Germans were killed trying to escape, and the others were tried by a vigilante court that was convened in the county seat

# EYEWITNESS
## Dennis E. Haynes

*Dennis E. Haynes (ca. 1819–?) was an Irish immigrant and Texas Unionist who was forced to flee to Louisiana when he tried to raise a company of Union men for military service. He spent months hiding out in the woods and swamps and was captured and escaped repeatedly. Haynes also briefly served as a captain of Union scouts in the 1864 Red River Campaign. After the war, he wrote his memoirs to publicize the Confederates' "Reign of Terror" against Louisiana Unionists. Two passages tell of Haynes being arrested and the activities of Howard "Dog" Smith, a mysterious man who came to Winn Parish to track down deserters and draft evaders.*

When we arrived at Manny [Many, Louisiana] I was put into the jail, and in the jail was an iron cage seven feet by five. . . . When [the guard] opened the cage to put me into it I asked him why he was putting me into such a place, and with what crime I was charged to merit such treatment as to put me in a cage, like a wild beast. . . . He answered he had orders to put me in close confinement. I asked him with what offence I was charged. He told me high treason. I denied having ever committed any; that I owed no allegiance to the Confederacy; that I was an adopted citizen, and had taken the oath of allegiance to the United States Government; that I was a Union man, and should never deny it; that I could not commit any political act which could be considered, justly, more than that of a belligerent, and consequently I should not be charged with anything more, and should be held only as a prisoner of war; that I could not be considered a spy, having lived in the Southern States twenty-five years before secession; that all that could be said against me was that I denounced the conscript act, and the exemption in that act of all persons owning twenty negroes or five hundred head of cattle from military duty in the Confederate army. He answered that, seeing from my conversation I was a man of education, he was astonished at my making use of such language; that he knew of several men being shot for speaking against the exemption in the conscript act. Then said I: "What are you fighting for?" He answered, "Liberty." "Liberty!" says I; "to hell with such liberty where a man is shot for criticising [*sic*] on an act of congress; I don't want such liberty.". . .

of Gainesville. In an atmosphere tinged with rancor and rumors, many of the Unionists were sentenced to death. Over a weeklong period, approximately forty Unionists were hanged, with nineteen being hanged in one day. Other arrests followed in nearby Grayson, Wise, and Denton counties, and six more men were hanged. The "Great Gainesville Hanging" was the worst Confederate attack on Unionists in the entire war. After the Civil War, a number of secessionists who had been involved in the hangings were tried for murder, but none was convicted.

A similar reaction to Southern Unionists took place on the opposite side of the Confederacy in the mountains of North Carolina. This region was particularly

The North side of Red river was also the scene of numerous atrocities; the chief perpetrator there was a Captain Smith, better known by the sobriquet of "Old Dog Smith." This wretch . . . was the terror of the Union men in Winn and Bienville parishes. He had a pack of bloodhounds to hunt conscripts with. A man by the name of Sandleford, being one of his company, his wife sent him word she had nothing to eat for herself and children. Sandleford asked leave of "Dog Smith" to go home to provide something to eat for his family. "Dog Smith" would not let him go. Sandleford said he would go at all hazards rather than his family should suffer. "Dog Smith" told him if he did go he would pay for it. Sandleford went, but when he returned he paid for it, sure enough; for this hyena had him tied and shot to death at Mount Lebanon, Bienville parish, leaving a heart-broken widow and six children in abject poverty and distress. He also shot a man in Natchitoches parish, out of a tree, whom his dogs ran down, he leaving three orphan children without a mother. He also hunted down, in Bienville parish, a mere lad, with his dogs; the dogs ran him up a tree. "He was the only son of his mother, and she was a widow." This inhuman wretch fired his pistols at him without effect, and then ordered his men to shoot him, which order was obeyed by the cowardly wretches. The poor boy being mortally wounded, fell from the tree. The dogs being enraged by the shooting and hallooing of the human bipeds, and smelling the blood from his wounds, before he fairly touched the ground they covered him, literally tearing him to pieces before they could be taken off.

*During the war, Haynes was wounded during one escape attempt, his home was burned by the Rebels, and he lost his wife and a child. "Dog" Smith did not fare much better. Winn Parish residents finally rose up against him and his tracking hounds "Rock" and "Ruler." After a woman poisoned the dogs, a Confederate soldier home on sick leave helped drive Smith out of the parish.*

Captain Dennis E. Haynes. Edited by Arthur W. Bergeron, Jr., *A Thrilling Narrative: The Memoir of a Southern Unionist* (Fayetteville: University of Arkansas Press, 2006), pp. 16, 84, 85.

divided in its loyalties and was the scene of numerous raids and skirmishes between Unionists and Confederates. In one incident, about fifty Unionists raided Shelton Laurel, a valley in the western mountains. Because some of the raiders were deserters from the Confederate 64th North Carolina, that regiment's commander was ordered to clear the area of all such guerrillas. In instructing Colonel Lawrence M. Allen, Brigadier General Henry Heth reportedly declared, "I do not want to be troubled with any prisoners and the last one of them should be killed." Allen's house was one of those looted by the Unionists, so he was in complete agreement with Heth's orders.

When the 64th North Carolina moved into Shelton Laurel, the men ransacked the houses of Unionists and beat men, women, and children. The Confederates also took fifteen men and boys prisoners, most of whom had not participated in the earlier Unionist raid. Two men managed to escape, but on January 18, 1863, the remaining thirteen were murdered while they were on their knees begging for mercy and then buried in a mass grave. Confederate officials were outraged when they learned of the massacre and demanded that those responsible be punished. Five officers were forced to resign their commissions, but no one else involved in the murders was punished.

## Confederate Nationalism

It is sometimes argued that the loyal opposition and discontent were so widespread in the Confederacy that the Southern people never formed a national identity that could sustain them through the trying times. According to this theory, white Southerners continued to view themselves as Americans and never forgot they had much more in common with the North than differences. As the Davis administration took more oppressive actions and Southern society began to crumble, many Confederates began to look back on the old Union with longing and nostalgia. By 1864, casualties were in the hundreds of thousands, slaves were running away, homes were destroyed, and starvation was a stark reality. A separate nation whose main difference was the support of slavery simply was not worth the sacrifice. The intense suffering and the loss of confidence in the administration caused soldiers to desert and the people to stop supporting the war effort, and this led directly to the Confederates' defeat on the battlefield.

But is this explanation of Confederate defeat supported by facts? Should Confederate nationalism be judged solely on victory or defeat, or should it be judged by the creation of a viable national government that survived four years under incredible military and economic pressure? If France had not joined America in the Revolutionary War, George Washington almost certainly would have been defeated and Great Britain would have been victorious. In that case, would historians today blame the colonies' defeat on their inability to form a national identity? Southerners made far more sacrifices than Northerners did to fight the Civil War or colonial Americans did to fight Great Britain. Approximately 80 percent of eligible Southern men served in the Confederate army, and almost one-third died, while about 50 percent of eligible Northern men served in the Union army, and about one-sixth died. In contrast, about 33 percent of Americans actively supported the independence movement in the Revolutionary War. Approximately 105,000 Confederate soldiers deserted in the Civil War, as did 278,000 Yankees.

In reality, Southerners had begun to develop a separate identity in the years preceding the war. Partisan newspapers and fire-eating politicians began creating an "us" versus "them" mentality in the 1830s. The countless references to "my country" and "our people" found in Confederate newspapers, letters,

# BIOGRAPHY

## William Gannaway Brownlow: The Fighting Parson

William G. Brownlow

William G. Brownlow (1805–1877) was born in Virginia but grew up near Knoxville, Tennessee, after being orphaned as a boy. Mostly self-educated, he became a hellfire-and-brimstone circuit minister for the Methodist Episcopal Church and a newspaper editor for the *Knoxville Whig*. Known as "Parson" Brownlow, he also published books highly critical of the Presbyterians, Baptists, Catholics, Democrats, and immigrants. Convinced the peculiar institution was divinely ordained, Brownlow strongly defended slavery. He described abolitionist Harriet Beecher Stowe as "ugly as Original Sin" and claimed slaveholders "who feed and clothe them well, and instruct them in religion, are better friends to them than [abolitionists]." Yet Brownlow hated the slaveholding aristocrats, whom he called "overbearing tyrants," and remained devoted to the common man.

Despite his support of slavery, Brownlow was a devout Unionist, and he used his newspaper to oppose secession. "I am for the Union," he proclaimed, "though every other institution in the country perish." After Tennessee seceded, Brownlow tried unsuccessfully to create a separate state in East Tennessee, and he infuriated the secessionist government by continuing his pro-Union writings. The *Knoxville Whig*, in fact, was the only Southern newspaper that openly opposed the Confederacy. The "Fighting Parson" declared he would "fight the Secession leaders until Hell freezes over, and then fight them on the ice." Brownlow was jailed on suspicion of bridge burning, and in October 1861 authorities closed his newspaper and secessionists vandalized the office building. Nonetheless, he continued to speak out against the Confederacy and defiantly flew a U.S. flag over his house. Brownlow finally was arrested and exiled to Union territory. On crossing the lines, he cried out, "Glory to God in the highest, and on earth peace, good will toward all men, except a few hell-born and hell-bound rebels in Knoxville." Brownlow became a popular speaker for the Union cause, but he returned to Knoxville in 1863, when Union forces occupied the city, and began publishing a new Union newspaper.

During Reconstruction, most white Tennesseeans hated Brownlow because he supported black voting rights and wanted to disenfranchise former Confederates. With only white Unionists voting, he was elected governor in 1865 by a vote of 23,352 to 35. Under his leadership Tennessee became the first Southern state readmitted to the Union. Brownlow was reelected governor in 1867 and then served one term in the U.S. Senate.

and diaries clearly prove Southerners viewed themselves as a separate nation. That does not mean, however, that they agreed with all of the Confederate government's policies. One reason the Confederacy was able to hold out for four long years was that the government began to abandon states' rights philosophy and centralize power as a wartime necessity, even though such measures were unpopular with many people. Conscription is a good example. While it is true that 80 percent of eligible Southern men served in the army, many did so only because the conscription act forced them to do so. Many also opposed the government's taxation and impressment policies and the suspension of habeas corpus. But most Southern whites continued to support the war, and they never lost their identity. Defeat did not occur because the Southern people failed to develop a sense of nationalism or exert enough effort to win. Defeat occurred because the Northern people had a *stronger* sense of nationalism and were just as committed to winning.

## FOR FURTHER READING

Confederate Constitution
U.S. Constitution preamble

# CHAPTER 14

# Advance and Retreat: The Chancellorsville and Gettysburg Campaigns

The Chancellorsville Campaign

The Gettysburg Campaign

Thousands of Confederate soldiers stood on the bank of the Potomac River and began stripping off their dirty uniforms and slinging their cartridge boxes and equipment over their shoulders in preparation for wading across. It was June 15, 1863, and Robert E. Lee was once again on the offensive. After defeating the enemy at Chancellorsville the month before, Lee believed a raid into Pennsylvania might turn the tide of war in favor of the South. That state was rich in horses and supplies his army desperately needed, and a major victory on Northern soil might strengthen the Union peace movement and force Lincoln to the negotiating table.

Lieutenant General Richard S. Ewell's corps had the honor of leading the Army of Northern Virginia, which was now poised to enter Union territory for the second time in the war. One Confederate officer who watched the men cross the Potomac wrote, "The [water] was very high and it was amusing to see the long lines of naked men fording it—their clothing and accoutrements slung to their guns and carried above their heads to keep them dry. The water was very cold and the men as they entered it would scream and shout most boisterously." Moving quickly through Maryland, Ewell's men soon reached the Pennsylvania state line. A Louisiana Tiger claimed that his brigade "shook M[arylan]d dust off of our feet and marched into the union to the tune of 'Dixie.'" Scores of civilians lined the road and watched in horror as the ragged Rebels confidently marched along. The Confederates enjoyed the moment, and one claimed they told the Yankees "that we had Eat up the last mule we had and had come over to get some beef & bacon. Others said we were going back into the union at last."

June 1863 was a critical time for both the North and South. In the western theater, Union General Ulysses S. Grant was laying siege to Vicksburg, Mississippi, and on the verge of gaining complete control of the Mississippi River. But in the eastern theater, Lee's victorious Rebels were moving farther north than any Confederate army had ever gone before in search of a decisive victory in Pennsylvania. If they were successful, the Confederates might capture Harrisonburg, Baltimore, or even Washington. The fate of the entire war might very well hang in the balance.

## THE CHANCELLORSVILLE CAMPAIGN

**January 26, 1863: Hooker takes command of the Army of the Potomac**
**April 27, 1863: Hooker begins Chancellorsville Campaign**
**May 1, 1863: Battle of Chancellorsville begins**
**May 3–4, 1863: Second Battle of Fredericksburg**
**May 5, 1863: Hooker retreats across the Rappahannock River**

1862 had been a nightmare for Union forces in Virginia as Lee's Army of Northern Virginia skillfully defeated one general after another. The disaster at Fredericksburg, in particular, shattered morale in the Army of the Potomac. Ambrose Burnside and his subordinates feuded over who was responsible for the debacle, and Burnside recommended to Lincoln that a number of generals be dismissed from the service. Among them was Major General Joseph "Fighting Joe" Hooker, an ambitious and conniving officer who wrote Lincoln a letter recommending a military dictator seize power to save the Union. To Burnside's horror, Lincoln relieved *him* of command in January 1863 and replaced him with none other than Joe Hooker. In his appointment letter, Lincoln addressed Hooker's call for a dictator. "Of course," he pointed out, "it was not for this, but in spite of it, that I have given you the command. Only those generals who gain successes can set up dictators. What I now ask of you is military success, and I will risk the dictatorship."

Lincoln was well aware of Hooker's shortcomings, but the general was also brave and aggressive. A native of Massachusetts, Hooker (1814–1879) was a West Point graduate and veteran of the Seminole and Mexican wars. While commanding a division during the Peninsula Campaign, he earned his nickname when a typographical error in a newspaper headline read "Fighting Joe Hooker" instead of the intended "Fighting: Joe Hooker." Hooker was an egotistical and opinionated officer who drank as hard as he fought. One officer claimed he was "a noisy, low-toned intriguer" and that army headquarters was "a place which no self-respecting man liked to go, and no decent woman could go. It was a combination of barroom and brothel." Hooker began with great promise when he restored morale by supplying badly needed equipment, fresh food, back pay, and furloughs. One of his most significant changes was to reorganize the cavalry into a single corps under Major General George Stoneman to increase its efficiency and power. Fighting Joe's innovations were impressive, and by the spring of 1863 the 134,000-man Army of the Potomac was in peak fighting condition.

## "My Plans are Perfect"

Following the Battle of Fredericksburg, Lee remained camped around Marye's Heights, but he sent Longstreet's corps to southeastern Virginia to gather supplies. This left him with only 60,000 men to face Hooker. Taking advantage of his superior numbers, Hooker devised a bold plan to force Lee to retreat. First, he would send Stoneman's cavalry on a raid toward Richmond to disrupt Lee's line of communications and draw away J. E. B. Stuart's cavalry. Stuart's absence would leave Lee blind and allow Hooker to carry out his main maneuver undetected. To keep Lee in position on Marye's Heights, Hooker ordered Major General John Sedgwick to remain in the winter camps with 40,000 men. While Lee was distracted by Stoneman's raid and Sedgwick's inaction, Hooker would lead 75,000 men upstream beyond Lee's left flank to cross over the Rappahannock River and sweep into the enemy's rear. Lee would then have to retreat from his strong position to avoid being cut off from Richmond.

Secrecy and speed were essential for success. Once across the river, Hooker had to march rapidly through the Wilderness, a tangled region of briar patches and thickets twelve miles west of Fredericksburg. A fight inside the Wilderness had to be avoided at all costs because the wooded terrain would negate Hooker's advantage in manpower and artillery. For his plan to succeed, he needed to get through the Wilderness before making contact with the enemy. Supremely confident, Hooker declared, "My plans are perfect and when I start to carry them out, may God have mercy on Bobby Lee; for I shall have none."

## DID YOU KNOW?

### Corps Badges

The modern American practice of using uniform patches to denote a soldier's branch of service and unit started during the Civil War. General Joseph Hooker adopted corps badges as a way to improve morale in the Army of the Potomac by promoting the pride soldiers had in their division and corps. Such badges also made it easier for officers to quickly identify a soldier's unit. Corps badges were usually made from flannel cloth and were attached to the cap or uniform. Each badge had a unique shape, such as a diamond for the III Corps, the Maltese cross for the V Corps, and a crescent for the XI Corps. Each division within the corps also used a different color based on the national flag. The 1st Division was red, the 2nd Division white, and the 3rd Division blue. Thus, a soldier wearing a red diamond was immediately recognized as belonging to the III Corps' 1st Division. Hooker's idea quickly caught on and spread to armies serving in the western theater. Soldiers liked the system and often wore their corps badges at postwar veterans' reunions and even placed them on their tombstones. In World War I, the practice of using colored patches to identify a specific unit was revived, and today they are standard on all American uniforms.

Unfortunately for Hooker, his grand plan was already going awry when he moved upriver on April 27, 1863. Hooker assumed he could cross the Rappahannock and move through the Wilderness undetected because the Confederate cavalry would be pursuing Stoneman. Lee, however, simply ignored Stoneman and kept most of Stuart's troopers on patrol. Stuart discovered Hooker's turning maneuver soon after he crossed the river, and Lee immediately made a daring decision. He left 10,000 men under Major General Jubal A. Early to watch Sedgwick at Fredericksburg, while Stonewall Jackson took the remaining 50,000 men to stop Hooker. Jackson attacked Hooker on May 1 just as his advance units reached high ground at the edge of the Wilderness and could see the open fields beyond. Hooker seemed shocked at the enemy's swift response and surprised his officers by ordering them to fall back into the thick woods and entrench. His generals were incredulous, but Hooker remained confident and told them, "The enemy is in my power and God Almighty cannot deprive me of them."

During this first day of fighting, Stuart's cavalry made the stunning discovery that Hooker's right flank was "in the air": It did not rest on entrenchments or a strong natural barrier but simply petered out in the dense thickets. Lee immediately began contemplating a counterattack and had Stuart scout out roads leading to the exposed flank, but it was almost daylight by the time he completed the mission. In the wee hours of morning, Lee and Jackson sat on cracker boxes around a fire and finalized their plans. Lee decided once again to split the army, with Jackson taking his 26,000-man corps to attack Hooker's flank while Lee held the front lines with just 20,000 men. Jackson's route was fourteen miles long and required the use of several narrow, twisting roads to remain hidden from enemy view. It would take him most of the day to reach the flank, leaving Lee and his small force to face Hooker's 75,000 men alone. If Hooker learned of the movement, he could attack Lee and Jackson while they were separated and defeat each in turn. The plan was risky and audacious, but it was a classic Lee maneuver.

## "Push Right Ahead"

As Jackson made his historic march on May 2, Union outposts spotted the long column snaking through the woods and reported the movement to Hooker. As Grant did at Shiloh, however, Hooker misinterpreted the warning signs of an impending attack and believed Lee was retreating. He did caution Major General Oliver O. Howard, whose XI Corps held the exposed right flank, to be prepared for an attack, but Hooker took no steps to ensure the order was carried out. Late that afternoon, Howard's men, many of whom were recent German immigrants, were preparing supper when deer and rabbits suddenly bounded from the thickets to their right. Surprised at the odd sight, they pointed and laughed at the fleeing animals until they saw what was following behind them. Thousands of Confederates arranged in three battle lines, each nearly a mile long, emerged from the seemingly impenetrable briar patches, raised the Rebel

Yell, and attacked. The Confederates crushed Howard's corps and chased the survivors through the woods. Pleased with his success, Jackson rode along with his men smiling and urging them to "Push right ahead."

Hooker's headquarters were not far away at the Chancellor House, but an acoustic shadow prevented him from hearing the battle distinctly. Officers were standing in the yard discussing the faint gunfire when one looked to the right and gasped, "My God—here they come!" As panicked Union soldiers broke from the woods in a run, Hooker reacted quickly to form a new defensive line with fresh troops. This stubborn stand, darkness, and confusion in the Confederate ranks saved Hooker from complete disaster. The Union line finally stabilized, but the fighting continued well after dark. As a full moon rose over the horizon, the Wilderness glowed eerily from woods fires ignited by gunfire and exploding shells. Standing on a hill overlooking the burning landscape, a Union cavalryman thought it looked "like a picture of hell."

## The Death of Stonewall

Jackson was determined to finish off the enemy and decided to take advantage of the full moon to launch a rare night attack. With a large entourage of officers and men, he rode out beyond the Confederate lines to reconnoiter the ground in front, but when the party returned, a jittery North Carolina regiment mistakenly believed the galloping horses were Union cavalry and opened fire. The volley cut down Jackson and several other men, with two bullets shattering Jackson's upper left arm and another tearing into his right hand. After much difficulty, he finally was taken to a house in the rear, where a physician amputated the arm.

Lee was shocked at the news and wrote Jackson a congratulatory note praising his victory and assuring him, "Could I have directed events, I should have chosen for the good of the country to have been disabled in your stead. . . ." When an aide read the note, Jackson whispered, "General Lee is very kind, but he should give the praise to God." At first, it appeared Jackson would recover from the wound, but he developed pneumonia about the time his wife, Anna, and infant daughter arrived. Drifting in and out of consciousness, he began calling out orders. "A. P. Hill, prepare for action!" "Pass the infantry to the front!" On May 10, Anna informed Jackson he would not survive, but he took the news well. Realizing it was a Sunday, he assured her, "It is the Lord's day. My wish is fulfilled. I have always desired to die on Sunday." Once again falling into a stupor, Jackson was heard to say softly, "Let us cross over the river and rest under the shade of the trees," and then he died.

## The Second Battle of Fredericksburg

Stuart was put in temporary command of Jackson's corps, and both he and Lee launched numerous frontal attacks throughout May 3 in an attempt to drive Hooker into the Rappahannock River. Lee's aggressive tactics failed him on this occasion, however, because by then the enemy had established strong defensive positions. While the Confederates did successfully reunite their two separated wings and force Hooker to withdraw closer to the Rappahannock, it was little reward for the massive casualties suffered in the attacks. The Yankees suffered fewer casualties, but Hooker was among them. While he was leaning against a porch pillar at the Chancellor House, a solid shot smashed the pillar just above his head and knocked him to the ground with a possible concussion.

Desperate to relieve some of the pressure from his front, Hooker ordered Sedgwick to cross the river at Fredericksburg and threaten Lee's rear. Sedgwick attacked, forced Early's Confederates off Marye's Heights, and began moving west toward Chancellorsville. To face this new threat, Lee divided his army for the third time in the campaign. Leaving Stuart and 25,000 men to continue the fight against Hooker, he returned to Fredericksburg with 20,000 men to confront Sedgwick. On May 4, Lee attacked Sedgwick near Salem Church and pushed him back toward the Rappahannock River, but the stubborn Yankees finally made a stand near the river and held their position until darkness ended the fight. Sedgwick then retreated across the Rappahannock, and Hooker followed suit on the night of May 5.

Lincoln was shocked when he learned the army was retreating and paced back and forth in the White House exclaiming, "My God, my God! What will the country say? What will the country say?" In the following months, many people sought to explain how the campaign could have ended so ingloriously when it had begun with such promise. Some falsely accused Hooker of being drunk, while others suspected his injury at the Chancellor House may have left him confused. General John Gibbon, former commander of the Iron Brigade, suspected Hooker simply lost his nerve on the first day when he could have pushed on to the open ground. He wrote General McClellan that Hooker "so well known to possess personal bravery, seems to have yielded entirely to his nerves and to have shown a complete want of backbone at the wrong moment, to the surprise of every one. . . ." After the battle, George Armstrong Custer summed up Hooker's initiation as army commander when he wrote, "Hooker's career is well exemplified by that of a rocket, he went up like one and came down like a stick."

## A Pyrrhic Victory

Historians consider Chancellorsville to have been Lee's greatest victory. Facing overwhelming odds, he seized the initiative from Hooker, divided his army three times, defeated two Union forces, inflicted 17,000 casualties, and forced the enemy to retreat. But the victory came at a high cost. Jackson's death was devastating, and approximately 13,000 Confederates were killed, wounded, or captured. Most casualties occurred on the second day when Lee tried to crush Hooker with frontal attacks. He was not content with simply defeating Hooker; he wanted to utterly destroy his army. While the public generally defined victory as driving the enemy from the field, Lee knew that tactic would not be enough to win the war. The enemy had to be dealt a blow strong enough to destroy Northern morale and make them willing to negotiate a peace. Only the

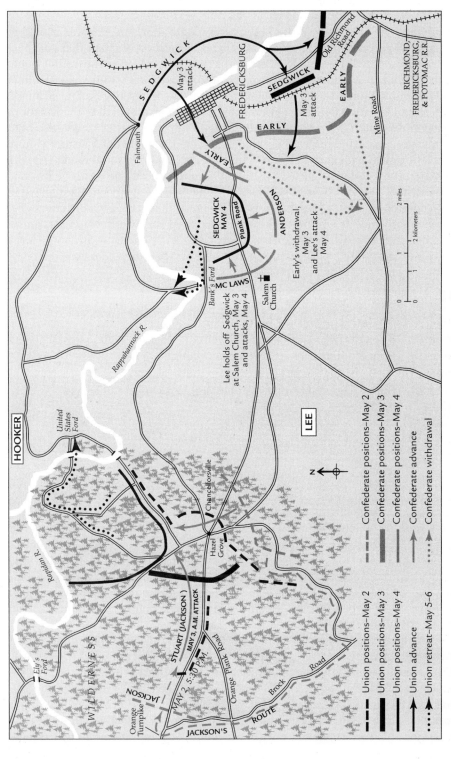

**The Chancellorsville Campaign, May 2–6, 1863.** The Chancellorsville Campaign involved three distinct battles. On learning that Hooker had crossed the Rappahannock River and was threatening to turn his flank, Lee left Early to hold Fredericksburg and sent the rest of the army west to intercept Hooker in the Wilderness. The Confederates stopped Hooker at Chancellorsville, but Stonewall Jackson was mortally wounded on May 2 after launching a devastating attack against the Union right flank. As fighting continued the next day, Sedgwick drove Early off Marye's Heights at Fredericksburg and began moving west to reinforce Hooker. On May 4, Lee left Stuart to continue the fight against Hooker while he took part of the army back toward Fredericksburg to stop Sedgwick at Salem Church. The entire Union army then retreated back across the Rappahannock River.

annihilation of the Army of the Potomac could do that, and Lee was willing to launch risky frontal attacks and suffer high losses to accomplish that goal.

Chancellorsville was a Pyrrhic victory for Lee because the Union could replace its losses, while the Confederacy could not. Hooker's army was still intact and undoubtedly would renew the offensive once it had recovered its strength. Other than boosting Southern morale and perhaps strengthening the Northern peace movement, Chancellorsville did little to improve the Confederates' military position. Lee and many of his officers realized it would not take many more such "victories" to ruin their cause. This sobering fact only reinforced his desire to maneuver the enemy into a position where they could be destroyed in one battle. Time, however, was of the essence. The Confederacy could not afford to keep fighting year after year, even when it won such battles as Chancellorsville. Simple mathematics was in the Union's favor, and the South would run out of men before the North. Nothing short of destroying the enemy army would force Lincoln to negotiate a peace and secure Confederate independence.

## THE GETTYSBURG CAMPAIGN

**June 9, 1863: Battle of Brandy Station, Virginia**
**June 10, 1863: Gettysburg Campaign begins**
**June 15, 1863: Confederates enter Pennsylvania**
**June 25–July 2, 1863: Stuart's Gettysburg Raid**
**June 28, 1863: Meade takes command of the Army of the Potomac**
**July 1–3, 1863: Battle of Gettysburg**
**July 4, 1863: Lee begins his retreat from Gettysburg**
**July 14, 1863: Gettysburg Campaign ends when Lee's army crosses Potomac River**
**November 19, 1863: Gettysburg Address**

After Chancellorsville, Lee wanted to keep the initiative and proposed launching a raid into Pennsylvania. He argued such a move would take the war out of Virginia and give its people a needed respite, and it would allow him to gather supplies in rich Pennsylvania. Also, a major victory on enemy soil would strengthen the Northern peace movement, and it might even convince Great Britain and France to extend diplomatic recognition to the Confederacy. Such pressure could force Lincoln to the negotiating table before the Union grew too strong to defeat.

While Lee's reasoning was sound, the deteriorating situation in the western theater threatened his strategy. On the very day Hooker marched through the Wilderness, General Ulysses S. Grant crossed the Mississippi River to begin his attack on Vicksburg, Mississippi (see Chapter 15). Vicksburg was vital to controlling the river, and Confederate officials were desperate to hold it. When Grant began his siege of the city in mid-May, President Davis called Lee to Richmond to discuss the western situation with him and the cabinet. Something had to be done quickly if Vicksburg was to be saved. One possibility was to transfer Lee to the western theater to take command and rescue the city. Another suggestion was for Lee to assume the defensive in Virginia and send Longstreet's corps west to join forces with Braxton Bragg and Joseph E. Johnston, defeat the enemy in Tennessee first, and then raise the siege on Vicksburg.

Lee, however, disagreed with both plans. He had no desire to leave Virginia and had little faith that the western commanders would use Longstreet's corps any more wisely than their own troops. Besides, Lee believed Johnston already had ample men to form a force large enough to defeat the enemy in Tennessee and relieve Vicksburg. Lee remained convinced he could serve the Confederacy best by moving into Pennsylvania. Davis was under tremendous political pressure to aid Vicksburg, and he preferred Lee follow a more defensive strategy in Virginia. But a majority of the cabinet members supported Lee's Pennsylvania raid, and Davis had come to trust him. As a result, Davis acquiesced and Lee began making plans for his offensive.

Lee first had to reorganize his army's command structure because so many officers had been lost at Chancellorsville. He appointed many new regimental, brigade, and division commanders, but his most important decision was to promote Richard S. Ewell to replace Jackson. Ewell, who had returned to duty after losing a leg in the Second Bull Run Campaign, had been Jackson's most dependable division commander, and he was popular with the men. Lee also created a new III Corps and put it under Lieutenant General A. P. Hill, a fiery officer who had won laurels on many battlefields. Longstreet had returned from southeastern Virginia to lend his experienced hand to the operation, but the army would be moving into Pennsylvania with two of its three corps commanders new to their jobs. Nonetheless, Lee was fully confident that his 75,000 men were up to any task he asked of them. Major Campbell Brown agreed. He returned from temporary duty in the west just as the army was preparing to move north. Brown remembered, "I found everything in the bustle & exhilaration of an expected move, on an unrevealed but brilliant campaign. Never was our Army in finer fighting trim than at this time. The sick of the winter & the slightly wounded of Chancellorsville had returned to camp—a good many recruits had been forwarded—the health & physical condition of the troops were excellent—& the prestige of a recent victory & a full knowledge of the depressed condition of the Federals, contributed to inspire confidence." Lee's veterans were anxious for a fight and had no doubt they would trounce the Army of the Potomac just as they had done so many times before.

## The Campaign Begins

Suspecting Lee was planning an offensive, Hooker sent his cavalry, now commanded by Major General Alfred Pleasonton, across the Rapidan River to probe the Confederates' position and gather intelligence. On June 9, 1863, Pleasonton splashed across the river and surprised Stuart's cavalry at Brandy Station. Thousands of troopers fought hand to hand in a wild and bloody engagement that proved to be the largest cavalry battle of the war. The Confederates eventually forced Pleasonton to withdraw and claimed victory, but the Battle of Brandy Station embarrassed Stuart, and it was an important turning point for Union cavalrymen. For two years, the Rebel horsemen had outfought them in virtually every clash, but during those two years of humiliating defeats the Yankee troopers had learned some valuable lessons. At Brandy Station, for the first time in the war, the Union cavalry caught Stuart by surprise and demonstrated that it was finally his equal in both skill and tenacity.

Fearing that Hooker had discovered his intentions, Lee hurried Ewell's corps to the Shenandoah Valley to clear the way to the Potomac River while Stuart's cavalry held the Blue Ridge Mountain passes to prevent the enemy from discovering the movement. In a maneuver reminiscent of Stonewall Jackson, Ewell swiftly marched into the Valley, defeated Union forces at the Second Battle of Winchester and Stephenson's Depot, and crossed the Potomac on June 15. His foot cavalry then marched rapidly through Maryland into southern Pennsylvania, with Hill's and Longstreet's corps following a few days behind.

With the offensive well under way, Stuart was eager to redeem his reputation from the surprise at Brandy Station and asked permission to make a cavalry raid behind Union lines. Lee acquiesced on the condition he leave behind two brigades to screen the army as it marched north and that he stay in contact with Ewell to keep the army informed of Union activity. Stuart rode out on June 25, but the enemy advanced sooner than expected, and he became trapped behind the Union army. Stuart was unable to communicate with Ewell, and Lee marched blindly into Pennsylvania completely unaware of the Union army's position. Stuart later became one of several scapegoats for the Confederate defeat at Gettysburg. His critics claim that if he had remained in contact with Ewell, Lee would have known the Union army was closing in, and he could have avoided the Battle of Gettysburg altogether. Stuart's supporters, however, place the blame on Lee himself. Had he used the two cavalry brigades left behind more effectively, he would have known the enemy's whereabouts. Stuart becoming trapped behind enemy lines was simply an unforeseen circumstance of war and not a result of his disobeying orders.

When Hooker realized Lee was marching north, he moved along a parallel course into Maryland and carefully kept his 93,000 men between the enemy and Washington. Convinced he was outnumbered, Hooker complained he was not receiving necessary reinforcements and requested that the garrison at Harpers Ferry, Virginia, be evacuated and assigned to him. It was a reasonable request, considering the Confederates had captured Harpers Ferry when they raided Maryland the year before. General-in-Chief Henry Halleck, however, had no confidence in Hooker's leadership and refused. An angry Hooker then sent Halleck a letter offering to resign and was surprised when President Lincoln quickly accepted. On June 28, Lincoln replaced Hooker with Major General George Gordon Meade.

The entire Rebel army was already in Pennsylvania when Meade took command, with elements of Ewell's corps reaching as far as York and the outskirts of Harrisburg. Lee gave strict orders not to mistreat civilians and reminded his men, "[W]e make war only upon armed men. . . ." Although Jubal Early's division burned abolitionist Thaddeus Stevens's ironworks and levied a $28,600 tribute on York, the Confederates generally obeyed Lee and treated the terrified civilians with respect. They politely, but firmly, took horses, food, clothing, and other needed goods and paid for them with Confederate money. An amazed General Ewell wrote his wife, "It is wonderful how well our hungry, foot sore, ragged men behave in this land of plenty—better than at home." African Americans, however, were not so lucky. The Confederates seized hundreds of runaway slaves and transported them back South, along with a number of free blacks. One Northerner described the Pennsylvania raid as a "regular slave hunt."

On June 28, the day Meade took command of the Army of the Potomac, a spy shocked Lee when he informed the general that the enemy had crossed the Potomac River and was in pursuit. Having heard nothing from Stuart, Lee had assumed the Yankees were still in Virginia, but he reacted quickly to the threat and ordered the army to assemble at Cashtown. When Meade realized Lee was preparing for battle, he decided to concentrate ten miles east of Cashtown at Gettysburg. Meade's decision was a wise one because nine roads intersected at Gettysburg, and whichever army controlled the town would control all of the major roads in the area.

On June 30, a Confederate unit

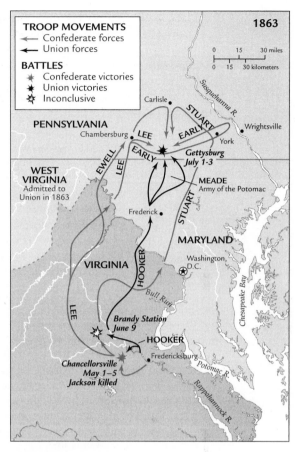

**The Virginia Theater, May–July 1863.** In May 1863, Hooker advanced on Richmond, but Lee left his Fredericksburg camps to intercept and defeat him at Chancellorsville. The following month, Lee launched the Gettysburg Campaign. After an initial clash at Brandy Station, Stuart's Confederate cavalry raided behind Union lines, but Stuart was unable to rejoin Lee when Hooker moved north in response to Lee's offensive. With Ewell leading the way, the Confederate army swept through the Shenandoah Valley and entered Pennsylvania. Just days after George Meade took command of Union forces, the two armies collided at Gettysburg.

approached Gettysburg from the west in search of supplies. When they reached some high ground (later known as McPherson's Ridge), the Rebels were surprised to find Brigadier General John Buford's cavalry division blocking the

# BIOGRAPHY

## George Gordon Meade: The "Old Goggle-Eyed Snapping Turtle"

Born in Spain the son of a Pennsylvania businessman, George G. Meade (1815–1872) graduated from West Point in 1835 and briefly served in the Seminole Wars before resigning his commission to become a railroad and civil engineer. He soon reentered the army, however, and served well in the Mexican War. During the Civil War, Meade rose rapidly through the ranks to become a major general and a corps commander in the Army of the Potomac. A highly competent officer, he fought in many battles and was severely wounded in the hip and arm during the Seven Days Campaign. When Lincoln made Meade the army's commander in June 1863, most soldiers approved the appointment because he was a steady and dependable general.

**George Gordon Meade**

Meade was never noteworthy in dress or demeanor. One general who witnessed his arrival at Gettysburg wrote, "There was nothing in his appearance or his bearing—not a smile nor a sympathetic word addressed to those around him—that might have made the hearts of the soldiers warm up to him, or that called forth a cheer. . . . But this simple, cold, serious soldier with his businesslike air did inspire confidence. The officers and men, as much as was permitted, crowded around and looked up to him with curious eyes, and then turned away, not enthusiastic, but clearly satisfied." The plain-looking Meade was famous for his volatile temper and legendary use of profanity. One officer referred to him as a "damned old goggle-eyed snapping turtle," and another wrote, "I don't know any thin old gentleman, with a hooked nose and cold blue eye, who, when he is wrathy, exercises less of Christian charity. . . ."

way. Buford was a hard-riding former Indian fighter from Kentucky who recognized the importance of the dominating ridge and placed his men along its crest. The Confederates withdrew, but Major General Henry Heth planned to return the next day with his entire division to see how large an enemy force was in Gettysburg. His decision set in motion the largest battle of the Civil War.

## Gettysburg: The First Day

Heth's infantry engaged Buford's cavalry at about 8:00 a.m. on July 1, but the outnumbered cavalrymen fought stubbornly and held their ground on McPherson's Ridge. At midmorning, Buford received badly needed reinforcements when Major General John F. Reynolds arrived with his I Corps and took command of the field. Unfortunately, a Confederate sharpshooter soon

Meade assumed army command in the midst of an enemy offensive and just three days before the Battle of Gettysburg. He had no time to create his own staff or adjust to his new duties, but he took the reins with confidence and fought with great skill. Robert E. Lee was correct when he declared, "General Meade will commit no blunder in my front, and if I make one he will make haste to take advantage of it." After defeating Lee at Gettysburg, however, Meade was criticized for not pursuing the enemy more aggressively. "Our army held the war in the hollow of their hand," Lincoln lamented, "and they would not close it." Stung by the criticism, Meade tendered his resignation, but the administration quickly backed down, and the Congress voted him its thanks.

When Ulysses S. Grant became general-in-chief in March 1864, he decided to personally direct the Army of the Potomac in the campaign against Lee. Meade graciously offered to step aside if Grant preferred one of his western officers to command the army, but Grant kept him in place. Grant was impressed by the selfless gesture and wrote in his memoirs that Meade "was brave and conscientious, and commanded the respect of all who knew him. He was unfortunately of a temper that would get beyond his control, at times. . . ." The last year of the war was difficult for Meade because Grant took control of strategy and tactics, and Meade was left simply to follow his orders. Adding to his misery was the fact that war correspondents intentionally avoided mentioning his name (unless it was in reference to a defeat) to punish him for his contemptible treatment of reporters. The reporters' conspiracy of silence prevented Meade from attaining the fame he deserved, but Grant did promote him to major general of regulars in August 1864 as a reward for his faithful service. However, the promotion came only after Grant's protégés, Philip Sheridan and William T. Sherman, were given that rank. Meade remained in the army after the war and commanded various military departments and districts during Reconstruction.

shot Reynolds dead, and his men were forced to retreat closer to Gettysburg to another strip of high ground known as Seminary Ridge. By noon, the Union soldiers were hard pressed, but more troops began arriving to help. Major General Oliver O. Howard's XI Corps marched into Gettysburg and rushed through the streets to take up a position on I Corps' right. One soldier later remembered that as they hurried through town the "citizens lined the street holding cups of water for the thirsty, but we had no time to stop. . . ."

Each side continued to commit more troops to the fight, and by midafternoon the battle was raging in an arc west and north of Gettysburg. Lee soon had A. P. Hill's entire corps engaged, but he seemed nervous and angry because he did not know the enemy's strength. To one officer, Lee complained about the missing Stuart and declared, "In the absence of reports from him,

I am in ignorance of what we have in front of us here. It may be the whole Federal army, or it may be only a detachment. If it is the whole Federal force, we must fight a battle here." Fortunately for Lee, Southern fortunes changed dramatically in the afternoon when Ewell's corps approached the field from the northeast along a road that brought it in perfect position to attack Howard's right flank. Ewell smashed Howard's flank, and the entire Union line collapsed when Hill joined in the attack. The disorganized Yankees fell back through Gettysburg, with the Rebels pursuing close behind and scooping up several thousand prisoners. Howard finally rallied his men on Cemetery Hill, a large prominence south of town, and was joined there by Major General Winfield Scott Hancock. Known as "Hancock the Superb" for his outstanding service in the Peninsula Campaign, Hancock had been sent ahead by Meade to take command of all the troops at Gettysburg. When he joined Howard on Cemetery Hill and saw its natural strength, Hancock declared, "I select this as the battlefield."

From his position northwest of town, Lee saw the Union soldiers gathering atop Cemetery Hill and ordered Ewell to advance and seize it "if practicable." While the order seemed simple enough, Ewell found it difficult to implement. His corps was completely disorganized after sustaining 2,000 casualties in the hard-fought battle, and the men were trying to round up thousands of prisoners. Ewell knew a fresh division was on the way to join him and decided to wait for it before attacking the strong Union position, but the division did not arrive until sundown. By then, it was too late to attack Cemetery Hill. At the time, Ewell's actions received little attention, but later they became a major part of the Gettysburg story because some Southerners blamed him for Lee's defeat. They claimed that if Ewell had taken Cemetery Hill as ordered, the enemy would have withdrawn, and the battle would have ended in victory.

Meade finally arrived at Gettysburg that night and met with his generals in the cemetery gatehouse on Cemetery Hill. Gathering around flickering candles, the officers assured Meade that the army occupied good defensive ground, and they advised him to stay and fight. "I am glad to hear you say so, gentlemen," quipped Meade, "for it is too late to leave it." As the various corps arrived that night, they were set up in a defensive line resembling an inverted fishhook. Culp's Hill, to the northeast, was the hook's barb, and the shank curved at Cemetery Hill and ran south along Cemetery Ridge. The eye of the hook was the far left (or southern) flank, anchored on two rugged hills known as Little Round Top and Big Round Top. The Confederate line roughly paralleled Meade's position, with Ewell on the left occupying Gettysburg and facing Culp's and Cemetery hills, and Hill and Longstreet in the center and right, respectively, along Seminary Ridge. The Union army spent the night strengthening its naturally strong position. One Confederate officer wrote, "All night long the Federals were heard chopping away and working like beavers, and when day dawned the ridge was found to be crowned with strongly built fortifications and bristling with a most formidable array of cannon."

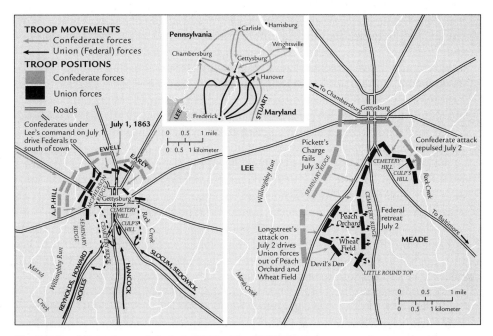

**The Battle of Gettysburg, July 1–3, 1863.** After Hill's Confederates made contact with Union cavalry west of Gettysburg on the morning of July 1, Lee and Meade rushed troops there and the fighting spread north of town. When Ewell's corps attacked the Union right flank that afternoon, the Union forces collapsed and fell back through town to Cemetery Hill. Meade then concentrated his men in a defensive line that resembled an inverted fishhook, with the right flank anchored on Culp's Hill, the center on Cemetery Hill and Cemetery Ridge, and the left flank on Little Round Top. On July 2, Lee launched unsuccessful attacks against both Union flanks and Cemetery Hill. The battle culminated on July 3 when Union forces on Cemetery Ridge beat back Pickett's Charge.

## Gettysburg: The Second Day

After consulting with his corps commanders, Lee decided to resume the offensive by having Longstreet attack the Union left flank while Ewell and Hill demonstrated along their fronts to pin down enemy troops. If there was a chance of success, they were to turn their demonstrations into full-scale attacks. Longstreet, however, did not think he could break the Union line and tried to convince Lee to disengage and move around the enemy's left flank to cut off Meade from Washington. But Lee, jabbing a fist toward Cemetery Ridge, proclaimed, "If the enemy is there tomorrow, we must attack him." "If he is there," replied Longstreet, "it will be because he is anxious that we should attack him—a good reason, in my judgment, for not doing so."

Historians continue to debate the wisdom of Lee's decision, but attacking was probably his best option. To follow Longstreet's advice would have required disengaging thousands of men, removing the wounded and prisoners, and transferring wagons, artillery, and equipment a long distance. Such a move would have required at least a full day, and it could not have been done in secret. Union cavalry certainly would have discovered the movement, and Meade could have attacked Lee's army while it was on the march. On the other hand, the battle was already developed, Lee knew the location of the Union forces, and he still held the initiative. Perhaps most important, Lee was absolutely convinced his men were up to the challenge.

It took Longstreet much of the day to get his men into an attack position. After the war, critics accused him of ignoring an order to strike at daylight and of deliberately delaying the attack because of his disagreement with Lee. Along with Stuart and Ewell, Longstreet became a scapegoat for the Confederates' defeat at Gettysburg, but the accusations against him are utterly false. Lee never gave an order to attack at daylight; he did not even finalize his plans until late morning. Longstreet was a professional soldier, and his personal feelings did not stop him from carrying out Lee's wishes. It took hours for him to get into position because he was slow and methodical by nature, and he had to take a circuitous route to stay out of sight of the enemy.

Meanwhile, Major General Daniel Sickles made a critical blunder on the Union side. Sickles was a former New York congressman who gained notoriety before the war by murdering Philip Barton Key, the son of Francis Scott Key, who was having an affair with Sickles's wife. Future secretary of war Edwin Stanton defended Sickles, and he became the first attorney in American history to win an acquittal by using the temporary insanity defense. Sickles had remained an influential congressman despite the scandal and was later made a Union general even though he had no military experience.

Sickles was ordered to hold the Union left flank, but he believed a ridge of high ground a half mile in front was a better position. Without proper orders, he moved his entire corps forward just as Longstreet attacked. The Confederates smashed his isolated corps and slowly pushed it back in some of the war's most vicious fighting. Areas soon dubbed the Wheat Field, Devil's Den, and the Peach Orchard were the scenes of terrible carnage. The terrain was rugged and covered with rocks, trees, and small streams that broke up formations and forced the men to fight in small groups. One Confederate general described it as "more like Indian fighting than anything I experienced during the war." Sickles rushed from point to point trying to rally his men until an exploding shell shattered his right leg. When stretcher bearers carried him off the field, the general lit a cigar, lifted himself up on one elbow, and calmly smoked to show the men he was still alive. He donated his amputated leg to the army's medical museum and sometimes paid it a visit. Despite his blunder, Sickles was later awarded the Medal of Honor.

The battle now entered a critical phase. Little Round Top was undefended, and if the Confederates captured it they could outflank the entire Union position. Meade's chief engineer, Brigadier General Gouverneur K. Warren, realized the significance of Little Round Top and ordered a brigade to hold it at all costs. One of the brigade's regiments was Colonel Joshua Lawrence

**Gettysburg's "Wheat Field."** This photograph of Union dead was taken three days after the Confederates smashed Daniel Sickles's corps in the Wheat Field. The Confederates controlled this part of the field long enough to rob the dead of their shoes.

Chamberlain's 20th Maine. Chamberlain was a professor at Bowdoin College who had joined the army while on sabbatical. Having seen little combat prior to Gettysburg, he now found himself holding the army's most important position. Chamberlain's regiment put up a heroic defense and repulsed numerous enemy attacks. One Confederate officer claimed that casualties in his regiment were so high, "The blood stood in puddles in some places on the rocks." Chamberlain's men eventually ran out of ammunition, but they were under strict orders not to retreat. Unable to withdraw and too weak to withstand another attack, the Maine men fixed bayonets and charged down the hill to drive off the remaining Confederates. Chamberlain's actions made him one of the Union's most popular heroes, and he was awarded the Medal of Honor for his defense of Little Round Top.

Throughout the fighting of July 2, Meade skillfully used his interior line to pull units from his right flank and rush them into the gap formed by Sickles's untimely advance. In the bloody fighting, Confederate Major General John Bell Hood was severely wounded in the arm, and Brigadier General William Barksdale was killed. On the Union side, Sickles lost a leg, and Brigadier Generals Stephen H. Weed and Samuel K. Zook were mortally wounded and killed, respectively. The 1st Minnesota, one of the Union regiments rushed into the melee, suffered 215 casualties out of 262 men in just ten minutes of combat. In the end, the Union army was pushed back to its original position around the Round Tops, but the line held. Despite his failure to break through, Longstreet was proud of his men's efforts and declared that it had been "the best three hours' fighting ever done by any troops on any battle-field."

Late in the day, more intense fighting broke out on the Union right. There, Ewell bombarded Cemetery and Culp's hills when he heard Longstreet's attack begin and then sent his men forward. In fierce fighting on Culp's Hill, the Confederates gained a foothold on the rocky slope, but a lone Union brigade prevented them from seizing the hill. General Jubal Early also sent his Louisiana Tigers and North Carolinians in a desperate twilight assault on Cemetery Hill. They came under intense artillery fire but managed to fight their way to the cemetery gates and briefly capture two artillery batteries after a fierce hand-to-hand clash, during which one artilleryman claimed "clubs, knives, stones and fists—anything calculated to inflict death or pain was resorted to." For a brief moment, the Confederates had finally pierced Meade's line, but they were unable to exploit their success because no units moved up in support. When the Union launched a determined counterattack, the Confederates had to retreat back down the hill.

The bloody fighting had accomplished little, and the two armies occupied almost the same positions they had held when the day began. When Meade met again with his generals that night, a junior officer noted how composed the ten generals were. They looked "as calm, as mild-mannered, and as free from flurry or excitement as a board of commissioners met to discuss a street improvement." Everyone agreed they should hold their ground and neither attack nor retreat. As the officers filed out of the room, Meade casually told General John Gibbon, "If Lee attacks tomorrow, it will be in your front." Gibbon's division occupied the center of Cemetery Ridge, and he asked Meade why he thought so. "Because," Meade explained, "he has made attacks on both our flanks and failed, and if he concludes to try it again it will be on our center."

## Pickett's Charge

Meade's prediction proved correct, for Lee believed the enemy had weakened their center to reinforce the flanks. Convinced one more push against the Union center would finally crack the line, he ordered Longstreet to organize an attack force of about 13,000 men. Lee's plan was risky, but it was not without merit. A frontal attack might surprise the enemy, and Cemetery Ridge would be their weakest point if Meade had, indeed, stripped it of troops to reinforce his flanks. To support Longstreet, Lee also ordered simultaneous attacks at other points. Ewell was to continue his fight on Culp's Hill, and Stuart, who had finally arrived on the field, was to ride behind the enemy lines to create as much havoc as possible.

Longstreet once again tried to convince Lee to use a turning movement instead of a frontal attack. "General," he argued, "I have been a soldier all my life. I have been with soldiers engaged in fights by couples, by squads, companies, regiments, division, and armies, and should know, as well as any one, what soldiers can do. It is my opinion that no fifteen thousand men ever arrayed for battle can take that position. . . ." Lee refused to change his orders, and Longstreet later wrote, "Never was I so depressed as upon that day." Despite his feelings, he assembled the divisions of George Pickett, John J. Pettigrew, and Isaac Trimble and a brigade under Cadmus Wilcox. Because his division was the largest, the attack became known as Pickett's Charge.

At daybreak on July 3, the fighting resumed on Culp's Hill when Union troops attacked the Confederates who had a foothold there. A fierce but indecisive battle raged on its slopes until about noon, during which time Longstreet prepared for his assault. Longstreet decided to use a massive artillery bombardment to wreck the Union artillery and infantry on Cemetery Ridge before sending in his infantry. It was the first time in history that such a preliminary bombardment was used, although it became standard practice in World War I. At 1:00 p.m. scores of Confederate cannons opened fire on Cemetery Ridge, and almost immediately the Union artillery responded. The noise was deafening. One soldier wrote, "Naught could be heard but the hoarse roar of the cannon, the screaming and bursting of shell, the dull *thud* of the solid shot as it buried itself in the ground, the crash of falling timber, the loud explosion of ammunition chests, the unearthly cries of wounded horses, and the loud shouts of defiance of the combatants. It was a most terrible scene and made one believe that truly 'Hell was empty, and all the devils were there.'" On Cemetery Ridge, General Hancock tried to steady his men's nerves by calmly riding his horse along the crest amidst the shot and shell. Surprisingly, the bombardment was not very effective because most of the shells overshot their targets. Dust and smoke obscured Cemetery Ridge from view and when the enemy's fire slackened after about two hours, Longstreet believed the bombardment had driven the artillery from the ridge. In reality, the Union guns were little damaged and had simply ceased fire to conserve ammunition for the infantry attack the gunners knew was coming.

When Pickett asked if he should advance, Longstreet could not answer but simply nodded his head. He later wrote, "My feelings had so overcome me that I could not speak, for fear of betraying my want of confidence." A long Confederate battle line swept over Seminary Ridge and began marching steadily across a mile of open ground toward a small clump of trees and a stone wall on Cemetery Ridge. Almost immediately the Union artillery opened fire and tore gaping holes in the formation. The Union soldiers on Cemetery Ridge were awestruck when the enemy periodically stopped to close the holes. "My God," one man declared, "they're dressing the line!" Soon, General Hancock's divisions opened fire and shot down hundreds of Confederates. The Rebels returned fire, and Hancock was wounded when a bullet tore through the saddle pommel and sprayed wooden splinters and a rusty nail into his groin. Although seriously wounded, he refused to leave the field until the attack was repulsed.

By the time the Confederates reached the stone wall, two of Pickett's three generals had fallen. Lewis Armistead, however, continued to lead the charge, guiding the men forward by putting his hat on the tip of his sword and holding it aloft. "Come on, boys!" he yelled, "Give them the cold steel!" Armistead

# BIOGRAPHY

## James Longstreet: Lee's War Horse

**James Longstreet**

"Pete" Longstreet (1821–1904) was a native of South Carolina, but he grew up in Georgia. After graduating from West Point in 1842, he was wounded once and brevetted twice during the Mexican War. Longstreet then married a cousin of Ulysses S. Grant's wife before resigning his commission and joining the Confederacy in June 1861. He quickly rose to lieutenant general and corps commander in the Army of Northern Virginia, but he suffered a personal tragedy when three of his children died from scarlet fever.

Longstreet's excellent service led Robert E. Lee to call him "the staff of my right hand" and "my old *war-horse*." Lee trusted him more than any other officer and made sure Longstreet's commission was dated so he would be the Confederacy's senior lieutenant general and second in command of the Army of Northern Virginia. Longstreet became Lee's most dependable corps commander, although he tended to be somewhat slow on the march because of his methodical nature. Always in the thick of the fighting, he was accidentally shot by his own men in the Wilderness and put out of action for months.

Longstreet was an imposing figure at six feet, two inches in height, but an officer claimed he was "one of the kindest, best hearted men I ever knew. Those not well acquainted with him think him short and crabbed and he does appear so except in three places: 1st, when in the presence of ladies, 2nd, at the table, and 3rd, on the field of battle. At any of those places he has a complacent smile on his countenance, and

crawled over the wall and was mortally wounded just as he reached a Union cannon. A Pennsylvania brigade broke and fell back as the enemy poured over the wall, but others quickly counterattacked and sealed the breach in vicious hand-to-hand fighting. The sound of battle was terrific. One soldier described it as "strange and terrible, a sound that came from thousands of human throats, yet was not a commingling of shouts and yells but rather like a vast mournful roar." Finally, the Confederates conceded defeat and began making their way back to Seminary Ridge as the victorious Union soldiers stood along the stone wall and taunted them with chants of "Fredericksburg! Fredericksburg!"

Having watched the charge from Seminary Ridge, Lee rode out to meet the survivors. When he met a sobbing Pickett, Lee told him, "Your men have done all that men could do; the fault is entirely my own. . . ." To others he said, "We'll talk it over afterwards. But in the meantime all good men must rally." One British officer who was serving as a foreign observer wrote, "Very few failed to answer his appeal, and I saw many badly wounded men take off their seems to be one of the happiest men in the world." Longstreet's men greatly admired him, and one said he "was like a rock in steadiness when sometimes in battle the world seemed flying to pieces." General John Bell Hood perhaps gave the best compliment when he declared, "Of all the men living, not excepting our incomparable Lee himself, I would rather follow James Longstreet in a forlorn hope or desperate encounter against heavy odds. He was our hardest hitter."

Longstreet was one of the first Civil War officers to recognize the strength of the tactical defense, and he became reluctant to launch frontal attacks. At Gettysburg, this brought him into conflict with Lee, and critics later blamed him for the defeat there. Lee, however, retained an absolute trust in Longstreet and came to rely on him greatly throughout the war. A fighter until the end, Longstreet advised Lee at Appomattox, "General, if [Grant] does not give us good terms, come back and let us fight it out."

After the war, Longstreet believed the North and South should reconcile, and he joined the Republican Party to work for peaceful Reconstruction. Settling in New Orleans, he led the Republican policemen in clashes against his former comrades, and President Grant later appointed him minister to Turkey. Many Southerners came to hate Longstreet and branded him a scalawag for joining the Republicans. Former Confederate generals also began attacking his war record—particularly his role at Gettysburg—and Longstreet did not help his cause when he defended himself in a number of clumsy, poorly argued articles and his memoir, *From Manassas to Appomattox*. Soldiers, however, never forgot Longstreet's valor. At his funeral, an old veteran silently stepped forward and laid on the coffin his enlistment papers and part of his uniform to be buried with his former general.

hats and cheer him." Lee took full responsibility for the failure, but the charge was clearly disastrous. Five generals were killed, wounded, or captured; all thirteen of Pickett's regimental commanders were casualties; and total losses may have reached 7,500, or just over half the attacking force. On the Union side, General Hancock lost about 1,500 men.

## The Retreat

Lee's last chance for victory had been dashed. Not only had Hancock's men repulsed Pickett's Charge on Cemetery Ridge, Union cavalry had also stopped Stuart behind the lines. Stuart had ridden several miles northeast of the battlefield and took up a position from which he could cut the roads Meade would have to use for retreat should Pickett's Charge be successful. Union Brigadier General David M. Gregg engaged Stuart in the rolling fields with his cavalry division and George Armstrong Custer's brigade. Wielding sabers and pistols,

# EYEWITNESS
## Frank Haskell

*Thirty-one-year-old Frank Haskell, a Dartmouth College graduate, entered the Civil War as a lieutenant in the 6th Wisconsin. The regiment was part of the famous Iron Brigade, and Haskell became a staff officer to brigade, and later division, commander John Gibbon. At Gettysburg, Gibbon's division was posted at the stone wall that was the focal point of Pickett's Charge. Shortly after the battle, Haskell wrote an account of the dramatic charge.*

Every eye could see his [the enemy's] legions, an overwhelming resistless tide of an ocean of armed men sweeping upon us! Regiment after regiment and brigade after brigade move from the woods and rapidly take their places in the lines forming the assault. . . . The first line at short interval is followed by a second, and that a third succeeds; and columns between support the lines. More than half a mile their front extends; more than a thousand yards the dull gray masses deploy, man touching man, rank pressing rank, and line supporting line. The red flags wave, their horsemen gallop up and down; the arms of eighteen thousand men, barrel and bayonet, gleam in the sun, a sloping forest of flashing steel. Right on they move, as with one soul, in perfect order, without impediment of ditch, or wall or stream, over ridge and slope, through orchard and meadow, and cornfield, magnificent, grim, irresistible.

All was orderly and still upon our crest; no noise and no confusion. . . . The click of the locks as each man raised the hammer to feel with his fingers that the cap was on the nipple; the sharp jar as a musket touched a stone upon the wall when thrust in aiming over it, and the clicking of the iron axles as the guns were rolled up by hand a little further to the front, were quite all the sounds that could be heard. Cap-boxes were slid around to the front of the body; cartridge boxes opened, officers opened their pistol-holsters. . . . General Gibbon rode down the lines, cool and calm, and in an unimpassioned voice he said to the men, "Do not hurry, men, and fire too fast, let them come up close before you fire, and then aim low and steadily." The coolness of their General was reflected in the faces of his men. . . .

Our skirmishers open a spattering fire along the front, and, fighting, retire upon the main line—the first drops, the heralds of the storm, sounding on our windows. Then the thunders of our guns, first Arnold's then Cushing's and Woodruff's and the rest, shake and reverberate again through the air, and their sounding shells smite the enemy. . . . [B]ut in spite of shells, and shrapnel and canister, without wavering or halt, the hardy lines of the enemy continue to move on. . . . And so across all that broad open ground they have come, nearer and nearer, nearly half the way, with our guns bellowing in their faces, until now a hundred yards, no more, divide our ready left from their advancing right. . . . All

the two sides charged and countercharged in a wild melee that eventually ended in a tactical draw. But Gregg's aggressiveness secured Meade's rear and eliminated Stuart as a threat. It was the second time in a month that the Union troopers had held their own against their Confederate counterparts and proven they were every bit equal to Stuart's vaunted horsemen.

along each hostile front, a thousand yards, with narrowest space between, the volleys blaze and roll; as thick the sound as when a summer hail-storm pelts the city roofs; as thick the fire as when the incessant lightning fringes a summer cloud. . . .

This portion of the wall was lost to us [when a Pennsylvania brigade retreated], and the enemy had gained the cover of the reverse side, where he now stormed with fire. . . . At this point little could be seen of the enemy, by reason of his cover and the smoke, except the flash of his muskets and his waving flags. These red flags were accumulating at the wall every moment, and they maddened us as the same color does the bull. . . . The jostling, swaying lines on either side boil, and roar, and dash their flamy spray, two hostile billows of a fiery ocean. Thick flashes stream from the wall, thick volleys answer from the crest. . . . The men do not cheer or shout; they growl, and over that uneasy sea, heard with the roar of musketry, sweeps the muttered thunder of a storm of growls. . . . My "Forward to the wall" is answered by the Rebel counter-command, "Steady, men!" and the wave swings back. Again it surges, and again it sinks. These men of Pennsylvania, on the soil of their own homesteads, the first and only to flee the wall, must be the first to storm it. . . . "Sergeant, forward with your color. Let the Rebels see it close to their eyes once before they die." The color sergeant of the 72d Pa., grasping the stump of the severed lance in both his hands, waved the flag above his head and rushed towards the wall. "Will you see your color storm the wall alone?" One man only starts to follow. Almost half way to the wall, down go color bearer and color to the ground—the gallant sergeant is dead. The line springs—the crest of the solid ground with a great roar heaves forward its maddened load, men, arms, smoke, fire, a fighting mass. It rolls to the wall—flash meets flash, the wall is crossed—a moment ensues of thrusts, yells, blows, shots, and undistinguishable conflict, followed by a shout universal that makes the welkin ring again, and the last and bloodiest fight of the great battle of Gettysburg is ended and won.

*In early 1864, Haskell was promoted to colonel and was given command of the 36th Wisconsin. He led his men in their first battle at Cold Harbor, Virginia, four months later. During the attack, the brigade's commander was killed, and Haskell took over. He had his men lie on the ground for protection, but he stood erect behind them. In moments, Haskell was shot through the brain and killed. General Gibbon bemoaned, "I have lost my best friend, and one of the best soldiers in the Army of the Potomac has fallen!"*

Excerpts from THE BATTLE OF GETTYSBURG by Frank A. Haskell, edited by Bruce Catton (Boston: Houghton Mifflin, 1957).

Hoping Meade would foolishly attack his strong position on Seminary Ridge, Lee kept his exhausted army in place on July 4. That Independence Day was a dark one for the Confederacy. As the Army of Northern Virginia hunkered down in defeat at Gettysburg, far to the west Union forces captured the key city of Vicksburg and gained control of the Mississippi River. When Meade wisely declined to attack, Lee gave his 17-mile-long wagon train of wounded a head start and then ordered the battered army to begin its retreat to Virginia. Meade moved out in pursuit, but it was less than swift. One Confederate officer claimed Meade "pursued us as a mule goes on the chase of a grizzly bear—as if catching up with us was the last thing he wanted to do." The slow chase was partially justified by the battered condition of Meade's own army and his healthy respect for the still-dangerous Rebel army. Lincoln, however, was angry and disappointed that Lee had managed to escape back to Virginia. "If I had gone up there, I could have whipped them myself," he lamented. Meade only made things worse when he congratulated the army for "driving the invader from our soil," apparently not appreciating the political implications of his poorly worded message. "The whole country is our soil," Lincoln exploded.

Gettysburg was the last large battle in the eastern theater that year. Although Lee and Meade probed each other's positions in Virginia during October and November in what became known as the Bristoe Station and Mine Run campaigns, there were no further major operations. Gettysburg was not only the largest battle of the Civil War, it was the largest battle ever waged in the Western Hemisphere. Together, the two armies had more than 50,000 casualties, with Lee losing perhaps 28,000 men to Meade's 23,000. Gettysburg also became the war's most controversial battle, mainly because Southerners sought to explain why Lee had been defeated. Stuart, Ewell, and Longstreet all became scapegoats, but Lee bore ultimate responsibility for insisting on fighting a battle in which the enemy had enjoyed a great tactical advantage. One fact many Confederates failed to grasp was that Meade and the Army of the Potomac had performed magnificently and essentially out-fought them. Several years after the war, this point was driven home by none other than General George Pickett. When asked why Lee lost the Battle of Gettysburg, Pickett replied, "I always thought the Yankees had something to do with it."

## High Tide of the Confederacy?

In the twentieth century, Gettysburg came to be seen as the turning point of the war, and some historians referred to it as the "High Tide of the Confederacy." It is true that Lee's army was at peak strength that summer of 1863 and marched farther north than any other Rebel army. The Army of Northern Virginia also never fully recovered from the defeat, and Lee never again launched a major offensive. But that does not mean Gettysburg was the war's high tide in the sense it ensured Confederate defeat. At the time, soldiers on both sides viewed it as an important battle but not a decisive one.

Captain Campbell Brown perhaps best summed up how the Confederates viewed Gettysburg. "It would be ridiculous to say that I did not feel whipped," he wrote, "or that there was a man in that Army who didn't appreciate the position just as plainly. But the 'fight' wasn't out of the troops by any means— they felt that the *position* & not the *enemy* had out done us. . . ." A Confederate chaplain echoed this sentiment when he wrote that his soldiers were

# NOTABLE UNIT: *Custer's Cavalry Brigade*

Brigadier General George Armstrong Custer (1839–1876) commanded the most famous cavalry unit in the Army of the Potomac. He spent much of his youth living with a sister in Michigan, and it was rumored that a young girl's father had secured his appointment to West Point because he wanted to be rid of Custer. "Fanny" Custer's academy career was a dismal one. Each year he was threatened with expulsion because of excessive demerits, and he barely graduated in last place in the 1861 class.

Lieutenant Custer served on George B. McClellan's staff during the Peninsula Campaign, and he sometimes gathered intelligence by going aloft in a hot air balloon. Although Custer was brash and arrogant, his superiors thought highly of him because he was also brave and capable. After joining General Alfred Pleasonton's staff, Custer received an astonishing promotion in June 1863 from captain to brigadier general. At age twenty-three, he was the youngest general in the Union army, and he was given command of the Michigan Cavalry Brigade even though he had never commanded troops in battle.

Custer's brigade, which had been formed in December 1862 under the command of Brigadier General Joseph T. Copeland, consisted of the 1st, 5th, 6th, and 7th Michigan Cavalry. After Custer replaced Copeland, the unit was commonly referred to as Custer's Cavalry Brigade. Custer nicknamed his brigade the "Wolverines" (from the "Wolverine State"), and the troopers came to idolize him (even adopting Custer's red necktie as their unofficial badge).

The brigade fought almost nonstop from June 1863 until war's end and suffered 524 fatalities, more than any other Union cavalry brigade. It earned great fame during the Gettysburg Campaign when it fought J. E. B. Stuart's cavalry in a number of battles. In 1864, the brigade participated in Philip Sheridan's raid against Richmond, and one of its members mortally wounded Stuart at the Battle of Yellow Tavern. In every fight, Custer was at the forefront of battle. At Gettysburg, he stood up in his stirrups, yelled "Come on, you Wolverines!" and led his men in a dramatic charge. In another clash, Custer's horse was killed from under him, and he was slightly wounded by a spent bullet. In yet another, he bravely saved one of the brigade's flags from capture by wrenching it from the mortally wounded color bearer. In September 1864, Custer left the brigade when he was promoted to division commander, but the Wolverines continued to perform admirably through the Shenandoah and Appomattox campaigns.

Custer was brevetted for gallantry five times in the war and had eleven horses shot from under him. After the war, he remained in the army as lieutenant colonel of the 7th U.S. Cavalry and was sent west to fight Indians. Custer's famous luck ran out in 1876 when he was killed at the Battle of the Little Big Horn.

"as cheerful a body of men as I ever saw and to hear them, you would think they were going to a party of pleasure instead of retreating from a hard fought battle." The Confederates continued to fight for nearly two more years, and the war in Virginia remained a stalemate to the bitter end. Blissfully ignorant of the war's final outcome, Lee's veterans retreated from Gettysburg in good

**The Gettysburg Address.** On November 19, 1863, a crowd of 15,000 spectators gathered in Gettysburg for the dedication of the national cemetery. After Edward Everett delivered the two-hour keynote address, President Lincoln stood to "make a few appropriate remarks." Lincoln spoke for only three minutes, but his Gettysburg Address was one of the greatest speeches in American history.

spirits because they knew there would be other opportunities to fight the Yankees and to win the war.

## The Gettysburg Address

On November 19, 1863, President Abraham Lincoln sat on a stage at Gettysburg, Pennsylvania, to help dedicate a cemetery for the Union soldiers who had been killed there four months earlier. Edward Everett, the nation's foremost public speaker, was to give the keynote address, but Lincoln had been asked to "make a few appropriate remarks." The Gettysburg ceremony came at a time when Northern morale was at a low point. Lee's army continued to block the way to Richmond and was as dangerous as ever, and Union forces had been trying unsuccessfully for months to capture Charleston, South Carolina. In the west, the Rebels had routed a Union army at the Battle of Chickamauga, Georgia, and were besieging it at Chattanooga, Tennessee, the very day Lincoln addressed the Gettysburg crowd. In the far west, two Union attempts to invade Texas had met humiliating defeats at Sabine Pass, Texas, and in southwest Louisiana.

About the only good news the Northern people had received in the past year were the spectacular victories won at Gettysburg and Vicksburg, Mississippi, on July 4. Lincoln appreciated the significance of the victories occurring on the eighty-seventh anniversary of the signing of the Declaration of Independence. Knowing that the cemetery dedication would draw a large crowd and newspaper coverage, he decided to use it to deliver a speech to link the events. Contrary to a popular myth, Lincoln did not scratch out his remarks on the back of an envelope while on the train to Gettysburg. The Gettysburg Address was a well-thought-out political statement, and Lincoln had worked on it diligently for several weeks.

Everett spoke first to the 15,000 spectators and delivered a two-hour speech that recounted the battle in great detail. When the applause died down, Lincoln walked to the podium, pulled out two sheets of paper and read them carefully in his high, somewhat squeaky, voice. Interrupted by applause five times, his brief remarks took only about three minutes. While some newspapers and audience members dismissed Lincoln's remarks as forgettable, most immediately recognized the speech as a brilliant oration. A *Harper's Weekly* editorial declared, "The few words of the President were from the heart to the heart. . . . as simple and felicitous and earnest a word as was ever spoken." In a manner similar to the Emancipation Proclamation, the speech claimed the moral high ground for the Union. In the most eloquent way, the Gettysburg Address called on the Northern people to persevere for a higher purpose. The war was not just a political struggle to reunite the Union and enforce constitutional law. It was a war to safeguard the noble experiment of democracy, to guarantee freedom and dignity for all people, and to fulfill the promise made by the Declaration of Independence "that all men are created equal." "It is rather for us to be here dedicated to the great task remaining before us," Lincoln told his audience, "that from these honored dead we take increased devotion to that cause for which they gave the last full measure of devotion—that we here highly resolve that these dead shall not have died in vain, that this nation, under God, shall have a new birth of freedom, and that government of the people, by the people, for the people shall not perish from the earth." Thanks to Abraham Lincoln's pen, Gettysburg helped bolstered the resolve of millions of Northerners to see the war through to victory.

## FOR FURTHER READING

Hooker's letter to Lincoln
Lincoln's appointment letter to Joseph Hooker
The Gettysburg Address
Lee's official report of the Battle of Gettysburg

## CHAPTER 15

# Pocketing the Key: The Vicksburg and Port Hudson Campaigns

Grant's Vicksburg Overland Campaign

Floods, Canals, and Yankee Raiders

The Vicksburg Campaign

The Port Hudson Campaign

Mary Ann Webster Loughborough stood quietly at the entrance of a cave dug into a hillside in Vicksburg, Mississippi. Union forces under General Ulysses S. Grant had driven the Confederate army into the city's defenses and were regularly bombarding the town. Loughborough was the 26-year-old wife of a Confederate officer, but she and her husband decided she and their 2-year-old daughter would remain in the city with him rather than separate. When the bombardment began, she and many other civilians quickly abandoned their homes in Vicksburg and sought refuge in hillside caves.

On this particular day, enemy shells suddenly began exploding all around Loughborough, kicking up geysers of dirt and smoke. As she hesitated a moment trying to decide whether it was safer to remain outside and face the flying shrapnel or retreat inside and risk a shell collapsing the cave, a deafening explosion rocked her senses. Loughborough wrote in her diary, "The cave filled instantly with powder, smoke and dust. I stood with a tingling, prickling sensation in my head, hands and feet, and with a confused brain. Yet alive!—was the first glad thought that came to me;—child, servants, all here, and saved!—from some great danger, I felt." Walking outside, Loughborough found her life had been spared because the mortar shell had hit the corner of the cave at an angle. It had torn the ground to bits and shredded nearby trees and rosebushes, "breaking large masses from the side of the hill—tearing away the fence, the shrubbery and flowers—sweeping all, like an avalanche, down near the entrance of my good refuge."

Friends who had gathered to look for Loughborough marveled that no one was injured. They then sat down and sang songs as one strummed a guitar, and shells continued to shriek overhead. "To me," Loughborough wrote, "it seemed like the crushing and bitter spirit of hate near the light and grace of happiness. How could we sing and laugh amid our suffering fellow beings—amid the shriek of death itself?" Loughborough noted in her diary that during the day an African American child found a shell in his yard and was killed when it exploded while he was playing with it. There was also a young girl who became bored in her cave and decided to run back to her house during a lull in the shelling. "On returning," Loughborough wrote, "an explosion sounded near her—one wild scream, and she ran into her mother's presence, sinking like a wounded dove, the life blood flowing over the light summer dress in crimson ripples from a death-wound in her side, caused by the shell fragment." Another fragment from the same shell broke a little boy's arm. Loughborough sadly recorded, "This was one day's account."

Loughborough and her family survived the siege of Vicksburg, which lasted forty-seven days. It was one of the Civil War's largest and most important battles. At stake was not only the fate of an entire Southern army but control of the mighty Mississippi River and the territorial integrity of the Confederacy. The entire campaign lasted seven months and killed hundreds of soldiers and an unknown number of civilians. But, in the end, the Vicksburg Campaign helped decide who would emerge victorious in the Civil War.

## GRANT'S VICKSBURG OVERLAND CAMPAIGN

**November 26, 1862: Grant begins his Vicksburg Overland Campaign**
**December 12, 1862: Confederates sink USS *Cairo* in the Yazoo River**
**December 20, 1862: Van Dorn destroys Grant's supply base**
  **at Holly Springs, Mississippi; Sherman leaves Memphis**
  **to attack Chickasaw Bayou, Mississippi**
**December 27–29, 1862: Confederates defeat Sherman at the Battle**
  **of Chickasaw Bayou**
**January 4, 1863: McClernand leaves Memphis to attack Arkansas Post,**
  **Arkansas**
**January 10–11, 1863: McClernand captures Arkansas Post**

After General Rosecrans's victory at the Battle of Stones River, Tennessee, in January 1863, Union forces in the west concentrated on seizing control of the Mississippi River. They had successfully pounded their way down the river to Memphis, Tennessee, and had pushed upstream from the Gulf of Mexico to Baton Rouge, Louisiana. The only strongholds the enemy still held on the river were

Vicksburg, Mississippi, and Port Hudson, Louisiana. Of the two, Vicksburg was more important. President Lincoln recognized its strategic significance when the war first began. During one strategy meeting, he swept his hand over a large map and declared, "See what a lot of land these fellows hold, of which Vicksburg is the key. The war can never be brought to a close until that key is in our pocket."

Vicksburg was Mississippi's second-largest city with a population of almost 5,000, and it served as a railroad hub with a ferry connecting the Vicksburg, Shreveport & Texas Railroad in Louisiana with the Southern Railroad in Mississippi. By late 1862, it was the only point on the Mississippi where the Confederates still had railroad heads on both river banks. Vicksburg and Port Hudson kept the eastern Confederacy connected to the western Trans-Mississippi Department. If the Union could capture these last strongholds, the Confederacy would be split in two, its interior line disrupted, and the Mississippi River opened once again to Northern trade.

Approximately 50,000 Confederates under Lieutenant General John C. Pemberton defended Vicksburg. Pemberton was a Pennsylvania native and West Point graduate who was wounded twice in the Mexican War. Married to a Virginia woman, he supported the South on political issues and resigned his captain's commission when Virginia seceded. Pemberton then joined the Confederacy, although two of his brothers fought for the Union. Since he was highly intelligent (he spoke Hebrew, Greek, and Latin) and a good administrator, Pemberton quickly rose through the ranks while serving in various administrative positions. He had little experience commanding large numbers of troops in battle, but that did not stop Jefferson Davis from appointing him commander of the Vicksburg defenses.

In October 1862, General Ulysses S. Grant was put in command of the Department of the Tennessee and began making plans to capture Vicksburg. Unfortunately, Major General John A. McClernand, a popular Democratic politician from Illinois who resigned his congressional seat to enter the army, soon threatened the operation. Lincoln admired the feisty McClernand and promoted his career because of McClernand's political connections and his staunch devotion to the Union. Grant, Halleck, and other professional soldiers, however, viewed the general with contempt because he was self-promoting, reckless, and conniving. Just as Grant was making plans to attack Vicksburg, Lincoln gave McClernand permission to raise a separate army in the Midwest and assemble it at Memphis for the same purpose. Grant shrewdly derailed this competition by pulling rank and assigning the troops to Major General William T. Sherman before McClernand arrived in Memphis. In explaining his motivation, Grant simply declared in his memoirs, "I doubted McClernand's fitness. . . . ."

## Chickasaw Bayou

Grant's strategy to capture Vicksburg seemed foolproof. He would personally lead the 40,000-man Army of the Tennessee from Grand Junction, Tennessee, south along the Mississippi Central Railroad into northern Mississippi to draw Pemberton away from Vicksburg. From Memphis, Sherman would take his (formerly McClernand's) 32,000 men down the Mississippi River on transports to enter the Yazoo River above Vicksburg and attack the city's northern defenses at Chickasaw Bayou. By then, most of the Confederates would be facing Grant, and Sherman could capture the city.

At first everything went as planned. Grant moved into Mississippi in November 1862, and, as expected, Pemberton left Vicksburg to meet him. Things then quickly fell apart. In December, Confederate cavalry under Nathan Bedford Forrest raided Grant's supply line in Tennessee, and Earl Van Dorn's cavalry destroyed his supply base at Holly Springs, Mississippi. Unable to supply his army, Grant was forced to withdraw back to Tennessee. On the retreat, his men lived off the land, taking what they needed from civilians. Grant wrote of the foraging, "I was amazed at the quantity of supplies the country afforded." It was a valuable lesson he would put to good use later in the Vicksburg Campaign.

Sherman assumed all was going well with Grant and left Memphis the very day Van Dorn attacked Holly Springs. Previously, Admiral David Porter's gunboats had been sent downstream to clear Confederate torpedoes from the Yazoo River. While on this duty, the *Cairo* hit one of the "infernal machines" and became the first warship in history to be sunk by an electrically detonated mine. One hundred years later, the *Cairo* was discovered and raised, and it now is on display at the Vicksburg National Military Park.

Unaware that Pemberton had sent troops back to Vicksburg, Sherman attacked Chickasaw Bayou on December 29 but was defeated by Brigadier General Stephen D. Lee. Even though he lost about 1,800 men to the Confederates' 200, Sherman decided to try again and reportedly quipped, "We will lose 5,000 men before we take Vicksburg, and may as well lose them here as anywhere else." Maneuvering was so difficult in the boggy swamps, however, that he quickly changed his mind and returned to Memphis. Sherman's curt message to Grant read, "I reached Vicksburg at the time appointed, landed, assaulted and failed."

## Arkansas Post

McClernand was furious at Grant for stealing his army for the Vicksburg operation. Jealous of West Pointers in general and Grant in particular, he sought fame and glory for himself and did not intend to sit idly by. Wielding considerable political muscle, McClernand took command of Sherman's force when it returned to Memphis and launched his own attack against Arkansas Post, a Confederate bastion on the Arkansas River fifty miles upstream from its juncture with the Mississippi. Grant thought the operation was an unnecessary sideshow, but McClernand argued it was necessary to prevent Confederate Major General Thomas J. Churchill's garrison from threatening Union movements on the Mississippi River.

# BIOGRAPHY

## David Dixon Porter: "Brave and Daring Like All His Family"

**David Dixon Porter**

A Pennsylvania native, David Dixon Porter (1813–1891) belonged to a famous family of officers. His father, Commodore David Porter, was a veteran of the Revolution and the War of 1812, and his brother William D. "Dirty Bill" Porter commanded gunboats during the Civil War. David G. Farragut, the nation's first admiral, was Porter's foster brother, and Union Major General Fitz John Porter was a cousin.

Porter went to sea with his father when he was ten years old, saw combat against Caribbean pirates, and was wounded and captured by the Spanish while his father briefly served in the Mexican navy. Joining the U.S. Navy in 1829, young Porter eventually married George Ann Patterson, the daughter of his commanding officer. After serving in the Mexican War, he left the military to captain various civilian vessels but returned to the navy in 1855.

Taking command of the USS *Powhatan* when the Civil War began, Porter reinforced Fort Pickens, Florida; served on blockade duty; and chased the Confederate raider *Sumter*. Promoted to commander, he led Farragut's mortar boats at Forts Jackson and St. Philip and was given command of the Mississippi River Squadron in September 1862 with the acting rank of rear admiral. At that time, Secretary of the Navy Welles summed up Porter's qualities as an officer: "[He has] stirring and positive qualities, is fertile in resources, has great energy, excessive and sometimes not over-scrupulous ambition, is impressed with and boastful of his powers, given to exaggeration of himself—a Porter infirmity—is not generous to older and superior living

Escorted by Porter's gunboats, McClernand moved up the Arkansas River. On January 9, 1863, he put the men ashore near Fort Hindman, the Confederates' main defensive works at Arkansas Post, and Porter began a two-day bombardment the next day. When Porter knocked out the fort's artillery on January 11, McClernand attacked, but his men were repulsed at the fort's outer defenses. Porter then renewed his bombardment, and the defenders along the river began to surrender. Although Churchill had actually repulsed every enemy attack, he finally surrendered the rest of the garrison when he saw his river defenses raise the white flag. The Confederates had suffered few battle casualties in the brisk fight but surrendered nearly 5,000 men. McClernand and Porter lost just over 1,000 men.

officers, whom he is too ready to traduce, but is kind and patronizing to favorites who are his juniors . . . but [he] is brave and daring like all his family. . . ."

Porter performed his most valuable service cooperating with Generals Grant and Sherman in the Vicksburg Campaign. The trio became fast friends and made a good team. Porter even claimed to have saved Grant's career when General Lorenzo Thomas arrived to relieve Grant as Lincoln began to doubt Grant's chances of success. He told Thomas, "Let an old salt give you a piece of advice. Don't let your plans get out, for if the army and navy should find out what you . . . came for, they would tar and feather you, and neither General Grant nor myself could prevent it." Grant kept his job and captured Vicksburg, while Porter was promoted over eighty more senior officers to the rank of rear admiral.

After reluctantly cooperating with General Nathaniel P. Banks in the failed 1864 Red River Campaign, Porter was given command of the North Atlantic Blockading Squadron to attack Fort Fisher, North Carolina. The first attempt failed, largely because of the bungling of General Benjamin F. Butler, but Porter demanded a change in command and the War Department sent Alfred H. Terry with a new landing force. Porter and Terry worked well together and successfully captured the important fort. Porter went on to command gunboats on Virginia's James River and played host to President Lincoln in the war's final weeks. When the Confederates evacuated Richmond, Porter accompanied the president into the city for a tour. He became one of Lincoln's greatest admirers, and at his funeral told a friend, "There lies the best man I ever knew or ever expect to know."

Porter earned the Thanks of Congress three times during the Civil War and afterward served as commandant of the U.S. Naval Academy and became the navy's senior admiral in 1870. Although arrogant, ambitious, and scheming, he was one of the Union navy's most successful officers.

## FLOODS, CANALS, AND YANKEE RAIDERS

**January 18, 1863: Grant begins the Vicksburg Campaign**
**January 23, 1863: Union forces start to work on Grant's Canal**
**March 7–April 5, 1863: Yazoo Pass Expedition**
**March 14–25, 1863: Steele's Bayou Expedition**
**March 29, 1863: Grant begins his march to New Carthage, Louisiana**
**April 17–May 2, 1863: Grierson's Raid**
**April 21–May 3, 1863: Streight's Raid**

McClernand's victory at Arkansas Post did little to change the overall strategic situation in the west because the Confederates still blocked the Mississippi

River at Vicksburg. Much to McClernand's chagrin, Lincoln chose Grant to command the operation to capture the city; and, in January 1863, Grant put his army aboard transports and moved downriver from Memphis to begin the campaign. The expedition was immediately beset by seemingly insurmountable problems. High floodwater inundated the Mississippi Valley and forced the Union army to camp along the narrow Louisiana levee. Pemberton's Confederates outnumbered Grant, and dozens of heavy cannons were positioned on the Vicksburg bluffs to blast any approaching ship. There seemed no way to even get to the city. Sherman's earlier attack at Chickasaw Bayou proved that a direct assault was impossible, floodwaters prevented maneuvering overland north of town, and it appeared suicidal to run the transports past Vicksburg to land downstream.

## Grant's Canals

Grant's solution to the dilemma was an inspired bit of strategy—he would bypass the bluffs altogether by digging a series of canals. One that became known as Grant's Canal had actually been started a year earlier by General Thomas Williams when he made the first Union attack on Vicksburg. Located across the river from Vicksburg, it was about a mile and a half long and ran across a peninsula known as DeSoto Point. Grant planned to complete the canal and then cut the upstream levee. Engineers assured him a wall of Mississippi River water would roar through the canal and scour out an entirely new channel. If successful, the canal would enable Porter's transports to take troops below the city without having to steam past the deadly batteries on the bluffs. Vicksburg would no longer even be on the river and thus unable to interfere with steamboat traffic at all.

Grant quickly put thousands of confiscated slaves and soldiers to work digging the canal. The process was slow and dangerous as the men struggled in the frigid mud and water digging and pulling up stumps. Pneumonia and other diseases ravaged the laborers, and the Confederates frequently fired artillery shells at them. Hundreds of soldiers and slaves died and were buried in the same levee on which the survivors camped. Fluctuating water levels washed out the shallow graves, and decomposed arms and legs began jutting from the soggy soil. A Union officer remembered, "The period . . . was on many accounts one of the gloomiest in the career of the regiment. At the time of its arrival the river was rapidly rising, and the turbid waters gradually crept up the slope of the high levee several feet above the level of the encampments. It was a winter of excessive rains and unusual floods. . . ."

While work progressed on Grant's Canal, other troops labored on similar projects elsewhere. Three more canals were dug in Louisiana to connect the Mississippi River with inland bayous. Grant hoped transports could take the army from the river through various Louisiana streams to connect with the Red River and then reenter the Mississippi below Vicksburg. At Lake Providence, Grant's engineers needed a steamboat to scout out the route.

A thirty-ton boat was made available to them, but there seemed no way to get it into the lake because the canal connecting it to the river was not yet completed. Undeterred, officers attached ropes to the ship and rounded up hundreds of soldiers and horses. It took the men ten days to drag the boat out of the river, over the levee, across a cotton field, and through the town of Lake Providence before finally putting it into the lake. After all their backbreaking labor, the soldiers were disgusted when their officers began using the steamer as a party barge. Commandeering a regimental band for musical accompaniment, the officers often boarded the steamboat at night and cruised the lake to loot the liquor cabinets of local plantations. With band blaring, the inebriated officers then returned to camp late at night to disrupt the sleep of their exhausted men.

Poor placement, thick cypress trees, and receding floodwater doomed all of Grant's canal projects. All they accomplished was to flood even more of northeast Louisiana. More than 900 square miles of land and scores of homes were inundated that winter and spring as the Yankees deliberately cut the levees along the Mississippi. Grant was criticized for his canal projects, but the engineering logic behind them was sound. In the flood of 1876, the Mississippi did cut a new channel across DeSoto Point very near Grant's Canal.

## The Yazoo Pass and Steele's Bayou Expeditions

While the canal projects continued in Louisiana, Grant also used Mississippi waterways to approach Vicksburg. One such expedition took place at Yazoo Pass, an abandoned Mississippi River channel whose intersection with the river had been blocked by a levee fifty miles downstream from Memphis. Cutting the levee there would allow Porter's gunboats and transports to enter Yazoo Pass and snake through several inland streams to enter the Yazoo River above Vicksburg. The troops could then be unloaded, and Grant could attack Vicksburg from the northeast.

When the levee was blown on February 3, the Mississippi River exploded through the breach. An engineer claimed it was "like nothing else I ever saw except Niagara Falls. Logs, trees, and great masses of earth were torn away with the greatest ease." When the cascade finally subsided, twenty-two Union ships entered Yazoo Pass. Everything went well until the ships reached the Yazoo River and unexpectedly encountered Fort Pemberton, a Confederate stronghold built by Major General William W. Loring. Constructed out of cotton bales, the fort was protected from infantry assault by surrounding floodwater, and it contained a powerful 6.5-inch rifled cannon. For nearly a month, the Yankees made numerous naval attacks and infantry probes against Fort Pemberton, but Loring held his position, and the enemy was finally forced to retreat. Relieved to escape the gloomy swamps, one Union soldier wrote, "When our boat reached the Mississippi river, we fired a 'grand salute' of all the muskets on board, and the one six-pound brass field piece on the bow, as a kind of greeting to the noble river."

While the Union gunboats were engaged at Fort Pemberton, another naval operation was underway farther down the Yazoo River. To prevent enemy ships from moving up the river to land troops in the rear of Vicksburg, the Confederates had blocked the lower Yazoo with strong artillery batteries. Porter proposed to bypass these defenses by entering the Yazoo River from the Mississippi, detouring into Steele's Bayou, and then steaming through a series of waterways to reenter the Yazoo upstream of the Confederate positions. Transports could follow him to land infantry behind these enemy strongholds and attack Vicksburg from the rear.

Accompanied by troops from Sherman's corps, Porter began the Steele's Bayou Expedition on March 14 with five gunboats and assorted other vessels. His optimism, however, proved ill-founded. The narrow, twisting streams were almost impassable, and low-hanging limbs swept away smokestacks and lifeboats. The Yankees also found the flooded timber was crawling with snakes, raccoons, and bobcats seeking refuge from the high water. Various creatures rained down on the decks whenever a ship collided with a tree, and sailors with brooms were detailed to sweep them over the side. Porter quipped the animals "were prejudiced against us, and refused to be comforted on board, though I am sorry to say we found more Union feeling among the bugs." The Confederates also harassed the ships by felling trees to impede their progress and by ambushing them wherever possible. One Union officer claimed, "Every tree and stump covered a sharpshooter ready to pick off any luckless marine who showed his head above deck." Soon, Porter was in danger of being trapped, but Sherman rushed troops to him through thigh-deep water. With Sherman as an escort, Porter turned his ships around and began retreating back downstream a week after the expedition started.

## The Move Downriver

For four months Grant had tried unsuccessfully to find a way to maneuver in the flooded Mississippi Delta. He was greatly relieved in April 1863 when the floodwater finally receded, the land dried out, and land movement was possible once again. Grant prepared to move downstream to New Carthage, Louisiana, and Porter agreed to send his ships past the Vicksburg bluffs to meet him there and ferry the army across the river. Grant and Porter had been trying to avoid running past the bluffs for months, but Porter discovered that the passage was not as dangerous as they had believed. On the night of April 16, eleven of twelve ships successfully made the passage despite a barrage of cannon fire. The captains found the enemy could not depress their cannons low enough to hit the ships if they hugged the bluffs on the east bank. When Porter ran another eighteen vessels downriver a few nights later, Grant was ready to make his move. To divert the Confederates' attention while he marched to New Carthage, Grant left Sherman behind to threaten Vicksburg and sent Colonels Benjamin H. Grierson and Abel D. Streight on cavalry raids behind enemy lines.

**Porter's Fleet Passing Vicksburg, April 16, 1863.** After Grant marched his army to New Carthage, Louisiana, Porter ran his ships past Vicksburg so he could ferry Grant across the Mississippi River. Porter came under heavy fire, but his captains found they could avoid much of the shot and shell by steaming close to the bluffs.

## Grierson's Raid

Grierson was ordered to disrupt Pemberton's supply line and draw his attention away from Grant's maneuvers by raiding Newton Station, Mississippi, a Southern Railroad depot about one hundred miles east of Vicksburg. The mission was kept secret from Grierson's 1,700 men; all they knew when they left La Grange, Tennessee, on April 17 was they were to "play smash with the railroads." Confederate cavalry immediately set out in hot pursuit when the raiders entered Mississippi, so Grierson confused the enemy by splitting his force and sending about one-third of the men to the east to threaten the Mobile & Ohio Railroad. This detachment later turned north and returned to La Grange, while Grierson continued south. Grierson captured Newton Station with little trouble and destroyed tracks, telegraph wires, and supplies. The Confederates expected him to return to Tennessee, but Grierson did the unexpected and continued south toward Baton Rouge, Louisiana.

Throughout the raid, Grierson kept a squad of men dressed in Confederate uniforms ahead of the column. Called Butternut Guerrillas, these men gathered intelligence from locals, scouted roads, and even sent telegrams with false information on the column's whereabouts. The scouts kept the pursuing enemy confused and greatly contributed to the raid's success. One of the Butternut Guerrillas later claimed, "[We] enjoyed ourselves very much at the expense of the deluded citizens." In southern Mississippi, the raiders destroyed another railroad and kept one step ahead of the enemy by riding day and night. Sleep was rare, and an officer remembered, "Men by the score, and I think by fifties, were riding sound asleep in their saddles. . . . Nothing short of a beating with the flat of a saber would awaken some of them."

On May 2, Grierson and his exhausted men finally rode into Baton Rouge. During the sixteen-day raid, they covered 800 miles and destroyed 50 miles of railroad tracks, as well as telegraph lines and enemy supplies. The Union troopers also fought numerous skirmishes, inflicted approximately 600 enemy casualties, captured 1,000 horses and mules, and destroyed 3,000 small arms at the loss of just 27 men. Grierson's Raid was one of the few successful Union cavalry raids during the first half of the Civil War. Sherman considered Colonel Benjamin H. Grierson to be "the best cavalry officer I have yet had," and Grant boasted, "Grierson has knocked the heart out of the state." Almost one hundred years later, John Wayne starred in Hollywood's version of the raid in a movie called *The Horse Soldiers*.

## Streight's Raid

While Grierson was riding through Mississippi, Colonel Abel D. Streight launched a similar raid toward the railroads in western Georgia. Major General William Rosecrans authorized the raid to disrupt the Confederates' supply line into Tennessee and to draw the enemy's cavalry away from Grierson. Unlike Grierson's Raid, however, Streight's Raid was plagued with problems from the beginning. First, Streight mounted his men on mules rather than horses. The mules supposedly were better suited for the mountainous terrain, but they were too worn out and stubborn to be of much use. Then, just before the raid began, the Confederates attacked Streight's base at Eastport, Mississippi, and drove off many of his mules.

Streight left Eastport on April 21, 1863, and moved to Tuscumbia, Alabama, where he received additional mules. Handpicking 1,500 men, he then entered the rugged mountains of north Alabama and rode toward the Western & Atlantic Railroad in western Georgia. Nathan Bedford Forrest's Confederate cavalry set out in pursuit and made an exhausting ride to catch up with the raiders at Sand Mountain. Forrest tried to surround the raiders, but Streight ambushed one of his columns and captured two cannons. Streight next headed for Rome, Georgia, where he planned to cross the Oostanaula River and burn the bridge behind him. Forrest, however, pushed his men to their limit, telling them, "Whenever you see anything blue, shoot at it, and do all you can to keep up the scare." When he caught up with Streight again near the Georgia state line, the raiders were completely exhausted, and Streight claimed, "A large portion of my best troops actually went to sleep while lying in line of battle under a severe skirmish fire."

Forrest had only 600 men, but he cleverly marched them in a circle through an open field in front of the enemy to make it appear that he had a much larger force. Forrest later recalled the scene as he and Streight negotiated between the lines. "I seen him all the time we was talking, looking over my shoulder and counting the guns. Presently he said: 'Name of God! How many guns have you got? There's fifteen I've counted already!'" "I reckon that's all that has kept up," Forrest calmly replied. Convinced his exhausted men were outnumbered,

Streight surrendered on May 3. Forrest claimed that when Streight realized he had been tricked, "[H]e did rear! Demanded to have his arms back and that we should fight it out. I just laughed at him and patted him on the shoulder, and said: 'Ah, Colonel, all is fair in love and war you know.'" At a loss of 65 men, Forrest captured 1,500 Yankees, but Streight's Raid did succeed in drawing Forrest out of Mississippi during a critical phase of the Vicksburg Campaign.

## THE VICKSBURG CAMPAIGN

**April 30, 1863: Grant's army begins crossing Mississippi River**
**May 1, 1863: Battle of Port Gibson**
**May 8, 1863: Grant begins marching toward Jackson**
**May 12, 1863: Battle of Raymond, Mississippi**
**May 14, 1863: Grant captures Jackson**
**May 16, 1863: Battle of Champion Hill**
**May 17, 1863: Battle of Big Black River Bridge; Pemberton retreats**
      **into Vicksburg defenses**
**May 19, 1863: Grant unsuccessfully attacks Vicksburg**
**May 22, 1863: Grant makes second unsuccessful attack on Vicksburg**
**June 7, 1863: Battle of Milliken's Bend, Louisiana**
**July 1, 1863: Johnston's army leaves Jackson and marches toward**
      **Vicksburg**
**July 4, 1863: Pemberton surrenders Vicksburg**

Grant's diversions succeeded, and Pemberton was unaware that the Union army had moved downstream toward New Carthage. Grant first planned to cross the river near Grand Gulf, Mississippi, but the enemy's defenses proved too strong when Porter tested them with his gunboats. When a slave informed the Yankees of a good road leading inland from Bruinsburg, Grant changed the landing site to that place. McClernand's and James B. McPherson's corps were ferried across the river on April 30, and Sherman was ordered to follow as soon as possible. Grant felt a tremendous relief once he crossed over. Years later, he recalled, "When this was effected I felt a degree of relief scarcely ever equaled since. Vicksburg was not yet taken it is true, nor were its defenders demoralized by any of our previous moves. I was now in the enemy's country, with a vast river and the stronghold of Vicksburg between me and my base of supplies. But I was on dry ground on the same side of the river with the enemy."

### The Battle of Port Gibson

There were few Confederates to contest Grant's march inland from Bruinsburg because Pemberton had dispersed his troops to chase Grierson and defend Vicksburg against Sherman. At Grand Gulf, Brigadier General John S. Bowen informed Pemberton of the crossing, and Pemberton sent reinforcements to meet the invaders. By sunrise of May 1, Grant had 23,000 men on Mississippi soil, and he pushed McClernand's corps inland along two parallel roads. McClernand smashed into Bowen's 8,000 Confederates near Port Gibson, and heavy fighting erupted on thick wooded ridges as the Rebels were slowly forced back. The firing was so intense, one soldier claimed, "The storm of leaden rain and iron hail which was flying through the air was almost sufficient to obscure the sunlight." In the Battle of Port Gibson, Bowen lost four cannons and about 800 men, while Grant lost 875 men.

Amazingly, Grant's twelve-year-old son, Fred, found himself alone in the middle of the battlefield. He accompanied Grant throughout the campaign and was sometimes left free to wander at will. At Port Gibson, the boy's adventure turned into a nightmare. He later wrote, "I joined a detachment which was collecting the dead for burial, but, sickening at the sights, I made my way with another detachment, which was gathering the wounded, to a log house which had been appropriated for a hospital. Here the scenes were so terrible that I became faint and ill, and making my way to a tree, sat down, the most woe-begone twelve-year-old lad in America." A few weeks later, Fred was slightly wounded by a Confederate sharpshooter at Vicksburg.

## Grant Moves Inland

With a beachhead finally established, Grant made a fateful decision. He had recently been ordered to move downriver to assist Major General Nathaniel P. Banks in capturing Port Hudson, but he had no desire to break off his own campaign and loathed the idea of serving under a political general. Thus, Grant decided to ignore the order and continue the Vicksburg operation.

By now, General Joseph E. Johnston, commander of the Confederate Department of the West, was concentrating troops at Jackson. Johnston could attack Grant's rear if he marched directly toward Vicksburg, so Grant decided to eliminate him as a threat. By moving against Jackson first, Grant could also gain control of the vital railroad over which Pemberton received supplies and reinforcements. Such a tactic was risky, for he would be placing his army deep inside enemy territory without support, and it would be impossible to keep the men supplied from the transports on the Mississippi River. Sherman vehemently objected and warned Grant he was voluntarily placing the army in a position the Confederates would have maneuvered for months to get it in. But Grant did not hesitate. He had learned months earlier during his retreat in northern Mississippi that there was plenty of food and fodder in the state. Convinced he could live off the land, Grant began the march toward Jackson on May 8. Before leaving, he wired General-in-Chief Halleck, "[Y]ou may not hear from me again for several days."

When McPherson's corps defeated a small Confederate force at Raymond on May 12, Johnston prepared to evacuate Jackson. Two days later, Grant's columns advanced on the city in a pouring rain and met stiff resistance from the Confederate rear guard that kept them at bay until Johnston completed his evacuation that afternoon. Grant then occupied Jackson and the next day turned most of the army toward Vicksburg while Sherman's corps remained behind to destroy enemy supplies, public buildings, and the railroad. Unfortunately, the destruction soon got out of hand, and the Catholic church and other private property were burned.

The Confederate response to Grant's invasion was weak and poorly handled. Johnston had 8,000 men at Jackson and Pemberton had 30,000 at Vicksburg, and with proper coordination they might have trapped Grant's small army between them. Unfortunately, President Davis disliked Joe Johnston and had the Confederate War Department instruct Pemberton to communicate directly to Richmond without going through his commanding officer. Johnston sometimes went days without hearing from Pemberton, and, when he did, the messages were hardly useful in planning strategy to stop Grant. The officer who deciphered Pemberton's messages at Johnston's headquarters remembered, "I never knew, in all my life, so provoking a stupidity as Pemberton's at this time. I remember

**John C. Pemberton.** A Pennsylvania native, Pemberton was a West Point graduate who sided with his wife's native South. He was highly intelligent and dedicated to the Confederate cause but proved no match for General Ulysses S. Grant.

translating a very long cipher dispatch from him, so utterly unimportant & ridiculous that Col. Ewell declared I must have made some mistake. . . . Then, all of a sudden, after telegraphing very vigorously for several days—showing himself totally misled by the enemy's movement, he reported their landing at [Bruinsburg]. Then silence for a couple of days. Then their defeat of Bowen [at Port Gibson]. Again silence—spite of vigorous questioning from our side." As disappointing as Pemberton's leadership was, Johnston did little better. He seemed content to stay in Jackson and let Grant seize the initiative and took few steps to stop his advancing army. Grant's march on Jackson succeeded because of his own audacity and the failure of Confederate leadership.

Throughout the course of Grant's long march from Bruinsburg, Johnston frequently ordered Pemberton to leave Vicksburg and engage the enemy while they were strung out on the road. President Davis, however, ordered Pemberton to hold the city at all costs. Faced with conflicting orders, Pemberton became indecisive. Messages flew back and forth between the two generals, but they could not agree on a plan of action, and when Pemberton finally decided to move toward Jackson it was too late. Grant had already concentrated his army and was marching west to confront him. By this time many of Pemberton's generals had lost all confidence in him. One junior officer recounted listening to several generals sitting under a tree discussing their commander. It was, he claimed, "quite an animated conversation. . . . They all said harsh, ill-natured things, made ill-tempered jests in regard to General Pemberton and when an order came from him, the courier who brought it was not out of hearing, before they made light of it and ridiculed the plan he proposed."

## – Champion Hill and Big Black River Bridge

Grant and Pemberton collided at Champion Hill, a prominent piece of high ground that controlled the main road to Vicksburg. Pemberton positioned 22,000 men on the hill and awaited Grant's 29,000-man army. The ensuing battle was vicious as several attacks and counterattacks were made. A Confederate wrote, "The battle here raged fearfully. . . . one unbroken, deafening roar of musketry was all that could be heard." The blood-soaked hill changed hands three times, but in the end Pemberton was outmaneuvered and forced to retreat. In the Battle of Champion Hill, the campaign's largest, Pemberton lost almost 4,000 men and 27 cannons, while Grant lost about 2,500 men.

Pemberton now had no recourse but to fall back to Vicksburg, and he ordered General Bowen to man the breastworks on the east bank of the Big Black River and hold the bridge until the last retreating Confederates had crossed. When Grant attacked Bowen on May 17, the Confederates panicked and fled after setting fire to the bridge. In the rout 1,700 of Bowen's men and 18 cannons were captured, while Grant suffered fewer than 300 casualties. The disaster forced Pemberton to file into the Vicksburg defenses to make his last stand.

By now the Confederates' confidence in their commander was shaken to the core, and one surgeon declared, "Pemberton is either a traitor, or the most incompetent officer in the confederacy. *Indecision, Indecision, Indecision.*" Pemberton had never had the full trust of his subordinates. He was a harsh martinet who seemed to assume his officers knew what he wanted to do, and his orders were often poorly worded, which led to misunderstandings and unnecessary marching and countermarching that exhausted the troops. In contrast, Grant kept his units well in hand within supporting distance of one another and issued clear, concise orders. The low opinion some generals had of Pemberton became abundantly clear when Major General William W. Loring's division was separated from the army at Champion Hill and made its way to join Johnston at Jackson. When he arrived, Loring began to curse Pemberton's incompetence in front of officers and enlisted men alike. One officer who witnessed the spectacle wrote, "The way Loring cursed Pemberton in speaking of the affair . . . was frightful to hear. . . . Loring's way of abusing Pemberton was unmilitary & by no means pleasant."

# NOTABLE UNIT: *8th Wisconsin: The Eagle Regiment*

This Union regiment, which saw combat at Vicksburg, entered Union service in September 1861. When the companies were first forming, a local man presented an eagle chick as a mascot to the volunteers from Eau Claire. A Chippewa Indian had captured the two-month-old chick earlier and traded it to a white settler for a bushel of corn. The men named the eagle "Old Abe" (for Abraham Lincoln), and the entire regiment soon adopted it. The soldiers even built a perch for the bird to sit on during marches, and it was always carried to the left of the regiment's flag. Because of its unique mascot, the 8th Wisconsin was nicknamed "The Eagle Regiment."

During battles, Old Abe often flew high overhead screeching and then returned to his perch when the shooting stopped (the men eventually clipped his wings and tail to keep him grounded). At the Battle of Corinth, Mississippi, Old Abe was slightly wounded. One soldier wrote, "[He] hopped off his perch to the ground and ducked his head between his carrier's legs. He was thoroughly demoralized and the same feeling suddenly extended itself to the line and they broke and ran . . . the carrier of the Eagle picking him up and carrying him under his arm as fast as he could run." When the regiment entered northern Mississippi during Grant's overland campaign against Vicksburg, one Southern woman stood in her yard and sneered at what she called the "*Yankee* Buzzard," but the men's threatening response sent her scurrying back into her house. Old Abe became well known in both armies, and the Confederates tried unsuccessfully to shoot him down in some battles.

At Vicksburg, the 8th Wisconsin participated in the doomed assault on May 22. As usual, Old Abe led the way, but the men became pinned down outside a Confederate fort and were finally forced to retreat. The Eagle Regiment went on to serve in the Red River Campaign and at the Battles of Nashville, Tennessee, and Spanish Fort, Alabama. Out of the 1,203 men who served in the unit, 195 died during the war. Old Abe survived his three-year "enlistment" and was said to have survived forty-two battles and skirmishes. When discharged in 1864, he weighed ten pounds and had a 6½-foot wingspan. Old Abe became a famous icon for the Union, and a group of Northern children sold his picture to raise $16,000 for the war effort. After mustering out of service, he was presented to the state of Wisconsin and was put on display at the state capital. Sadly, Old Abe died of smoke inhalation when the capitol burned in 1881. Today, his replica sits in Madison's Memorial Hall and in the Assembly Chamber.

## The Siege of Vicksburg

The Confederates' morale lifted once they took refuge inside Vicksburg, largely because two fresh divisions, that had not fought at Champion Hill, arrived to give Pemberton just over 30,000 men. There also were miles of strong trenches, earthworks, and fortifications around the city, and fronting these works was a tortured landscape of deep gullies, thickets, and tangles of obstructions that made any advance difficult. For good reason, Vicksburg was known as "The Gibraltar of the West." The Confederate defenders had little doubt they could

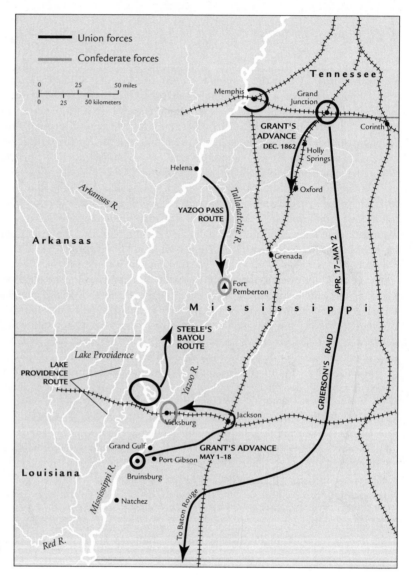

**The Vicksburg Campaign, December 1862–May 1863.** It took Grant six months to get into position to attack Vicksburg. In December 1862, Confederate cavalry turned back his advance from Grand Junction, Tennessee, by destroying the supply base at Holly Springs, Mississippi. Grant then moved down the Mississippi River and tried unsuccessfully to approach Vicksburg by water. Louisiana canal projects at Lake Providence and De Soto Point failed, as did two attempts to attack Vicksburg by way of Yazoo Pass and Steele's Bayou, Mississippi. While Grierson's Raid distracted the enemy, Grant marched farther downstream, crossed the Mississippi River at Bruinsburg, and attacked Vicksburg from the rear.

hold their position until Johnston lifted the siege by attacking Grant's rear from Jackson.

Grant reached Vicksburg on May 18 and finally reestablished his supply line with Porter's fleet. Emboldened by his recent victories, he believed the city could be taken by storm and ordered a frontal assault for the next day. Grant, however, badly underestimated the enemy's strength and position. When his men attacked, they were met by a solid wall of lead and iron. One Union soldier remembered how "the very sticks and chips, scattered over the ground, [were] jumping under

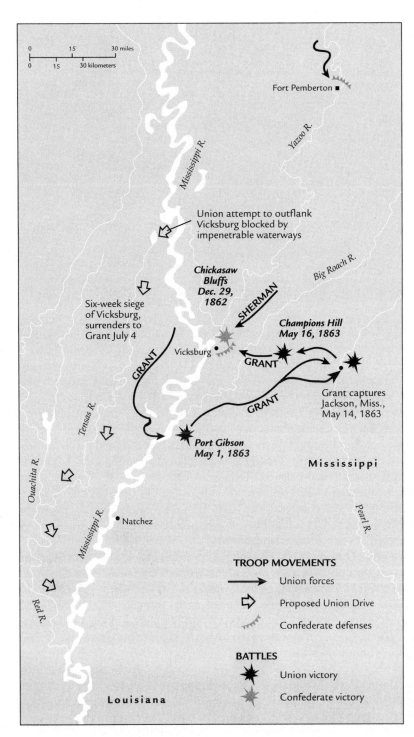

0   15   30 miles
0   15   30 kilometers

Fort Pemberton ■

*Yazoo R.*

*Mississippi R.*

Union attempt to outflank
Vicksburg blocked by
impenetrable waterways

*Big Roach R.*

**Chickasaw
Bluffs
Dec. 29,
1862**

SHERMAN

**Champions Hill
May 16, 1863**

Six-week siege
of Vicksburg,
surrenders to
Grant July 4

GRANT

Vicksburg •

GRANT

Grant captures
Jackson, Miss.,
May 14, 1863

GRANT

*Tensas R.*

**Port Gibson
May 1, 1863**

**Mississippi**

*Ouachita R.*

*Mississippi R.*

• Natchez

*Pearl R.*

**TROOP MOVEMENTS**

→ Union forces

⇨ Proposed Union Drive

Confederate defenses

**BATTLES**

✸ Union victory

✸ Confederate victory

*Red R.*

**Louisiana**

**The Siege of Vicksburg,
May–July 1863.** All of
Grant's initial attempts
to reach Vicksburg failed.
Sherman was defeated in
December 1862 when he
attacked the enemy defenses
at Chickasaw Bluffs, and
Confederate Fort Pemberton
stopped Union gunboats
in March 1863 during the
Yazoo Pass Expedition.
Several Louisiana canal
projects were also failures.
In late April, Grant marched
downstream and crossed
the Mississippi River near
Port Gibson. After defeating an enemy force there,
he moved to Jackson and
destroyed that Confeder-
ate base. Afterward, Grant
headed west, defeated the
Confederates at Champion
Hill, and then trapped them
inside Vicksburg's defenses.
After a 47-day siege, the
Confederates surrendered
on July 4, 1863.

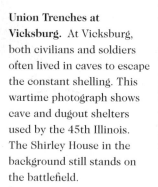

**Union Trenches at Vicksburg.** At Vicksburg, both civilians and soldiers often lived in caves to escape the constant shelling. This wartime photograph shows cave and dugout shelters used by the 45th Illinois. The Shirley House in the background still stands on the battlefield.

the hot shower of rebel bullets." Little ground was gained, and Grant lost almost 1,000 men, while Pemberton lost fewer than 200.

After the failed attack, General McClernand claimed his men were partially successful and convinced Grant to order a second attack on May 22. When the signal was given, thousands of Union soldiers rose from their trenches and charged toward the ominous earthworks. In describing the attack on his front, one Confederate wrote, "Suddenly the roar of the guns ceased. . . . I sprang to my feet and looked in the direction of the enemy, when they seemed to be springing from the bowels of the earth a long line of indigo a magnificent line in each direction. . . . It was a grand and appalling sight." To capture one of the main Confederate fortifications, 150 volunteers called the "Forlorn Hope" led the charge to throw ladders across the ditch in front of the enemy's works. The men bravely pressed forward, only to be shot down by the score. The attack failed, but 78 members of the Forlorn Hope were awarded the Medal of Honor.

Grant lost more than 3,000 men on May 22, while Pemberton counted fewer than 500 men lost. In his memoirs, Grant claimed that this second attack—and one a year later at Cold Harbor, Virginia—were the only two he regretted making in the entire war. He blamed the defeat on McClernand, whose misleading claims convinced him to make the charge. When McClernand later published newspaper reports praising his corps at the expense of the others, Grant replaced him with Major General Edward O. C. Ord.

Realizing the city could not be taken by direct assault, Grant settled into a siege. For the next six weeks, artillery and sharpshooter fire was constant. Citizens trapped in Vicksburg were terrified and began living in caves dug into the hillsides to escape the shellfire. Soldiers on both sides endured the misery of oppressive heat, water-filled ditches, and frequent thunderstorms. During the siege, the Union army grew to 77,000 men as reinforcements and supplies poured in. At night, they dug their trenches closer to the Confederates and during the day shot at everything that moved. Grant was able to rotate his men off the front line for occasional rest, but Pemberton's soldiers remained in the muddy ditches suffering shortages of food, medicine, and ammunition. The Confederates eventually ate mule meat and held rat hunts in the trenches to supplement their meager rations. Through it all, they maintained a dark sense of humor and sometimes warned the Yankees to "look out as we have a new general . . . General Starvation."

During the weeks of siege, Johnston built up a 31,000-man army near Jackson and urged Pemberton to break out of the city and join him. Pemberton refused, however, choosing to obey Davis's orders to hold the city—and Johnston took no steps to rescue him. The only Confederate attempts to raise the siege were two small attacks at Milliken's Bend, Louisiana, in early June, and Helena, Arkansas, in July. They were intended to disrupt Grant's supply line and divert Union attention away from Vicksburg, but both failed.

The strain of constant combat and supply shortages finally broke the spirit of many Confederates. In early July, Pemberton received an anonymous note that stated, "If you can't feed us, you had better surrender us, horrible as the idea is, than suffer this noble army to disgrace themselves by desertion. . . . MANY SOLDIERS." With the situation hopeless, Pemberton arranged a cease-fire. One Union soldier remembered how eerie the quiet was. "The silence began to be fearfully oppressive. For so many long days and nights it had been a continuous battle. Not a minute but the crack of the rifle or the boom of the cannon had been in our ears. And much of the time it had been deafening. Now it was still, absolutely still. . . . It was leaden. We could not bear it; it settled down so close; it hugged us with its hollow, unseen arms till we could scarcely breathe." Pemberton began negotiating with Grant on the afternoon of July 3 and surrendered the city and its garrison the next day. The 47-day siege was over. Three days earlier, Johnston had finally moved out of Jackson and began advancing toward Vicksburg to make a diversionary attack so Pemberton could escape. He got as far as the Big Black River when he learned of the surrender. When Sherman moved his corps to meet him, Johnston retreated, and for the second time abandoned Jackson to the enemy.

The choice of surrender dates caused many Southerners to denounce the northern-born Pemberton as a traitor, but Pemberton defended his actions by explaining that he had thought Grant would be in a festive mood on Independence Day and would give him more generous surrender terms. The terms were not generous, however, for Grant demanded unconditional surrender. Grant had no way to feed 30,000 prisoners, so he paroled most of the Confederates. Some went to camps to await exchange, while others simply went home, never to return to service. His reputation ruined, Pemberton resigned his general's commission a year later and asked to be allowed to reenter service as a private. Jefferson Davis refused, however, and appointed him a lieutenant colonel of artillery. Pemberton served until war's end commanding an artillery battery defending Richmond.

# EYEWITNESS
## William H. Tunnard

*Sergeant William H. Tunnard was a 26-year-old New Jersey native who grew up in Louisiana. After graduating from college in Ohio, he returned home and joined the 3rd Louisiana Infantry when the Civil War began. The regiment served in several bloody battles before it entered Vicksburg to defend one of the most important parts of the line. Tunnard's diary gives a graphic description of life in the trenches:*

May 25th: Another clear and hot day, and a continuation of the usual music along the lines. In the afternoon, a flag of truce was sent into the lines, requesting a cessation of hostilities for the purpose of burying the dead. The effluvia from the putrefying bodies had become almost unbearable to friend and foe, and the request was granted, to continue for three hours. Now commenced a strange spectacle in this thrilling drama of war. Flags were displayed along both lines, and the troops thronged the breastworks, gaily chatting with each other, discussing the issues of the war, disputing over differences of opinion, losses in the fight, etc. Numbers of the Confederates accepted invitations to visit the enemy's lines, where they were hospitably entertained and warmly welcomed. They were abundantly supplied with provisions, supplies of various kinds, and liquor. . . . The hours of peace had scarcely expired ere those who had so lately intermingled in friendly intercourse were once again engaged in the deadly struggle. Heavy mortars, artillery of every caliber, and small-arms, once more with thunder tones awakened the slumbering echoes of the hills surrounding the heroic city of Vicksburg. . . .

June 8th: Clear and warm. The struggle raged with unabated fury. The enemy's lines were slowly but surely approaching nearer to our own breastworks, and the struggle was daily becoming more fierce and deadly. The Federals procured a car-frame, which they placed on wheels, loading it with cotton-bales. . . . Protected by this novel, movable shelter, they constructed their works with impunity, and with almost the certainty of eventually reaching our intrenchments. Rifles had no effect on the cotton-bales, and there was not a single piece of artillery to batter them down. . . .

June 9th: . . . All night long the fight was kept up. The moveable breastwork in front of the intrenchments of the Third Louisiana, became a perfect annoyance to the regiment, and various plans were proposed for its destruction. . . . Finally, a happy invention suggested itself to the mind of Lieutenant W. M. Washburn, of Company

In addition to capturing almost 30,000 prisoners at Vicksburg, Grant also seized 172 cannons, 60,000 stands of arms, and more than 2 million rounds of ammunition. Earlier in the campaign, the Confederates lost another 88 cannons and sustained an additional 8,000 casualties, while Grant sustained a total of about 10,000 casualties (approximately 5,000 during the siege). The capture of Vicksburg confirmed Grant as the most successful Union general. His campaign was brilliant and demonstrated how a smaller army could defeat a larger one through audacity and swift marching. Some

B. . . . procuring turpentine and cotton, he filled the ball with the latter, thoroughly saturated by the former.

A rifle was loaded, and, amid the utmost curiosity and interest, fired at the hated object. The sharp report was followed by the glittering ball, as it sped from the breast-works straight to the dark mass of cotton-bales, like the rapid flight of a fire-fly. . . . Suddenly some one exclaimed, "I'll be d——d if that thing isn't on fire!" Sure enough, smoke was seen issuing from the dark mass. The inventive genius of Lieutenant Washburn had proved a complete success. . . .

June 17th: . . . [T]he enemy's lines were now so near, that scraps of paper could be thrown by the combatants into each other's ranks. Thus, a Yankee threw a "hard-tack" biscuit among the men of the regiment, having written on it "starvation."

June 19th: . . . The rations issued at this time were: flour, one-quarter of a pound: rice flour, one-quarter of a pound; peas one-quarter of a pound; rice, sugar and salt, in equally small proportions. Tobacco and bacon, one-quarter of a pound. It was a small allowance for men to sustain life with. . . .

June 27th: . . . Vicksburg presented a fearful spectacle. . . . The avenues were almost deserted, save by hunger-pinched, starving and wounded soldiers . . . Fences were torn down, and houses pulled to pieces for fire-wood. Even the enclosures around the remains of the revered dead, were destroyed. . . . and men using the tombstones as convenient tables for their scanty meals, or a couch for an uncertain slumber. Dogs howled through the streets at night; cats screamed forth their hideous cries; an army of rats, seeking food, would scamper around your very feet, and across the streets, and over the pavements. Lice and filth covered the bodies of the soldiers. Delicate women, and little children, with pale, care-worn and hunger-pinched features, peered at the passers-by with wistful eyes, from the caves in the hill-sides . . . Human language is impotent to portray the true situation of affairs. . . .

*Tunnard was one of nearly 30,000 Confederates captured at Vicksburg, but he avoided prison camp by being paroled and exchanged in December 1863. He remained in the army until the bitter end but saw no further combat.*

people came to see July 4, 1863, as the turning point of the war, because the capitulation occurred on the same day Robert E. Lee began his retreat from Gettysburg, Pennsylvania. With the capture of Vicksburg, the Union was on the verge of seizing the entire Mississippi River, and Sherman boasted to his brother, "The fall of Vicksburg has had a powerful effect. They are subjugated. I even am amazed at the effect. . . ." All that remained to secure the mighty river was to complete the capture of Port Hudson, Louisiana, farther downstream.

## DID YOU KNOW?

### Vicksburg: City of Sadness

Both the Confederate soldiers who defended Vicksburg and the civilians trapped there were horrified that General Pemberton chose to surrender on July 4, 1863. After the war, many of Vicksburg's citizens viewed Independence Day as a day of sadness and humiliation—not a day to be celebrated. As a result, Vicksburg did not officially observe Independence Day for eighty years, but that is not to say no one recognized the holiday. African Americans and some Unionists continued to celebrate even if the city did not. Black veterans, for example, gathered in the National Cemetery on July 4 to read the Declaration of Independence. The city's official snub only ended on July 4, 1945, two months after Germany surrendered in World War II. Deciding the time was right, Vicksburg officials agreed to celebrate Independence Day to commemorate V-E Day. Apparently, the holiday was skipped the next year, but a small ceremony was held on July 4, 1947, to coincide with a visit by General Dwight D. Eisenhower. Eisenhower encouraged the people to recognize Independence Day, but even today some Vicksburg residents refuse to do so.

## THE PORT HUDSON CAMPAIGN

**March 25, 1863: Banks begins the Bayou Teche Campaign**

**April 12–13, 1863: Battle of Fort Bisland, Louisiana**

**April 14, 1863: Battle of Irish Bend**

**May 22, 1863: Banks surrounds Port Hudson**

**May 27, 1863: Banks makes unsuccessful attack on Port Hudson**

**June 14, 1863: Banks makes second unsuccessful attack on Port Hudson**

**July 9, 1863: General Gardner surrenders Port Hudson**

While Grant battled for Vicksburg, another Union army under Major General Nathaniel P. Banks began operations against Port Hudson, Louisiana, located about twenty-five miles north of Baton Rouge. The main purpose of Banks's campaign was to assist Grant's attack on Vicksburg by tying down Confederate soldiers so they could not reinforce Pemberton or threaten Grant's rear. If he captured Port Hudson quickly, Banks could then join Grant at Vicksburg. The Confederates recognized the importance of Port Hudson early in the war and spent a year ringing it with 4½ miles of earthworks and dozens of powerful cannons. Within this strong perimeter were about 7,500 Confederate troops under Major General Franklin Gardner. A New York native, Gardner was a West Point graduate and Mexican War veteran. He married a former Louisiana governor's daughter and resigned from the U.S. Army to join the Confederates when the Civil War began. Although Gardner had a history of drunkenness, he was a capable commander and was determined to defend his post.

## The Bayou Teche Campaign

Before he attacked Port Hudson, Banks first had to clear the Rebels out of Louisiana's Bayou Teche (TESH) region. This was necessary because Major

General Richard Taylor's small Confederate army might threaten Banks's rear once he became engaged at Port Hudson. Banks also wanted to capture Alexandria in central Louisiana to prevent the enemy from reinforcing Port Hudson by way of the Red River. On March 25, 1863, Banks left Baton Rouge and headed to Brashear City (modern-day Morgan City). From there, he sent part of his army by transports through Grand Lake to Irish Bend, located behind Taylor's position at Fort Bisland on Bayou Teche. Banks then led the rest of the army up Bayou Teche to attack Taylor and trap him between the two converging columns.

Taylor had a few thousand infantrymen and the gunboat *Diana* in position at Fort Bisland on Bayou Teche to stop Banks's advance. After enduring a two-day artillery bombardment, Taylor learned the other Union force had landed behind him at Irish Bend and began evacuating his position on the night of April 13 to escape the closing trap. The following day, Taylor attacked the enemy at Irish Bend with the *Diana* and part of his infantry while the rest of the army escaped up Bayou Teche. After holding the Yankees at bay in a short, sharp fight, the Confederates abandoned and blew up the *Diana* and then disengaged to continue the retreat northward. Banks ultimately reached Alexandria, but the enemy got away.

Banks's campaign had mixed results. Bayou Teche had been cleared of Confederates and Port Hudson's supply line was cut, but Taylor's army remained intact. A Union officer complained, "We had the rebels in a bag . . . but the damn string was rotten, and they slipped through." The entire Bayou Teche region was left devastated as both armies stripped the land of supplies, and the Yankees engaged in wholesale vandalism. One Union soldier admitted, "We have left an awful scene of desolation behind us. In spite of orders not to pillage, burned and sacked houses mark our course."

## The Siege of Port Hudson

Banks soon abandoned Alexandria and moved down the Red River to start the Port Hudson Campaign while another two divisions marched north from Baton Rouge to join him. On May 22, his 30,000 men encircled the enemy garrison, while Admiral David Farragut maintained a naval presence on the Mississippi River. Hoping to avoid a long siege, Banks ordered a general assault on May 27, but poor execution and rough terrain foiled his plan. The attack was made in piecemeal fashion, which allowed Gardner to take advantage of his interior line and skillfully shift troops to defend threatened positions. One defender wrote, "We moad them down and made them disperse[,] leaving there dead and wounded on the field to stink." A Union war correspondent claimed the Confederates fired "shot and shells, and pieces of railroad iron twelve to eighteen inches long." Among Banks's attacking troops were the 1st and 3rd Louisiana Native Guards, two of the Union's first black regiments. The Native Guards fought bravely and advanced as far as their white counterparts, but they, too, ultimately failed. In the disjointed attacks, Banks lost approximately 2,000 men, while Gardner counted fewer than 500 lost.

# BIOGRAPHY

## Nathaniel Prentiss Banks: "Bobbin Boy of Massachusetts"

**Nathaniel P. Banks**

Nathaniel P. Banks (1816–1894) was a self-made man who became known as the "Bobbin Boy of Massachusetts" because he began working in the state's textile industry at a young age. He often bragged to have graduated "from a college with a water-wheel in the basement." Although Banks had little formal education, he became a successful lawyer and was elected to the state legislature, where he served as the Speaker of the House before being elected to Congress. A moderate on the slavery issue, Banks was known for changing his political positions and was affiliated with five different parties during his career.

Banks was the consummate politician. An acquaintance claimed he was "not a warm-hearted person, and was never known to go out of his way an inch to confer a favor on a friend or supporter, unless another and a greater favor was expected at a future period." Although slightly shorter than average, Banks cut an impressive figure, but he was described as being arrogant and a "pretentious humbug." After switching from the Democrats to the Republicans because of his opposition to the Kansas-Nebraska Act, he was elected Speaker of the House in 1856 on the 133rd ballot. Banks was elected governor of Massachusetts the following year and was reelected twice, but he resigned his post in January 1861 to replace George B. McClellan as director of the Illinois Central Railroad.

When the Civil War began, President Lincoln appointed Banks a major general of volunteers because he needed Banks's political support. Although he had no military experience, Banks looked like a successful general. One newspaper reporter wrote he was "by all odds the most impressive man, in countenance, language and demeanor, whom I have seen since the war commenced." But looks were deceiving. A subordinate captured the general's essence when he declared Banks "means well, but I fear that he lacks a little either of education or confidence to push things through."

Over the next two weeks, Banks's army grew to about 40,000 men. When Gardner refused a surrender demand, Banks launched a second attack on June 14, but once again his men were flung back with heavy losses. This time Banks lost 1,800 men to Gardner's 200. Banks then settled into siege work, and the battle became a miniature Vicksburg with constant artillery and sharpshooter fire. Gardner's men went hungry, while Banks's men suffered tremendously from exposure and disease. To set an example for his men, General Gardner became the first soldier in the trapped garrison to eat mule meat, and he later dined on rats and dried magnolia leaves. One Confederate wrote, "Rats, which are very numerous in our camps, are considered a dainty dish, and are being considerably sought after . . . I have eaten a piece of horse this morning. I do not fancy it, but will eat it as long as I can sustain life upon it, before I will give any consent to surrender. The whole army exhibit the same spirit."

Banks was given command of the Department of the Shenandoah. His combat career started auspiciously enough when he defeated Stonewall Jackson at the Battle of Kernstown in March 1862. Within months, however, Jackson chased Banks out of the area in his famous Valley Campaign. Adding insult to injury, the Confederates nicknamed Banks "Commissary Banks" because they captured so many supplies from him. The defeat did little damage to Banks's reputation, however, because many believed he had not been supported properly and because he did not complain. Secretary of War Stanton wrote "on this occasion as at all other times Gen. Banks has obeyed the orders from the War Department without one selfish complaint and was the only General of his rank of whom it could be said."

Banks next was sent to Louisiana to replace Benjamin F. Butler in command of the Department of the Gulf. He was victorious in the Bayou Teche and Port Hudson campaigns, although his leadership and tactical abilities were uninspiring. Nonetheless, Banks received the Thanks of Congress and was put in charge of the 1864 Red River Campaign to capture Shreveport, Louisiana. He mishandled the invasion, however, and was defeated by Richard Taylor's much smaller Confederate army. Banks's soldiers became disgusted with his leadership and one man declared, "The sooner Banks goes home, the better will it be for the service." Superior officers tended to agree. Banks was removed in September 1864, and his military career essentially ended. He resigned from the army in August 1865, resumed his political career in Massachusetts, and later served twelve years in Congress.

Although not a brilliant general, Banks was a capable politician, and he worked diligently to implement Lincoln's Reconstruction plan in Louisiana. He enrolled voters, held new elections, and helped draw up a new constitution that abolished slavery. Banks's political work was much more effective and had a longer-lasting impact than any of his military achievements.

Despite the near-starvation conditions, the Confederates held on until Gardner learned Vicksburg had fallen. Realizing it was hopeless to continue the fight, he surrendered Port Hudson on July 9.

At forty-nine days, Port Hudson was the longest siege in American history, but it finally ended the Union's bloody struggle to secure the Mississippi River. The campaign cost Banks nearly 10,000 casualties, while Gardner had about 1,000 men killed or wounded and surrendered 6,500. Lincoln, who was disappointed that Meade allowed Lee to escape after Gettysburg, was particularly ecstatic over the twin victories at Vicksburg and Port Hudson. He was almost giddy with excitement when he learned of Vicksburg's capture on July 7 and told Secretary of the Navy Welles, "I cannot, in words, tell you my joy over this result." As Lincoln eloquently put it, the victories ensured the "Father of Waters again goes unvexed to the sea." Although some of the war's bloodiest

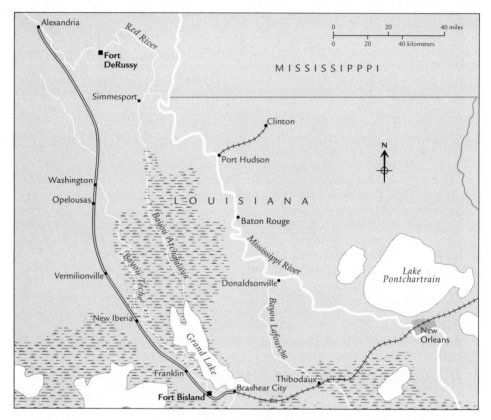

**South Louisiana, 1863.** In the spring of 1863, both the Bayou Teche and Port Hudson campaigns took place in South Louisiana. In March, Banks left New Orleans and invaded the Bayou Teche region to clear out Taylor's Confederate army. Small battles were fought around Fort Bisland, and Banks chased Taylor to Alexandria, but the Confederates escaped. Banks then moved down the Red River and laid siege to Port Hudson.

battles still lay ahead, the capture of Vicksburg and Port Hudson was a major achievement for the Union. The rebelling states were now split in two, and the war in the west had permanently turned in the Union's favor. The key to the Confederacy was finally in Lincoln's pocket.

## FOR FURTHER READING

Soldiers' Anonymous Letter to Pemberton

## CHAPTER 16

# Shifting Fortunes in the West: The Chickamauga and Chattanooga Campaigns

The Tullahoma Campaign

The Chickamauga Campaign

The Chattanooga Campaign

The Knoxville Campaign

The Trans-Mississippi Department

November 25, 1863, dawned crisp and clear as thousands of Union soldiers in the Army of the Cumberland took up attack positions outside Chattanooga, Tennessee. Their target was Missionary Ridge, a long, 400-foot-high, rocky ridge southeast of the city. On top of the ridge waited General Braxton Bragg's grimly determined Army of Tennessee. For weeks the Confederates had besieged Chattanooga, but now the Union armies were on the offensive. When the main Union attack against the northern tip of Missionary Ridge failed, the Army of the Cumberland was sent forward with orders to capture the rifle pits at the base of the ridge. The Yankees attacked and quickly took the rifle pits but then found themselves exposed to a deadly fire from the Confederates on the ridge above. To stay in the rifle pits seemed certain death, but it was just as dangerous to retreat back across the open ground from which they had come. It seemed suicidal, but the only alternative was to keep going forward. One Union officer wrote, "Here and there a man leaps the works and starts towards the hilltop; small squads follow. Then someone gave the command, 'Forward!' after a number of men began to advance. Officers catch the inspiration. The mounted officers dismount and stone their horses to the rear. The cry, 'Forward!' is repeated along the line, and the apparent impossibility is undertaken. . . ."

In the rear, Major Joseph Fullerton stood with Generals Ulysses S. Grant, George H. Thomas, and others watching the attack. All were taken aback when the men surged up Missionary Ridge without orders. Grant was furious because the attack would obviously fail. Fullerton recalled, "Grant quickly turned to Thomas, who stood by his side, and I heard him say angrily: 'Thomas, who ordered those men up the ridge?' Thomas replied, in his usual slow, quiet manner: 'I don't know; I did not.' Then, addressing General Gordon Granger, he said, 'Did you order them up, Granger?' 'No,' said Granger; 'they started up without orders. When those fellows get started all hell can't stop them.' General Grant said something to the effect that somebody would suffer if it did not turn out well, and then, turning, stoically watched the ridge. He gave no further orders."

Against all odds, the Union soldiers fought their way to the top. Major James A. Connolly of the 123rd Illinois described the dramatic ascent: "One flag bearer, on hands and knees, is seen away in advance of the whole line. . . . [I]n a few moments another flag bearer gets just as near the summit at another point. . . . [A]ll eyes are turned there; the men away above us look like great ants crawling up. . . . One of our flags seems to be moving; look! Look! Look! Up! Up! Up! It goes and is planted on the rebel works. . . . Our men, stirred by the same memories, shouted 'Chickamauga!' as they scaled the works at the summit, and amid the din of battle the cry 'Chickamauga!' 'Chickamauga!' could be heard."

Waving one of the Union flags atop Missionary Ridge was eighteen-year-old Lieutenant Arthur MacArthur of the 24th Wisconsin. As he clawed his way toward the summit, the regimental color bearer was bayoneted, and a second soldier who picked up the fallen flag was decapitated by a cannonball. Already wounded and covered in blood, Lieutenant MacArthur picked up the tattered flag, raised it above his head, and yelled to the men, "On Wisconsin!" He then led them to the top and planted his colors on the summit. MacArthur survived the Civil War, rose to lieutenant general in the post-war army, and was awarded the Medal of Honor for his heroics at Missionary Ridge. Years later, his son General Douglas MacArthur also received the Medal of Honor, for his defense of the Philippine Islands in World War II. Lieutenant MacArthur and his comrades had accomplished the seemingly impossible feat of forcing the enemy off the high ground and lifting the siege of Chattanooga. The victory at Missionary Ridge kept Chattanooga and its important railroad junction in Union hands, thus disrupting the Confederates' transportation system. It also forced the Southern Army of Tennessee to retreat back into Georgia and go on the defensive. Missionary Ridge was one of the Union's most important victories because it regained the initiative for Union forces in the West.

## THE TULLAHOMA CAMPAIGN

**June 23, 1863: Rosecrans begins the Tullahoma Campaign**
**June 24, 1863: Wilder's Brigade forces the Confederates out of Hoover's Gap**
**June 27, 1863: Union forces occupy Manchester**
**June 30, 1863: Bragg withdraws from Tullahoma, ending the campaign**

In the western theater, the bloody Battle of Stones River ushered in 1863, but that Union victory did little to change the strategic situation in Tennessee. Afterward, Major General William S. Rosecrans's 65,000-man Army of the Cumberland remained encamped around Murfreesboro, while General Braxton Bragg's 44,000-man Army of Tennessee retreated farther south to the Duck River. There Bragg established a defensive line stretching from Shelbyville in the west, through Wartrace and Manchester, and all the way to McMinnville in the east, from which he continued to protect Middle Tennessee's vital agricultural area that provided food and fodder for much of the Confederacy. Bragg's Duck River position also prevented Rosecrans from advancing on the important rail center of Chattanooga, Tennessee. Chattanooga had a population of about 2,500 and was one of the Confederacy's most strategic points because its three railroads helped provide the Confederacy with its advantageous interior line: The East Tennessee & Georgia Railroad linked Virginia with the western theater, the Nashville & Chattanooga ran all the way to Kentucky, and the Western & Atlantic linked Chattanooga with Atlanta and points south. Not only were troops moved along these lines, but the Confederates also used them to ship Tennessee's vital supplies all across the Confederacy. President Abraham Lincoln recognized the city's significance and declared capturing Chattanooga was "fully as important as the taking and holding of Richmond."

Tennessee remained rather quiet militarily throughout the spring of 1863 as both sides concentrated on the Vicksburg and Port Hudson Campaigns along the Mississippi River. This worried Union officials because Bragg might take advantage of the inactivity and send reinforcements to relieve Vicksburg. To prevent such an occurrence, authorities urged Rosecrans to launch an offensive in Tennessee to keep Bragg in place. Rosecrans responded with a brilliantly executed offensive known as the Tullahoma Campaign.

## "A Great Disaster"

On June 23, 1863, Rosecrans split his army into four columns to threaten various sections of the Confederate line. Heavy rains fell in torrents and slowed travel, but Rosecrans's troops pushed forward and thoroughly confused Bragg. In the left center, Colonel John T. Wilder's brigade spearheaded Major General George H. Thomas's column. Wilder was the officer who surrendered 4,000 men at Munfordville, Kentucky, during the Kentucky Campaign after seeking advice from Confederate General Simon Buckner. Having been exchanged, he now commanded a brigade of mounted infantry that was the first western unit to be armed with the seven-shot Spencer carbine. Wilder himself, not the federal government, procured these modern rifles. He personally signed a guarantee for the bank loan to buy them, and his men agreed to have their pay docked each month to pay back the money.

In a driving rainstorm, Wilder's men put their rapid-firing carbines to good use and quickly drove the Confederates out of Hoover's Gap and cleared the way to Manchester. This obscure but important clash was clear evidence that the Union's superiority in manufacturing numerous and modern weaponry gave its troops an edge on the battlefield. Thanks to Wilder's brigade, Thomas was now in a position to move into Bragg's rear and cut him off from Chattanooga. To avoid being trapped, Bragg had to abandon his Duck River line and retreat south to Tullahoma. After concentrating his army at Manchester, Rosecrans next sent Wilder's fast-moving brigade to destroy the Elk River railroad bridge in Bragg's rear and cut his line of retreat. Confederate cavalry under Nathan Bedford Forrest stopped Wilder before he could destroy the bridge, but Bragg realized his position was untenable and quickly retreated from Tullahoma and crossed to the south side of the Tennessee River.

The Tullahoma Campaign had been a brilliant campaign of maneuver. With little fighting, Rosecrans forced the Confederates to abandon one of their most important agricultural areas, and he could now threaten Chattanooga. The weeklong campaign cost Rosecrans fewer than 600 men while costing Bragg about 2,000. Bragg was devastated and admitted, "This is a great disaster."

## A Hollow Victory

Instead of receiving the accolades he deserved, Rosecrans's achievement was barely noticed by the Northern people because the great victories at Vicksburg and Gettysburg occurred at the same time. To make matters worse, Union officials criticized him for not pursuing Bragg and destroying his army before it crossed the Tennessee River. Few people in Washington seemed to appreciate the extent to which the heavy rains ruined the few existing roads and made rapid pursuit impossible. Rosecrans was furious and wrote his superiors, "You do not appear to observe the fact that this noble army has driven the rebels from Middle Tennessee. I beg in behalf of this army that the War Department may not overlook so great an event because it is not written in letters of blood." Rosecrans had forced the enemy out of Middle Tennessee, but the fact remained that the Confederate army was still intact and ready to fight, and Union victory depended on destroying the enemy's armies, not just occupying its territory. The Tullahoma Campaign simply assured that the next large battle would occur somewhere in northern Georgia when Rosecrans resumed his pursuit.

## THE CHICKAMAUGA CAMPAIGN

**September 9, 1863: Union forces occupy Chattanooga; Longstreet's corps leaves Virginia to reinforce Bragg**

**September 10–11, 1863: Confederates fail to destroy isolated Union corps at McLemore's Cove**

**September 18, 1863: Longstreet's corps reaches Bragg**

**September 19–20, 1863: Battle of Chickamauga**

Rosecrans was under tremendous pressure to engage and destroy the Confederate army protecting Chattanooga, and General-in-Chief Henry Halleck even hinted at removing him from command because of his lack of aggression. Rosecrans responded by informing his superior, "I say to you frankly that whenever the Government can replace me by a commander in whom they have more confidence, they ought to do so, and take the responsibility of the result." When Rosecrans finally did advance in mid-August, he once again split the Army of the Cumberland into several columns, with one marching west toward Chattanooga while the other two moved south to threaten Bragg's left flank. To avoid being trapped, Bragg withdrew from Chattanooga on September 7, and Union forces occupied the city two days later.

## A Rebel Surprise

As Bragg retreated into northern Georgia, reinforcements were forwarded to him. Among the new arrivals was Major General Daniel Harvey Hill, an old acquaintance, who discovered Bragg had little support in the army and was haunted by the recent reversals. "He was silent and reserved and seemed gloomy and despondent. . . ." wrote Hill. "He had grown prematurely old since I saw him last, and showed much nervousness. . . . His relations with his next in command (General Polk) and with some others of his subordinates were known to be not pleasant. His many retreats, too, had alienated the rank and file from him, or at least had taken away that enthusiasm which soldiers feel for the successful general . . . ." Bragg had reason to be depressed, but he still had plenty of fight left in him and was planning a counterattack. In fact, thousands of troops from the vaunted Army of Northern Virginia were already on their way to join him.

By September 1863, Lee's army had recuperated from the Battle of Gettysburg and Lee was contemplating taking the offensive once again. Jefferson Davis, however, was more concerned about turning the war around in the western theater. In August and September, he called Lee to Richmond to discuss strategy and informed his most trusted general that he wanted to send him west to retrieve the military fortunes lost at Vicksburg and in Tennessee. But Lee was no more eager to go west than he had been before the Gettysburg Campaign. He argued that he knew nothing about the Army of Tennessee and that poor health prevented him from undertaking such a mission. No doubt, Lee also was reluctant to go west because it would have meant working with generals he had transferred there from Virginia because he thought they were incompetent. Lee informed the president that he still hoped to take the offensive in Virginia but that he would obey whatever orders Davis issued. Although disappointed by Lee's decision, Davis refused to force the issue. Instead, the two reached a compromise in which Lee would temporarily transfer Longstreet and most of his corps to the west to help retrieve the situation there. For his part, Longstreet was in complete agreement with the decision. For some time he had recommended assuming the defensive in Virginia and sending part of the army

**Lee and Gordon's Mill.** Lee and Gordon's Mill was located on the bank of Chickamauga Creek and served as an important landmark during the Battle of Chickamauga.

to reinforce the west. Longstreet's men began boarding trains in Richmond for the long trip to Georgia on September 9, the same day Rosecrans's soldiers marched into Chattanooga.

Completely unaware of the enemy buildup, Rosecrans pushed his two columns into Georgia's rugged mountains. Bragg set up an ambush to destroy one of the columns when it emerged from a mountain pass at McLemore's Cove, but his subordinates executed the plan poorly, and the enemy escaped. Although disappointed and angry that his officers had missed their opportunity, Bragg immediately planned another attack. Intelligence placed Rosecrans's left flank about ten miles south of Chattanooga at Lee and Gordon's Mill on Chickamauga Creek. Bragg would concentrate his forces south of Chattanooga, move west across Chickamauga Creek, and then turn south to strike the exposed enemy's northern flank. Rosecrans would be cut off from Chattanooga, and his army could be pushed back into the mountains and destroyed. Because the longer he delayed, the more likely Rosecrans would discover he was in danger, Bragg decided to make his move immediately even though he was unsure if Longstreet would arrive from Virginia in time to participate in the fight.

Before Bragg could attack, Rosecrans realized his separated columns were vulnerable and began concentrating his army along Chickamauga Creek. In what proved to be a critical decision, he extended his left flank three miles north of Lee and Gordon's Mill to protect the road back to Chattanooga. Bragg was unaware of this shift and assumed his army still extended far beyond Rosecrans's flank when actually the two armies were nearly parallel. Instead of enveloping the Union left flank, a Confederate attack near Lee and Gordon's Mill would actually be heading into a solid defensive line.

As both sides prepared for battle on September 18, the advanced units of Longstreet's corps began arriving on the field. The train ride from Virginia had been quite an experience for Lee's veterans. One soldier claimed, "Never before were such crazy cars—passenger, baggage, mail, coal, box, platform, all and every sort wobbling on the jumping strap-iron—used for hauling good soldiers. But we got there nevertheless." A civilian who witnessed the troop trains pass by wrote, "It was a strange sight. What seemed miles of platform cars, and soldiers rolled in their blankets lying in rows with their heads all covered, fast asleep. In their gray blankets packed in regular order, they looked like swathed mummies. . . . A feeling of awful depression laid hold of me. All those fine fellows going to kill or be killed, but why?"

## The Battle of Chickamauga

The Battle of Chickamauga began early on the morning of September 19 when Union forces on Rosecrans's left flank attacked a detachment of Confederates that had crossed Chickamauga Creek. The battle soon spread south along the entire front as each side committed more troops. The fighting was extremely confusing because the entire region was covered in thick woods with only a few scattered small fields. Union Colonel John Wilder recalled, "All this talk about generalship displayed on either side is sheer nonsense. There was no generalship in it. It was a soldier's fight purely, wherein the only question involved was the question of endurance. The two armies came together like two wild beasts, and each fought as long as it could stand up in a knock-down and drag-out encounter." The fighting was brutal, and both sides suffered heavy casualties without gaining much advantage. One Confederate described the clash as "one solid, unbroken wave of awe-inspiring sound . . . as if all the fires of earth and hell had been turned loose in one mighty effort to destroy each other."

The first day of fighting ended with the armies' positions little changed, but Bragg decided to continue his attacks the next day and divided the army into two wings, with Lieutenant Generals Leonidas Polk and James Longstreet commanding the right and left wings, respectively. Bragg then ordered Polk to attack Rosecrans's left wing at daylight. That same night Rosecrans held a meeting with his generals, in which they advised him to withdraw from the thick woods and take up a more defensible position closer to Chattanooga. Rosecrans, however, dismissed the advice and decided to stay and fight. Soldiers along the firing line that night waited nervously for the clash they knew was coming. One Union soldier wrote, "All looked with anxiety for the coming of the dawn; for although we had given the enemy a rough handling, he had certainly used us very hard."

To everyone's surprise, the battlefield remained quiet when the sun rose on the morning of September 20. Bragg anxiously listened for Polk

# NOTABLE UNIT: *Washington Artillery*

This New Orleans artillery unit was organized in 1838 as part of the Louisiana militia. Composed of men from the city's most prominent families, it first gained fame while fighting in the Mexican War. When the Civil War began, four of the unit's companies were sent to Virginia and became part of James Longstreet's command.

The Washington Artillery fought with the Army of Northern Virginia in almost every major battle. At Second Bull Run, it helped repulse an enemy attack, and two weeks later engaged the enemy at Antietam. When the men became so exhausted they could barely continue to fight, Longstreet had his staff work the guns while he corrected their aim. A battalion officer remembered, "Longstreet was on horseback at our side, sitting side-saddle fashion, and occasionally making some practical remark about the situation. He talked earnestly and gesticulated to encourage us, as the men of the detachments began to fall around our guns. . . ." The Washington Artillery received more notoriety when it defended Marye's Heights during the Battle of Fredericksburg and helped repulse the famous Irish Brigade. One artilleryman later wrote, "We hammered away at them as fast as we could load and fire, but on they came. . . . A note from Longstreet declared the firing of the battalion to be splendid." The Washington Artillery remained on Marye's Heights during the Chancellorsville Campaign and lost six cannons and thirty-three men when Union forces overran their position during the Second Battle of Fredericksburg. The battalion then accompanied the army to Gettysburg and participated in the artillery bombardment that preceded Pickett's Charge. In fact, the signal to begin the charge was two quick shots fired by

to begin his attack, but there was only silence. An officer sent to find the reason for the delay found Polk three miles in the rear at a farmhouse calmly reading a newspaper and waiting for breakfast. When he finally did attack at midmorning, Polk's troops engaged in savage fighting but made only temporary gains against the stubborn Union defenders. Rosecrans was successfully holding his ground, but just before noon a catastrophic mistake doomed his army. During the confused fighting, Rosecrans was told a gap had developed in the right wing, and he ordered Brigadier General Thomas John Wood to withdraw from the line and move his division to seal the breach. Earlier in the day, Rosecrans had cursed Wood for moving into position too slowly. Wood, a West Point professional, was still smarting from the berating and moved immediately without questioning Rosecrans's order. Unfortunately, the report forwarded to Rosecrans was incorrect. There was no gap until Wood created one when he pulled out of line and marched off as ordered.

It was sheer luck that Longstreet happened to launch a massive attack at the very point Wood left vacant. The screaming Rebels poured through the gap and shattered Rosecrans's right wing. Thousands of Union soldiers the Washington Artillery. After Gettysburg the battalion helped defend Richmond and Petersburg, and the men destroyed their gun carriages and most of them walked home to Louisiana when they learned Lee had surrendered at Appomattox.

A fifth company of the Washington Artillery was assigned to the western theater. At Shiloh it participated in bombarding the Hornet's Nest and then joined the Army of Tennessee for most of its major campaigns. The company saw heavy combat at Chickamauga and lost all its cannons after the Confederates were overrun at Missionary Ridge. Receiving new guns, the company served well in the Atlanta Campaign and accompanied the army in its 1864 Tennessee campaign. After the Battle of Franklin, the artillerymen were sent to Mobile, Alabama, and fought there in early 1865 at Spanish Fort.

During Reconstruction, federal authorities permitted the Washington Artillery veterans to form a charitable and benevolent association. Secretly they began to arm themselves to drive the Radical Republicans out of Louisiana. At the 1874 Battle of Liberty Place, the artillerymen joined White League forces and manned two small cannons in a bloody street battle against the New Orleans police (commanded, ironically, by James Longstreet). After Reconstruction, the Washington Artillery once again became part of the state militia. It fought in the Spanish-American War, World War I, and World War II, and it is still an active unit in the Louisiana National Guard.

---

panicked and ran, and many who were willing to fight became caught up in the rout and were swept from the field "like flecks of foam upon a river." Charles Dana, who accompanied Rosecrans as an observer for the War Department, heard the attack begin and declared, "Never in any battle had I witnessed such a discharge of cannon and musketry." Nearby, the devout Rosecrans seemed to know what was happening and fervently crossed himself. "Hello!" Dana recalled. "If the general is crossing himself, we are in a desperate situation." When Rosecrans saw the Union line collapse, he turned to Dana and calmly advised, "If you care to live any longer, get away from here." Dana claimed that at that moment the entire headquarters disappeared as Rosecrans and his staff were caught up in the swirling mass of men running for Chattanooga.

Rosecrans's departure left Major General George H. Thomas the ranking officer on the field. The Virginia-born soldier was stubborn and resolute—precisely the type of man needed in such a crisis. Thomas quickly appraised the situation, gathered up what troops he could, and decided to make a stand on Snodgrass Hill (later renamed Horseshoe Ridge) long enough for the fleeing army to escape. In the rear, Major General Gordon Granger and his corps had

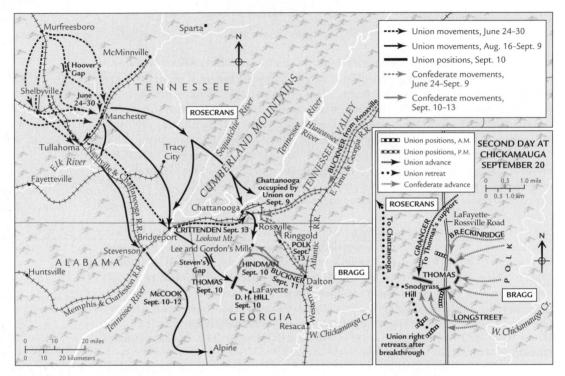

**The Tullahoma and Chickamauga Campaigns, June–September 1863.** In June 1863, Rosecrans advanced several columns in Middle Tennessee to force Bragg's Confederate army to retreat to Tullahoma. Bragg later continued his retreat and even abandoned the important railroad town of Chattanooga. With reinforcements from Virginia at hand, however, he turned and attacked Rosecrans on September 19 at Chickamauga Creek, Georgia. The next day, the Confederates drove most of the Union army from the field, but Thomas's stubborn stand on Snodgrass Hill held the Confederates back and saved the Union army from annihilation.

no orders from Rosecrans to engage the enemy and could only listen to the battle roar as the victorious Confederates battered Thomas's position with attack after attack. Finally, Granger declared to an aide, "I am going to Thomas, orders or no orders"; but the officer cautioned him, "And if you go, it may bring disaster to the army and you to a court martial." "Don't you see Bragg is piling his whole army on Thomas?" Granger spit back. "I am going to his assistance." When Granger arrived, Thomas smiled, shook his hand, and then sent in the fresh troops to push back the enemy and stabilize the line. Soon afterward, future president James A. Garfield arrived with new orders from Rosecrans. Unsure of the situation on Snodgrass Hill, Rosecrans instructed Thomas to use his discretion on whether to fight or retreat. Without hesitation, Thomas informed Garfield, "It will ruin the army to withdraw it now. This position must be held until night."

The Confederates continued to attack Thomas and slowly bent back the Union line until it formed an eastward-pointing "V." Although pressured from three directions, Thomas and Granger held Snodgrass Hill and prevented the enemy from overtaking the retreating army as it fell back to Chattanooga. When the fighting finally died out about dark, thousands of Confederates realized the hard-luck Army of Tennessee had finally won its first clear-cut victory and raised the Rebel Yell in celebration. When unit after unit picked up the yell (which one Yankee called "the ugliest any mortal ever heard") and the unearthly screams slowly spread around Snodgrass Hill, the exhausted Yankees realized how close they were to being completely surrounded. That night Thomas withdrew to Chattanooga, but three unfortunate regiments that had expended all of their ammunition were sacrificed by being left behind to hold Snodgrass Hill so the rest of the men could escape. They surrendered the next day when the Confederates advanced again. For his heroic efforts in saving the Army of the Cumberland, Thomas became known as the "Rock of Chickamauga."

## The Price of Victory

The Battle of Chickamauga holds several distinctions in Civil War history. It was the largest battle fought in the western theater, one of the few engagements where the Confederates outnumbered the Yankees, and it was the only large victory ever won by the Confederate Army of Tennessee. Casualties on both sides were horrendous; in fact, only Gettysburg was bloodier. Bragg lost approximately 18,500 men out of 66,000 engaged and 9 generals who were killed or wounded. Rosecrans lost about 16,000 men, and 1 general, out of 58,000 engaged. Chickamauga was a major tactical victory for the Confederates, and it briefly lifted their morale, but its strategic effect was only temporary because Rosecrans escaped to fight another day. Cavalry commander Nathan Bedford Forrest and others pressured Bragg to follow up his victory and strike a decisive blow against the retreating enemy. Bragg, however, thought it unwise to advance from his base of supplies and declined. "General Bragg," Forrest pleaded, "we can get all the supplies our army needs in Chattanooga." When Bragg still refused to move forward, Forrest angrily left him muttering, "What does he fight battles for?"

Chickamauga also demonstrated a hard truth that few generals at the time appreciated. Forrest, Robert E. Lee, and most Civil War commanders sought to annihilate the enemy's army. Lee, in particular, believed the war could be won by destroying the Union army in one spectacular battle and forcing Lincoln to negotiate a peace. Chickamauga, however, joined a long list of battles that revealed this as a pipe dream. Unless they were trapped in a siege like Vicksburg, Civil War armies were simply too large and resilient to be destroyed in a single battle. Armies were divided into several corps that could act independently of one another, and each corps was subdivided into many semi-autonomous divisions, brigades, and regiments. Even if one part

# BIOGRAPHY

## George Henry Thomas: The Rock of Chickamauga

**George H. Thomas**

George H. Thomas (1816–1870) was a native Virginian whose earliest childhood memory was hiding in the woods to escape marauding slaves during Nat Turner's Rebellion. After graduating from West Point in 1840, he served in the Seminole and Mexican wars and won two brevets for gallantry in the latter. Thomas also fought on the frontier and was severely wounded in the chest by an Indian arrow. When Virginia seceded in 1861, Thomas declined a state commission and chose to remain in the U.S. Army, even though his family permanently disowned him.

As a brigadier general, Thomas was sent to Kentucky and secured one of the Union's first victories at Mill Springs. Promoted to major general, he went on to fight well at Perryville and Stones River. Thomas's finest moment came at Chickamauga when he successfully fought off the enemy and earned the nickname "Rock of Chickamauga." After the battle, Lincoln proclaimed, "It is doubtful whether [Thomas's] heroism and skill, exhibited last Sunday afternoon, has ever been surpassed in the world." In October 1863, Grant made Thomas commander of the Army of the Cumberland while it was besieged at Chattanooga, and his men stormed Missionary Ridge and forced Bragg to retreat.

Standing six feet tall and weighing more than two hundred pounds, Thomas was described as having a "full rounded, powerful form" that "gradually expands upon you, as a mountain which you approach." One soldier claimed he was "not scrimped anywhere, and square everywhere—square face, square shoulders, square step; blue eyes with depths in them, withdrawn beneath a pent-house of a brow, features with

of the army was destroyed, the rest could fight on under its own command system, as Thomas did at Snodgrass Hill. Also, unlike European battlefields, most Civil War battles were fought on terrain unsuited for a battle of annihilation. Like Chickamauga, they usually were fought in thick woods where it was impossible to launch intricate maneuvers that might surround and destroy an army. If an army suffered a disastrous defeat, there was always good defensible ground such as Snodgrass Hill or some nearby river on which part of the army could make a stand to buy time for the other units to escape. The Civil War was not to be won in one giant clash. It would be won through endurance. Whichever government could maintain the support of its people and soldiers and keep its armies supplied with men and material would eventually grind down the other and win what had become a war of attrition.

legible writing on them, and the whole giving the idea of massive solidity, of the right kind of man to 'tie to.'" One officer noticed Thomas was so calm in battle his mood could only be determined by how he stroked his whiskers. "When satisfied he smoothes them down; when troubled he works them all out of shape."

Like Confederate General James Longstreet, Thomas had a reputation for being a slow and plodding officer. At Chattanooga, Grant complained Thomas's men "could not be got out of their trenches to assume the offensive," and Sherman once declared, "A fresh furrow in a plowed field will stop the whole column, and all will begin to entrench." On the other hand, Thomas paid meticulous attention to detail and never attacked until he believed all was ready. He made few mistakes, was completely reliable in a fight, and never lost a battle in which he commanded. In the field, Thomas pushed himself hard, but he then had a tendency to fall asleep at nighttime war councils. When Rosecrans met with his generals one night during the Battle of Stones River, Thomas fell asleep in a chair and only stirred to mutter, "This army doesn't retreat." He did the same thing at Chickamauga, waking long enough to advise, "I would strengthen the left."

Thomas fought well under Sherman during the Atlanta Campaign and was then sent to Nashville, where he crushed John Bell Hood's Confederate army when it raided into Tennessee. In recognition of his victory, Thomas was promoted to major general of regulars and received the Thanks of Congress.

After the war, Thomas became embroiled in Reconstruction politics by refusing to cooperate with President Andrew Johnson when he tried to remove Grant as the army's commander and replace him with Thomas. At his own request, Thomas was sent west in 1869 to command the Division of the Pacific. The following year, he suffered a stroke and died in San Francisco, California.

## THE CHATTANOOGA CAMPAIGN

October 23, 1863: Grant arrives in Chattanooga

October 27, 1863: Grant opens the "Cracker Line"

October 28, 1863: Battle of Wauhatchie

November 4, 1863: Longstreet leaves Chattanooga to attack Knoxville

November 24, 1863: Battle of Lookout Mountain

November 25, 1863: Battle of Missionary Ridge

November 27, 1863: Chattanooga Campaign ends with Battle
of Ringgold Gap, Georgia

November 29, 1863: Burnside defeats Longstreet at Fort Sanders

Braxton Bragg's Army of Tennessee followed Rosecrans to Chattanooga and occupied the dominating high ground around the city. By seizing Raccoon

# EYEWITNESS
## William Franklin Gore Shanks

*W. F. G. Shanks (1837–1905) was a Kentucky native who became a Union war correspondent for the* New York Herald. *The Civil War was the first American conflict where large numbers of war correspondents reported on the fighting in great detail. Union correspondents proudly referred to themselves as the "Bohemian Brigade" because they were a close-knit group who led an unusual lifestyle. Living off expense accounts, they tagged along with the armies drinking and playing as hard as they worked. Unless they angered high-ranking generals by revealing military secrets or writing unflattering articles, reporters usually had tremendous freedom of movement. Shanks spent time in Chattanooga during the autumn of 1863 and witnessed the only Union army ever to become besieged and hungry. After the war, he wrote an article about conditions there.*

Life in Chattanooga during the two months of the siege was dreary enough. There was no fighting to do; the enemy daily threw a few shells from the top of Lookout Mountain into our camps, but they were too wise to attack with infantry the works which soon encircled the city. Bragg preferred to rely for the final reduction of the garrison upon his ally Famine, and a very formidable antagonist did our men find him in the end. . . . [Rosecrans was compelled] to haul his provisions in wagon trains from Stevenson across the Cumberland Mountains. . . . The animals of the army were overworked and ill-fed, and thousands died from exhaustion. It was almost impossible to obtain forage for those in Chattanooga, and the quarter-masters reported that ten thousand horses and mules died of actual starvation during the siege. Thousands were turned loose in the mountains and perished. . . . They would frequently gather in groups around a small pool at which they could quench the thirst that consumed them, and lie down to die. Finding it impossible to obtain forage for an animal which I had . . . I turned

Mountain to the west, Lookout Mountain to the southwest, and Missionary Ridge to the east, the Confederates effectively severed the enemy's main supply lines. Only a long, difficult wagon road stretching from Chattanooga to Bridgeport, Alabama, remained open to bring Rosecrans supplies, but it required a twenty-day trip. When Confederate cavalry under Major General Joseph Wheeler raided into Tennessee and burned huge amounts of Union supplies destined for Chattanooga, Rosecrans was forced to cut his soldiers' rations in half.

Rosecrans failed to take any action to lift the siege and even made plans to evacuate Chattanooga. Fortunately for the Union, General Ulysses S. Grant intervened quickly to hold the city. In October, Grant was promoted to command the Military Division of the West, which put Rosecrans and the entire western theater under his direction. Grant relieved Rosecrans from command of the Army of the Cumberland and replaced him with Major the poor animal loose to graze near a small stream in the town. He was too exhausted to stray away from it; lying down he picked the few blades of grass within his reach, stretched his neck to the pool for the few drops of water which it gave, and at length gave up the ghost.

The other heroes in the beleaguered town hardly suffered less. Famine became a familiar fiend [*sic*]; they laughed in his face, as crowds will laugh in the face of great dangers and disasters, but it was a very forced laugh. . . . After the third week of the siege the men were put on quarter rations, and only two or three articles were supplied in this meager quantity. The only meat to be had was bacon, "side bacon" or "middling," I think it is called, and a slice about the size of the three larger fingers of a man's hand, sandwiched between the two halves of a "Lincoln Platform," as the four inches square cake of "hard bread" was called, and washed down by a pint of coffee, served for a meal. . . . I have often seen hundreds of soldiers following behind the wagon trains which had just arrived, picking out of the mud the crumbs of bread, coffee, rice, etc., which were wasted from the boxes and sacks by the rattling of the wagons over the stones. . . . The hundreds of citizens who were confined in the town at the same time suffered even more than the men. They were forced to huddle together in the centre of the town as best they could, and many of the houses occupied by them during the siege surpassed in filth, point of numbers of occupants, and general destitution, the worst tenement-house in New York city.

*After the war, Shanks worked as a playwright, correspondent, editor, and publisher. He served as Washington correspondent for the* New York Times *and foreign editor for the* New York Tribune.

W. F. G. Shanks, "Chattanooga, And How We Held It," *Harper's New Monthly Magazine*, Vol. 36 (January 1868), pp. 145–46.

General George H. Thomas. Grant then ordered Thomas to hold the city "at all hazards," to which Thomas replied, "We will hold the town till we starve." Shortly afterward, Grant personally went to Chattanooga to direct the relief operations.

Grant first had to reopen the supply line. In late October, he drove the enemy from Brown's Ferry, a Tennessee River crossing west of Chattanooga, and opened the "Cracker Line." This was a precarious supply line that ran from Brown's Ferry westward to Alabama. In the predawn of October 28, elements of Longstreet's Confederate corps tried to break the Cracker Line by attacking a Union division guarding the road at Wauhatchie, Tennessee. The Battle of Wauhatchie was one of the few nighttime Civil War battles, and it was particularly ferocious, close quartered, and confusing. The Confederate attack was repulsed, however, and supplies began to trickle into Chattanooga.

## An Army in Disarray

Despite having won an impressive victory at Chickamauga and besieging the enemy in Chattanooga, the Army of Tennessee was in complete disarray. Bragg blamed his subordinates for failing to carry out his orders at Chickamauga, and he even placed General Polk under arrest for failing to launch the early-morning attack on the battle's second day. For their part, the subordinates accused Bragg of exercising little control over the battle and of failing to pursue the defeated enemy. The nominal leader of the anti-Bragg movement was James Longstreet. He wrote the War Department, "I am convinced that nothing but the hand of God can save us or help us as long as we have our present commander." Bragg learned of the letter and condemned it as "disrespectful and insubordinate." It appeared Longstreet was maneuvering to win army command for himself, and Bragg declared it would be a "great relief to me" to get rid of the old war horse. The feuding was so intense, President Davis visited the army in October to try to smooth things over, but he had no success.

After spending weeks doing little more than besieging Chattanooga, Bragg decided to send Longstreet's corps to attack Knoxville, Tennessee, where Major General Ambrose Burnside had assembled 20,000 men to reinforce Chattanooga. Longstreet opposed the decision, but Bragg argued it was necessary to defeat Burnside to prevent him from reinforcing Grant. If Longstreet captured Knoxville quickly, he could return to Chattanooga before a decisive battle was fought there. If it required a long siege, Grant would have to weaken his forces in Chattanooga to reinforce Burnside and thus make it easier for the Confederates to capture the city. Although he couched the order in terms of military necessity, there is little doubt Bragg was largely motivated by a desire to send Longstreet away. But doing so was a critical mistake because it reduced the Confederates' fighting strength at a time when Grant was receiving steady reinforcements to attempt a breakout. When Grant learned of Longstreet's departure in early November, he had 70,000 men on hand and decided it was time to lift the siege of Chattanooga.

## The Battle Above the Clouds

Grant's first objective was to capture Orchard Knob, a high hill located between the opposing lines that served as the Confederates' forward position. For an hour on November 23, 1863, Gordon Granger paraded his corps in plain sight in front of Orchard Knob. Thinking the display was nothing more than a parade, the Confederates came out of their trenches and sat down to watch the spectacle. At 1:30 p.m., a signal cannon was fired, and the Yankees suddenly rushed forward and drove the surprised Rebels off the hill.

Having secured the high ground between the lines, Grant next prepared to assault the main enemy positions on Lookout Mountain and Missionary Ridge. Rising 1,400 feet above the valley floor, Lookout Mountain runs southwest to northeast and terminates southwest of Chattanooga on a bend of the Tennessee River. The position seemed impregnable, so Bragg had placed only a few thousand men to defend it. Major General Joseph "Fighting Joe" Hooker, the former commander of the Army of the Potomac, had been transferred west with a detachment from that army to reinforce Rosecrans. He was given the task of taking Lookout Mountain and then pushing on to Rossville. From there, Hooker could attack Bragg's left flank on Missionary Ridge while Sherman attacked his right flank.

On the morning of November 24, Hooker's three divisions attacked Lookout Mountain from the west. The Confederates were concentrated on the northern side facing Chattanooga so the Union soldiers had to clear them off by moving around the mountain's slope, not directly over it. Soon after making contact, a thick layer of fog, drizzle, and smoke enveloped the rocky slopes and hid the fight from the thousands of soldiers watching from Chattanooga. Those below could only listen to the battle roaring on the mountainside and try to judge its progress by the cheers of the combatants. When the Confederates realized they could not stop the onslaught, they withdrew to Missionary Ridge that night. The Union soldiers around Chattanooga endured a long night unsure of the battle's outcome, and they did not learn of the victory until morning. One wrote, "As the morning sun rose it discovered the national banner floating out in the mountain air from Lookout Point, and the soldier below caught up a shout from the regiment on the summit which rang through the crags and valleys and was borne to their comrades below, who were standing to arms behind the defenses of Chattanooga." What became known as the "Battle Above the Clouds" secured Lookout Mountain for the Union.

## Missionary Ridge

Missionary Ridge was the Confederates' last bastion. This ridge on the eastern side of Chattanooga also runs southwest to northeast. Jutting up several hundred feet from the valley floor, Missionary Ridge provided Bragg's army with a commanding view of the entire area. Grant's plan called for Sherman to make the main attack against the ridge's northern flank, while Hooker attacked the southern flank from Rossville. Since the center of Missionary Ridge was the strongest part of Bragg's line, Grant did not wish to attack there. Instead, he ordered Thomas's army to simply demonstrate against the center to pin down the enemy and prevent them from reinforcing their flanks. Unfortunately, Hooker was unable to participate in the climactic battle. The retreating enemy from Lookout Mountain destroyed a vital bridge across a creek and he could not get into position in time.

About 11:00 p.m. on November 25, Sherman attacked Confederate Major General Patrick Cleburne's division at Tunnel Hill on Missionary Ridge's northern tip. Cleburne's division was the best in Bragg's army, and his men fought tenaciously, even rolling rocks down on the advancing enemy. Sherman made no

**View from Lookout Mountain.** In this photograph taken from atop Lookout Mountain, the Tennessee River and Chattanooga area can be seen in the background. In the Battle Above the Clouds, Union troops moved along the slope between this summit and the river below.

headway at all, even after Grant sent him considerable reinforcements from Thomas. When Grant realized Bragg was reinforcing Cleburne, he knew something had to be done before the Rebels could launch an attack on Sherman. Sherman, too, was becoming concerned and requested a diversion be made against the Confederate center to relieve the pressure on his front.

In late afternoon, Grant ordered Thomas to advance and capture some enemy rifle pits at the base of the ridge. Thomas sent forward two divisions that succeeded in taking the rifle pits, but they then came under a heavy plunging fire from the Confederates farther up the ridge slope. Desperate to escape the bullets and shells, junior officers on the scene seized the initiative and without orders led their men straight up the ridge. To everyone's surprise, the attack succeeded, largely because Bragg's defensive line was poorly laid out on the highest crest of the ridge rather than the military crest that provided a view down the slope. This meant the defenders often could not even see the Yankees as they struggled up the ridge. When Thomas's men poured over the crest, the Confederates panicked and fled, and one Union soldier claimed they saw "the sight of our lives—men tumbling over each other in reckless confusion, hats off, some without guns, running wildly."

Bragg retreated down the Western & Atlantic Railroad into northern Georgia, with Cleburne's division covering the withdrawal. Cleburne took up a position at Ringgold Gap and mauled a detachment under Hooker's command when it tried to push through. Cleburne's rearguard action stopped

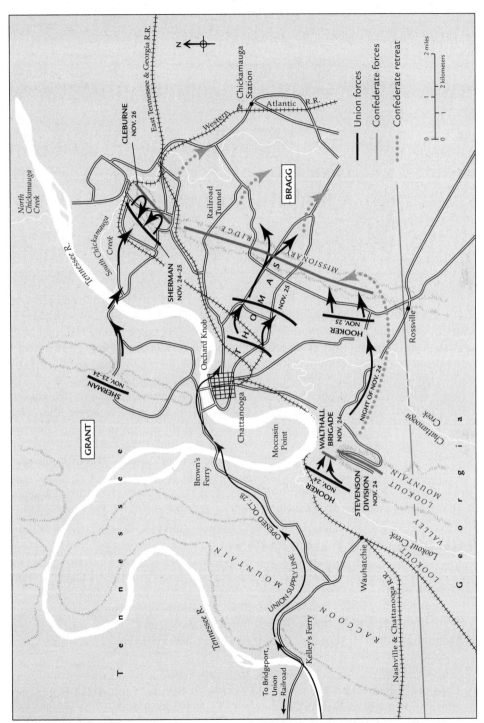

**The Chattanooga Campaign, November 1863.** After the Battle of Chickamauga, Bragg's Confederates besieged Chattanooga by taking up positions on Lookout Mountain and Missionary Ridge. On November 24, Grant began his breakout from the city by sending Hooker to clear the Confederates off Lookout Mountain. The next day Sherman and Thomas attacked Missionary Ridge, and Thomas made a dramatic breakthrough that forced Bragg to retreat into northwest Georgia.

**Missionary Ridge.** This photograph of Missionary Ridge was taken after the battle from George Thomas's position. Note how the Confederates had cut down most of the timber to open up fields of fire and to create entanglements to slow down attacking infantry.

Grant's pursuit and allowed Bragg's army to retreat safely to Dalton, Georgia. The disaster at Missionary Ridge ended Bragg's career as an army commander. Realizing his reputation was ruined, he requested to be relieved, and Jefferson Davis appointed Joseph E. Johnston to take command of the Army of Tennessee.

The Chattanooga Campaign once again demonstrated Grant's skill as a tactician and secured his position as the Union's premier general. Normally in the Civil War, the attacking force suffered much heavier losses than the defenders, but at Chattanooga Grant lost 5,800 men to Bragg's 6,700. To add to the loss, the Confederates left behind 37 cannons (one-third of the army's total) and 7,000 rifles when they fled from Missionary Ridge. The Chattanooga Campaign was an unmitigated disaster for the Southerners. The victory at Chickamauga had raised their hopes, but now they were back on the defensive in northern Georgia to await the enemy's next move.

## THE KNOXVILLE CAMPAIGN

November 4, 1863: Longstreet leaves Chattanooga to begin Knoxville
   Campaign
November 16, 1863: Battle of Campbell's Station, Tennessee
November 29, 1863: Battle of Fort Sanders, Tennessee
December 4, 1863: Longstreet retreats from Knoxville

When Grant attacked at Chattanooga, Bragg sorely missed the 17,000 men Longstreet had taken with him to capture Knoxville. Longstreet began his campaign in early November, but bad luck plagued him from the beginning. The march through eastern Tennessee was exhausting because rains turned the roads to mud, supplies were scarce, and an attempt to cut off and destroy part of Burnside's command outside of Knoxville at Campbell's Station failed. Longstreet finally reached Knoxville and prepared to attack Fort Sanders, the main Union bastion protecting the city. Fronted by a deep ditch, its nearly vertical fifteen-foot walls were topped by cotton bales. The approximately 400 Union defenders also had positioned a dozen cannons in the fort and strung telegraph wire between stumps out front to trip up any attacking Rebels.

While studying Fort Sanders from a distance, Longstreet observed a lone Union soldier cross over the ditch and commented to bystanders that it "catches him to his waist." Actually, the ditch was twelve feet deep and eight feet wide—the soldier had walked across an unseen board. Convinced his men could storm Fort Sanders in a frontal assault, Longstreet prepared to attack with Major General Lafayette McLaws's division. Because he thought the ditch was only waist deep, he made no provisions for the men to carry ladders to scale the fort's wall.

In sleet and bitterly cold weather, McLaws moved into position and launched his attack at dawn of November 29. One soldier admitted he and his comrades rushed forward "without a doubt in our minds of going right over." The 3,000 Confederates quickly made their way through the wire entanglements and jumped into the ditch. Only then did they realize they had entered what one described a "death pit." The sleet and freezing rain coated the steep walls with a thin layer of ice, making them impossible to scale. With no ladders, the men were stuck in the bottom of the ditch and were slaughtered when the Union defenders fired volleys of musketry into their packed mass and even rolled lighted cannon shells on top of them. A few color bearers stood on the shoulders of comrades and managed to plant three flags on top of the wall, but few Confederates ever made their way into the fort. After only twenty minutes of fighting, Longstreet realized it was hopeless and recalled the men. To some, retreating across the bullet-swept field seemed more dangerous than staying in place. Most of the men took the risk and dashed back to their lines, but about 200 refused to leave the shelter of the ditch and were captured. McLaws lost some 800 men in the failed attack, while Burnside lost only 15 men. An Ohio artilleryman wrote of the one-sided fight, "They just piled in there on top of one another dead wounded and dying and the living to get away from the fire of our troops. . . . As soon as the firing stopped I went up and got on the parapet to look at them. And such a sight I never saw before nor do I care about seeing again. The ditch in places was almost full of them piled one on top of the other. . . . They were brave men."

After the failed attack, Longstreet received a telegram informing him of Bragg's defeat at Missionary Ridge and his retreat into Georgia. Instead of rejoining the army, however, Longstreet remained at Knoxville to prevent the enemy from sending reinforcements against Bragg. It was not until early December that he finally withdrew and spent the winter in eastern Tennessee before returning to Virginia in March 1864.

# BIOGRAPHY

## Patrick Ronayne Cleburne: Stonewall of the West

**Patrick Cleburne**

Pat Cleburne (CLAY-burn) (1828–1864) was born in County Cork, Ireland, to a prominent Protestant family and served for a while in the British army. Immigrating to the United States, he settled in Helena, Arkansas, and became a partner in an apothecary before becoming a lawyer and entering Arkansas' rough and tumble politics. Cleburne was once shot through the right lung in a politically motivated shoot-out.

When the Civil War began, Cleburne was elected colonel of the 1st Arkansas Infantry and by year's end was in command of a brigade. Because of his British army experience, he trained his men incessantly. Many of them resented the constant drill and Cleburne's shy and aloof demeanor, but they appreciated his caring manner and sense of humor. One aide wrote, "Although he was rigid in the enforcement of discipline, the soldiers whom he commanded loved him as a man, and trusted him implicitly."

Promoted to brigadier general in March 1862, Cleburne was highly praised for his conduct at Shiloh and during the Kentucky Campaign. In the latter, he was wounded in the mouth at Richmond and in the ankle at Perryville. Cleburne became one of only two foreign-born men to become Confederate major generals, and many soldiers considered him to be the best division commander in the Army of Tennessee. Sometimes referred to as the "Stonewall Jackson of the West," his bravery in battle was legendary. One soldier with him at Stones River claimed, "Genl. Cleburne . . . fought, as usual, like a lion." Another who saw him personally lead a charge at the Battle of Atlanta wrote, "His sword was drawn. I heard him say, 'Follow me, boys.' He ran forward, and amid the blazing fires of the Yankee guns was soon on top of the enemy's works." Cleburne's outstanding

## THE TRANS-MISSISSIPPI DEPARTMENT

**July 17, 1863: Northern victory at Honey Springs secures Indian Territory for the Union**
**September 8, 1863: Battle of Sabine Pass, Texas**
**September 10, 1863: Union forces occupy Little Rock, Arkansas**
**October 3, 1863: Union forces begin the Texas Overland Expedition**
**November 3, 1863: Battle of Bayou Bourbeau, Louisiana**
**November 6, 1863: Union forces capture Brownsville, Texas**

Union forces marched from one victory to another in the western theater throughout 1863, but they enjoyed far less success in the Trans-Mississippi Department. Confederate Lieutenant General Edmund Kirby Smith commanded that vast Rebel region. A native of Florida, Kirby Smith was a West Point graduate and Mexican War veteran who began his Civil War career leading a combat record was further enhanced at Chickamauga, Missionary Ridge, and in the Atlanta Campaign. His division inflicted four times its own casualties at Pickett's Mill, and at Kennesaw Mountain it lost only eleven men while inflicting one thousand enemy casualties. Such service earned Cleburne the Thanks of Congress twice.

In many soldiers' eyes, the one blot on Cleburne's record occurred in January 1864 when he advocated the enlistment of slaves into the army. Cleburne claimed slavery was "our most vulnerable point, a continued embarrassment, and in some respects an insideous [*sic*] weakness . . . . As between the loss of independence and the loss of slavery, we assume that every patriot will freely give up the latter—give up the negro slave rather than be a slave himself." Virtually all of the army's senior commanders condemned the proposal, and Braxton Bragg, Cleburne's superior, claimed Cleburne and his supporters were "agitators, and should be watched. We must mark the men." Although he was the most successful general in the Army of Tennessee, Cleburne never received another promotion. Many suspected his controversial plan to enlist slaves was the reason.

Cleburne's last battle was at Franklin, Tennessee, on November 30, 1864, when General John Bell Hood ordered a suicidal attack against a well-entrenched enemy. In the attack, Cleburne led his men on horseback until the horse was killed under him. He attempted to mount another, but it, too, was killed. General Daniel Govan claimed Cleburne then "moved forward on foot, waving his cap; and I lost sight of him in the smoke and din of battle." Cleburne's body was discovered the next day, and Govan remembered, "He was in his sock feet, his boots having been stolen. His watch, sword belt and other valuables all gone, his body having been robbed during the night." Cleburne was engaged to Susan Tarleton, and an embroidered handkerchief she had presented him was laid over his face when his body was placed on a nearby porch.

brigade in Virginia. Now he was responsible for the largest military department in the Confederacy, and that responsibility increased after the capture of Vicksburg and Port Hudson. In mid-1863, Kirby Smith became cut off from the rest of the Confederacy and was forced to defend his department with little help or advice from Richmond. Acting largely on his own, he ruled over an almost autonomous area from his headquarters in Shreveport, Louisiana. His authority was so complete some people came to refer to the Trans-Mississippi Department as "Kirby Smithdom." Late in the war, Kirby Smith even appointed his own generals, even though they were never official because the Senate did not approve the appointments. No other department commander on either side held such power, but Jefferson Davis had to acquiesce to the arrangement because there was nothing he could do about it.

Victory was elusive for Union forces operating in the Trans-Mississippi. Their only significant accomplishments there in 1863 were gaining control of the Indian Territory in July by defeating the Confederates at Honey Springs and capturing Little Rock, Arkansas, in September. These victories, however, had little effect on the war because the Indian Territory was so remote and the Yankees made no serious attempt to expand their control over the rest of Arkansas. Missouri continued to be wracked by cavalry raids and guerrilla fighting that made life miserable for everyone. The most important military activity occurred in Texas and Louisiana, where the outnumbered Confederates succeeded in winning most clashes. Despite their isolation, the Confederates in the Trans-Mississippi Department proved to be a tough, resilient enemy.

## The Battle of Sabine Pass

After the 1863 Port Hudson Campaign, Union Major General Nathaniel P. Banks wanted to join Grant and David Farragut for an attack on Mobile, Alabama. President Lincoln, however, had other ideas. Union forces had been driven out of Texas on New Year's Day when the Confederates attacked and captured Galveston. Now Lincoln was desperate to reestablish a presence in the Lone Star State to stop Confederate trade with Maximilian's Mexico and to dissuade the French from recognizing the Confederacy. Although General-in-Chief Henry Halleck preferred to invade Texas by way of the Red River, he allowed Banks discretion in choosing his avenue of attack. Banks was convinced that an invasion by sea had the best chance of success and targeted Sabine Pass, Texas, the waterway that separates Louisiana and Texas near the Gulf of Mexico.

The Confederates had constructed Fort Griffin to defend Sabine Pass, but it was hardly an impressive fortification. The fort was commanded by Lieutenant Richard W. "Dick" Dowling and had just six cannons and forty-three members of the Davis Guards, 1st Texas Heavy Artillery. Dowling, however, was determined to hold his position and spent considerable time carefully honing his men's skills. In particular, he placed white poles in the pass to serve as range markers and had his artillerymen engage in regular gunnery practice so they could easily estimate distances and hit any point in the pass with deadly artillery fire.

In September, Banks sent Major General William B. Franklin from New Orleans with 4,000 men aboard sixteen transports and four gunboats to begin the Texas invasion by capturing Sabine Pass. Four additional gunboats were to rendezvous with him at the pass. On the morning of September 8, four of Franklin's gunboats engaged Fort Griffin, but Dowling used his range markers effectively and quickly riddled two of the ships with cannon fire and forced their surrender. After witnessing the enemy's devastating accuracy, the army commanders on the transports panicked and threw overboard 200,000 rations and two hundred mules and withdrew to the Gulf of Mexico. Dowling's forty-three men had turned back a massive invasion force and inflicted about four hundred casualties on the enemy without suffering a single loss. Jefferson Davis was so impressed with the victory he later referred to the Battle of Sabine Pass as the "Thermopylae of the Civil War."

## The Texas Overland Expedition

With Sabine Pass effectively blocked, Banks changed tactics and tried to invade Texas by way of south Louisiana. On October 3, he sent General Franklin with 20,000 men up Bayou Teche toward Vermilionville, and from there Franklin was to make his way west to Texas. Richard Taylor's small Confederate army skirmished with the advancing Yankees along Bayou Teche, but Taylor was unable to prevent Franklin from reaching Opelousas and Washington. By that time, however, the Union soldiers were plagued by serious supply problems. Taylor's army had stripped the countryside of forage and fodder, and low water and muddy roads made it difficult to bring supplies up Bayou Teche. Fearing he could not sustain his men in the barren country, Franklin canceled the invasion and began to retreat in late October. Taylor followed up and attacked Franklin's rear guard at Bayou Bourbeau and captured nearly 700 men. After constant skirmishing with the enemy, Franklin finally reached New Iberia on November 17. The Union army's second attempt to invade Texas had been turned back by a Confederate force half its size.

---

### DID YOU KNOW?

#### Davis Guard Medal

The only medal officially issued by the Confederate government was to honor Dick Dowling and the forty-three men of the Davis Guards who won the Battle of Sabine Pass. Sponsored by Sabine City, Texas, the Davis Guard Medal was made from a silver dollar and was suspended by a green ribbon to be worn around the neck. A Maltese Cross with the letters "DG" (Davis Guards) were on one side of the medal, and the battle's name and date were inscribed on the other side. One of the Davis Guard Medals was presented to Jefferson Davis, and he kept it until the medal was confiscated during his imprisonment at war's end.

---

## Brownsville, Texas

While Franklin struggled through the bayou country, General Banks personally led a third Texas invasion. His target was Brownsville, a popular port for blockade runners located at the mouth of the Rio Grande. Banks sailed from New Orleans with 4,000 men and captured Brownsville on November 6 after the few hundred Confederate defenders decided not to oppose the landing. Andrew Jackson Hamilton soon joined him there. Hamilton was a prominent Texas politician who remained loyal to the Union and fled to the North when the Civil War began. Lincoln appointed him military governor of Texas, and Hamilton came to Brownville to establish his provisional Union government. Little was accomplished, however, because the Yankees did not really control Texas, and Hamilton and Banks could not get along. The two clashed over authority, and Banks had a low opinion of the governor because he and his cronies were involved in questionable cotton speculation. As a result, Hamilton's influence in Texas was barely noticeable.

Thrilled over his success at Brownsville, Banks quickly sent troops to occupy Point Isabel, Aransas Pass, and Pass Cavallo. Once he gained control of the Texas coast, he planned to move inland and either occupy Houston or go up the Rio Grande to join Union forces in New Mexico. Nothing ever came of his grand plan, however. The Confederates continued to hold the more important areas of Sabine Pass and Galveston, and most of Banks's forces were withdrawn in the summer of 1864 to reinforce the major campaigns farther east. Among those who left Brownsville was Governor Hamilton, who did not return to Texas until after the war ended. The only tangible benefit of Banks's operations along the Texas coast was the disruption of Confederate trade. The Confederates tried to continue their trade through Matamoros, Mexico, but had little luck. Interference from bandits, French and Mexican troops, and extremely rugged terrain conspired against the Rebels to limit the war material coming in from Matamoros to a mere trickle.

The small Confederate victories in the Trans-Mississippi Department did nothing to offset the catastrophic reversals suffered in the western theater throughout 1863. Even the great victory at Chickamauga could not undo the damage caused by the defeats at Stones River, Vicksburg, Port Hudson, Tullahoma, Chattanooga, and Knoxville. Despite the embarrassing setbacks at Sabine Pass and south Louisiana, the mighty Union war machine was steadily conquering the west. In the coming year, if the Army of the Potomac could maintain the stalemate in Virginia and prevent Lee from reinforcing the west, the Union stood a good chance of destroying the Confederates there and essentially ending the conflict. The spring campaigns would undoubtedly result in massive casualties as the Union attacked well-prepared enemy positions. Final victory depended on whether the Northern people had the will to see the bloody business through. On the other hand, if the Confederates could conserve their strength, protect their heartland for another year, and inflict more casualties than the Union could stand, the Northern people might become disillusioned and force the government to negotiate a peace. In any case, the coming year was likely to be decisive.

## FOR FURTHER READING

General George H. Thomas's report on the Battle of Chickamauga
General Braxton Bragg's report on the Battle of Chattanooga

## CHAPTER 17

# The Other Participants

Women in the Civil War

Children in the Civil War

Native Americans in the Civil War

---

On a beautiful spring afternoon in 1863, 22-year-old Kate Stone walked into her Louisiana home carrying some lilacs from the garden when one of the family's slaves called out the dreaded warning—"Yankees!" When Kate, her widowed mother, and siblings walked onto the porch, they were confronted by what Kate described as "two most villainous-looking" Union soldiers. With pistols in hand, the men offered to "swap" one of their worn-out mounts for Kate's beloved horse, Wonka. The family begged the soldiers not to take Wonka, and Mrs. Stone even offered to pay them his worth. One Yankee then flew into a "towering rage" while the other rode over to catch the horse. Livid, Kate ordered a servant to open the gate so Wonka could escape, but he was frozen with fear. She then ran over and opened the gate herself despite a warning from the soldier to stop. Kate wrote in her diary, "He then dashed up with the pistol pointed at my head . . . and demanded in the most insolent tone how I dared to open a gate when he ordered it shut. I looked at him and ran on to open the other gate." Kate's heroics were fruitless, and the Yankees quickly caught Wonka and rode away, leaving one of their broken-down horses in his place. Before leaving, one of them cursed Kate and sneered, "I had just as soon kill you as a hoppergrass." It was only then that Kate realized she still held the lilacs she had picked ten minutes earlier. "I cried the rest of the day and half of the night," she wrote. "I think I will never see lilac blooms again without recalling this sad incident."

Kate Stone's harrowing ordeal during the Vicksburg Campaign was shared by countless other civilians who lived in the war zone, and her story is a reminder that the Civil War affected everyone because it turned all of society upside down. The experiences of women, children, and Native Americans, however, are often overlooked because they did not leave as many written accounts as soldiers or because some earlier historians simply were not interested in them. Their participation in the Civil War, however, is an important part of the conflict's history.

## WOMEN IN THE CIVIL WAR

**May 29, 1861:** U.S. War Department appoints Dorothea Dix superintendent of Union nurses
**February 1862:** *Atlantic Monthly* publishes "Battle Hymn of the Republic"
**July 7, 1863:** *Idahoe* transports Nashville prostitutes out of the city

The Civil War occurred at the beginning of the Victorian era, a conservative period named after Great Britain's Queen Victoria. During that time everyday behavior was governed by strict rules. Sexual topics were avoided in conversation, women were shielded against sights and events that might shock their sensibilities, public affection such as kissing was frowned on, men provided for their families while women took care of the house and children, and divorce was almost unheard of. Although some women worked outside the home and even became involved in politics (although they could not vote), most people believed a woman's life should revolve around her role as a wife and mother. Middle- and upper-class women were expected to marry, bear and raise children, and maintain an orderly household for their husbands. The home was seen as a refuge from the male-dominated, business-oriented outside world. Women were thought to have a stronger moral character than men, and their influence at home thus improved their husband's and children's morals and, through them, society as a whole. This popular view of a woman's role has been labeled the "cult of domesticity."

The Civil War dramatically changed gender roles because women were forced to take on new responsibilities when the men left home to serve in the military. For the first time in American history, large numbers of white women performed manual labor on farms, worked as nurses and in factories, raised money for the war effort, and joined relief societies. Many others became directly involved in the Civil War by accompanying the armies into the field. Such activity was somewhat easier for Northern women because the North had undergone more social changes than the South during the antebellum period. Quakers played a particularly important role in these changes. There was more sexual equality in Quaker communities because their belief in the Inner Light meant everyone was equal in God's eyes. As a result, Quaker women enjoyed more freedom to become involved in matters outside the home. Quakers such as Lucretia Mott joined Elizabeth Cady Stanton to organize the first women's rights convention at Seneca Falls, New York, in 1848. The Convention adopted a Declaration of Sentiments (based on the Declaration of Independence) that declared "all men and women are created equal" and called for women to pursue expanded political and social rights. Many people ridiculed the Convention, but it did mark an important moment in the women's rights movement. At the same time, Quaker Susan B. Anthony championed equal educational opportunities for women, and Sojourner Truth (who was helped by Quakers) furthered the women's rights cause with her famous "Ain't I a Woman" speech at the Ohio Women's Rights Convention in 1851.

Northern women were also more educated than Southern women, which allowed them to pursue a wider range of outside opportunities. Writing books and poetry and short stories for magazines were popular activities, and a number of women became successful authors. In New England, women also began to dominate the teaching field during the antebellum period, and Northern women in general had more political experience than Southern women because they had long been involved in the abolitionist and temperance movements. All of these changes in Northern antebellum society affected how women there reacted to the Civil War. While the cult of domesticity still held sway, it was easier for them to challenge standard conventions and participate in the war effort outside their roles as wives and mothers.

The Victorian ideal of the woman and the cult of domesticity were not as strong in the antebellum South. There the plantation society and rural setting helped reinforce a traditional patriarchal system where the husband dominated both the field and the home. Rather than being a moral refuge from the outside world, the Southern home was simply an extension of the plantation—a visible symbol of the husband's success. In addition, slaves worked inside the home, and supervising slaves was a man's job, not a woman's. Southern women were also tied more to the home because they tended to marry at an earlier age and to have more children. This more rigid social system meant middle- and upper-class Southern women had fewer opportunities to become active outside the home during the antebellum period and Civil War.

## Changing Roles

The Civil War presented unique hardships for women that cut across sectional, racial, and class lines. As men marched off to fight, women had to take up the slack. In letters to absent husbands, wives frequently revealed the difficulties they faced and sought advice on collecting debts or selling livestock. Women in the North and South found themselves managing family farms, plowing fields, repairing fences, treating sick livestock, keeping books, and harvesting grain. Southern women were also forced to search for substitutes and home remedies when coffee, medicine, and other essential items were in short supply.

For the first time in American history large numbers of women took on jobs outside the home to support their families and began moving into such traditional male professions as teaching and government service. Before 1861, women made up approximately 7 percent of all teaching positions (although the percentage was much higher in New England), but by 1865 they accounted for about 50 percent. Teaching was an appealing profession, but the pay was poor. Some teachers in Vicksburg, Mississippi, were paid in goods such as wood for their stoves, potatoes, butter, and pumpkins. Government positions paid more, but neither side was particularly supportive of hiring women until it became necessary because of the acute shortage of men. The U.S. Treasury Department and the Confederate Post Office and Treasury Departments finally hired hundreds of women.

For some Southern women, the Civil War was the first time they had ever had the opportunity to work outside the home, and they found that their social status greatly influenced which job they received. Higher-status women were much more likely to win a prized government job because literacy and good penmanship were often required skills. Women who worked for the Confederate Treasury Department had to sign every piece of paper money printed. One woman's quota was 3,200 signatures in a six-hour shift. Such Treasury girls were indispensable and were paid about six times the wages of an army private. Lower-class women lacking education were more likely to find work in textile and ammunition factories where the pay was far less. Much has been made of Rosie the Riveter of World War II fame, but the Civil War was the first American conflict in which large numbers of women worked in the war industries.

Whether they worked outside the home or not, women found it difficult to adjust to the new demands placed on them because Victorian values did not change. Often, they were trapped in a no-win situation. Caring for a husband was central to a nineteenth-century woman's identity, so when a husband left home to join the military much of the wife's self-worth went with him. The husband's focus shifted from wife and family to his patriotic duty. He also entered a new and exciting male world where the army took over the wife's traditional role in caring for him. The wife, however, was left at home alone, caring for a brood of demanding children and doing the work of two people. If she wrote to her husband complaining of her loneliness and the difficulty of managing the family by herself, he might write back accusing her of being unpatriotic and selfish. Husbands far removed from the family could alleviate their loneliness by drinking, gambling, or taking advantage of the myriad vices of army life, but women could not socialize as freely as men. Wives were left under the prying eyes of nosy neighbors, and if they socialized outside the family, they might be accused of inappropriate behavior and become the target of gossip.

While working outside the home was more novel for Southern women, losing domestic authority when their husbands left for war was not as big a concern. They had much more practical things to worry about—such as having to assume the physical labor previously performed by their husbands and to protect their personal safety when armies, deserters, and Jayhawkers were in the area. The most difficult adjustment fell to those women whose families owned slaves. Upper-class women had spent their entire lives cultivating the Victorian ideals of genteelness and submissiveness to their husbands—traits that were the complete opposite of what was needed to be a successful slave master.

Despite the difficulties white women faced in the Civil War, they paled in comparison to those of African Americans. Unfortunately, their story is less well known because few left a written account of their experiences. Slave women also saw their husbands and sons go off to war as soldiers, servants, cooks, and teamsters, and frequently both armies confiscated family members and took them away as laborers. White women could look forward to receiving word from their relatives in the army, but slave women could not. The most they could expect was the master mentioning in his letters that the family's slaves were safe and well. "Willis does finely— is attentive & faithful" is typical of such comments.

## Patriotic Women

Patriotism in the Civil War knew no gender boundaries, and women on both sides were caught up in the initial enthusiasm. They encouraged young men to enlist, and, if encouragement did not work, coercion usually did. Reluctant soldiers were ostracized and shunned; one Alabama woman even sent her fiancé a petticoat and skirt with an accompanying note that read "wear these, or volunteer." Women frequently made flags for departing units and presented them to the men in a rousing patriotic ceremony. They also formed sewing circles to make uniforms, socks, and other clothing for the volunteers. Such enthusiastic support of the soldiers played an important role in maintaining army morale.

**Patriotic Women.** Hundreds of women like this one, who apparently is posing with her husband and children, accompanied the armies to cook, nurse, and wash clothes.

In the North, two women in particular played a role in boosting morale. Poet John G. Whittier popularized the heroism of Barbara Frietschie (1766–1862) in his famous, although misspelled, 1863 poem, "Barbara Fritchie." In Whittier's version of the story, Frietschie defied Stonewall Jackson's soldiers when they marched through Frederick, Maryland, during the Antietam Campaign. When the Confederates shot at a Union flag, she reportedly shouted, "Shoot if you must this old gray head, but spare your country's flag." Jackson was impressed with Frietschie's bravery and told his men, "Who touches a hair of yon gray head Dies like a dog! March on!" The Rebels moved on without incident, and 95-year-old Frietschie died a few weeks later. Whittier's poem captured Northerners' imagination and came to symbolize the patriotism of Union women, but the story of Barbara Frietschie is probably entirely apocryphal. It is now known that she was bedridden at the time of the campaign, and Jackson did not march past her house. Some residents later claimed the defiant woman was actually Mary S. Quantrill, a Unionist relative of Confederate guerrilla William Quantrill (see Chapter 20).

Prominent New York native Julia Ward Howe (1819–1910) also strengthened Northern resolve. A published author and U.S. Sanitary Commission agent (see Chapter 18), she once toured Union army camps around Washington, D.C., with Massachusetts Governor John A. Andrew. Howe was impressed with the military spectacle she witnessed and wrote a poem entitled "Battle Hymn of the Republic." It became popular in the North after *Atlantic Monthly* published it in February 1862. Later put to the tune of "John Brown's Body," "Battle Hymn of the Republic" became one of the Union army's most popular marching songs.

Southern women also influenced army morale because they viewed the conflict from a more personal perspective. If the Confederates were defeated, their homes and children would be subjected to the enemy's wrath. As a result, Southern women encouraged their men to fight for their sake. When the war began to go badly and food shortages and threats from Jayhawkers increased, however, many women believed the family would be better served if their husbands were back home to provide for them. They then often encouraged the men to desert. Confederate Lieutenant General Stephen D. Lee noted the connection between women's patriotism and soldiers' morale and admitted his men frequently lost the will to fight when the women began to lose heart. Colonel Walter Taylor, General Robert E. Lee's aide, claimed desertions increased late in the war when women began to complain of worsening conditions at home. He wrote that "hundreds of letters addressed to soldiers were intercepted and sent to army headquarters, in which mothers, wives and sisters, told of their inability to respond to the appeals of hungry children for bread, or to provide proper care and remedies for the sick; and in the name of all that was dear, appealed to the men to come home and rescue them from the ills which they suffered and the starvation that threatened them."

## Nursing in the Civil War

Nursing was one of the most visible roles women played in the Civil War. In the nineteenth century, nursing was not a profession but a vague term used for any type of work in the medical field. Nursing in a military setting was a man's job because of Victorian sensibilities and the exhausting nature of the work. While women did have experience serving as midwives and herbalists and tending sick relatives, that was not the same as being an army nurse. Civil War nurses bathed nude soldiers, undressed mutilated bodies, held down screaming patients, cleaned up after chronic diarrhea, changed dressings on maggot-filled wounds, and washed down tables after bloody amputations. They also had to cook, wash laundry, change linen, write letters, collect firewood, and scrub floors. It was almost unthinkable in the Victorian era to use women for such work, and most surgeons did not think they could mentally cope with the trauma or perform the strenuous physical labor. One physician declared, "Imagine a delicate refined woman assisting a rough soldier to the closet-stool, or supplying him with a bed-pan, or adjusting the knots on a T-bandage employed in retaining a urinary catheter

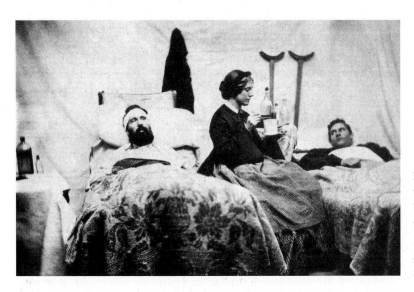

**Nursing the Wounded.** This wartime photograph shows Union nurse Anne Bell with two of her patients. It was probably taken in a Nashville, Tennessee, military hospital.

in position. . . . Women, in my humble opinion, are utterly and decidedly unfit for such service."

Women, however, wanted to serve in some fashion, and nursing seemed a logical way to do it. Northern women soon got their chance when Congress was forced to authorize the hiring of females in August 1861 when the Union military proved unable to muster enough male nurses to treat the tremendous number of sick and wounded. The Confederates were more reluctant to hire female nurses. Many Southern women volunteered for such work, but the government did not authorize them until a year after the Union's decision.

Hundreds of women took advantage of the new policies by hiring out to the government or working for various relief organizations. Many followed the armies in the field, while others simply showed up at hospitals after a battle to lend a hand for a few days. Letters and diaries indicate these women volunteered to become nurses for the same reasons men joined the army. They were motivated by patriotism, a sense of adventure, to make money, and to be with friends and relatives in the service. Female nurses cut across social lines to include young and old, rural and urban, black and white, upper and lower class, and wives and nuns. As more women flocked to the armies, surgeons feared their presence would create sexual friction and cause turmoil among male patients. Such fears were unfounded because most patients appreciated the women's efforts and treated them with respect. A Confederate in Richmond declared, "The ladies of Richmond, may God ever bless them, from the maiden of sixty to the young girl in her teens, moved like ministering angels among these sufferers, doing all in their power to relieve the soldiers' pain and sufferings." As it turned out, male surgeons sexually harassing nurses was a greater problem than nurses creating sexual tension. One nurse warned,

"[A hospital] is no place for young girls. The surgeons are young and look upon nurses as their natural prey."

Despite military authorities' initial opposition, female nurses quickly proved proficient in their work. In some cases, the mortality rate in hospitals run by women was half that of hospitals run by men. Being female also allowed them to work outside normal military channels and use their charm to accomplish things male workers could not. A highly respected nurse could sometimes improve hospital food or living conditions by simply appealing in a ladylike manner to a ranking officer or influential politician. And, for the most part, female nurses handled the horrors of war just as well as the men. On one occasion, a U.S. Sanitary Commission official witnessed the offloading of a train filled with wounded men. The cars were crammed with the dead and dying bearing maggot-filled wounds. Some veteran male nurses vomited when they entered, but the official wrote, "Shall I tell you that our noble women were always ready and eager, and almost always the first, to press into these places of horror, going to them in torrents of rain, groping their way by dim lantern light, at all hours of the night, carrying spirits, ice and water, calling back to life those who were in the despair of utter exhaustion, or catching for mother or wife the last priceless words of the dying."

## Civil War Nurses

Clara Harlowe Barton and Dorothea Lynde Dix were the two most famous Civil War nurses. Barton (1821–1912) was a native of Massachusetts who worked as a teacher before taking a position with the U.S. Patent Office (she is said to have been the first female civil service employee). When the Civil War began, she organized a relief program for the Massachusetts soldiers who were attacked in the Baltimore Riots and later appealed for medical supplies for the wounded at First Bull Run. Barton was so successful in raising and distributing privately donated supplies to hospitals that the Surgeon General presented her with a pass to travel with army ambulances. She became known as the "Angel of the Battlefield" and performed a valuable service for the Army of the Potomac and other Union forces. A hard-driving woman, Barton had little patience with those who were less committed. When some women shunned wearing fancy dresses as a show of sacrifice for the war effort, Barton was not impressed and declared, "They must go beyond wearing apparel before it will reach me, when they get down to bread and water, I will listen to them. . . . I have no time to join in dress festival."

At war's end, President Lincoln commissioned Barton to identify soldiers missing in action so the families could be informed of their fate. She was completely dedicated to the task and even took a team to Andersonville prison to exhume nearly 12,000 graves. The remains of all but 451 soldiers were identified and reburied with headboards. Barton eventually identified 22,000 previously unknown Union bodies. In later years, she also served with the

International Red Cross in the Franco-Prussian War, organized the American Red Cross, lobbied for the U.S. to sign the Geneva Agreement, and worked in Cuba during the Spanish-American War.

Dorothea Lynde Dix (1802–1887) was a native of Maine who spent her antebellum years teaching, writing, and caring for the mentally ill. Because of her popularity as a social worker, she was appointed the superintendent of women nurses to secure trained nurses and badly needed medical supplies for the Union military. Although Dix was competent and refused to be paid for her work, she also was dictatorial and outspoken and was resented by many surgeons, soldiers, and nurses. Frequently referred to as "Dragon Dix," she adopted strict rules for hiring nurses and did not accept any women who might create a sexual distraction. "No woman under thirty need apply to serve in government hospitals," Dix declared. "All nurses are required to be plain looking women. Their dresses must be brown or black, with no bows, no curls, no jewelry, and no hoops." Dix frequently turned down potential nurses because they were "too young" or "too attractive," and she forbid her nurses from going "to any place of amusement in the evening." Despite her hard manners, Dix's untiring efforts greatly improved the Union medical service.

Although technically not a nurse, Sally Louisa Tompkins (1833–1916) became the only female commissioned officer in the Confederate army while working in the medical field. A native of Virginia, the well-to-do widow opened and financed the privately owned Robertson Hospital in Richmond. It was regarded as one of the city's best medical facilities because it returned a higher percentage of its patients to duty than any other hospital and had the lowest mortality rate. Out of 1,333 patients treated there, only 73 died. When officials adopted a policy requiring all hospitals to be run by military personnel, President Davis commissioned Tompkins a captain of cavalry, making her the only female officer in the Confederate army. The five-foot-tall "Captain Sally" never married, habitually carried a Bible, and required her patients to listen to temperance lectures, but the soldiers greatly respected her work. Colonel Walter Taylor once wrote, "I declare she is an angel on earth—or I should say she is a true woman. If every one strived to do good as she does how different matters would be. . . ." Tompkins spent much of her fortune on the hospital and was forced to live in Richmond's Confederate Women's Home after the war. When she died in 1916, she was buried with full military honors.

Thousands of women served as nurses in the Civil War, but the exact number is unknown because many were volunteers and not carried on official rosters, and others were enrolled as cooks or laundresses. Whatever the number, they performed heroic service but were never given the credit they deserved. After the war, the federal government published *The Medical and Surgical History of the War of the Rebellion*, an exhaustive twelve-volume medical study of the Civil War. It covers the role of all female hospital workers in just 200 words.

# EYEWITNESS
## Louisa May Alcott

*Louisa May Alcott (1832–1888) grew up in Massachusetts and led a sheltered life with her parents and three sisters. Determined to make something of her life, she became a published author and then volunteered as a Union nurse and was sent to Washington, D.C., without any training. After Alcott had been on duty for just three days, someone cried out, "THEY'VE come! They've come! Hurry up, ladies—you're wanted." The wounded from Fredericksburg had just arrived.*

Presently, Miss Blank tore me from my refuge . . . with these appalling directions: "Come, my dear, begin to wash as fast as you can. Tell them to take off socks, coats and shirts, scrub them well, put on clean shirts, and the attendants will finish them off, and lay them in bed."

If she had requested me to shave them all, or dance a hornpipe on the stove funnel, I should have been less staggered; but to scrub some dozen lords of creation at a moment's notice, was really—really—. However, there was no time for nonsense, and, having resolved when I came to do everything I was bid, I drowned my scruples in my wash-bowl, clutched my soap manfully, and, assuming a business-like air, made a dab at the first dirty specimen I saw, bent on performing my task *vi et armis* if necessary. I chanced to light on a withered old Irishman, wounded in the head. . . . He was so overpowered by the honor of having a lady wash him, as he expressed it, that he did nothing but roll up his eyes, and bless me, in an irresistible style which was too much for my sense of the ludicrous; so we laughed together, and when I knelt down to take off his shoes, he "flopped" also, and wouldn't hear of my touching "them dirty craters. May your bed above be aisy darlin', for the day's work ye ar doon!—Whoosh! There ye are, and bedad, it's hard tellin' which is the dirtiest, the fut or the shoe." It was; and if he hadn't been to the fore, I should have gone on pulling, under the impression that the "fut" was a boot, for trousers, socks, shoes and legs were a mass of mud. This comical tableau produced a general grin, at which propitious beginning I took heart

## Women at War

Civil War military history concentrates on the bravery and suffering of soldiers and usually ignores the fact that thousands of women were also affected by military operations. They had to protect their homes from looting, risked being imprisoned on suspicion of supporting guerrillas, and frequently had to take refuge from battles being fought in their backyards. Some did not survive. Mrs. Judith Henry, an 85-year-old invalid widow, was killed in her home during the First Battle of Bull Run, and 20-year-old Jennie Wade became the only civilian killed at Gettysburg when she was shot while kneading dough in a Gettysburg house.

Northern women did not face as many physical risks as Southerners because they usually were far removed from the battlefield. One notable exception was and scrubbed away like any tidy parent on a Saturday night. Some of them took the performance like sleepy children, leaning their tired heads against me as I worked, others looked grimly scandalized, and several of the roughest colored like bashful girls. . . .

The next scrubbee was a nice looking lad, with a curly brown mane, and a budding trace of gingerbread over the lip, which he called his beard. . . . He lay on a bed, with one leg gone, and the right arm so shattered that it must evidently follow: yet the little Sergeant was as merry as if his afflictions were not worth lamenting over. . . . "Now don't you fret yourself about me, miss; I'm first rate here, for it's nuts to lie still on this bed, after knocking about in those confounded ambulances. . . ." "Is this your first battle, Sergeant?"

"No, miss; I've been in six scrimmages, and never got a scratch till this last one; but it's done the business pretty thoroughly for me, I should say. Lord! What a scramble there'll be for arms and legs, when we old boys come out of our graves, on the Judgment Day: wonder if we shall get our own again? If we do, my leg will have to tramp from Fredericksburg, my arm from here, I suppose, and meet my body, wherever it may be."

The fancy seemed to tickle him mightily, for he laughed blithely, and so did I; which, no doubt, caused the new nurse to be regarded as a light-minded sinner by the Chaplain. . . .

*After serving as a nurse for only a few weeks, Alcott contracted typhoid fever. Treated with mercury-based calomel that caused her teeth and hair to fall out, she was forced to return home and never completely recovered from the mercury poisoning. Alcott went on to become a popular writer and is best known for her novel* Little Women, *which was based on her own childhood experiences.*

Louisa May Alcott, *Hospital Sketches* (Boston: James Redpath. Publisher, 1863), pp. 35–37.

when the Confederates entered Pennsylvania in 1863. At Gettysburg, Catherine Elizabeth Thorn, the wife of the cemetery caretaker, showed incredible bravery after her home on Cemetery Hill began filling up with wounded soldiers seeking a place of refuge. Wanting to help, she agreed to show one officer around the hill so he could plan a proper defense. There was heavy enemy fire, and the officer had Thorn walk on the opposite side of his horse on the way back so she would not be shot. Soldiers who witnessed Thorn's bravery gave her three rousing cheers. When she entered the house, a shell smashed through the window and went through the ceiling, but Thorn stepped gingerly around the bloody soldiers on her kitchen floor and began cooking the men supper.

**Fort Sumter, South Carolina.** When Confederate forces opened fire on Fort Sumter in the predawn hours of April 12, 1861, many women crowded onto Charleston's rooftops to witness the historic event. Few realized to what extent the war would affect their lives.

When large numbers of soldiers occupied a place like Gettysburg, a woman's greatest fear was being sexually assaulted. Rape, however, was not as common in the Civil War as in more modern times. One English observer concluded that such crimes were rare because "the privates [were] mostly married, and all men of some kind of education. . . ." When rape did occur, the victim was usually black. African Americans were more frequently targeted partly because Victorian attitudes protected white women from physical violence (but not their property) and partly because soldiers knew they were less likely to be punished for attacking a slave or a free black than a white woman. The frequency of rape can partially be judged by examining military court records. The Union army held 350 rape trials during the war, but that is not an accurate figure because many sexual crimes were tried as assault or battery. Confederate records were burned at war's end, so it is impossible to make an accurate estimate for them.

## Daughters of the Regiment

Many women actually accompanied Civil War armies into the field. Some were the visiting wives of officers, but most were wives of enlisted men or army employees who served as laundresses, cooks, and nurses. A few, called vivandiéres (vee-vahn-DYAIRS), were even carried on a regiment's roll. All were affectionately known as "daughters of the regiment."

European armies were the first to use vivandiéres to wash soldiers' clothes, nurse the sick and wounded, and perform other needed duties. These women were recognized as members of the regiment and often had their own distinctive uniforms. Vivandiéres were popular in both the North and South, but Louisiana regiments, in particular, employed them. One New Orleans newspaper reported a Zouave battalion "had the good taste" to bring women with it to the training camp at Pensacola, Florida, to wash, cook, and clean the men's quarters. At least one Louisiana vivandiére fought in the First Battle of Bull Run. Rose Quinn Rooney joined her company as a nurse and cook, but at Bull Run she tore down a rail fence under fire to allow the Washington Artillery to

**A Vivandiére.** Some women, known as vivandiéres, marched off to war in uniform. In this photograph of a Louisiana Zouave battalion, a vivandiére can be seen standing fourth from the left. She is wearing a sword and what appears to be a plumed hat.

pass through. Rooney also worked as a nurse at Gettysburg, where a witness claimed she "served with the undaunted bravery which led her to risk the dangers of every battle-field where the regiment was engaged, unheeding the zip of the miniés, the shock of shells, or the horrible havoc made by the solid shot, so that she might give timely succor to the wounded or comfort the dying." Rooney was still listed as an official company member when the survivors surrendered at Appomattox.

Two of the most famous Union vivandiéres were Bridget Divers and Annie (or Anna) Etheridge. Divers was an Irish native who followed her husband into the 1st Michigan Cavalry of Custer's Cavalry Brigade. Known as "Irish Biddy" or "Michigan Bridget," her bravery was legendary. Divers served as a U.S. Sanitary Commission agent and sometimes nursed the sick and wounded under fire. She also accompanied the regiment into battle and had several horses shot from under her while serving alongside the men. A male nurse wrote that Divers "has probably seen more of the danger and hardship than any other woman during the war. She has been riding with the cavalry all the time, going out with them on their cavalry raids—always ready to succor the wounded on the field—often getting men off who, but for her, would be left to die, and fearless of shell or bullet among the last to leave." After the war civilian life did not suit Divers, so she rejoined the army as a laundress and served in the western Indian campaigns.

Annie Etheridge enlisted as a nurse in a Michigan regiment to be with her husband, but when he deserted she refused to go along and eventually transferred to the 5th Michigan. Adopted as a daughter of the regiment, Etheridge was known as "Michigan Annie" or "Gentle Annie" and was described as being "decidedly good looking." She kept medical supplies stuffed in her horse's saddlebags and carried two pistols for protection. Etheridge served in the Army of the Potomac for the entire war and was sometimes exposed to enemy fire while treating the wounded or riding along the lines encouraging the men to fight and shaming those who ran away. A Maine soldier wrote in his diary, "When danger threatens, she never cringes. At the battle of Fredericksburg she was binding the wounds of a man when a shell exploded nearby, tearing him terribly, and removing a large portion of the skirt of her dress." Etheridge was awarded the Kearny Cross for bravery, received a pension for her wartime service, and is one of the few women buried in Arlington National Cemetery.

## Women Warriors

Some women were not content to serve as daughters of the regiment and disguised themselves to fight as men. Approximately 300 women can be documented as serving as Civil War soldiers, and about half were wounded in battle. Most were motivated by adventure, patriotism, and money, but some joined to be near their husbands or boyfriends. Women avoided detection during their initial physical exams because the exams were so lax that recruits often were not required to take off their shirts. Soldiers rarely undressed completely in camp or bathed very often, and calls of nature could be addressed by walking off into the woods. Thus, fellow soldiers invariably were shocked to discover the true identity of a female comrade. One Indiana cavalryman wrote to his wife, "We discovered last week a soldier who turned out to be a girl. She had already been in service for 21 months and was twice wounded. Maybe she would have remained undiscovered for a long time if she hadn't feinted. She was given a warm bath which gave the secret away." Another surprising discovery occurred in Johnson's Island prison camp. In December 1864, a local newspaper reported, "We are credibly informed that one day last week, one of the rebel officers in the 'bull pen' . . . gave birth to a 'bouncing boy.'"

Sarah Emma Edmonds (1842–1898) and Jennie Hodgers (1844–1915) are two of the best documented women who disguised themselves as men. Edmonds was a Canadian who ran away to avoid a marriage arranged by her father, disguised herself as "Franklin Thompson," and joined the 2nd Michigan. Trained as a nurse, she participated in the First Battle of Bull Run and in the Peninsula Campaign before being appointed her regiment's postmaster. Edmonds contracted malaria in 1863, deserted out of fear her secret would be discovered in the hospital, and then joined the U.S. Christian Commission—as a woman. In 1865, she wrote a highly embellished account of her life entitled *Nurse and Spy in the Union Army* under the name Sarah E. Edmundson. Edmonds married in 1867 but never revealed her secret until she attended an 1884 regimental reunion. As might be expected, the veterans were shocked. One remembered "Frank" as a "whole-souled, enthusiastic youngster, frank and fearless." Edmonds's comrades supported her coming out and encouraged her to apply for a veteran's pension. She eventually received the pension and became the only woman ever granted membership in the Union veterans' organization, Grand Army of the Republic (see Chapter 26).

Irish native Jennie Hodgers came to America as a stowaway, settled in the Midwest to work as a farmer and shepherd, and enlisted in the 95th Illinois as "Albert Cashier." One fellow soldier shed light on how Hodgers avoided detection. "When we were examined [during enlistment] we were not stripped.... All that we showed was our hands and feet. I never did see Cashier go to toilet nor did I ever see any part of his person exposed by which I could determine the sex. He was of very retiring disposition and did not take part in any of the games. He would sit around and watch, but would not take part." Hodgers fought in the Vicksburg, Red River, and Mobile campaigns, and today her alias "Albert Cashier" is etched on the Illinois monument at the Vicksburg battlefield. After the war, she was awarded a pension (which required another medical examination), but her real identity was not discovered until 1911 when a physician treated her injured leg after she was accidentally struck by an automobile. When the news spread, Hodgers's former comrades visited her and reflected on the long deception. One said the men never suspected "Cashier" was a woman, although he did recall she "seemed to be a little funny." After her accident, Hodgers lived for two years in an Illinois Soldiers' and Sailors' Home and then was admitted to an insane asylum. No evidence was given in court papers to explain the incarceration so it is assumed her posing as a man was considered sufficient evidence of her unbalanced mental state. However, some who visited Hodgers suspected she really did suffer from mental illness. When she died, the veterans in the local Grand Army of the Republic post buried Hodgers in a Union uniform with military honors.

## Prostitution

One way in which the Civil War affected women was by forcing more of them to become prostitutes to sustain themselves and their families after their husbands went into the army or were killed or maimed. With thousands of lonely soldiers confined in camps, these working women found themselves in great demand. One Confederate officer serving in Tennessee claimed "female virtue if it ever existed in this Country seems now almost a perfect wreck. Prostitutes are thickly crowded through mountain & valley, in hamlet & city. . . ." Some prostitutes even accompanied units into the field by assuming the title of cook or laundress. This subterfuge became such an open secret in Vicksburg that Confederate officers ordered "company laundresses who do not actually wash for them must be discharged."

Most prostitutes worked in large cities that served as staging and training areas. By 1862, Washington had more than 7,000 prostitutes working in 450 houses of ill repute bearing such names as "Hooker's Headquarters" and "Mother Russell's Bake Oven." Richmond, too, was similarly plagued, and in 1864 Mayor Mayo declared, "Never was a place more changed than Richmond. Go on the Capital Square any afternoon, and you may see these women promenading up and down the shady walks jostling respectable ladies into the gutters." One Richmond hospital superintendent complained when a house of

## DID YOU KNOW?

### Hookers

General Joseph Hooker, commander of the Army of the Potomac during the Chancellorsville Campaign, was a notorious womanizer, and after the Civil War it was widely believed his name gave rise to the word "hookers" as a synonym for prostitutes. However, the word was actually used before Hooker became famous, although he did make it popular. To regulate prostitution better, the general segregated Washington's prostitutes into one district that became known as "Hooker's Division."

prostitution opened across the street because the convalescing men sneaked out at night to visit.

Prostitutes posed a serious threat to armies because thousands of soldiers became too ill to fight after contracting venereal diseases. There were 183,000 reported cases of syphilis and gonorrhea in the Union army (the number of infected Confederates is unknown). Surgeons spent much of their time treating venereal disease and often took drastic measures against the prostitutes. In July 1863, a Union officer seized the steamboat *Idahoe* and forcibly transported about one hundred "soiled doves" from Nashville to Louisville, Kentucky. When the boat docked, however, Louisville officials refused to accept them, and the military commander placed guards on the wharf to prevent any women from disembarking. The *Idahoe* steamed on to Cincinnati but met the same cool reception and was forced to return the prostitutes to Nashville.

Unable to get rid of the prostitutes, Union officers in Nashville decided to regulate them, and Nashville became the first city in America to license the profession. To obtain a license, prostitutes were required to pass a bi-monthly physical exam administered by a military surgeon. If they passed they could practice their profession; if they failed they were put in a hospital established specifically to treat venereal diseases. The army's licensing program reduced venereal diseases among the men, but it also attracted more prostitutes to Nashville because it was a much healthier place to work. Memphis, Tennessee, copied the Nashville program and enjoyed similar positive results. Other cities, however, refused because licensing prostitutes seemed to encourage immoral activity. Both Nashville and Memphis abandoned their programs when the Civil War ended, and diseased prostitutes once again became the norm.

## CHILDREN IN THE CIVIL WAR

**February 17, 1864: Confederates begin conscripting seventeen-year-olds**
**May 15, 1864: Virginia Military Institute cadets fight at the Battle of New Market**

The Civil War directly affected more American children than any other conflict—they accounted for one-third of the population when the war began. Adults had some control over how the war affected them by choosing to enlist or volunteer as nurses or seek jobs in war industries, but children had no control over how the war affected their lives. Just as the women's rights movement took hold in America during the antebellum period, so did changes in the status of children. As women gained some control over their lives, marriage became more about romantic love and less about an economic union. Household dynamics also changed as families became more loving and child oriented. Fathers, in particular, were expected to be attentive and loving and spend time with their children. This stronger bond made it even more traumatic for children when their fathers marched off to war. Just like adults, older children were quite aware of the dangers their family members faced and eagerly read newspapers and magazines to keep abreast of the war's progress, and they scanned with dread the lengthy casualty lists that appeared in newspapers after major battles.

The Civil War affected every aspect of a child's world. Numerous towns in the North and South were forced to close schools when male teachers and older students joined the army, and communities were often left barren of adult male residents when fathers, brothers, and friends marched off to war. Politics also split families, particularly in the Border States, and children found favorite relatives suddenly becoming the enemy overnight. As patriotic fervor swept both sections, children began playing with military toys, reading books with a martial theme, singing patriotic songs, and drilling or marching at playtime to emulate their fathers and older brothers. In the classroom and church, teachers and ministers imparted morality lessons based on the war and the respective cause for which they fought, military campaigns were followed on wall maps, and classes were sometimes dismissed so students could attend fundraising events, political speeches, and parades. Children also volunteered their time, just like the adults, to roll bandages or collect lint for aid societies or community relief organizations.

In the antebellum period, children were nurtured and pampered more than before, and childhood became a distinctive stage of life before one entered the workforce. That changed for many during the Civil War. With so many male relatives absent, children were often forced to take on adult chores at home or even work in factories to supplement the family's income. Working in munitions factories or the textile industry was extremely dangerous, and scores of children were killed in explosions and accidents. Southern boys and girls faced the additional burden of food shortages, which were revealed in some heartrending letters. "Before God, Edward," wrote one desperate mother to her husband, "Unless you come home we must die. Last night I was aroused by little Eddie's crying. . . . He said 'Oh, mamma, I'm so hungry!' And Lucy, Edward, your darling Lucy, she never complains but she is growing thinner and thinner every day." For many children, the Civil War was as hellish an experience as it was for adults.

## Children at War

Some of the most poignant Civil War stories involve children caught in the path of opposing armies. Thousands saw their homes looted or burned, and

428 The American Civil War

all lived in dread. The suffering of Vicksburg's children is particularly well documented. Lida Lord, the daughter of the local Episcopal minister, took refuge in the church basement with the rest of the family during bombardments. Once, as the shells exploded nearby, she began to cry. Lida's mother tried to comfort her by promising, "God will protect us." "But, momma," Lida wailed, "I'm so afraid that God's killed too." Like many other Vicksburg families, the Lords eventually took refuge in a cave—along with eight other families. The parents furnished the dwelling with furniture from home, flowers, books—and the children's toys. Lida claimed sixty-five people were "packed in, black and white, like sardines in a box" during one bombardment. Among the group were several wounded men and a woman who went into labor as the shells began to explode. One shell collapsed part of the cave's ceiling and buried Lida. "They pulled me from under the mass of earth," she recalled. "The blood was gushing from my nose, eyes, ears, and mouth . . . but there were no bones broken. . . . During all this excitement there was a little baby boy born in the room dug out of the back of the cave. . . ." Despite the hardships, Lida and other children showed remarkable resilience and often adapted more quickly to war than the adults. During the siege, Mrs. Lord proudly wrote, "The children bear themselves like little heroes. At night when the balls begin to fly like pigeons . . . and I call them to run to the cave, they spring up . . . like soldiers, slip on their shoes without a word and run up the hill to the cave."

Because the Civil War was mostly fought in the South, Northern children were much less likely to encounter enemy soldiers or personally witness war's destructiveness. Pennsylvania children were an exception during the Gettysburg Campaign. By all accounts, the Confederates rarely physically mistreated the white civilians they encountered, although they did seize hundreds of African Americans and confiscate livestock, food, and supplies. Nonetheless, the very presence of Rebels terrified most families, and some of Lee's soldiers even promoted such fear. When members of Ewell's corps marched through one town, they overheard children standing on the street corner ask their father, "Why Papa I thought the Rebs had horns, where are they?" Imagining what stories the father most have spun, the soldiers jabbed their bayonets at the children when they marched by and sneered, "Here are our horns!" Such threats were just jest, and most parents came to realize the Confederates posed no great threat to their children. One Gettysburg father was horrified when his five-year-old daughter poked her head out the window and began singing "Hang Jeff Davis on a Sour Apple Tree" to a group of Confederates gathered on the street. Much to his relief, the soldiers paid her no heed.

## Young Warriors

Just as women slipped into the army disguised as men, some young children also managed to enlist. When the war began both sides required recruits to be at least age eighteen, but the Union War Department soon began enlisting boys younger than eighteen with the parents' permission. Contrary to popular belief, however, there were never many boy soldiers. Officials were uncomfortable recruiting youngsters, and the law was changed in 1864 to prohibit the enlistment of boys under sixteen. One study of approximately one million Union soldiers found only about 1 percent of soldiers were under eighteen when they enlisted. Confederate records are incomplete, but the Rebels probably had a slightly larger percentage of boy soldiers because the conscription act was amended to draft seventeen-year-olds.

Most young boys who did enter service became drummers, buglers, and musicians. The older men usually looked after them the best they could, but the boys were exposed to the same battlefield dangers, disease, and camp vices as anyone. Judging by letters and diaries, most of them performed their duties well. A member of the 22nd Wisconsin praised the regiment's twelve-year-old drummer, Johnnie Walker. He claimed, "Everybody in the regiment likes Johnnie because he is a good little boy, is always pleasant and polite and not saucy like a great many boys." Sometimes these boy soldiers actually engaged in combat. One Ohio soldier claimed at the Battle of Perryville "a little drummer-boy, having lost his drum, took a musket and fought manfully in the line." Fifteen-year-old Nathaniel Gwynne was awarded the Medal of Honor for bravery at Petersburg. When the Union army attacked the Confederate defenses, Gwynne was told not to enter the fight because he was too young and had not officially been mustered into the regiment. A comrade claimed he "indignantly protested," joined in the attack anyhow, and lost an arm. Fourteen-year-old Orion P. Howe, a drummer boy for the 55th Illinois, was also awarded the Medal of Honor for his service at Vicksburg. On the Confederate side, General P. G. T. Beauregard once commended Private John Sloan of the 9th Texas for his role in a small battle. Sloan, Beauregard wrote, was "a lad of only 13 years of age who having lost a leg in the affair. . . . exclaimed 'I have but one regret I shall not soon be able to get at the enemy.'"

The most famous incident involving young soldiers occurred at the Battle of New Market, Virginia, on May 15, 1864. Union Major General Franz Sigel raided the Shenandoah Valley that spring and was confronted by a small Confederate army under Major General John C. Breckinridge. Breckinridge scraped up every man he could find to stop the enemy, including 257 cadets from the Virginia Military Institute. The veteran soldiers referred to them as "Katydids," because some were as young as fifteen. Breckinridge did not want to expose the cadets to combat unless it was absolutely necessary so he held them in reserve until Union artillery began battering his line. Breckinridge then reluctantly ordered, "Put the boys in." The Katydids joined other units in attacking the enemy artillery and captured one Union cannon. Breckinridge won the battle, but ten cadets were killed and fifty-one were wounded.

# BIOGRAPHY
## John "Johnny" Lincoln Clem: Johnny Shiloh

**Johnny Clem**

The most famous Civil War boy soldier was Ohio native Johnny Clem (1851–1937), who became known as "Johnny Shiloh" and the "Drummer Boy of Chickamauga." In explaining his determination to join the Union army, Clem wrote, "My mother was dead; my father had no notion of allowing me to go to war. Accordingly I decided to run away. The spirit of adventure gripped me. It was necessary that the Union be preserved, and my help was obviously needed. . . ." Clem made his move one Sunday morning in May 1861 when he walked out of church and told the family he was going swimming. His sister recalled, "That was the last we saw of him for two years." Clem first tried to join an Ohio regiment, but a captain looked at him, laughed, and said "he wasn't enlisting infants." The 22nd Michigan also rejected him, but he remained with that regiment as an unofficial drummer boy. The officers donated Clem's monthly pay, the regiment's tailor cut down a uniform to fit him, and the soldiers provided him with a shortened musket.

Clem's initiation to combat occurred at Shiloh, where he earned the nickname Johnny Shiloh after an exploding shell destroyed his drum. After Shiloh, Clem abandoned his drum and began carrying a musket because "I did not like to stand and be shot at without shooting back." He fought at Stones River and Perryville and was finally allowed to enroll in the regiment officially. Clem's enlistment papers indicate he was four feet tall and thirteen years old, but they are in error. He actually was eleven. One of Clem's most harrowing experiences occurred at the Battle of Chickamauga when the Confederates overran his regiment's position, and a mounted Rebel colonel

## NATIVE AMERICANS IN THE CIVIL WAR

November 19, 1861: Battle of Round Mountain
December 19, 1861: Battle of Chusto-Talasah
December 26, 1861: Battle of Chustenahlah
August 18, 1862: Sioux Uprising begins in Minnesota
July 1–2, 1863: Battle of Cabin Creek
July 7, 1863: Battle of Honey Springs
November 29, 1864: Sand Creek Massacre

The Civil War posed a particularly difficult problem for Native Americans. They, too, had to confront issues such as slavery and sectional loyalty and decide which government would best serve their interests. Sometimes these issues split apart Indian tribes just as they did their white neighbors. Approximately 3,000 to 4,000 Native Americans fought in the war, and they played a significant role in such western battles as Pea Ridge and Poison Springs, Arkansas, and rode up and barked, "Surrender, you damned little Yankee!" Clem raised his musket and shot the officer from his horse. Later in the battle, Clem was captured, but he managed to escape by playing dead when his captors came under heavy fire. For his heroics, Clem was promoted to sergeant and became known as the "Drummer Boy of Chickamauga."

In October 1863, Clem was captured again while guarding a wagon train. "[To w]hat sore straits the Yankees are driven," the Confederates quipped, "when they have to send their babies to fight us." After being exchanged, Clem became an orderly for Major General George H. Thomas. He was mustered out of service in September 1864, but not before being slightly wounded when his horse was killed under him while he was delivering orders. After the war, President Grant appointed Clem to West Point, but he was unable to pass the entrance exam. Grant then made him a 2nd lieutenant, and Clem remained in the army until retiring in 1916 as a major general. When the United States entered World War I, he asked to be reactivated to fight in France, but President Woodrow Wilson refused.

Johnny Clem was one of the most popular Civil War heroes. Unfortunately, a great deal of his story is suspect. He claimed to have joined the 22nd Michigan in 1861 and fought with it at Shiloh, but the regiment was not organized until nearly five months after the battle. He also said he served with the regiment at Perryville and Stones River, but the 22nd Michigan did not fight in either battle. Clem was at Chickamauga, where he was said to have wounded a Confederate colonel, but there is no record of any Confederate colonel being shot at the time and place Clem claimed. In short, much of Johnny Clem's wartime record may have been a fabrication, but that does not detract from the fact that he was a boy soldier who bravely served in the Civil War.

in the Indian Territory (modern-day Oklahoma). Indians made good guerrilla fighters and scouts, but they often deserted because they were too independent to accept military discipline.

## Native American Soldiers

When the Southern states seceded, most of the Indians living east of the Mississippi River and in Indian Territory had adopted farming, Christianity, modern dress, and even slaveholding. The Native American population was widely scattered because of Andrew Jackson's Indian removal policy, and few all-Indian units were formed. Exceptions included a North Carolina Cherokee battalion, the 1st Mississippi Choctaw Infantry Battalion, and some small Louisiana Koasati and Alabama units. Most of the Indians who enlisted east of the Mississippi did so as individuals. One of these was Ely Parker (1828–1895), a Seneca lieutenant colonel who served as General Grant's personal secretary. When Parker was introduced to General Lee at Appomattox, Lee quipped he was glad to see one "real American" in the gathering of officers. Parker responded that they were now all Americans once again and then sat down to write out copies of the surrender terms for each general.

One Native American rose to the rank of brigadier general. Stand Watie (1806–1871), who was half Cherokee, was Christianized and educated at a Georgia mission school and became a planter and influential tribal member. He and three other Eastern Cherokee leaders believed it was useless to oppose Georgia when it tried to seize tribal land in the 1830s. Watie and his supporters signed a treaty to sell the land and migrated to Indian Territory to join the Western Cherokee who had moved there some years earlier. Chief John Ross led the majority of the Eastern Cherokees in opposing the treaty, but the United States ratified it and forced them to move to Indian Territory in the infamous "Trail of Tears." By that time, Watie had allied himself with the minority Western Cherokees. The Cherokee Nation remained deeply divided because of the treaty, loss of their homeland, and even slavery, and the three men who joined Watie in signing the treaty were executed in 1839 by members of the majority Eastern Cherokees. When Watie's brother was murdered a few years later, Watie became the leader of the minority faction.

When the Civil War began, Watie supported the Confederacy and even convinced John Ross to do the same, although Ross was less than eager. Watie formed a company of soldiers that protected Indian Territory from Kansas Jayhawkers and fought at Wilson's Creek, Missouri. He then became the most important Indian leader when he was appointed colonel of the Cherokee Mounted Rifles. Watie's men fought Unionist Indians and Yankee soldiers in Indian Territory and at the Battle of Pea Ridge, Arkansas. When John Ross abandoned the cause and fled to Kansas, the Cherokees recognized Watie as their leader in August 1862. Two years later, he was promoted to brigadier general, making him the only Native American general in the Civil War. Watie fought in Shelby Price's Missouri Raid (see Chapter 23) and made the last significant Confederate surrender on June 23, 1865, in Indian Territory.

## Indian Territory

Most of the 64,000 people living in Indian Territory were Native Americans who had been pushed out of their homelands during the antebellum period. They included the Five Civilized Tribes (Cherokee, Choctaw, Chickasaw, Creek, and Seminole), Quapaw, Seneca, Shawnee, Osage, Comanche, Caddo, and Wichita. The majority sided with the South because many were slaveholders, the Confederacy offered more concessions, and the Union government had a long history of broken treaties and Indian removal policies. Nevertheless, several tribes—most notably the Cherokee, Creek, and Seminole—were divided in their loyalties, and many members fought for the Union.

The Confederate Congress created a Bureau of Indian Affairs and sent Albert Pike to Indian Territory in March 1861 to negotiate treaties. In return for the Indians' allegiance, the Confederates agreed to assume the financial obligations made by the Union government in previous treaties, guarantee slavery, not organize Indian land into territories, allow Indians access to Confederate courts, and admit one non-voting Indian delegate per tribe to Congress. Pike successfully negotiated treaties with most of the tribes, although some individual leaders led significant numbers of Unionist Indians.

## The Indians' Civil War

While Stand Watie became the leader of the Confederate Indians, Creek Chief Opothleyahola (Oh-POTH-luh-yuh-HO-luh) led about 3,500 Unionist Creeks and Seminoles. In November 1861, Colonel Douglas Cooper and approximately 1,400 Confederate Indians and Texans attacked Opothleyahola at Round Mountain while the Unionists were trying to escape to Kansas. Opothleyahola retreated to Chusto-Talasah (CHOOS-toe-tuh-LAH-suh), but Cooper followed up and attacked again in mid-December. Opothleyahola withdrew during the night and eventually camped at Chustenahlah (CHOOS-tuh-NAH-lah). The Confederates attacked Chustenahlah on the day after Christmas and finally drove the Unionist Indians away after heavy fighting. Although pursued by Watie, Opothleyahola made it to Kansas, but not before many of his followers died from exposure during the trek.

The victories at Chusto-Talasah and Chustenahlah only gave the Confederates temporary control of Indian Territory. In early 1863, Union Major General James G. Blunt assembled a large number of Creeks and Seminoles at Fort Gibson to return them to their Indian Territory homes. A long wagon train of supplies was sent from Kansas in July to feed the gathering, but Stand Watie and 2,000 Confederate Cherokees and Texans blocked its path at Cabin Creek. In a sharp battle, the 1st Kansas Colored Infantry escorting the wagon train fought its way through the Rebels and delivered the supplies to Fort Gibson. Blunt then assumed the offensive with his mostly Indian and black troops and routed Cooper's Indians at Honey Springs on July 17. Although casualties were light, Honey Springs proved to be the decisive battle that gave the Union control of Indian Territory for the rest of the war.

## The 1862 Sioux Uprising

Unlike those in Indian Territory, the northern plains Indians were united in their opposition to the United States. In Minnesota, the Civil War presented an opportunity for the Sioux to take back their land when Union soldiers were withdrawn to fight the Confederates. The Sioux had long suffered from disease and starvation, and they received little sympathy from government officials. When tribal leaders asked one Indian agent for help, he simply sneered, "So far as I am concerned, if they are hungry, let them eat grass." The situation exploded on August 17, 1862, when a group of Sioux attacked and killed a white family while stealing chickens. Realizing the incident would lead to retaliation, Chief Little Crow of the Santee Sioux (also known as the Dakota) launched a preemptive strike the next day against the Indian agent's headquarters. After killing the agent and about twenty other people, the Sioux stuffed grass into the agent's mouth. Over the next six weeks, the Minnesota River Valley was awash in blood as the Indians attacked Fort Ridgely, isolated homesteads, and small towns.

Henry Hasting Sibley took command of the Minnesota militia to fight the Sioux. Colonel Sibley was a former congressman and trader who had been friends with Little Crow and many of the hostile Indians. In September, President Lincoln also sent Major General John Pope to take charge of federal forces in the area. Pope, the former commander of the Army of Virginia, had been disgraced by his defeat at Second Bull Run, but he now promised to "utterly exterminate the Sioux." Before Pope arrived, Sibley led 1,400 men to Fort Ridgely to put down the uprising, but his troops were poorly trained and were defeated in several battles.

Realizing the assemblage of white forces would ultimately defeat him, Little Crow led his supporters west to the Dakota Territory. Sibley then was able to convince the remaining Sioux to release their white captives and lay down their arms. Approximately 800 white settlers and 150 Sioux had been killed in the fighting, and about 1,500 Indians were held as prisoners. Over the next few months, 303 Indians were found guilty of murder and sentenced to death, but most were pardoned when a clergyman convinced Lincoln of their innocence. On a huge gallows specially constructed for the occasion, thirty-eight Indians were publicly hanged simultaneously on December 26, 1862, in the largest mass execution in American history. Physicians later exhumed their bodies and used them for medical studies.

After the Sioux Uprising was quelled, the federal government voided all Sioux treaties and used the money still owed the Indians to aid white victims. In June 1863, General Pope launched a two-pronged attack into the Dakota Territory to give the Sioux "a whipping they would long remember." The army enjoyed little success, however, and the Indians simply retreated farther west. Little Crow escaped to Canada but returned to Minnesota in July and was shot dead while picking raspberries. His body was scalped, and the scalp was kept on display by the Minnesota State Historical Society until 1971.

## The Far West

In the far west, military campaigns were also waged against Native Americans living in the New Mexico and Colorado territories. In New Mexico, the Union army sent Christopher "Kit" Carson (1809–1868) to force the Navajo onto reservations in 1863. Carson was a native of Kentucky but grew up in Missouri and eventually ran away to New Mexico where he became a famous Rocky Mountain guide, mountain man, and Indian agent. Returning to the army in 1861, he was appointed colonel of the 1st New Mexico Infantry and participated in the Battle of Glorieta Pass before being sent on the Navajo expedition.

Carson generally was sympathetic toward Indians, but he could be ruthless when necessary. With the aid of Ute, Pueblo, and Hopi warriors, he defeated

**An Uneasy Truce.** Following the 1863 Sioux Uprising, more U.S. forts were constructed in the Northern Plains to keep the peace. This photograph of a Union officer and Plains Indians was taken at Fort Rice, Dakota Territory, during a tense interlude before renewed fighting erupted after the Civil War.

the Navajo by destroying their crops, villages, and livestock in a brutal campaign that essentially starved out the Indians. At the same time, Carson protested the harsh treatment of the Navajo who surrendered and he refused to obey orders to shoot any Indian who resisted resettlement. The 8,000 surviving Navajo were forced to walk 300 miles from Arizona to Fort Sumner, New Mexico, and many died on what was remembered as the "long walk." Several months later, Carson launched a punitive expedition against the Comanche and Kiowa who had been attacking wagon trains on the Santa Fe Trail. He destroyed one Kiowa village, but in November 1864 several thousand Indians attacked his men at Adobe Walls, Texas. Carson successfully defended his position in one of the West's largest Indian battles, but he eventually retreated back to New Mexico.

Three days after the fight at Adobe Walls, one of the most controversial events in Native American history occurred in Colorado. The territory's Cheyenne and Arapaho remained peaceful when the Civil War began, but officials still viewed them as a threat. Colonel John M. Chivington, commander of the Military District of Colorado, particularly hated Indians, and in April 1863 he ordered his soldiers to shoot all Cheyenne on sight. The Cheyenne and Arapaho fought back, taking a number of white captives and successfully cutting the Overland Trail to Denver. Chief Black Kettle of the Southern Cheyenne and Chief Left Hand of the Southern Arapaho tried to restore peace by releasing their white captives and agreeing to remain in a camp on Sand Creek. The chiefs thought peace had been restored, but in reality Colonel Chivington and Governor John Evans were planning to exterminate them.

With Evans's approval, Chivington marched on the Sand Creek encampment with two cannons and nearly 1,000 soldiers. Ordering his men to take no prisoners, Chivington attacked on the morning of November 29, 1864. The Colorado soldiers showed no mercy, even though Black Kettle flew a U.S. flag and a white flag over his tipi as a sign of peace. Chivington's men destroyed the village and its supplies and killed and mutilated a large number of Indians, many of whom were women and children. Estimates of the Indian dead in the Sand Creek Massacre range from 150 to 600, while Chivington lost 48 men. Chivington returned to Denver and placed many Indian scalps on public display. With winter approaching, Black Kettle led his surviving people north to safety without adequate food or clothing. A congressional investigation later condemned Chivington, and General-in-Chief Henry Halleck ordered his arrest, but the colonel was allowed to leave the service in January 1865 without facing trial. Governor Evans eventually resigned his position at the request of President Andrew Johnson.

## The Hidden Cost of War

Women, children, and Native Americans played a significant role in the Civil War, and their story is one of immense courage, sacrifice, and suffering. Unlike the military, no government agency kept detailed records on the deaths or property losses of civilians, so historians may never accurately calculate this hidden cost of the war. Even to make an estimate would require an exhaustive search of census records, newspapers, and church and family documents in every state. What we do know is that the Civil War was national in scope, and it touched the lives of all Americans, even those who lived far from the battlefields.

An Englishman traveling in America during the Civil War marveled at how active women were and wondered "whether either ancient or modern history can furnish an example of a conflict which was so much of a 'woman's war' as this." Many women who worked in factories were killed or injured in industrial accidents, and others were traumatized by the loss of family members or from having suffered depredations at the hand of enemy soldiers or Jayhawkers. Thousands of women also witnessed the true horror of war while working in the medical field. Mary Ann Bickerdyke, one of the North's most famous hospital workers, viewed the work women performed in hospitals as a type of military duty. She spoke for many nurses when she asked rhetorically, "Are we not all soldiers?" In a sense nurses were, indeed, like soldiers because they ate the same poor rations, faced the same mental trauma, became just as lonely, were just as susceptible to falling ill with countless camp diseases, and died for the same cause.

Children also paid an enormous cost in the Civil War. About 80 percent of all the white adult Southern males served in the Confederate military, and several hundred thousand died. This meant the children in approximately one Southern family out of three lost a father or brother. Undoubtedly, thousands of children also died of disease, malnutrition, wounds, and in industrial accidents, but there is no way to estimate an accurate number. It is not even known exactly how many children served in the armies. What is known is that the Civil War traumatized children across the North and South.

How many Native Americans died or were displaced during the war is also unknown. The best available data comes from the Indian Territory where perhaps 20 percent of the Native American population died. For Indians there, the war was an internecine conflict that split apart tribes and families and left them at odds for decades. Thousands lost homes and property and were displaced, but the Indians' suffering did not end with the fighting. After the war, Union authorities voided all Confederate treaties and forced the tribes to sign new ones giving the federal government additional Indian land and allowing railroads to be constructed across tribal territory. The Civil War may have killed more American soldiers than any other war, but it also devastated the lives of countless people of every age, sex, and race.

## FOR FURTHER READING

Seneca Falls "Declaration of Sentiments"
Sojourner Truth's "Ain't I a Woman" speech
Dorothea Dix, "Requirements for Union Army Military Nurses"

## CHAPTER 18

# Medical Care in the Civil War

**Civil War Medicine**

**U.S. Sanitary Commission**

**Rising to the Challenge**

Major General Richard S. Ewell's Confederate division was fighting desperately in the fields and pine thickets near Groveton, Virginia, during the Second Bull Run Campaign. Stonewall Jackson had ambushed a Union column at sundown on August 28, 1862, but the enemy put up a stubborn fight, and a vicious close-quartered battle ensued. Ewell's horse became unmanageable in the melee, so he dismounted to direct his men on foot. Heavy fire was coming from a thicket one hundred yards in front, and the general knelt on his left knee to peer under the limbs for a better look when a 500-grain soft lead minié ball skimmed the ground and struck him on the left kneecap. Some nearby Alabama soldiers lay down their muskets and hurried over to carry him from the field, but the fiery Ewell barked, "Put me down, and give them hell! I'm no better than any other wounded soldier, to stay on the field."

Ewell remained conscious and lay on a pile of rocks while two badly wounded soldiers nearby cried out for help until stretcher bearers finally arrived on the scene. Despite their own painful wounds, the two men insisted Ewell be carried off first, but he declined and instructed the stretcher bearers to take them away and send back a surgeon to amputate his leg on the field. The surgeon eventually arrived and after a quick examination told the general the leg might be saved. Ewell argued with him to amputate immediately, but Brigadier General Jubal A. Early convinced him to follow the surgeon's advice. Finally, hours after being wounded, Ewell was gingerly placed on a stretcher and taken behind the lines.

Dr. Hunter McGuire, Stonewall Jackson's medical director, examined Ewell's wound, but he postponed amputating until the following afternoon in a fruitless attempt to save the leg. Campbell Brown, Ewell's aide and future stepson, witnessed the operation. McGuire and his assistants sedated Ewell with chloroform and used a scalpel to cut around his leg just above the knee before applying the bone saw. In his drug-induced fog, Ewell spoke in a hurried manner and issued orders to troops, but he did not appear to feel any pain until McGuire began sawing. Ewell then "stretched both arms upward & said: 'Oh! My God!'" McGuire opened up the amputated limb to show Brown and others why the operation had been necessary. Brown later wrote, "[The bullet] pierced the joint & followed the leg down for some inches. . . . When the leg was opened, we found the knee-cap split half in two—the head of the tibia knocked into several pieces—& that the ball had followed the marrow of the bone for six inches breaking the bone itself into small splinters & finally had split into two pieces on a sharp edge of bone." Brown and a servant wrapped the bloody limb in an oilcloth, and the servant "decently buried" it in the home's garden. Brown kept the two pieces of bullet as souvenirs for his mother, who was engaged to Ewell, although he "always avoided letting the Gen'l know that I had them."

Rank was no protection from such brutal operations, and General Ewell was just one of many high-ranking officers to face the surgeon's saw. In fact, statistically speaking, a Confederate general was more likely to require medical treatment than a private. Almost one out of four died in the war, and an even larger percentage fell ill or was wounded, while only one out of ten Union generals died. Of the 250 Confederate generals who were wounded, 24 underwent amputations. General Ewell was one of the lucky ones who survived and returned to duty many months later with an artificial leg.

## CIVIL WAR MEDICINE

**1842: Surgeons first use ether as an anesthetic**
**1847: Researchers discover chloroform to be an anesthetic**
**1864: Louis Pasteur discovers germs cause diseases**
**1867: Joseph Lister publishes paper on the use of disinfectants**

Civil War medicine may have been primitive by today's standards, but it improved in many areas and put American medicine on the road to modernity. In the words of U.S. Sanitary Commission founder Dr. Henry Bellows, the Civil War was "God's method of bringing order out of chaos." Medical officers developed innovative methods to handle mass casualties, large numbers of female nurses were used for the first time, America's first maxillofacial surgery hospital was opened in Atlanta, orthopedics developed as a separate specialty, and surgical techniques were developed that are still used today. For example, Civil War surgeons were the first to discover that compound fractures had to be debrided quickly, cleaned, and sewn shut to avoid infection. The war led to the development of better-designed hospitals and convinced Americans that hospitals were not just for the mentally ill. Many cities copied the military hospital system and constructed municipal hospitals after the war. City officials also took note of the military's discovery that sanitation improved health and began addressing the problems of sewage and other pollutants.

## The Medical System

As Union Surgeon General William A. Hammond observed, the Civil War "was fought at the end of the medical Middle Ages." In 1864, Louis Pasteur found that germs caused diseases, but his discovery was not widely accepted until years later. Joseph Lister began using antiseptics in 1865, but he did not publish his findings until two years after the Civil War ended. Early in the war, most military physicians (called surgeons) practiced medicine in pretty much the same fashion as they had in the Mexican War. One admitted years later, "We operated in our blood-stained and often pus-stained coats. . . . We operated with clean hands in a social sense, but they were undisinfected hands. . . . If a sponge or an instrument fell on the floor, it was washed and squeezed in a basin of tap water and used as if it were clean." Some surgeons may have felt pangs of guilt when they later realized how primitive Civil War medicine had been, but one Confederate surgeon spoke for most when he declared, "We did not do the best we would, but the best we could."

The Union and Confederate medical systems were similar. Both had a surgeon general who supervised the entire military medical department, and every army in the field had a medical director who supervised the army's surgeons. Each regiment had a surgeon and assistant surgeon to care for the men, and each brigade and division had a chief surgeon to supervise the surgeons under him. To combat the myriad diseases found in camp, regimental surgeons held daily sick calls and examined complaining soldiers. Without modern diagnostic tools, however, they were hard-pressed to distinguish between the malingerer and the soldier who was really sick. Most patients were given medicine and sent back to their quarters, and the surgeon checked on them from time to time. Only the most desperately ill were admitted to the hospital.

Civil War surgeons' medical training varied greatly. Most of the older physicians had been trained through apprenticeship to experienced doctors. Medical schools became fairly common in the decade before the war, but most had only a two-year course of study, with the second year essentially being a refresher course of the first. There was virtually no laboratory training, and the study of anatomy was hampered by the fact that dissection was illegal in some states. Younger surgeons who attended these medical schools may have attained the skills needed to become a respected community doctor, but they were ill-prepared to face the types and numbers of wounds and diseases seen in a military setting.

At the time, medical practice was divided into several competing systems. Physicians at the time believed the body had four "humors"—blood, yellow bile, black bile, and phlegm. Most diseases were caused by the humors getting out of balance, so it was necessary to purge the patient of a particular humor for the body to heal itself. Those who might be described as orthodox physicians practiced "heroic therapy," which included liberal bloodletting and the use of strong drugs and enemas containing toxic agents such as mercury, strychnine, and opium to purge the body of the harmful humors. But there were also unorthodox systems based on therapies that generally avoided toxic drugs and bloodletting. Homeopathy and the Thomsonian System (also known as botanical medicine) were two of the more popular.

German physician Samuel Hahnemann (1755–1843) began homeopathy ("like cures like"), which is still practiced today. It treats ailments by using minute amounts of drugs that in massive doses actually cause the symptoms of the disease being treated. Samuel Thomson (1769–1805) began the Thomsonian System. Instead of the toxic medicines prescribed by orthodox physicians, it used natural herbs such as lobelia (Indian tobacco or puke weed) to purge the body, as well as steam baths to counter the ill effects of cold. All of the unorthodox systems had their own schools of instruction (that generally admitted women), but there was no real licensing process. When the Civil War began, it was mostly older physicians who still practiced the unorthodox systems because they had fallen out of favor with the younger university-trained physicians. But all of these competing systems provided Civil War surgeons, although the orthodox physicians dominated Civil War medicine and often tried to purge the unorthodox practitioners from the military.

## The Surgeons

Neither side was prepared for the medical nightmare brought on by the Civil War. After the Southern states seceded, the U.S. Army had just ninety-eight surgeons on duty. There were so few Union physicians at the First Battle of Bull Run that one surgeon performed seventy-five amputations in a single morning. Both governments frantically recruited additional physicians and hired contract surgeons, but they never had enough trained doctors. A few days after the Battle of Gettysburg, the Union's surgeon-to-patient ratio on the battlefield was about 1 per 900. Throughout the entire war, the Union military had nearly 12,000 surgeons, while the Confederates had about 3,000. Those relatively few physicians treated approximately 275,000 Union and 226,000 Confederate wounded men and 6 million cases of sickness (about 3 episodes per soldier).

Most soldiers had little respect for surgeons because some became alcoholics from having easy access to medicinal liquor, and some were simply incompetent because of poor training. Others made critical mistakes because of exhaustion. One Union soldier bled to death because his surgeon was too drunk to sew up his bleeding arteries, and a Confederate surgeon once tried to set the wrong leg of his patient. Such cases did little to earn the men's respect. In a letter home, a sick Confederate summed up many soldiers' feelings when he wrote, "I believe these damn quacks we have got for Drs. in this regt. are doing me more harm than good."

The poor reputation of Civil War surgeons is largely undeserved because the vast majority were dedicated and caring (albeit poorly trained) physicians who labored under almost unimaginably poor conditions. It should be noted that surgeons had a higher mortality rate in the war than any other military specialty. Surgeons sometimes worked days on end with little or no rest. At

# BIOGRAPHY

## Mary Edwards Walker: Medal of Honor Recipient

**Mary Edwards Walker**

Mary Edwards Walker (1832–1919) was a New York native who became one of the few antebellum female physicians after graduating from Syracuse Medical College (she was the only woman in the class). Her gender and subsequent divorce made it difficult for people to accept her as a physician, but she practiced medicine in Ohio until the Civil War began. When Walker sought a surgeon's commission, the Union army refused but offered her a nurse's appointment. Insulted, Walker refused and chose, instead, to work as a volunteer nurse in hospitals around Washington. Although she received free room and board, she was never paid for her service and even refused one surgeon's offer to share his salary. The soldiers highly respected Walker for volunteering to serve in Fredericksburg hospitals after that bloody battle and for saving some limbs from amputation by treating the wounds with her own remedies. She became something of a celebrity in the Army of the Potomac and wore an altered uniform of trousers with suspenders and knee-length coat with brass buttons, but she kept her hair long so she would be recognized as a woman.

Dr. Walker offered to raise a regiment called "Walker's U.S. Patriots" with her serving as the medical officer, but the War Department refused to consider the idea. Instead, Major General George H. Thomas appointed her a civilian contract surgeon for the 52nd Ohio in 1863 when the regiment's assistant surgeon died. Walker was the

the Battle of Fredericksburg, the Army of the Potomac had just 40 surgeons to treat 7,000 wounded men. A New York physician wrote his wife, "We are almost worked to death. My feet are terribly swollen; yet we cannot rest for there are so many poor fellows who are suffering. All day yesterday I worked at those terrible operations since the battle commenced, and I have also worked at the tables two whole nights and part of another. Oh! It is awful. It does not seem as though I could take a knife in my hand to-day, yet there are a hundred cases of amputation waiting for me. Poor fellows come and beg almost on their knees for the first chance to have an arm taken off. It is a scene of horror such as I never saw." Nurses and other hospital workers generally praised the surgeons' dedication, although they often criticized their dictatorial demeanor and sexist sentiments. Confederate nurse Fannie Beers wrote, "I never saw or heard of a more self-sacrificing set of men than the surgeons."

## Treating Wounds

Nearly all of the wounds treated by Civil War surgeons were caused by rifle fire. Although they did occur on occasion, violent hand-to-hand clashes with first woman to hold such a position in the U.S. Army. Male surgeons were horrified, calling her a "medical monstrosity" and branding her dress a "hybrid costume." In 1864, the Confederates captured Walker while she was treating civilians in Tennessee. One officer wrote they were "all amused and disgusted too at the sight of a thing that nothing but the debased and depraved Yankee nation could produce—a 'female doctor.'" This particular Confederate suggested Walker should either be returned to the Union army in proper female attire or be put in an insane asylum. After being kept four months in a Richmond prison, she was exchanged and served as chief surgeon of a women's prison in Kentucky.

When the war ended, authorities refused to allow Walker to stay in the army as a surgeon, but she was awarded the Medal of Honor for her wartime service. She was active in several postwar reform movements, including the direct election of senators and women's rights. Walker's zealous nature and radical beliefs (she eventually adopted male attire) caused many friends and relatives to shun her. Her creation of a women's colony known as Adamless Eden did not help her popularity, and later in life she was reduced to living on a small veteran's pension. Walker was proud of her Medal of Honor and wore it regularly, but in 1919 the government revoked the medal in a general purge of recipients who did not earn it in combat. She reportedly declared officials could have it back "over my dead body" and died in poverty less than a week later. The medal was restored to Walker in 1977, making her the only female recipient of the nation's highest award.

bayonets and swords were not as common as popularly believed. Union records indicate swords, bayonets, and knives accounted for less than .5 percent of all wounds treated. Even artillery fire caused relatively few wounds because most men hit by shells and canister were killed outright. A postwar study found that artillery fire caused only 1.3 percent of the wounds treated by Union surgeons. A Union surgeon at the Battle of the Wilderness noted that 250 cannons were employed in the fight, but only 12 Union soldiers were wounded by artillery shells or shrapnel (although many others were wounded by flying wood splinters when shells hit trees).

Treatment of wounds depended on several variables. If the bullet or shell fragment went through the body without striking bone, the wound was simply cleaned and bandaged. If the projectile was lodged in the body, the surgeon used his bare finger or a porcelain probe to ascertain the extent of damage and locate the object. A porcelain probe was used because it made a tapping noise when it contacted the projectile, and lead from the bullet would be left on its tip. If possible, the surgeon extracted the projectile with forceps, but deeply embedded bullets were simply left in place. Little could be done for penetrating head wounds, although surgeons did cut away pieces of the skull to relieve pressure on a swelling brain in a procedure called trepanning. One man who witnessed Dr. Hunter McGuire perform such an operation wrote, "I have seen him break off one prong of a common table fork, bend the point of the other prong, and with it elevate the bone in a depressed fracture of the skull and save life." Once the initial treatment was completed, all wounds were cleaned of any foreign debris and debrided by cutting away dead or badly damaged tissue. Sometimes bromine or another antiseptic was used to wash the wound before it was bandaged with clean, although unsterilized, strips of linen. These linen bandages were rinsed and used again and again on different patients.

Sticking bare fingers and probes into wounds and using contaminated bandages always introduced bacteria into the body and guaranteed some type of infection. Hospital gangrene was one of the most deadly, with a mortality rate of about 50 percent. Once a wound was infected, the flesh began to die at a rate as fast as half an inch per hour. Surgeons usually amputated infected limbs or used a particularly torturous procedure that involved pouring hydrochloric or nitric acid directly onto the decaying flesh to eat it away. Surgeons eventually found bromine was effective in treating hospital gangrene, and they learned to use fresh sponges and bandages to reduce the number of cases. Confederate surgeons also discovered quite by accident that maggots cleaned out dead tissue and began introducing them to infected wounds with great success.

No matter what the wound or treatment, survival often seemed completely random. Some men suffered horrible wounds and lived; others died from what appeared to be minor injuries. One Union surgeon was amazed by a soldier who was struck in the neck by a bullet that shattered his vertebra. He wrote, "Nearly the entire body of the third cervical vertebra has come away. . . What supports his head anteriorly, I can't conceive. . . ." Not only did the man survive, he was put to work in the hospital. Another miracle was an 18-year-old Confederate who was shot through the head at Gettysburg. His brother, the company commander, found him and was horrified by what he saw. The bullet had entered the boy's left cheek and popped his right eye out of the socket as it passed through his head to exit the right temple. He too survived, although he was blinded in the right eye. Then there was the case of two Michigan soldiers who served in the same company during the Atlanta Campaign. In one battle, both were shot in the index finger. One man treated himself by using his pocket knife to cut off the mangled finger at the middle joint. He wrapped it in a handkerchief and waited until the battle was over to have the wound dressed at the field hospital. The other soldier went immediately to the surgeon for a proper amputation. Gangrene set in within days, and the surgeon amputated his arm at the shoulder, but the man died soon afterward. The soldier who treated himself made a full recovery.

## Resections and Amputations

Approximately two out of every three wounds treated by surgeons involved the extremities. This was because more than 90 percent of the soldiers killed

**Union Field Hospital.** This is the field hospital used by the 16th New York after the Battle of Savage's Station, Virginia, during the 1862 Seven Days Campaign. The officer squatting in the foreground is a surgeon examining one soldier's wound.

in the Civil War were shot in the head, neck, chest, or stomach. Relatively few soldiers hit in those critical areas lived long enough to make it back to a field hospital. From a technical point of view, damaged limb bones presented the greatest challenge to surgeons. The large oblong minié balls often tumbled when they hit the body and caused much more damage to bone than smooth-bore musket balls. One Confederate surgeon observed, "The shattering, splintering, and splitting of a long bone by the impact of a minié or Enfield ball were, in many instances, both remarkable and frightful. . . ." When bone was damaged, surgeons had to decide quickly on one of three possible treatments: If it was a simple fracture, a wooden or plaster splint was applied, but if the bone was shattered the surgeon performed either a resection or an amputation.

Resection involved cutting open the limb, sawing out the section of damaged bone, and then closing the incision. It was a time-consuming procedure, requiring considerable surgical skill, but some surgeons became quite proficient. After the Battle of Savage's Station, one Union surgeon completed twenty-six resections of the shoulder and elbow in a single day. He was said to be able to eat and drink coffee at the operating table while pieces of bone, muscle, and ligaments piled up around him. Besides being a difficult procedure, resection carried a high risk of profuse bleeding, infection, and postoperative necrosis of the flesh. Successful resections, however, allowed the patient to keep his limb, although it was limp and useful only to "fill a sleeve." Because of the time required, resections were not always practical when there were large numbers of patients to treat, but they were used more frequently after surgeons learned amputations had a much higher mortality rate.

Amputation was the most common surgical procedure in the Civil War, with Union surgeons performing more than 30,000 (compared with just over 16,000 by American surgeons in World War II). The procedure was fairly simple. After a circular cut was made completely around the limb, the bone was sawed through, and the blood vessels and arteries sewn shut with silk or cotton ligatures. To prevent future pain, nerves were then pulled out as far as possible with forceps, cut, and released to retract away from the end of the stump. Finally, clippers and a rasp were used to smooth the end of the exposed bone. Sometimes the raw and bloody stump was left uncovered to heal gradually, and sometimes excess skin was pulled down and sewn over the wound. Speed was essential in all amputations to lessen blood loss and prevent shock. An amputation at the knee was expected to take just three minutes.

Because surgeons preferred to operate outdoors where the lighting and ventilation were better, thousands of soldiers witnessed amputations firsthand. Passersby and even wounded men waiting their turn watched as surgeons sawed off arms and legs and tossed them onto ever-growing piles to be buried later. Poet Walt Whitman witnessed such a scene when he visited Fredericksburg in search of his wounded brother. "One of the first things that met my eyes in camp," he wrote, "was a heap of feet, arms, legs, etc., under a tree in front of a hospital." At the Battle of Fredericksburg, Union surgeons performed almost 500 amputations.

Early in the war surgeons earned the nickname "Saw-bones" because they seemed eager to amputate. This eagerness stemmed not from overzealousness but from the knowledge that infections developed quickly in mangled flesh, and amputation was the most effective way to prevent it. Those limbs removed within forty-eight hours of injury were called primary amputations, and those removed after forty-eight hours were called secondary amputations. The mortality rate for primary amputations was about 25 percent, while that for secondary amputations was about 50 percent. The increased mortality rate was due to the fact that most secondary amputations were performed after gangrene or blood poisoning had developed in the wound. Surgeons learned that amputating the limb after it became infected actually caused the infection to spread, and patients frequently died. Thus, the patient was much more likely to survive if a primary amputation was performed before infection set in. Primary amputations were also preferred because it was easier and less painful to transport an amputee than a soldier whose broken bones and inflamed tissue made the slightest jostle sheer torture. One surgeon admitted that an excessive number of amputations may have been performed, but he added, "I have no hesitation in saying that far more lives were lost from refusal to amputate than by amputation."

Where the amputation was made on the limb was as vital to survival as when it was done. Generally, the higher up the amputation was made, the higher the mortality rate. This was especially true for thigh wounds. A little more than 50 percent of soldiers who suffered a femur injury died, and amputations at or near the hip joint had a 66-percent mortality rate in the Confederate army. Nonetheless, it is estimated that about three out of four soldiers who had

**Amputation.** This photo depicts surgeons preparing to amputate a man's lower right leg at a Gettysburg field hospital. The two men to the left of the surgeon appear to be administering chloroform.

amputations survived the surgery. Amazingly, some soldiers, like Confederate Brigadier General Francis T. Nicholls, endured more than one. His lower left arm was amputated after he was shot at the First Battle of Winchester and his lower left leg was taken off when he was wounded at Chancellorsville. After the war, Nicholls was a popular Louisiana governor who was said to ask voters to vote for "all that's left of General Nicholls" and to support him for governor because he "was too one sided to be a judge."

Taking care of amputees put a significant strain on both governments. The Union provided its disabled soldiers with prosthetic limbs made from cork wood, metal, or rubber and gave amputees pensions of $8 a month. The Confederacy was unable to match such generosity and by 1864 was providing just 10 percent of needed prostheses. Amputees were a visible reminder of the Civil War for decades. One postwar British traveler noted they were "everywhere in town and farm communities through the South." Incredibly, Mississippi's single greatest state expenditure a year after the war ended was the purchase of artificial limbs for its war veterans. Supplying prostheses consumed 20 percent of the state's budget. Some amputee veterans were forced to look after themselves and paired up to form a "shoe exchange," where they could buy a pair of shoes together and keep the appropriate one needed.

## Anesthesia

Contrary to popular belief, Civil War surgeons usually had supplies of chloroform or ether to anesthetize patients before surgery. Both had been used during the Mexican War, but Civil War surgeons overwhelmingly preferred chloroform. It was nonflammable and easier to transport, and ether caused blood pressure to drop dangerously low and worsened shock. Chloroform was dripped onto a piece of cloth held over the patient's face until he was unconscious. Although not an exact science, the procedure worked well, and few patients died from its use. Opium pills, opium dust, and injections were also available to control postoperative pain or for changing dressings.

The common belief that surgery was routinely performed without anesthetics can be partially attributed to the fact that patients were not put into a deep unconscious state. As in the case of General Ewell, patients often reacted to the scalpel and bone saw as if in pain but did not remember it afterward. Bystanders who saw struggling patients crying out or being held down on the table wrongly assumed no anesthetic was being used. However, there were a few occasions when supplies did run out, and surgeons were forced to perform amputations without anesthesia. Minié balls have been found at some field hospital sites with bite marks on them, proving surgeons did sometimes have patients "bite the bullet" during operations.

## Civil War Diseases

Although Civil War medical studies often concentrate on the treatment of wounds, disease caused two out of three deaths. Cramming thousands of men into small areas led to regular outbreaks of measles, pneumonia, and smallpox. Conditions were perfect for the spread of contagious diseases because men were shut up together for long periods of time in small tents and huts. A New Hampshire soldier wrote, "It is fearful to wake at night, and to hear the sounds made by the men about you. All night long the sounds go up of men coughing, breathing heavy and hoarse with half-choked throats, moaning and groaning with acute pain. . . ." Those soldiers from rural areas were especially susceptible to mumps and measles, which often developed into pneumonia, because they had never been exposed to them as had soldiers who grew up in cramped cities. Measles nearly wiped out entire regiments early in the war when many soldiers were first exposed. A Mississippi surgeon described his visit to a makeshift hospital during a measles epidemic: "About one hundred sick men crowded in a room sixty by one hundred feet in all stages of measles. The poor boys lying on the hard floor, with only one or two blankets under them, not even straw, and anything they could find for a pillow. Many sick and vomiting, many already showing unmistakable signs of blood poisoning." That particular regiment had 204 men die in this one epidemic.

Unsanitary living conditions caused diseases such as dysentery, diarrhea, typhoid, and cholera. Both armies issued orders requiring that long latrines be dug and the contents be covered daily with a fresh layer of dirt. However, little thought was given sometimes to the placement of latrines, and they often were dug close to wells or upstream from freshwater sources. Many modest soldiers disliked using the open latrines and simply relieved themselves wherever they found a secluded place. Regulations also required men to bathe once a week, but soldiers almost universally ignored that rule and remained filthy. Tons of manure from cows, horses, and mules and entrails from slaughtered animals only added to the filth in a typical Civil War encampment. Dysentery and typhoid flourished in such conditions, with dysentery being the single greatest killer. It differed from common diarrhea because it was caused by a bacterial infection that gave a soldier loose, bloody bowel movements. Both dysentery and diarrhea were commonly called the "flux," "Tennessee Trots," or simply the "runs," and probably all Civil War soldiers suffered from them at one time or another. As one surgeon put it, "No matter what else a patient had, he had diarrhea." Bacteria also caused typhoid and cholera. Typhoid was spread by soldiers coming in contact with flies that landed on feces or contaminated food, while cholera was caused by ingesting food or water contaminated by particular bacteria. The latter bacteria caused diarrhea, vomiting, and cramps and could kill a person within hours of the infection's first onset.

Malaria and yellow fever added to the misery of camp life. Both were commonly found in the mosquito-infected regions of the Deep South. Malaria, or the "ague," accounted for about 20 percent of all patients treated. A soldier with malaria first developed a high fever called the "shakes," followed by debilitating weakness that could leave him bedridden for days or weeks. The symptoms gradually subsided and the soldier returned to duty, but the fever periodically returned and the process was repeated. Soldiers infected with yellow fever also developed a high fever, followed by headache and the "black vomit" caused by internal hemorrhaging. In the latter stages of the disease, the liver stopped functioning and the patient took on a jaundiced hue, thus giving the fever its name. Physicians at the time did not know malaria and yellow fever were carried by mosquitoes and believed they were caused by harmful fumes emitted by swamps, the breath of infected men, or camp excrement.

Smallpox was another dreaded disease in Civil War camps, but soldiers were fortunate that a vaccine had been developed that helped prevent widespread epidemics. The vaccine was primitive and dangerous, however, and soldiers dreaded being inoculated. Surgeons took a small amount of pus from an infected cow and injected it into a soldier's arm by making a cut through the skin. In describing his regiment's vaccination, a Massachusetts soldier wrote, "Such a wholesale slashing and cutting of arms never was witnessed before. The commanding officer of each company would march up the men, all with bared arms. The doctor would make three or four passes with his knife, cutting through the skin, punch a little of the vaccinating matter into the wound, and the thing was done. The doctors went through the thousand men in about three hours, and the sore arms for ten days afterwards was a sight to behold."

Venereal diseases plagued both armies and became such a medical threat to the Union army that generals were forced to take action to regulate prostitution. Syphilis and gonorrhea were common. During the war, 8.2 percent of Union soldiers contracted some sort of venereal disease, but this reflects only those soldiers who sought medical treatment (Confederate records are incomplete). Few soldiers, however, were hospitalized or died from such infections. Physicians treated most soldiers on an outpatient basis with mercury-based compounds that were applied to the skin. Poke roots, elderberries, mercury, sarsaparilla, zinc sulfate, silver nitrate, sassafras, Jessamine, and even cauterization were also popular treatments. Often the surgeons never knew what actually worked—whenever the symptoms disappeared they assumed the last treatment had cured the patient.

One final indignity endured by soldiers was infestations of fleas and body lice, commonly called "graybacks." An Iowa soldier claimed, "I have seen men literally wear out their underclothes without a change and when they threw them off they would swarm with Vermin like a live Ant hill when disturbed." Soldiers learned to live with the lice and even entertain themselves by dropping them onto a heated plate and betting on which one would crawl off first.

## Treating Disease

Soldiers often complained that the treatment surgeons prescribed for diseases was worse than the disease itself. Malaria and other fevers were treated quite effectively with quinine, but it had the severe side effect of loosening one's teeth. Quinine was also used to treat diarrhea and dysentery, as was opium to ease abdominal spasms and pain. Calomel, blue mass, strychnine, castor oil, turpentine, silver nitrate, and ipecac were also popular treatments for dysentery and diarrhea, but they all had extreme side effects. Turpentine could damage the nervous system and kidneys and induce bloody vomiting. Calomel, castor oil, and blue mass *caused* diarrhea, and ipecac induced vomiting. Calomel in particular caused explosive diarrhea and projectile vomiting, which dehydrated dysentery patients even more. Calomel and blue mass were mercury-based drugs that caused mercury poisoning, extreme salivation, inflamed gums, and loose teeth. Ulcers sometimes formed in the mouth and ate away bone and tissue and caused hideous facial deformities.

Other types of medical treatment seemed almost medieval torture. Incredibly, some surgeons were known to cauterize the anus to treat dysentery or the penis to treat venereal disease. Pneumonia was often treated by bleeding the patient or using heated mustard plasters to draw out fluid from the lungs. Surgeons once used heat to treat a soldier's stomach ailment by applying hot bricks to his feet and hot cloths to his stomach. The man wrote home, "Oh such hours of suffering, but the Lord was with me praise his name."

The Union was blessed with ample supplies of medicine, but the Confederates were forced to look for substitutes when the blockade cut off medical supplies from Europe. All across the South, drug manufacturing and research facilities were established to produce medicine and search for viable alternatives. Virtually all drugs at the time came from plants, such as quinine from South American tree bark, opium from poppies, and turpentine from tree resin. Therefore, the Confederates believed they could find substitutes growing naturally in the Southern forests. Dr. F. P. Porcher published the booklet *Resources of Southern Fields and Forests* that provided information on indigenous Southern plants with medicinal properties, and he and Confederate Surgeon General Samuel P. Moore published similar articles in the *Confederate States Medical and Surgical Journal*. The bark of dogwood, poplar, blackberry, willow, and sweet gum were among the substitutes Confederates tried for quinine. They also planted poppies in an attempt to produce opium. Soldiers were even sent into the woods to search for wild onion, garlic, mustard, sassafras, pokeweed, artichoke, peppergrass, and dandelion as a citrus substitute to treat scurvy. Such efforts, however, were largely fruitless, and the Confederates had little success in developing medicines from their own resources.

## U.S. SANITARY COMMISSION

**April 29, 1861: Dr. Elizabeth Blackwell helps establish the Woman's Central Relief Association**
**June 13, 1861: Union officials establish the U.S. Sanitary Commission**
**October 27, 1863: Chicago Sanitary Fair begins**

Civilians on both sides frequently made clothing and collected supplies for soldiers in the field, but the Northern people took this popular involvement a step further and created several large relief societies. Dr. Elizabeth Blackwell, reputedly the first American woman to earn a medical degree, was one of the first to realize that Northern women's efforts to gather supplies were rather ineffective because they were disorganized and only helped local soldiers. She helped create the Woman's Central Relief Association in 1861 to recruit and train nurses and coordinate women's efforts to aid the entire Union army, not just local volunteer companies. The U.S. Christian Commission, created by the New York City Young Men's Christian Association (YMCA), was another relief society. Its members promoted Christian values in the army, provided free meals and reading and writing material to soldiers, and performed nursing duties in numerous hospitals. Both organizations worked hard to support Union soldiers, but they never attained the power and influence of the U.S. Sanitary Commission.

The Sanitary Commission was the brainchild of Drs. Henry W. Bellows and Elisha Harris. They lobbied the government to sanction one large relief organization to oversee the military's medical program and coordinate the relief efforts of local groups. Government officials were leery of the idea because they did not want civilians to supervise the military's medical services, and they opposed using female nurses. Charles Tripler, the Army of the Potomac's medical director, was a leading opponent of the plan, and he dismissed Bellows, Harris, and their supporters as "sensation preachers, village doctors, and strong minded women." Bellows and Harris persevered, however, and finally secured the administration's reluctant approval in June 1861. Frederick Law Olmsted, antebellum reformer and architect of New York City's Central Park, was made executive secretary, and George Templeton Strong served as treasurer. Olmsted, known to his agents as "Old Boss Devil," was sometimes heavy-handed in his struggle to keep branch commissions subordinate to the national office and limit the influence of competing organizations, but he did an admirable job before resigning in 1863.

# DID YOU KNOW?

## The U.S. Sanitary Commission

The U.S. Sanitary Commission, which was patterned after the British Sanitary Commission that proved so effective in the Crimean War, was America's first civilian relief organization sanctioned by the federal government. Besides providing nurses and medical supplies, it helped disabled soldiers collect government pensions, provided lodging for discharged or furloughed soldiers, wrote letters for patients, and set up refreshment stands for hungry soldiers. Although disbanded in 1878, the Commission's success was not forgotten. It inspired the creation of the American Red Cross and United Services Organization (USO), which today continue the work begun by the U.S. Sanitary Commission.

## The Sanitary Commission's Work

The Sanitary Commission's mission was to provide services to Union soldiers that the government would not or could not undertake. Although military medical officers were conservative by nature and loathe to tinker with the antiquated system that had been in place since the Mexican War, the Sanitary Commission brought new ideas to the army and began to modernize medical care. Agents inspected military camps and hospitals and gave advice on how to improve sanitary conditions and diet. The Sanitary Commission also set up hospitals, provided nurses, and collected food, supplies, and ambulances. The amount of supplies distributed to the army was staggering. After the Battle of Gettysburg, commission agents provided 11,000 pounds of meat; 12,500 gallons of milk; 6,430 pounds of butter; and 2,316 bottles of whiskey and wine to the wounded men of both sides. One of its greatest services was compiling and publishing the names of more than 600,000 men in more than 200 hospitals so family members could locate their loved ones.

At its peak strength, the Sanitary Commission had branches in ten major Northern cities and approximately 500 field agents. Recognizing their accomplishments, one army surgeon declared, "But for the timely arrival of these [agents], many lives would, undoubtedly, have been sacrificed." Over the course of the war the Commission spent more than $7 million on relief efforts and provided $15 million worth of supplies. While the Confederates never developed anything to rival it ("We were too poor," explained one Southerner), Southern civilians were active on an individual and community level to raise money and supplies for their hospitals.

## Sanitary Fairs

The huge amount of food, medicine, supplies, and money required by the Sanitary Commission came entirely from private donations. Much of the money was raised at what were called sanitary fairs. Agents Mary A. Livermore and Jane Hoge organized the first sanitary fair at Chicago, Illinois, in October 1863 to assist the northwestern branch of the Sanitary Commission. To draw a good crowd, local businesses and schools closed for the fair's opening, and a three-mile-long parade snaked through the city. Captured enemy flags were put on display; prominent officials made speeches; and jewelry, clothing, war relics, race horses, and autographs were donated to be sold at auction. The original draft of Lincoln's Emancipation Proclamation brought $3,000. The Chicago sanitary fair was a huge success, raising more than $75,000, and other Sanitary Commission branches soon began holding their own fairs.

## Sanitary Commission Workers

Men occupied all of the leadership positions in the Sanitary Commission, but women volunteers performed most of the fieldwork. Two of the better-known workers were Mary Ashton Rice Livermore (1820–1905) and Mary Ann Ball Bickerdyke (1817–1901). A native of Massachusetts, Livermore was a former teacher who became active in various antebellum reform issues with her minister husband. They moved to Chicago before the Civil War and published the *New Covenant,* a religious and reform-oriented newspaper. Livermore gained some notoriety by being the only female reporter to cover the 1860 Republican National Convention. When the Civil War began, she used the newspaper to encourage women to become active in soldiers' relief work and helped form a Sanitary Commission branch in Chicago. As one of the national directors, Livermore raised money and supplies and used her writing skills to expose negligence and create sympathy for sick and wounded soldiers. After the war, she championed women's suffrage, became active in women's educational issues, and wrote her popular memoirs, *My Story of the War.*

Mary Ann Ball Bickerdyke was a widowed Ohio native who supported her family by becoming a botanic physician. Living in Illinois when the Civil War began, she and her neighbors became concerned when local soldiers began to complain about poor hospital conditions. The community quickly gathered medical supplies and chose Bickerdyke to take them to the army. "Mother Bickerdyke," as she became known, spent the entire war working in field hospitals, collecting medical supplies, and caring for soldiers. She served as a Sanitary Commission agent in both U.S. Grant's Vicksburg Campaign and William T. Sherman's Atlanta Campaign. Mother Bickerdyke became a beloved figure to Union soldiers and claimed to have served in three armies and nineteen battles. At war's end, she was allowed to ride in the armies' Grand Review in Washington and was given a government pension in 1886.

## RISING TO THE CHALLENGE

October 17, 1861: Chimborazo Hospital opens

April 25, 1862: U.S. government appoints William A. Hammond Surgeon General

June 10, 1862: USS *Red Rover* commissioned first U.S. hospital ship

July 4, 1862: Jonathan Letterman becomes medical director of the Army of the Potomac

**August 2, 1862: Union adopts the Letterman System**
**March 11, 1864: Congress creates the U.S. Ambulance Corps**

Civil War medicine should be studied in the context of its time and not compared with today's medical treatment. Although frequently described as primitive and barbaric, it actually was quite sophisticated by nineteenth-century standards and improved steadily throughout the war. Both sides rapidly built new hospitals, recruited female nurses, and established examining boards to test and certify surgeons and weed out the incompetents. Medical personnel also gained a great deal of knowledge about diseases, wounds, and the need for improved camp sanitation and changed their methods when better ways were discovered. Amputations, for example, became less frequent as surgeons learned more about the risks involved and developed more effective resection techniques. Surgeon General Hammond was correct to boast that the mortality rate in the U.S. Army was "lower than had been observed in the experience of any army since the world began." A testament to the surgeons' skills was the fact that Union hospitals saw only an 8-percent mortality rate in the approximately one million patients treated.

## The Letterman System

The speedy removal of wounded men from the battlefield was one of the greatest challenges for medical personnel. When the war began, regiments used musicians, cooks, or other nonessential personnel as litter bearers to take the wounded to field hospitals. It was a haphazard system at best, and men often lay on the field for hours or even days before being evacuated. Sometimes soldiers fell in isolated places and died because they were never found. Knowing this, men frequently dropped out of ranks in the midst of battle to take a wounded friend back to the field hospital so he could be treated quickly. Such action seriously weakened a unit's fighting strength, and officers usually gave specific orders before a battle that no one was to leave his place to help the wounded.

Even when a wounded man was found, the trip back to a field hospital was a nightmarish ordeal. Civil War ambulances were crude wagons without springs, and they jostled patients mercilessly. Most became caked in blood and gore, and one soldier recalled the "blood trailed from the ambulances like water from an ice cart." A Confederate cavalry officer who escorted Lee's ambulances back to Virginia after Gettysburg wrote of the wounded, "[T]heir torn and bloody clothing, matted and hardened, was rasping the tender, inflamed, and still oozing wounds. Very few of the wagons had even a layer of straw in them, and all were without springs. . . . From nearly every wagon as the teams trotted on, urged by whip and shout, came such cries and shrieks as these: 'Oh, God! Why can't I die?' 'My God, will no one have mercy and kill me?' 'Stop! Oh, for God's sake, stop just for one minute; take me out and let me die on the roadside!'. . . . During this one night I realized more of the horrors of war than I had in all the two preceding years." It took eighteen days to get some of the wounded to Virginia hospitals. Traveling by train was little better. Frederick Law Olmsted, secretary of the U.S. Sanitary Commission, once described the wounded he saw on a hospital train. "They were packed as closely as they could be stowed in the common freight cars, without beds, without straw, at most with a wisp of hay under their heads. They arrived, dead and alive together, in the same close box, many with awful wounds festering and alive with maggots. The stench was such as to produce vomiting with some of our strong men, habituated to the duty of attending the sick & wounded of the army."

While the Confederates always sent out noncombatants to remove the wounded, the Union greatly improved its retrieval system. Some changes were made in the Army of the Potomac soon after the First Battle of Bull Run, but significant progress was not made until Jonathan Letterman became the army's medical director in 1862. He created the "Letterman System" by subdividing the army's medical department into separate units to supervise ambulances, medical supplies, and field hospitals. Each surgeon was required to maintain a standard surgical kit, and each brigade had to have a surgical wagon fully equipped with dressings, medicine, instruments, bedpans, basins, and food. The Letterman System also revamped the field hospital system by requiring each regiment to place an assistant surgeon at a forward aid station to perform triage and send the most critically wounded patients to a division hospital in the rear.

Letterman's greatest innovation was creating a separate ambulance corps and using trained personnel to recover the wounded. Previously, individual medical officers controlled ambulances, but during a battle they became too busy to supervise properly the retrieval of wounded men. Letterman took the ambulances out of the medical department and placed them under the command of field officers. Each corps had a captain who was in charge of the unit's ambulances, and he had a number of lieutenants and noncommissioned officers to supervise the ambulances for each division, brigade, and regiment. These officers recruited litter bearers and ambulance drivers from the various units to be trained specifically to evacuate the wounded.

Progress in removing the wounded was slow but steady. It was estimated that 3,000 wounded men still lay on the battlefield three days after Second Bull Run. A few weeks later, however, it took just twenty-four hours to retrieve all the wounded from the Antietam battlefield, and this was cut to twelve hours at Fredericksburg. Training and experience perfected the system until it worked to near perfection at Gettysburg. There, 1,000 ambulances retrieved 14,000 wounded men within half a day after the Confederates retreated. Despite considerable opposition from officers who wanted to keep ambulances under the control of medical officers, Congress passed a law in 1864 creating a separate ambulance corps for all the Union armies. The Letterman System and ambulance corps were so successful that many other nations adopted them for their armies.

## EYEWITNESS
## Carl Schurz

*Carl Schurz (1829–1906) was a Prussian native who earned a doctorate at the University of Bonn and became involved in the failed 1848 European revolutions. Forced to flee the continent, he eventually settled in Wisconsin and became a popular abolitionist speaker and Republican Party member. Schurz briefly served as Lincoln's minister to Spain before the president appointed him a brigadier general of volunteers to gain the support of German Americans. After the war, he wrote a descriptive account of his visit to a Gettysburg field hospital.*

A heavy rain set in during the day—the usual rain after a battle—and large numbers [of wounded] had to remain unprotected in the open, there being no room left under roof. I saw long rows of men lying under the eaves of the buildings, the water pouring down upon their bodies in streams. Most of the operating tables were placed in the open where the light was best, some of them partially protected against the rain by tarpaulins or blankets stretched upon poles. There stood the surgeons, their sleeves rolled up to the elbows, their bare arms as well as their linen aprons smeared with blood, their knives not seldom held between their teeth, while they were helping a patient on or off the table, or had their hands otherwise occupied; around them pools of blood and amputated arms or legs in heaps, sometimes more than man-high. Antiseptic methods were still unknown at that time. As a wounded man was lifted on the table, often shrieking with pain as the attendants handled him, the surgeon quickly examined the wound and resolved upon cutting off the injured limb. Some ether was administered and the body put in position in a moment. The surgeon snatched his knife from

## Field Hospitals

After being picked up by an ambulance, a wounded man's next stop was at a field hospital, which was often set up in a tent, barn, home, or church near the front lines. Conditions in such facilities were primitive, with little more than hay for bedding. As casualties arrived, some of the surgeons performed triage to determine the severity of the wounds and decide whom to treat first. Less-experienced physicians cleaned and bound the noncritical wounds, while the most skilled physicians performed amputations and other types of surgery. Their operating table often was nothing more than a door taken off its hinges and placed across two chairs near a window or out in the open air. Patients often waited for hours to be treated, in full view of surgeons going about the grisly business of hacking off arms and legs.

Needless to say, field hospitals were horrifying, and soldiers frequently recorded their impressions after seeing one. A Union officer who visited a field hospital after the Battle of Malvern Hill wrote, "On every side we heard the appeals of the unattended, the moans of the dying, and the shrieks of those under the knife of the surgeon." An Ohio soldier wrote an even more between his teeth, where it had been while his hands were busy, wiped it rapidly once or twice across his blood-stained apron, and the cutting began. The operation accomplished, the surgeon would look around with a deep sigh, and then—"Next!"

And so it went on, hour after hour, while the number of expectant patients seemed hardly to diminish. Now and then one of the wounded men would call attention to the fact that his neighbor lying on the ground had given up the ghost while waiting for his turn, and the dead body was then quietly removed. Or a surgeon, having been long at work, would put down his knife, exclaiming that his hand had grown unsteady, and that this was too much for human endurance—not seldom hysterical tears streaming down his face. Many of the wounded men suffered with silent fortitude, fierce determination in the knitting of their brows and the steady gaze of their bloodshot eyes. Some would even force themselves to a grim jest about their situation or about the "skedaddling of the rebels." But there were, too, heart-rending groans and shrill cries of pain piercing the air, and despairing exclamations, "Oh, Lord! Oh, Lord!" or "Let me die!" or softer murmurings in which the words "mother" or "father" or "home" were often heard.

*After Gettysburg, Schurz was transferred west, where he commanded a division under Joe Hooker in the Chattanooga Campaign. He resigned his commission at war's end and devoted his life to writing and championing liberal causes such as racial equality, a civil service system, and anti-imperialism. Schurz also served one term as a U.S. Senator from Missouri and one year as the Secretary of the Interior.*

Carl Schurz, *The Reminiscences of Carl Schurz*, 3 Vols. (New York: McClure, 1907–1908), Vol. 3, pp. 39–40.

disturbing account of another hospital. "Wounded men are lying everywhere. What a horrible sight they present! Here the bones of a leg or an arm have been shattered like glass by a Minnie ball. Here a great hole has been torn into an abdomen by a grape shot. Nearby see that blood and froth covering the chest of one choking with blood from a wound of the lungs. By his side lies this beardless boy with his right leg remaining attached to his body only by a few shreds of blackened flesh. This one's lower jaw has been carried entirely away. . . . Over yonder lies an old man, oblivious to all his surroundings, his grizzly hair matted with brain and blood slowly oozing from a great gaping wound in the head. . . . All are parched with thirst, and many suffer horrible pain; yet there are few groans or complaints." Few who witnessed a Civil War field hospital ever forgot the experience.

## Permanent Hospitals

From a field hospital, badly wounded men eventually ended up in a permanent hospital. Hospitals were not common in antebellum America, and the few that

**Table 4**    *Casualties in Civil War Armies and Navies*

Confederate records are incomplete; the Confederate data listed here are therefore estimates. The actual Confederate totals were probably higher.

| | Killed and Mortally Wounded in Combat | Died of Disease | Died in Prison | Miscellaneous Deaths* | Total Deaths | Wounded, Not Mortally | Total Casualties |
|---|---|---|---|---|---|---|---|
| Union | 111,904 | 197,388 | 30,192 | 24,881 | 364,345 | 277,401 | 641,746 |
| Confederate (estimated) | 94,000 | 140,000 | 26,000 | No Estimates | 260,000 | 195,000 | 455,000 |
| Both Armies (estimated) | 205,904 | 337,388 | 56,192 | 24,881 | 624,365 | 472,401 | 1,096,766 |

* Accidents, drownings, causes not stated, etc.

existed were small and mostly used to care for the indigent and the mentally ill. When they became ill or injured, people were usually treated by physicians, midwives, or self-trained healers who came to their homes. Even major military hospitals contained only a few dozen beds. As in the case of surgeons, both the Union and Confederate governments vastly underestimated the need for large hospitals and were overwhelmed by the sheer number of casualties. Armies constantly struggled to care for the sick and wounded, and nearby towns were always swamped with casualties after battles. Gettysburg, Pennsylvania, had an 1863 population of 2,000 people, but it housed 20,000 wounded men after the battle. Considerable progress was made in setting up temporary field hospitals on battlefields and large permanent hospitals near major cities, but the system was far from adequate. Finding facilities in large cities to provide long-term care for the sick and wounded was difficult. At first the two armies simply improvised and housed patients in government buildings, churches, and warehouses. Even the halls of the U.S. Congress were turned into an infirmary. Soon, however, large permanent hospitals began to spring up around both capitals and in other major cities.

Union Surgeon General William Alexander Hammond (1828–1900) performed wonders in improving the Union hospital system. A native of Maryland, he was a New York University Medical College graduate and former army surgeon who published a widely read treatise on nutrition before accepting a professorship at the University of Maryland. Through the influence of Major General George B. McClellan and the U.S. Sanitary Commission, Hammond was appointed surgeon general in 1862. He quickly brought order to the military medical department, but he was tactless and often clashed with Secretary of War Edwin Stanton.

One of Hammond's innovations was the adoption of the European pavilion-style hospital. The British first used these large complexes, which were

**Armory Square Hospital, Washington, D.C.** Washington's Armory Square Hospital was one of many pavilion-style hospitals the Union constructed. It was one of the North's best medical facilities.

composed of a central structure with long buildings radiating outward like spokes on a wheel. Because it was commonly believed infections and diseases were airborne, Hammond made sure the pavilions were well ventilated with high ceilings and numerous windows. He also limited the hospitals to one story so the "exhalations and secretions of the ill would be rapidly dissipated and not rise to affect patients on a second story." To increase efficiency and provide surgeons with learning laboratories, Hammond subdivided the hospitals into wards where specific types of wounds and illnesses were treated. Later, this policy was expanded by establishing specialty hospitals, such as one in St. Louis that treated smallpox and one in Philadelphia that treated nervous maladies. By war's end, the Union had 204 permanent hospitals with nearly 140,000 beds. Washington alone boasted 25 hospitals, and Philadelphia's Mower General Hospital, the North's largest, had 4,000 beds.

Hammond's abrupt manner and lack of political skill finally led to his downfall. Secretary of War Stanton eventually maneuvered him out of Washington and named an acting surgeon general in his place. Hammond demanded reinstatement or a trial by court-martial, but the powerful Stanton prevailed, and Hammond was dismissed from the army in August 1864 after being found guilty of ungentlemanly conduct. After the war, he was a leading figure in the treatment of mental disorders and published many medical works. In 1879, Hammond was cleared of his court-martial conviction and was placed on the army's retired list as a brigadier general.

The Confederates were never able to match the Union's resources and had only thirty-four permanent hospitals by war's end. Of these, Chimborazo (chim-buh-RAH-zoh) was by far the largest; in fact, it was believed to be the largest hospital in the world. Constructed on a prominent plateau outside Richmond, Virginia, Chimborazo served as the prototype for future Confederate hospitals. It contained seventy-five long barracks buildings called wards, each housing up to forty patients. Among the hospital's 120 buildings were soup houses, icehouses, kitchens, mess halls, morgues, bathhouses, a bakery (capable of making 10,000 loaves of bread a day), and even a brewery. Directed by Dr. James Brown McCaw, and treating some 3,000 patients at any given time, Chimborazo had approximately one surgeon for every seventy-five patients, plus scores of hospital stewards and nurses. Although Chimborazo was one of the most modern and efficient Civil War hospitals, about 16,000 of its 78,000 patients still died. One chaplain described it as a "charnel house of living sufferers."

## Hospital Ships

One of many advantages the Union had over the Confederacy in medical treatment was the availability of ships to use as hospitals. Hospital ships proved particularly useful because many battles were fought along rivers or on the coast. Hospital ships included U.S. Navy vessels, privately owned ships contracted by the government, and boats funded by individual states to treat their soldiers. Some hospital ships were simply used to transport patients to permanent land-based hospitals, while others were true floating hospitals, complete with operating rooms. A total of thirty-two vessels were used as Union hospital ships, and they transported or treated 150,000 patients.

Early in the war, the U.S. Sanitary Commission supervised most Union hospital ships, provided surgeons, and distributed government medical supplies. In 1863, however, the army's medical department assumed responsibility. The ships' service record was outstanding, and they often had a lower mortality rate than land-based hospitals. One vessel transported nearly 24,000 patients and had a mortality rate of just over 2 percent (Chimborazo's mortality rate was about 20 percent). The first commissioned U.S. Navy hospital ship was the *Red Rover,* which was converted from a captured Confederate vessel and used on the Mississippi River. It had operating rooms, an elevator to move patients between decks, two kitchens, a cold locker with ice, bathrooms, and a laundry. Described as a floating palace, the *Red Rover* was also the first U.S. Navy hospital ship to have female nurses.

## Medical Personnel

One of the first steps taken to improve the medical treatment of soldiers was to recruit hundreds of additional personnel, some of whom were commissioned officers and some civilian contract workers. Physicians were particularly sought out, but a wide variety of other trained personnel were also needed.

Among these were dentists. Dentists did not have the same status as surgeons, although they did perform such demanding surgical procedures as repairing shattered jaws. Confederate dentists were classified as mere hospital stewards, but they provided their soldiers better dental treatment than did the Union. Confederate dentists even established America's first maxillofacial hospital in Atlanta, Georgia, specifically to treat facial wounds, and they performed some of America's first plastic surgery.

Apothecaries (pharmacists) and veterinarians also served in Civil War armies. Union apothecaries were civilian contract employees who had to pass a board of examiners just as surgeons did. Sometimes using the honorary title of "captain," they worked in hospitals to collect, store, and dispense medical supplies. Although rarely mentioned in Civil War studies, veterinarians were critical in the medical field. Huge numbers of draft animals were required to transport the wounded and keep an army functioning, and trained veterinarians were needed to keep the animals healthy. However, veterinarians were in short supply because the United States had only one veterinary school when the war began. This shortage forced both armies to depend on farriers to work with the draft animals that pulled ambulances. A farrier was a self-trained layman who served as a combination veterinarian and blacksmith. Many Confederate farriers were soldiers taken from the ranks, while Union farriers were civilian employees who were given the honorary rank of sergeant major.

## The Medical Legacy of the Civil War

One way to judge the quality of Civil War medicine is to compare it with the care soldiers received in wars of the same time period. In the Civil War, approximately 206,000 soldiers died in battle and 418,000 died from disease and other noncombat causes, for a ratio of about 1:2.4. In the Mexican War (1846–48), 1,549 Americans were killed in battle and 10,986 died from noncombat causes, for a ratio of about 1:7. In the Spanish-American War (1898), 968 soldiers were killed in battle and 5,438 died from noncombat causes, for a ratio of about 1:5.5. In overall mortality, approximately 19.5 percent of all Civil War soldiers died. In comparison, about 16 percent of British soldiers died in the Crimean War (1853–56) and 15 percent of French soldiers in the Franco-Prussian War (1870). Such statistics seem to indicate that Civil War soldiers had better medical care than American soldiers received in other nineteenth-century wars and comparable treatment to European soldiers.

Despite the often primitive working conditions and overwhelming numbers of patients, Civil War surgeons made significant strides in their profession and discovered new techniques that changed how medicine was practiced. Innovative splints and traction were developed using screws, plates, wires, and rods. New and more modern prostheses, including artificial hands, feet, arms and legs, complete with artificial joints, were also created for amputees. Between 1861 and 1873 nearly 150 patents were granted for such prosthetic limbs, or about triple the number issued in the previous fifteen years.

One of the greatest steps Union officials took to further medical knowledge was creating the Army Medical Museum to preserve physical specimens of wounds and diseases for future surgeons to study. Curator John Brinton scoured numerous battlefields to secure the specimens, sometimes going so far as to dig up fresh corpses to retrieve shattered limbs or damaged and diseased organs. The specimens were placed in barrels of alcohol or whiskey and shipped to Washington where they were cleaned, catalogued, and put on public display. The museum became a popular tourist attraction, and it included Major General Daniel Sickles's leg that was amputated at Gettysburg. Sickles's limb was placed in a makeshift coffin, complete with the general's calling card. Brinton's museum is now the National Museum of Health and Medicine of the Armed Forces Institute of Pathology at Walter Reed Army Medical Center in Maryland.

Officials also made sure the knowledge gained by Civil War surgeons was recorded for posterity to help modernize medicine. In 1888, the federal government completed publication of *The Medical and Surgical History of the War of the Rebellion,* which described in illustrated detail the thousands of wounds and myriad diseases that confronted wartime physicians. The 600-page *Treatise on Hygiene* by William Hammond was the first English-language work on military hygiene ever published. Hammond also wrote a 350-page text on human physiology, and other military physicians produced such groundbreaking works as *The Hospital Steward's Manual* and *On Bandaging and Other Operations of Minor Surgery.* Far from being the drunken, scalpel-happy surgeons often portrayed in movies, Civil War physicians were, for the most part, highly dedicated professionals who deserve great respect for improving America's medical system.

## FOR FURTHER READING

General Orders No. 147 of McClellan establishing Ambulance Corps for Army of the Potomac

Confederate Surgeon General Samuel P. Moore's letter on using indigenous plants for medicinal purposes, July 22, 1862

General Orders, No. 20, outlining duties of brigade surgeons of Army of the Potomac

# CHAPTER 19

# In the Hands
# of the Enemy

**Prisoners in the Civil War**

**Prisons in the Civil War**

**Escaping Prison**

**Placing the Blame**

---

Something was not right. While taking the morning roll call, the Confederate guards at Libby Prison found their count was short. "They were excited and counted again," recalled one Union prisoner. "In a twinkling, church bells were ringing, cavalrymen were out with horns blaring, and all hounds obtainable were yelping. The excitement was at white-heat. . . ." Amazingly, 109 Yankee officers had simply disappeared from the heavily guarded prison located in the heart of the Confederates' capital city.

Civil War prisoners were desperate in early 1864. The agreement between the Union and Confederacy governing the exchange of captives had broken down because the Confederates refused to treat black Union soldiers as prisoners of war. Conditions in most prisons were horrid, and it seemed the inmates were condemned to languish there until hostilities ceased. In Libby Prison, Colonel Thomas E. Rose of the 77th Pennsylvania decided to take action. After Rose enlisted the help of Major Andrew G. Hamilton, the pair began making plans to break out. One night, Hamilton borrowed a knife, moved a stove in the kitchen, and pried up the loose hearthstones to gain access to the prison's abandoned basement. He and other officers soon realized an escape tunnel could be dug from the basement without attracting the guards' attention. Working around the clock in three teams of five, the prisoners began the laborious task using nothing but a table knife, an old chisel stolen from the carpenter shop, a wooden box made from a spittoon, some string, and candles. To reach freedom, they had to dig approximately fifty feet to get beyond a wooden fence that would hide them from guards when they broke through to the surface.

Colonel Harrison Hobart of the 21st Wisconsin described the work. "But two persons could work at the same time. One would enter the hole with his tools and a small tallow candle, dragging the spittoon after him attached to a string. The other would fan air into the passage with his hat, and with another string would draw out the novel dirt cart when loaded, concealing its contents beneath the straw and rubbish of the cellar." Colonel Hamilton claimed, "The only difficulties experienced in making this excavation resulted from a lack of tools and the unpleasant feature of having to hear hundreds of rats squeal all the time, while they ran over the diggers almost without a sign of fear."

After digging many days, the prisoners believed they had cleared the fence. To make sure, one man cut a small hole to the surface at night and stuck his shoe in it. Colonel Hamilton recalled, "The next morning at daylight we looked out the window and to our disappointment found that the shoe was on the wrong side of the fence." The men resumed digging and when they finally made it past the fence, Rose decided to make the breakout on the night of February 9. As a diversion, some of the prisoners would put on a loud, boisterous musical to drown out any noise made. Leading the first batch of prisoners into the tunnel, Colonel Rose dug through the last few inches of topsoil and disappeared into Richmond's dark streets. Watching from upstairs windows, the prisoners could actually see their comrades scurrying away in pairs and small groups. Colonel Hobart explained how he blended into the night. "My face being very pale and my beard long, clinging to the arm of Col. West, I assumed the part of a discrepit [sic] old man who seemed to be in exceeding ill-health and badly affected with a consumptive cough. In this manner we passed beneath the glaring gas lights, and through the crowded streets, without creating a suspicion as to our real character."

Some of the men made their way to known loyalists who assisted them, while others headed straight for the Union lines to the north and east. Hamilton walked to Williamsburg and later recalled, "While traveling I was in ice and water to my knees the greater part of the time, and often it was up to my waist." Fifty-nine of the officers made it safely to Union lines, 48 were captured, and 2 drowned. Among those caught was the ringleader, Colonel Rose. Reporting on the daring escape, the Richmond *Examiner* declared, "It is fortunate that the leak was discovered when it was, or the exodus would have been continued last night, and night after night, until there would have been no Yankees to guard."

The Libby Prison escape was the most spectacular of the Civil War, but such large breakouts were rare. It is estimated that approximately 195,000 Union soldiers and 215,000 Confederates (not counting those who surrendered at war's end) were captured—or about one in seven men. Early in the war, most were paroled on the battlefield and never saw the inside of a prison. Those who were incarcerated later in the conflict had little hope of being released until the war ended. Their story is one of incredible hardship, suffering, and death. The treatment of prisoners of war was a shameful blot on the record of both the Union and Confederacy.

# PRISONERS IN THE CIVIL WAR

**July 18, 1862: U.S. and Confederate officials sign the Dix-Hill Cartel**
**July 3, 1863: Stanton orders halt to routine paroles and exchanges**
**July 4, 1863: Grant paroles prisoners captured at Vicksburg**
**October 27, 1863: Secretary of War Stanton halts most prisoner exchanges**
**March 15, 1865: North and South resume prisoner exchanges**

Prisoners' fates varied greatly and depended largely on when and where they were taken and their captor's character and frame of mind. The most dangerous time was the moment of capture. Some soldiers became enraged in combat or harbored extreme hatred of the enemy and simply killed men who surrendered. Confederates sometimes murdered black soldiers rather than take them prisoner, and Union troops often killed captured guerrillas. When Confederate Brigadier General Thomas B. Smith was captured and disarmed at the Battle of Nashville, an enraged Union colonel repeatedly hacked him in the head with a sword. The vicious blows fractured Smith's skull and exposed his brain. To the surgeon's surprise, Smith survived the attack but was left with permanent brain damage and spent his last forty-seven years in an insane asylum.

If soldiers survived the first few hours of captivity, the enemy usually did not further mistreat them except, perhaps, to strip them of food and personal belongings. However, there was always some danger during transportation to rear areas. Anecdotal evidence indicates guards who had been through the trial of combat generally treated prisoners better than militiamen or support troops who had never been under fire. One Michigan soldier whose unit was captured by Nathan Bedford Forrest's cavalry wrote, "In justice to the active and fighting elements of the Confederacy I must say we were seldom mistreated by them, but we did dred [*sic*] to be left in the hands of the non-combatants." This soldier and his comrades were so appreciative of their Mississippi cavalry guards protecting them from irate civilians they gave the Confederates a loud cheer when they were relieved by other troops.

The prisoners' greatest suffering occurred once they were put into a prison camp. No one envisioned the Civil War lasting as long as it did or considered the possibility of having to care for tens of thousands of prisoners of war. This shortsightedness led to overcrowded camps where disease and hunger were commonplace. Prisoners also suffered because the opposing governments used them as pawns to protect their own soldiers captured by the enemy. If one government believed the other was mistreating prisoners, it frequently retaliated against the men it held. And, perhaps most important, both governments focused most of their attention on fighting the war. Caring for prisoners simply was not a priority, and few resources were dedicated to that purpose.

The Union did develop a code of conduct that offered some limited guidance for handling prisoners in a humane manner, but it was sometimes ignored. Officials quickly discarded the code when the war ended and treated

Native American captives harshly during the western Indian wars. Americans were not forced to address large-scale domestic prison camps again until World War II. By that time, the United States had signed the Geneva agreements that provided for the humane treatment of prisoners. As a result, enemy prisoners held in America during World War II were treated much better than American prisoners held by Americans during the Civil War.

## The Lieber Code

The Civil War was the first conflict in which a nation drew up a code of conduct that instructed its soldiers how to act in the field and addressed the treatment of prisoners of war. As seen in earlier chapters, the war posed many legal questions for President Lincoln as to whether the Confederates were traitors and pirates or legitimate soldiers of a warring nation. Therefore, Lincoln asked Francis Lieber (1798?–1872) to prepare a manual on how Union soldiers should conduct themselves in relation to Confederate soldiers and civilians. Lieber was a Prussian native and veteran of several European wars who once was imprisoned for his liberal ideas. After leaving prison, he earned a doctorate, served in the Greek war of liberation, and continued to champion liberal causes in Europe. Lieber eventually immigrated to the United States and lived in South Carolina as a slaveholder, writer, and teacher before joining the faculty at New York's Columbia University.

Lieber's 1863 report was entitled *Instructions for the Government of the Armies of the United States in the Field,* but it was commonly referred to as the Lieber Code. The code not only addressed such matters as martial law and military law, it also established rules on how to treat civilians, prisoners, deserters, and spies. In general, the code stressed acting in a humane and ethical manner at all times, and it forbade "no quarter" unless it was necessary for a military unit to survive. Civilians were to be treated humanely as long as they remained peaceful. However, soldiers were allowed to act more harshly to combat guerrilla activity, including confiscating or destroying private property and arresting, imprisoning, or exiling suspects. The Lieber Code even authorized the immediate execution of any combatant captured out of uniform, and it permitted retaliation against prisoners if it was necessary to protect one's own prisoners from abuse. The Lieber Code was not always adhered to, but it became the standard on which other nations based their codes, and it was used by the Geneva Conventions in the twentieth century to standardize the treatment of prisoners of war.

## The Parole and Exchange System

Union and Confederate authorities realized immediately after the first few battles that some plan had to be devised to care for the thousands of prisoners taken. There were no prison camps to house them, and it was difficult to provide food and medical care for such large numbers of men. The simplest solution was to use a traditional European method of releasing prisoners on parole. Soon after being captured, a prisoner took an oath and signed a parole document promising he would not fight again until he had been exchanged for an enemy prisoner. The prisoner kept one copy of the parole oath to prove he was a parolee and not a deserter, and the paroling officer kept a copy for his government. While on parole, a soldier could not perform any duty that would benefit his government, such as manning a fort to allow another soldier to fight. If a soldier violated the parole and returned to the war before being properly exchanged, he could be executed if captured a second time. The parole system was based entirely on a soldier's honor to keep his promise and the opposing governments trusting each other to not abuse the system.

In the first months of war, the Union was leery of using the parole system because officials feared an agreement with the Confederacy would be de facto recognition of its independence. As one Union general declared, "To exchange prisoners would imply that the United States government admitted the existing war to be one between independent nations. This I cannot admit." Because of this Union reluctance, the parole and exchange system began as an informal arrangement made by local commanders. By 1862, however, prisoners overwhelmed both armies, and a more formal policy had to be formulated. Such an agreement was made easier by the fact that a Supreme Court ruling in the *Enchantress* Affair allowed Lincoln to treat captured Confederates as prisoners of war without recognizing Southern independence.

In July 1862, John A. Dix and Daniel H. Hill, generals in the Union and Confederate armies, respectively, worked out a formal parole and exchange procedure known as the Dix-Hill Cartel. It required prisoners to be paroled and exchanged within ten days of capture (although in practice it sometimes took longer) and created a formula for the exchange. For example, equal ranks would be swapped on a one-for-one basis, two privates for one sergeant, eight privates for one major, or sixty privates for one major general. If one side held an excessive number of prisoners that could not be exchanged, they would be turned over to the prisoners' own army and kept in parolee camps until they could be exchanged. In an important loophole, the cartel also allowed local military commanders to make special arrangements when necessary. Colonel William Hoffman was chosen to supervise the Union's prisoner exchange and Colonel Robert Ould the Confederates'. City Point, Virginia, and Vicksburg, Mississippi, were designated as exchange points because they had adequate water and rail transportation that could easily serve the eastern and western theaters.

## Breakdown

For the most part, the parole and exchange system was an effective way to keep prisoners from returning to the war while relieving the governments of the responsibility of maintaining large prison camps. Although the system worked fairly well for two years, both sides became increasingly frustrated with recurring problems. The Confederates were furious when they learned the Union sometimes violated the Dix-Hill Cartel by using parolees to guard prisoners or fight Indians on the frontier to free up soldiers to fight the South. Both Union and Confederate officials also complained that some soldiers allowed themselves to be captured because sitting in a parolee camp was safer than fighting on the front lines. Union parolees even accused officials of intentionally making Northern parolee camps overcrowded, disease ridden, and poorly supplied to discourage soldiers from allowing themselves to be captured.

The parole and exchange system was first threatened in 1862 when Major General Benjamin F. Butler issued his infamous Woman's Order in New Orleans. In retaliation, Jefferson Davis branded him a war criminal and declared no Union officers would be paroled until the "Beast" was captured and hanged. Accepting the challenge, Secretary of War Stanton quickly halted the parole and exchange of Confederate officers. A more serious problem arose in 1863 when large numbers of black Union soldiers were captured. The Confederates refused to recognize African Americans as soldiers or treat them as prisoners of war. According to Confederate policy, blacks captured in Union uniforms were to be treated as escaped slaves and turned over to state authorities. Captured white officers commanding black soldiers could be executed for inciting slave insurrection. After the Battle of Milliken's Bend, Louisiana, in June 1863, Confederate Secretary of War James Seddon left little doubt as to his sentiments when he wrote, "[A]s to the white officers serving with negro troops, we ought never to be inconvenienced with such prisoners."

When the Confederates refused to treat black soldiers as prisoners of war, Secretary of War Stanton halted routine prisoner exchanges on July 3, 1863. The next day, General Grant captured 30,000 Confederates at Vicksburg. Unable to guard or care for them, he got around Stanton's order by taking advantage of the Dix-Hill Cartel's loophole allowing local commanders to make special arrangements when necessary. Grant paroled the prisoners and allowed most of those living west of the Mississippi River to go home rather than report to Confederate parolee camps. This was a clear violation of the Dix-Hill Cartel, but Grant knew it was a sound strategic move. Many of the Rebels who went home would probably be unable to cross back over the river to rejoin their commands even after being exchanged.

Grant's actions angered Confederate authorities, and the Vicksburg parolees who dutifully reported to the camps became restless because they, too, wanted to go home. Fearing the parolees might simply desert, Colonel Ould unilaterally declared most of them exchanged a few months later as an expedient way to return them quickly to the army. Union authorities cried foul because there was no equal number of Union prisoners in Northern parolee camps to exchange for the Confederates. Colonel Hoffman, therefore, declared all Union parolees were exchanged, as well, but federal authorities estimated the Confederates still made a net gain of 10,000 soldiers in the process.

The Vicksburg incident caused much bitterness and considerable distrust between the belligerents, and a year later Grant was still demanding that the

Confederates release the estimated 10,000 prisoners owed the Union. He also was angry at the Confederate treatment of black soldiers. Determined to take a firm stand, Grant declared in April 1864, "Until there is released to us a sufficient number of officers and men as were captured and paroled at Vicksburg and Port Hudson not another Confederate prisoner of war will be paroled or exchanged. . . ." Thus, large-scale exchanges came to a halt, although some prisoners (especially the sick and wounded) continued to be paroled and exchanged by local commanders exercising their right to make special arrangements under the Dix-Hill Cartel. Officially, Grant stopped paroles and exchanges because of the Vicksburg incident and the mistreatment of African American soldiers, but he also had another motive. The exchange system actually strengthened the Confederates because the returned prisoners helped them replace battlefield losses. The North had a huge population to draw conscripts from, so its returning prisoners did not significantly aid the Union. Stopping the exchanges meant condemning thousands of Union prisoners to languish in squalid prison camps, but Grant believed it would end the war sooner and save lives in the long run.

The Confederates also knew the exchange system worked in their favor, and they desperately sought ways to change Union policy. Colonel Ould hoped the growing publicity of Union soldiers' suffering in Confederate prisons might help. He wrote Secretary of War Seddon, "We can only hope that the pressure brought to bear upon the Federal authorities by the friends and relatives of the prisoners held by us may force a change of policy." The Northern press and public did, in fact, put considerable pressure on Grant to resume exchanges to save the prisoners, but he held firm. The Confederates even offered to exchange white prisoners on a one-to-one basis with no regard to rank, but they still refused to exchange black prisoners. As one Confederate officer declared, they would "die in the last ditch before giving up the right to send slaves back to slavery as property recaptured."

In early 1865, Grant finally agreed to resume exchanges. By that time he was confident the war was all but won. Lee's army was starving at Petersburg, the Shenandoah Valley was in ruins, and Sherman was marching through the Carolinas. Resuming exchanges would not materially change the military situation, and Grant was eager to relieve the suffering of Union prisoners. He reopened prisoner negotiations with the Confederates and exchanges resumed in March, just one month before Lee surrendered at Appomattox.

## Retaliation

One of the more disturbing aspects of the Civil War was how authorities on both sides used prisoners as pawns in a war of retaliation. Sometimes captured guerrillas or civilian sympathizers were summarily executed as an intimidation tactic. Other times, innocent prisoners were chosen by lot to be executed as a retaliatory measure for executions carried out by the enemy. Both governments embraced a clause in the Lieber Code that condoned the latter practice if it was necessary to protect one's own prisoners from abuse. In 1861, President Davis warned, "[T]his Government will deal out to the prisoners held by it the same treatment and the same fate as shall be experienced by those captured [by the Union]." Abraham Lincoln echoed that sentiment when he promised, "[F]or every soldier of the United States killed in violation of the laws of war a rebel soldier shall be executed." Such retaliation against prisoners began early in the war when fourteen Confederate privateers were captured in the *Enchantress* Affair. Placed in chains and treated as common criminals, they were convicted of piracy and sentenced to be hanged. Confederate authorities immediately put into chains fourteen Union officers being held in Libby Prison and prepared to hang them if authorities executed the privateers. Fortunately, the tense standoff was defused when Union courts finally ruled Confederate privateers could be treated as prisoners of war. All of the prisoners involved were eventually exchanged.

The most celebrated case of prisoners being used for retaliatory purposes involved what Southerners came to call the "Immortal 600." In 1864, Union cavalryman George Stoneman made an unsuccessful raid to free the Union prisoners being held at Macon and Andersonville, Georgia. Fearing more raids, the Confederates sent hundreds of those prisoners to Charleston, South Carolina, which was being shelled by Union artillery batteries located on Morris Island. The prison camps there were already overcrowded, so officials placed the new prisoners inside the city. Union authorities believed the Confederates were intentionally putting prisoners in harm's way and selected 600 Southern prisoners at Fort Delaware for transport to Morris Island. The passage was horrible because the men were crammed into the ships' broiling, unventilated holds with little water. Union guards placed with them fainted from the heat and stench, and one declared, "A dog couldn't stand this." At Morris Island, the 600 prisoners were put in a stockade and guarded by members of the black 54th Massachusetts. Over the next several weeks, Union and Confederate gunners exchanged fire regularly but went to great lengths to avoid areas with prisoners. Eventually, the Confederates moved the Union prisoners out of Charleston, and the Immortal 600 on Morris Island were shipped back to Fort Delaware. Incredibly, none of the prisoners was killed during the forty-four days of bombardment.

Other prisoners were not so fortunate. In 1864, General Grant, eager to stop the raids by John S. Mosby's Confederate rangers, instructed Philip Sheridan, "When any of Mosby's men are caught, hang them without trial." Sheridan's officers, particularly George Custer, carried out the orders with enthusiasm, and Sheridan soon informed Grant, "We hung one and shot six of [Mosby's] men yesterday." Robert E. Lee was outraged and informed his superiors, "I have directed Colonel Mosby to hang an equal number of Custer's men in retaliation for those executed by him." About the same time in Missouri, a Confederate cavalry colonel executed seven members of the Missouri militia in an apparent revenge killing for seven men he lost in capturing them. A few weeks later, Union officials picked out six Confederate prisoners from a

St. Louis prison and shot them. One of the victims was a four-year combat veteran. He wrote his family, "I am now to be shot for what other men have done, that I had no hand in, and know nothing about." A seventh prisoner was to be shot later, but President Lincoln finally intervened and stopped the execution.

One act of retaliation involved Robert E. Lee's son, Brigadier General W. H. F. "Rooney" Lee. In the spring of 1863, two captured Confederate officers were executed in Kentucky as spies even though they claimed they were simply recruiting. In what was becoming a routine procedure, Confederate officials then chose two Union officers in Libby Prison to be executed, despite Colonel Ould's fears that the incident might spiral out of control and plunge the two sides into an "awful vortex" of retaliation. About that time, "Rooney" Lee was captured in a rural Virginia home while recuperating from a wound. He and another Confederate officer were set aside for execution if the Libby prisoners were killed. Another tense standoff ensued because everyone feared the consequences of executing such a prominent officer as Lee. When Union officials learned that Rooney Lee's wife had died, they exchanged him on humanitarian grounds as a convenient way to settle the matter with honor. All the prisoners involved were then quickly exchanged, and the crisis passed.

## PRISONS IN THE CIVIL WAR

**February 25, 1864: First Union prisoners arrive at Andersonville**
**July 6, 1864: First Confederate prisoners arrive at Elmira**
**November 10, 1865: U.S. government hangs Henry Wirz as a war criminal**

As long as the parole and exchange system worked, large prison camps were not needed because prisoners were held only long enough to be paroled. This changed in 1863 when the Dix-Hill Cartel broke down, and both sides were forced to care for tens of thousands of prisoners for months at a time. Eventually, more than 150 prison camps were used. Some were warehouses, state penitentiaries, or forts converted to hold prisoners of war, while others were constructed by putting up a log or plank palisade with catwalks and towers for guards. Within these enclosures were barracks and other buildings and an area of open ground the prisoners called the "bull pen." To discourage escape attempts, most prisons also had an infamous "dead line," a marked line running along the inside of the wall's perimeter. Any prisoner who crossed the line was shot without warning. Most prisons were notorious for their overcrowded conditions, scant food, and rampant disease. A few, however, were made bearable by caring commandants who did everything in their power to care for the inmates. The Confederate prisoners at Camp Morton, Indiana, appreciated the commandant so much that they commissioned a bust of him that was put on display in the state capitol.

**Camp Morton, Indiana.** Camp Morton was transformed from a training camp to a prison after the Union captured thousands of Confederates at Fort Donelson, Tennessee. It was one of the better Civil War prisons and had a lower death rate than most.

## Union Prisons

Union prison camps were scattered across the Northern states, and many were converted from existing state and local facilities. Alton Prison, Illinois' first state prison, was reopened in 1862 to house Confederate prisoners. Camp Chase, Ohio; Camp Douglas, Illinois; and Camp Morton, Indiana, were former state militia training camps. The Old Capitol Prison in Washington, D.C. (located at the modern day Supreme Court building), once served as the nation's capitol building and as a hotel before being pressed into service as a prison to hold deserters, spies, and political prisoners.

Some Union prisons were converted U.S. Army forts. Fort Warren, Massachusetts, was located on an island in Boston Harbor. Used mainly to hold Confederate officers, it was considered one of the more comfortable Northern prisons. Inmates enjoyed better accommodations, exercise opportunities, and food than most, and only twelve deaths were recorded among its inmates. One officer who was kept there in the war's closing weeks with a number of generals had few complaints and noted the prisoners got along well with their keepers, especially with the commandant's three-year-old daughter, Mabel. Mabel once told the officers she would be sailing in the bay on a particular day and would wave her handkerchief at them. A dozen or so of the most feared Rebel generals lined the parapet at the appropriate time and watched as Mabel waved her handkerchief. Brigadier General Eppa Hunton remembered, "We gave her as fine a 'Rebel yell' as ever was heard."

Fort Delaware, Delaware, was another converted army fort, but it was one of the war's worst prisons. Located on an island in the Delaware River, this stone structure was used as a holding pen for Confederate prisoners on their way to City Point, Virginia, for exchange. When the exchange system broke down in 1863, Fort Delaware became a permanent prison camp. In 1864, it held more than 9,000 inmates in barracks designed to hold 5,000. The overcrowded conditions were made worse by poor and scant food and the damp and unhealthy location. The boggy land inside the fort was lower than the river, and some barracks actually sank into the mud. Union surgeons condemned the fort's living conditions, but nothing was ever done to improve things. Epidemics of scurvy and smallpox sometimes ravaged the prisoners, and nearly 2,500 men died. Fort Delaware became known as the "Andersonville of the North," and one Alabama prisoner wrote, "A respectable hog would have turned up his nose in disgust at it."

Most of the Union prisons built during the war were nearly as bad as Fort Delaware. One was constructed on Johnson's Island, Ohio, a 300-acre island in Lake Erie near Sandusky, Ohio. Union officials naively believed it would be adequate to house all of the Confederate prisoners captured in the war. A plank fence enclosed a forty-acre plot, and several two-story barracks and other buildings were constructed inside. Almost immediately, thousands of prisoners overwhelmed Johnson's Island, and at one point nearly 10,000 men were held in the small compound. Prisoners suffered from intense cold during the winter and lived in squalid conditions because the shallow bedrock prevented the digging of adequate latrines. Food was in such short supply the inmates routinely hunted rats to eat. One prisoner claimed, "We traped for Rats and the Prisoners Eat Every one they Could get. I taken a mess of Fried Rats. They was all right to a hungry man, was liked Fried squirrels. . . ."

Another dreaded Yankee prison was Point Lookout, Maryland, located on a peninsula where the Potomac River enters Chesapeake Bay. Constructed to hold Confederate enlisted men, it covered about forty acres of low, sandy ground. Point Lookout was the Union's largest prison camp with more than 50,000 prisoners being housed there during its two-year existence. By war's end, nearly 20,000 inmates were crammed into the small enclosure, living in tents and suffering from unsanitary living conditions, bitter winter cold, and swarming summer mosquitoes. A Virginian claimed hunger was so prevalent, "I have heard men pray to be made sick that the appetite might be taken away." Adding insult to injury, the Union army used black soldiers to guard the prisoners. One inmate declared this "made our Southern blood boil." When the guards learned of the Fort Pillow massacre, some of them fired randomly into the bull pen and killed several men. Officially, about 3,600 deaths were recorded at Point Lookout, but the total may have surpassed 4,000.

In the far west, few prisons rivaled Rock Island, Illinois, for inhumane conditions. This Mississippi River island was low and swampy, most of its drinking water came directly from the muddy Mississippi, and each of the crude barracks had only two stoves to ward off the biting cold. Some prisoners actually froze to death inside the barracks when the temperature once dipped to –32°. One Tennessee soldier summed up conditions at Rock Island when he wrote, "[T]he hardest service ever tendered by a soldier was to be my lot for the next sixteen months—Rock Island." He was more fortunate than the approximately 2,000 prisoners who died there.

Topping the long list of the Union's worst prison camps was Elmira, New York, known to its inmates as "Hellmira." A Texan explained the nickname when he wrote, "If there was ever hell on earth, Elmira prison was that hell." The Elmira camp consisted of a simple palisade erected around some old army barracks. When the barracks proved inadequate to house the large number of prisoners, many men were forced to live in tents. Elmira's ground was low and poorly drained, and a pond inside the wall caught the drainage from the prisoners' latrines. The putrid pond smelled so foul, hardened inmates frequently vomited. Prisoners also suffered from the intense winter cold. A Virginian remembered how they had to fight for a place near the barrack's stove each morning. "God help the sick or the weak," he declared, "as they were literally left out in the cold." All the prisoners suffered from malnutrition, and one Union official described them as being "pale and emaciated, hollow-eyed and dispirited in every act and movement." Hellmira had the highest death rate of any Northern prison camp, with 775 men dying in one three-month period. Death was so commonplace, one Union surgeon found cause to boast when the death rate *dropped* to forty per week. Elmira was in existence for only one year, but in that time nearly 3,000 Confederate prisoners (or 25 percent) died.

## Confederate Prisons

Confederate prisons also ran the gamut from being reasonably tolerable to outright nightmares. Castle Pinckney, an old U.S. government installation in the harbor at Charleston, South Carolina, was one of the better ones where guards and prisoners treated one another with respect. Another relatively healthy prison was located at the opposite end of the Confederacy in Texas. Camp Ford was constructed near Tyler and consisted of an open square stockade built on high, dry ground that had a good water supply. Union prisoners usually had adequate food and housing, and there was no need even to build a camp hospital. Camp Ford did become overcrowded and less healthy when hundreds of new prisoners were brought in during the 1864 Red River Campaign, but it remained one of the better Confederate camps. Fewer than 300 men died, even though it sometimes held as many as 5,000 inmates.

In truth, Castle Pinckney and Camp Ford were the exceptions. Most Confederate prisons were notorious hellholes where Union prisoners suffered horribly from disease, exposure, and starvation. Two of the worst were located in Richmond, Virginia. Belle Isle, an eighty-acre island in the James River, was designed to hold 3,000 prisoners but housed more than 8,000 by 1864. It was finally closed, but the unfortunate survivors were sent to the even less hospitable prison at Andersonville, Georgia. Libby Prison, a converted three-story tobacco warehouse located on the banks of the James River, was even more notorious. Since it was close to City Point, Virginia, Libby housed large numbers of Union prisoners for short periods of time before they were exchanged. As many as 125,000 men were detained there during the war (this is believed to be more inmates than any other Civil War prison), with as many as 3,000 being held at one time.

Conditions at Libby Prison were filthy, cramped, and unbearable. One prisoner wrote, "The floor is an inch deep in thick black greasy slime which we cannot remove. A horrible odor pervades the apartment. An open privy is on one side of the room for the common use of this crowd, exhaling most dreadful smells. The walls are smeared from the floors above with the slops & excretions of the hundreds of men confined overhead. . . . The floors, walls, clothes, and the bodies of the men swarm with vermin." Lying on the floor in rows at night, the men were packed so tightly they could only roll over in one mass on command of a squad leader. Common complaints included a cold damp atmosphere, rats, poor ventilation, and cruel guards. Surprisingly, deaths were not as common at Libby as might be expected because the prisoners (who were mostly officers) were allowed to purchase supplemental food and supplies.

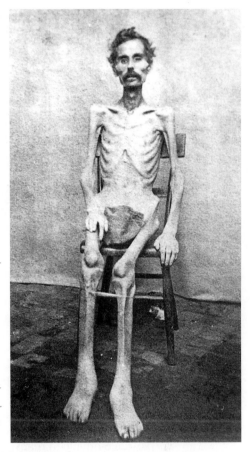

**The Living Dead.** One can only imagine the horrific conditions that existed in Civil War prisons when examining this photograph of a just released Union prisoner of war.

The two largest Confederate prison camps outside Richmond were Salisbury, North Carolina, and Andersonville, Georgia. Salisbury Prison was formed around an old cotton factory and held both Union prisoners of war and Confederate deserters and political prisoners. At first, the inmates had ample food, water, recreation, and housing, but Salisbury became terribly overcrowded in 1864 after the exchange system broke down. Although designed to hold 2,500 inmates, the stockade eventually housed nearly 9,000, including several hundred black prisoners. This huge increase turned Salisbury from a relatively comfortable facility into a crowded, unhealthy death pit. Inmates suffered from contaminated water supplies, unsanitary living conditions, cold temperatures, and food shortages. Some men were forced to eat acorns to survive or live in holes dug in the ground.

**Andersonville.** This photograph of Andersonville was taken in August 1864 when it was at its most crowded. Note the latrine in the foreground is located on the same sluggish stream prisoners used for water.

Salisbury was the only Civil War prison actually destroyed by the opposing army. In April 1865, Union cavalry under George Stoneman burned the buildings, but by that time all the inmates had already been moved. Of the camp's approximately 15,000 inmates, almost 4,000 died and were buried in unmarked graves. This death rate was comparable to the better-known Confederate prison at Andersonville. After the war the commandant was tried for intentionally mistreating prisoners, but he was released after convincing the court the breakdown of the Confederate supply system was to blame for the miserable conditions.

By far, the most infamous Civil War prison was Andersonville. Officially known as Camp Sumter, it was constructed in southwest Georgia near the town of Andersonville to relieve the overcrowded Richmond prison system. A secondary reason was to remove prisoners from the Richmond area before the Union army could liberate them. Andersonville covered about sixteen acres when the first prisoners arrived in February 1864, but it was later enlarged to twenty-six acres when the population swelled to nearly 33,000. Polluted drinking water, poor rations, and unsanitary, overcrowded living conditions led to nightmarish conditions and a high death rate. By war's end, at least 13,000 men died at Andersonville, sometimes at the rate of one hundred per day. After the war, camp commandant Heinrich (Henry) Wirz was convicted of abusing the prisoners and hanged. He was one of the few Civil War soldiers to be executed for his wartime activities.

Numerous Union prisoners left graphic accounts of their stay at Andersonville. One wrote, "The lexicographers of our language have not yet invented the words of proper strength to express condemnation of the studied inhumanities of Andersonville." Inmates lived in lean-tos or in holes in the ground covered with blankets. A small stream sarcastically referred to as "Sweet Water Branch" flowed through the camp and served as a combination garbage dump, latrine, and source of drinking water. Prisoners hated the

Georgia militia who served as guards and accused them of shooting and mistreating inmates for their own amusement. One prisoner wrote, "[W]e are under the Malishia & their ages range from 10 to 75 years & they are the Dambdst set of men I ever have had the Luck to fall in with yet . . . God help the Prisoner when they fall into the hands of the Malishia." Not all of the terror at Andersonville came from the guards, however. A gang of prisoners called the "Raiders" regularly preyed on their weaker comrades to steal food and clothing. The other inmates finally tired of the mayhem, formed their own group called the "Regulators," and seized the thugs. Wirz agreed to hold the Raiders under guard until the prisoners could form a vigilante court. The prisoners convicted the Raiders on numerous charges and hanged six, who were then buried dishonorably in a separate cemetery plot. Eighteen others were forced to run a gauntlet formed by fellow prisoners, and three of them died from the beatings.

> ## DID YOU KNOW?
> ### Libby Prison
> The Civil War's notorious Libby Prison enjoyed a second life as a popular Chicago tourist attraction. A group of investors purchased the building in 1888 for $23,000 and had it dismantled brick by brick and timber by timber, with each piece carefully marked so it could be reconstructed accurately. It required 132 railroad cars to haul the material to Chicago, where it was resurrected as the Great Libby Prison War Museum. The museum drew thousands of tourists and turned a considerable profit before being closed in 1899.

## ESCAPING PRISON

**July 25, 1862: Thirty-five Confederate prisoners escape from Alton Prison**
**November 27, 1863: John Hunt Morgan escapes from Ohio Penitentiary**
**February 9, 1864: 109 Union prisoners escape from Libby Prison**
**June 27, 1864: George Stoneman begins unsuccessful raid to liberate Andersonville**

The length of time spent as a prisoner depended on several factors. Early in the war, many captured soldiers never saw the inside of a prison because they were paroled on the battlefield, and others were held for a short period of time before being exchanged. Unfortunately, some unlucky soldiers went through the system several times by being captured, exchanged, and then captured again. There were Confederate soldiers, in particular, who were captured as many as three times. After the parole and exchange system broke down, most prisoners of war could expect to spend the duration incarcerated. Some refused to accept their fate and freed themselves by taking oaths of allegiance and switching sides or by making daring escapes. Both armies also made several attempts to free prisoners through bold cavalry raids, although none was successful.

# BIOGRAPHY

## Heinrich Hermann (Henry) Wirz: War Criminal or Innocent Victim?

**Henry Wirz's Hanging**

A native of Switzerland, Henry Wirz (1823–1865) hoped to become a physician, but he followed his father's wishes and became a businessman. Although the details are unknown, he served a short prison sentence over some financial dealings before immigrating to the United States in 1849 and settling in Louisiana as a homeopathic physician.

Wirz entered Confederate service in June 1861 as a private in the 4th Louisiana Battalion. After guarding prisoners in Richmond, Virginia, he joined the staff of Brigadier General John H. Winder, who commanded all of the city's prisons. Although Wirz never rose above the rank of captain, he was frequently referred to as "Major" and enforced martial law and supervised the city's prisons. Wirz also claimed to have been wounded in the wrist at the Battle of Seven Pines, but it is more likely he was injured in a stagecoach accident. Whatever the cause, his arm was partially paralyzed and it pained him for the rest of his life.

After serving on a European diplomatic mission, Wirz was put in command of Georgia's Andersonville Prison in February 1864. A German accent, violent temper, and profane manner made it easy for prisoners to hate Wirz and hold him accountable for the prison's horrible conditions and cruel guards. In reality, he was only in charge of the prison's interior and had little control over food, supplies, or personnel. A common accusation against Wirz was that he used vicious dogs to hunt down escapees or turned dogs loose on helpless prisoners. One prisoner claimed he was "a most savage

## The "Galvanized" Prisoners

Taking an oath of allegiance to the enemy was a quick way a prisoner could win his freedom. This policy was first developed by Colonel William Hoffman, who supervised the Union's parole and exchange system. Hoffman realized a number of Confederate prisoners did not want to be exchanged and returned to the war. These men had been coerced into joining the Rebel army, were disillusioned with military life, or simply did not relish the idea of returning to combat. Hoffman took advantage of this discontent by giving Confederate prisoners the opportunity to take an oath of allegiance to the United States and join the Union army. It was a rather shrewd policy because it relieved overcrowded prisons and weakened the Confederacy by siphoning off some of its manpower.

looking man, and who was as brutal as his looks would seem to indicate." Another inmate claimed a one-legged prisoner once asked Wirz to allow him out of the bull pen for fresh air. A guard then blew his head off when Wirz yelled, "Shoot the one-legged Yankee dog!" Wirz was even accused of injecting prisoners with poison while claiming it was smallpox vaccine. Historians, however, find many of the stories about Wirz's cruelty suspect. Most surfaced during his trial, and enough of the charges can be disproved to cast doubt on the more sensational ones.

Wirz was arrested at war's end, and Union officials denied his request to be allowed to take his family to Europe. In a letter to Major General James Wilson, Wirz wrote, "The duties I had to perform were arduous and unpleasant, and I am satisfied that no man can or will justly blame me for things that happened here and which were beyond my power to control. . . . Still I now bear the odium, and men who were prisoners here seem disposed to wreak their vengeance upon me for what they have suffered. . . . My life is in danger, and I most respectfully ask of you help and relief." Instead of receiving help, Wirz was sent to Washington under guard. On the way, some of Andersonville's survivors unsuccessfully tried to kill him.

To Northerners, Wirz came to personify the horror of Rebel prisons. Illustrations in books and magazines even depicted him as a winged demon. Walt Whitman spoke for most Northerners when he declared, "There are deeds, crimes that may be forgiven, but [Andersonville] is not among them." Wirz was tried for murder and the inhumane treatment of prisoners. Given little opportunity to defend himself, he was found guilty despite conflicting testimony and was hanged on November 10 at the Old Capitol Prison. Before the sentence was carried out, Wirz was offered a reprieve if he would sign a document implicating Jefferson Davis in a conspiracy to kill Union prisoners. He refused. A common misconception is that Wirz was the only Civil War soldier executed for war crimes. In fact, Confederate guerrilla Champ Ferguson also was hanged for his role in the Saltville, Virginia, Massacre.

Hoffman preferred recruiting Confederate deserters rather than soldiers captured in battle. The latter were in prison involuntarily, and he assumed they were still loyal to the Confederacy and might take the oath just to get out of prison to seek an opportunity to desert and return to their units. Deserters, on the other hand, had already renounced their allegiance to the Confederacy by running away. Taking the oath and serving in the Union army was a way to restore their loyalty and citizenship, but Hoffman realized the policy was risky and moved cautiously. He insisted on reviewing the case of every prisoner who applied for the oath, and Secretary of War Stanton gave final approval for their release and enrollment in the Union army. About 6,000 Confederate prisoners and deserters accepted the offer and became known as "Galvanized Yankees."

Many Galvanized Yankees were foreign-born soldiers who probably were not committed to the Confederacy in the first place. A case in point were the forty-two prisoners from the 10th Louisiana who took the oath and joined the Union army. That particular regiment was composed of men of twenty-four different nationalities. Most Galvanized Yankees were sent west of the Mississippi River to free up Union soldiers to fight in the Civil War. Among their duties were delivering mail, guarding stage lines, escorting wagon trains, guarding telegraph lines, fighting Indians, and searching for white captives taken by Indians. Some Galvanized Yankees, however, did join in the fight against the Confederates and faced severe punishment if captured by their former comrades. Several of the victims of the Shelton Laurel, North Carolina, massacre (see Chapter 20) were Confederate deserters who had joined the Union army. Not only did the Confederates hate Galvanized Yankees and execute them when captured, most Northern soldiers also viewed them with suspicion and generally treated them poorly. Galvanized Yankees were even refused membership in the postwar veterans' organization Grand Army of the Republic. Despite the discrimination they faced, most Galvanized Yankees proved to be loyal soldiers and served well. While a few deserted their new army, the desertion rate was only slightly higher than that of regular Union soldiers.

The Confederates also had some success in persuading Union prisoners to switch sides. About 500 Andersonville inmates took the Confederate oath of allegiance and joined the Rebel army. Many were members of the notorious Raiders, who, one prisoner claimed, naturally "did that which was wrong in preference to what was right." But most "Galvanized Rebels" probably took the oath just to survive. As one inmate explained, "Before them they saw nothing but weeks of slow and painful progress towards bitter death. The other alternative was enlistment in the Rebel army." Many Galvanized Rebels had no qualms about violating their oaths and deserting at the first opportunity. As one prisoner explained, "No oath administered by a Rebel can have any binding obligation. These men are outlaws who have not only broken their oaths to the Government, but who have deserted from its service, and turned its arms against it. They are perjurers and traitors, and in addition, the oath they administer to us is under compulsion and for that reason is of no account."

Like their Union counterparts, Confederate authorities also discovered many foreign-born men could be persuaded to swap uniforms to escape prison. An astute Louisiana Catholic chaplain first raised the idea when he wrote President Davis, "I understand that there are now in our hands a large number of Irish Catholic prisoner of war, who I think may be induced to enlist in the Confederate Army." The chaplain suggested putting all Catholic prisoners in one location where he and other priests could minister to their religious needs. He believed it would then be possible to convince some of them to join the predominantly Catholic Louisiana regiments. Davis approved the plan, but prison officials found it impractical to move all Catholic prisoners to one location. However, there were hundreds of German- and Irish-born soldiers already held at Salisbury Prison, so officials concentrated their efforts there. Brigadier General Zebulon York and two Catholic priests were sent to Salisbury to recruit the immigrants for a Louisiana Tiger brigade in Virginia. Prison officials set up a separate camp to isolate the Catholic prisoners, and the experiment seems to have been successful. The prisoners appreciated having the priests attend to their religious needs, and many were desperate to leave Salisbury. Records indicate approximately 1,700 Salisbury inmates did join the Confederate army, but it is not clear how many of those served with the Louisiana Tigers. At one point, York reported having about 800 prisoners interested in becoming "galvanized," but one of the priests claimed "few availed themselves of the opportunity."

## Escapes

Escape was constantly on prisoners' minds, and some went to extraordinary lengths to make a break for freedom. Few were more determined than Confederate Colonel Ebenezer Magoffin, brother of Kentucky Governor Beriah Magoffin. Before being sent to Alton Prison, Colonel Magoffin had already made two escapes and killed three men in the process. At Alton, he made his third escape by leading a group of prisoners in tunneling under the wall. On July 25, 1862, Magoffin and thirty-four fellow inmates donned civilian clothing, crawled through the tunnel, and scattered into the night. With the aid of Southern sympathizers, all but two made it back safely to Confederate territory.

Tunneling was, by far, the preferred method of escape. Prisoners usually used such simple digging tools as knives and spoons and placed the dirt in a box that was pulled out of the tunnel with a rope. Other prisoners then put the dirt in their pockets and scattered it while walking around the bull pen. The men were quite ingenious in hiding their tunnel activity. At Elmira, Confederate prisoners secretly made a wooden floor for their tent and then packed dirt on top to conceal it. Using a single knife, fifteen men took turns hiding under the false floor and digging out of the prison. Guards were never the wiser, even when the tent was taken down each day for inspection. At Andersonville, enterprising Union prisoners dug several tunnels, but not all were successful. One sergeant was buried when a tunnel collapsed. Forced to dig himself out, he popped to the surface right next to a guard and was taken into custody and put into stocks as punishment. Four days later, an inmate wrote in his diary, "11 of the Boys left last night & 2 more were going out this morning & they were shot. Poor Boys such is life. Some die one way & some another." Another Andersonville tunneling incident makes an interesting commentary on conditions there. A prisoner noted, "This morning it was ascertained that fourteen of our men had 'tunneled out,' and that seven guards had accompanied them, taking their arms and accoutrements." The single greatest escape by tunnel occurred on February 9, 1864, when 109 Union officers dug their way out of Libby Prison.

John Hunt Morgan, who was captured during an 1863 cavalry raid into Indiana and Ohio, led the Confederates' most famous tunnel escape. He was considered such a desperado that Union officials incarcerated him and a number of his officers in Ohio Penitentiary. Morgan and six of his men immediately began digging a tunnel beneath the floor of their cell. When one guard started making unscheduled inspections, Morgan crumbled up coal

# EYEWITNESS
## Marcus B. Toney

*Marcus B. Toney was twenty years old when he joined the 1st Tennessee Volunteers in 1861. He fought in many western battles and was captured at Perryville but was quickly paroled. Transferring to the 44th Virginia to serve with a cousin, Toney was captured again at Spotsylvania when his regiment was overrun at the famous Mule Shoe. Imprisoned at both Point Lookout and Elmira, he later described his Elmira experiences in his memoir,* The Privations of a Private.

Until I reached prison I did not know what a slave to habit man was. I have seen men go hungry a day and save their rations and trade them for tobacco. I have seen a prisoner discharge a quid of tobacco from his mouth and other one pick it up, dry, and smoke it. . . . We had all kinds of trade and traffics, and tobacco was one of the mediums of exchange. We had many barbers, and they would shave you for five chews of tobacco. When the barber would get more tobacco than he needed, he would sell five chews for a small loaf of bread, valued at five cents, or he could purchase a small piece of meat or a fresh rat, each valued at five cents. . . .

Each man had a plate and spoon, in the plate were his bean soup and beans, by the side of his plate was a small piece of light bread, and on the bread a thin ration of salt pork. . . . A prisoner eating this diet will crave any kind of fresh meat.

Marching through the camp one day was a prisoner in a barrel shirt, with placard, "I eat a dog," another one bearing a barrel with placard "Dog Eater.". . . It appeared that these prisoners had captured a lapdog owned by the baker who came into camp daily to bake the bread. . . . A prisoner carrying a barrel shirt, "I stole my messmate's rations," was hissed all around the camp, and deservedly so, because a man who would steal from his messmates in prison deserved the most severe punishment; while the ones who carried the placard, "Dog Eater," had the sympathies of the entire camp, because many of them would have enjoyed a piece of the fresh meat. When twitted about it, they said: "It was not a common cur, but a Spitz, and tasted like mutton."

On account of the waste from the commissary a great many rodents from Elmira ran into the prison. As there were not any holes in which they could hide, it was an easy catch for the boys by knocking them over with sticks, and there was quite a traffic in them. As there was very little currency in prison, tobacco, rats, pickles, pork, and light bread were mediums of exchange. Five chews of tobacco would buy a rat, a rat would buy five chews of tobacco, a loaf of bread would buy a rat, a rat would buy a loaf of bread, and so on.

*Toney refused to take the oath of allegiance to gain an early release and remained at Elmira until June 1865. After the war, he returned home and survived a steamboat accident by swimming to shore when almost 150 other people were killed. Toney later married and became a leading citizen of Nashville, where he helped found the Masonic Widows and Orphans Home.*

Marcus A. Toney, *The Privations of a Private* (Nashville: Printed for the author, 1905), pp. 96–100.

and scattered it outside the cell so he could warn the diggers when he heard the guard approach. The men dug for twenty-three days and managed to cut through a six-foot thick granite wall. Morgan led the men out on a dark, rainy November night when he knew the guard dogs would be in their kennels. The men broke through to the surface, clambered over the prison's outer wall, and split up into small groups to make their escape. Theirs was the only successful escape from Ohio Penitentiary during the entire nineteenth century.

## Liberation Attempts

Both armies made several attempts to raid prison camps and free the inmates, but none was successful. The first such raid was carried out in early 1864 by Brigadier General H. Judson Kilpatrick, who received permission from Abraham Lincoln to free the Union prisoners held at Richmond's Libby Prison and Belle Isle (see Chapter 20). But it failed miserably and many of the would-be liberators found themselves in the very prisons they sought to open. Another Union prison raid was made during the Atlanta Campaign. When Major General William T. Sherman sent his cavalry to cut the Confederates' supply line south of Atlanta, Major General George Stoneman was given permission to free the prisoners at Macon and Andersonville after the railroad had been cut. Stoneman set out on July 27, 1864, but he immediately disobeyed orders and headed for Andersonville first. Joe Wheeler's Confederate cavalry had little difficulty surrounding Stoneman and capturing the general and seven hundred of his men (Stoneman was later exchanged). The entire scheme was ludicrous because Stoneman never would have been able to escort thousands of sick and ema-ciated prisoners to safety even if his raid had been successful. In April 1865, Stoneman earned the distinction of being the only cavalry raider to destroy an enemy's prisoner of war camp when he burned Salisbury Prison.

The Confederates also made several attempts to free their men from Northern prisons. Three weeks before Stoneman's raid, Major General Jubal A. Early was beginning his raid on Washington, D.C., when he received orders from Robert E. Lee to send a cavalry brigade to free Confederate prisoners at Point Lookout, Maryland. Early sent the brigade, but the cavalry commander called off the mission when he discovered Union authorities had learned of the plan and had strengthened the camp's defenses. Two more attempts were made to free Confederate prisoners later that summer. In August 1864, Union authorities uncovered the Northwest Conspiracy, a plot involving Confederate agents in Canada who planned to liberate prisoners at Camp Douglas. A month later, Confederate agent John Yates Beall led a raid to free prisoners on Johnson's Island. He and his twenty men successfully captured two steamboats on Lake Erie and were outfitting a third when Canadian authorities arrested one of the men. The others feared the plan had been uncovered and backed out when they failed to receive an agreed-on signal from shore to proceed with the attack. Later in the year, Beall made another attempt to free some

Confederate generals who were being transferred to prison by rail. During that mission, he was captured in New York and hanged as a spy.

## PLACING THE BLAME

Virtually all Civil War prisons were horrid places with overcrowded and unsanitary living conditions, and prisoners on both sides suffered from malnutrition, exposure, disease, and mistreatment. Throughout the war the belligerents blamed each other for deliberately creating such conditions to kill prisoners. Union authorities eventually hanged Henry Wirz for intentionally starving and mistreating the inmates at Andersonville, but his guilt is questionable. If he was, indeed, guilty of willful neglect, he certainly was not alone. There were cruel guards and prison officials on both sides who enjoyed mistreating prisoners, and neither government fed their captives adequately.

### Union Blame

When the war began, both the North and South endorsed a policy to feed prisoners the same rations as active soldiers and to allow them to purchase supplemental food from prison sutlers or receive packages from home. Soon, however, Union officials began to violate this agreement to save money and to retaliate against abuses in the Confederate prison system. In July 1862, Colonel William Hoffman ordered prisoners' rations reduced because inmates were more sedentary and did not require as much food as soldiers in the field. This new policy was designed to save the government money because the surplus food could be sold back to the army's commissary department, and the money put into each camp's prison fund to buy necessary goods. Fort Delaware built up a $17,000 prison fund from the money it saved on food, but the commandant refused to buy fresh vegetables even when scurvy wracked many prisoners.

Conditions worsened for Confederate captives when the Northern people learned more about the squalid conditions in Southern prisons and General-in-Chief Henry Halleck authorized retaliatory measures to be taken. By early 1864 Confederate inmates were no longer allowed to buy extra rations from sutlers or receive food packages. Colonel Hoffman cut rations several times that year, particularly after more was learned about conditions at Andersonville. Eventually, the daily ration for a Confederate prisoner was only one-fourth of what it had been in 1862. "My God," remembered one inmate, "it was terrible." Confederate prisoners began eating rats and dogs, and thousands died. Describing a typical meal, a South Carolinian wrote, "For breakfast, half-pint coffee, or, rather, slop water; for dinner; half-pint greasy water (called soup for etiquette), also a small piece of meat, perhaps three or four ounces. For bread we were allowed eight ounces per day; this you could press together in your hand and take at a mouthful. . . . The writer has known large, stout men to lay in their tents at night and cry like little babies from hunger. . . ."

## Confederate Blame

Union prisoners of war were the responsibility of Commissary General Lucius B. Northrup, a hard-bitten man who did not believe in feeding prisoners of war the same as soldiers in the field. As a result, Northrup reduced prisoners' rations despite complaints by his own camp commanders and medical officers. The plight of Union prisoners became desperate in 1864, and prison commandants repeatedly warned government officials that the overcrowded conditions and lack of food were causing a large number of unnecessary deaths—particularly at Andersonville. Instead of addressing their concerns, however, Secretary of War Seddon insisted on sending even more prisoners to Andersonville.

Conventional wisdom has always held that the chronic food shortages inside Confederate prisons were mostly caused by Union armies overrunning Southern agricultural regions and the Confederate railroad system becoming too dilapidated to move supplies to where they were needed. In reality, it was not so much the Confederates' inability to provide food to prisoners as it was their choice to use the available food to feed their own soldiers. Records indicate there was a significant amount of supplies in the South even late in the war. In May 1864, the commissary department managed to send 500,000 rations (one serving for one man) of bread and nearly 1 million rations of meat to Lee's army during the Wilderness Campaign. One week before Lee surrendered at Appomattox, officials still had a couple of million rations of meat and bread stockpiled at various places in Virginia and North Carolina. Of course, these supplies were reserved for the army, and one cannot really blame the Confederates for stockpiling surpluses for future military use. However, if they could gather such a huge amount of food even at war's end, one has to wonder if they could have done more to gather supplies for their starving prisoners. And while it is true the railroads were badly damaged and worn out, trains continued to run until war's end. In the spring of 1864, the Confederates were able to transfer thousands of prisoners from Richmond to Andersonville to remove them from the reach of Grant's advancing armies. Later in the year, thousands of Andersonville prisoners were moved again by rail to Virginia, Georgia, North Carolina, and Alabama to remove them from the reach of Sherman's armies. If the Southern railroads were able to transport thousands of prisoners hundreds of miles, they should have been able to ship more food to the prisons.

For prisoners on both sides, it mattered little if the starvation and mistreatment were deliberate or not. The end result was misery and death. The North and South never agreed on how many men died in captivity, but a good estimate is about 30,000 Union soldiers and 26,000 Confederates, or about one in seven prisoners. As years passed, former Rebels and Yankees were able to forgive each other for most of their Civil War actions. The mistreatment of prisoners, however, was not one of them. The suffering of Union prisoners was an important component of the postwar political tactic known as "waving the bloody shirt" (Republicans blaming the war on Democrats). When an amnesty bill was introduced in 1876 to pardon the former Rebels, one Northern congressman demanded that Jefferson Davis be excluded because of his supposed complicity in the horrid conditions at Andersonville. In turn, a Southern congressman stood up to defend Davis and blamed the inmates' plight on the North's refusal to resume exchanging prisoners.

## The *Sultana* Disaster

As the war drew to a close, hundreds of sick, emaciated, and exhausted former Union prisoners of war were collected at Vicksburg, Mississippi, to be placed aboard steamboats and taken home. The *Sultana* was one of several steamboats contracted by the federal government to take the men north. Since the ships' owners were paid five dollars for each soldier transported, they wedged as many men as possible onto the boats and bribed supervising officers to turn a blind eye. When the *Sultana* left Vicksburg, there were 2,300 men aboard even though it was built to carry just 400 passengers. "Take good care of them," an officer called out from the dock. "They are deserving of it."

The *Sultana* was only two years old, and it had the most modern engines, boilers, and firefighting equipment available. But all was not well. On the trip upriver from New Orleans, the engineer discovered that one of the four boilers was leaking. Unwilling to delay his voyage to repair it properly, the captain ordered the boiler patched at Vicksburg and then shoved off. All went smoothly until the predawn hours of April 27 when the *Sultana*'s boilers exploded seven miles above Memphis, Tennessee. The escaping steam scalded hundreds of men to death, while collapsing smokestacks crushed others. Most of the soldiers who jumped into the chilly Mississippi River to escape the fires drowned. One man on board the burning vessel remembered, "On looking down and out into the river, I would see men jumping from all parts of the boat into the water until it seemed black with men, their heads bobbing up and down like corks, and then disappearing beneath the turbulent waters, never to appear again." A few who survived the explosion, fire, and swift current made it to shore or were plucked out of the water by other ships. A precise death toll was never calculated, but estimates ran as high as 1,700. The sinking of the *Sultana* was the worst maritime accident in American history, eclipsing even the *Titanic* disaster that would occur forty-seven years later. It also was a tragic last chapter in the story of Civil War prisoners of war.

## *FOR FURTHER READING*

Lieber Code
Report of Confederate Chief Surgeon E. J. Eldridge on conditions
   at Andersonville Prison, May 6, 1864

# CHAPTER 20

# The Irregular War

Espionage in the Civil War

Partisans and Guerrillas

Cavalry Raids

The Effectiveness of Irregular Warfare

---

In late winter 1864, Union Brigadier General H. Judson Kilpatrick launched an audacious cavalry raid to liberate Union prisoners from Richmond's Belle Isle and Libby Prison. Twenty-two-year-old Colonel Ulrich Dahlgren commanded one of the columns. Dahlgren was the son of Union Admiral John Dahlgren and a daring officer who earned considerable fame while serving on several generals' staffs. He lost his right leg during the Gettysburg Campaign but was fitted with an artificial limb and returned to duty. Kilpatrick's raid accomplished nothing because stiff enemy defenses and rain-swollen rivers forced him and Dahlgren to retreat after reaching the outskirts of Richmond. Kilpatrick made it back safely to Union lines, but Dahlgren did not. On March 2, 1864, the Confederates ambushed Dahlgren's detachment and killed the colonel and several of his men. The rest took to the woods, but the Confederates used tracking hounds to round up most of them.

After shooting Dahlgren from his horse, the Confederates stripped his body, took his papers, carried off his artificial leg as a trophy, and hacked off a finger to steal his ring. Northern people were outraged when they learned of the abuse, but their protests were cut short when the Rebels revealed the contents of Dahlgren's papers. In a speech to be delivered to his men, Dahlgren had written, "We will cross the James River into Richmond, destroying the bridges after us and exhorting the released prisoners to destroy and burn the hateful city; and do not allow the rebel leader Davis and his traitorous crew to escape. . . . The men must keep together and well in hand and once in the city it must be destroyed and Jeff Davis and cabinet killed."

For the first time in the Civil War, a belligerent government was implicated in an assassination plot. Robert E. Lee called the Kilpatrick-Dahlgren Raid a "Barbarous and inhuman plot." "My own inclinations," he wrote, "are toward the execution of at least a portion of those captured at the time." Lee demanded that General Meade explain Dahlgren's orders, and Meade interrogated Kilpatrick, but he denied any knowledge of the assassination plot. Meade assured Lee that neither he nor Kilpatrick had been aware of Dahlgren's intentions, but privately he thought otherwise. Meade admitted to his wife, "Kilpatrick's reputation, and collateral evidence in my possession, rather go against this theory." Union officials branded the Dahlgren papers forgeries, but the Confederates insisted they were genuine and threatened to execute Dahlgren's men as criminals. Not wishing to engage in an unending war of retribution, however, the Southerners finally accepted Meade's denial and treated the raiders as prisoners of war.

For decades, historians viewed the Dahlgren papers with suspicion because his signature seemed to be misspelled, and it was in a style he did not normally use. Modern tests conducted at the National Archives, however, proved the apparent misspelling was actually caused by ink leaking through the paper—Dahlgren's signature was, indeed, authentic. Nonetheless, no proof has ever been discovered linking Meade, Lincoln, or other high-ranking Union officials to the assassination plot. The Dahlgren incident remains a mystery, but it illustrates a darker side of the Civil War. Cavalry raids were a common tactic to disrupt the enemy's lines of communication and distract the opposing army, but assassinating opposing political leaders was not the American way of waging war. Whether or not Dahlgren was acting under orders may never be known, but the fact that he intended to kill Confederate officials and set fire to Richmond illustrates how vicious the Civil War became. Soldiers on both sides believed they were fighting to defend a sacred way of life and came to accept such irregular warfare as espionage, sabotage, guerrilla raids, arson, and even assassination as acceptable tactics.

## ESPIONAGE IN THE CIVIL WAR

**April 13, 1862: The Great Locomotive Chase begins**
**November 27, 1863: U.S. authorities hang Sam Davis as a Confederate spy**
**November 25, 1864: Confederate agents try to burn New York City**

Spies and saboteurs were active throughout the war and were not limited to any particular race or gender. Because English was the common language and security was often lax, secret agents moved about rather freely and blended into society unnoticed. Respectable white women made successful agents because Victorian customs allowed them considerable freedom of movement and protection from bodily searches. One Southern woman smuggled 50,000 percussion caps across Union lines, and others hid medicine in their clothing and delivered it to Confederate armies. Southern women proved such effective secret agents that Union authorities were forced to hire female detectives to catch them. At least 200 Southern women were tried as spies, and some were hanged.

## Confederate Spies

Because most Civil War spies were anonymous, relatively few have ever been identified. One Confederate agent who gained some notoriety was the mysterious James Harrison (1834–1913), a Maryland actor who sometimes worked with John Wilkes Booth before the war. Harrison enlisted in the Confederate army as a private and became a trusted spy for Lieutenant General James Longstreet. Some of Longstreet's officers had doubts about Harrison's effectiveness, however, because of his fondness for liquor and women. One officer was surprised to see him performing in a play at the same time he was working for the general. Despite these misgivings, Harrison proved his worth when he rode into Longstreet's camp on the night of June 28, 1863, and warned him that Meade's army was moving into Pennsylvania. Jeb Stuart's cavalry was absent on a raid, and this was the first reliable information the Confederates received on the whereabouts of the Union army. Harrison's report allowed General Lee time to concentrate his forces prior to the Battle of Gettysburg. The spy then dropped out of sight until he resumed his acting career after the war.

Belle Boyd (1843–1900) was a better-known Confederate spy. A native Virginian and staunch secessionist, she once killed a Union soldier who broke into her home. Boyd entertained Union officers to gain military information to pass on to the Confederates and in May 1862 provided critical intelligence to Stonewall Jackson as his army approached Front Royal during the Shenandoah Valley Campaign. One Confederate officer remembered being startled to see Boyd running "like mad" down a hill toward them. Taken to Jackson, she told him there was only a small enemy force in town. The officer recalled how Boyd "begged him to push on & he could take them all—& then ran back to the town." Jackson did attack and capture the town and was so impressed with Boyd's bravery that he made her an honorary member of his staff. In 1863, Boyd was captured on a blockade runner, and a Union officer was placed in charge of the vessel. The two fell in love, and the Yankee officer allowed her to continue on to Great Britain. He was dismissed from the army but then proceeded to Great Britain and married Boyd. After the war, Boyd became an actress and published her memoirs.

**Belle Boyd.** Many women engaged in Civil War espionage but few became celebrities like Confederate spy Belle Boyd. During the war she killed one Union soldier and provided critical military intelligence to Stonewall Jackson. After the war, Boyd moved to Great Britain and became an actress.

Rose O'Neal Greenhow (1817?–1864) was another successful Confederate agent. A Maryland native nicknamed "Wild Rose," she was a pretty, charming, and intelligent Washington socialite and the widow of a former State Department employee. Because of her late husband's position, Greenhow was acquainted with numerous Union officials and was able to pick up useful intelligence while visiting them. One of her greatest coups was discovering the Union army's marching orders prior to the First Battle of Bull Run.

Union agent Allan Pinkerton finally discovered Greenhow's spying activities and she and her eight-year-old daughter were put in the Old Capitol Prison. A Union general interrogated her and asked how she communicated with the Confederates. "That is my secret, sir," Greenhow declared, "and, if it be any satisfaction to you to know it, I shall, in the next forty-eight hours, make a report to my government at Richmond of this rather farcical trial for treason." True to her word, Greenhow continued to smuggle out information by using visitors as couriers. After being paroled, she was exiled to enemy territory and arrived in Richmond to a heroine's welcome. Greenhow then traveled to Europe as an unofficial Confederate representative and published a book about her adventures. She returned to the South aboard a blockade runner in October 1864, but a Union warship gave chase and ran it aground in North Carolina. While being transported to shore, Greenhow drowned when the heavy surf foundered the boat. Witnesses claimed she was dragged underwater by the weight of $2,000 in gold she carried.

## Union Spies

Allan Pinkerton (1819–1884) was the best-known of all Civil War espionage agents. He immigrated to the United States from Scotland and became a cooper in Chicago, Illinois. While moonlighting as a detective, Pinkerton broke up a counterfeiting ring and was appointed Cook County's deputy sheriff. In 1850, he organized the Pinkerton National Detective Agency, the nation's first private detective agency. His men were quite skilled and gained considerable fame tracking down and capturing train robbers and counterfeiters. In early 1861, they also uncovered the plot to assassinate president-elect Abraham Lincoln in Baltimore, and Pinkerton helped him slip into Washington unharmed.

When the Civil War began, Pinkerton served under Major General George B. McClellan and established a Secret Service unit to gather military intelligence for the Army of the Potomac. He assumed the code name Major E. J. Allen and used spies, slaves, and other informants to keep McClellan apprised of the Confederates' strength. The system was flawed, however, because the uneducated slaves did not have a good concept of numbers, and Pinkerton's agents sometimes simply counted Confederate flags to estimate the size of the enemy force. Erring on the side of caution, Pinkerton also had the habit of inflating the enemy numbers before forwarding them to McClellan. As a result, his figures often were two or three times larger than the Confederates' actual strength, which made the cautious McClellan even more timid. Pinkerton's military

**Allan Pinkerton.** Allan Pinkerton, head of McClellan's secret service, is seen here in a checkered shirt with some of his agents.

career was tied directly to McClellan, and when the general was relieved of command Pinkerton returned to his Chicago agency.

The Union also found that women made excellent espionage agents. Pauline Cushman (1833–1893), a Louisiana native who grew up in Michigan, was one actress turned spy. While she was performing in a Louisville, Kentucky, play some paroled Confederate prisoners bribed her to make a toast to Jefferson Davis. Cushman accepted the money but informed Union officials before making the toast. This bit of acting convinced the Confederates she was a Southern sympathizer and provided her with the opportunity to travel openly in the South. By 1863, Cushman was performing for Confederate troops in Tennessee while secretly gathering intelligence for the Union. She finally was caught carrying incriminating papers, was convicted of spying, and sentenced to hang. Fortunately, when the Union army made an advance, Cushman's captors retreated and left her behind. Such exploits made her a popular hero in the North, and Lincoln appointed her an honorary major in the Union army. Cushman earned a living giving lectures on her exploits, and she published a much exaggerated account of her life entitled *Life of Pauline Cushman*. After the war, she moved to California and worked as a seamstress before committing suicide by overdosing on opium. Cushman's popularity as a spy was resurrected in the early twentieth century when silent movies were made depicting the "Perils of Pauline."

Elizabeth Van Lew (1818–1900) was one of the most successful Union spies. A New York native, she settled in Richmond, Virginia, and became something of an oddity because she was both an abolitionist and a Unionist. When the war began, Van Lew began to act in an eccentric, even insane, manner to appear harmless to her secessionist neighbors. Richmond residents referred to her as "Crazy Bet" because she dressed in shabby clothes and muttered to herself on the street. They never realized Van Lew and a few accomplices gathered vital intelligence for the Union and helped hide soldiers who escaped from Libby Prison. She also carried supplies to Libby's inmates, but Confederate officials thought little of it because of her eccentric ways. One of her most dramatic exploits was retrieving Colonel Dahlgren's body from its secret grave and reburying it in a safe place. During the Overland Campaign, Van Lew's spy network was so effective she sometimes smuggled flowers from her garden to place on General Grant's table, along with secret information hidden in hollowed-out eggs.

Richmond's residents never realized the extent of Van Lew's activities until Grant visited her house at war's end and provided guards to protect her. "You have sent me," the general admitted, "the most valuable information received from Richmond during the war." The Civil War ruined Van Lew financially, and the people of Richmond forever shunned her as a traitor. "No one will walk with us on the street, no one will go with us anywhere," she wrote in her diary, "and it grows worse and worse as the years roll on." Van Lew, however, always considered herself a true Southerner who had simply remained loyal to the Constitution.

Union authorities also relied heavily on slaves to gather military intelligence because they had an intimate knowledge of the people and terrain, raised no suspicion around enemy camps, and had considerable experience operating in a clandestine manner. Confederate Major General Patrick Cleburne recognized the importance of slaves to the Union secret service and wrote, "It is an omnipresent spy system, pointing out our valuable men to the enemy, revealing our positions, purposes, and resources." One reason Cleburne proposed enlisting slaves into the Confederate army in 1864 was to prevent them from spying for the Union (see Chapter 9).

Runaway slaves proved to be valuable informants and were responsible for some of the Union's most important intelligence coups. Pinkerton, in particular, always trusted information gained from contrabands more than that from Confederate deserters because deserters sometimes were sent into Union lines with false information. Slaves who had been servants for officers, laborers for the Rebel army, or lived near military installations provided particularly useful intelligence. One slave helped confirm the Confederate army's withdrawal from Yorktown during the Peninsula Campaign when he reported enemy wagons were being sent to the rear. Another accurately identified four enemy regiments that were stationed near Manassas and provided information on area gun emplacements, fortifications, roads, bridges, and even the rotation schedule of the Rebels' picket posts. He was able to gather the information because his owner sent him

**Professor Lowe's Balloon.** During the Peninsula Campaign, Professor Thaddeus Lowe used a balloon to spy on the Confederates and gather intelligence. This photograph shows the *Intrepid* being prepared for launch.

throughout the area performing errands. When the Confederates evacuated Manassas in early 1862, General Philip Kearny learned of it first through runaway slaves. General Lee was quite aware of the value of slaves to the Union in gathering intelligence. While planning the Gettysburg Campaign, he worried that the enemy might discover his movement prematurely. "The chief source of information to the enemy is through our Negroes," he wrote.

Unfortunately, few slave informants' names are known today. An exception is Charley Wright, a young man who learned a great deal about the Army of Northern Virginia while he was the servant of a Confederate quartermaster. At the beginning of the Gettysburg Campaign, he made his way into Union lines and accurately reported the units within Lee's army and informed General Hooker that Ewell's Confederate corps was moving into the Shenandoah Valley toward Maryland. If it had not been for Charley Wright, the Union army's pursuit of Lee might have been delayed several days.

Harriet Tubman, who worked in South Carolina for Major General David Hunter, was another successful African American spy. She established a network of black scouts and spies throughout South Carolina, Georgia, and Florida. On one occasion Tubman guided a detachment of black soldiers along the Combahee River on a raid that destroyed bridges and railroads and freed 750 slaves. One Union general reported to Secretary of War Stanton, "This is the only military command in American history wherein a woman, black or white, led the raid and under whose inspiration it was originated and conducted." General Hunter described Tubman as "a valuable woman" and gave her a pass to travel throughout the department on government ships. Despite the high regard in which she was held at the time, Tubman received little pay for her wartime service and was denied a federal pension afterward.

## Counterintelligence Activities

Both governments made considerable efforts to catch enemy spies, but the Union developed the most sophisticated system. The head of the Union counterintelligence efforts was the much-feared Lafayette Curry Baker (1826–1868). Baker was a New York native, but he moved to California before the Civil War and became a member of the Vigilance Committee of San Francisco to bring frontier justice to that crime-ridden city. Having an interest in espionage, he returned east when the war began and volunteered to spy on Confederate forces around Manassas, Virginia. Baker was captured during this mission, but, incredibly, he convinced Confederate authorities he was actually sympathetic to their cause. They sent him back North as a double agent, but Baker remained loyal to the Union and delivered his valuable intelligence to the proper authorities. He performed various intelligence duties over the next two years, and in May 1863 was commissioned colonel of the 1st D.C. Cavalry. This special regiment was organized specifically to gather intelligence and suppress Confederate activity around Washington, and it answered only to Secretary of War Stanton. Stanton trusted Baker and later allowed him to establish the National Detectives to replace Allan Pinkerton's espionage organization. Again answering only to Stanton, Baker's detectives hunted spies, disloyal citizens, counterfeiters, and corrupt contractors. Baker was the most feared man in Washington because of his almost unlimited power of arrest and imprisonment, and he had a reputation for being as corrupt as the criminals he hunted. One official wrote, "Baker became a law unto himself. He instituted a veritable Reign of Terror. He always lived in the first hotels [and] had an abundance of money." President Andrew Johnson finally dismissed him for being corrupt and for conducting secret espionage operations against the White House.

Spies were frequently captured either through the persistent efforts of such counterintelligence agents as Baker or simply through bad luck. Sometimes the evidence against them was quite clear, and sometimes it was questionable. One of the more controversial cases involved Sam Davis (1842–1863), a young Tennessee Confederate soldier who was captured in 1863 and jailed for spying while serving as a courier for a company of scouts. During the interrogation, a Union general offered leniency if Davis revealed the source of his information and the identity of the scouts' leader. If he refused to cooperate, he would be hanged. A Union officer claimed that when Davis was given this opportunity to escape execution, "He stood before me, an uncrowned hero, his eyes flashing, and said: 'I will die a thousand deaths rather than betray my cause.' We were both moved to tears. . . ." Although his captors were impressed with the young man's dedication and bravery, Davis was convicted of spying and hanged. Unknown to the Yankees, they had already captured the commander whose identity Davis so loyally protected. He watched the execution from his own jail cell. Davis's young age and brave demeanor made him a Confederate counterpart of Nathan Hale, the twenty-one-year old American spy in the Revolutionary War who told his British captors, "I only regret that I have but one life to lose for my country." Davis's home in Smyrna, Tennessee, was later turned into a museum.

## Secret Codes

The use of cryptic codes is absolutely necessary in espionage because officials have to be certain the enemy cannot decipher orders sent to field commanders or intelligence reports transmitted by spies. In the Civil War, such reports were sent by telegraph, signal flags, or couriers, and they were frequently intercepted. Telegraphs were particularly vulnerable because enemy agents could simply tap into a line and listen in on messages.

Anson Stager, the former general superintendent of the Western Union Company, developed the Union's secret code. Stager was a skilled telegrapher and served on General McClellan's staff before being promoted to colonel and put in command of the U.S. Military Telegraph Corps. Stager's department controlled the Union's entire telegraph system, and he developed a code based on one used by the Scots to deceive the British. Words were written in English and transmitted by Morse Code, but they were jumbled out of order so the message was nonsensical unless one knew how to arrange them properly. The first word in the message was the key that told the reader how to arrange the words in a predetermined manner. Some words were standard code words for important cities and individuals, and some were nulls, meaningless words designed to confuse any Confederates trying to decipher the message.

The Confederates adopted a variation of the sixteenth-century Vigenére code. This code used a cipher table consisting of a block of twenty-six alphabetized letters across and twenty-seven down. All coding and decoding was based on the key phrase, "Manchester Bluff." Messages were encoded by using the first line of horizontal letters to match the letters in Manchester Bluff and

**Cutting Wires.** Telegraphs were essential for communication during the Civil War, and spies and saboteurs frequently targeted them for destruction. This wartime photograph apparently depicts a spy cutting a telegraph wire.

the first line of vertical letters to match the coded message. For example, if a spy wanted to encode the word "Jackson" he would find the first letter of the key phrase ("M") in the first horizontal line and then the first letter of the encoded word ("J") in the first vertical line. Where these lines intersected gave the first letter of the coded word: "V." By following this formula, the coded word "Jackson" would be spelled "VAPMZSF." When Vicksburg surrendered in 1863, Union intelligence officers examined captured decoded Confederate messages and successfully broke the Vigénere. The Confederates, however, realized the code was broken and simply changed the key phrase. A Vigénere cipher table was found among John Wilkes Booth's possessions after he assassinated Lincoln and in the office of Confederate Secretary of State Judah P. Benjamin after Richmond was evacuated. These discoveries convinced many Union authorities that the Confederate government was involved in the assassination.

## Saboteurs

Saboteurs were active on both sides and frequently burned bridges, destroyed railroads, and cut telegraph wires. Confederate saboteurs were also quite effective in blowing up ships by using such infernal machines as bombs disguised as lumps of coal. Single individuals could easily carry out acts of sabotage and were virtually impossible to stop. If caught, however, they were usually hanged.

James J. Andrews, a rather mysterious Union agent from Kentucky, led one of the first sabotage missions. Andrews and a band of twenty-one disguised soldiers sneaked into northern Georgia and boarded a train in Marietta on the night of April 12, 1862. When the passengers and crew debarked for breakfast, the Yankees brazenly stole the locomotive, "The General," and several cars. Andrews's plan was to head for Chattanooga, Tennessee, and burn railroad bridges along the way. Unfortunately, he did not foresee the train's conductor and a shop foreman setting out in a relentless pursuit. First on foot, then by handcar, the tenacious Southerners followed Andrews down the track until they finally commandeered the locomotive "Texas" and began a 90-mile pursuit that became known as "The Great Locomotive Chase." Just eighteen miles shy of Chattanooga and safety, "The General" literally ran out of steam, and Andrews' men bolted for cover. They had failed to destroy a single bridge because of the enemy's dogged pursuit, and recent rains had soaked the bridge timbers. Soon captured, Andrews and seven of his men were convicted of spying and hanged in June; the others were imprisoned, but seven later escaped. The remaining raiders were paroled and eventually released. Some of Andrews's men became the first soldiers ever awarded the Medal of Honor.

One of the most ambitious sabotage raids of the war occurred in 1864 when Confederate agents tried to burn down several hotels in New York City in retaliation for the Union armies' destruction in Georgia and the Shenandoah Valley. Colonel Robert M. Martin and seven men slipped into the city on the night of November 25 and checked into various hotels with 402 bottles of combustible material hidden in their luggage. Later that night, they set fire to the buildings, but the flames did not spread as expected, and all were quickly extinguished. Although P. T. Barnum's Museum suffered considerable damage, the hotels survived intact. One man was captured and executed, but Martin and the others escaped safely.

The Confederates even resorted to biological warfare in their sabotage campaign. In Georgia and Mississippi, Union officers accused retreating Confederates of killing animals and dumping their bodies into ponds to pollute the water so Union soldiers could not drink it. One Confederate physician, Dr. Luke Blackburn, also tried to spread panic when he shipped trunkloads of clothing and linen to the North that were infected with yellow fever. Nothing happened because yellow fever is only spread by mosquitoes, but Blackburn did not know that at the time. Ironically, Blackburn spent much of his life after the war trying to eradicate yellow fever. He also was elected the governor of Kentucky.

## PARTISANS AND GUERRILLAS

September 22, 1861: Lane's Jayhawkers raid Osceola, Missouri
August 21, 1863: Quantrill raids Lawrence, Kansas
August 25, 1863: Ewing issues General Orders No. 11
October 13, 1864: Mosby makes the Greenback Raid
September 27, 1864: "Bloody Bill" Anderson raids Centralia, Missouri

Guerrilla warfare is waged by irregular forces that operate in small, independent groups and use speed and surprise to harass the enemy. To be successful, guerrillas must have the support of the local people to provide them with food, shelter, and intelligence. This type of warfare is an effective way for a small force to tie down large numbers of enemy troops and weaken the enemy's morale by inflicting significant casualties. Guerrillas also hamper major military operations by disrupting lines of communication and threatening rear staging areas. In the Civil War, the Confederates resorted to guerrilla warfare more frequently than the Union because the enemy occupied so much Southern soil.

Recognizing the usefulness of guerrilla warfare, the Confederate Congress passed the Partisan Ranger Act in April 1862. Unlike other guerrillas, partisan

# NOTABLE UNIT: *Mosby's Rangers*

After gaining great renown as a scout for Jeb Stuart's cavalry, John S. Mosby (1833–1916) raised a partisan ranger unit in late 1862. In March 1863, he slipped into Fairfax Court House with twenty-eight men and captured Union Brigadier General Edwin H. Stoughton, a Vermont officer who had a reputation for enjoying drink, women, and a comfortable headquarters' life. When Mosby entered his room, Stoughton awoke and shouted, "What is this! Do you know who I am, sir?" "I reckon I do, General. Did you ever hear of Mosby?" Thinking the man before him was a Union officer, Stoughton asked excitedly, "Yes, have you caught him?" "No," replied Mosby, "but he has caught you." Recruits flocked to Mosby after this raid, and he soon had enough men to form an army battalion. Officially named the 43rd Virginia Cavalry Battalion (another battalion was added later), the partisans were usually referred to as Mosby's Rangers. Approximately 1,900 men served in Mosby's command, but there never were more than about 800 at any one time, and they usually split up into small bands.

Mosby's Rangers were based in Fauquier and Loudoun counties, which became known as "Mosby's Confederacy," but they operated as far away as the Shenandoah Valley and Maryland. Protected and fed by local civilians and hiding out in woodlots, they seemingly appeared out of nowhere to attack Union outposts, railroads, and wagon trains. The rangers harassed Union commanders, tied down thousands of enemy troops, and provided Robert E. Lee with valuable intelligence. Lee, in fact, commended Mosby more times than any other officer. Although a small, thin man, Mosby was

rangers were official members of the army who wore regulation uniforms. They were committed to the Confederate cause and wanted to serve in the military but preferred staying close to home, and they liked the lax discipline usually found in ranger units as opposed to the regular army's strict discipline. Because they were enrolled in the army, partisan rangers were supposed to be treated as prisoners of war if captured, although many were executed anyhow. Some West Point–trained officers condemned the partisans for being too independent and lax in discipline, and the Confederate Congress finally repealed the Partisan Ranger Act, with the stipulation that the secretary of war could authorize partisan units on a case-by-case basis.

## The Virginia Rangers

Some of the most successful Confederate partisans operated in Virginia. John Hanson "Hanse" McNeill (1815–1864) was a Virginia native who led McNeill's Rangers, whom General Philip Sheridan declared were "the most daring and dangerous" of all the partisans. McNeill's company was so effective raiding the Baltimore & Ohio Railroad and harassing Union troops that federal authorities briefly imprisoned his wife and two children to intimidate him. In October 1864, McNeill was accidentally shot and wounded by one of his own men during a raid. He was left behind and captured, but the rangers rescued him shortly absolutely fearless and was wounded three times on his daring exploits. In the 1864 Greenback Raid, he burned a train on the Baltimore & Ohio Railroad near Harpers Ferry, West Virginia, but not before relieving two Union paymasters of $178,000 in greenbacks (Mosby divided the money with his men). Such bold raids infuriated Union commanders, and they waged a brutal war of retaliation. Grant ordered all supplies in Loudoun County destroyed, stating that Mosby and his men would be executed without trial if captured (Grant also considered imprisoning their families but decided against it). When Brigadier General George Armstrong Custer hanged six captured rangers, Mosby retaliated by hanging seven of Custer's men. The Yankees hated Mosby, who became known as the "Gray Ghost," but they begrudgingly recognized his skill. One Union officer declared, "[A] more harassing enemy could not well be imagined," and another wrote of the Rangers, "They were a most dangerous element, and caused perhaps more loss than any single body of men in the enemy's service."

Mosby's Rangers never officially surrendered at war's end. When Mosby learned of the surrenders, he quietly disbanded his men and sent them home. When some suggested continuing the fight, Mosby replied, "Too late! It would be murder and highway robbery now. We are soldiers, not highwaymen." More than one-third of the rangers were killed or wounded during the war, and nearly 500 were captured. After the war, Mosby lost some of his popularity in the South when he supported Grant for president. Grant, in turn, appointed him the American consul to Hong Kong.

before he died. McNeill's son, Jesse, then assumed command and led the company on its most famous exploit. In February 1865, sixty rangers slipped into Cumberland, Maryland, past 10,000 Union soldiers and captured Generals George Crook and Benjamin F. Kelley in a hotel.

As impressive as their exploits were, McNeill's Rangers were overshadowed by fellow Virginia Colonel John S. Mosby, who led a partisan band known as Mosby's Rangers. Union authorities eventually formed partisan units to counter Mosby. Led by Captain Richard Blazer, Blazer's Scouts were armed with repeating Spencer rifles and enjoyed some initial success. Mosby, however, finally lured Blazer into battle, wiped out his rangers, and replaced his men's muzzle-loading rifles with the highly prized Spencers. The Loudoun Rangers was another Union partisan unit organized to fight Mosby. They frequently clashed with the Confederates but were almost always beaten. In April 1865, the Loudoun Rangers ceased to exist when Mosby's partisans captured virtually every man during a raid on their camp.

## The Missouri Guerrillas

While partisan rangers were regular Confederate soldiers, other guerrilla units were composed of civilians who independently conducted war against the enemy. Labeled bushwhackers by Union soldiers, they were not officially affiliated with the Confederate army and generally were hanged as common criminals if captured. These guerrillas were often motivated by personal revenge against Union soldiers or sympathizers who had committed acts of violence against them or their families, or they were seeking opportunities to rob and loot under the guise of fighting the enemy. Such guerrillas were particularly active in Missouri, where much of the fighting was the result of vendettas carried over from the days of Bleeding Kansas. The Union formed regular army units to counter these guerrillas, but they were often just as brutal in their treatment of Southern sympathizers.

Missouri's population was badly split between secessionists and Unionists, and their infighting gave rise to many guerrilla units. Some, like those led by M. Jeff Thompson, fought in a civilized manner, but most waged a violent war of revenge and retribution. Of these, none was more notorious than William Clarke Quantrill (1837–1865). An Ohio native who taught school before settling in Kansas, Quantrill became a gambler and bandit and was active with the proslavery "border ruffians" in Bleeding Kansas. He enlisted in the Confederate army and fought at the Battle of Wilson's Creek before being commissioned a captain. Quantrill was not assigned to any particular regiment, so he organized a personal band of guerrillas that terrorized both Missouri and Kansas. Included among his men were such notorious figures as Bloody Bill Anderson and future western outlaws the Younger brothers and Frank and Jesse James. Quantrill's tactics were ruthless and shocked even Confederate authorities. When he murdered twelve teamsters after capturing their wagon train, officials refused his request to raise a unit under the Partisan Ranger Act. Inexplicably, they did promote him to colonel.

On August 21, 1863, Quantrill carried out one of the most brutal massacres of the war when his men raided Lawrence, Kansas, a town noted for its abolitionism. The raid supposedly was in retaliation for the collapse of a Union prison in Kansas City, Missouri, that killed several women who were related to members of Quantrill's band. In three hours of murder, robbery, and mayhem, the raiders killed 150 men and boys and burned much of the town. Quantrill lost only one man. A Lawrence minister wrote of the aftermath, "The dead lay along the street, some of them so charred that they could not be recognized, and could scarcely be taken up. . . . As [I] passed along the street, the sickening odor of burning flesh was oppressive." After the Lawrence Raid, Quantrill's band broke up because of internal bickering. He then raised another, smaller, unit and headed to Kentucky, but Union troops cornered him and shot him. Paralyzed, Quantrill died in Union captivity on June 6, 1865, shortly after a deathbed conversion to Catholicism.

Quantrill may have been the most famous Missouri guerrilla, but William "Bloody Bill" Anderson (1840–1864) was more vicious. He rode with Quantrill and habitually took the scalps of his victims and tied them to his horse's bridle. Anderson once explained, "I have chosen guerrilla warfare to revenge myself for wrongs that I could not honorably revenge otherwise. . . . [T]he Yankees sought my life, but failed to get me. Revenged themselves by murdering my father, destroying all my property, and since that time murdered one of my

**Quantrill's Victims.** This photograph shows the members of Union General James G. Blunt's headquarters band. Several weeks after the Lawrence, Kansas, raid, Quantrill's guerrillas attacked Blunt at Baxter Springs, Kansas, and massacred many of his men. Every band member in this photograph was killed.

sisters and kept the other two in jail twelve months." Anderson's sisters were among those imprisoned in the Kansas City jail that collapsed. One was killed, and the other was severely injured.

Quantrill and Anderson parted ways after the Lawrence Raid when Quantrill had one of Anderson's men shot for killing a civilian. Anderson formed his own guerrilla band and on the morning of September 27, 1864, raided Centralia, Missouri, and looted and robbed the town for several hours. When a train pulled into the station, the guerrillas surrounded it and took off twenty-five unarmed Union soldiers. They stripped the soldiers of their uniforms, robbed the train's passengers, and murdered two men who tried to hide their valuables. Bloody Bill then burned the train and ordered the soldiers to line up. When he asked if any were officers or noncommissioned officers, Sergeant Thomas Goodman bravely stepped forward. Surprisingly, Anderson released him in apparent respect for his bravery and then killed the other twenty-four.

That afternoon, the 39th Missouri Infantry arrived in Centralia. Despite warnings from citizens, the commander rashly divided his unit by leaving part of the regiment in town and taking the rest to pursue Anderson. The inexperienced officer rode into an ambush and was killed, along with most of his men. The guerrillas then went back to Centralia and killed nearly all the soldiers there. In little more than an hour, the 39th Missouri lost 124 men, all but 8 of whom were killed. One witness claimed the men were "shot through the head, then scalped, bayonets thrust through them, ears and noses cut off." A month later, Bloody Bill Anderson's rampage ended when he was killed in a clash near Richmond, Missouri. Union soldiers propped up his body in a chair to take a photograph and then tied it to a horse and dragged it through the streets before hacking off the head and impaling it on a nearby telegraph pole.

These bloody raids caused Union officers to take more draconian measures against the guerrillas and their supporters. Brigadier General Thomas Ewing, Jr.

**Bloody Bill Anderson.** No Missouri guerrilla was feared as much as William "Bloody Bill" Anderson. When he was killed in 1864, his body was posed for this photograph. Afterward, Union soldiers tied it to a horse and dragged it through the streets before hacking off the head and impaling it on a nearby telegraph pole.

(1829–1896), a well-connected officer, was particularly harsh. Ewing had two brothers who also served as Union generals, and Major General William T. Sherman was his brother-in-law. It was Ewing who jailed the guerrillas' female relatives in Kansas City to use as hostages, leading to their deaths and Quantrill's subsequent attack on Lawrence, Kansas. In retaliation for that raid, Ewing issued General Orders No. 11. Convinced most of the people in southwest Missouri supported the guerrillas, he ordered the forced exile of nearly all the civilians living in four western counties. Anyone who violated the order was to be executed.

Colonel Charles R. Jennison's Union cavalry, known as Jennison's Jayhawkers and as "Redlegs" because they wore distinctive red leggings, carried out Ewing's order. Jennison also considered most Missouri civilians to be secessionist sympathizers and ordered them to be "treated as traitors and slain" if they refused to give up their arms and property. Despite his ruthless ways, Jennison was popular in the North because his tactics were seen as effective in battling the equally brutal guerrillas. With great enthusiasm, Jennison not only removed the people from the four counties, he also burned most of their homes, barns, and crops. Even the 1864 burning of the Shenandoah Valley paled in comparison. Ewing's order was unprecedented in the Civil War, and the brutality shocked many Northerners. A Union officer wrote his wife, "It is heartsickening to see what I have seen. . . . A desolated country and men & women and children, some of them all most [sic] naked. Some on foot and some in old wagons. Oh God." The population of Cass County dropped from 10,000 to 600, and many people reportedly died of starvation and exposure on the exodus from what was called the "Burnt District."

Brigadier James Henry Lane (1814–1866) was another Union officer who engaged the Missouri guerrillas. This Indiana native and Mexican War veteran was a popular Democrat who served as lieutenant governor and congressman before moving to Bleeding Kansas. There he became a leader of the antislavery forces and personally carried the free-state constitution to Washington, where he unsuccessfully challenged Stephen A. Douglas to a duel when the Senate rejected it. Returning to Kansas, Lane worked with John Brown, and was elected to the U.S. Senate as a Republican in 1861. He quickly gained the trust and admiration of President Lincoln, who recognized Lane as the de facto leader of Kansas. Returning home, Lane organized a 1,500-man Kansas brigade, also known as Jayhawkers, that plundered farms, killed innocent civilians, and freed slaves in nearby Missouri. On September 22, 1861, Lane's Jayhawkers destroyed the secessionist town of Osceola, Missouri. Nine men were murdered and the town was stripped of horses, cattle, and other valuables to be carted back to Kansas. The Confederates retaliated by burning Lane's house, and he only escaped being murdered in the raid on Lawrence, Kansas, by hiding out until the guerrillas departed.

# CAVALRY RAIDS

**October 10, 1862: Stuart begins his Chambersburg Raid**
**July 2, 1863: Morgan begins his Ohio Raid**
**July 26, 1863: Union troops capture Morgan in Ohio**
**October 2, 1864: Saltville Massacre**
**November 4, 1864: Forrest raids Johnsonville, Tennessee**
**April 2, 1865: Wilson captures Selma, Alabama**

Cavalry in the Civil War carried out reconnaissance missions to locate the enemy, guarded an army's flanks against surprise attack, and raided behind the lines to destroy supplies and distract enemy commanders from more important movements on the front. Such raids gained considerable attention because they usually surprised the enemy with their audacity and created fear in areas that were normally safe from attack. Two classic cavalry raids occurred during the Vicksburg Campaign. In late 1862, Confederate troopers under Earl Van Dorn destroyed Grant's supply base at Holly Springs, Mississippi, and forced him to retreat. A few months later, Union Colonel Benjamin Grierson raided central Mississippi to draw the Confederates' attention away from Grant's maneuvers along the Mississippi River.

## Rebel Raiders

Confederate cavalry launched more raids than the Union and were more successful early in the war. This was because the long Union supply lines were more vulnerable to attack and the rural Southerners were better horsemen than their Yankee counterparts. Western Confederate raiders included such figures as Major Generals Joseph "Fighting Joe" Wheeler (1836–1906) and Sterling Price (1809–1867). Wheeler destroyed railroads and supplies and captured hundreds of prisoners in raids during the Stones River and Chattanooga Campaigns. In 1864, Price covered 1,500 miles and traversed Arkansas, Missouri, Kansas, Indian Territory, and Texas in what proved to be the war's longest cavalry raid. Neither, however, instilled the same fear among Northerners as did John Hunt Morgan and Nathan Bedford Forrest.

John Hunt Morgan (1825–1864) was a Kentucky militia officer who became a Confederate brigadier general and cavalry commander. He made several raids

# EYEWITNESS
## Gurdon Grovenor

*Gurdon Grovenor (1830–1914) was a successful businessman and community leader in Lawrence, Kansas. Early on the hot, dusty morning of August 21, 1863, he was startled awake by the sound of galloping horses and shouts coming from the street. When Grovenor looked out the window he was shocked to see William C. Quantrill's guerrillas attacking the town. Good fortune saved him from death that day, and he later wrote an account of the devastating attack.*

Just on the north of our house, a half a block away and in full view was a camp of recruits twenty-two in all, not yet mustered into service and unarmed. They were awakened by the noise, got up and started to run but were all shot down but five. I saw this wholesale shooting from my window, and it was a sight to strike terror to a stouter heart than mine. But we had not long to wait before our time came. Three of the guerrillas came to the house, stepped up on the front porch, and with the butt of a musket smashed in one of the front windows; my wife opened the door and let them in. They ransacked the house, talked and swore and threatened a good deal, but offered no violence. They set the house on fire above and below, took such things as they fancied, and left. After they had gone I put the fire out below, but above it had got too strong a hold, and I could not put it out.

Not long after a single man rode up to the front gate; he was a villainous looking fellow, and was doubly villainous from too much whiskey. He saw me standing back in the hall of the house, and with a terrible oath he ordered me to come out. I stepped out on the piazza, and he leveled his pistol at me and said: "Are you union or secesh?" It was my time of trial; my wife with her little one in her arms, and our little boy clinging to her side, was standing just a little ways from me. My life seemingly hung on my answer, my position may be imagined but it cannot be described. The thought ran through me like an electric shock, that I could not say that I was a secessionist, and deny my loyalty to my country; that I would rather die than to live and face that disgrace; and so I answered that I was a union man. He snapped his pistol but it

into Kentucky in 1862 that captured hundreds of prisoners and destroyed valuable enemy supplies. The most famous of these was the Christmas Raid, in which he destroyed Union railroads and supply bases and captured 2,000 prisoners while losing just 26 men. Morgan's successes made him overconfident, however, and led to disaster in July 1863. That summer General Braxton Bragg was forced out of Middle Tennessee in the Tullahoma Campaign, and he ordered Morgan to raid behind Union lines to slow the enemy's advance toward Chattanooga. Morgan suggested pushing across the Ohio River in the belief that it would strengthen the Northern peace movement, but Bragg rejected his plan and authorized a raid only into Kentucky.

failed to fire. I stepped back into the house and he rode around to the north door and met me there, and snapped his pistol at me again, and this time it failed. Was there a providence in this? Just then a party of a half dozen of the raiders came riding towards the house from the north, and seeing my enemy, hallooed to him "Don't' shoot that man." They rode up to the gate and told me to come there; I did so and my would-be murderer came up to me and placed the muzzle of his revolver in my ear. It was not a pleasant place to be in, but the leader of the new crowd told him not to shoot, but to let me alone until he could inquire about me, so he asked me if I had ever been down in Missouri stealing niggers or horses; I told him "No that I never had been in Missouri, except to cross the state going and coming from the east." This seemed to be satisfactory so he told my old enemy to let me alone and not to kill me. This seemed to make him very angry, and he cursed me terribly, but I ventured to put my hand up and push away his revolver. The leader of the party then told me if I did not expect to get killed, I must get out of sight, that they were all getting drunk, and would kill everybody they saw; I told him that that was what I had wanted to do all the morning, but I could not; "Well," he says, "you must hide or get killed." And they all rode away. . . . Such was my experience during those four or five terrible hours. Our home and its contents was in ashes, but so thankful were we that my life was spared that we thought but little of our pecuniary loss. After the raiders had left and the people could get out on the street, a most desolate and sickening sight met their view. The whole business part of the town, except two stores, was in ashes. The bodies of dead men, some of them partly burned away, were laying in all directions. A large number of dwellings were burned to the ground, and the moaning of the grief stricken people was heard from all sides.

*Grovenor was elected mayor of Lawrence twice after the raid and remarried when his wife died. He also joined the Baptist Church, became a deacon, and was active in the state's Baptist organization. Grovenor died in 1914, and his will bequeathed $4,000 each to the Lawrence Public Library and the First Baptist Church.*

William Elsey Connelly, *Quantrill and the Border Wars* (Cedar Rapids: Torch Press, 1910), pp. 363–365.

With 2,500 men, Morgan disobeyed Bragg's orders and crossed the Ohio River on July 2. Sweeping through Indiana, he destroyed supplies, plundered the countryside, and captured and paroled Union prisoners, but the raid did not strengthen the Northern peace movement as he predicted. Instead, it galvanized the people in resisting the Confederates. Soon, both men and mounts began dropping from exhaustion, and Morgan's strength dwindled. Crossing into Ohio, he galloped through the suburbs of Cincinnati and set a Civil War record by riding ninety miles in thirty-five hours. By then Union authorities were closing in on the raiders and placed troops to intercept Morgan if he tried to cross back over the Ohio River. On July 19, Morgan attempted to fight his way across the river at Buffington Island, but the Yankees badly mauled his command and captured most of the men. With a small band of survivors, he continued east toward Pennsylvania with the enemy in hot pursuit, but Union forces finally caught up with Morgan at Salineville, Ohio, and forced his surrender after a sharp fight.

Morgan's Ohio Raid covered 700 miles and spread panic throughout Indiana and Ohio. He captured and paroled 6,000 prisoners, tied down approximately 135,000 Union soldiers, destroyed 34 bridges and a large amount of supplies, and cut railroads at more than 60 places. Yet the raid had no effect on the war's outcome because the enemy quickly repaired the damage. Nonetheless, Union officials considered Morgan such a threat that they put him and several officers in the Ohio Penitentiary as common criminals, but they made a daring escape several months later. Morgan then launched another unauthorized raid into Kentucky that was marked by even more looting because Brigadier General Basil Duke, Morgan's brother-in-law and disciplinarian, remained in prison. By that time, many people recognized Duke as the real genius behind Morgan's raids, and one newspaper editor even predicted, "Someone might hit Duke on the head and knock Morgan's brains out." On September 3, Morgan's career came to an abrupt end when Union troops surprised and killed him at Greeneville, Tennessee.

No Confederate cavalryman was more feared than Nathan Bedford Forrest. His first raid in July 1862 gave an indication of his shrewdness. While attacking Union outposts around McMinnville, Tennessee, Forrest resorted to trickery to persuade the enemy to surrender. He enticed one outpost commander to lay down his arms by threatening to take no prisoners if he was forced to attack. At another, Forrest convinced an officer to surrender by allowing him to view his cavalrymen, who were riding in circles through a clearing to give the appearance of a much larger force. In December 1862, Forrest led another successful raid into Tennessee to disrupt General Grant's railroad supply line as he advanced overland toward Vicksburg. Union cavalry pursued and there was heavy fighting around Lexington, but Forrest won the battle. He then moved into Kentucky, destroying railroads as he went. By then, 10,000 Union soldiers were closing in on the raiders, and gunboats patrolled the Tennessee River. When he became trapped on New Year's Eve by enemy forces to the front and rear, Forrest ordered his men to "charge them both ways" and escaped across the Tennessee River.

Forrest's most successful raid was against the Tennessee River port of Johnsonville, Tennessee, in the autumn of 1864. After making his way to the river undetected, he set up his cannons and captured two Union vessels after a short artillery duel. Moving downstream, Forrest again quietly placed his artillery and opened fire on the unsuspecting enemy on the morning of November 4. The Union commander was so unnerved that he ordered three gunboats and seven transports run aground and burned to keep them out of enemy hands. Forrest continued firing into numerous ships and completely wrecked the docks before withdrawing. The Johnsonville Raid secured Forrest's reputation as the Confederacy's premier cavalryman. The Yankees suffered few casualties but lost 4 gunboats, 14 transports, 20 barges, and millions of dollars in supplies. It was this raid that prompted William T. Sherman to brand the Confederate raider "that devil Forrest."

In the east, successful Confederate raiders included John D. Imboden, William E. "Grumble" Jones, and Thomas Lafayette Rosser, but Jeb Stuart was the undisputed champion. Stuart rode roughshod over the enemy throughout Virginia and Maryland in the first half of the war. His thigh-high boots, ostrich-plumed hat, and brave, charismatic personality made him the epitome of the romantic cavalier. Stuart's skill as a raider was proven in the spring of 1862 when he rode completely around the Union army on the Peninsula and brought Lee critical intelligence that allowed him to plan the Seven Days Campaign.

In August 1862, Union cavalry surprised and nearly captured Stuart, and he lost his plumed hat, sash, and gloves. To get revenge, he raided Catlett's Station, an important supply base in the rear of General John Pope's army. In a driving rainstorm Stuart's troopers routed the Union soldiers and seized several officers, more than $500,000 in cash, and much of Pope's official papers and personal possessions. Stuart later put Pope's uniform on display in a Richmond shop window. Two months later, he raided Chambersburg, Pennsylvania, and rode around McClellan's army for the second time. Lincoln relieved McClellan of army command a few weeks later. Stuart added insult to injury in late December when he attacked two Union supply bases in Virginia and captured prisoners and draft animals within twelve miles of Washington. Afterward, he playfully wired Union Quartermaster General Montgomery C. Meigs to complain about the poor-quality mules the Union army was supplying its men.

## Yankee Raiders

Union cavalry raiders never received the same attention as the Confederates because they were not as successful until late in the war. Also, much of the Union raiding activity was part of larger military campaigns and not the rapid hit-and-run tactics the Confederates used so successfully. For example, Philip Sheridan's raid in the Overland Campaign was to draw the enemy's cavalry into battle and not simply to destroy lines of communication. Franz Sigel's and David Hunter's Shenandoah Valley raids involved mostly infantry units and were ponderous affairs that targeted large areas rather than a specific point.

With Grierson's Raid the exception, most Union cavalry raids were not very successful until late in the war when the Confederates were weak. George Stoneman launched raids in the Chancellorsville and Atlanta campaigns, but both failed and he was captured in the latter. In October 1864, Brigadier General Stephen G. Burbridge made another disastrous raid into southwestern Virginia against the salt works at Saltville. A small but determined force of Confederates defeated him, and Burbridge abandoned his wounded

# BIOGRAPHY

## Nathan Bedford Forrest: "That Devil Forrest"

**Nathan Bedford Forrest**

Nathan Bedford Forrest (1821–1877) was born in Tennessee, but his impoverished family moved to northern Mississippi when he was thirteen, and he assumed responsibility for his family when his father died three years later. After marrying, he settled in Memphis, Tennessee, where he became a city alderman and a wealthy trader in slaves, cotton, and land before moving back to Mississippi to become a planter.

Forrest entered Confederate service as a Tennessee private, but he soon raised a cavalry battalion at his own expense. Promotions came regularly as he and his "critter cavalry" proved their worth fighting Yankees. Forrest fought skillfully in most of the Army of Tennessee's campaigns, made raids behind enemy lines, captured Abel Streight's Union raiders, and defeated the enemy on numerous occasions. His most controversial battle was at Fort Pillow, Tennessee, in April 1864, where many of the fort's black soldiers were massacred. Forrest was accused of ordering the killings, but his defenders claimed the murders were just the result of individual acts of brutality.

A large man at six feet, two inches in height, Forrest had a violent temper and little patience with the lazy, timid, or incompetent. He once whacked a young lieutenant in the face with a pole because the officer refused to help push a boat across a stream. "Now, damn you," Forrest screamed, "get hold of the oars and go to work! If I knock you out of the boat again I'll let you drown." On another occasion, he saw one of his soldiers running away in battle. One general claimed Forrest ripped a branch off a nearby tree, grabbed the man, and gave him "one of the worst thrashings I have ever seen a human being get."

and retreated. Confederate guerrilla Champ Ferguson murdered some of those unfortunate men. At the time it was claimed more than one hundred members of the 5th U.S. Colored Infantry were executed, but the number was probably closer to a dozen. Major General John C. Breckinridge arrested Ferguson for the "Saltville Massacre," but he was never punished. After the war, however, federal authorities hanged him for murdering a number of people, including the black soldiers at Saltville.

Brigadier General Lovell Harrison Rousseau (1818–1869) did make one successful raid in July 1864 when he attacked Alabama during the Atlanta Campaign. Rousseau covered 400 miles, captured prisoners, and destroyed Confederate supplies and the Montgomery & West Point Railroad and lost just forty-two men. But it was not until the war was almost over that the Union cavalry began to have steady successes. After being exchanged, General Stoneman made a second raid against Saltville in December 1864. He left Knoxville,

Extremely self-confident, Forrest disliked serving under others and clashed with nearly all of his superiors. He once exchanged harsh words with Joseph Wheeler, drew his sword against Earl Van Dorn, and threatened Braxton Bragg after he turned Forrest's cavalry over to Wheeler. Forrest burst into Bragg's tent without saluting and brushed aside his outstretched hand. "You have played the part of a damned scoundrel, and are a coward," Forrest snarled, "and if you were any part of a man I would slap your jaws and force you to resent it. . . . [I]f you ever again try to interfere with me or cross my path it will be at the peril of your life."

Forrest truly loved to fight. His philosophy of warfare was simple and best summed up in his famous advice to "get there fustest with the mostest." Forrest was wounded four times in battle and was even shot by one of his own officers in a personal altercation. Lieutenant General Richard Taylor doubted whether "any commander since the days of lion-hearted Richard has killed as many enemies with his own hand as Forrest." When asked how many Yankees he killed in hand-to-hand combat, Forrest declared he had slain one more than the twenty-nine horses killed under him.

After the war, Forrest returned to his Mississippi plantation and in 1867 was elected Grand Wizard of the Ku Klux Klan. He then returned to Memphis and worked in insurance and railroading until his death. Forrest was a violent man who had little regard for African Americans or his own men whom he thought were ineffective soldiers. Nonetheless, he was one of the most remarkable generals of the war and rose from private to lieutenant general. William T. Sherman called him "that devil Forrest" and ordered his men to "go out and follow Forrest to the death if it costs 10,000 lives and breaks the Treasury." When Robert E. Lee was asked whom he thought was the war's greatest soldier, he replied, "A man I have never seen, sir. His name is Forrest."

Tennessee, in bitterly cold, wet weather and rode toward Virginia, destroying the railroad as he went. Brushing aside the few Confederate defenders, Stoneman advanced on Wytheville, Virginia, where General Breckinridge was assembling a small force to defend the mines. Stoneman captured Wytheville, wrecked some mines and foundries, and then destroyed the salt works and stockpiled salt at Saltville. The Confederates successfully reopened the salt works a short time later, but the railroad remained out of service for two months.

Brigadier General James Harrison Wilson (1837–1925) conducted one of the most successful Union raids. A native of Illinois, Wilson graduated in the upper ranks of his 1860 West Point class and became Grant's chief topographical engineer in the Army of the Tennessee. Although Wilson was an engineer, Grant gave him a cavalry division under Philip Sheridan, and he served for a while in the Army of the Potomac before returning west to become Sherman's chief of cavalry. Wilson performed excellent service, and in March 1865 he led 13,500 troopers in a raid against the important Confederate munitions depot and manufacturing center of Selma, Alabama. Nathan Bedford Forrest had only 8,000 men and could do little to stop the enemy. Wilson quickly occupied modern-day Birmingham and sent troopers to Tuscaloosa to burn the University of Alabama. Wilson and Forrest then fought furiously over the next two days, but Wilson won both clashes. Forrest suffered his fourth wound of the war in these fights and retreated to Selma, where he was joined by Lieutenant General Richard Taylor. Outnumbered almost two to one, the Confederates manned strong entrenchments but were overrun when Wilson attacked on April 2. He seized Selma and its vital warehouses and foundries and forced Forrest and Taylor to flee. In the short struggle, Wilson captured 2,700 prisoners, 102 cannons, and a large amount of munitions and supplies. From Selma, he pushed on to capture the capital of Montgomery and Macon, Georgia. Wilson's Selma Raid was one of the war's most successful. Penetrating 300 miles into enemy territory, he lost 725 men but captured nearly 7,000 prisoners and inflicted an estimated 1,200 casualties on the Confederates. Soon afterward, a unit of Wilson's command captured fleeing Confederate President Jefferson Davis in Georgia.

## THE EFFECTIVENESS OF IRREGULAR WARFARE

Irregular warfare such as cavalry raids, espionage, and guerrilla attacks played an important role in the Civil War. Spies, guerrillas, and cavalrymen gathered intelligence and harassed enemy armies, but it is rather difficult to judge their overall effectiveness. Undoubtedly they forced the opposing armies to expend a considerable amount of resources to defend against such activity, but did they materially affect the war's outcome?

### The Intelligence War

Military commanders frequently used the intelligence gathered by cavalry raids and spies to plan strategy. In his raid around McClellan's army on the Peninsula, Stuart provided information to Lee that allowed him to plan the Seven Days Campaign and save Richmond, but the campaign did not destroy McClellan's army as Lee intended. Grant claimed Van Lew's spy network provided him with vital intelligence on Richmond's defenses, but he gave no specific details on what he learned so it is not known if the information was used effectively. The spy Harrison informed Lee of the Union army's proximity during the Gettysburg Campaign, which allowed him time to concentrate the army. One could argue that Harrison's information saved Lee's army, but that is speculation since no one knows what would have happened if Lee had not learned of the enemy's presence when he did. And even after learning of the Union army's location, Lee still failed to defeat Meade.

Two of the greatest victories involving intelligence coups were Antietam and Vicksburg. McClellan discovered Lee's campaign plans during the Antietam Campaign and was able to drive him out of Maryland, but the information was accidentally found wrapped around cigars and was not uncovered by spies. In the Vicksburg Campaign, Grant chose to cross the Mississippi River at Bruinsburg because he knew a good road led inland from there. That intelligence, however, came not from a secret agent but from an anonymous slave who gave the information to a Union patrol. Slaves also informed Union officers of the Confederate evacuations of Yorktown and Manassas, but the officers did not use the information to launch any attacks. Charley Wright may have provided the most useful information given by a slave when he informed the Union that Lee's army was heading toward Maryland at the beginning of the Gettysburg Campaign. That information was put to good use and allowed the Army of the Potomac to begin its pursuit of the enemy.

## Cavalry Raids and Guerrillas

Unlike the war's known espionage activities, cavalry raids and guerrilla activity were effective at times in distracting the enemy and hampering their ability to fight. They destroyed huge amounts of supplies and railroad track, pinned down thousands of troops, and sometimes changed entire campaigns. Van Dorn and Forrest forced Grant to abandon his first Vicksburg campaign by destroying his supply line, and Grierson's Raid helped Grant cross the Mississippi River unmolested. Guerrilla fighters such as Mosby also provided important intelligence information. Unfortunately, most guerrillas operated more like Quantrill and Bloody Bill Anderson. While they did tie down a significant number of enemy troops, their lawless activity also angered many Southerners. It is questionable whether their contribution to the war effort justified the suffering they caused and their weakening effect on Confederate morale.

Some Confederates believed Lee should have disbanded his army at Appomattox and carried out a prolonged guerrilla war rather than surrender. Lee rejected the notion even though he had personally encountered guerrillas in the Mexican War and was well aware of the difficulty of defeating them. Sitting on a log with Brigadier General Edward Porter Alexander, he asked Alexander what he thought they should do. Alexander suggested the army "scatter like rabbits & partridges in the woods & [the enemy] could not scatter so to catch us." Lee disagreed, however, because he concluded it would hurt the South more than help. Without supplies or a command structure, the men would be forced to survive by plundering civilians, and they would become little more than outlaws. The Yankees, in turn, would be ruthless in hunting them down. "[W]hile you young men might afford to go to bushwhacking," he told Alexander, "the only proper & dignified course for me would be to surrender myself & take the consequences of my actions." Because of Lee's sense of honor and astute assessment of the military situation, the Civil War ended quickly as other Confederate armies put down their arms as well. If Lee had chosen the guerrilla option, an irregular war of unimaginable destructiveness might have swept across the South for years afterward.

## FOR FURTHER READING

Confederate Vigenére cipher code
General Ewing's General Orders No. 11

## CHAPTER 21

# The Bloody Road to Richmond: From the Wilderness to Petersburg

**The Overland Campaign**

**Jubal Early's Washington Raid**

**The Move to Petersburg**

On the cold, windy afternoon of March 8, 1864, a nondescript middle-aged man and a 13-year-old boy checked into the posh Willard Hotel in downtown Washington. A bystander described the stranger as a "short, round-shouldered man in a very tarnished major general's uniform [with] rough, light-brown whiskers, a blue eye, and rather a scrubby look withal . . . as if he was out of office and on half pay, with nothing to do but hang round the entry of Willard's, cigar in mouth." The haggard officer's identity was revealed when he signed the registry "U.S. Grant & Son—Galena, Illinois." As word spread, the hotel's lobby was soon buzzing with activity as people jostled to catch a glimpse of the general who had been summoned to Washington to win the war. Immediately, the clerk changed Grant's accommodations from the small room on the top floor—the only room available just minutes before—to the hotel's best suite. Unsettled by the commotion, Grant and his son, Fred, immediately went upstairs.

The next day, Grant and Fred went to the White House to meet President Lincoln, the cabinet, and other dignitaries. When Grant was ushered into the East Room, a silence descended on the crowd, but there was scattered applause and a few cheers when he and Lincoln shook hands. Many in the back were unable to see, and an embarrassed Grant was forced to mount a sofa so they could get a look at him. One journalist wrote, "Ladies suffered dire disaster in the crush and confusion; their laces were torn and crinolines mashed, and many got up on sofas, chairs, and tables to be out of harm's way or to get a better view of the spectacle. . . . The little, scared-looking man who stood on a crimson-covered sofa was the idol of the hour." Grant was anything but scared, but it remained to be seen whether he could do what no other Union general had done before—defeat Robert E. Lee in battle and force his surrender.

## THE OVERLAND CAMPAIGN

May 4, 1864: Overland Campaign begins
May 5–6, 1864: Battle of the Wilderness
May 8–20, 1864: Battle of Spotsylvania
May 9–14, 1864: Sheridan's Richmond Raid
May 12, 1864: Grant temporarily breaks Lee's line at the Bloody Angle
June 1–3, 1864: Battle of Cold Harbor

When Grant was promoted to lieutenant general and general-in-chief in March 1864, the Union clearly had the upper hand, but the Confederates were not yet defeated. In the far west, Union armies had won control of the Mississippi River and isolated the Confederates' Trans-Mississippi Department. However, General Kirby Smith's Southern forces still occupied most of that vast region and had defeated several Union invasion attempts. Elsewhere in the west, the Yankees controlled most of Tennessee, but little else. Nathan Bedford Forrest's Rebel cavalry had virtual free rein over the region, and the Army of Tennessee remained defiant in northern Georgia despite its defeat at Chattanooga. The coastal cities of Mobile, Alabama; Savannah, Georgia; and Charleston, South Carolina, also remained in Confederate hands. In the eastern theater, the war was a stalemate. Although battered at Gettysburg, Lee's Army of Northern Virginia remained strong and the men's morale high. After three years of bloody fighting, it still barred the way to Richmond and was a dangerous threat to any Union army operating in Northern Virginia. The Confederates were on the defensive for sure, but Grant would soon discover there was plenty of fight left in them and the war's ultimate outcome was far from certain.

### Grant's Strategy

The Union's greatest strategic error in the first three years of war was failing to coordinate all of its armies to strike the Confederates at one time and crush them. Generals McClellan and Halleck could have done so when they served as general-in-chief, but McClellan had his hands full directing the Army of the Potomac, and Halleck refused to assume the responsibility. Both were content to let the department commanders operate separately, which in turn allowed the Confederates to take advantage of their interior line and concentrate troops where needed. Grant's arrival in Washington marked a turning point in Union strategy. Lincoln and the Congress believed Grant was up to the challenge to lead all the armies in a final push for victory because he was the only Northern general who could boast of consistent success. Grant had captured two Confederate armies at Fort Donelson and Vicksburg, and he had defeated the enemy's main western army twice at Shiloh and Chattanooga. In February 1864, Congress revived the rank of lieutenant general with the clear understanding that Grant would be given the appointment and made general-in-chief to devise a winning strategy.

Grant had planned to return west after the White House ceremony to direct operations from familiar ground far removed from Washington's political intrigue. He changed his mind, however, and later explained, "[W]hen I got to Washington and saw the situation it was plain that here was the point for the commanding general to be. No one else could, probably, resist the pressure that would be brought to bear upon him to desist from his own plans and pursue others." Grant decided to direct the Army of the Potomac personally and promoted Sherman to take charge of the huge Military Division of the West. Grant brought his loyal staff of westerners with him to Virginia, but he made no major changes in the Army of the Potomac except to appoint Philip Sheridan (another westerner) to lead the cavalry. He left Meade in command of the army even though Meade graciously volunteered to step down if Grant preferred a western officer in whom he had more confidence. Meade, however, had little to do with making strategic decisions and was left simply to carry out Grant's orders.

Grant wasted no time in implementing a comprehensive strategy. In the past, the Union had concentrated on capturing territory rather than targeting the Confederate armies, and it had never launched coordinated attacks in both theaters of operation. Grant realized the key to victory was to destroy the Rebel armies and the Southerners' ability to wage war, not to just capture cities. His strategy was to make simultaneous advances on many different fronts to keep pressure on the enemy. Each advance would target a particular Southern city or critically important geographical area, but the main focus was the enemy's armies. Attacking the cities was simply a way to force the Confederates into open battle so they could be crushed. In the west, Sherman would move against Atlanta, Georgia, to destroy Joseph E. Johnston's Army of Tennessee, and Nathaniel P. Banks would advance up Louisiana's Red River to threaten Shreveport. In Virginia, Benjamin F. Butler's Army of the James would move up the James River to attack Richmond from the east while Franz Sigel would invade the Shenandoah Valley to destroy Lee's vital source of supplies.

Grant would personally direct the most important offensive, an advance on Richmond, Virginia, that became known as the Overland Campaign. Meade's Army of the Potomac and Ambrose E. Burnside's IX Corps—120,000 men strong—would march toward Richmond to draw out Lee's 60,000-man Army of Northern Virginia from its winter camps around Gordonsville. By moving rapidly past Lee's right flank, Grant hoped to lure the enemy onto open ground and destroy them with his superior firepower. Lee, too, wanted to engage Grant before he reached Richmond. The disasters at Fort Donelson and Vicksburg clearly demonstrated that an outnumbered army could not successfully defend a city against Grant, and Lee planned to avoid that hopeless situation. He put it succinctly to General A. P. Hill when he declared, "This army cannot stand a siege." Thus, the stage was set for the Civil War's bloodiest fighting.

## The Battle of the Wilderness

The Overland Campaign began on May 4, 1864, when Grant crossed the Rapidan River and pushed into the Wilderness. Exactly one year earlier at Chancellorsville, "Fighting Joe" Hooker met disaster in this same area of dense woods and thickets. Grant was determined not to suffer a similar fate. He knew the heavy cover largely negated his superior numbers and urged his generals to push through quickly before Lee learned of their movement and attacked. Unfortunately, Lee had already discovered Grant's march and was rushing his men toward the Wilderness to give battle.

On May 5, the Confederates moved east along two roughly parallel roads: Ewell's corps was on the left following the Orange Turnpike, and Hill's corps was on the right using the Orange Plank Road. Longstreet's corps was farther behind with orders to follow Hill and join the fight as quickly as possible. Lee's veterans were completely confident of victory. In a letter home, one soldier claimed the men were "anxious to meet the Yankees' greatest general under the immortal Robert E. Lee." A chaplain later recalled that it was a beautiful spring morning and spirits were high. "I never saw our men so cheerful," he wrote. "The poor fellows had little idea of the terrible conflict in which they were about to engage."

Hesitant to attack without Longstreet, Lee ordered Ewell and Hill to avoid a general battle until the entire army was concentrated. This order caused all of the Confederate commanders to act cautiously, but Grant and Meade were spoiling for a fight. They hoped to pass through the Wilderness without a clash but knew it was impossible once contact was made with Ewell that morning. In the early afternoon, Meade sent Gouverneur K. Warren's corps straight down the Orange Turnpike in a devastating attack against Ewell's corps. A Union soldier wrote, "The incessant roar of the rifle; the screaming bullets; the forest on fire; men cheering, groaning, yelling, swearing, and praying! All this created an experience in the minds of the survivors that we can never forget." Ewell's right flank broke in confusion, but reinforcements were rushed to the front and pushed the enemy back. Meade then sent John Sedgwick's corps to help Warren, and the bloody battle continued along Ewell's front for the rest of the day.

Meanwhile, heavy fighting also broke out on the Confederate right wing between A. P. Hill and George W. Getty's and Winfield S. Hancock's Union corps. Hill pushed forward through the woods and nearly seized a crucial intersection with the Brock Road that would have given the Confederates a clear path to Grant's rear. In turn, a heavy Union counterattack by Hancock's corps nearly broke Hill's line, but stubborn Confederate resistance and darkness finally ended the battle. The fighting along the Orange Plank Road had been desperate, and a North Carolinian declared the Wilderness "roared like fire in a canebreak." One Pennsylvania officer wrote, "[T]he noise of the musketry, multiplied and re-echoed by the thick woods, was often frightful, and many a stout heart which had passed unshrinkingly through the dangers of well-fought fields quailed before the leaden blast which cut and stripped the young pines as if a cyclone had swept over them. . . . It was a fearful experience."

After dark, the two armies dug in along parallel lines through thick brush. Lee had stalled Grant's advance, but he now was in a precarious position. A dangerous gap existed between his army's two wings because Ewell and Hill were unable to link up in the woods. If Grant discovered the gap and attacked, he might very well split Lee's army in two and maul it much as Hood had done to Rosecrans at Chickamauga. Adding to Lee's worries was the fact that Longstreet had not yet arrived to reinforce Hill's corps, which was completely exhausted and in disarray after the fierce fighting. Hill wanted to pull back and reform, but Lee ordered him to stay in place until he was relieved. Assured that Longstreet would arrive before morning, Hill allowed his men to rest and did not take any significant precautions to reinforce his line. On the Union side that night, Grant was optimistic of victory. Scouts informed him of the gap in Lee's line, and he ordered Burnside's corps to push through it the next morning and split the enemy while the rest of the army made a coordinated attack along the entire front.

When the eastern sky began to brighten on May 6, Lee found himself in a desperate situation. Longstreet failed to arrive during the night as expected, and Hill's exhausted and unprepared men were still on the firing line when Hancock's corps attacked at 5:00 a.m. Once again the entire Wilderness exploded with the sound of battle. John Gibbon, former commander of the Iron Brigade, wrote, "The roar of musketry was incessant and prolonged. . . . The whole forest was now one mass of flame." Hancock crushed Hill's corps and sent it fleeing back down the Orange Plank Road past Lee. Unusually excited and using uncharacteristically harsh language, Lee rode among the men pleading with them to stop and make a stand. Few of the men rallied, but a lone artillery battery did hold its ground and slowed the enemy's advance with double loads of canister.

The fate of the battle hung in the balance when Longstreet dramatically arrived. A Confederate artilleryman captured the moment when he wrote, "Like a fine lady at a party, Longstreet was often late in his arrival at the ball, but he always made a sensation . . . with the grand old First Corps, sweeping behind him, as his train." Hood's Texas Brigade led the corps, and Lee immediately ordered it to counterattack to stop the Union advance. So desperate was the moment, Lee joined the Texans for the charge. When they realized he was advancing with them, the Texans stopped and refused to go any farther. Some began to yell, "Lee to the rear!" and others grabbed Traveller's reins to turn Lee around physically. Reluctantly, Lee finally complied, and the Texans raised the Rebel Yell, charged, and stopped Hancock's advance.

Soon after this "Lee to the Rear" incident, the battle's momentum shifted in favor of the Confederates. Burnside foundered lost through the woods and failed to attack through the gap in the enemy's line. His failure allowed Longstreet to push his divisions to the left to make contact with Ewell's corps and unite the two Confederate wings. Scouting parties also made the surprising discovery that both of Grant's flanks were in the air and open to attack. Longstreet moved against the enemy's left flank first. Late that morning, he hid several brigades behind a convenient unfinished railroad embankment and used it to approach the Yankees unseen. The surprise attack crushed the Union flank and, as one Confederate claimed, "rolled them up like a scroll." Victory seemed at hand, and Longstreet was preparing to push on when Brigadier General Micah Jenkins joined him flushed with victory. Moments later, a nearby Confederate regiment opened fire on another it mistakenly believed was the enemy. Longstreet and Jenkins were caught between them. Two men in their party were killed outright, and Jenkins was shot through the head and mortally wounded. Another bullet tore through Longstreet's throat and shoulder, destroying the nerves in his right arm. Bleeding badly, Longstreet was helped from his horse and propped up against a tree. Bloody froth spewed from his mouth when he tried to speak, but he was evacuated to the rear and survived. Eerily, it was almost a year to the day—in almost the same spot—that Confederate soldiers mortally wounded Stonewall Jackson.

On the other end of the line, Brigadier General John B. Gordon discovered the undefended Union right flank that morning, but for reasons that are still unclear, Ewell did not give him permission to attack until nearly dark. When Gordon finally did move forward, he, too, caught the enemy by surprise as they were boiling coffee and preparing supper. A Union surgeon recalled, "Suddenly out of the dusk in front, and to the rear of us, burst the Ki-yi Ki-yi [Rebel Yell] close to us, and with it the rebels were seen crossing the breastwork we had just put up. The men in front of us were so much surprised that they immediately ran, leaving the pork in the pan and the coffee on the fire and their arms." Part of Sedgwick's corps was routed, and Grant's right flank was pushed back some distance, but timely reinforcements and darkness finally ended the fight. Except for the Union flanks being pushed back, the two armies remained in about the same positions they had occupied when the battle began.

The fighting in the Wilderness had been among the war's most savage, and the battle ignited fires that burned many wounded men alive. Union Brigadier General Horace Porter remembered the Wilderness as an "unutterable" terror. "Forest fires raged; ammunition trains exploded; the dead were roasted in the conflagration; the wounded, roused by its hot breath, dragged themselves along, with their torn and mangled limbs, in the mad energy of despair, to escape the ravages of the flames; and every bush seemed hung with shreds of blood-stained clothing. . . . It seemed as though Christian men had turned to fiends, and hell itself had usurped the place of earth." Even today, the death toll remains uncertain because officers on both sides apparently underreported the casualties so as not to lower morale. Officially, the Army of the Potomac lost about 17,500 men, but the actual number may have been 20,000. Lee's losses were put at 7,500, but modern research indicates the number may have been 11,000.

The Battle of the Wilderness was the first clash between the war's two best generals. No one knew how Grant would match up against Lee because many of Grant's victories had been against less than impressive Rebel generals (the same thing could be said of Lee, but no one pointed that out at the time). All who saw him in the Wilderness noted Grant's calm demeanor and confidence. Throughout the battle, he often sat on a stump whittling and issuing orders while the fighting raged nearby. By end of the first day he had worn out the tips of his gloves, and his fingertips poked through. When the Confederates attacked the flanks on the second day, an unidentified officer came to Grant in great excitement and exclaimed, "General Grant, this is a crisis that cannot be looked upon too seriously. I know Lee's methods well by past experience; he will throw his own army between us and the Rapidan, and cut us off completely from our communications." The officer's defeatism was too much for Grant. "Oh, I am heartily tired of hearing about what Lee is going to do," he roared. "Some of you seem to think he is suddenly going to turn a double somersault and land in our rear and on both of our flanks at the same time. Go back to your command, and try to think what we are going to do ourselves, instead of what Lee is going to do." It was obvious Grant was not the type to panic easily.

## DID YOU KNOW?

### Coffee

Coffee was a mainstay of the Civil War soldier's diet, and it was prized by Southern soldiers and civilians after the Union blockade caused supplies to run low. Some Southern women were even said to have traded sex for coffee. When available, coffee was a part of every meal, and a type of instant coffee was created by Civil War soldiers. The men pre-mixed coffee and sugar in a bag so they could quickly spoon some out in a cup of water and boil it during short rests on the march. Hundreds of thousands of soldiers became addicted to coffee and continued to drink it after returning home. Thanks to the Civil War, the United States is now the only former British colony where coffee is preferred over tea.

## The Race to Spotsylvania

After the two-day bloodletting in the Wilderness, Grant decided to disengage rather than continue attacking the formidable Confederate defenses. Withdrawing on the night of May 7, he moved southeast toward Spotsylvania Court House. If he got there first, Grant could turn the enemy's right flank and place his army between Lee and Richmond and force Lee to leave his trenches and attack at a disadvantage. When the withdrawal began, the Union soldiers thought Grant was retreating as all their previous generals had done after engaging Lee. When they realized they were heading for the Confederates' flank instead, morale soared and men cheered and tossed their caps in the air.

# EYEWITNESS
## Robert Campbell

*Robert Campbell (1844–1892) was an 18-year-old Texan who joined the 5th Texas Infantry in the Army of Northern Virginia. He saw extensive combat and was wounded six times—the most of any soldier in Hood's Texas Brigade. In 1866, Campbell wrote an account of his war experiences for his family and gave a firsthand account of the famous "Lee to the Rear" episode at the Wilderness.*

As we stood upon this hill, Lee excited and in close consultation with Longstreet—our batteries thundering into the Wilderness below, the roar of musketry from the undergrowth below—our men retreating in a disorganized mass, and the Yankees pressing on and within musket shot, almost, of the hill upon which stood our idolized chief, indeed was an exciting time, and the emergency called for *immediate* and *determined* action upon the part of the Confederate General. Lee was equal to the hour. Action must *not* be delayed, for in less than five minutes the enemy would be upon the hill. . . . The cannon thundered, musketry rolled, stragglers were fleeing, couriers riding here and there in post-haste, minnies began tossing, the dying and wounded were jolted by the flying ambulances, and filling the road-side, adding to the excitement the terror of death. The "Texas Brigade" was in front. . . . About this time, Gen. Lee, with his staff, rode up to Gen. [John] Gregg—"General what brigade is this?" said Lee. "The Texas Brigade," was General G's. reply. "I am glad to see it," said Lee. "When you go in there, I wish you to give those men the cold steel—they will stand and fire all day, and never move unless you charge them. . . ." And now comes the point upon which the interest of this "o'er true tale" hangs. *"Attention Texas Brigade"* was rung upon the morning air, by Gen. Gregg, *"the eyes of General Lee are upon you, forward, march."* Scarce had we moved a step, when Gen. Lee, in front of the whole command, raised himself in his stirrups, uncovered his grey hairs, and with an earnest, yet anxious voice, exclaimed above the din and confusion of the hour, *"Texans always move them."* Reader, for near four years I followed the fortunes of the Virginia army, heard, saw and experienced much that saddened the heart or appealed in one form or

This emotional display demonstrated just how committed Union soldiers were to victory. That spring the three-year enlistments of the 1861 volunteers expired. All could have gone home content in the knowledge that they had done their part to preserve the Union. But, remarkably, more than half reenlisted to see the war through, even though they knew there was a good chance they would not survive the spring campaign. Several factors motivated this decision. The federal government offered a $400 bonus to those who reenlisted (and state and local authorities sometimes added more), plus a 35-day furlough. For some soldiers, the furlough meant more than the money. They calculated the odds were against their surviving until their enlistment expired so it was better to reenlist, go home for one last visit, and then come back to be killed.

another to human passions, but never before in my lifetime or since did I ever witness such a scene as was enacted when Lee pronounced these words, with the appealing look that he gave. A yell rent the air that must have been heard for miles around, and but a few eyes in that old brigade of veterans and heroes of many a bloody field was undimmed by honest, heartfelt tears. Leonard Gee, a courier to Gen. Gregg, and riding by my side, with tears coursing down his cheeks and yells ensuing from his throat exclaimed, "I would charge hell itself for that old man." It was not what Gen. Lee said that so infused and excited the men, as his tone and look, which each one of us knew were born of the dangers of the hour. . . .

After moving over half the ground we all saw that Gen. Lee was following us into battle—care and anxiety upon his countenance—refusing to come back at the request and advice of his staff. If I recollect correctly, the brigade halted when they discovered Gen. Lee's intention, and all eyes were turned upon him. Five and six of his staff would gather around him, seize him, his arms, his horse's reins, but he shook them off and moved forward. Thus did he continue until just before we reached the undergrowth, not, however, until the balls began to fill and whistle through the air. Seeing that we would do all that men could do to retrieve the misfortunes of the hour, accepting the advice of his staff, and hearkening to the protest of his advancing soldiers, he at last turned round and rode back to a position on the hill.

*Campbell's vivid description of the "Lee to the Rear" episode demonstrates the close bond soldiers sometimes formed with their commanders. Generals like Lee who willingly shared the danger of battle and exposed themselves to enemy fire were always respected more than those who remained in the rear, out of harm's way. Campbell received his sixth wound during the Petersburg Campaign and was sent home on furlough to spend the rest of the war recruiting in Houston.*

Reprinted from *Lone Star Confederate: A Gallant and Good Soldier of the Fifth Texas Infantry* by George Skoch and Mark W. Perkins, eds., by permission of the Texas A&M University Press. © 2003 Texas A&M University.

Unit pride also played a role. If 75 percent of a regiment reenlisted, the unit would not be disbanded. Instead, it would be designated a Veteran Volunteer regiment, and its members could wear distinctive red and blue chevrons on their arms to proudly show their veteran status. In addition to these perks, another powerful motivation was a determination to finish the job they had started. One lieutenant who reenlisted in the 57th New York wrote home that half of the regiment's original members were dead. "Amongst the survivors," he wrote, "the excitement and enthusiasm of the early days has long since passed away, but the resolve still remains." Much has been made of die-hard Rebels, but the determination shown by those Union soldiers who reenlisted in 1864 proves they were every bit the Southerners' equal in grit.

# NOTABLE UNIT: *Hood's Texas Brigade*

Hood's Texas Brigade was one of the most renowned units in Lee's army. It included the 1st, 4th, and 5th Texas Infantry, with the 18th Georgia, Hampton Legion Infantry, and 3rd Arkansas sometimes serving with it as well. Brigadier General John B. Hood led the brigade for about six months early in the war, and it forever carried his name. The Texans were wild and reckless and did not conform well to military discipline, but they were absolutely devoted to Hood. During the Antietam Campaign, Hood was arrested in a dispute with another general and was relieved of command and forced to ride in the army's rear. The Texans were angry and yelled to Lee, "Give us Hood!" when they prepared to enter battle at South Mountain. Lee appreciated Hood's ability and immediately raised his hat in salute and responded, "You shall have him, gentlemen!"

The brigade first earned fame during the Seven Days Campaign when it cracked the tough Union defenses at Gaines' Mill after several other Confederate assaults had failed. Hood was promoted to a division command afterward, and several different officers led the brigade for the rest of the war. The Texans' fame only increased on other battlefields. At Antietam, the brigade arrived after an exhausting march and was allowed to stay in the rear to cook breakfast on the condition that it would immediately enter the battle if needed. When the enemy attacked through the infamous cornfield, the Texans had to leave their simmering food to counterattack the same New York troops they had faced at Gaines' Mill. Although badly outnumbered, they surged through the corn, drove back the enemy, and captured several cannons, but the brigade lost two-thirds of its men in the process. Hood wrote, "It was here that I witnessed the most terrible clash of arms, by far, that has occurred during the war." At Gettysburg, the brigade was also in the thick of the fighting around the Peach Orchard and the Wheat Field. To prepare them for battle, Hood rode to the front, stood in his stirrups, and cried out, "Fix bayonets, my brave Texans; forward and take those heights!" Hood's arm was shattered in the fighting, and the 1st Texas Infantry lost more than 82 percent of its men. This reportedly was the highest percentage loss of any Confederate regiment in one day of battle.

In the autumn of 1863, the Texas Brigade went west with James Longstreet's corps and fought at Chickamauga. Returning to Virginia, it was involved in the famous "Lee to the Rear" episode when the men refused to launch a counterattack in the Battle of the Wilderness until Robert E. Lee left the front lines. When Lee finally removed himself from danger, the Texans charged and drove back the enemy, but they lost more than 400 men out of 711 engaged. Afterward, the brigade served in the Petersburg Campaign, and in October 1864 its commander, Brigadier General John Gregg, was killed. That very day, Lee complimented the unit when he was told only the Texas Brigade was prepared for battle. "The Texas Brigade is *always* ready," he responded. During the war, Hood's Texas Brigade fought in thirty-eight engagements and compiled a combat record second to none. But its losses were staggering. In a single three-month period during the Seven Days, Second Bull Run, and Antietam campaigns the brigade lost 1,780 men.

## Sheridan's Richmond Raid

Anticipating that Grant might make a move toward Spotsylvania, Lee used his interior line to get Stuart's cavalry and an infantry corps there first. Arriving on May 8 just minutes before the enemy, the Confederates turned back several Union attacks before both armies arrived and strongly entrenched. Meanwhile, an ongoing argument between Meade and cavalry commander Philip Sheridan came to a head. Sheridan had chafed under Meade's command since the campaign began because Meade had relegated the cavalry to guarding wagon trains, screening the army, and gathering intelligence. Sheridan, who wanted to be turned loose to destroy Stuart's Confederate cavalry, became frustrated at Meade's lack of aggressiveness. He later complained, "The trouble with the commanders of the Army of the Potomac was that they never marched out to 'lick' anybody; all they thought of was to escape being 'licked' themselves." The disagreement finally exploded in a heated argument at Meade's headquarters, during which Sheridan promised he would defeat Stuart if given the chance. One witness described Sheridan's language as "highly spiced and conspicuously italicized with expletives." Furious, Meade stormed over to Grant's tent and reported Sheridan's disrespectful behavior. Expecting Grant to support his position, Meade was disappointed when Grant simply replied, "Well, he generally knows what he is talking about. Let him start right out and do it."

Sheridan left Spotsylvania with 12,000 men and headed for Lee's rear to disrupt his railroad supply line. Instead of riding rapidly like most cavalry raiders, Sheridan moved slowly and deliberately to draw Stuart into battle. Accepting the challenge, Stuart rode hard with 4,500 troopers and blocked Sheridan's path at Yellow Tavern on the morning of May 11. Stuart repulsed several Union attacks, but late in the afternoon George Custer's Wolverine Brigade broke through the Confederate line. Stuart launched a successful counterattack, but he was mortally wounded during the fighting and died the next day. Sheridan finally disengaged and returned to Union lines, but his raid was a disappointment. Although his men did kill Stuart and destroy some valuable supplies, Sheridan failed to disrupt Lee's supply line for any length of time, and he did not annihilate the Confederate cavalry as promised.

## The Battle of Spotsylvania

While Sheridan was away on his raid, heavy fighting continued around Spotsylvania as the armies probed each other's positions. Sharpshooters were particularly active in picking off officers and artillery crews. On one occasion, Union Major General John Sedgwick visited an artillery battery that was under constant fire. He found the men trying to dodge the bullets and chided them, "What! What! Men, dodging this way for single bullets! What will you do when they open fire along the whole line? I am ashamed of you. They couldn't hit an elephant at this distance." One man walked in front of Sedgwick and dropped to the ground when a minié ball zipped past his head. Amused at the soldier's

# BIOGRAPHY

## James Ewell Brown Stuart: "I Had Rather Die than Be Whipped"

**James Ewell Brown "Jeb" Stuart**

After graduating from West Point in 1854, Virginia native "Jeb" Stuart (1833–1864) was shot in the chest while fighting Indians on the frontier. He also served as Robert E. Lee's aide at Harpers Ferry and ferried messages between Lee and John Brown. In May 1861, Stuart resigned his U.S. Army commission and joined the Confederacy. Appointed colonel of the 1st Virginia Cavalry, he became famous for leading a charge at First Bull Run that routed an enemy regiment. Promoted to brigadier general (and later major general), Stuart earned more accolades when he rode around the Union army on the Peninsula and set the stage for the Seven Days Campaign by discovering the enemy's flank was unprotected. Stuart's father-in-law, General Philip St. George Cooke, led the Union cavalry and unsuccessfully pursued him during this mission.

Stuart was a vain man who became a caricature of the romantic cavalier. An aide described him as "a gallant figure to look at. The gray coat buttoned to the chin; the light French saber balanced by the pistol in its black holster; the cavalry boots above the knee, and the brown hat with its black plume floating above the bearded features, the brilliant eyes, and the huge moustache, which curled with laughter at the slightest provocation—these made Stuart the perfect picture of a gay cavalier." Stuart was daring and brave on the battlefield, flirtatious around women, and playful with his men. He also was something of a braggart, and he loved attention. One officer who

attempt to dodge an unseen bullet, Sedgwick nudged him with his foot and said, "Why, my man, I am ashamed of you, dodging that way." He then repeated his assertion, "They couldn't hit an elephant at this distance." The soldier got up, saluted, and walked away, and Sedgwick turned to talk to an aide. Suddenly, there was the unmistakable thud of a bullet hitting bone. The aide remembered, "The general's face turned slowly to ice, the blood spurting from his left cheek under the eye in a steady stream." Sedgwick dropped to the ground, dead from a sharpshooter's bullet fired from more than half a mile away.

At Spotsylvania, Lee's line was laid out in haste and generally followed a ridge of high ground. In the center it bulged out toward the enemy forming a salient the Confederates dubbed the Mule Shoe. This salient was vulnerable to attack because it could not be properly supported by the troops on either side, but Lee ordered Ewell's corps to hold the position because it controlled the high ground. Union Colonel Emory Upton (1839–1881) studied the Mule Shoe and saw an opportunity. One of the rising stars in the Army of the Potomac, Upton saw Generals Lee, Hill, Ewell, and Longstreet ride into a Virginia town without fanfare recalled how moments later Stuart galloped through with "a large cavalcade of staff and courier" and two buglers "blowing most furiously." Stuart's vanity, however, did not detract from the fact that he was an outstanding cavalry officer. Even the enemy admired his skill. Union General John Sedgwick once declared Stuart was "the greatest cavalryman ever foaled in America."

Stuart's reputation preceded him in battle, and a Union minister admitted, "Wherever Stuart rides, he carries terror with him. His victories are half won before he strikes a blow. Our soldiers feel that he may pounce on them at any minute, and that he is as resistless as a hawk in a fowl yard." In a fight, Stuart usually commanded from the front. At Chancellorsville, he personally led the infantry in frontal attacks after taking over the corps when Stonewall Jackson was wounded. One soldier remembered, "He leaped his horse over the breastworks near my company, and when he had reached a point about opposite the center of the brigade, while the men were loudly cheering him, he waved his hand toward the enemy and shouted, 'Forward men! Forward! Just follow me!'"

In September 1863, Stuart's cavalry was organized into a corps, but he was never promoted to the appropriate rank of lieutenant general. His stellar career ended on May 11, 1864, when he engaged the Union cavalry at Yellow Tavern. When a Confederate counterattack forced the enemy to retreat, Stuart pulled out his pistol and began shooting at the Yankees as they ran past him. One Union soldier turned and fired back and hit Stuart in the stomach. As he was being taken to the rear, Stuart noticed some of the men were retreating, and, despite his great pain, yelled out, "Go back! Go back! And do your duty, as I have done mine, and our country will be safe. Go back! Go back! I had rather die than be whipped." He died the next day in Richmond.

was a New York native and West Point graduate who commanded a brigade in Sedgwick's VI Corps. He had served well in numerous battles as both an artillery and infantry officer and had come to realize that the traditional method of attacking strong entrenchments along a wide front was useless. The attacking line moved forward too slowly because it stopped to exchange fire with the enemy, and it lacked depth to break through the defenses. All too often the long lines of infantry were simply shot to pieces before they even reached the enemy. Upton suggested a bold new tactic of attacking in a narrow column and not stopping to return fire. The fast-moving column would punch a small hole through the enemy line, and the mass of men following behind could fan out to the left and right to expand the opening.

On May 10, Upton was given twelve regiments to try his new tactic against the Mule Shoe. He issued strict orders to the men not to slow down or return fire until the enemy trenches were taken. One soldier vividly recalled Upton's last-minute instructions "not to fire a shot, cheer or yell, until we

**War Council.** This candid photograph of a strategy session was taken during the fighting around Spotsylvania. Union officers sit on pews in a churchyard while Grant (on the left) leans over Meade's shoulder to examine a map.

struck their works." The plan worked brilliantly and the compact column sliced right through the Confederate line, but Upton was forced to withdraw when other Union units failed to move forward to support the breakthrough. Nonetheless, Grant was impressed, and Upton was rewarded with a promotion to brigadier general of volunteers. At twenty-four, he became one of the youngest generals in the Union army. Upton was wounded in the war, but he survived to become a major figure in the postwar army by developing modern tactics, instituting new training methods, and serving as the commandant of cadets at West Point.

## The Bloody Angle

Grant decided to use Upton's innovative tactic again on a much larger scale. In the predawn hours of May 12, he massed Hancock's corps in front of the Mule Shoe to lead another attack, while additional units moved up to support it. In all, some 40,000 men were committed to the effort. It was a rainy and

**Burial Party.** Photographer Timothy O'Sullivan captured this scene of a Union burial party at Spotsylvania.

miserable night, but the Mule Shoe's defenders could clearly hear the rumble of troops out in the darkness and sent a warning to Lee. Lee, however, initially believed the noise indicated Grant was retreating and ordered Ewell's twenty cannons withdrawn from the Mule Shoe so he could move quickly in pursuit. As more information trickled in, however, he realized an attack was coming and ordered the artillery to move back into position.

When Hancock attacked at 4:30 a.m. the Confederates were awestruck. One Confederate remembered, "Never have I seen such an exciting spectacle as then met my gaze. As far as the eye could reach, the field was covered with the serried ranks of the enemy, marching in close columns to the attack." Hancock's men actually met little resistance because the rain had soaked the Confederates' muskets and prevented many from firing. Behind the trenches, Ewell's missing artillery returned to its original position just in time to be swallowed up and captured. With little fighting, the Yankees overran an entire Confederate division. Among the units shattered were the famous Stonewall Brigade and a brigade of Louisiana Tigers, and Generals Edward Johnson and General George H. Steuart were captured. When a Union soldier demanded Steuart's sword in surrender, the general declined with the explanation, "Well, sir, you all waked us up so early this morning that I didn't have time to get it on."

After breaking the enemy's line, Hancock's men fanned out to both sides and began clearing the entrenchments to widen the breach. Only then did the Confederates begin fighting back ferociously. A New York colonel declared, "Then ensued one of those hand-to-hand encounters with clubbed rifles, bayonets, swords, and pistols which defies description." Lee and Ewell desperately assembled the brigades of Generals Stephen D. Ramseur,

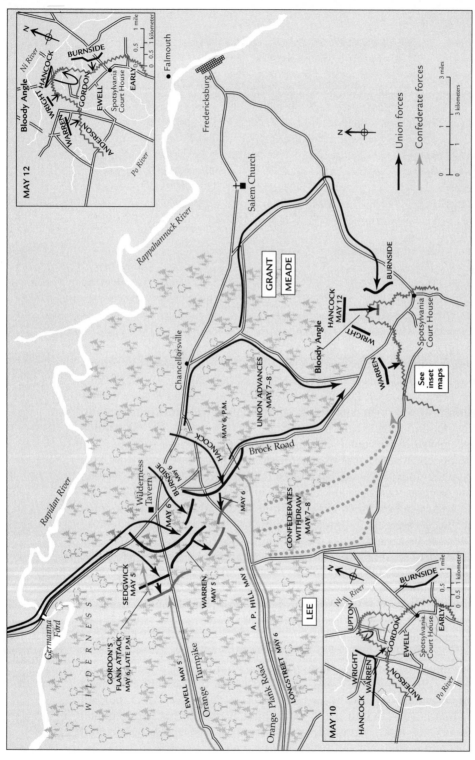

**The Battles of the Wilderness and Spotsylvania, May 5–12, 1864.** When Grant's army crossed the Rapidan River and entered the tangled Wilderness, Lee's men rushed in from the west along the parallel Orange Turnpike and Plank Road. After two days of brutal fighting in the thick woods, Grant disengaged and moved southeast to Spotsylvania Court House to turn Lee's position. Lee, however, used his interior line to get there first. On May 10 (lower insert), Emory Upton led an attack that temporarily broke through Lee's line at a salient dubbed the Mule Shoe. On May 12, the battle climaxed at the Mule Shoe's "Bloody Angle" (upper insert) when Grant launched a massive attack.

Robert Rodes, and John B. Gordon for a counterattack. At this critical moment, Lee joined Gordon and a second "Lee to the Rear" episode ensued. The army's survival was at stake, and Lee was determined to lead Gordon's brigade personally. Gordon, however, refused to go forward. Cutting Lee off with his horse, he assured the general his men would succeed. In a loud voice to get his men's attention, Gordon declared, "They will not fail you here. Will you, boys?" His question was met with wild cheering, and Gordon turned to Lee and said, "You must go to the rear." Gordon later described how several men surrounded Traveller and "turned his horse in the opposite direction, some clutching his bridle, some his stirrups, while others pressed close to Old Traveller's hips, ready to shove him by main force to the rear. . . ." Finally relenting, Lee moved back as Gordon's brigade shouted, "Lee, Lee, Lee to the rear! Lee to the rear!"

Gordon, Ramseur, and Rodes charged into Hancock's men, stopped their advance, and pushed them back over the entrenchments at the salient's apex. The battle then stalemated as both sides rushed in reinforcements. For the next twenty hours the armies fought like wounded animals in a small confined space that became known as the "Bloody Angle." The rain poured down, and Yankees and Rebels shot, bayoneted, and clubbed each other to death while separated by only a few feet of earthworks. A woman living nearby listened to the battle roar and wrote, "It sounded as if the very earth was breaking up from the direction of Captain Brown's old place in one continuous line to Miss Pritchetts. The earth shakes. Great God, how more than awful. Shells whizzing oh so fearfully. My very soul almost dies within me." Soldiers described the rifle fire as the war's heaviest. Minié balls killed an entire forest behind the Confederates' position, and one oak tree twenty-two inches in diameter was shot down (its stump was later collected by the U.S. Army as a souvenir). Some Confederates were actually crushed to death when trees were shot down on top of them. In the trenches, some men attached bayonets to rifles and tossed them over the earthworks like javelins, while some reached over to grab an enemy by the hair and drag him across as a prisoner. Soldiers tried to prop up the wounded, but many were trampled into the mud and blood and drowned. One survivor wrote, "The breastworks were slippery with blood and rain, dead bodies lying underneath half trampled out of sight." A chaplain who visited the sight after the battle exclaimed, "May God grant that I may never again experience such sensations or witness such scenes. The sights are shocking. The smell is still more offensive."

While the fighting raged, Lee prepared a new defensive position behind the Mule Shoe. Finally, late that night, Ewell's survivors withdrew to the new line. This one day of battle cost Grant about 9,000 men to Lee's 8,000. When the Battle of Spotsylvania finally ended a few days later, Lee had lost approximately 10,000 men and 8 generals, while Grant lost 18,000 men and 5 generals. The most tragic thing about Spotsylvania was that it accomplished little because neither army had struck a decisive blow, and the campaign remained a stalemate.

## A Changing War

Strong entrenchments helped save Lee's army from destruction at Spotsylvania. By this phase of the war, armies in both theaters had learned the value of such earthworks. An army positioned in trenches and behind breastworks enjoyed a tactical advantage because the enemy usually could not dislodge it with a frontal attack. A Union staff officer claimed "the strength of an army sustaining an attack was more than quadrupled . . . there is scarcely any measure by which to gauge the increased strength. . . ." Both sides realized the benefits of entrenchments and habitually began digging in as soon as they stopped marching. With nothing more than a few shovels, bayonets, tin cups, and plates, veteran soldiers learned how to throw up strong works in a matter of hours. One of Meade's aides observed, "It is a rule that, when the rebels halt, the first day gives them a good rifle-pit; the second, a regular infantry parapet with artillery in position; and the third a parapet with an abatis in front and entrenched batteries behind." If an army was in place for a few days, the defensive positions became more elaborate with log walls, side trenches, and covered sleeping areas. A reporter who studied the works wrote, "They are intricate, zig-zagged lines within lines, lines protecting flanks of lines, lines built to enfilade an opposing line, lines within which lies a battery . . . a maze and labyrinth of works within works and works without works, each laid out with some definite design either of defense or offense." Such massive earthworks would not be seen again until World War I.

Grant also came to recognize another important fact at Spotsylvania. Although newspapers and politicians were starting to criticize his growing casualty list, he realized Lee was losing a proportionate number of men. The South had already enlisted nearly every available man, and the breakdown of the prisoner exchange system meant that Lee would not be able to replace his losses while the Union could. Grant's aggressive tactics were steadily wearing down Lee's army, and the Rebels would eventually break if the pressure could be maintained. The important question was whether the Northern people had the will to see this attrition strategy through to victory. Hopefully, Lee's army would collapse before the November presidential election. If not, voters might abandon the administration and elect a Peace Democrat.

Grant was well aware of the political risks involved in fighting such a war, but he was willing to accept them because his strategy would eventually bring victory. His grim determination was evident when he wired Lincoln from Spotsylvania, "I propose to fight it out on this line if it takes all summer." After being disappointed by so many timid generals, Lincoln appreciated Grant's fighting spirit and was determined to support him to the end. Across the lines, the Confederates also began to realize that Grant was not the typical Yankee general they were used to fighting. One soldier wrote home, "We have met a man this time who either does not know when he is whipped, or who cares not if he loses his whole Army, so that he may accomplish an end. . . . [Grant] seems determined to die game if he has to die at all."

## The North Anna River

Grant finally recognized the futility of continuing the fight at Spotsylvania and disengaged on the night of May 20. Repeating his previous maneuver, he headed southeast to turn Lee's right flank, but Lee again skillfully countered the move by taking up a blocking position at the North Anna River. Lee was frustrated at being forced on the defensive for so long and desperately sought an opportunity to strike back and defeat Grant before he moved any closer to Richmond. The North Anna offered such an opportunity. There, Lee placed his army in an inverted "V" position, with the angle resting on the river at the Union center. If Grant continued to advance, he would split his army at the angle and place his two wings on opposite sides of the inverted "V" where they would be unable to support each other. Lee then could hold one side of the "V" with a small force behind strong breastworks and concentrate the bulk of his army to destroy Grant's isolated wing on the other side.

When Grant resumed his advance, he moved straight into the trap. At that critical moment, however, Lee fell ill with severe diarrhea and was confined to his tent. His subordinates had to supervise the attack, but they accomplished little more than mauling some individual Union units before Grant realized the danger he faced and ordered his men to entrench. Lee was deeply disappointed in his own weakening constitution and his lieutenants' failure to deliver the knockout blow he planned. The danger of becoming besieged at Richmond was increasing, and he became even more desperate to find a way to stop Grant. In frustration, Lee told his officers, "We must strike them a blow—we must never let them pass us again—we must strike them a blow."

## Cold Harbor

Having barely escaped Lee's trap at the North Anna River, Grant once more withdrew and marched to the southeast. This time he attempted to turn Lee's right flank at Cold Harbor, a small hamlet just ten miles northeast of Richmond, but once again Lee got there first. Furious attacks and counterattacks were made over the next few days as the armies dug their elaborate defensive works. By now, Grant was convinced Lee's army was so badly battered that one more determined attack would finish it. Winning a decisive victory at Cold Harbor would shatter the Confederate army, open the way to Richmond, and perhaps end the war. Unfortunately for Grant, Lee's men were braced behind almost impregnable fortifications by the time he was ready. The Union soldiers knew a frontal attack was suicidal, and many spent the night sewing their names and addresses to their uniforms so their bodies could be identified.

At 4:30 a.m. on June 3, 40,000 Union soldiers surged forward. The massive assault overran some advanced Confederate positions, but Lee's main line held firm, and his men slaughtered the enemy. A New Hampshire survivor wrote, "To those exposed to the full force and fury of that dreadful storm of lead and iron that met the charging column, it seemed more like a volcanic blast

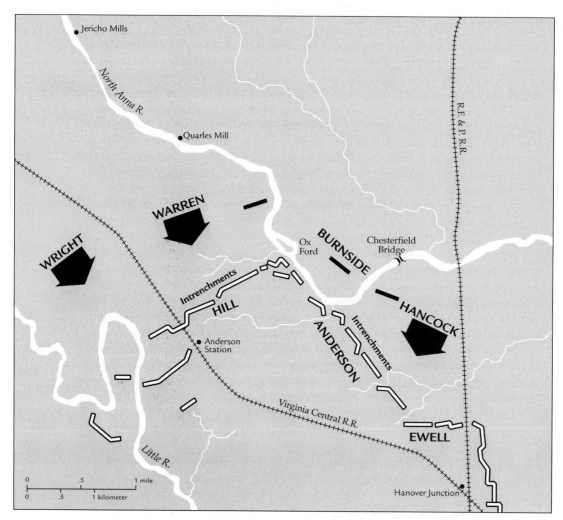

**North Anna River, May 22–26, 1864.** At the North Anna River, Lee set a clever trap by positioning his units in an inverted "V" to split Grant's army if he attacked. Grant moved into the trap, but Lee fell ill and his subordinates were unable to carry out his plan.

than a battle, and was just about as destructive." The doomed attack lasted less than thirty minutes, but Grant lost 7,000 men to Lee's 1,500. To make matters worse, Grant refused to ask for a truce under a white flag to recover his wounded because to do so would be an admission of defeat. Not until two days later did he send a message to Lee stating rather disingenuously, "[I]t is reported to me that there are wounded men probably of both armies, now lying exposed and suffering between the lines." Both sides had listened to the wounded moaning and screaming for days, but Lee knew none of them were Confederates and refused a truce unless Grant formally asked for one under

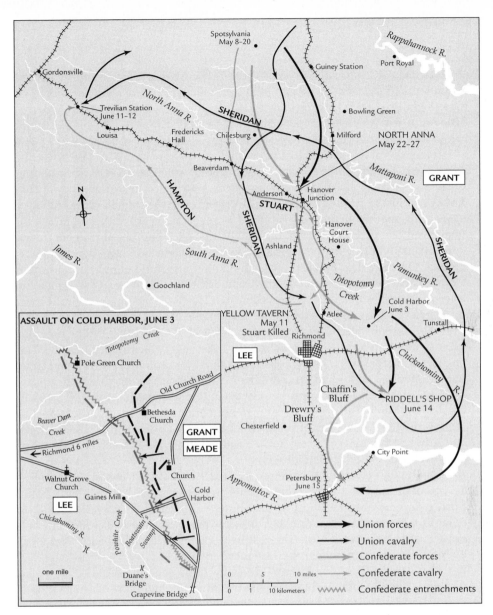

**From Spotsylvania to Petersburg, May–June 1864.** During the Battle of Spotsylvania, Sheridan's cavalry raided toward Richmond and killed Jeb Stuart at Yellow Tavern. Soon afterward, Grant once again disengaged and moved southeast to turn Lee's right flank, but Lee blocked his path at the North Anna River. Grant then moved on to Cold Harbor, where he made an ill-advised attack on June 3 (see insert) that resulted in heavy casualties. To break the stalemate, Grant made plans to withdraw from Cold Harbor, quickly cross the James River, and attack Richmond's supply base at Petersburg. To distract the enemy, Sheridan's cavalry rode northwest toward the Shenandoah Valley. Wade Hampton's Confederate cavalry stopped Sheridan at Trevillian Station, but Grant's plan succeeded and he reached Petersburg unopposed on June 15. Grant, however, failed to capture the city, largely because his generals did not press home the attack.

a white flag. Grant finally did so on June 7, but by that time all but two of the wounded had died under the broiling summer sun. In his post-war memoirs, Grant admitted the Cold Harbor attack was one of two he regretted ordering (the other was at Vicksburg), but his and Lee's decision to let the men suffer while they argued protocol does not reflect well on either general.

Historians have sought to understand why Grant failed to see what the lowliest private seemed to know—that a frontal attack at Cold Harbor had no chance to succeed. Apparently, he thought there was no alternative. Grant could not just sit idle in front of the Rebel army so it was either attack or start all over again with another maneuver. By now, however, there was little room left for maneuver. The swampy Chickahominy River blocked another movement on the left flank, and moving by the right flank would mean backtracking over hard-won ground. On the other hand, the Chickahominy also ran behind Lee's army. If Grant attacked and defeated Lee, the Confederates would be trapped against the river and perhaps could be destroyed. When weighing the options, Grant must have believed a frontal attack was the only course of action open to him.

Cold Harbor was the last battle of the Overland Campaign. Unlike previous campaigns when armies had fought only a day or two before disengaging, Lee and Grant had been in almost constant combat for a month. During that time, both armies lost about half their original strength, with Grant suffering approximately 60,000 casualties and Lee 30,000. Reinforcements replaced most of the losses, but both armies sustained permanent damage because the new men were often conscripts or inexperienced troops. The Army of the Potomac and Army of Northern Virginia never regained the same fighting élan they had possessed when the campaign began.

Shock and mourning spread across America in the early summer of 1864 as the enormity of the Overland Campaign losses became evident. Some Northerners referred to Grant as the "Butcher" because he seemingly had no regard for his men's lives, and Southerners began to question whether Lee's army could survive the year (interestingly, Lee was never called a "butcher" by Southerners even though he lost more men than Grant proportionately). But Presidents Lincoln and Davis stood by their generals because they had the utmost confidence in them. Of the two, Lincoln had more reason for optimism. Despite incurring unforeseen losses, Grant's strategy of simultaneous attacks on all fronts was working. Lee's army was pinned down near Richmond and unable to take major offensive action, and in the west Sherman's armies were slowly but surely advancing on Atlanta. It seemed only a matter of time before Lee would become besieged in Richmond's defenses and Atlanta would fall. If the Northern people had the fortitude to see things through, the Union would ultimately prevail. No one knew this better than Robert E. Lee. Although the odds were greatly against him, his only hope of victory was to find a way to defeat Grant before he reached Richmond. "We must destroy this army of Grant's before he gets to James River," Lee explained to Jubal Early. "If he gets there, it will become a siege, and then it will be a mere question of time."

# JUBAL EARLY'S WASHINGTON RAID

**May 15, 1864: Battle of New Market**
**July 9, 1864: Battle of the Monocacy**
**July 11–12, 1864: Early attacks Washington**
**July 30, 1864: Confederate cavalry burn Chambersburg, Pennsylvania**

While Lee fought desperately to keep Grant away from Richmond, events were unfolding in the Shenandoah Valley that gravely endangered his entire army. As part of the spring offensive, Grant sent Major General Franz Sigel into the Valley to cut off the supplies being sent to Lee, but Major General John C. Breckinridge's smaller force defeated Sigel at New Market and forced him to retreat. Grant then appointed Major General David Hunter to lead a second raid to destroy the Shenandoah Valley and then join Grant, if possible.

## David Hunter's Valley Campaign

Hunter began his Valley campaign in late May and was soon confronted by a small Confederate force under Brigadier General William E. "Grumble" Jones. Jones tried to block Hunter's advance at Piedmont, but his men were crushed in heavy fighting and Jones was killed. Hunter pushed on to Staunton and wrecked the Virginia Central Railroad, factories, stores, and other property. His lumbering army then occupied Lexington and burned the Virginia Military Institute and the home of Governor John Letcher, looted Washington College, and plundered and set fire to the entire area.

Outraged at Hunter's unrestrained destruction and gravely concerned that his vital Shenandoah Valley supply line might be cut forever, Lee took steps to stop the Yankee raiders. General Breckinridge was sent back to the Valley with a small force, but he soon called for reinforcements. By this time, General Ewell had fallen ill and Lieutenant General Jubal A. Early had taken command of the II Corps. In a bold move, Lee sent Early to destroy Hunter's army in the Valley and then threaten Washington, if possible. Lincoln was protective of the capital, and Lee believed he would order Grant to send some of his units to defend the city from such a threat. If so, Lee might be presented with an opportunity to assume the offensive and strike a decisive blow against the weakened Union army.

## The Race to Washington

Early's corps withdrew from Cold Harbor on June 12 and headed toward the Valley. When he and Breckinridge joined forces at Lynchburg, Hunter retreated all the way to West Virginia without a major fight. Hunter's lack of aggressiveness essentially surrendered the Shenandoah Valley back to the Confederates and restored Lee's supply line. Early's 14,000 men then entered Maryland. There, he forced the residents of Hagerstown and Frederick to pay $20,000 and $200,000 ransoms, respectively, to save their towns from destruction. The only Union troops available to confront Early were 6,000 men under Major General Lew Wallace (who wrote the novel *Ben Hur* after the war). Wallace took up a blocking position behind the Monocacy (muh-NOK-acy) River outside Frederick. He knew his small army could not defeat the Confederates, but he was determined to slow them down long enough for reinforcements from the Army of the Potomac to reach the capital.

In the early morning of July 9, Early attacked Wallace and pushed across the Monocacy. The fighting was bitter, with numerous attacks being made, and losses were heavy on both sides as the Confederates slowly forced Wallace back. A number of soldiers claimed that the relatively small battle was the most intense fight they had experienced in the entire war. One Confederate who saw the battlefield wrote, "On the crest of the hill where our men first attacked the enemy, we saw a regular line of dead Yankee bodies. A little in the rear they were to be seen lying in every direction and position. . . ." Early claimed so many men were shot down along the river that a 100-yard stretch of water turned red with blood. Wallace lost about 1,300 men at the Monocacy, while Early lost perhaps 800, but it was a pyrrhic Confederate victory. Wallace successfully delayed Early, and the few hours it took the Confederates to cross the river was the time needed for Union reinforcements to reach Washington.

Early's vanguard reached the outskirts of Washington on July 11 and skirmishing began near Fort Stevens, a large defensive position outside the city. Both Abraham and Mary Lincoln visited the fort that day and witnessed some of the fighting, and Lincoln returned the next day. Bullets whistled around his top hat, and one man standing near him was shot down. Years after the war, Chief Justice Oliver Wendell Holmes, Jr., who was a captain at the time, claimed he did not realize the standing figure was Lincoln until after he persuaded him to take cover by shouting, "Get down, you damn fool, before you get shot!"

Early was eager to capture Washington, but he realized his chance had passed and wisely withdrew on the night of July 12. The Confederates burned the house of Postmaster General Montgomery Blair on their way out and returned to Virginia the next evening. Early's raid succeeded in temporarily clearing the enemy from the Shenandoah Valley and drawing some Union troops from Lee's front, but it had no lasting strategic impact. Early best summed up the operation when he declared to one officer, "Major, we haven't taken Washington, but we've scared Abe Lincoln like hell!"

## The Chambersburg Raid

Early remained in the Shenandoah Valley after the Washington raid and decided to take revenge for David Hunter's destruction of the region. In late July, he ordered Brigadier General John McCausland to take his cavalry brigade to Chambersburg, Pennsylvania, and demand $100,000 in gold or $500,000 in greenbacks as compensation for Virginians whose property Hunter destroyed.

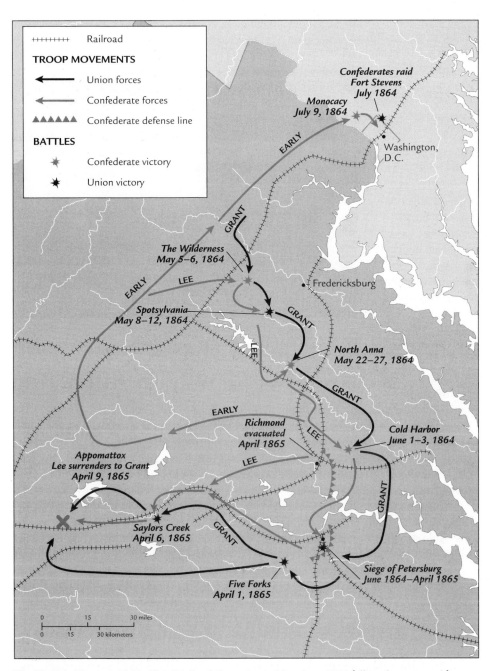

**The Virginia Theater, 1864.** The Overland Campaign in May–June 1864 followed a pattern. After each large battle, Grant disengaged and tried to move around Lee's right flank, only to be stopped by the Confederates and forced to fight again. By the time Grant reached Petersburg, he and Lee had sustained a combined 90,000 casualties. During the campaign, Jubal Early led an audacious Confederate raid to the outskirts of Washington, but he was unable to capture the enemy capital.

**Chambersburg, Pennsylvania.** On July 30, 1864, General John McCausland's Confederate cavalry torched 400 buildings in Chambersburg, Pennsylvania, after its residents refused to pay a ransom demand. This photograph shows some of the destruction.

If the demand was not met, McCausland was to burn the town. McCausland was sitting on his horse talking to an officer when a courier brought the order. "I opened it up," he recalled, "and when I read those first lines I nearly fell out of the saddle. He ordered me in a very few words to make a retaliatory raid and give the Yankees a taste of their own medicine."

McCausland reached Chambersburg on July 30 and gave the townspeople six hours to comply with the demand. While waiting for a reply, many Confederates spent their time robbing the civilians and looting their homes. The residents finally refused to pay because there was not that much money in town and, as one remembered, "[T]he citizens did not feel like contributing aid in the overthrow of their government." McCausland torched Chambersburg, destroying 400 buildings and causing nearly $1,500,000 in damages. It was a terrible act of destruction that was not supported by all of McCausland's men. One officer was temporarily arrested for refusing to carry out the order, and other Confederates helped save several houses. Jacob Hoke, a town resident, left a graphic account of the destruction and the Rebels' mixed feelings. He claimed some Confederates "entered into this work with evident delight, and to the entreaties and tears of the aged, the infirm, of women and children, they turned a deaf ear. . . . In some cases, after fire had been kindled, others would come in extinguishing it. Some sections of the town were entirely saved because the officers sent there refused to execute their barbarous orders, and in a few cases officers and soldiers worked with citizens at the fire engine to extinguish the flames." Hunter's destruction of the Shenandoah Valley and McCausland's Chambersburg Raid were clear evidence that both armies were plunging into a war of violent retribution.

# THE MOVE TO PETERSBURG

**May 5, 1864: Butler lands on Bermuda Hundred**
**May 6–7, 1864: Battle of Port Walthall Junction**
**June 11–12, 1864: Battle of Trevilian Station**
**June 14, 1864: Grant crosses the James River**

By July, Lee's army was battered and weakened, and it had been pushed back to within a few miles of Richmond, but the Confederates still fielded a potent fighting force that continued to block the way to the capital. Although the Shenandoah Valley had been ravaged by Union forces, Lee continued to get supplies from there, and both armies had received substantial reinforcements to replace their horrendous losses. Despite the stalemate, Grant was cautiously optimistic because he had seriously weakened Lee's army and was closer to the enemy's capital than any Union army had been since McClellan's Peninsula Campaign. If it had not been for Ben Butler's abject failure on his front, Richmond might have already been captured.

## The Bermuda Hundred Campaign

Butler had the best chance of achieving a quick and stunning victory during the spring offensive. While Grant hammered away at Lee in Northern Virginia, Butler was to take his Army of the James by sea to Bermuda Hundred, Virginia. This peninsula, formed by the juncture of the James and Appomattox rivers, was located fifteen miles southeast of Richmond. Bermuda Hundred was important strategically because it was located between Richmond and Petersburg, a vital railroad hub that funneled supplies to the capital by way of the Richmond & Petersburg Railroad. Butler was to secure a foothold on Bermuda Hundred and then cut the Richmond & Petersburg Railroad to sever Lee's southern supply line.

On May 5, the same day Lee and Grant made contact in the Wilderness, Butler successfully landed 39,000 men on Bermuda Hundred. A speedy advance would have captured the railroad before the Confederate's department commander, P. G. T. Beauregard, had time to react. Butler, however, moved slowly and cautiously and even stopped to entrench the next day. This inexcusable delay gave Beauregard time to rush Major General George Pickett's division to the threatened area. That afternoon, Butler pushed on toward the railroad at Port Walthall Junction, but the division commander on the scene thought he was outnumbered and withdrew after a short clash. The fighting continued over the next several days and Butler managed to tear up some track, but the damage was later repaired and Beauregard skillfully held the enemy in check. If Butler had moved quickly and decisively after landing at Bermuda Hundred, he might very well have captured Richmond. Instead, the campaign fizzled out when he retreated back to the peninsula and took up a defensive position behind a strong line of works built across the narrow neck of land. Beauregard followed and constructed his own line of entrenchments fronting Butler. Butler thus seemed, in Grant's words, as if he were in a bottle "strongly corked."

## Crossing the James River

After the debacle at Cold Harbor and Butler's failure at Bermuda Hundred, Grant decided it was time to change tactics. For a month, he had repeatedly tried to turn Lee's right flank, only to meet entrenched Confederates each time. With the Chickahominy River now blocking another short slide to the left, Grant settled on a new plan. He would withdraw from Cold Harbor, make a longer sweep to the left than usual to cross the James River, and march swiftly to the south to capture the important railroad center of Petersburg before Lee could react. If the plan was successful, the supply line to Richmond would be severed, and the Confederates would have to evacuate the city. It was an inspired strategy, but success depended on secrecy and speed. If Lee discovered the movement, he could either attack Grant's army while it was astride the James River or take advantage of his interior line and reach Petersburg first.

To distract Lee while he crossed the river, Grant sent Sheridan's cavalry on a raid toward Charlottesville to join forces with David Hunter's army rampaging through the Shenandoah Valley and to destroy the Virginia Central Railroad and James River Canal. Major General Wade Hampton, who had replaced the fallen Stuart, immediately set out in pursuit and engaged Sheridan at Trevilian Station on June 11–12. The two-day battle was close-quartered and bloody, but Sheridan was unable to fight his way through the Confederates, although he did destroy several miles of track. A few days later, Jubal Early stopped Hunter's advance and drove him completely out of Virginia.

Although Sheridan was unable to join Hunter, he did distract Lee's cavalry at the critical time Grant was crossing the James River. The Army of the Potomac suddenly disappeared from Cold Harbor on the night of June 12 and began crossing the river two days later on a pontoon bridge. Grant accomplished what few Union generals had ever done—slip away and steal a march on Lee. When Grant arrived at Petersburg on June 15, there were virtually no Confederates defending the city because Lee was still at Cold Harbor. Once again, a swift attack might have captured Petersburg and forced Lee to abandon Richmond, but none of Grant's corps commanders was up to the task. Major General William F. Smith advanced cautiously with his corps because he had heard rumors Lee had arrived on the scene, and he received little support from Hancock. Ambrose Burnside did force Beauregard to retreat a short distance, but the Creole general and his small band of men held back the overwhelming Union force long enough for Lee to learn of the danger and rush his army to Petersburg. Lee's veterans arrived on June 18 just in time to stop Burnside's attack. The series of clashes outside Petersburg cost Grant another 10,000 casualties, and all he accomplished was to overrun a few forward enemy positions. Grant had missed an excellent opportunity to capture Richmond, and now he and Lee had to settle into a protracted siege that neither wanted.

## FOR FURTHER READING

General Grant's discussion of his strategy from his *Personal Memoirs,* Vol. II, pp. 127–32.
General Richard S. Ewell's report on the Overland Campaign

# CHAPTER 22

# From Meridian to Atlanta

The Meridian and Florida Expeditions

The Red River Campaign and Camden Expedition

The Atlanta Campaign

William T. Sherman, the newly appointed commander of the Military Division of the Mississippi, was a bundle of energy in the spring of 1864 as he prepared for his campaign against Atlanta, Georgia. Organizing his various departments and making command changes occupied much of his time, but nothing worried him as much as logistics. "The great question of the campaign," Sherman wrote, "was one of supplies." There were 136 miles of railroad track from his staging area at Chattanooga to his supply base at Nashville, Tennessee, that had to be guarded constantly against Rebel cavalry raids. This single line was all Sherman had to supply the tons of food, ammunition, and medicine needed for the campaign. Not only did he have to secure enough supplies for daily needs, he also had to stockpile a surplus in case the enemy did cut the railroad. To do this, Sherman restricted train cargoes to essential military supplies and cut off all civilian traffic. He also ordered troops and cattle coming out of Nashville to use the roads rather than take the train. "This was a great help," Sherman recalled, "but of course it naturally raised a howl." Some East Tennessee Unionists complained to President Lincoln, and he asked Sherman to reconsider his orders. Sherman wrote in his memoirs, "I answered him that a great campaign was impending, on which the fate of the nation hung; that our railroads had but a limited capacity, and could not provide for the necessities of the army and of the people too; that one or the other must quit, and we could not. . . ." Lincoln understood and did not interfere.

Stockpiling the necessary supplies for the Atlanta Campaign required 130 railroad cars per day, but Sherman did not have that many available. Undeterred, he began commandeering trains as they arrived in Nashville. When the railroad companies complained, Sherman explained his predicament and they volunteered to ferry more locomotives and rolling stock across the Ohio River. Sherman later wrote, "I was amused to see, away down in Georgia, cars marked 'Pittsburg & Fort Wayne,' 'Delaware & Lackawanna,' 'Baltimore & Ohio,' and indeed with the names of almost every railroad north of the Ohio River." He appreciated the railroads' selflessness and declared, "How these railroad companies ever recovered their property, or settled their transportation accounts, I have never heard, but to this fact, as much as to any other single fact, I attribute the perfect success which afterward attended our campaigns. . . ."

On May 4, 1864, the same day Grant started his Overland Campaign, Sherman began moving toward Atlanta. The operation was made possible by his careful planning and stockpiling of supplies, which allowed his armies to keep attacking the enemy without having to stop and resupply. The Atlanta Campaign would prove to be a resounding success, and the Union's superiority in logistics was just as responsible for victory as were the men on the battlefield.

# THE MERIDIAN AND FLORIDA EXPEDITIONS

**February 3, 1864: Sherman begins the Meridian Campaign**
**February 14, 1864: Sherman reaches Meridian**
**February 20, 1864: Battle of Olustee, Florida**
**February 22, 1864: Battle of Okolona, Mississippi**

In early 1864, the Confederates in the west were reeling from their defeat at Chattanooga, and Lincoln was putting them under increasing political pressure by organizing loyal state governments in areas under Union control. In January, an Arkansas constitutional convention adopted a resolution abolishing slavery, and the Thirteenth Amendment was proposed in the U.S. Senate to abolish slavery nationwide. Determined to keep up this pressure, Union forces launched two military expeditions that February in Mississippi and Florida. The pendulum of war seemed to be swinging in favor of the Union, but the Confederates had a habit of doing the unexpected, and it remained to be seen if the Northern optimism was warranted.

## The Meridian Expedition

To sever the enemy's interior line and weaken Southern morale, William T. Sherman led 26,000 infantry east from Vicksburg, Mississippi, in February 1864. At the same time, Brigadier General William Sooy Smith was to take 7,000 cavalrymen from Tennessee and head south. The two columns were to create as much havoc as possible and rendezvous at Meridian. Moving along a wide front, Sherman destroyed barns and houses and confiscated food and livestock; but, on arriving at Meridian he discovered that the Confederates had already removed most of the supplies and railroad cars, and Smith was nowhere to be seen. After spending several days destroying tracks and bridges, Sherman returned to Vicksburg with approximately 5,000 freed slaves in tow. He was satisfied with the raid and proudly reported, "Meridian, with its depots, storehouses, arsenals, hospitals, offices, hotels, and cantonments no longer exists.

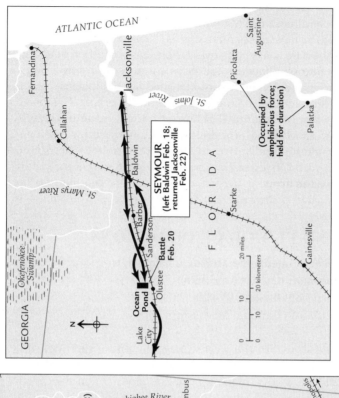

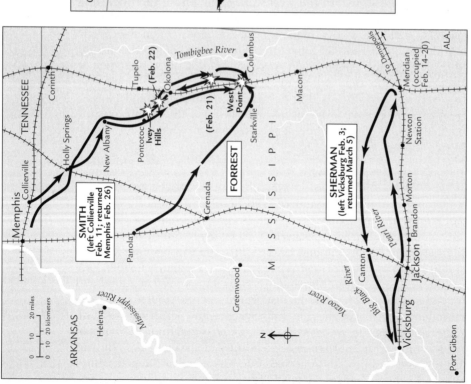

**The Meridian and Florida Expeditions, February 1864.** In the Meridian Expedition (left), two Union columns advanced on Meridian, Mississippi, to destroy the Confederate railroad. Marching from Vicksburg, Sherman wrecked the railroad at Meridian, but Forrest defeated Smith at Okolona and forced his retreat. In Florida (on right), Seymour advanced from Jacksonville to recruit slaves and destroy an enemy railroad, but Finegan's Confederates defeated him at Olustee and drove him back to Jacksonville.

I have no hesitation in pronouncing the work as well done." Farther north, however, Smith had met disaster at the hands of Nathan Bedford Forrest.

Smith was two weeks late leaving Tennessee because he took too much time gathering reinforcements. This delay gave Forrest the opportunity to concentrate his 4,000 cavalrymen to meet the invaders. Smith destroyed some railroad track, cotton, and supplies, but he quickly retreated when he encountered the enemy. At dawn on February 22, Forrest attacked and pushed Smith back to the outskirts of Okolona (OH-kuh-LON-uh). Heavy fighting continued throughout the day, but Smith finally disengaged and withdrew to Tennessee. The expedition was an embarrassing failure, and Smith soon resigned his commission and retired from the army.

Purely in military terms, Sherman's Mississippi expeditions accomplished little because they failed to destroy the Confederates' vital rolling stock, and the damaged track was back in operation a month later. However, the Meridian Expedition did provide Sherman with a valuable lesson. To his surprise, he discovered the Confederate interior was rich in forage but nearly devoid of enemy troops. A large Union army could operate almost at will in the very heart of enemy territory and spread terror by taking the war to the people with little risk of being annihilated in battle. Later in the year, Sherman's March to the Sea would gain much attention, but the Meridian Expedition planted the seeds of that famous march.

## The Florida Expedition

While Sherman was destroying railroads in Mississippi, another Union raid was made in Florida. Anxious to form a loyal state government there, President Lincoln authorized an invasion to liberate Florida's Unionists, recruit troops among the slaves, and cut Confederate supply lines. A large force landed at Jacksonville, and in early February, Brigadier General Truman Seymour advanced 5,500 men inland and engaged Brigadier General Joseph Finegan's Confederates near the railroad depot of Olustee (oh-LUS-tee). Although the two forces were about equal in strength, many of Seymour's men were recently recruited black soldiers who had no training. Seymour attacked on the afternoon of February 20, but the enemy drove him back in hard fighting and captured several cannons. He then brought up the 54th Massachusetts to reinforce the battered line and help cover his retreat to Jacksonville. The newly formed 8th U.S. Colored Troops also saw combat at Olustee. Its proud commander wrote, "I was afterward told that they had never had a day's practice in loading and firing. Old troops, finding themselves so greatly over-matched, would have run a little and re-formed—with or without orders. . . . [They] stood to be killed or wounded—losing more than three hundred out of five hundred and fifty." In the Battle of Olustee, Seymour lost almost 1,900 men, while Finegan lost nearly 1,000 men. The Yankees returned safely to Jacksonville and held it for the rest of the war, but the Confederate victory stopped the invasion of Florida and prevented the Union from establishing a loyal government there.

## THE RED RIVER CAMPAIGN
## AND CAMDEN EXPEDITION

**April 8, 1864: Battle of Mansfield, Louisiana**
**April 9, 1864: Battle of Pleasant Hill, Louisiana**
**April 18, 1864: Battle of Poison Spring, Arkansas**
**April 30, 1864: Battle of Jenkins' Ferry, Arkansas**
**May 13, 1864: Burning of Alexandria, Louisiana**

As the newly appointed general-in-chief, General Grant planned simultaneous offensives on all fronts in 1864 to overwhelm the Confederates. He intended Mobile, Alabama, to be one target, but political concerns over Mexico forced him to alter his plans. In 1862, Napoleon III took advantage of the American Civil War to reestablish the French empire in North America. French troops invaded Mexico, overthrew Benito Juárez's government, and created a puppet government under Austrian Archduke Ferdinand Maximilian. Both Napoleon and Maximilian were sympathetic to the Rebel cause, and Lincoln wanted to establish a strong Union presence in Texas to prevent Maximilian from aiding the Confederacy or expanding into the American southwest. Bowing to the president's wishes, Grant cancelled the Mobile operation and ordered Major General Nathaniel P. Banks to invade Texas.

Banks, a former Massachusetts congressman and Speaker of the House, saw political opportunity in such an invasion. His state's economy was suffering because textile mills were being deprived of Southern cotton, and a move up the Red River into Texas would give him the opportunity to confiscate Rebel cotton, save the economy, and secure his political future. A Red River route also would enable Banks to capture Shreveport, Louisiana, an important manufacturing site close to the Texas border that served as both the Confederates' state capital and the headquarters for General Edmund Kirby Smith's Trans-Mississippi Department.

To ensure success, Major General Frederick Steele was ordered to advance on Shreveport from Little Rock, Arkansas, as a diversion to draw away as many Confederate defenders as possible. Sherman also attached Brigadier General Andrew Jackson Smith's 10,000 men to the expedition, but he made it clear to Banks that Smith was simply on loan and had to be returned in time for the Atlanta Campaign in early May. Smith's men were battle-hardened veterans and were good to have in a fight, but their poor discipline and outrageous behavior led Banks to refer to them as "gorillas." Admiral David Porter's fleet of ninety ships would transport Smith's command from Vicksburg to the Red River and cooperate with Banks's 30,000 men.

Defending Louisiana was Major General Richard Taylor's 7,000-man Confederate army. "Dick" Taylor (1826–1879) was a Louisiana native, the son of former President Zachary Taylor, and the brother of Jefferson Davis's first wife. A Yale University graduate, he had been a planter and state senator before the

**Alexandria, Louisiana.** Alexandria was an important staging area for Banks and Porter during the Red River Campaign. The downtown area, shown in this wartime photograph, was burned several weeks later when Union forces retreated after their defeat at Mansfield.

war. Although Taylor had no prior military experience, he was a natural soldier and was promoted to major general after commanding a Louisiana Tiger brigade under Stonewall Jackson. One veteran said Taylor was "a very quiet, unassuming little fellow, but noisy on retreats, with a tendency to cuss mules and wagons which stall in the road." Among Taylor's many admirers was Nathan Bedford Forrest, who said of him, "He's the biggest man in the lot. If we'd had more like him, we would have licked the Yankees long ago."

In early March 1864, the Red River Campaign began when Banks marched out of South Louisiana and Porter's fleet sailed from Vicksburg. Porter and Smith engaged the enemy first on March 14 when they attacked and easily captured Fort DeRussy, a Confederate stronghold on the Red River. Soon afterward, the Yankees occupied Alexandria, confiscated as much cotton as possible, and then moved upstream to Grand Ecore. There Banks made a serious blunder by leaving the protection of Porter's gunboats and taking a narrow woods road that snaked west and north to Shreveport through what one cavalryman called a "howling wilderness."

## The Battles of Mansfield and Pleasant Hill

Taylor retreated before the massive invasion, but he slowly gathered reinforcements to increase his army to about 9,000 men. Now ready to fight, he repeatedly requested permission from General Kirby Smith to attack. When Kirby Smith hesitated, Taylor decided to act on his own and blocked the road to Shreveport near the town of Mansfield. On April 8, Banks's vanguard under Brigadier General Thomas E. G. Ransom entered a large field, but heavy enemy

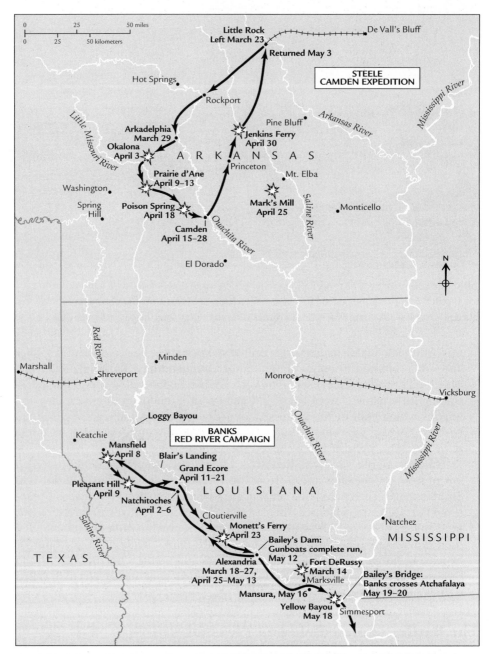

**The Red River Campaign and Camden Expedition, March–May, 1864.** In the spring of 1864, Union forces launched a two-pronged attack against Shreveport, Louisiana. In the south, Banks and Porter moved up the Red River but were forced to retreat when Taylor's Confederates attacked Banks at Mansfield and Pleasant Hill. In Arkansas, Steele's Union army advanced southwest out of Little Rock to Camden. After running short of supplies and being attacked by growing enemy forces, Steele, too, abandoned the operation and retreated to Little Rock.

fire forced him to fall back behind a rail fence. About 4:00 p.m., Major General Alfred Mouton's (MOO-tahn's) Louisiana division attacked across the field and came under a murderous fire from the Union infantry and artillery. The rest of Taylor's army quickly joined in and pressure mounted all along Ransom's line. Mouton and all three of his regimental colonels were killed, but Brigadier General Camille Prince de Polignac (poe-leen-YAK) snatched up a fallen flag and pressed on the attack. The Confederates finally overran Ransom and forced him back to a second position. When the Rebels drove them from there, the Yankees panicked, and the orderly retreat became a rout. A Union reporter who was caught up in the confusion wrote, "Suddenly, there was a rush, a shout, the crashing of trees, the breaking down of rails, the rush and scamper of men. . . . I turned to my companion to inquire the reason of this extraordinary proceeding, but before he had the chance to reply, we found ourselves swallowed up, as it were, in a hissing, seething, bubbling whirlpool of agitated men." Only darkness and the arrival of a fresh Union division stopped the retreat, three miles from where the battle began.

The Battle of Mansfield was a stunning Confederate victory and one of the largest Civil War battles west of the Mississippi River. Besides stopping Banks's invasion and saving Shreveport, Taylor inflicted 2,200 Union casualties (while sustaining 1,000) and captured 20 cannons, hundreds of rifles, and nearly 200 wagons filled with supplies. While basking in his victory that night, he received a note from Kirby Smith ordering him to avoid a general engagement. "Too late, sir," Taylor replied, "the battle is won."

Banks retreated that night to Pleasant Hill and took up a strong defensive position in thick woods. After receiving several thousand fresh troops, Taylor attacked again on the afternoon of April 9. A furious battle raged throughout the day, but the Confederates were unable to break the tough Union defenses before darkness finally ended the fight. Banks could claim a tactical victory at Pleasant Hill because he successfully defended his position and inflicted about 1,600 casualties on Taylor while losing about 1,400 men. But two days of fighting had rattled his nerves because he had not expected a battle until he reached Shreveport. As a result, Banks decided to abandon his dead and wounded and fall back to Grand Ecore to regroup. By this time, subordinate officers were losing confidence in his leadership because the retreat was unnecessary, and it turned a tactical victory into a strategic defeat. The Confederates had also suffered heavy losses, and Banks still had a much larger army than Taylor. If he had resumed the advance, he probably could have pushed Taylor aside and marched on to Shreveport.

Taylor was ready to pursue the enemy and attack again, but Kirby Smith took most of his infantry and sent them to Arkansas to stop Steele's advance from Little Rock. This left Taylor with so few men that all he could do was follow Banks and harass his rear guard. Taylor fumed over Kirby Smith's decision for years and later called him "stubborn" and "obstinate" in his memoirs. The generals' rift was so great that Taylor refused to serve under Kirby Smith after the campaign ended and was transferred to the east side of the Mississippi River.

**Foreign Observers.** A number of European officers accompanied Civil War armies as observers. Here, the three men on the left are the Duc de Chartres, the Prince de Joinville, and the Comte de Paris. They were attached to the Army of the Potomac during the Peninsula Campaign. (The two men on the right are unidentified.)

## The Retreat

While Banks was fighting for his life in the piney woods, Porter was having difficulty moving up the Red River because the normal spring rains had failed and the water level was steadily falling. The Confederates had also shrewdly opened a clogged distributary to drain even more  water out of the river, and they blocked the channel with a sunken steamboat. Porter was forced to retreat downstream, but Brigadier General Thomas Green's Rebel cavalry constantly harassed his ships. Green frequently peppered the vessels with artillery and rifle fire from concealed positions, and he even made one bold attack at Blair's Landing when he found several boats run aground. Green led his dismounted men against the heavily armored ships, but the troopers withdrew when he was killed by a cannonball that nearly decapitated him. A Union soldier who saw the ships arrive at Grand Ecore wrote in his diary, "[T]he sides of some of the transports are half shot away, and their smoke-stacks look like huge pepper boxes."

From Grand Ecore the retreat turned ugly. Frustrated at withdrawing unnecessarily and completely disgusted with Banks, the Yankees burned several small towns and numerous plantation houses and outbuildings. Louisiana's Governor Henry Watkins Allen claimed, "From Mansfield to the Mississippi River the track of the spoiler was one scene of desolation. . . . You can travel for miles . . . and not see a man, nor a woman, nor a child, nor a four-footed beast. The farm-houses have been burned. The plantations deserted. . . . A painful melancholy, a death-like silence, broods over the land, and desolation reigns supreme." One Union general agreed with this assessment and declared the retreat was "disgraceful to the army of a civilized nation."

Taylor tried to cut off Banks's retreat at the Cane River crossing of Monett's (MAH-nets) Ferry, but the superior Union force ran roughshod over his men and continued on to Alexandria. Porter also reached the city safely after losing several ships to artillery ambushes and torpedoes, but the low water stopped him at a stretch of shallow rapids. Porter's fleet was trapped, and he was preparing to destroy the ships to keep them out of enemy hands when Lieutenant Colonel Joseph Bailey proposed a daring plan. Bailey was a Wisconsin lumberman turned engineer. He confidently declared that he could build a series of wing dams to raise the water level enough for Porter to extract the ships. Having no better plan, Banks provided Bailey with thousands of soldiers to construct the dams over a two-week period. In early May, the dams began to give way from the growing water pressure, and Porter ordered his fleet to make a dash for safety. All the ships managed to escape, and Porter and Banks prepared to abandon Alexandria.

As the army departed Alexandria on May 13, Andrew Jackson Smith's gorillas were spotted carrying buckets of turpentine and boasting they were "preparing the place for Hell!" Flames suddenly engulfed the city, and one Union soldier recalled, "Cows went bellowing through the street. Chickens flew out from yards and fell in the streets with their feathers scorching on them. A dog with his bushy tail on fire ran howling through, turning to snap at the fire as he ran. . . ." Residents grabbed what they could and ran for the levee. With their meager goods piled at their feet, hundreds of people stood along the river and watched twenty-two city blocks burn to the ground. As Smith's gorillas marched out of

# DID YOU KNOW?

## The Foreign Participants

When the Civil War began, many Europeans served with the opposing armies. Some were professional soldiers sent by their governments as observers to study tactics, while some actually enlisted out of a sense of adventure or because they were truly committed to the cause. British Lieutenant Colonel James Fremantle accompanied Lee's army at Gettysburg and wrote a popular account of his experiences entitled *Three Months in the Southern States.* Brothers Duc de Chartres and Comte de Paris and their uncle Prince de Joinville were members of the French royal family who traveled with McClellan and the Army of the Potomac. The Comte de Paris later wrote the 8-volume *History of the Civil War in America,* and the Prince de Joinville published *The Army of the Potomac.* Heros von Borcke was a Prussian who joined Jeb Stuart's staff and wrote *Memoirs of the Confederate War for Independence.*

Camille Armand Jules Marie, Prince de Polignac (1832–1913) was unique in becoming a Confederate major general. A French native and Crimean War veteran, Polignac abandoned his scholarly studies in Central America to offer his services to the Confederacy. With jet-black hair, white teeth, and waxed moustache, he was one of the Rebels' most colorful figures. Polignac spoke fluent English, drank like a sailor, and cursed "like a trooper." His extraordinary bravery earned him a promotion to brigadier general and command of a Texas brigade in Richard Taylor's army. The Texans at first disliked their general and called him "a damn frog-eating Frenchman." Unable to pronounce his name, they referred to him as "General Polecat" and held their noses when he passed by. But Polignac proved himself in battle and became a popular officer in the Trans-Mississippi Department. He was the last surviving Confederate major general, dying in Europe in the early twentieth century.

**Bailey's Dam.** To dam up the Red River and rescue Porter's stranded fleet, Union soldiers loaded barges with debris and sunk them in the river. Note the swirling whitewater rapids in the foreground.

town, some walked along the levee and stole what little the people had saved. While the burning of Alexandria was blamed on individual arsonists, there is little doubt General Smith encouraged it. One soldier claimed he was seen riding through streets yelling, "Hurrah, boys, this looks like war!"

Taylor continued to harass Banks's rear guard as the Union army marched to the Atchafalaya (uh-CHAF-uh-LIE-uh) River. There the Yankees again found themselves momentarily trapped because there was no bridge across the wide, turbulent stream. For the second time in the campaign, however, Colonel Bailey saved the day by building a pontoon bridge across the river with lumber stripped from nearby barns and houses. To keep the enemy from interfering with the work, Banks placed Brigadier General Joseph A. Mower's division in the rear along Yellow Bayou. Bailey completed his bridge while Mower held back Taylor in a small firefight on May 18, and the campaign came to an end when the Union army successfully crossed over the Atchafalaya and left Taylor stranded on the west bank.

The Red River Campaign was a Union disaster. Banks failed to capture Shreveport or invade Texas, he was defeated by a smaller Confederate force at Mansfield, and he then retreated unnecessarily after winning the Battle of Pleasant Hill. Banks also failed to return Smith's 10,000 men in time to participate in the Atlanta Campaign. In hindsight, it would have been better had Banks moved against Mobile to tie down its defenders rather than allow them to reinforce

Joseph E. Johnston in the Atlanta Campaign. The only gain made in the ill-fated campaign was the few thousand bales of cotton that were confiscated. However, that hardly offset the 15,000 additional troops the Confederates were able to muster from Mobile to help defend Atlanta. When asked his opinion, William T. Sherman declared that the Red River Campaign had been "One damn blunder from beginning to end." Such stubborn fighting on the part of the Rebels and poor leadership on the part of the Yankees left most of the Trans-Mississippi Department under Confederate control until the end of the war.

## The Camden Expedition

In Arkansas, Major General Frederick Steele's expedition to Shreveport was also turned back because he took so long to prepare that the Confederates were able to defeat Banks in Louisiana and then concentrate their forces against Steele. Leaving Little Rock on March 23, Steele first made his way to Elkin's Ferry, where he was reinforced by 10,000 men from Fort Smith. Confederate Major General Sterling Price expected the enemy then to attack the Confederate capital at Washington, so he put his 5,000 men in a blocking position. Steele, however, surprised Price by moving toward Camden, where he hoped to gather badly needed supplies. By the time the Union soldiers entered town, they had been living on half rations for three weeks and were desperate. From Camden, Steele dispatched 200 wagons to forage for supplies in the countryside, but nearly 4,000 Confederates ambushed and overwhelmed the wagon train and its 1,200-man escort at Poison Spring on the morning of April 18.

Although a modest affair, the Battle of Poison Spring was quickly engulfed in controversy when Union survivors accused the Rebels of murdering members of the 1st Kansas Colored Volunteers who were wounded or trying to surrender. With 117 dead and only 65 wounded, the Kansas soldiers had an unusually high ratio of killed to wounded. Most of the Confederates claimed the black soldiers simply fought to the death, but one Texan admitted, "The havoc among the negroes had been tremendous. . . . Over a small portion of the field we saw at least 450 dead bodies lying in all conceivable attitudes, some scalped & nearly all stripped. . . . No black prisoners were captured."

Two days after the fight at Poison Spring, General Edmund Kirby Smith arrived with thousands of Confederate troops from Richard Taylor's Louisiana army. Conditions only worsened for Steele when the Rebels attacked another of his supply trains at Marks' Mills on April 25. In a short, bloody battle, the Confederates killed about 100 Union soldiers, seized all 240 wagons, and captured approximately 1,300 prisoners while losing only 300 men. Several hundred runaway slaves were following the wagon train seeking freedom, and many of them were slaughtered. A Confederate officer confirmed the atrocity when he wrote, "The battle-field was sickening to behold. No orders, threats, or commands could restrain the men from vengeance on the negroes, and they were piled in great heaps about the wagons, in the tangled brushwood, and upon the muddy and trampled road."

# NOTABLE UNIT: *1st Kansas Colored Volunteers*

This regiment's origins can be traced to noted abolitionist General James H. Lane, who began recruiting black soldiers in Kansas in the summer of 1862. On October 29, some of the new recruits became the first African American soldiers to engage in combat. Captain Henry Seaman took about 250 blacks and a few white soldiers to Island Mound, Missouri, in search of guerrillas and defeated them in a fierce hand-to-hand fight. One of the white soldiers wrote, "For some ten or fifteen minutes the conflict raged with demoniacal fury—a hand to hand fight—the first crucial test in our Civil war which proved the courage of the ex slave to meet his former master on the field of battle. With bayonet and clubbed gun he there did a deadly work unmoved apparently by a sign of fear."

Formation of the regiment was completed in early 1863 and James M. Williams was made colonel. Four additional companies were added in May. The regiment served the entire war west of the Mississippi River and spent much of its time fighting guerrillas. It was extremely dangerous duty. In May 1863, guerrillas ambushed a foraging party made up of twenty-five black soldiers and twenty white artillerymen in Jasper County, Missouri. Sixteen men were killed and three of the whites and two blacks were captured. The white soldiers were exchanged, but the Rebels refused to release the blacks and even murdered one. Outraged, Colonel Williams demanded the guilty party be executed, but the Confederates refused. He then retaliated by shooting one of his prisoners. Afterward, the colonel viewed the ambush scene and wrote, "Men were found with their brains beaten out with clubs, and the bloody weapons left by

When Steele learned that Banks was retreating in Louisiana, he withdrew from Camden and headed back to Little Rock with Kirby Smith in close pursuit. On April 30, the Confederates attacked again when Steele crossed the Saline River at Jenkins' Ferry. Rebel cavalry engaged the Union rear guard for most of the day but was unable to fight its way to the river. Both sides lost approximately 500 men in the clash, but Steele escaped. Kirby Smith then called off his pursuit, and the exhausted, half-starved Yankees stumbled into Little Rock on May 3. For them, the Camden Expedition had been a nightmare.

## THE ATLANTA CAMPAIGN

May 14–15, 1864: Battle of Resaca
May 25–27, 1864: Battle of New Hope Church
June 10, 1864: Battle of Brice's Cross Roads
June 27, 1864: Battle of Kennesaw Mountain
July 14–15, 1864: Battle of Tupelo
July 20, 1864: Battle of Peachtree Creek
July 22, 1864: Battle of Atlanta
August 5, 1864: Battle of Mobile Bay

their sides, and their bodies most horribly mutilated." Williams then razed the region within a five-mile radius and executed another prisoner who was suspected of violating his parole.

On July 2, 1863, Colonel Williams was escorting a wagon train in Indian Territory when he encountered Confederate General Stand Watie blocking his way at Cabin Creek. Eight of Williams's men were killed and twenty-five wounded when they had to make a frontal attack across the stream to dislodge the enemy. On July 17, they hit the enemy again at Honey Springs, and lost five killed and thirty-two wounded. Colonel Williams was among the latter, being wounded in the face, chest, and both hands. Of this fight, he declared, "I had long been of the opinion that this race had a right to kill rebels, and this day proved their capacity for the work. Forty prisoners and one battle flag fell into the hands of my regiment on this field." In the spring of 1864 the regiment joined the Camden Expedition and suffered very high losses at Poison Spring, Arkansas. Shortly after this disaster, Williams was promoted to brigade command and left the regiment. In September, forty-two of the Kansas men were sent to guard a hay-making party at Flat Rock in Indian Territory. The Confederates attacked the detachment and killed twenty-two men and took ten prisoners. Again, some of the captured were reportedly murdered.

When the 1st Kansas was mustered out of service in October 1865, it had served in twelve battles and ranked 21st among Union regiments for the highest percentage of men killed in action.

## August 31–September 1, 1864: Battle of Jonesboro
## September 2, 1864: Sherman captures Atlanta

The failures in Louisiana and Arkansas were an inauspicious start for Grant's spring offenses. Fortunately for the Union, those operations were of marginal importance and would not have materially altered the course of the war if they had succeeded. Much more important was Sherman's march on Atlanta to destroy Joseph E. Johnston's Army of Tennessee. Atlanta was a vital Confederate railhead and industrial center, and its loss would be a devastating blow to the South. Sherman knew Johnston would fight to defend it, and he planned to use the city as the anvil against which he would hammer the Rebel army.

On May 4, 1864, Sherman began the 100-mile march to Atlanta. He had 110,000 men divided among Major General George H. Thomas's Army of the Cumberland, Major General James B. McPherson's Army of the Tennessee, and Major General John M. Schofield's Army of the Ohio. To oppose this massive onslaught, Johnston could muster about half as many men, but he had the tactical advantage. Northern Georgia was laced with rivers and mountain ranges that ran perpendicular to Sherman's route and gave Johnston numerous places to make a defensive stand. Frontal assaults against these nearly impregnable

## BIOGRAPHY
# William Tecumseh Sherman: "Uncle Billy"

**William T. Sherman**

Known to his friends as "Cump," William Tecumseh Sherman (1820–1891) was the son of an Ohio supreme court justice whose death left the family destitute. Friends and relatives raised the family's eleven children, with Senator Thomas Ewing taking in Sherman (who later married Ewing's daughter). After graduating from West Point in 1840, Sherman served in the Mexican War before resigning his commission and engaging in a number of failed business ventures. In 1859, he was appointed superintendent of the Louisiana Seminary of Learning and Military Academy and became quite popular. Sherman supported slavery and was content to live in Louisiana as long as there was peace, but his love of the Union remained paramount. When South Carolina seceded, he sadly resigned his position to join the Union army. After leading a brigade at First Bull Run, Sherman was promoted to brigadier general of volunteers and sent to Kentucky.

Tall and angular, with a rough face and short red hair and beard, Sherman had a brilliant intellect and an abundance of nervous energy. He was constantly in motion and spoke in a rapid-fire style while frequently changing the subject of conversation. This natural nervousness and the stress of command eventually led to an emotional collapse in Kentucky when he began predicting imminent disaster. The assistant secretary of war declared, "Sherman's gone in the head, he's luny," and reporters claimed he was insane. Sherman was soon relieved of command, but a lengthy rest restored his spirits, and he became a division commander under Ulysses S. Grant.

Although surprised by the attack at Shiloh, Sherman fought well and was slightly wounded in the hand. An admiring reporter saw him "dashing along the line, encouraging

positions would be suicidal. Sherman would have to find another way to force the Confederates out of their entrenchments.

## Snake Creek Gap and Resaca

Sherman's advance into Georgia came to an abrupt halt when he found Johnston's army dug in on the nearly vertical 500-foot Rocky Face Ridge. A frontal attack against what Sherman called a "door of death" would be foolhardy, so he began a turning movement that set the pattern for the entire campaign. Thomas and Schofield were left in front of Rocky Face Ridge to hold the enemy's attention while McPherson moved south beyond Johnston's left flank to Snake Creek Gap, a gap the Confederates had inexplicably neglected to guard. If he moved quickly, McPherson could move through the gap into the Confederates' rear, cut their railroad supply line, and trap the enemy.

them [his troops] everywhere by his presence, and exposing his own life with the same freedom with which he demanded their offer of theirs." After the battle, Sherman was promoted to major general of volunteers and performed perhaps his most valuable wartime service when he convinced Grant not to resign after he and General Halleck clashed. Sherman recalled, "I argued with him that, if he went away, events would go right along, and he would be left out; whereas, if he remained, some happy accident might restore him to favor and his true place." Grant stayed, and he and Sherman continued their successful partnership. Sherman commanded a corps in the Vicksburg Campaign, led the Army of the Tennessee at Chattanooga, and took over the Military Division of the West when Grant became general-in-chief.

In all of his assignments Sherman was popular with his men, and they bestowed on him the affectionate nickname "Uncle Billy." But he often appeared to be a cold-hearted killer because of some outrageous statements he made and his targeting of civilians to destroy the enemy's morale and ability to wage war. Sherman once boasted, "To secure the safety of the navigation of the Mississippi River, I would slay millions," and his 1864 eviction of civilians from Atlanta, Georgia, infuriated the enemy. When Confederate General John Bell Hood complained that such action was inhuman, Sherman simply retorted, "War is cruelty and you cannot refine it." However, Sherman did not wage a war of annihilation, and he did not hate Southerners. He sometimes allowed enemy armies to escape complete destruction, and he used his influence to help rebuild the South after the conflict ended.

After the war, Sherman replaced Grant as general-in-chief and directed the postwar Indian campaigns. After retiring in 1884, he remained a popular figure, but he shunned politics. When considered for the presidency, Sherman warned, "If nominated I will not run; if elected I will not serve." Despite his war record, he was always greeted warmly in the South and helped reopen the Louisiana Seminary, which eventually became Louisiana State University.

The maneuver worked perfectly. McPherson passed through Snake Creek Gap at dawn on May 9, easily pushed aside a small enemy force, and cut the vital railroad. Just when it appeared he had trapped Johnston, however, he withdrew after learning there were Confederate forces in the nearby town of Resaca (rih-SAHK-uh). When it was later discovered there actually were few Rebels in Resaca, a disappointed Sherman chided his friend, "Well, Mac, you have missed the greatest opportunity of your life." Sherman thought there might still be time to trap Johnston and rushed more troops to the gap, but it was too late. Johnston realized his position was being turned and withdrew to Resaca before Sherman could trap him.

After being reinforced by Lieutenant General Leonidas Polk, Johnston placed nearly 70,000 men in strong entrenchments around Resaca, which was located on the Oostanaula (OOH-stah-NAW-luh) River. Intense fighting took place on May 14–15, but neither side made any appreciable gains. Unable to

# BIOGRAPHY

## Joseph Eggleston Johnston: "The Very Picture of a General"

**Joseph E. Johnston**

An 1829 West Point graduate, Virginia native "Joe" Johnston (1807–1891) saw extensive combat in two wars. After Johnston was shot in the head fighting the Seminole Indians and wounded five times in Mexico, General Winfield Scott quipped, "[Johnston] is a great soldier, but he had an unfortunate knack of getting himself shot in nearly every engagement." Johnston went on to serve as quartermaster general with the staff rank of brigadier general, but he resigned his commission in 1861 and became a Confederate brigadier general. After First Bull Run, he was promoted to full general and was given command of Confederate forces in Northern Virginia.

Johnston immediately became embroiled in a bitter feud with Jefferson Davis over military seniority, which was based on the rank officers had previously held in the U.S. Army. Johnston believed his position as staff brigadier general made him senior to all others, but Davis placed him fourth because his permanent rank in the old army was lieutenant colonel. For the rest of the war, the two proud men constantly argued over strategy, logistics, and responsibility.

The relationship between Johnston and Davis was strained further when Johnston continually retreated during the 1862 Peninsula Campaign. Johnston lost command of the Virginia army when he was wounded at Seven Pines, but Davis made him commander of the Department of the West when he recovered. Unfortunately, he proved reluctant to assume responsibility and once told the president he could

crack the tough Confederate lines, Sherman decided to use another turning movement to force Johnston to retreat. Sherman constructed two pontoon bridges across the Oostanaula River downstream from town and pushed one division over the river to threaten Johnston's rear, while the cavalry moved farther south and captured the Confederate supply base at Rome. With his line of retreat again threatened, Johnston abandoned Resaca that night and withdrew farther south to Cassville. Resaca was the first large battle of the Atlanta Campaign, and it cost Sherman an estimated 4,000 casualties to Johnston's 3,000.

As Sherman approached Cassville, he made a potentially fatal error by spreading his three armies widely apart, with Schofield dangerously exposed far to the east of McPherson and Thomas. Taking advantage of this mistake, Johnston ordered part of his army to keep McPherson and Thomas occupied while John Bell Hood's corps smashed Schofield. Hood was preparing to ambush the unsuspecting Schofield on May 19 when he was told an enemy not defend both Tennessee and Mississippi and demanded that Davis decide which state he should abandon. Johnston also failed to take any significant action to save the trapped garrison at Vicksburg in 1863 even though he had a sizable army at Jackson, Mississippi.

Davis was convinced Johnston was useless as a field commander, but the general had strong military and political support, and he was popular with the troops. One officer declared, "Few men that I have met—none in fact that I remember—possess the same *personal*, purely personal, influence. To my mind, he surpasses Genl Lee as far in the power of attaching his subordinates & his troops devotedly to himself. . . ." A private attributed part of Johnston's popularity to his flamboyant style. "In his dress he was a perfect dandy. . . ," the man recalled. "His hat was decorated with a star and feather, his coat with every star and embellishment, and he wore a bright new sash, big gauntlets, and silver spurs. He was the very picture of a general." Partly because of Johnston's popularity, Davis reluctantly appointed him commander of the Army of Tennessee after the Missionary Ridge debacle. Johnston quickly restored the men's morale by providing fresh supplies, equipment, and furloughs. He then fought skillfully in the Atlanta Campaign, but his constant retreating angered Davis, and the president replaced him with John Bell Hood. In February 1865, Davis put Johnston in command of the Confederate forces in the Carolinas, but he could do little to stop Sherman and finally surrendered in late April 1865.

After the war, Johnston worked in various business ventures, was elected to Congress, and was appointed a federal railroad commissioner. In 1891, he was asked to serve as an honorary pallbearer in the funeral of his old adversary William T. Sherman (Johnston also had served as a pallbearer in U.S. Grant's funeral). Joe Johnston walked bareheaded in the funeral procession, contracted pneumonia, and died a few weeks later.

column was advancing on *his* flank. Convinced he was about to be attacked, Hood repositioned his corps to face this reported threat, but it turned out to be nothing more than a small Union cavalry brigade that had taken a wrong turn. Just as McPherson's caution at Snake Creek Gap prevented Sherman from trapping Johnston, Hood's caution at Cassville prevented Johnston from destroying one of Sherman's columns.

## The Battle of New Hope Church

Johnston retreated once more and fell back to another formidable mountain ridge at Allatoona. Sherman again declined to attack and headed southwest to turn the enemy's left flank. Reacting quickly to block the maneuver, Johnston shifted his army to New Hope Church and Dallas. On May 25, Major General Joseph "Fighting Joe" Hooker's corps engaged the Confederates at Pumpkinvine Creek and pushed them back three miles, but he then was stopped by the

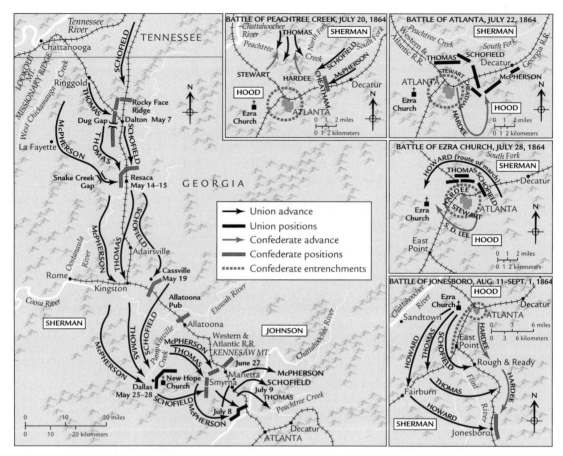

**The Atlanta Campaign, May–September 1864.** Unlike the bloodbath that occurred in Virginia, the Atlanta Campaign was based more on maneuver. Sherman repeatedly pinned down Johnston with part of his force and then sent the rest around the enemy's flanks to threaten Johnston's supply line and force him to withdraw. Major battles were fought at Resaca, New Hope Church, and Kennesaw Mountain, but Johnston steadily retreated. When Hood replaced Johnston, he lashed out at Sherman at Peachtree Creek and Atlanta but was unable to stop the Union juggernaut. Late in the campaign, Sherman moved south of Atlanta and cut Hood's supply line at Ezra Church and Jonesboro and forced him to abandon Atlanta.

Rebels' main defenses around New Hope Church. From behind nearly impregnable earthworks, the Confederates easily repulsed Hooker's attacks in an area the soldiers dubbed the "Hell Hole." Heavy fire, including "shells, grapeshot, canister, railroad spikes, and every deadly missile" pinned the Yankees to the ground. During the battle, lightning cracked overhead and a torrent of rain fell on the men as a thunderstorm passed through. After the fight, one Confederate wrote, "The trees looked as if they had been cut down for new ground, being mutilated and shivered by musket and cannon balls. Horses were writhing in their death agony, and the sickening odor of battle filled the air."

That night and the following day more units arrived to extend the lines in the thick timber and deep ravines, and fierce fighting continued through May 26. To break the stalemate and turn Hood's left flank, Sherman sent McPherson to the southwest toward Dallas. He was stopped by William J. Hardee's entrenched Confederates, as was Oliver O. Howard's corps the next day when it ran into Patrick Cleburne's division at Pickett's Mill while trying to turn the Confederate right flank. The last battle around New Hope Church occurred on May 28 when Confederate Major General William B. Bate misunderstood his orders and made futile attacks against McPherson's entrenched men near Dallas. In the four days of fighting, Sherman lost 3,500 men and Johnston about 2,300. Sherman finally gave up on June 1 and moved back east to his railroad supply line. When Union cavalry captured Allatoona Pass a few days later and threatened Johnston's right rear, the Confederates retreated once again.

## The Battle of Kennesaw Mountain

Johnston eventually formed a new defensive line on Kennesaw Mountain, but not before General Polk was killed atop Pine Mountain by a well-aimed Yankee shell. By this stage of the campaign, Sherman was frustrated and angry that his men were becoming reluctant to attack entrenched positions. He was particularly irritated at General Thomas. "A fresh furrow in a plowed field will stop [his] whole column," fumed Sherman, "and all will begin to entrench." Previously when he encountered strong earthworks, Sherman used turning movements to force Johnston to retreat, but that was impossible at Kennesaw Mountain because heavy rains had turned the roads into quagmires. Instead, he decided to make a rare frontal attack because he was convinced the enemy's line was stretched thin, and he wanted to show his troops they sometimes had to attack fortified positions.

McPherson and Thomas attacked on June 27, but the men were mowed down by the hundreds, particularly in front of Cleburne's division at a position known as the "Dead Angle." Years after the war, Confederate Sam Watkins wrote, "My pen is unable to describe the scene of carnage and death that ensued in the next two hours. . . . The sun beaming down on our uncovered heads, the thermometer being one hundred and ten degrees in the shade, and a solid line of blazing fire right from the muzzles of the Yankee guns being poured right into our very faces, singeing our hair and clothes, the hot blood of our dead and wounded spurting on us, the blinding smoke and stifling atmosphere filling our eyes and mouths, and the awful concussion causing the blood to gush out of our noses and ears. . . ." Sherman lost 3,000 men in the futile attack, while Johnston lost fewer than 1,000 men. Sherman never admitted he made a mistake at Kennesaw Mountain, and he seemed almost indifferent to the losses when he wrote his wife, "I begin to regard the death and mangling of a couple

# EYEWITNESS
## Ambrose Bierce

*Raised in a poor Indiana family, Ambrose Bierce (1842–1914?) worked for an abolitionist newspaper before joining the 9th Indiana as a private. He saw extensive service in the western theater and became a lieutenant and topographical engineer for Major General William B. Hazen, who led a brigade in General Thomas J. Wood's division. During the Atlanta Campaign, Wood was ordered to attack what was thought to be the exposed Rebel flank at Pickett's Mill. In reality, Patrick Cleburne's division was strongly posted there behind earthworks. Hazen's men were slaughtered when they were sent forward without support just to test the enemy's strength. Embittered by the experience, Bierce later described the debacle in a short story entitled "The Crime at Pickett's Mill."*

The attack, it was understood, was to be made in column of brigades, Hazen's brigade of Wood's division leading. . . . But after a march of less than a mile an hour and a further delay of three hours at the end of it to acquaint the enemy of our intention to surprise him, our single shrunken brigade of fifteen hundred men was sent forward without support. . . . "We will put in Hazen and see what success he has." In the words of General Wood to General Howard we were first apprised of the true nature of the distinction about to be conferred upon us. . . . [When Hazen] heard Wood say they would put him in and see what success he would have in defeating an army—when he saw Howard assent—he uttered never a word, rode to the head of his feeble brigade and patiently awaited the command to go. Only by a look which I knew how to read did he betray his sense of the criminal blunder. . . .

That, then, was the situation: a weak brigade of fifteen hundred men, with masses of idle troops behind in the character of audience, waiting for the word to march a quarter-mile up hill through almost impassable tangles of underwood, along and across precipitous ravines, and attack breastworks constructed at leisure and manned with two division of troops as good as themselves. . . . We moved forward. In less than one minute the trim battalions had become simply a swarm of men struggling through the undergrowth of the forest, pushing and crowding. . . . Horses were all sent to the rear; the general and staff and all the field officers toiled along on foot as best they could. . . . Suddenly there came a ringing rattle of musketry, the familiar hissing of bullets, and before us the interspaces of the forest were all blue with smoke. Hoarse, fierce yells broke out of a thousand throats. . . . The uproar was deafening; the air was sibilant with streams and sheets of missiles. In the steady, unvarying roar of small-arms the frequent shock of the cannon was rather felt than heard, but the gusts of grape which they blew into that populous wood were audible enough, screaming among the trees and cracking against their stems and branches. . . . Our brave color-bearers were now all in the forefront of battle in the open, for the enemy had cleared a space in front of his breastworks. They held the colors erect, shook out their glories, waved them forward and back to keep them spread, for there was no wind. From where I stood, at the right of the line . . . I could see six of our flags at one time. Occasionally one would go down, only to be instantly lifted by other hands. . . .

Early in my military experience I used to ask myself how it was that brave troops could retreat while still their courage was high. As long as a man is not disabled he can go forward; can it be anything but fear that makes him stop and finally retire? Are there signs by which he can infallibly know the struggle to be hopeless? . . . In many instances which have come under my observation, when hostile lines of infantry engage at close range and the assailants afterward retire, there was a "dead-line" beyond which no man advanced but to fall. Not a soul of them ever reached the enemy's front to be bayoneted or captured. It was a matter of the difference of three or four paces—too small a distance to affect the accuracy of aim. In these affairs no aim is taken at individual antagonists; the soldier delivers his fire at the thickest mass in his front. The fire is, of course, as deadly at twenty paces as at fifteen; at fifteen as at ten. Nevertheless, there is the "dead-line," with its well-defined edge of corpses—those of the bravest. . . .

I observed this phenomenon at Pickett's Mill. Standing at the right of the line I had an unobstructed view of the narrow, open space across which the two lines fought. It was dim with smoke, but not greatly obscured: the smoke rose and spread in sheets among the branches of the trees. Most of our men fought kneeling as they fired, many of them behind trees, stones and whatever cover they could get, but there were considerable groups that stood. Occasionally one of these groups, which had endured the storm of missiles for moments without perceptible reduction, would push forward, moved by a common despair, and wholly detach itself from the line. In a second every man of the group would be down. There had been no visible movement of the enemy, no audible change in the awful, even roar of the firing—yet all were down. Frequently the dim figure of an individual soldier would be seen to spring away from his comrades, advancing alone toward that fateful interspace, with leveled bayonet. He got no farther than the farthest of his predecessors. . . .

No command to fall back was given, none could have been heard. Man by man, the survivors withdrew at will, sifting through the trees into the cover of the ravines, among the wounded who could draw themselves back; among the skulkers whom nothing could have dragged forward. . . . As it was, just forty-five minutes had elapsed, during which the enemy had destroyed us and was now ready to perform the same kindly office for our successors. . . .

*With William Randolph Hearst's support after the war, Bierce published the popular books* Tales of Soldiers and Civilians *and* The Devil's Dictionary *and such short stories as "An Occurrence at Owl Creek Bridge" and "The Coup De Grace." While reporting on the bandit Pancho Villa in the early twentieth century, he disappeared in Mexico and is presumed to have been killed.*

Ambrose Bierce, "The Crime at Pickett's Mill," in *The Collected Works of Ambrose Bierce*, Vol. I (New York: Neale Publishing Company, 1909), pp. 283–294.

**Trench Warfare.** By 1864, armies in both the eastern and western theater had learned the advantages of well-prepared defensive positions. This photograph of some Confederate defensive works around Atlanta, Georgia, illustrate how elaborate those positions became.

of thousand men as a small affair, a kind of morning dash—and it may be well that we become so hardened."

## "That Devil Forrest"

Early in the campaign, Sherman worried that Nathan Bedford Forrest's marauding cavalry might disrupt the advance by breaking his supply line in Tennessee. To prevent this, he ordered Brigadier General Samuel D. Sturgis to invade northern Mississippi and defeat Forrest. Sturgis left Memphis with 8,500 men in early June, but his march was slowed by continuous rain, deep mud, and blistering heat. On the morning of June 10, he finally made contact with Forrest's 3,500 troopers at Brice's Cross Roads, and Brigadier General Benjamin Grierson pushed the Confederates' vanguard across Tishomingo Creek. Although forced to retreat, Forrest shrewdly used the muddy road and hot weather to his advantage. To his officers, he explained how the Union cavalry would rapidly outpace the infantry in the mud and could be easily defeated first. "As soon as the fight opens," Forrest declared, "they will send back to have the infantry hurried up. It is going to be as hot as hell, and coming on a run for five or six miles over such roads, their infantry will be so tired out we will ride right over them."

Forrest's plan worked flawlessly. He defeated Grierson by noon and then turned on Sturgis's exhausted infantry as it limped onto the field. In bitter fighting, the Confederates pushed Sturgis back across Tishomingo Creek, and the Union retreat soon became a rout. Forced to abandon much of their artillery and wagons, the Yankees fled back to Tennessee with Forrest in close pursuit. In the humiliating defeat at Brice's Cross Roads, Sturgis lost more than 2,200 men, 16 cannons, and nearly 200 wagons, while Forrest lost fewer than 500 men. An incredulous Sherman wrote Secretary of War Stanton, "Forrest is the very devil, and I think he has got some of our troops under cower. . . . I will order [others to] go out and follow Forrest to the death if it costs 10,000 lives and breaks the Treasury. There will never be peace in Tennessee till Forrest is dead."

Sherman chose Major General Andrew Jackson Smith, recently returned from the Red River Campaign, to lead the next expedition. In early July, Smith left La Grange, Tennessee, with 14,000 men and burned a wide swath as he slowly advanced into Mississippi. When Grierson's cavalry reached Tupelo, they began destroying railroad track while Smith's main body stopped and entrenched a mile west of Harrisonburg. Nearby, Lieutenant General Stephen D. Lee had Forrest and 9,500 cavalrymen ready to engage the Yankees, but he and Forrest disagreed on tactics. Forrest wanted to harass the enemy while they were on the march and gradually weaken them before fighting a major battle. Lee, however, was being pressured by his superiors to send reinforcements to Mobile, Alabama, and decided to attack Smith immediately.

Lee engaged Smith on the morning of July 14, but all of his assaults were disjointed and unsuccessful, even a rare night attack made by Forrest. The Battle of Tupelo was one of the few fights in which Forrest suffered a tactical defeat, but he was serving under Lee and did not direct the battle. Low on rations, Smith abandoned his position the next day and retreated back to La Grange. He had inflicted more than 1,300 enemy casualties while sustaining fewer than 700 himself, but his raid had mixed results. While Smith did keep Forrest away from Sherman's supply line during the Atlanta Campaign, he failed to destroy Forrest's command, and the fearsome cavalryman continued to play havoc with Union forces for the rest of the war.

## Johnston's Dismissal

In early July, the roads dried out and Sherman once again turned Johnston's right flank and forced him to abandon Kennesaw Mountain. Two weeks later, the Confederates withdrew across the Chattahoochee River, the last natural barrier protecting Atlanta. Sherman followed and reached a position only seven miles from the city. President Davis had now reached the end of his patience with Johnston. Throughout the campaign, he had fretted over Johnston's inability to stop the Union advance. Not once had he counterattacked, and nothing in his telegrams indicated he had any strategy to save the city. Davis saw it as a repeat of Johnston's disappointing defense of Richmond during the 1862 Peninsula Campaign and sent General Braxton Bragg, late commander of the Army of Tennessee and now the president's military adviser, to Georgia to assess the situation. When Bragg was unable to draw any specific information from Johnston, Davis asked Robert E. Lee what he thought of having Hood replace Johnston. Lee's reply undoubtedly disappointed the president. "Hood is a bold fighter," he wrote. "I am doubtful as to the other qualities necessary." Undeterred, Davis forced the issue by asking Johnston to tell him specifically how he planned to save Atlanta. Johnston replied that the army would stay on the defensive, and his plans "must therefore, depend upon that of the enemy." The evasive answer was the last straw, and Davis relieved Johnston on the night of July 17 and put Hood in command of the Army of Tennessee. Davis's decision shocked the troops because the men adored Johnston. One of them remembered the news "came like a flash of lightning, staggering and blinding every one. It was like applying a lighted match to an immense magazine. . . . It was like the end of the Southern Confederacy."

## The Battles of Peachtree Creek and Atlanta

Hood attacked Sherman almost immediately. As the Union armies approached Atlanta along a wide front, Thomas became separated on the right from Schofield and McPherson. Hood knew Thomas's army would be vulnerable when it began crossing the 40-foot-wide Peachtree Creek and prepared to strike. As Hardee's and Stewart's corps moved into position on July 20, however, Hood received an alarming report that McPherson was approaching Atlanta from the east. This news forced him to delay the attack while he shifted troops to block McPherson. By the time Hardee and Stewart advanced, Hooker's Union corps was already across Peachtree Creek and ready for battle.

A lone Union soldier picking blackberries saw the Confederates coming and alerted his superiors, who quickly drew up a battle line and rushed forward to meet the attack. An officer who witnessed the charging Rebels wrote, "Pouring out from the woods they advanced in immense brown and gray masses (not lines), with flags and banners, many of them new and beautiful, while their general and staff officers were in plain view, with drawn sabers flashing in the light, galloping here and there as they urged their troops on to the charge." Rushing down a hill, the Yankees fired a volley of musketry at just fifty feet. The Union soldiers held their ground for four hours and sustained 1,800 casualties in the bloody fight, but they inflicted 2,500 enemy casualties. A Michigan soldier walked across the field after the Confederates retreated and was shocked to find a uniformed woman among the wounded. He recalled, "She was shot in the breast and through the thy & was still alive & as gritty as any reb I ever saw."

Hood withdrew into Atlanta's main defenses, but he made one more attempt to avoid a siege by attacking McPherson's exposed left (or southern) flank as he approached Atlanta from the east. Hood positioned Cheatham's corps to attack the Union center while Hardee's corps circled to the south and attacked McPherson's left flank and rear. At the same time, Wheeler's cavalry was to attack the enemy wagon train far in the rear at Decatur. Hood's plan was well conceived on paper, but it quickly fell apart on execution. Hardee began his 15-mile march toward the enemy flank on the night of July 21, but he did not get into position until midday on July 22 because the terrain was thick with undergrowth and briars. When Hardee finally did attack, he discovered that a Union corps had extended McPherson's left wing. Instead of hitting the exposed enemy flank as planned, Hardee was charging straight into the main Union line.

After the Confederates attacked, McPherson realigned some of his units and then rode off through the woods with two aides to make contact with another part of his line. Suddenly, a Rebel captain and small party of soldiers stepped out of the woods and demanded their surrender. The captain recalled, "[McPherson] checked his horse slightly, raised his hat as politely as if he were saluting a lady, wheeled his horse's head directly to the right, and dashed off to the rear in a full gallop." The Confederates immediately shot and killed McPherson and captured the others. When the general's wounded horse returned to Union lines, soldiers advanced into the woods and found his body lying on the ground. Sherman was shocked at the news and exclaimed, "McPherson dead! Can it be?" Although Fighting Joe Hooker had seniority and expected to assume command of the Army of the Tennessee, Sherman replaced McPherson with Major General Oliver O. Howard. Hooker was so incensed that he asked to be relieved and returned north.

Heavy fighting continued after McPherson's death, and only the timely arrival of a fresh brigade stopped the Confederates when they poured through a gap that opened in the Union line. While the fight raged, all remained quiet in the center because Hood failed to send Cheatham's corps against McPherson's front until midafternoon. When he did advance, Cheatham overran some forward Union units, but massed artillery fire and a determined counterattack by John A. Logan's corps quickly forced him back. Poor coordination between units, stubborn enemy resistance, and bad luck had conspired against Hood's seemingly foolproof battle plan. Even Wheeler's cavalry was driven off before it could destroy the Union wagon train at Decatur. The Confederates had killed General McPherson and inflicted 3,700 Union casualties in the Battle of Atlanta, but that was little compensation for the 8,000 casualties they had sustained. Afterward, when a Union picket asked his Rebel counterpart, "How many men have you fellows got left?" the Confederate glumly replied, "About enough for another killin'."

## The Fall of Atlanta

Hood had taken the offensive as Davis expected, but all he accomplished was further weakening the army. Now he was pinned inside Atlanta's defenses, and the enemy was close enough to bombard the city. A Michigan soldier who witnessed the cannonade felt little sympathy for the civilians. "It is terrible what those people are going through," he wrote home, "but they deserve everything they are getting! . . . It is a beautiful sight to see the shells burst over the houses."

To avoid a long siege and force the Rebels to abandon Atlanta, Sherman moved against the railroad supply lines south of the city. In late July, he sent Major General George Stoneman's and Brigadier General Edward M. McCook's cavalry around opposite sides of Atlanta to destroy the railroad at Lovejoy's Station. McCook reached the station and inflicted some temporary damage on the track, but Wheeler's cavalry captured Stoneman and 700 of his men. Sherman also sent Howard's army around the west side of Atlanta to cut the Atlanta & West Point Railroad. Hood rushed troops to Ezra Church to cut off the enemy's advance, but the Yankees established a strong defensive position and slaughtered the Confederates when they attacked on July 28. The Battle of Ezra Church was a testament to the futility of making frontal attacks against strong earthworks. Howard lost 500 men in the fight, while the Confederates lost ten times as many. Hood temporarily saved the railroad at Ezra Church, but the tremendous bloodletting only further reduced his dwindling army.

In early August, Hood retaliated by sending Wheeler's cavalry to attack Sherman's supply line. Over a 30-day period, Wheeler destroyed railroad tracks and bridges in Georgia and Tennessee, but he could not force Sherman to loosen his grip on Atlanta. If anything, the raid weakened Hood because it deprived him of his cavalry during the campaign's final crucial weeks. Sherman took advantage of Wheeler's absence by sending H. Judson Kilpatrick's cavalry to raid the Atlanta & West Point Railroad and the Macon & Western Railroad south of Atlanta. Kilpatrick destroyed some track and enemy supplies, but he was forced to retreat when he was attacked at Lovejoy's Station on August 20. Although Kilpatrick boasted that he had put the railroad out of service for ten days, the Confederates had it back in operation in two.

These unsuccessful raids convinced Sherman it would take a massive infantry force to cut Hood's supply line permanently. In a final push, he left one corps north of Atlanta to distract the enemy, while the armies moved south and west to cut the Atlanta & West Point Railroad. When he realized Sherman's intentions, Hood sent General Hardee with his and Stephen D. Lee's corps to stop the Yankees at Jonesboro. Hardee attacked Howard's army on August 31, but the attack was poorly coordinated and Howard successfully held his ground. That night, Hood discovered another Union column was threatening the railroad at Rough and Ready and sent Lee there. Sherman reinforced his position at Jonesboro and on September 1 launched a massive attack on Hardee's weakened line that forced the Confederates to retreat to Lovejoy's Station.

Sherman suffered 1,100 casualties at Jonesboro, but the victory was decisive. Not only did he inflict 2,000 Confederate casualties, Sherman severed Hood's last supply line and made his position in Atlanta untenable. After setting fire to military supplies, trains, and warehouses, Hood evacuated the city that night, and Union soldiers entered Atlanta on the morning of September 2. Hood dug in around Lovejoy's Station expecting Sherman to make one last attack to annihilate his army, but, in a controversial decision, Sherman chose not to engage and allowed Hood to escape. Satisfied with his victory, a jubilant

Sherman wired Chief of Staff Halleck, "Atlanta is ours, and fairly won." The destruction of Hood's army would be left for a later day.

## The Battle of Mobile Bay

Sherman's telegram to Halleck came on the heels of another Union victory at Mobile Bay. Mobile, Alabama, was critical to the Confederacy because it was one of the last ports open to blockade runners. Its bay was heavily defended by three forts and Admiral Franklin Buchanan's small fleet, which included the powerful ironclad ram *Tennessee*. The most important Confederate position was Fort Morgan, which guarded the bay's entrance.

On August 15, Admiral David Farragut led eighteen ships into Mobile Bay. Farragut shrewdly lashed his wooden ships together in pairs, with the stronger ones facing Fort Morgan, while four ironclad monitors steamed between them and the fort to lay down covering fire. Soon after entering the channel, the lead monitor *Tecumseh* struck a torpedo and sank. The explosion unnerved the captain of the next vessel, and he threatened to disrupt the formation by backing up to avoid the torpedoes. Lashed to the rigging of his flagship *Hartford,* Farragut reportedly yelled, "Damn the torpedoes. . . . Go ahead . . . full speed!" and took the lead to pass boldly through the minefield and engage the enemy fleet. One Confederate ship was disabled, one surrendered, and another steamed away to leave Buchanan and the *Tennessee* to fight alone. The ironclad was repeatedly rammed and raked by broadsides in a furious one-hour engagement with the entire Union fleet. Finally, with the ship dead in the water and Buchanan suffering a broken leg, the *Tennessee* surrendered. Over the next few days, two of the Confederate forts were either abandoned or captured, and Fort Morgan surrendered to Major General Gordon Granger's infantry on August 23 after enduring a prolonged bombardment.

Besides closing down one of the Confederacy's last ports, the capture of Mobile Bay placed Union forces in position to take the city itself. This victory and Sherman's capture of Atlanta a week later marked a decisive moment in the Civil War. With Grant still besieging Petersburg and the war in Virginia a bloody stalemate, these western victories were crucial in boosting Northern morale. Had Sherman become bogged down in a long siege at Atlanta like Grant at Petersburg and had Farragut been defeated at Mobile Bay, the Northern people might have become completely disillusioned and elected a Peace Democrat in the November presidential election. Instead, they were greatly encouraged by Sherman's and Farragut's victories. Soldiers, in particular, rallied to Lincoln's side. In a remarkable display of determination, more than three-fourths of the military vote went to Lincoln even though the soldiers knew his reelection meant continued fighting and dying. They were completely dedicated to final victory, and the capture of Atlanta and Mobile Bay clearly demonstrated that the tide of war was turning steadily in their favor.

The Confederates had little hope of victory after Atlanta and Mobile Bay, but they continued to fight out of desperation. Every Southern man who donned a gray uniform and every civilian who supported him had committed treason against the United States. As long as they fought there was always a possibility that some unforeseen happenstance might turn the tide of war, or the Northern people might tire and force Lincoln to negotiate a peace. But to stop fighting meant certain defeat and possible arrest, imprisonment, or even execution. Many soldiers believed it was better to die with honor fighting the enemy than surrender and face the unthinkable. Jefferson Davis was one who continued to believe victory was possible if the Southern people simply committed themselves totally to the war. If the western generals would perform as well as Lee in Virginia, if the tens of thousands of soldiers who had deserted or were absent without leave would return to duty, and if politicians would spend more effort fighting the Yankees than each other, the Confederacy could survive. Davis made his feelings quite clear to two Northerners who took it on themselves to pass through the lines and visit him in Richmond to discuss the possibility of a negotiated peace. He told them, "The war . . . must go on till the last man of this generation falls in his tracks, . . . *unless you acknowledge our right to self-government*. We are not fighting for slavery. We are fighting for Independence—and that, or extermination, we *will* have." The war would continue until the Confederates no longer had the capacity to resist.

## FOR FURTHER READING

General Sherman's report on the Atlanta Campaign
Correspondence between Jefferson Davis and General Johnston on defense
  of Atlanta

## CHAPTER 23

# The Rebellion's Last Gasp

Price's Missouri Raid

Hood's Tennessee Campaign

The March to the Sea

When a weary Jefferson Davis stepped from his train at Palmetto, Georgia, on Sunday, September 25, 1864, the wet, stormy afternoon reflected his mood. The tide of war seemed to be turning inexorably against the Confederacy. Lee was still successfully defending Richmond and Petersburg, but Hood had abandoned Atlanta, and Mobile Bay had been closed to blockade runners. The western Confederacy was so demoralized rumors spread that Georgia's Governor Joseph Brown had crossed the lines to discuss making a separate peace with Sherman. The rumors were false, although Sherman had, indeed, invited the governor to meet with him in Atlanta. Davis also had received a letter from one of Hood's division commanders reporting low morale among the officers and men. Clearly the Army of Tennessee was in trouble, so the president decided to make a personal visit to decide on Hood's fitness to command and to make some encouraging speeches.

Davis first met with Hood to discuss future operations in the west, and he agreed to a new strategy the general had developed. Hood had already sent Forrest to attack Sherman's supply lines in Tennessee and was preparing to move the entire army into northern Georgia on a similar expedition. Threatening Sherman's lines of communication might force him to abandon Atlanta and either move north to confront Hood or head south to collect supplies. In either case, it could present an opportunity to attack and destroy the enemy. After their meeting, Davis and Hood reviewed the troops, and the president learned firsthand the men's mood when some soldiers yelled out, "[G]ive us General Johnston."

After his visit to the army, Davis made several speeches in Georgia and Alabama "to arouse all classes to united and desperate resistance." At every stop, he stressed there would never be any reconciliation with the Yankees—this was a fight to the death. Davis put up a brave front and predicted eventual victory, but many Southerners believed his confidence bordered on fantasy.

At Augusta, he told the crowd, "We must beat Sherman; we must march into Tennessee. There we will draw from 20,000 to 30,000 to our standard, and, so strengthened, we must push the enemy back to the banks of the Ohio and thus give the peace party of the North an accretion no puny editorial can give." In Montgomery, Davis pleaded, "Let no one despond. . . . I have striven to behold our affairs with a cool and candid temperance of heart, and, applying to them the most rigid test, am more confident the longer I behold the progress of the war. . . . We should marvel and thank God for the great achievements which have crowned our efforts."

Davis's speeches changed few opinions, and in some cases he made things worse. He frequently blamed Joe Johnston for the loss of Atlanta and criticized Governor Brown for failing to support the war effort properly. Such outbursts (particularly on Brown's home soil) outraged both soldiers and politicians. Most Southerners realized that Davis's optimism was completely unrealistic, but the die had been cast. There would be no negotiating with the enemy, and the Confederates would continue to fight. In the Trans-Mississippi Department, one army was already advancing toward the Yankees, and Hood was preparing to head north on the Confederacy's last great offensive.

## PRICE'S MISSOURI RAID

**September 19, 1864: Price enters Missouri**
**September 26–27, 1864: Battle of Pilot Knob, Missouri**
**October 21–23, 1864: Battles of Little Blue and Big Blue Rivers**
**October 23, 1864: Battle of Westport**
**October 25, 1864: Battle of Mine Creek, Kansas**

Despite Davis's claims to the contrary, the Confederacy was on its last legs in the autumn of 1864. Lee was pinned down at Richmond and Petersburg, and Hood's army had been driven out of Atlanta. Union forces had closed or captured all but a few Southern ports to blockade runners, and Confederate desertions were mounting as soldiers answered the pleas of starving families. The late summer victories at Atlanta and Mobile Bay had raised Northern morale, and it appeared Lincoln would be reelected in November to push the war to final victory. But these military reversals did not mean the Confederacy was ready to capitulate. Rebel armies were still in the field with thousands of men, much of the South had been spared the war's destruction, and most white Southerners were willing to continue fighting for independence. That autumn the Northern people were reminded just how dangerous the enemy was when Sterling Price's Confederate army launched a major raid in the Trans-Mississippi Department.

Sterling Price (1809–1867) was a Virginia native who moved west and became, according to a friend, "unquestionably the most popular man in Missouri." He served in the state legislature and resigned a seat in Congress to become colonel of a Missouri regiment during the Mexican War. In that conflict, an acquaintance noted that Price exhibited the same personal qualities he would later show in the Civil War. He "displayed a laxness in enforcing discipline, a tendency to quarrel with other officials, and a penchant for acting in a highly independent, almost insubordinate fashion. . . . " Price went on to serve two terms as Missouri's governor and become a reluctant secessionist. Appointed a major general in the Missouri State Guard after the Civil War began, he later became a major general of Confederate troops. Known to his soldiers as "Old Pap," Price was personable and one of the most popular Confederate commanders in the Trans-Mississippi Department. Always eager to operate against the enemy in his home state, he was receptive when exiled Governor Thomas C. Reynolds proposed a raid into Missouri in late summer 1864. Price received permission to take 12,000 mounted men from Arkansas and capture St. Louis. From there, he intended to cross the Mississippi River and move into Illinois. Price was convinced such a raid would "throw off the yoke of oppression" in Missouri and relieve pressure on General Hood in Georgia by forcing the enemy to strip away some of Sherman's men to defend Illinois.

## The Battle of Pilot Knob

After entering Missouri on September 19, 1864, Price immediately moved against a 1,500-man Union garrison near Pilot Knob. To prevent the enemy from receiving reinforcements from St. Louis, he ordered Jo Shelby's cavalry to destroy the connecting railroad while he marched on Pilot Knob with the main force. Shelby, however, disapproved of the attack and argued that it was more important to keep pushing north as fast as possible. "I favored moving rapidly into St. Louis and seizing it," Shelby later declared. "I then and there . . . stated what the result would be if we attacked Pilot Knob. I could see nothing as an inducement; they had nothing we required. It would only cripple and retard our movements, and I knew too well that good infantry, well entrenched, would give us Hell, and Hell we did get. . . . "

Commanding the Pilot Knob garrison was Brigadier General Thomas Ewing, Jr., one of the most hated Yankees in the Trans-Mississippi because of the brutal campaign he had waged against Confederate guerrillas and their families. Ewing could have retreated before Price's overwhelming force, but he decided to stay and delay the enemy's advance on St. Louis as long as possible. On the evening of September 26, Price made contact with Ewing near Pilot Knob, and Ewing retreated into Fort Davidson. The fort was a formidable position protected by a deep ditch and numerous cannons, but Price attacked the next day after Ewing refused to surrender. Ewing's men raked the enemy with shot and shell and finally forced them to retreat. Price intended to renew the assault using scaling ladders to climb the walls, but Ewing evacuated Pilot Knob before dawn and moved undetected past a Confederate brigade that was supposed to block his escape route. Price did not even realize the enemy had fled until after daylight, and he then made an unsuccessful pursuit. Pilot Knob was an inauspicious beginning for the Confederates' raid. Price lost nearly 1,000 men and achieved nothing, while Ewing lost only 200 men.

Price pursued Ewing until he learned that Union Major General Alfred Pleasonton was on his way from St. Louis with reinforcements. This growing enemy threat convinced Price to abandon his original campaign strategy. He decided St. Louis was too strongly protected to be captured and chose, instead, to head west up the Missouri River toward Jefferson City. Price believed thousands of Missourians would enlist in his army along the way, and threatening the capital might strengthen the Northern peace movement in the upcoming presidential election. Unfortunately for the Confederates, nothing went as planned. The men were forced to live off the land and few recruits materialized. Price managed to destroy some railroad track and bridges, but he had to bypass heavily defended Jefferson City, and Pleasonton's cavalry constantly pressured his rear guard. After skirting the capital, the raiders turned northwest to capture Boonville on October 9. From there Price sent Shelby's and M. Jeff Thompson's cavalry north to Glasgow and southwest to Sedalia, respectively, on minor raids that captured several hundred Union prisoners.

## Little Blue and Big Blue Rivers

From Boonville, Price continued toward the northwest, but his progress was slowed by a 500-wagon supply train and Pleasonton's harassing cavalry. This plodding pace allowed Union authorities time to bring together several columns to trap the raiders. Pleasonton's cavalry continued slashing Price's rear guard, and Major General Samuel Curtis assembled a large Union force on the Missouri-Kansas border. When Curtis sent Major General James G. Blunt with 2,000 men to Lexington, Price was in danger of being surrounded by thousands of Yankees.

Price entered Lexington on October 19 and pushed back Blunt's vanguard, but he could still be trapped if the enemy united their forces. Turning to the southwest, he hurried to get between the converging columns and defeat each in turn. Two days later, the Confederates encountered Blunt's force at the Little Blue River, and a fierce fight erupted between the numerically superior Confederates and Blunt's better-armed soldiers using rapid-firing, breech-loading rifles. Greater numbers finally prevailed, and Blunt retreated to join Curtis a few miles southeast of Kansas City at the Big Blue River. There Curtis took up a defensive position to prevent the Confederates from entering Kansas.

When Price reached the Big Blue River on October 22, he split his army into three columns. Marmaduke's division remained in the rear to keep Pleasonton's aggressive cavalry at bay, while other units kept Curtis occupied along the front lines. Price then sent Jo Shelby's cavalry south to Bryam's Ford. Shelby fought his way across the river, turned the enemy's right flank, and forced Curtis to retreat toward Westport. Despite his success, Price was still in danger of being trapped between Curtis in his front and Pleasonton's troopers in his rear so he called off his advance on Kansas City and hurried south. Price's only hope was to defeat Curtis first at Westport and then turn and defeat Pleasonton's cavalry in the rear.

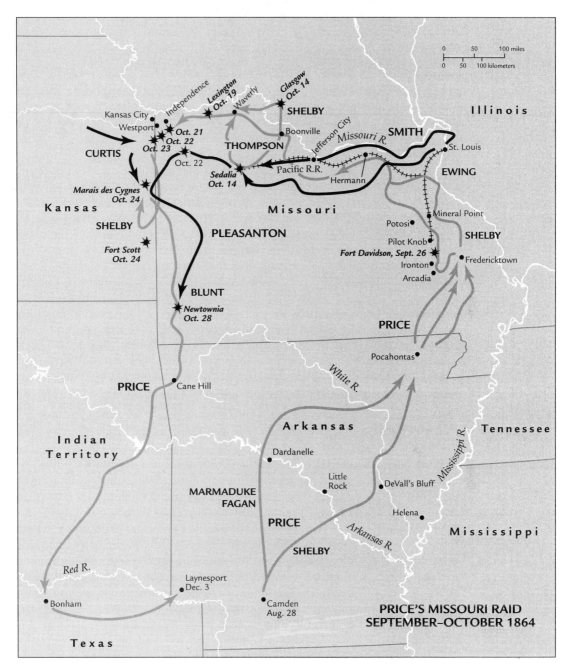

**Price's Missouri Raid, September–October 1864.** In September 1864, Sterling Price raided Missouri with the intentions of capturing St. Louis and moving into Illinois to force the Union to withdraw some of its troops from the South. When he discovered that St. Louis was too heavily defended, however, Price moved west to threaten Kansas City, but converging Union columns forced him to retreat. Although the Confederates won some small battles during the 1,500-mile raid, the operation did nothing to alter the war's strategic situation.

## The Battle of Westport

Adopting a plan proposed by Shelby, Price left Marmaduke's cavalry at Byram's Ford to keep Pleasonton in check while sending the long wagon train south out of harm's way. He then attacked Curtis at Westport on October 23 with Shelby's and James F. Fagan's cavalry. At first Price drove the enemy back, but Curtis managed to regroup his forces and launch a counterattack that sent the Confederates reeling. In describing the scene, a Colorado officer wrote, "I never saw such havoc. The line was strewed with dead and wounded men and horses." In the town of Westport, terrified families hid in their root cellars as the battle raged. One youngster wrote, "Every once in awhile, a cannonball would strike our yard with a thud that shook the house. Once in the day, mother ventured outside to look around. A cannonball passed so close behind her head that the wind from it tore her hair down and left it streaming."

After several hours of fierce fighting, Price received disastrous news from Byram's Ford. Pleasonton had smashed Marmaduke and captured hundreds of prisoners and now was in a position to attack Price from the rear. To keep from being crushed between Curtis and Pleasonton, Price disengaged at Westport and marched rapidly south. Confederate morale was shattered, and only Shelby's skillful rearguard action prevented the withdrawal from becoming a rout. Approximately 36,000 men were engaged at Westport, making it the largest Civil War battle west of the Mississippi River. Although exact casualty figures are unknown, each side lost approximately 1,500 men.

## Mine Creek

Crossing into Kansas, the retreating Confederates covered 61 miles in the next two days before camping on the Marais des Cygnes (MAIR-duh-SEEN) River. On October 25, Pleasonton's cavalry attacked and drove the exhausted Rebels to Mine Creek. Price was struggling to get his cumbersome wagon train across the creek when 2,600 Union troopers suddenly arrived. Price began deploying 7,000 men on the north side of the stream under Fagan and Marmaduke, but Pleasonton attacked before they could prepare a defense. The ensuing fight was fierce and close quartered. One Kansas colonel wrote, "For a time the fire was incessant and terrific. Both lines seemed like walls of adamant—one could not advance; the other would not recede." Colonel Frederick Benteen, who later served under Custer at the Little Big Horn, claimed it was a "fierce hand-to-hand fight, one that surpassed anything for the time it lasted [that] I have ever witnessed." Price's cavalry was quickly defeated and forced to continue their retreat in what he described as "utter and indescribable confusion." The Battle of Mine Creek was one of the largest cavalry clashes of the war, and it was the only large battle fought in Kansas. Pleasonton sustained 150 casualties in the fight, but he inflicted 800 enemy casualties and captured Brigadier General William L. Cabell and a wounded General Marmaduke. Confederate survivors also claimed a number of their men were murdered by the enemy for wearing captured Union uniforms.

After the defeat at Mine Creek, Price burned many of his wagons so he could move more quickly. The fighting retreat continued for several more days, with a last rearguard action occurring at Newtonia on October 28. After that, most of the Union soldiers were recalled because the Confederates no longer threatened Kansas. Curtis was left with too few men to continue the pursuit, and Price was allowed to withdraw. In a nightmarish march, the Confederates passed through Indian Territory and finally reached the safety of Texas in November. By the time the survivors returned to Arkansas, they had covered nearly 1,500 miles, fought in 43 engagements, and lost approximately 4,000 men (most of whom were deserters). Hundreds of soldiers fell by the wayside during the retreat, and all nearly starved because they had little more than corn to eat. Curtis boasted that Price "entered Missouri feasting and furnishing his troops on the rich products and abundant spoils of the Missouri Valley, but crossed the Arkansas destitute, disarmed, disorganized, and avoiding starvation by eating raw corn and slippery-elm bark."

Many of the Confederates who survived the retreat blamed the general they now called "God damn Old Pap!" While he did gather a few thousand recruits and captured some prisoners, Price failed to liberate Missouri, capture St. Louis, or weaken Sherman's armies in Georgia (although the raid did tie down a large number of Union troops that had been slated to reinforce Sherman). Even the recruits who did enlist proved worthless because many were violent guerrillas whose lawless activities turned Missourians away from the Confederate cause. Governor Reynolds, who accompanied the army on the raid, bitterly criticized Price's leadership, and Confederate officials investigated accusations of the general's "glaring mismanagement and distressing mental and physical military incapacity." Price's Missouri Raid had been an abject failure, and it essentially ended organized Confederate resistance in the Trans-Mississippi Department, although most of the Trans-Mississippi remained under Confederate control until war's end.

## DID YOU KNOW?

### Os Confederados

When the Civil War ended, Generals Jo Shelby and Sterling Price joined an estimated 8,000 other Southerners who chose self-exile to Yankee rule. Some did so because they hated the Union, while others fled for economic reasons or to avoid possible prosecution. Shelby and Price moved to Mexico and lived there for a while, and Confederate Secretary of State Judah P. Benjamin vowed to go to "the farthest place from the United States, if it takes me to the middle of China." He eventually settled in Great Britain and never returned to America. The most famous Confederate exiles were those who moved to Brazil and became known as "Os Confederados." Establishing such communities as Little Texas and Santa Bárbara (also known as Americana), the former Rebels and their families became farmers and Brazilian citizens. Today the descendants of Os Confederados continue to maintain Southern traditions in Brazil and have established a Sons of Confederate Veterans camp.

**Confederate Exiles.** When the war ended, Sterling Price and several other Confederate generals chose exile over Yankee rule. Some of them posed for this photograph while in Mexico. Price sits in the middle, flanked on the left by Cadmus Wilcox and on the right by Thomas C. Hindman. Standing, from the left, are John B. Magruder and William P. Hardeman. All eventually returned to the United States.

# HOOD'S TENNESSEE CAMPAIGN

September 8, 1864: Sherman orders
civilians out of Atlanta
October 5, 1864: Battle of Allatoona
November 16, 1864: Hood enters
Tennessee
November 28, 1864: Spring Hill
Incident
November 30, 1864: Battle of
Franklin
December 15–16, 1864: Battle of
Nashville

While Price was preparing for his Missouri Raid, Sherman was taking drastic measures to solidify his control of Atlanta, Georgia. On September 8, 1864, he shocked the residents by ordering them out of the city. In a telegram to General Halleck, Sherman explained, "I am not willing to have Atlanta encumbered by the families of our enemies. I want it a pure Gibraltar." When city officials complained about the draconian measure, Sherman declared, "War is cruelty and you cannot refine it; and those who brought war into our country deserve all the curses and maledictions a people can pour out. . . . You might as well appeal against the thunderstorm as against those terrible hardships of war." Sherman evicted the civilians partly to turn Atlanta into a military stronghold and partly to weaken the Confederate army by forcing it to feed the refugees. General Hood, however, considered it barbaric and claimed the order "transcends, in studied and ingenious cruelty, all acts ever brought to my attention in the dark history of war." Hood complained to Sherman in several messages, but Sherman held firm and the city's residents began leaving on September 12.

## "Hold the Fort, I Am Coming"

After Sherman banished Atlanta's citizens, Hood moved into northern Georgia and threatened the Union supply base at Allatoona. Sherman expected such a maneuver and ordered Brigadier General John M. Corse to reinforce the small garrison. Union signal officers on Kennesaw Mountain used signal flags to inform the men at Allatoona that reinforcements were coming and to hold on. Corse arrived just a few hours before the enemy cut the roads into town. When he refused a surrender demand on October 5, the Confederates attacked from three sides, but the Union soldiers held their position and the Rebels finally withdrew. Corse, who was grazed by a bullet during the battle, sent a grandiose message to Sherman declaring, "I am short a cheek-bone and an ear, but am able to whip all h——l yet." When Sherman finally arrived and saw Corse was barely wounded, he quipped, "Why, Corse they came damned near missing you, didn't they?" Although a small affair, the Battle of Allatoona became a famous Civil War story. The message sent by the Kennesaw Mountain signal station was corrupted into "Hold the fort; I am coming!" and it led to a popular hymn entitled "Hold the Fort."

## The Spring Hill Incident

Hood's move into northern Georgia was intended to draw the enemy out of Atlanta, but Sherman foiled the strategy by refusing to give chase beyond Allatoona. More concerned with planning his March to the Sea, Sherman returned to Atlanta and sent Major General George H. Thomas to Nashville to gather forces to stop the Confederates. Even though Sherman was not cooperating, Hood decided to continue north into Tennessee. In what proved to be a critical delay, he was forced to wait three weeks in Alabama to give Forrest time to join him for the offensive. While Hood waited, Thomas used the time to gather his troops in Nashville. Not until November 16 did Hood's 40,000-man Army of Tennessee began crossing the Tennessee River. Despite their late start, morale was high, and the men cheered when they saw a sign at the state line declaring, "TENNESSEE—A FREE HOME OR A GRAVE."

As the Confederates moved north, Major General John M. Schofield withdrew his 30,000 Union soldiers from Pulaski, Tennessee, and hurried toward Nashville to avoid being trapped. He reached Columbia shortly before the Confederates, but Hood acted quickly to cut him off. On November 29, Hood moved his army around the east side of town and established his headquarters in a local plantation house. That evening, he ordered Cheatham to take his corps a few miles farther and block the Columbia-to-Nashville road at the small hamlet of Spring Hill. What happened next became one of the war's greatest controversies.

When Cheatham approached Spring Hill, he encountered a larger than expected Union force and positioned his corps parallel-to-the road instead of across it. Thinking Cheatham had blocked the road as ordered, Hood sent more units forward with orders to extend Cheatham's right. Hood thought this would lengthen his line across the enemy's front, when it actually stretched his units parallel to the road. It was not until some time later that Forrest and Lieutenant General Alexander Stewart informed Hood the road was not blocked. According to one witness, Hood was shocked and asked, "Gen'l. Stewart, it is

# BIOGRAPHY

## John Bell Hood: The Wounded Knight

John Bell Hood

John Bell Hood (1831–1879) came from a prominent Kentucky family and was appointed to West Point by a congressman uncle. Hood struggled at the academy, where he was given the nickname "Sam," but managed to graduate in 1853 and was sent to fight Indians in Texas. Resigning his commission to join the Confederacy, he was colonel of the 4th Texas before being promoted to brigadier general of the Texas Brigade in the Army of Northern Virginia.

The six-foot, two-inch Hood was unequaled as a brigade commander, but he did not look like a fierce warrior. Noted Richmond diarist Mary Chesnut described him as having a "sad Quixote face, the face of an old crusader who believed in his cause, his cross, his crown. . . ." Hood's appearance belied the fact that he genuinely loved to fight. One of Lee's aides claimed that in battle, "The man was transfigured. The fierce light of his eyes—I can never forget." Promoted to major general and a division command, Hood earned a reputation for launching fierce attacks, but that very trait eventually caused his downfall as an army commander.

At Gettysburg, Hood was badly wounded in the upper left arm. Surgeons resected the bone rather than amputate, but the limb remained limp and useless. Two months later, a bullet shattered his right thigh at Chickamauga, and surgeons amputated the leg at the hip. Hood eventually acquired two artificial limbs (complete with boot and spurs) and kept the spare one tied to his horse, but he never learned to use them well and usually hobbled around on crutches. He also kept two aides close at all times to help him mount his horse and tie him to the saddle.

of great importance that a brigade should be put on the road to-night. Can you send one?" "Well, Gen'l," answered Stewart, "my men have had nothing to eat all day & are very tired & . . ." Hood cut him off abruptly and asked Forrest, "Genl'l Forrest, can *you* put a brigade there?" "Yes, Gen'l," Forrest replied, "if I can get ammunition—tho my men have been fighting all day with nothing to eat besides." Hood then told Stewart to supply Forrest with ammunition, and the two generals departed.

Hood never went to Spring Hill or took any personal action to see his orders were carried out. Instead, he simply went to bed assuming Schofield was trapped. About 3:00 a.m., an exhausted, barefooted private came to the house and asked to see Hood. The general was roused from bed to hear a shocking tale. The soldier told him he had been cut off from his unit and had wandered through the enemy camp that night. The Yankees were rapidly leaving Spring Hill down the very road Hood assumed was blocked, and they were in such confusion they paid him no heed. Hood wakened his aide and told him to send

Hood was promoted to lieutenant general in February 1864 and was given a corps command in the Army of Tennessee. He did not perform particularly well during the Atlanta Campaign, however, and some believed either his crippling wounds had taken the fire out of him, or he simply did not have the ability to command large units. Nonetheless, Jefferson Davis appointed Hood to replace Joe Johnston in July 1864 and gave him the temporary rank of general. Hood lashed out at Sherman in a series of battles around Atlanta but simply bled down the army and eventually had to abandon the city. After being defeated at Franklin and Nashville, Hood resigned his command in January 1865 and returned to Richmond.

Hood was a changed man when he returned to the capital and sank into depression. Mary Chesnut recalled how at one party he ignored the usual small talk and stared into the fire with "huge drops of perspiration that stood out on his forehead." Chesnut told a mutual friend, "He is going over some bitter hour. . . . He feels the panic at Nashville and its shame." "And the dead on the battlefield at Franklin," replied the friend. Chesnut referred to Hood as the "wounded knight" and declared, "[He was] the *simplest,* most transparent soul I have met yet in this great revolution." Hood earlier had become engaged to 18-year-old Sally Buchanan "Buck" Campbell Preston, a prominent South Carolina socialite. The match seemed odd from the beginning because Hood was unsophisticated and rather abrupt. After his resignation, their engagement was called off.

Hood married after the war, became a prosperous New Orleans businessman, and wrote his memoirs, *Advance and Retreat.* His life was tragic to the end. In 1879, Hood's wife died in a yellow fever epidemic, and two days after the funeral his eldest child contracted the dreaded fever and also died. Hood then became ill and died two days later. His funeral drew only a small crowd.

---

the soldier to Cheatham with an order to attack at once with one regiment. He then returned to bed and went to sleep.

When morning dawned, Hood was furious to discover nothing had been done. He immediately blamed Cheatham for disobeying orders, but the aide later admitted to Tennessee Governor Isham Harris, "Govr, Gen'l Cheatham is not to blame for that. I never sent him the order . . . I fell asleep again before writing it." The aide finally admitted his error to Hood, and Hood made an apology of sorts to Cheatham, but the entire incident remains a mystery. Cheatham later claimed he *did* receive the order but was only able to harass the enemy since Hood called for a single regiment to attack. The only thing certain about the Spring Hill incident is that the entire Confederate command system broke down. Every general must have known the importance of cutting the road, but no one took any initiative to see it done. The only one who seemed to appreciate the situation was Schofield, who marched to safety right past the Confederate campfires. After the war, Schofield bragged, "Hood was in bed all night and I was in the saddle all night."

## The Battle of Franklin

On the morning of November 30, Hood called his generals to headquarters for breakfast and, according to one witness, "lashed out" at them. Voices were raised, and accusations of who failed at Spring Hill flew around the table. One general claimed Hood was "wrathy as a rattlesnake . . . striking at everything." Hood ordered an immediate pursuit of Schofield, and hundreds of civilians cheered the men as they hurried up the road to catch the enemy. One officer remembered that both young and old "lined the fences, cheering and crying out: 'push on, boys; you will capture all of the Yanks soon. They have just passed here on the dead run.'" General Cleburne rode at the head of his division, but he was moody and depressed. He told a fellow general he had heard "through a very reliable channel" that Hood blamed him for allowing the enemy to escape. Cleburne, the officer claimed, was "quite angry and evidently was deeply hurt."

That afternoon, Hood found Schofield had strongly entrenched at Franklin to cover his wagon train as it crossed the Harpeth River in his rear. Forrest informed Hood he could take a force of infantry behind the enemy and trap them, but Hood insisted on making a frontal attack. Shocked at the decision, Forrest begged, "Give me one strong division of infantry with my cavalry and within two hours time I will agree to flank the Federals from their works," but Hood waved him off and said he would attack the Yankees where they were. General Cheatham soon arrived and admitted, "I don't like the looks of this fight. The Federals have an excellent position, and are well fortified." Again Hood dismissed his subordinate and declared, "I would prefer to fight them here where they have only eight hours to fortify, than to strike them at Nashville where they have been strengthening themselves for three years and more." Still more generals rode up to express their concerns, and Cleburne offered the bold opinion that a frontal attack would be "a terrible waste of life." Despite the opposition, Hood was unmoved, and Brigadier General Daniel C. Govan claimed the generals rode away fully realizing "the desperate nature of the assault we were about to make." Later Govan found General Cleburne staring across the open ground his men would have to cross to close with the enemy. After some conversation, Govan took his leave and told his commander, "Well, General, few of us will ever return to Arkansas to tell the story of this battle." "Well, Govan," Cleburne replied, "if we are to die, let us die like men."

The Confederate attack at Franklin was perhaps the most spectacular of the war. Larger than Pickett's Charge at Gettysburg, it involved eighteen brigades and covered two miles of open ground. A blood-red sun was setting when the order was given to advance, and an eerie quiet descended on the field. "[I]t was simply awful," wrote one man, "reminding one of those sickening lulls which preceded a tremendous thunderstorm." As the brigades moved forward, regimental bands added to the drama by playing "The Bonnie Blue Flag" and "Dixie." The advancing Confederates then faintly heard the tunes of "Yankee Doodle" and "Battle Hymn of the Republic" coming from the enemy's bands in Franklin. In town, the Union soldiers were awed when thousands of Rebels headed toward them. "It was a grand sight!" a captain wrote. "For the moment we were spellbound with admiration, although they were our hated foes. . . . On they came, and in the center their lines seemed to be many deep and unbroken, their red-and-white tattered flags, with the emblem of St. Andrew's Cross as numerous as though every company bore them, flaring brilliantly in the sun's rays."

The Confederates crushed some Union units that had been left too far in front of the main line and chased them to Franklin. Unable to wait until all the men reached safety, the soldiers on the main line finally opened fire. One recalled how "the long line of blue-coats within the trenches rose, and a flash of flame shot out in a sinuous line, and the white smoke rose like the foam on the crest of a breaker. The few straggling blue-coats and the long line of gray went down like over-ripe grain before a blast of wind and hail." The Confederates crashed into Schofield's center and briefly broke through, but reinforcements were rushed in to plug the hole. Among them was Colonel Arthur MacArthur, who earned a Medal of Honor at Missionary Ridge. He led the 12th Wisconsin into the fray but fell to the ground when his horse was shot out from under him. Already wounded in the shoulder, MacArthur fought his way to a Rebel officer, who promptly shot him in the chest. MacArthur stabbed the officer in the stomach, but the Confederate shot him again in the knee as he fell. Similar fights raged around them. A Union officer remembered "seeing one man, with blood streaming down his face from a wound in the head, with a pick axe in his hands, rushing into a crowd of the enemy and swinging his pick." Many of the Confederates became trapped in a ditch running along the base of the Union line. All were finally forced either to surrender or make a dash for safety. One of the men claimed, "Sixteen of our soldiers sprang up and ran out of the ditch . . . a whole volley of musketry killed them to the last man." A Union artillery officer claimed the enemy was so close to his cannon, "At every discharge of my gun there were two distinct sounds, first the explosion, then the bones [breaking]."

When the Confederates finally retreated about 9:00 p.m., Hood's Army of Tennessee was wrecked. More than 6,000 men and twelve generals had been lost. Of these, Generals Patrick Cleburne, John Adams, Otho Strahl, and Hiram Granbury were killed on the field. Generals John C. Carter and States Rights Gist were mortally wounded, and six others were wounded or captured. In a sobering scene, the bodies of five of the generals were laid out on the veranda of a local home. After the battle, General Cheatham was seen walking across the grisly ground. A witness claimed "great big tears ran down his cheeks and he began to sob like a child." "You could have walked all over the field upon dead bodies without stepping upon the ground," Cheatham wrote. "I never saw anything like that field, and I never want to again."

Schofield lost 2,300 men at Franklin, but he retreated safely to Nashville that night. A final anguishing chapter of the battle occurred the next morning when Hood chose to march his surviving men through the battlefield rather than around it. Years later, Private Sam Watkins wrote, "O, my God! What did we see! It was a grand holocaust of death. Death had held high carnival there that night. The dead were piled the one on the other all over the ground. I never was so horrified and appalled in my life."

## The Battle of Nashville

When he reached Nashville, Hood took up a defensive position along the hills south of the city. Chances of victory against Thomas were slim, but Hood thought he might receive reinforcements or lure Thomas into attacking him on favorable ground. In a questionable decision, Hood sent one infantry division and Forrest's cavalry to Murfreesboro to prevent Union troops there from reinforcing Thomas. This expedition further weakened the army and accomplished nothing because Major General Robert H. Milroy defeated Forrest and Bate when they attacked Murfreesboro on December 7. It was an omen of worse things to come.

While Hood waited passively in his defensive position, Thomas assembled almost 70,000 men to crush the invaders. The methodical "Rock of Chicka-mauga" took his time preparing for the attack and refused to be hurried even after Grant pressured him to strike immediately. Grant's patience was wearing thin when he wired Thomas, "Hood should be attacked where he is. Time strengthens him, in all probability, as much as it does you." The next day, Grant issued direct orders to attack Hood at once. "There is great danger," he warned, "of delay resulting in a campaign back to the Ohio River." Thomas still refused to move and privately thought it was hypocritical of Grant to demand an immediate attack at Nashville while the general-in-chief was still sitting outside Petersburg. Expecting to be relieved, Thomas replied, "If you should deem it necessary to relieve me, I shall submit without a murmur." Grant's patience snapped when Thomas informed him that a heavy ice storm had blanketed Nashville, making troop movements impossible. Grant sent Major General John Logan to relieve Thomas, but Logan refused to deliver the order when he learned the ice was melting and Thomas was finally ready to fight.

On the morning of December 15, 1864, Thomas attacked Hood in a thick fog. He first sent part of his army against the Confederate center and right flank to pin down the enemy and then sent the rest of his men to crush the Rebels' left flank. The African American soldiers of Major General James B. Steedman's division led the attack against the Confederate right. One witness said the men advanced against the enemy "as if on dress parade," but the Confederates in Cheatham's corps repulsed them with great slaughter. Soon afterward, Thomas made his attack on Hood's left and overran one position after another. As the Confederates fell back in hasty retreat, civilians ran onto the field to plead with them to stay. In a letter to his wife, an officer wrote of one woman who "ran out under heavy fire and did all she could to induce the men to stop and fight, appealing to them and begging them, but in vain. . . ." Another soldier noticed a woman who lived in a house where "bullets were clipping the shrubbery and striking the house." She stood on her doorstep waving her handkerchief and implored the men to fight. "She looked like a goddess," the soldier declared. "She was the gamest little human being in all the crowd."

Hood's routed army withdrew a few miles to a new position, but the next day Thomas renewed his attack and crushed Hood's left flank with cavalry. Once again, black troops were in the thick of the fighting. Confederate Brigadier General James T. Holtzclaw wrote, "Placing a negro brigade in front they gallantly dashed up to the abatis, forty feet in front, and were killed by hundreds. Pressed on by their white brethren in the rear they continued to come up in masses to the abatis, but they came only to die. I have seen most of the battle-fields of the West, but never saw dead men thicker than in front of my two right regiments." Despite the horror, one of the black soldiers' white officers claimed the fight was inspiring because "the blood of the white and black men has flowed freely together for the great cause which is to give freedom, unity, manhood and peace to all men, whatever birth or complexion."

After suffering two disastrous defeats in two days, Hood's men disengaged and headed back to Alabama. The Battle of Nashville had essentially destroyed the Army of Tennessee, with Hood losing 6,000 men in the battle and retreat and Thomas reporting 2,600 men lost. Fewer than 19,000 men reported for duty when Hood assembled the army's survivors at Tupelo, Mississippi, a few weeks later. Hood's reputation was ruined, and he resigned his command in January 1865. The remnants of the Army of Tennessee were scattered to various points in the Confederacy, with some units being sent to join Joseph E. Johnston for the Carolinas Campaign.

## THE MARCH TO THE SEA

**November 15, 1864: Sherman burns Atlanta and begins the March to the Sea**
**November 22, 1864: Battle of Griswoldville**
**November 24, 1864: Burning of Milledgeville**
**December 21, 1864: Sherman captures Savannah**

While Hood assembled his forces in Alabama that autumn for the Tennessee campaign, Sherman was planning his next move in Georgia. Etched in his mind was the earlier Meridian Expedition. In that campaign, Sherman was surprised to find that much of the Confederacy was actually a hollow shell almost devoid of Rebel troops and that there were huge amounts of food and fodder in enemy territory that could support an invading Union army. Since Hood was no longer a threat in Georgia, Sherman was convinced he could forage off the land and march to the Atlantic coast with little risk. Such a raid would destroy Georgia's considerable military stores and industries, and it would greatly demoralize Southerners by demonstrating they could not even protect their heartland. Sherman explained to Grant, "If we can march a well-appointed army right through his territory, it is a demonstration to the world, foreign and domestic, that we have a power which Davis cannot resist. This may not be war but rather statesmanship, nevertheless it is overwhelming to my mind that there are thousands of people abroad and in the South who reason thus: If the North can march an army right through the South, it is proof positive that the North can prevail." Sherman also argued it was useless to occupy enemy territory because victory depended on destroying the South's ability to wage war. "Until we can repopulate Georgia," he wrote, "it is useless to occupy it, but the utter destruction of its roads, houses, and people will cripple their military resources. . . . I can make the march and make Georgia howl!"

Grant was not convinced such a march was wise because there would be no way to rescue Sherman if he became trapped in enemy territory. Grant preferred defeating Hood first and asked Sherman, "Do you not think it is advisable, now that Hood has gone so far north, to entirely ruin him before starting out on your proposed campaign? With Hood's army destroyed, you can go where you please with impunity." Sherman disagreed and noted that any pursuit of Hood would be playing into the enemy's strategy of drawing him out of Georgia. Although not entirely convinced by Sherman's arguments, Grant trusted his subordinate and gave his reluctant approval for the "March to the Sea."

## The Burning of Atlanta

Sherman had his officers pick 62,000 of the most physically fit soldiers to make the march. His command consisted of Major General Henry W. Slocum's Army of Georgia, Major General Oliver O. Howard's Army of the Tennessee, and Major General H. Judson Kilpatrick's cavalry division. With Hood out of Georgia, the Rebels could barely muster 8,000 men in Major General Gustavus W. Smith's state militia and Joseph Wheeler's small cavalry corps to stop the raid.

Before leaving Atlanta, Sherman made sure the city could never again be used by the enemy for military purposes. On November 15, he torched all of the public and commercial buildings and anything else of military use. Nearly 2,000 buildings were burned, most of which were private homes and businesses. Sherman referred to the latter destruction as "accidental." Fortunately, there was no apparent loss of life because most of the population had been forced out of Atlanta in September. Most of those who remained kept quiet and viewed the destruction as revenge for Jubal Early's burning of Chambersburg, Pennsylvania, a few months earlier, but one Union soldier remembered a particular civilian who spoke up as he prepared to burn a house. "[A]s I was about to fire one place," he wrote, "a little girl about ten years old came to me and said, Mr soldier you would not burn our house would you. If you do where are we going to live and She looked into my face with such a pleading look that I could not have the hart to fire the place So I dropped the torch and walked away." Atlanta's residents never forgave the Yankees for the destruction, and one wrote, "Hell has laid her egg, and right here it hatched."

As Atlanta burned, the confident Union solders headed south toward the sea. Sherman later recalled, "Behind us lay Atlanta, smoldering and in ruins,

**The Burning of Atlanta.** Before starting his March to the Sea, Sherman burned much of Atlanta so the enemy could never again use it for military purposes. This photograph of a railroad yard shows some of the destruction.

the black smoke rising high in the air, and hanging like a pall over the ruined city." An Illinois officer hinted at things to come when he wrote in his diary, "It is evident our soldiers are determined to burn, plunder and destroy everything in their way on this march." In an odd coincidence, Hood crossed the Tennessee River the very next day to begin his Tennessee campaign. In a strange twist of events, the two opposing armies in the west were marching in completely opposite directions at the same time.

## The March

Sherman shrewdly forced the Confederates to spread their troops thin by marching his armies in separate columns along roughly parallel roads. Covering a 60-mile-wide front, he kept the enemy confused by waiting until the last possible moment before converging on a particular target. This successful tactic and the paucity of Confederate troops kept the fighting to a minimum. The campaign's largest clash occurred at Griswoldville. Kilpatrick captured the town on November 21, burned the railroad depot and some buildings, and then took up a strong defensive position when he was reinforced by an infantry brigade. The next day, elements of the Georgia militia made several attacks, but all were repulsed. The Confederates were mostly inexperienced young boys and old men, who were said to have charged with "more courage than discretion." Estimates of Confederate losses at Griswoldville range as high as 600, while Kilpatrick lost just 62 men. One Union soldier lamented, "I hope

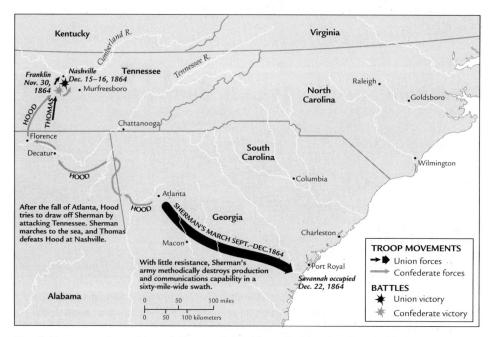

**Hood's Tennessee Campaign and Sherman's March to the Sea, October–December 1864.** In the autumn of 1864, the opposing armies in the western theater marched away from Atlanta in opposite directions. Hood first moved into Tennessee to threaten Nashville in an attempt to draw Sherman out of Georgia. Sherman, however, refused to follow and ordered Thomas to engage Hood. Union forces wrecked Hood's army at Franklin and Nashville and forced his retreat. Meanwhile, Sherman burned Atlanta and began his March to the Sea. After destroying a 60-mile-wide swath through southern Georgia, he safely reached Savannah on December 22.

we will never have to shoot at such men again. They knew nothing at all about fighting. . . ."

Kilpatrick's troopers had frequent clashes with Wheeler's cavalry, but few of Sherman's infantrymen ever fired a shot during the long march. Their greatest hardships were the constant marching and looking for food in the countryside. Sherman's orders called for the army to travel light with few wagons. The men were to live off the land, but strict rules were drawn up to govern foraging. Soldiers were not to enter homes, but they could confiscate vegetables and livestock within sight of their camp. Only corps commanders were authorized to destroy any buildings, and appointed officers were to supervise all foraging expeditions. These officers were to leave behind enough food for the families' use, but one admitted, "The question is never asked how much the farmer needs for his subsistence, but all is taken—literally everything." Despite these strict orders, civilians living in Sherman's path suffered greatly. In addition to the formal foraging parties, soldiers dubbed "bummers" roamed

# NOTABLE UNIT: *Terry's Texas Rangers*

Organized in September 1861 by Benjamin Franklin Terry and Thomas S. Lubbock, this unit was officially designated the 8th Texas Cavalry with Terry serving as colonel and Lubbock as lieutenant colonel. The men wore civilian clothing instead of uniforms (one captain wore buckskin and a Mexican sombrero) and were armed with a variety of weapons. Department commander Albert Sydney Johnston was frustrated trying to supply the unit with ammunition and once claimed there were twenty different types of firearms in the regiment. Rather than using traditional cavalry weapons, the Texans preferred bowie knives to sabers and shotguns and pistols to carbines. Knowing it could be fatal to stop and reload during a wild melee, some of the troopers carried as many as six revolvers.

The 8th Texas Cavalry became famous for its prowess at both scouting and fighting. Its first combat occurred in December 1861 when Terry led a charge at Woodsonville, Kentucky. The Union commander wrote, "With lightning speed, under infernal yelling, great numbers of Texas Rangers rushed upon our whole force. They advanced as near as fifteen or twenty yards to our lines, some of them even between them, and then opened fire with rifles and revolvers." Unfortunately, Terry was killed in the attack, and Lubbock assumed command. To honor its fallen leader, the regiment adopted the name "Terry's Texas Rangers" because many of the officers were former Rangers.

Serving under Nathan Bedford Forrest and Joseph Wheeler, Terry's Texas Rangers fought at Shiloh, Perryville, Stones River, Chickamauga, Knoxville, and in the Atlanta Campaign. The combat was often at very close range. Describing a charge made in the Shiloh Campaign, one Ranger wrote, "Forrest ordered forward. Without waiting to be formal in the matter, the Texans went like a cyclone. . . . In a twinkling of an eye almost, both barrels of every shotgun in our line . . . was turned into that blue line and lo! What destruction and confusion followed. . . . After the shotguns were fired, the guns were slung on the horns of our saddles and with our six shooters in hand we pursued those fleeing. . . . " Late in the war, the Texas Rangers were among the few Confederate units to oppose Sherman's March to the Sea, and they spread fear in the Union ranks by hunting down and killing Yankee bummers. Before the final surrender, about 160 men avoided capture by slipping away to join other Confederate units still in the field. Only ninety troopers remained with the regiment when it surrendered in April 1865. Those who joined other units returned home without formally surrendering.

the countryside without permission to gather food and loot houses. One man wrote that bummers were "a rough looking set of soldiers and care for nothing," and a reporter claimed, "They appear to be possessed with a spirit of 'pure cussedness.'" Wheeler's cavalry naturally hated the bummers and killed them on sight. During the march, Union soldiers found the bodies of sixty-four bummers who had been shot, had their throats slit, or been hanged.

By all accounts, the destruction wrought by Sherman's men was heavy. Public property (including the state capitol building at Milledgeville), buildings,

**Sherman's Hairpins.** Sherman's armies especially targeted Confederate railroads for destruction during the March to the Sea. They heated railroad iron atop bonfires made from crossties and then twisted it around trees or poles into "Sherman's Hairpins." Here, soldiers are prying up a rail to be placed on the crossties piled up on the right.

and railroads were routinely destroyed. An Illinois sergeant admitted, "The men worked with a will, seeming to take savage delight in destroying everything that could by any possibility be made use of by their enemies." One Michigan soldier wrote to his brother, "You can have but a faint idea of the effect of an army passing through a country like this when there is no good feeling toward the inhabitants and when it becomes necessary to live upon the substance of these people." On one occasion, Sherman issued orders to one of his columns to "Dress to the right of the Seventeenth Corps, whose progress you can rate by the smokes." The raiders took particular delight in tearing up more than 300 miles of railroad track. After ripping up the rails, the soldiers made huge bonfires from the crossties, and then laid the rails across them. When the iron was hot and pliable, they grabbed each end of the rail and wrapped it around a tree or pole to create a useless, twisted loop called "Sherman's Hairpins."

Despite the widespread destruction of railroads, gins, and public buildings, it occurred along a rather narrow path affecting about 12 percent of Georgia, and not as many private homes were burned as is commonly believed. Most of those destroyed were owned by prominent Confederate officials or were in areas where Union soldiers came under fire. Private homes were far more likely to be looted or vandalized by the bummers—or by Wheeler's poorly disciplined cavalry that was supposed to be protecting the people. From near Savannah, one Confederate soldier wrote, "[T]he people say it is a question of which they should prefer, Wheeler's cavalry or the Yanks."

White families were not the only Georgians affected by Sherman's march. Unknown thousands of slaves left the plantations to follow along, as one man wrote, "like a sable cloud in the sky before a thunderstorm." A Minnesota soldier was impressed with their determination and observed, "Men, women and children are willing to endure all the hardships of a long march to secure their liberty, yet the slave owners say that the slaves are contented and do not wish to be free." The reception the slaves received by the soldiers varied. Many of Sherman's men cared little for African Americans, and treated them with contempt. One wrote how the soldiers in his regiment entertained themselves by making slaves on the side of the road "pull off their hats and coats and dance while we were passing." Others, however, tried to help the runaways by letting them ride in army wagons and informally putting them to work to carry equipment, cook, or act as servants.

Sherman viewed the slaves as a nuisance for "clogging my roads and eating my subsistence." He tried to discourage the elderly and women with children from coming along by informing them of the dangers ahead and the long distance they would have to travel. Able-bodied men, however, were allowed to join the march and were provided rations in return for serving as pioneers to clear roads and build bridges. Brigadier General Jefferson C. Davis, commander of the XIV Corps, also believed the slaves were slowing down the march. To discourage his soldiers from aiding the runaways, he forbade the use of army wagons to transport the slaves or their baggage. "Useless negroes," Davis declared, "are being accumulated to an extent which would be suicide to a column which must be constantly stripped for battle and prepared for the utmost celerity of movement."

One of the march's most controversial events involved General Davis and the slaves following his column. When Davis approached Ebenezer Creek, he was being hard pressed from the rear by Joe Wheeler's cavalry. To get his men across a pontoon bridge as quickly as possible, Davis moved the slaves aside to clear the road. Officers then began selecting black men who could be of useful service and sent them across the bridge. Panic ensued when some families became separated and the slaves realized most were to be left behind. Cries and wails rent the air, and many drowned when they tried to swim across the stream. After marching his men across the pontoon bridge, Davis ordered it taken up, leaving hundreds of slaves stranded on the far bank. It was later claimed the Confederates killed many of them, but this was never proven (Wheeler, in fact, had a policy of returning all captured slaves to their owners).

Many soldiers bitterly criticized Davis for his seemingly heartless behavior at Ebenezer Creek. One officer wrote, "If I had the power, I would have him [hanged] as high as Haman. There is great indignation among the troops. I should not wonder if the valiant murderer of women and children should meet with an accident before long." Another soldier wrote home, "Let the 'iron pen of history' write the comment on this action of a Union General." On the other hand, Davis's supporters pointed out that the general's primary responsibility was protecting his men. Abandoning the slaves was a military necessity because it was imperative to get the corps across the river before the enemy attacked. Justified or not, leaving the slaves to their fate at Ebenezer Creek was one of the march's great tragedies.

## EYEWITNESS
### Eliza Frances Andrews

*"Fanny" Andrews (1840–1931) was twenty-four-years old when Sherman's armies swept through southern Georgia. The daughter of a prominent judge who opposed secession, she and her sister left their home to escape the invaders. In late December 1864, Andrews returned to the war zone and described in her diary the destruction left in Sherman's wake.*

December 24, 1864—About three miles from Sparta we struck the "Burnt Country," as it is well named by the natives, and then I could better understand the wrath and desperation of these poor people. I almost felt as if I should like to hang a Yankee myself. There was hardly a fence left standing all the way from Sparta to Gordon. The fields were trampled down and the road was lined with carcasses of horses, hogs, and cattle that the invaders, unable either to consume or to carry away with them, had wantonly shot down to starve out the people and prevent them from making their crops. The stench in some places was unbearable; every few hundred yards we had to hold our noses or stop them with the cologne Mrs. Elzey had given us, and it proved a great boon. The dwellings that were standing all showed signs of pillage, and on every plantation we saw the charred remains of the gin-house and packing-screw, while here and there lone chimney stacks, "Sherman's Sentinels," told of homes laid in ashes. The infamous wretches! I couldn't wonder now that these poor people should want to put a rope round the neck of every red-handed "devil of them" they could lay their hands on. Hay ricks and fodder stacks were demolished, corn cribs were empty, and every bale of cotton that could be found was burnt by the savages. I saw no grain of any sort, except little patches they had spilled when feeding their horses and which there was not even a chicken left in the country to eat. A bag of oats might have lain anywhere along the road without danger from the beasts of the field, though I cannot say it would have been safe from the assaults of hungry people. Crowds of soldiers were

## The Capture of Savannah

After Sherman marched out of Atlanta in mid-November, no one in the North was certain of his whereabouts—or condition—until he reached Savannah on December 10. For a month, Sherman simply disappeared into enemy country, and Lincoln and Grant were greatly relieved when they learned he was safe. Sherman immediately set out to capture Savannah, although it was strongly defended by fortifications and 10,000 men under Lieutenant General William J. Hardee.

After surrounding Savannah on the north, west, and south, Sherman had Brigadier General William B. Hazen's division attack and capture Fort McAllister on December 12. Fort McAllister was located south of the city on the Ogeechee River, and its capture allowed Union vessels positioned offshore to run needed supplies and ordnance to Sherman by way of the river. When tramping over the road in both directions; it was like traveling through the streets of a populous town all day. They were mostly on foot, and I saw numbers seated on the roadside greedily eating raw turnips, meat skins, parched corn—anything they could find, even picking up the loose grains that Sherman's horses had left. I felt tempted to stop and empty the contents of our provision baskets into their laps, but the dreadful accounts that were given of the state of the country before us, made prudence get the better of our generosity. . . .

Before crossing the Oconee [River] at Milledgeville we ascended an immense hill, from which there was a fine view of the town, with Gov. Brown's fortifications in the foreground and the river rolling at our feet. The Yankees had burnt the bridge, so we had to cross on a ferry. . . . On our left was a field where thirty thousand Yankees had camped hardly three weeks before. It was strewn with the *débris* they had left behind, and the poor people of the neighborhood were wandering over it, seeking for anything they could find to eat, even picking up grains of corn that were scattered around where the Yankees had fed their horses. We were told that a great many valuables were found there at first, plunder that the invaders had left behind, but the place had been picked over so often by this time that little now remained except tufts of loose cotton, piles of half-rotted grain, and the carcasses of slaughtered animals, which raised a horrible stench.

*After the war, Andrews wrote numerous novels, poems, editorials, and even a textbook on botany. Sometimes she wrote under a male pen name because newspapers and magazines often did not take female writers seriously. Andrews also became a prominent educator and opened a school for girls before joining the faculty at Wesleyan College to teach French and literature. In 1908, her excellent Civil War diary was published.*

Eliza Frances Andrews, *The War-Time Journal of a Georgia Girl, 1864–1865* (New York: D. Appleton and Company, 1908), pp. 32–38.

Hardee refused a surrender demand, Sherman next sent troops to the east side of Savannah to cut the Confederates' last avenue of retreat into South Carolina. Before they arrived, however, Hardee escaped across the Savannah River on a pontoon bridge. The Yankees occupied the city on December 21, and the next day Sherman jubilantly wired President Lincoln, "I beg to present you as a Christmas-gift the city of Savannah. . . ."

The March to the Sea was a resounding success. Losing just over 2,000 men, Sherman destroyed a considerable amount of enemy railroad track and war industries and greatly demoralized the Southerners by demonstrating that Union armies could raid with impunity deep inside the Confederacy. In a congratulatory telegram, Lincoln declared that the march "brings those who sat in darkness, to see a great light." And Sherman was not yet finished. From Savannah he wrote to General Halleck, "We are not only fighting hostile armies, but a hostile people, and must make old and young, rich and poor, feel the hard hand of war, as well as their organized armies." With a few months' rest, he would be ready to move into South Carolina—the cradle of secession—and continue his path of destruction all the way to Virginia.

By New Year's Day, 1865, the war seemed virtually over in the west. While the Confederates continued to occupy most of the Trans-Mississippi Department, they could no longer seriously threaten the Union, and the Army of Tennessee was virtually destroyed. Sherman had a free hand to take his "hard hand of war" into South Carolina and knock that state out of the war. Nothing short of a miracle seemed able to save the Confederacy from the Yankees' wrath.

## FOR FURTHER READING

Correspondence between Generals Hood and Sherman over the eviction of Atlanta's civilians

Sherman's Special Field Orders, No. 120, with instructions for the March to the Sea

## CHAPTER 24

# From Petersburg
to Appomattox:
The Final Campaigns

Jefferson Davis was sitting alone in his reserved pew at Richmond's St. Paul's Episcopal Church on Sunday, April 2, 1865, when the sexton gently tapped him on the shoulder and handed him a note. The man then walked over to Secretary of War John C. Breckinridge and whispered into his ear. All eyes were on the president as he calmly opened the envelope and silently read a message from General Lee informing him that the enemy had broken through Petersburg's defenses, and Richmond would have to be evacuated that night. Showing no emotion, Davis stood up, put on his overcoat, and walked out of the church. Over the next thirty minutes the sexton repeatedly returned to whisper mysteriously to other government officials, who also quietly exited. Realizing something of great importance was unfolding, the congregation began leaving in small groups to hurry home and prepare for what was to come.

Davis retained a "calm and manly dignity" throughout the day as he began transferring the government to Danville, Virginia. The city, too, remained calm until the president left by train just before midnight. Richmond then descended into chaos when General Ewell began carrying out orders to destroy the city's warehouses and military supplies. Weeks earlier, Mayor Joseph Mayo and others asked Secretary of War Breckinridge to not burn the warehouses because the fires might spread through town. To the officials' shock, Breckinridge seemed little concerned and declared "that he didn't care a d—n if every house in Richmond was consumed, the warehouse[s] must be burned." Ewell asked Mayo to provide extra security against looters, but the mayor did little. As Ewell feared, mobs ransacked the city and torched more buildings when the Confederate troops began departing before dawn on April 3. Stopping on a hill outside the city, the general looked back in horror to see the flames spreading across Richmond. Firefighters bravely rushed to contain the conflagration, only to find that the drunken mobs had cut their hoses. Ewell knew he, not Breckinridge, would be held responsible for the city's destruction. When he was captured three days later, Ewell grumbled to a Union surgeon, "I acted under orders, but regret that those orders did not include Breckinridge, who should have been thrown into the hottest of the flames." The burning of Richmond was the beginning of the end for the Confederacy. What no one foresaw was just how quickly that end would come.

## THE PETERSBURG CAMPAIGN

**July 30, 1864: Battle of the Crater**
**August 14–18, 1864: Battle of Deep Bottom**
**August 18–21, 1864: Battle of Globe Tavern**
**September 29–30, 1864: Battles of Fort Harrison and New Market Heights**
**February 5–7, 1865: Battle of Hatcher's Run**

The evacuation of Richmond ended the ten-month-long Petersburg Campaign. After failing to take Richmond and Petersburg at the end of the Overland Campaign, Grant besieged the cities and began extending his left flank westward to cut Lee's railroad supply lines. Lee was forced to extend his defensive line to block Grant, and his smaller army was stretched thinner and thinner to cover the necessary ground. The long Petersburg Campaign involved both monotonous siege work and large bloody battles that tested both armies' endurance. As the months passed, miles of trenches and fortifications stretched around the cities, and the battlefield began to resemble what would be seen in World War I.

### The Battle of the Crater

One of the most tragic episodes of the campaign started with great promise. Lieutenant Colonel Henry Pleasants believed the coal miners in his 48th

**The Petersburg Campaign, June 1864–April 1865.** After Beauregard thwarted Grant's initial attempt to take Petersburg in June 1864, Lee arrived with his army and took up a strong defensive position to protect both Richmond and Petersburg. Over the next nine months, Grant made numerous attacks and slowly stretched his left flank toward the west to cut the railroads that kept Lee's army supplied.

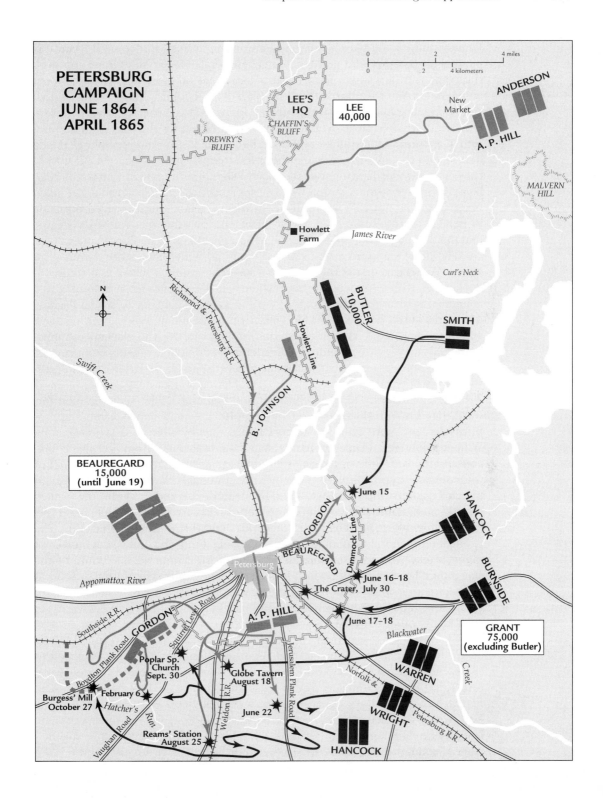

PETERSBURG
CAMPAIGN
JUNE 1864 –
APRIL 1865

LEE'S
HQ
*CHAFFIN'S
BLUFF*

*DREWRY'S
BLUFF*

LEE
40,000

New
Market

ANDERSON

A. P. HILL

*MALVERN
HILL*

Howlett Farm

*James River*

*Curl's Neck*

*Richmond & Petersburg R.R.*

BUTLER
10,000

SMITH

Howlett Line

B. JOHNSON

*Swift Creek*

N

BEAUREGARD
15,000
(until June 19)

June 15

GORDON

Dimmock Line

HANCOCK

BURNSIDE

Petersburg

BEAUREGARD

June 16–18

The Crater, July 30

*Appomattox River*

*Southside R.R.*

GORDON

A. P. HILL

June 17–18

*Blackwater*

GRANT
75,000
(excluding Butler)

*Squirrel Level Road*

*Boydton Plank Road*

Poplar Sp.
Church
Sept. 30

Globe Tavern
August 18

WARREN

*Jerusalem Plank Road*

*Norfolk &*

Burgess' Mill
October 27

February 6

*Hatcher's*

*Run*

*Weldon R.R.*

June 22

WRIGHT

*Petersburg R.R.*

*Vaughan Road*

Reams' Station
August 25

HANCOCK

*Creek*

0   2   4 miles
0   2   4 kilometers

Pennsylvania could blow a hole in Lee's line by mining underneath it and exploding an 8,000-pound powder charge. Generals Meade and Grant approved the plan, and Pleasants's men began digging the 600-foot-long tunnel. Corps commander Ambrose Burnside chose Brigadier General Edward Ferrero's division of black soldiers to lead the attack. To avoid being trapped, the men were specifically trained to go around the gaping hole left by the explosion and not into it. Ferrero's men trained zealously, but at the last minute Grant and Meade had second thoughts about using the black troops. Grant explained, "If we put the colored troops in front and [the attack] should prove a failure, it would then be said, and very properly, that we were shoving those people ahead to get killed because we did not care anything about them." When Grant ordered Burnside to replace Ferrero's unit with a white division, the other generals drew straws, and the dubious honor fell to Brigadier General James H. Ledlie.

The mine exploded at 4:45 a.m. on July 30. One officer who witnessed it wrote, "A slight tremor of the earth for a second, then the rocking as of an earthquake, and, with a tremendous blast which rent the sleeping hills beyond, a vast column of earth and smoke shoots upward to a great height, its dark sides flashing out sparks of fire, hangs poised for a moment in mid-air, and then, hurtling down with a roaring sound, showers of stones, broken timbers and blackened human limbs, subsides." Three hundred Confederates were killed when two entire regiments were blown into the air, and many others fled in terror. Where once impressive earthworks stood, there now was a smoldering 30-foot-deep crater.

The Confederate line was broken, and General Ledlie sent his men forward, but his untrained division moved into the hole and became trapped. Burnside sent more units to support Ledlie, but by that time Major General William Mahone's Confederate division had recovered from its shock and counterattacked. Burnside next ordered Ferrero's black troops into action, but their officers simply funneled them into the crater as well. Infuriated at the sight of black soldiers, the Rebels stood on the crater's rim and fired into the packed mass of men. Some soldiers lobbed artillery shells into the crater like hand grenades while others fixed bayonets onto rifles and threw them like javelins. The Confederates shot down hundreds of men packed into the crater and murdered many blacks who tried to surrender. A surviving Union soldier wrote of the slaughter, "Dismembered bodies, legs, arms, and heads strewed the ground in every direction, and this horrible butchery explains why the men's clothes were covered with blood and fragments of human flesh and brains to a degree never seen in any other battle of the war."

By 1:00 p.m. it was over. Virtually all the Union soldiers trapped in the crater were killed or captured, and the other battered divisions returned to their lines. Burnside lost 3,800 men in the disaster, while the Confederates lost 1,500 men. Grant declared it was "the saddest affair I have witnessed in the war." A military court of inquiry later blamed Burnside, Ledlie, and Ferrero for the fiasco, with Ferrero being singled out for the most criticism because he remained safely in the rear drinking rum with Ledlie while his men were slaughtered. Burnside was relieved of his corps command, and he and

# NOTABLE UNIT: *Berdan's Sharpshooters*

Sharpshooters, or snipers, played an important role throughout the Overland and Petersburg Campaigns. The most famous unit of these highly skilled riflemen was Berdan's Sharpshooters. Hiram Berdan (1824–1893), a New York City engineer and weapons inventor, was ranked the nation's top sport shooter before the Civil War. Taking advantage of his fame as a marksman, Burdan (bur-DAN) organized the 1st and 2nd U.S. Sharpshooters in 1861 and was appointed colonel of the former regiment. Sport shooters from across the North volunteered to join Berdan's Sharpshooters, but they first had to qualify in a rigorous shooting competition.

Berdan's Sharpshooters were among the few truly elite Civil War units. Besides being armed with breech-loading .52-caliber Sharps Rifles, they also underwent extensive physical training that was rare for soldiers of the day and dressed in distinctive green uniforms for camouflage. Assigned to the Army of the Potomac, the sharpshooters were usually placed in advance of the front lines to shoot enemy officers and artillerymen or to slow infantry advances with their rapid-firing rifles. At Yorktown some of the men crept beyond the front lines and in less than an hour silenced every Confederate cannon within 1,000 yards of their position. At Chancellorsville the sharpshooters overwhelmed a Georgia regiment and captured nearly 400 prisoners. When one of Berdan's officers asked the prisoners why they did not run away, "They replied that the balls came too close whenever they showed themselves. . . . It was a most splendid affair and the praise of the Sharpshooters was in everybody's mouth."

Two legendary members of Berdan's Sharpshooters were Chaplain Lorenzo Barber and California Joe. One officer wrote of Barber at Chancellorsville, "The sight of a butternut looking through a barn window at four hundred yards was too much for him. . . . [H]e blazed away and the rebs dropped out of sight like so many prairie dogs. . . ." The men flocked to hear the chaplain's sermons, because, as one said, "The chaplain practices what he preaches. He tells us what we should do, and goes with us to the very front to help us in battle." California Joe was actually Truman Head, a grizzled, 42-year-old bear hunter who had been a Forty-niner during the California gold rush. *Harper's Weekly* published stories of California Joe's sniper exploits and claimed he could pick off enemy soldiers from 1,500 yards. Rather oddly, he was discharged from the service in late 1862 because of senility and poor vision.

Berdan's Sharpshooters were disbanded during the Petersburg Campaign when their enlistments expired. They had fought in sixty-five engagements and had 1,008 men killed or wounded out of 2,570 who served in the two regiments.

Ledlie eventually resigned their commissions. Incredibly, Ferrero retained command of his division and at war's end was breveted major general of volunteers for his Petersburg service.

## The Longest Campaign

The Petersburg Campaign was the war's longest and fighting was constant, but the most intense battles took place on both flanks. On his right flank fronting

Richmond, Grant repeatedly tried to capture important enemy defensive positions, and on his left flank south of Petersburg he tried to cut Lee's railroad supply lines. Operations on the right began in August 1864 when Grant sent Winfield Scott Hancock north of the James River to attack Richmond's defenses at Deep Bottom. Hancock attacked on the morning of August 14, but the Confederates were stronger than expected and thick woods confused many of his units. Both sides launched attacks and counterattacks over several days, but the Confederates held firm. Six weeks later, Grant attacked Richmond's defenses again with Butler's Army of the James. In heavy fighting on September 29–30, Butler captured enemy positions at Fort Harrison and New Market Heights and successfully held them against a determined counterattack on the Darbytown Road a week later. As a result, Lee was forced to construct a new defensive line closer to Richmond. These battles north of the James River cost Grant more than 8,000 men, while costing Lee 5,000.

Grant's campaign against Lee's supply lines south of Petersburg began in June. James Wilson's and August Kautz's cavalry temporarily damaged some track that month, but two infantry corps were defeated when they attacked the force their government to demand it." After his Valley victory, Sheridan rejoined Grant, smashed the Confederates at Five Forks, and led the pursuit of Lee during the Appomattox Campaign.

Northerners credited Grant, Sherman, and "Little Phil" Sheridan with winning the Civil War, but Sheridan never looked like a war hero. Lincoln described him as "a brown, chunky little chap [with] not enough neck to hang him." Sheridan was wide through the shoulders, but he had short bowed legs that made him awkward on a horse. One soldier claimed the general "rolled and bounced upon the back of his steed much as an old salt does when walking up the aisle of a church after a four years' cruise at sea." Sheridan also had an odd-shaped head that reminded one man of a flattened-out minie ball. Despite Sheridan's looks, soldiers adored their red-faced, cigar-smoking commander. Sheridan knew how to inspire men on the battlefield, and Grant admitted he "had that magnetic quality of swaying men which I wish I had—a rare quality in a general." Sheridan's popularity was largely due to the fact he did not waste men's lives needlessly. He once wrote, "Soldiers are averse to seeing their comrades killed without compensating results, and none realize more quickly than they the blundering that often takes place on the field of battle."

During Reconstruction, Sheridan served as the military governor of Texas and Louisiana, but President Andrew Johnson removed him because he believed Sheridan was thwarting his policies. Sheridan then commanded the western armies against the Plains Indians, during which time he reportedly declared, "The only good Indians I ever saw were dead." He died just three days after completing his memoirs, *Personal Memoirs of Philip H. Sheridan, General, United States Army.*

Weldon Railroad. In August, Gouverneur K. Warren's corps captured the railroad at Globe Tavern, but Hancock's corps was driven out of Reams' Station a few days later. Having permanently cut the Weldon Railroad, Grant spent the next several months trying to capture the South Side Railroad and Boydton Plank Road farther west, but Lee's veterans drone off the enemy in desperate fighting at Peebles' Farm, Burgess' Mill, and Hatcher's Run. These operations south of Petersburg dragged on for months and cost Grant 15,000 men to Lee's 5,000.

## SHERIDAN'S SHENANDOAH VALLEY CAMPAIGN

**September 19, 1864: Third Battle of Winchester**
**September 22, 1864: Battle of Fisher's Hill**
**October 6–8, 1864: "The Burning"**
**October 19, 1864: Battle of Cedar Creek**

Since the beginning of the war the Shenandoah Valley had served as a major source of supplies for Lee's army. During the Overland Campaign, Grant sent expeditions under Franz Sigel and David Hunter to sever that supply line, but the Confederates defeated both. Adding insult to injury, Jubal Early then marched through the Valley and threatened Washington. Determined to destroy the region as an enemy supply base, Grant put Philip Sheridan in command of the 40,000-man Army of the Shenandoah and ordered him to "put himself south of the enemy and follow him to the death. Wherever the enemy goes let our troops go also."

## The Third Battle of Winchester

Sheridan moved out on the morning of September 19, but his advance slowed to a crawl when the wagon train clogged the road through a narrow gorge. Taking advantage of the delay, Early assembled his men and attacked with John B. Gordon's and Robert Rodes's divisions. The Confederates mauled two Union divisions, but Sheridan launched a successful counterattack that stopped their advance and mortally wounded General Rodes. Soon afterward, Union horsemen routed the Confederate cavalry guarding Early's left flank, and the entire Rebel line collapsed when Sheridan ordered a general advance. When the Confederates streamed through Winchester, Mrs. Gordon and other women tried to stop the retreat by joining hands across the street. The women's brave gesture was futile, however, and Early's army retreated after losing 3,600 men.

Although Sheridan lost 5,000 men at Winchester, he chased Early twenty miles to Fisher's Hill. The Confederates made a stand there, but Sheridan attacked on September 22 and once again crushed Early's left flank. The Southerners ran for their lives, and only darkness and pockets of stubborn resistance prevented Sheridan from completely annihilating Early's army. In the disaster, Early lost 1,200 men while Sheridan lost only 450. Sheridan pursued the Confederates to Staunton but then withdrew to Strasburg on the assumption that Early's offensive capability had been destroyed.

## "The Burning"

Sheridan next turned his attention to destroying the Valley as a source of Confederate supplies. Earlier, Grant had advised him, "[I]t is desirable that nothing should be left to invite the enemy to return. Take all provisions, forage, and stock wanted for the use of your command; such as cannot be consumed, destroy." Sheridan gave the assignment to Brigadier General Alfred T. A. Torbert, and from October 6 to 8 his cavalry methodically killed or confiscated livestock and burned hundreds of structures along a 92-mile path.

Torbert destroyed more than 2,000 barns and 70 flour mills and confiscated more than 4,000 head of livestock, while slaughtering another 3,000. Afterward, Sheridan claimed, "A crow would have had to carry its rations if it had flown across the valley." In describing the destruction, one Vermont soldier wrote, "The march from Harrisonburg was memorable on account of the sight of burning barns, mills, stacks of hay and grain. Pillars of smoke surrounded us through all the three days." The destruction of the Shenandoah Valley was complete, and residents afterward referred to the three days as "The Burning."

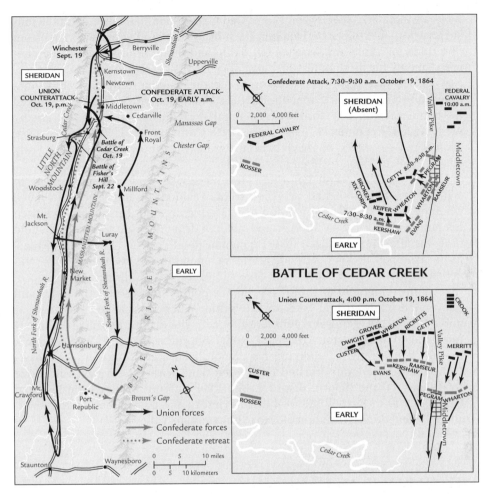

**Sheridan's Shenandoah Valley Campaign, September–October, 1864.** In September 1864, Sheridan advanced up the Shenandoah Valley to destroy Early's Confederate army, but Early attacked him first at Winchester on September 19. Early enjoyed some initial success but was eventually defeated and forced to retreat. Early tried to make a stand at Fisher's Hill, but Sheridan drove him from that position and chased him all the way to Staunton. Sheridan then destroyed much of the Valley in what became known as "The Burning." Believing Early was no longer a threat, Sheridan retreated and attended a meeting in Washington. While he was gone, Early launched a surprise attack on the Union army at Cedar Creek on October 19. Once again, Early enjoyed initial success, but he failed to press the enemy, and Sheridan was able to rejoin his men and win the battle.

## The Battle of Cedar Creek

Confident that Early's small army no longer posed a serious threat, Sheridan camped his men along Cedar Creek and left Major General Horatio G. Wright in command while he traveled to Washington to attend strategy meetings. While he was gone, Early secretly moved to Cedar Creek and launched an audacious surprise attack at dawn on October 19. John B. Gordon led three divisions out of a thick fog, smashed Wright's left flank, and he and Early chased the panicked enemy for three miles. Just as it appeared Early had won a stunning victory, his advance began to slow as units became disorganized in the chase, and famished Confederates stopped to loot the Union camps. Early was convinced the battle was won, but Gordon urged him to push on and annihilate the enemy while he had the chance. "That is the Sixth Corps, general," Gordon advised. "It will not go unless we drive it from the field." The overly confident Early simply replied, "Yes, it will go too, directly."

Early came to regret ignoring Gordon's advice. Fourteen miles away in Winchester, Sheridan had returned from Washington and was still in bed when he heard the distant cannon fire. Getting dressed, he quickly mounted his famous black horse, Rienzi, and made a dramatic ride to the battlefield that was later immortalized in T. Buchanan Read's poem, "Sheridan's Ride." As he galloped down the road, Sheridan encountered retreating men and yelled to them, "Boys turn back; face the other way. I am going to sleep in that camp tonight or in hell." Sheridan's confidence turned the tide, and many men followed him back to the battle. When he reached the army at midmorning, one general volunteered to form the army's rear guard while it retreated to Winchester. "Retreat—Hell!" Sheridan barked. "We'll be back in our camps tonight." Rallying his demoralized men, Sheridan counterattacked that afternoon, crushed Early's left flank with his cavalry, and drove the enemy off the field in disorder. Sheridan suffered more casualties than Early—5,700 to Early's 3,000—but the victory at Cedar Creek ended virtually all Confederate resistance in the Shenandoah Valley.

## THE CAROLINAS CAMPAIGN

**January 14, 1865: Union forces capture Fort Fisher**
**February 17, 1865: The burning of Columbia**
**February 18, 1865: Union forces occupy Charleston**
**March 19–21, 1865: Battle of Bentonville**

Southerners had little to celebrate on New Year's Day, 1865. Lee's army was starving at Petersburg, and the Confederates in the Shenandoah Valley had been routed. The Army of Tennessee was wrecked after Hood's disastrous Tennessee campaign, and Sherman stood poised to wreak the same havoc in the Carolinas as he had in Georgia. In the Trans-Mississippi, the war had virtually ground to a halt after Sterling Price's failed Missouri Raid. The Confederates were on the verge of collapse, and Southerners wondered if they would survive the year. Their woes only deepened when the enemy closed the port at Wilmington, North Carolina.

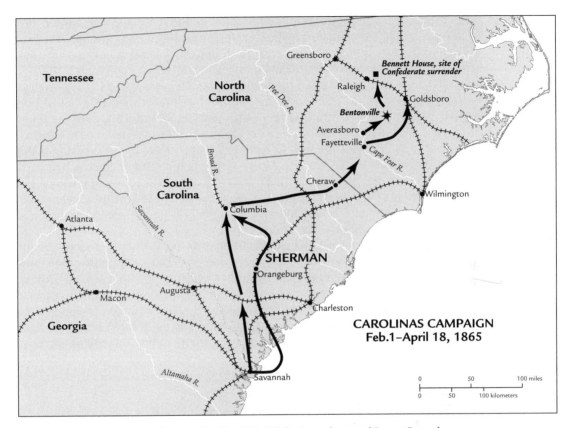

**The Carolinas Campaign, February–April, 1865.** While Grant besieged Lee at Petersburg, Sherman moved through the Carolinas to join him. As he had done during the March to the Sea, Sherman wreaked havoc on Confederate railroads, industries, and towns such as Columbia. Johnston's Confederates attacked the enemy at Averasboro and Bentonville, North Carolina, but were unable to stop Sherman's advance. When he learned of Lee's surrender at Appomattox, Johnston surrendered to Sherman at the Bennett House near Raleigh.

## Fort Fisher

Wilmington was the last Atlantic port open to blockade runners, and its connecting railroads made it critical in supplying both Lee's army and Confederate forces in the Carolinas. The city was well protected by earthworks, a small river fleet, cannons, and Fort Fisher's 1,400 troops. The fort, known as the "Gibraltar of the Confederacy," guarded the port's main inlet and was commanded by Colonel William Lamb. In December 1864, Grant sent Benjamin F. Butler with 6,500 men to capture Fort Fisher and close the Wilmington harbor, but the expedition ended in humiliating defeat. Before Butler arrived, Admiral David Porter tried to destroy the fort by detonating an explosives-laden barge next to it, but the barge ran aground too far away to inflict any damage. Butler then unsuccessfully attacked Fort Fisher on Christmas Day. Grant ordered Butler to besiege the fort if he could not capture it, but the general simply gathered up his men and sailed away. Furious, Grant relieved Butler of command.

Grant turned to the more capable Brigadier General Alfred H. Terry to lead a second expedition. Terry and Porter worked well together and attacked Fort Fisher on January 14, 1865. After a heavy naval bombardment, Terry attacked on one side with 2,000 men while a detachment of Marines and sailors attacked from the beach. Inside the fort, Colonel Lamb was joined by his superior, Major General William H. C. Whiting, whose requests for reinforcements had been denied. Lamb and Whiting successfully stopped the attack from the beach, but Terry's infantry stormed the parapet after fierce fighting. Whiting personally entered the fray, but he was mortally wounded in hand-to-hand combat, and the Yankees captured the fort after dark.

The fall of Fort Fisher closed Wilmington's port, but Confederate units under General Braxton Bragg continued to defend the city from other positions. When Sherman began his Carolinas Campaign in February, he ordered Major General John M. Schofield to capture Wilmington to give Sherman a shorter line of communications to the sea. Schofield attacked Bragg on February 16 and forced him to evacuate the city four days later. Schofield then occupied Wilmington and prepared to move inland to link up with Sherman.

## The Campaign Begins

Grant wanted Sherman to join him in Virginia to help defeat Lee, but he let Sherman choose the method of transportation. Sherman decided to march overland so he could continue his destructive tactics to spread terror and demoralize the Southern people. The Carolinas Campaign began on February 1, 1865, when Sherman left Beaufort, South Carolina, with 62,000 men in Major General Henry W. Slocum's Army of Georgia, Major General Oliver O. Howard's Army of the Tennessee, and Brigadier General H. Judson Kilpatrick's cavalry. Repeating the tactics he had used in Georgia, Sherman moved in two columns to confuse and disperse the enemy. Slocum and Kilpatrick marched on the left, while transports carried Howard to Port Royal Sound, from which he moved inland on Sherman's right. To stop Sherman, the Confederates had just 22,500 men.

Charleston was the first city to fall. Well defended by Forts Sumter and Wagner, it had withstood constant Union attacks for more than two years. The Yankees first tried to land troops near the city at Secessionville but were defeated there in June 1862, and Rear Admiral Samuel F. Du Pont failed in an April 1863 attack on Fort Sumter. Three months later, Union forces successfully landed on Morris Island, and the navy began a 587-day bombardment of the forts and city. Among the Union artillery was a massive 200-pound Parrott rifle dubbed the "Swamp Angel." Placed on Morris Island, it fired projectiles filled with combustibles in an unsuccessful attempt to burn down Charleston. Fortunately for the city's residents, a shell exploded prematurely in the Swamp Angel's barrel and disabled it.

Furious, but unsuccessful, infantry assaults were made on Fort Wagner in July 1863. The stubborn Confederate defenders finally abandoned the fort, but they continued to hold Fort Sumter and Charleston. Charleston remained in Rebel hands until Sherman threatened the city from the rear in February 1865. Confederate General William J. Hardee was then forced to withdraw to avoid being trapped, and Union troops occupied the city. Robert Anderson, the hero of Fort Sumter, was invited to return to Charleston, and on April 14, 1865, he had the pleasure of raising over the fort the very flag he had taken down in surrender four years earlier to the day.

## The Burning of Columbia

When Sherman began the Carolinas Campaign, he declared, "Every house, barn, fence and cotton gin gets an application of the torch. That prospect is revolting, but war is an uncivil game and can't be civilized." Reveling in this duty, Union soldiers set fire to at least a dozen South Carolina towns, and one officer admitted, "The country behind us is left a howling wilderness, an utter desolation." This wrath intensified as the Yankees approached Columbia—the state capital and cradle of secession.

When Howard reached Columbia on February 17, Sherman ordered him to destroy all public buildings, railroads, and war industries, but not to harm private property. What happened next is indisputable, but those involved bitterly disagreed over who was responsible. Within twenty-four hours of Howard's arrival, one-third of Columbia, nearly 460 buildings, had burned to the ground. Sherman blamed the Confederates for the destruction, claiming they set fire to cotton bales piled in the streets and that high winds and arsonists spread the flames. While it is true the Confederates set fire to cotton, there is also overwhelming evidence that the Union soldiers intentionally allowed the fires to spread and even started new ones. During their approach to the city, the soldiers openly talked of their intentions to destroy the city. One from Ohio admitted, "Our men had such a spite against the place they swore they would burn the city, if they should enter it, and they did." City residents accused the Yankees of getting drunk and setting fire to buildings and cutting water hoses so the flames could not be extinguished. A Minnesota soldier agreed and claimed his comrades not only intentionally cut the hoses, they even turned them on firemen trying to contain the conflagration. Some Union officers and men did try to stop the fires, but one captain wrote, "[I]t was no use for there was as many men setting fires as there was trying to put them out." The burning of Columbia was one of the war's great tragedies, and to those who lost their homes it mattered little who was to blame.

## The Battle of Bentonville

After the Confederates abandoned Charleston, General Joseph E. Johnston began concentrating his forces along the North Carolina border. When Sherman entered the state in early March, Schofield pushed two columns inland from Wilmington to join him at Goldsboro. To prevent the enemy from uniting their forces, General Braxton Bragg attacked one of Schofield's columns at Wyse Fork on March 8. The battle raged for three days, but Bragg finally had to withdraw and the Yankees captured Goldsboro. Sherman occupied Fayetteville at the same time and spent five days ransacking that city before sending Slocum to threaten Raleigh and Howard to join Schofield at Goldsboro.

Joe Johnston had steadily retreated before the massive enemy juggernaut, but now he saw an opportunity to destroy Slocum's isolated column before he could reunite with Howard. Johnston sent General Hardee to engage Slocum near Averasboro, but Slocum forced Hardee to retreat after heavy fighting on March 16. Johnston then concentrated his army near Bentonville and attacked Slocum on the afternoon of March 19. The Confederates pushed the Yankees back, but they took cover in some hastily built breastworks and held out until Sherman brought up reinforcements the next day. On March 21, Sherman counterattacked, but Johnston held his position until he was able to retreat safely at dark. Johnston's army was on the verge of collapse, but Sherman chose not to pursue and the defeated Confederates escaped. The three-day Battle of Bentonville was the largest, and last, battle of the Carolinas Campaign, with Sherman losing 1,500 men to Johnston's 2,600.

The Carolinas Campaign had been a resounding success, and Sherman was pleased with the 45-mile-wide swath of destruction from Savannah to Goldsboro. More attention has been given to his March to the Sea in Georgia, but the destruction Sherman wrought in South Carolina was far worse. Sherman noted this when he later wrote, "The march to the sea seems to have captured everybody, whereas it was child's play compared with the other." After Bentonville there was nothing Johnston could do to prevent Sherman from joining Grant in Virginia. To make matters worse, the Confederates in North Carolina learned two weeks later that the war had taken a disastrous turn at Richmond and Petersburg.

## THE COLLAPSE

February 3, 1865: Hampton Roads Peace Conference
March 25, 1865: Battle of Fort Stedman
April 1, 1865: Battle of Five Forks

When Sherman began his Carolinas Campaign, the war in Virginia remained a stalemate. Lee's battered Army of Northern Virginia was exhausted, sick, and hungry, but it was successfully defending Richmond and Petersburg. Although it was fairly apparent the Confederates would ultimately be beaten, no one knew how much more blood and treasure a final Union victory would cost. During these dark days, officials on both sides were willing to explore the possibility of a negotiated settlement to save lives. Peace talks, in fact, were held a couple of times in the last year of war, but they were doomed because neither president was willing to compromise. Both were convinced their cause was right, and they were quite prepared to see the war through to its final bloody conclusion.

## Peace Feelers

One peace feeler was made in July 1864 when Jubal Early was threatening Washington. At that time, *New York Tribune* editor Horace Greeley informed Lincoln he had learned that Confederate envoys were waiting in Niagara Falls, Canada, to negotiate a peace. Lincoln, however, was suspicious. He had already made it clear that any negotiations must be based on the Southern states returning to the Union and was aware that the Confederates might accept this condition in theory just to gain a ceasefire. Lincoln believed the negotiations would eventually break down, and it might be impossible to convince the war-weary Northern people to renew the fighting. "An armistice—a cessation of hostilities—is the end of the struggle," he declared, "and the insurgents would be in peaceable possession of all that has been struggled for." No doubt the November election was also on his mind. If Lincoln agreed to a ceasefire and tried to renew the war after talks broke down, Northern voters might turn to the Peace Democrats in the presidential election.

In the end, Lincoln had his personal secretary, John Hay, accompany Greeley to Niagara Falls and present the Confederates with a letter offering to entertain any peace proposal that was based on reuniting the Union *and* abolishing slavery. The Confederates expected the reunification demand, but emancipation came as a shock, particularly because the U.S. Congress had just voted down the proposed Thirteenth Amendment to abolish slavery nationwide. The Rebel envoys rejected Lincoln's conditions and made his letter public in an attempt to show he was not serious about negotiating a peace. The incident gave Peace Democrats considerable ammunition for the November election because they could claim that the president was being unreasonable. He was demanding that the Southerners do something even the Congress had refused to do—grant universal emancipation. One Democratic editor wrote, "All he has a right to require of the south is submission to the Constitution." Lincoln's tying emancipation to peace was a bold move, and it demonstrated just how much he detested slavery.

## The Hampton Roads Peace Conference

Horace Greeley was also involved in a peace conference held during the 1865 Petersburg Campaign. He and Francis P. Blair, Sr., the 73-year-old patriarch of a powerful Missouri family and one of Lincoln's closest advisers, believed a ceasefire should be arranged so the North and South could join forces to drive Maximilian out of Mexico. When the Confederate envoys were in Niagara Falls months before, Lincoln had worried such a ceasefire might eventually lead to Southern independence because it would be difficult to renew the fighting once talks broke down. In early 1865, however, there was no such danger. Lincoln was safely reelected and the Confederates were all but defeated. If anything, a ceasefire might benefit the Union more than the Rebels because General Grant estimated that half of Lee's army would desert if an armistice was declared. Therefore, Lincoln was willing to take a chance on talking to the enemy even though he still did not believe it would lead to anything positive. Blair was allowed to pass through the lines to meet with Davis in January 1865. Intrigued by the proposal, Davis informed Lincoln he was prepared to appoint a commission to discuss "securing peace to the two countries." Lincoln, in turn, said he would meet the Confederate envoys but only "with the view of securing peace to the people of our one common country." Obviously, neither president was prepared to compromise, but they agreed to the conference largely to silence critics who thought a political settlement was possible.

On February 3, 1865, Confederate Vice President Alexander H. Stephens, president pro tem of the senate Robert M. T. Hunter, and Assistant Secretary of War John A. Campbell met with Lincoln and Secretary of State William Seward aboard a ship at Hampton Roads, Virginia. Stephens suggested declaring an armistice, but Lincoln said that it could happen only after the Southerners disbanded their armies and recognized federal authority. Lincoln also dismissed a suggestion that he and Davis sign a secret treaty to stop the fighting and unite their armies to drive Maximilian out of Mexico. Stephens claimed such a cooperative effort would rekindle a nationalist spirit and lead to reunification, but Lincoln reminded him that only Congress could ratify such a treaty or declare war. Besides, Lincoln would never sign a treaty with Davis because such an act would recognize the Confederacy as an independent nation.

Lincoln had never wavered in his opposition to slavery, although political considerations had forced him to move slowly toward emancipation. Somewhat surprisingly, at Hampton Roads he reversed his position and stated that abolition was not necessary for the South to rejoin the Union. The Emancipation Proclamation had only freed about 200,000 slaves by early 1865, and Stephens asked what would happen to those still enslaved should the Southern states rejoin the Union. Lincoln replied that while the courts would ultimately have to decide, he believed the proclamation was a wartime measure that would expire when the war ended. The Southerners might have interpreted this rather vague answer to mean they could keep the millions of slaves still in their possession. Lincoln also mentioned the possibility of compensating slaveowners for slaves lost to emancipation. Seward was similarly cryptic about the Thirteenth Amendment when he declared that the proposed amendment might be withdrawn once the "revolutionary passions" had calmed. On the surface, such statements seemed to indicate Lincoln was backing away from his long-held opposition to slavery, but that is probably not the case. He likely said such things just to give the Southerners an incentive to end the war and rejoin the Union to save their property. In reality, Lincoln knew there was little likelihood the federal courts would ever allow slavery to survive, and it was certain the Radicals would never back away from the Thirteenth Amendment.

The four-hour conference failed because there was no middle ground on which to base a settlement. Although the two leaders were willing to compromise on some secondary issues, Lincoln demanded reunification while Davis insisted on independence. On the other hand, the conference strengthened both presidents' political positions. Critics who had been calling for a negotiated peace were silenced because the meeting proved conclusively that the enemy would never compromise. Northern and Southern people alike were left with just two options—accept defeat or redouble their efforts to win a military victory.

## Fort Stedman

Just weeks after the Hampton Roads Peace Conference, Lee realized he could not stay in Petersburg much longer. On March 2, Philip Sheridan defeated Jubal Early's small army in a battle at Waynesboro. Now Sheridan was on his way from the Shenandoah Valley to reinforce Grant, and Sherman was marching steadily toward Virginia from the south. When Grant united these armies in one command, he would simply overwhelm Lee with superior numbers. Lee's only hope was to break out of Petersburg before the enemy could join forces. In a desperate gamble, he gave John B. Gordon nearly half the army to punch a hole through Grant's lines so it could escape and join Johnston in North Carolina. The target was Fort Stedman, a Union stronghold about 150 yards from the Confederate line. Once the fort was taken, Gordon was to continue toward the Union rear to capture additional positions and open the hole large enough for Lee to extract the army.

At 4:00 a.m. on March 25, the Confederates stormed Fort Stedman in a short hand-to-hand fight, but the fortunes of war turned almost immediately. Unfamiliar with the confusing labyrinth of trenches and earthworks that lay in the rear of the fort, the Confederates were unable to find their next target. By sunrise, the enemy had recovered from their shock, and two divisions swarmed in to close the gap. Pounded by artillery and rifle fire, Gordon's men could go no farther and faced inevitable defeat. Lee finally ordered him to withdraw to save the men, but that proved far more dangerous than the assault itself. Many Confederates were shot down as they ran back to their lines, while hundreds more surrendered rather than run the gauntlet of fire. Gordon had lost 4,000 men by the time he returned to his starting position shortly after 8:00 a.m. Grant suffered about 1,500 casualties in the short, vicious fight. One Union soldier attested to the ferocity of the battle when he wrote that Fort Stedman "was the first place I saw footprints of men in puddles of human blood. Blood was on my boots when the fighting ended. It was hell!"

## The Battle of Five Forks

The attack on Fort Stedman led to the collapse of the Petersburg defenses. Correctly assuming Lee had stripped troops from his flanks to use in the attack, Grant sent Sheridan to turn the Confederate right flank on March 29. Lee expected such a maneuver and rushed Major Generals George Pickett's and Fitzhugh Lee's divisions to the threatened area. Heavy rains made movement difficult, but Sheridan's infantry pressed forward and pushed Pickett back to Five Forks, an important crossroads beyond Lee's flank. The capture of Five Forks would make Lee's position in Petersburg untenable because the enemy would then control the roads in his rear. Desperate, Lee ordered Pickett to hold Five Forks "at all hazards."

Incredibly, when Sheridan attacked on April 1, both Pickett and Fitzhugh Lee were away from their men enjoying a fish bake far in the rear. Sheridan crushed Pickett's division, and the Confederate position at Five Forks melted away. Pickett lost more than 5,000 men in the disaster, while Sheridan reported about 1,100 casualties. After the war, one of Pickett's men declared, "Pickett ought to have been shot. . . . I saw him at the close of the fight, thoroughly 'rattled,' & telling his officers in disarrayed tones to 'get out the best way they could.'" Instead of shooting Pickett, Lee relieved him of command, but he did not punish his nephew Fitzhugh.

# THE APPOMATTOX CAMPAIGN

**April 2, 1865: Lee begins evacuating Richmond**
**April 6, 1865: Battle of Sailor's Creek**
**April 9, 1865: Lee surrenders at Appomattox Court House**

After turning Lee's right flank at Five Forks, Grant launched a general assault along the entire Petersburg line the next day. Lee informed Davis he would have to abandon his position and made arrangements for supplies to be sent to Amelia Court House, about thirty miles to the west. After reuniting his men there, he planned to move south along a railroad to join Joe Johnston in North Carolina. Success depended on holding Richmond and Petersburg until nightfall to give the army a chance to escape and then remaining at least a day's march ahead of the pursuing enemy to have time to gather the supplies at Amelia Court House. It was going to be a footrace, something at which the Confederates had always excelled.

## Richmond Abandoned

Grant battered the Rebels on April 2, but the Confederates managed to keep their line of retreat open throughout the day. Davis and other officials fled that night to

Danville, Virginia, while General Ewell burned government warehouses and property. During the evacuation, wind and mobs spread the flames, and much of Richmond was destroyed. A Massachusetts officer who entered the smoldering city on April 3 wrote, "The scene that met our eyes here almost baffles description. . . . Tumult, violence, riot, pillage, everywhere prevailed, and as if these were not enough to illustrate the horrors of war, the roar of the flames, the clanging of bells, and general uproar and confusion were sufficient to appall the stoutest heart."

Lincoln happened to be visiting Admiral Porter on the James River when Richmond was evacuated. On April 4, he told Porter, "Thank God I have lived to see this. It seems to me that I have been dreaming a horrid dream for four years, and now the nightmare is gone. I want to see Richmond." With an escort of Marines, Porter, Lincoln, and the president's son Tad (on his twelfth birthday) entered Richmond on an odd sight-seeing excursion. Thankful slaves soon swamped the president, and one cried out, "Bless the Lord, the great Messiah!" and knelt down before him. "Don't kneel to me," Lincoln implored. "That is not right. You must kneel to God only, and thank Him for the liberty you will enjoy hereafter." The party continued down the street, and Lincoln had the pleasure of sitting at Davis's Confederate White House desk before returning to the safety of Porter's ships.

**Death in the Trenches.** When Grant launched his last Petersburg assault on April 2, 1865, the Confederates in Fort Mahone made a last-ditch stand to buy enough time for Lee to evacuate his army. This photograph taken the next day shows some of the Confederate soldiers who died in Fort Mahone's trenches.

## The Retreat

Lee reached Amelia Court House the same day Lincoln toured Richmond, only to find the trains were loaded with ammunition instead of food. This breakdown in communication forced the Confederates to spend an entire day gathering supplies from the countryside. The delay gave Sheridan's cavalry time to catch up and cut the railroad to the south. It was now impossible for Lee to join

Johnston, and the exhausted Confederates had to march west all the next day and night to reach another railroad supply depot at Farmville.

On April 6, George Custer's cavalry cut the Confederate column and isolated General Ewell's command. Ewell took up a defensive position along Sailor's Creek but was overwhelmed by superior numbers. In the debacle, Ewell and five other generals were captured, along with more than 3,000 men. The entire area was crawling with Yankees, who scooped up thousands of additional prisoners in two more clashes. Arriving just as these disasters unfolded, Lee sat on his horse atop a tall hill and exclaimed, "My God! Has the army been dissolved?" In just a few hours on what the Confederates came to call "Black Thursday," he had lost nearly 8,000 men, or almost one-fourth of the entire army.

## Lee Surrenders

Lee reached Farmville that night and continued fighting his way west on April 7. During the day, he rejected a surrender request from Grant, but on April 8 Sheridan cut off Lee's retreat at Appomattox Court House, and Custer's cavalry wreaked havoc capturing wagons and prisoners. The next morning, Lee ordered Gordon to make one last attempt to break out of the encirclement. Gordon made the Army of Northern Virginia's last attack, but after finding himself outflanked and outnumbered, he informed Lee that a breakout was impossible without heavy reinforcements. Realizing there were none to send, Lee muttered, "Then there is nothing left me but to go and see General Grant, and I would rather die a thousand deaths."

Grant awoke before daylight suffering from a blinding two-day headache, and his aide General Horace Porter found him "pacing up and down in the yard holding both hands to his head." A short time later, as Grant was drinking coffee and munching on a cucumber with vinegar, a letter arrived from Lee requesting a meeting. As they rode away, Porter asked Grant how he felt, and the general reported the headache had evaporated "the moment I got Lee's letter." Arrangements had been made to meet at Wilmer McLean's house that afternoon. When Grant and his large entourage arrived, they found Lee waiting for them. Dressed in a new uniform, Lee stood in stark contrast to Grant in his mud-spattered private's coat. After some small talk, the two got down to business, and Lee quickly agreed to the generous surrender terms Grant offered. Lee's men would be paroled and allowed to return home, where they would not be molested by federal authorities as long as they obeyed the law and did not take up arms again until all prisoners had been properly exchanged. The officers were allowed to keep their sidearms and men their privately owned horses, but all flags and government animals, weapons, and equipment had to be surrendered. When Lee mentioned the near-starving condition of his men, Grant also agreed to provide ample rations to feed the famished Confederates.

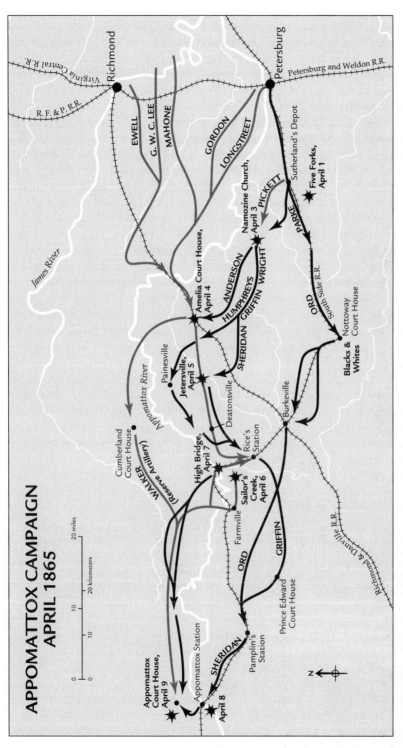

**APPOMATTOX CAMPAIGN APRIL 1865**

**The Appomattox Campaign, April 1865.** After the failed Confederate breakout at Fort Stedman, Grant attacked on April 1, 1865, and crushed the enemy at Five Forks. Lee then abandoned Richmond and Petersburg and fled westward in hopes of turning south to join Johnston in North Carolina. Union forces gave chase and captured a large part of Lee's army at Sailor's Creek on April 6. The advancing Union army cut off Lee's escape route to North Carolina and trapped him at Appomattox Court House. Lee surrendered there on April 9.

615

When Lee returned to camp, weeping soldiers surrounded him, and one man cried out, "Farewell, General Lee. I wish for your sake and mine that every damned Yankee on earth was sunk ten miles in hell!" The surrender ceremony was held on April 12, but Lee did not attend. After issuing a farewell address to the men, he and some close aides returned to Richmond that day—escorted by a Union honor guard.

Brigadier General Joshua Chamberlain, the hero of Gettysburg's Little Round Top, presided over the surrender ceremony and drew up his men on each side of the road on which the Rebels would march. Deeply impressed by the moment, Chamberlain was determined to honor the brave Confederates who had fought for so long. He wrote after the war, "Before us in proud humiliation stood the embodiment of manhood: men whom neither toils and sufferings, nor the fact of death, nor disaster, nor hopelessness could bend from their resolve; standing before us now, thin, worn, and famished, but erect, and with eyes looking level into ours, waking memories that bound us together as no other bond. . . ." When each Confederate division approached, Chamberlain had a bugle sound the order to "carry arms," a salute to marching soldiers. When the Union soldiers saluted their defeated foe, Chamberlain noted the effect it had on the Confederates. "[John] Gordon at the head of the column, riding with heavy spirit and downcast face, catches the sound of shifting arms, looks up, and, taking the meaning, wheels superbly, making with himself and his horse one uplifted figure, with profound salutation as he drops the point of his sword to the boot toe; then facing to his own command, gives word for his successive brigades to pass us with the same position of the manual—honor answering honor." During the emotional ceremony, approximately 26,000 survivors of the Army of Northern Virginia were formally surrendered. Another 25,000 had been lost during the weeklong campaign. Grant had lost nearly 11,000 men bringing the Rebels to bay.

## THE LINCOLN ASSASSINATION

**April 14, 1865: John Wilkes Booth shoots Lincoln in Ford's Theater**
**April 15, 1865: President Lincoln dies**
**April 26, 1865: U.S. soldier kills Booth in Virginia**
**July 7, 1865: U.S. authorities hang four assassination conspirators**

After his tour of Richmond, Lincoln returned to Washington and soon learned Lee had surrendered. The mood in the capital was upbeat, but Lincoln and other officials were not aware that John Wilkes Booth and a small band of conspirators were preparing one last murderous act to salvage a Confederate victory. Booth (1838–1865) was a Maryland native and belonged to a prominent, and peculiar, family of actors. Junius Brutus Booth, his alcoholic and somewhat mentally unstable father, and Edwin, his eldest brother, were two of the nation's leading Shakespearean actors. After Junius died in 1851, 14-year-old John Wilkes took to the stage and also became famous. Although unpredictable like his father, Booth was handsome and athletic, and he had a charismatic personality that made him popular with women. A staunch secessionist, he hated the federal government and wished it "would go to hell."

Despite his secessionist feelings, Booth continued acting in Washington when the war began rather than joining the Confederate army. When defeat seemed inevitable, however, he assembled a loose collection of associates and hatched a scheme to kidnap Lincoln and turn him over to Confederate authorities to hold as a hostage for the release of prisoners of war. Booth put his plan into action after listening to the president's second inaugural speech in March 1865. When Lincoln hinted he might support black suffrage, Booth turned to a companion and muttered, "Now, by God, I'll put him through." Two weeks later, the conspirators tried to kidnap Lincoln, but they were foiled by the unexpected presence of an armed escort.

## Ford's Theater

When Lee surrendered, Booth changed his plan from kidnapping Lincoln to murdering him and several other prominent Union officials. Booth hated the president for his racial policies, and he apparently believed the death of Union leaders would throw the North into disarray and provide an opportunity for a negotiated peace. Recently uncovered evidence indicates Booth may have had the support of the Confederate government. Just before the assassination,

**John Wilkes Booth.** Although a popular actor in Washington theaters, John Wilkes Booth was a Confederate sympathizer. When Lee surrendered at Appomattox, Booth made plans to assassinate Lincoln and other officials to throw the Union government into chaos.

Confederate officials dedicated a substantial amount of money for covert operations, and Booth took a mysterious trip to Canada, where many known Rebel agents operated. The Confederates' secret cipher was also found in Booth's possession after the murder, and he escaped along a route frequently used by Southern spies and smugglers.

Booth struck on the night of April 14 (Good Friday) after newspapers reported Lincoln would be attending Ford's Theater to watch the play "Our American Cousin." Because Booth was an actor, his presence would arouse no suspicion, and his familiarity with the facilities would help him carry out the assassination and escape afterward. An exhausted Lincoln considered staying home that night but finally relented to go to the play because he knew the crowd was expecting him. Accompanied by Mary and Major Henry Rathbone

# EYEWITNESS

## Horace Porter

*A Pennsylvania native and son of a former governor, Horace Porter (1837–1921) served on George B. McClellan's staff after graduating from West Point in 1860. Transferred west, he fought in several battles and was awarded a Medal of Honor for rallying men at Chickamauga. Grant took notice of Porter's diligent service, promoted him to lieutenant colonel, and attached him to his staff. Porter served with Grant through the Overland and Petersburg Campaigns and was in the McLean House when Lee surrendered.*

We walked in softly, and ranged ourselves quietly about the sides of the room, very much as people enter a sick-chamber when they expect to find the patient dangerously ill. . . . General Lee said: "I suppose, General Grant, that the object of our present meeting is fully understood. I asked to see you to ascertain upon what terms you would receive the surrender of my army . . . I would suggest that you commit to writing the terms you have proposed, so that they may be formally acted upon. . . ."

[Grant] wrote very rapidly. . . . Then he looked toward Lee, and his eyes seemed to be resting on the handsome sword that hung at that officer's side. He said afterward that this set him to thinking that it would be an unnecessary humiliation to require the officers to surrender their swords, and a great hardship to deprive them of their personal baggage and horses. . . . Lee pushed aside some books and two brass candle-sticks which were on the table, then took the book [with Grant's terms] and laid it down before him, while he drew from his pocket a pair of steel-rimmed spectacles, and wiped the glasses carefully with his handkerchief. He crossed his legs, adjusted the spectacles very slowly and deliberately, took up the draft of the terms, and proceeded to read them attentively. . . .

Lee felt in his pocket as if searching for a pencil, but he did not seem to be able to find one. Seeing this, I handed him my lead-pencil. During the rest of the interview he kept twirling this pencil in his fingers and occasionally tapping the top of the table with it. When he handed it back, it was carefully treasured by me as a memento of the occa-

and his fiancée Clara Harris, the president arrived after the play had begun. Ford's Theater was bedecked with Union flags and bunting, and the mood was festive. The actors halted the play out of respect when Lincoln entered, and the audience applauded loudly as the presidential party walked to the box. When the play resumed, Booth approached the closed door and apparently waited for an actor to deliver a particularly humorous line that would bring peals of laughter to muffle the gunshot. When the dialogue began about 10:30 p.m., Booth slipped quietly into the box and shot Lincoln once behind the left ear with a .44-caliber derringer. Major Rathbone jumped from his chair to confront the assassin, but Booth pulled out a knife and slashed open his arm from elbow to shoulder. Dramatically, he then leaped to the stage below, breaking his lower sion. When Lee came to the sentence about the officers' side-arms, private horses, and baggage, he showed for the first time during the reading of the letter a slight change of countenance, and was evidently touched by this act of generosity. It was doubtless the condition mentioned to which he particularly alluded when he looked toward General Grant, as he finished reading, and said with some degree of warmth in his manner, "This will have a very happy effect upon my army. . . . The cavalrymen and artillerists own their own horses in our army. Its organization in this respect differs from that of the United States." This expression attracted the notice of our officers present, as showing how firmly the conviction was grounded in his mind that we were two distinct countries. . . .

A little before four o'clock General Lee shook hands with General Grant, bowed to the other officers, and with Colonel Marshall left the room. One after another we followed, and passed out to the porch. Lee signaled to his orderly to bring up his horse, and while the animal was being bridled the general stood on the lowest step, and gazed sadly in the direction of the valley beyond, where his army lay—now an army of prisoners. He thrice smote the palm of his left hand slowly with his right fist in an absent sort of way, seemed not to see the group of Union officers in the yard, who rose respectfully at his approach, and appeared unaware of everything about him. All appreciated the sadness that overwhelmed him, and he had the personal sympathy of every one who beheld him at this supreme moment of trial. The approach of his horse seemed to recall him from his reverie, and he at once mounted. General Grant now stepped down from the porch, moving toward him, and saluted him by raising his hat. He was followed in this act of courtesy by all our officers present. Lee raised his hat respectfully, and rode off at a slow trot to break the sad news to the brave fellows whom he had so long commanded.

*Porter remained in the army after the war and served on both Grant's and Sherman's staffs before resigning his commission in 1873 to work in the railroad industry. He later served as ambassador to France.*

General Horace Porter, *Campaigning With Grant* (New York: The Century Company, 1897). pp. 473–86.

left leg on landing. Unsure what had happened, the crowd was stunned when Booth screamed, "sic semper tyrannis" ("thus always to tyrants") and limped offstage to a waiting horse in the alley.

Pandemonium ensued as Mary began wailing from the box. Two army surgeons rushed upstairs, and one restored Lincoln's breathing with artificial resuscitation. After a hurried examination, the president was carried across the street to a boarding room that soon became crowded with Mary, government officials, and surgeons. Describing the scene in his diary, Secretary of the Navy Welles wrote, "The giant sufferer lay extended diagonally across the bed which was not long enough for him. He had been stripped of his clothes. . . .His slow, full respiration lifted the clothes with each breath that he took. His features were calm

## DID YOU KNOW?

### Wilmer McLean

Grant and Lee used the Appomattox home of Wilmer McLean for the surrender negotiations. McLean previously lived on Bull Run, and his home there served as General Beauregard's headquarters during the 1861 battle. After serving briefly in the Confederate quartermaster department, McLean sold his Bull Run home and settled at Appomattox Court House to get his family as far away as possible from the combat zone. Ironically, the war that began at the McLean house in 1861 came to an end in the family's parlor four years later.

and striking. . . .The night was dark, cloudy, and damp, and about six it began to rain." Word soon arrived that Secretary of State Seward had also been attacked. Booth had sent Lewis Powell and George Atzerodt to assassinate Seward and Vice President Andrew Johnson, respectively, but Atzerodt became frightened and took no action. Powell, however, gained entrance to Seward's house by claiming to be delivering medicine for the secretary, who was bedridden after suffering a carriage accident. Forcing his way upstairs, Powell jumped into Seward's bed and began stabbing him. A thick neck brace saved Seward's life, but he suffered severe cuts, as did five other people who were slashed when Powell made his escape.

The attacks seemed well planned to those watching over Lincoln, and all agreed when Welles muttered, "Damn the Rebels, this was their work." Fearing the entire government was under attack, Secretary of War Stanton boldly took charge and began bringing order out of chaos. He had the hysterical Mary removed, ordered the roads out of Washington sealed, and brought in a clerk to take down the testimony of witnesses who had been in Ford's Theater. Meanwhile, a somber deathwatch ensued in the boarding room, and a large crowd gathered in the street. Lincoln never regained consciousness, and his breathing became more labored as morning approached. At 7:22 a.m., Senator Charles Sumner stood by the bed with his arm around Lincoln's son Robert while a surgeon checked the president's pulse. Looking up, the surgeon quietly said, "He is gone." A heavy silence fell on the room, and Stanton asked a minister to say some appropriate words. Everyone knelt around the bed in prayer, and then Stanton stood, and with tears running down his face, declared, "Now he belongs to the ages."

### Retribution

Booth and fellow conspirator David Herold made their escape from Washington and stopped in Maryland to have Dr. Samuel Mudd set Booth's broken leg. A massive manhunt was under way, and Union cavalry finally cornered the pair in a tobacco barn on Richard Garrett's Virginia farm. Herold quickly surrendered, but Booth refused. The Yankees then set the barn on fire, and moments later Sergeant Boston Corbett shot Booth in the neck as Booth hobbled around inside. When the paralyzed and dying Booth was dragged out, he whispered to the soldiers standing around him, "Tell my mother I die for my country."

Federal authorities quickly arrested a number of Booth's associates, including Mary Surratt, mother of co-conspirator John Surratt and the owner

**Retribution.** Four people were sentenced to hang for their involvement in the Lincoln assassination. As soldiers line the Old Capital Prison wall to watch, officials on the gallows prepare the condemned prisoners for execution. On the far left, a kneeling officer can be seen attending a seated Mary Surratt.

of the boarding house in which Booth's men had met. Tried by a military court, Powell, Herold, Atzerodt, and Surratt were convicted as accessories and sentenced to death. Of the group, Surrat's execution was the most controversial. She maintained her innocence throughout the ordeal, even to a priest who comforted her in prison. While the court was convinced of her guilt, the members were uneasy about executing a woman and barely mustered the necessary two-thirds vote required for a death sentence. As a sort of compromise, they attached a request for clemency to the execution order sent to President Johnson. Johnson, however, claimed he never saw it and signed the order. All four of the prisoners were hanged on July 7 at the Old Capital Prison. Surratt was the first woman executed by the federal government, and her Victorian-era executioners thought it best to tie down her dress so it would not fly up when the trap door was sprung. Samuel Arnold, Michael O'Laughlin, and Dr. Mudd were sentenced to life in prison, and Edward Spangler was sentenced to six years. O'Laughlin died in prison two years later, and Arnold and Mudd were pardoned

**Lincoln's Funeral.** Lincoln was mortally wounded in Ford's Theater on a Good Friday. Thousands of mourners lined Pennsylvania Avenue to witness his funeral procession.

in 1869. John Surratt fled to Egypt and was the only one who escaped punishment. Extradited in 1866, he was tried for murder but acquitted.

## The Martyred President

The assassination transformed Abraham Lincoln from a successful wartime president into a Union martyr. The symbolism of his being shot on Good Friday was not lost on Northerners. Lincoln was viewed as a Christ-like figure who was killed just weeks after he had reached out to the Southerners "with malice toward none" in his second inaugural address. He died at the height of his popularity and at the very moment of victory.

For four years Lincoln had held together a fragile alliance of Northerners and persevered in the face of staggering difficulties. Always pragmatic, he never became tied to one policy, but was willing to try new things as long as they helped achieve his goals. Compromising when he could and being ruthless when necessary, Lincoln never wavered in his opposition to secession and slavery, although political considerations forced him to move slowly toward emancipation. He once observed, "The pilots on our Western rivers steer from *point to point* as they call it—setting the course of the boat no farther than they can see; and that is all I propose to myself in this great problem." Lincoln was the Union's pilot and he successfully steered it through a bloody nightmare, but it was not until after his death that most people appreciated his stunning achievements. Not only did Lincoln save the Union and free the slaves, he did so within the framework of the Constitution and safeguarded America's republican form of government.

## PEACE

**April 26, 1865: Joseph E. Johnston surrenders in North Carolina**
**May 4, 1865: Richard Taylor surrenders in Alabama**
**May 10, 1865: Union forces capture Jefferson Davis**
**June 2, 1865: Edmond Kirby Smith surrenders in Texas**
**June 23, 1865: Stand Watie surrenders in Indian Territory**
**November 6, 1865: CSS *Shenandoah* surrenders in Great Britain**

Lee's surrender at Appomattox has traditionally been seen as the end of the Civil War, but it was not. Other Confederate armies were still in the field, and some die-hard Rebels wanted to continue the war in the west. Most high-ranking Confederates, however, realized there was no longer any hope of victory, particularly after the Union continued to defeat them on the battlefield. Appomattox did not end the Civil War, but it did mark the beginning of the end.

## The Capture of Mobile

Two days after Lee's failed attack at Fort Stedman, 45,000 Union soldiers under Major General E. R. S. Canby began a final push against Mobile, Alabama. There, Confederate Major General Dabney H. Maury's 10,000 men held strong defensive positions at Spanish Fort and Fort Blakely. Canby bombarded Spanish Fort for two weeks and captured the position in a successful night assault on April 8. He then joined Major General Frederick Steele, who was besieging Fort Blakely. On April 9 (the same day Lee surrendered at Appomattox), Canby attacked the small Confederate garrison and captured it in twenty minutes. Hundreds of black soldiers participated in this last major battle of the Civil War, and they were among the first to enter the fort. One officer claimed many Confederates tried to surrender to white Union soldiers "to save from being butchered. . . . [black soldiers] did not take a prisoner, they killed all they took to a man." Three days later, Maury evacuated Mobile, and the Yankees took possession of the city. The fall of Mobile and James H. Wilson's successful cavalry raid against Selma, Alabama, demonstrated the futility of continuing the war. Over the next six weeks, the Confederates' remaining armies began surrendering from east to west.

## The Final Surrenders

Joseph E. Johnston was one of those who realized victory was impossible after Appomattox. He met with Sherman on April 17 at James Bennett's farmhouse near Durham Station, North Carolina, and agreed to surrender his 30,000 men, but Sherman overstepped his authority by agreeing to allow the Southern state governments to continue to function until a final peace settlement was reached. Angry that Sherman had encroached on his political authority, President Andrew Johnson rejected the agreement, and Grant ordered Sherman to offer Johnston the same terms he had given Lee. Sherman and Johnston met again, and Johnston agreed to terms on April 26. Farther west at Citronelle, Alabama, Lieutenant General Richard Taylor surrendered approximately 12,000 men in Alabama, Mississippi, and eastern Louisiana to General Canby on May 4.

When Johnston surrendered, Jefferson Davis and his entourage were making their way west to continue the war from the Trans-Mississippi Department. On May 10, Union cavalry discovered their camp near Irwinville, Georgia, and surrounded it before daylight. Realizing they were trapped, Davis's wife, Varina, and his companions convinced him to escape into a nearby swamp. In the dark, the president mistakenly put on Varina's coat and she draped a shawl over his shoulders, which gave rise to false accusations that Davis intentionally disguised himself as a woman to make his escape. Stopped by a cavalryman just short of the swamp's safety, Davis muttered, "God's will be done" and surrendered. Defiant to the end, he told a companion, "I cannot feel like a beaten man."

Had Davis made it to the Trans-Mississippi Department, he would have found a kindred spirit in department commander Edmund Kirby Smith. Like Davis, he was not yet ready to make peace with the enemy, and he appealed to both civilians and soldiers to continue fighting. In May 1865, Kirby Smith headed for Houston, Texas, to rally his troops, but as knowledge of the eastern surrenders spread, most of his soldiers began disbanding their units or deserting in large numbers. When Kirby Smith arrived in Houston, he found himself a general without an army. Meeting with Canby in Galveston, Texas, he surrendered on June 2. Three weeks earlier, the final battle of the Civil War took place at Palmito Ranch, Texas, where Private John Williams of the 34th Indiana became, on May 13, the last soldier killed in action.

Stand Watie was the last Confederate general to surrender. At a council meeting in June, the Indian Territory's leading Confederate chiefs called on their officers to surrender. Watie was the last to do so, on June 23, when he surrendered his Indian battalion at Doaksville, Indian Territory. The final Confederate surrender, however, did not occur until five months later. On November 6, 1865, after a long voyage from the Arctic Ocean, the commerce raider *Shenandoah* surrendered to British officials in Liverpool. The Civil War was finally over.

## FOR FURTHER READING

"Sheridan's Ride"
Lee's Farewell
Appomattox surrender document

# CHAPTER 25

# Reconstructing the Nation

On May 10, 1865, the day Jefferson Davis was captured in Georgia, President Andrew Johnson declared that Confederate resistance was "virtually at an end." Although not all of the Rebels had surrendered, the announcement spurred officials to order the Union's principle armies to Washington to hold a Grand Review to celebrate victory and end the mourning for Abraham Lincoln. On the sunny morning of May 23, a signal gun fired at 9:00 a.m., and Major General George Meade's 80,000-man Army of the Potomac began marching down Pennsylvania Avenue. Thousands of people cheered them, and Meade proudly raised his sword in a silent salute when the crowd shouted "Gettysburg! Gettysburg! Gettysburg!" One woman was touched by the spectacle and wrote, "And so it came, this glorious old army of the Potomac, for six hours marching past, eighteen or twenty miles long, their colors telling their sad history. Some regiments with nothing but a bare pole, a little bit of rag only, hanging a few inches, to show where their flag had been . . . all the rest shot away."

The next morning, the 65,000 men in Sherman's Army of the Tennessee and Army of Georgia took their turn. When they arrived in Washington, the soldiers wore tattered uniforms and worn-out shoes after months of campaigning. Fearing they would appear as ragamuffins compared to the neatly attired Army of the Potomac, Sherman made sure the men received new clothing before the review. When the regimental bands struck up "Marching Through Georgia," spectators immediately noticed a difference. These hard-bitten westerners had more of a swagger than Meade's soldiers, and thousands of runaway slaves, cooks, and captured Rebel livestock marched with them. Sherman recalled, "When I reached the Treasury-building, and looked back, the sight was simply magnificent. The column was compact, and the glittering muskets looked like a solid mass of steel, moving with the regularity of a pendulum." It was, he said, "the happiest and most satisfactory moment of my life."

In their excitement, few people probably noticed that something was absent in the Grand Review. Although Sherman allowed his African American pioneers to march in the procession, African American combat soldiers were nowhere to be seen. There is no evidence that such battle-tested units as the 54th Massachusetts, Louisiana Native Guards, or 1st Kansas Colored Volunteers were even invited to attend. The guns had not yet fallen silent, yet the contribution black soldiers had made to final victory was already being forgotten. This slight did not bode well for Southern blacks, as the turbulent period of Reconstruction was just beginning.

## THE CHALLENGE OF RECONSTRUCTION

When the Civil War sputtered out in 1865, everyone knew there would be difficulties reconstructing the devastated South. Approximately 260,000 white Southern men, more than 20 percent of the total forces, were dead, as well as 360,000 Northerners. Many more suffered crippling wounds or broken health, and virtually every family mourned the loss of loved ones. Emancipation had wiped out half of the South's financial worth, but former slaveholders received no compensation for their loss. Two-fifths of the South's livestock and half the farm machinery was destroyed, along with towns, levees, bridges, railroads, houses, barns, and businesses. Repairing the physical damage was relatively easy, because Northern businessmen eagerly supplied investment capital in search of profits. Much more difficult was adjusting to the political and social changes brought about by military defeat and the emancipation of the slaves.

### Reconstruction's Problems

Reconstruction's problems were truly daunting. Should everyone who served the Confederacy be punished as traitors or just the leaders? If spared prison, should former Rebels be allowed to participate in politics or should they be stripped of their civil rights? And what of the former slaves, now called freedmen? Approximately 180,000 blacks had fought for the Union, but that did not make them citizens. Should they be kept in a subservient position, or should the Constitution be amended to grant them full citizenship?

White Southerners had to accept both defeat and emancipation, but they were determined to remain in political control and keep the freedmen subservient. The freedmen, on the other hand, were just as determined to acquire land, education, and political rights so they could live independently of their former masters. Both Southern whites and freedmen would exert influence over Reconstruction but they would not control it—that task fell to the victorious Northerners. While most Northerners did not care much about the economic

**Aftermath.** After the Civil War much of the South lay in ruins. Baton Rouge, Louisiana, was just one of many towns that were either burned deliberately or destroyed during the fighting. This photograph was taken in Baton Rouge shortly after Union gunboats shelled it in 1862.

and social plight of the freedmen, they did want to prevent the former secessionists from regaining power. The Republicans also wanted to protect such wartime measures as the transcontinental railroad; higher tariff; Homestead Act; and education, banking, and currency reform. If the Southern states were readmitted under their old leaders, the Democrats might take control of Congress and repeal the Republican legislation. Reconstruction would prove to be a turbulent and violent time because Southern whites, freedmen, and Northern whites all had their own agendas. Democrats were pitted against Republicans, blacks against whites, former Confederates against Southern Unionists, and black Republicans against white Republicans.

## Presidential or Congressional Reconstruction?

From the outset, Reconstruction was a political struggle within the Republican Party between the legislative and executive branches of government. Radical Republicans believed the Southern states had committed "state suicide" when they seceded. The South now was simply conquered territory, and the people were no longer U.S. citizens. Because Congress had the authority to admit new states, it was Congress's responsibility to bring them back into the Union. Lincoln and moderate Republicans, however, disagreed because secession was unconstitutional. The Southern states may have *rebelled* against the federal government, but they never seceded. The Confederacy was never a legitimate nation, and the South was still states and the people were still citizens. Therefore, Lincoln thought he, not Congress, had the responsibility to reestablish loyal state governments in the South and restore them to their rightful place in the Union.

Control over Reconstruction was not the only issue that fractured the Republican Party. All Republicans agreed slavery should be abolished nation-wide, the freedmen be granted some rights, and the former secessionists never be allowed back in power, but they disagreed on the details. Radicals wanted to disenfranchise all former Rebels, enfranchise the freedmen, and revolutionize Southern society by redistributing land to elevate freedmen to the same status as white owners of small farms. Moderate Republicans were willing to enfranchise blacks to counter the Southern white vote, but they were uncomfortable with vengeful measures and social revolution. Lincoln, in particular, preferred a lenient policy because it might draw anti-secessionist Southerners into the Republican Party and help prevent the former Rebels from dominating the new South. Of paramount importance to Lincoln, however, was to mend the nation quickly. Freedmen should be given a chance to live independently of their former masters, and perhaps even the right to vote, but their rights were secondary to the greater issue of restoring the Union.

## LINCOLN'S RECONSTRUCTION

**December 8, 1863: Lincoln announces his Ten Percent Plan**
**July 2, 1864: U.S. Congress passes the Wade-Davis Bill**

Lincoln began implementing a reconstruction policy as soon as Union armies occupied Southern territory. Since the Confiscation Acts authorized him to pardon secessionists, he issued a Proclamation of Amnesty and Reconstruction on December 8, 1863, offering a pardon and the restoration of non-slave property to all who took the oath of allegiance (except high-ranking Rebels, who could apply for pardons individually). In this proclamation, Lincoln also put forth a reconstruction program that became known as the Ten Percent Plan.

### The Ten Percent Plan

Lincoln declared that a seceded state could return to the Union when just ten percent of the 1860 voters took the oath of allegiance and established a loyal government that abolished slavery. This lenient policy reflected his belief that the fire-eating slaveholders had dragged most Southerners into the war and these reluctant Rebels could be persuaded to abandon the fight. The plan was quickly put into effect in Louisiana, Arkansas, and Tennessee because Union forces controlled much of those states. By early 1864, all three states had satisfied Lincoln's requirements and elected loyal governors and congressmen.

The Radicals bitterly opposed the Ten Percent Plan, and the ensuing debate revealed a fundamental difference of opinion among the Republicans. The Radicals were not convinced that the Southerners who took the oath of allegiance were really loyal. They believed the only way to ensure Southern loyalty was to radically reorganize Southern society. Everyone who had supported secession should be disenfranchised, and the slaves should be freed and granted political rights and land so they could control their own destinies. Lincoln's plan was too lenient on those who had started the war, and it did not provide rights to the freedmen who had helped defend the Union. As one Radical declared, "Loyal negroes must not be put down while disloyal white men are put up."

## The Wade-Davis Bill

On July 2, 1864, the Radicals passed their own Reconstruction policy. The Wade-Davis Bill, sponsored by Senator Benjamin F. Wade and Congressman Henry W. Davis, called for the president to appoint provisional governors in the seceding states once they were occupied by Union forces. When a majority of white male citizens signed an oath of allegiance swearing they had never supported the Confederacy, the state could hold a constitutional convention to reform its government. Former Confederates could not participate in the process or hold any state office. When qualified voters ratified a constitution that abolished slavery, repudiated the Confederate debt, and barred former Confederates from holding important political positions, the state could be readmitted. Because voting was a state right, not a federal right, the Wade-Davis Bill did not enfranchise the freedmen, but the Radicals expected the new state governments to do so. Lincoln supported parts of the bill, but he believed it was too vindictive so he used the pocket veto to prevent it from becoming law. In this process, the president simply refused to sign the bill, and Congress adjourned a few days later. Angry at the veto, the Radicals refused to seat the congressional delegations or count the electoral votes of the three Southern states that had been reconstructed under Lincoln's Ten Percent Plan.

## The Thirteenth Amendment

During the Civil War, all Republicans united behind a constitutional amendment to abolish slavery permanently because the confiscation acts and Emancipation Proclamation were wartime measures the Democrats might someday be able to repeal. The Senate passed the Thirteenth Amendment in April 1864, but the House refused to follow suit because Democrats believed it encroached on states' rights. This emancipation amendment became a major issue in the 1864 presidential election. The Democrats supported each state having the right to decide on slavery within its borders, while the Republicans called for the abolition of slavery nationwide. Lincoln's victory indicated most Northerners supported the amendment, and afterward he became personally

# BIOGRAPHY

## Andrew Johnson: The Tennessee Tailor

**Andrew Johnson**

North Carolina native Andrew Johnson (1808–1875) came from humble beginnings. Apprenticed to a tailor as a boy, he ran away and eventually opened his own shop in Greeneville, Tennessee. A rather rough, tactless man, Johnson reportedly did not receive an education until he married schoolteacher Eliza McCardle. He became a Jacksonian Democrat who championed the working class, opposed both the slaveholding aristocrats and the abolitionists, and reveled in playing the crude commoner to appeal to the eastern Tennessee mountain folk. Proud of his work as a tailor, Johnson continued to practice his profession after entering the U.S. Senate, and as president he sometimes visited tailors to talk shop.

With the mountaineers' support, Johnson embarked on a remarkable political career, serving as an alderman, mayor, legislator, state senator, congressman, governor, and U.S. senator. As a senator, Johnson was a moderate who supported slavery and states' rights but opposed secession. During the secession crisis, other Southerners hated him for his staunch Unionism. Johnson frequently was burned in effigy, and one Virginia mob was dissuaded from hanging him only because it was unfair to deprive Tennessee of the honor. Death threats increased as Johnson bravely campaigned against secession in the spring of 1861. While he was riding on a train, an armed mob rushed aboard, and one man declared he was going to tweak Johnson's nose. Johnson whipped out a pistol, forced the men off, and shouted defiantly, "I am a Union man!" as the train pulled away from the station. When Tennessee seceded, Johnson refused to resign his Senate seat and became the only one of twenty-two Southern senators to remain loyal to the Union. After being forced to leave Tennessee, he became a Northern hero for his staunch allegiance to the Constitution.

involved in getting it through the House. His effective use of patronage and persuasive political skills secured passage on January 31, 1865. The necessary twenty-seven states finally ratified the amendment in December, but even then the Republicans counted the votes of some Southern states whose congressional delegations they refused to seat. The Thirteenth Amendment was the first amendment to make a radical change in society rather than simply limit the federal government's power or make election rule changes. Nonetheless, the Radicals were not satisfied because it did not grant the freedmen civil rights or the vote.

When the Thirteenth Amendment was ratified, Frederick Douglass declared, "Verily, the work does not end with the abolition of slavery, but only begins." African Americans appreciated their newfound freedom but knew it meant little if they could not earn a living on their own. They expected the federal government to provide them with confiscated Rebel property so they

Johnson's loyalty never wavered. On one occasion, he declared, "Robbery is a crime; rape is a crime; murder is a crime; treason is a crime and crime must be punished. . . . Treason must be made infamous and traitors must be impoverished." Lincoln rewarded Johnson's brave stand by appointing him military governor of Tennessee in March 1862. As governor, Johnson required oaths of allegiance from civilians, tried to restrict the vote to loyalists, and supported the enlistment of black troops. He also supported the Emancipation Proclamation but only as a military necessity to win the war. In explaining his lukewarm support of African Americans, Johnson declared, "Damn the Negroes, I am fighting those traitorous aristocrats, their masters." Many Northerners came to admire Johnson's grit, and Lincoln chose him as his Union Party running mate in 1864.

By the time Johnson moved to Washington, he had become more radical in his rhetoric. He said of slaveholding Rebels, "I would arrest them—I would try them—I would convict them and I would hang them." Unfortunately, Johnson's tenure as vice president began inauspiciously when he appeared drunk on inauguration day and spoke incoherently. Enemies branded him an alcoholic, but friends claimed he was adversely affected by a small amount of alcohol after being weakened by typhoid.

When Johnson assumed the presidency after Lincoln's assassination, he clashed with the Radicals over Reconstruction policies. Johnson opposed black suffrage and the Fourteenth and Fifteenth Amendments, and he once declared, "White men alone must manage the South." Impeached in 1868, he was acquitted by one vote, but the Republicans' control of Congress prevented him from being a strong executive. When his term expired, Johnson returned to Tennessee, and in 1874 he became the only former president ever elected to the U.S. Senate. He died from a stroke four months later and was buried in Tennessee with a copy of the Constitution under his head.

could become independent farmers, but most white Northerners envisioned the freedmen emulating the North's free labor system and remaining on the plantations to work for wages. This difference in expectations spelled trouble for Reconstruction policies.

# THE FREEDMEN

**January 16, 1865: Sherman issues Special Field Orders No. 15**
**January 31, 1865: Congress passes the Thirteenth Amendment**
**June 19, 1865: Slaves in Texas learn they have been freed**

By the time Andrew Johnson assumed the presidency, millions of slaves had been freed and had become actively involved in determining their future. Labor strikes spread across the South when the war ended as freedmen

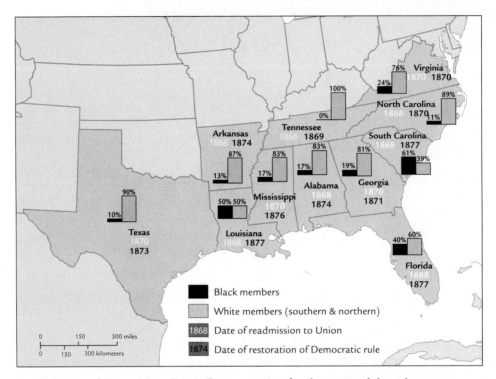

**Readmission and Restoration.** During Reconstruction, freedmen gained the right to vote and began to participate in Southern politics. This map shows the percentages of black and white participants in the Southern states' 1867–1868 constitutional conventions, the year in which each state was readmitted to the Union, and the year the former Confederates restored Democratic rule.

demanded better wages, and thousands simply left the plantations to seek opportunities elsewhere or to look for lost loved ones. More than one hundred years before the modern Civil Rights Movement, Southern blacks began to fight segregation laws and quickly forced Richmond, Charleston, and New Orleans to integrate their transportation systems. Freedmen sometimes held political rallies to promote the Republican Party and to pressure state governments to extend them more rights. African Americans proved so effective as political speakers the Republicans financed eighty of the most popular ones to travel across the South in 1867–1868 to drum up support for the party. Such political activity left little doubt where the freedmen stood on Reconstruction issues. Delegates at one Alabama political convention put it succinctly when they declared, "We claim exactly *the same rights, privileges and immunities as are enjoyed by white men*—we ask nothing more and will be content with nothing less. . . ."

African Americans from all walks of life became involved in the struggle for equality. Many were former slaves, while others were skilled workers who had always been free or former Union soldiers who had decided to remain in the South after the war. Black ministers were among the most effective political activists because they had a history of serving in leadership positions, and they often were the only literate blacks in the community. It sometimes was difficult to separate religion from politics because ministers used their pulpits to spread political messages based on God's word. This blending of religion and politics led to more than 100 ministers being elected to the Southern state legislatures when freedmen won the right to vote.

> ## DID YOU KNOW?
>
> ### Juneteenth
>
> On June 19, 1865, Union forces landed at Galveston, Texas, and informed the slaves they were free. This day became known to Texas African Americans as "Juneteenth" and was celebrated afterward as a holiday. The Juneteenth celebration spread after the Civil War and today it is an observed holiday in many states.

## The Question of Land

Owning land was one of the freedmen's greatest goals because they wanted to benefit from their own labor and be free from white domination. However, many well-meaning Northerners believed the blacks' best interests would be served by transforming them into wage laborers like Northern whites. This difference in expectations led to conflict when several experiments were begun during the war to uplift the freedmen.

When Union forces captured Port Royal, South Carolina, in November 1861, most of the whites living on the surrounding Sea Islands fled. In March 1862, abolitionist missionaries and teachers, government agents, and businessmen flocked to the area to take advantage of the whites' absence to transform the abandoned slaves into self-sufficient laborers. It quickly became apparent, however, that they and the slaves had different goals. The abolitionists wanted to uplift the slaves through education and religion, while the businessmen wanted them to work for wages on the abandoned plantations. The slaves, although eager to be educated, wanted to live independently from *all* whites, but that was not to be. The businessmen had the slaves sign contracts to perform daily tasks for wages, but the slaves disliked being tied to a plantation and having no control over what crops they grew. Living conditions did improve and many slaves began to be educated, but denial of their request to obtain land was a great disappointment.

While the Port Royal experiment received a great deal of attention in the North, an even larger initiative occurred along the Mississippi River. In Louisiana, several southern parishes opposed secession and a number of planters took the oath of allegiance when Union General Benjamin F. Butler occupied New Orleans in early 1862. Butler forced slaves to continue working for those planters who took the oath so the army would not have to feed them. The planters had to pay the slaves wages and provide them with food and medical care, and they were forbidden to use corporal punishment (although the army could flog those who refused to work). Abandoned plantations were seized and leased to Northern investors under the same rules. General Nathaniel P. Banks expanded the program north along the Mississippi River after Vicksburg and Port Hudson were captured in 1863. Banks required the freedmen to sign labor contracts that bound them to a particular plantation for a specific period of time. The freedmen thought the program was little better than slavery, but by war's end 700,000 blacks were working abandoned plantations on the Mississippi River under the army's supervision.

## Forty Acres and a Mule

The freedmen never gave up hope of receiving a share of the planters' land. After all, as one explained, "The property which they hold was nearly all earned by the sweat of our brows." They were supported by such Radicals as Charles Sumner and Thaddeus Stevens, who wanted to confiscate the South's large plantations and distribute the land to the freedmen as a way to destroy the planters' power and influence while ensuring the freedmen could survive on their own. One such land redistribution program was carried out late in the war, not by the Radicals, but by conservative General William T. Sherman.

As Sherman prepared his Carolinas Campaign in January 1865, Secretary of War Stanton joined him in Savannah, and the two met with twenty black leaders. They found that the men were well informed on politics and quite opinionated. One pointedly told Sherman and Stanton, "The way we can best take care of ourselves is to have land, and . . . till it by our labor. . . . We want to be placed on land until we are able to buy it, and make it our own." The black leaders' strong opinions impressed Sherman, and four days later he issued Special Field Orders No. 15, which confiscated plantations along the Atlantic coast from Charleston, South Carolina, to St. John's River, Florida, and reserved them for the freedmen. Each head of family received forty acres, and Sherman later agreed to loan them surplus army horses and mules to work their land. This order gave rise to the belief that the federal government had promised every freedman family "forty acres and a mule." The order, however, only gave them use of the land, not title to it, because it was intended to be a temporary arrangement until a permanent solution could be made to address their needs. Although Sherman bowed to the freedmen's wishes, he was motivated by military, not humanitarian, concerns. Thousands of runaway slaves had joined his armies during the March to the Sea and had put a strain on supplies. Redistributing Rebel land was a way to provide the freedmen with a means to support themselves and to prevent a similar occurrence in the Carolinas Campaign. Eventually, about 40,000 freedmen benefited from Sherman's order.

Several months after the war ended, Congressman Thaddeus Stevens proposed another plan to give freedmen title to land. He wanted to confiscate the land of all Southerners who owned more than 200 acres (about 70,000 people) and give the head of each freedman family forty acres. The rest of the land would be sold at auction and the money used to pay for veterans'

**A Freedmen's School.** One of the greatest social changes brought about by Reconstruction was the opening of schools to educate African Americans. Most of the early teachers were white Northern women, but more African American women became involved as Reconstruction progressed. This teacher poses with her students in a typical freedmen's school.

pensions, compensate Unionists for damages sustained at the hands of the Rebels, and fund the national debt. Stevens claimed his plan would reward those slaves who had supported the government during the war and punish Southern traitors at little cost to the Treasury. Congress, however, refused to undertake such a radical reorganization of Southern society.

## The Freedmen's Bureau

The Freedmen's Bureau was greatly involved in the Sea Island and Mississippi Valley land redistribution programs. Established by Congress in March 1865, this federal agency was intended to be a one-year experiment to consolidate all freedmen aid programs into one agency. The Freedmen's Bureau was the federal government's first large welfare agency, and it was placed in the War Department under Major General Oliver O. Howard. The Freedmen's Bureau was designed to assist both blacks and whites to adjust to the South's new social order, feed the poor, set up schools and hospitals, find jobs for the unemployed, help freedmen with labor contracts, negotiate labor disputes, and place freedmen on their own land under the guidelines of the land redistribution projects. Agents had to seem impartial and protect both the freedmen's and landowners' rights, maintain law and order, enforce federal policies, supervise elections, settle disputes, work out labor contracts, and educate freedmen.

# EYEWITNESS
## Henry Adams

*In 1880, the U.S. Senate held hearings on why so many African Americans left the South during Reconstruction. Henry Adams was one of those who testified at length. Adams, a former Louisiana slave, told the senators about the conditions freedmen faced in the months after the Civil War.*

[T]he white men read a paper to all of us colored people, telling us that we were free, and that we colored people could go where we pleased and manage our own affairs, and could work for who we pleased. The man I belonged to . . . told me it was best to stay there with him. . . . He said the bad white men was mad with all the negroes, because they were free, and they would kill you all for fun. . . . He said it was no use of that, to stay where we were living, and we could get protection from our old masters. I told him I thought that every man when he was free, could have his rights and protections and protect himself. He said that was true, but the colored people could never protect themselves among the white people. "So you all had better stay with the white people who raised you, and not leave them, but make contracts with them to work by the year for one-fifth of you all make. . . ."

On the same day after all had signed the papers, we went to cutting oats. I asked the boss could we get any of the oats; He said no; the oats were made before you were free. . . . We made five bales of cotton, but we did not get a pound of that. We made two or three hundred gallons of molasses and we only got what we could eat. . . . We made about seven or eight hundred bushels of potatoes; we got a few to eat. We split rails three or four weeks, and got not a cent for that; so in September I asked the boss to let me go to Shreveport. . . . [I met] four white men about six miles south of Keachie, De Soto Parish. One of them asked me who I belonged to. I told him no one; so him and two

The Freedmen's Bureau had a checkered record. On the positive side, it saved many people from near starvation and resettled about 10,000 black families on their own land. Within months after Appomattox, the bureau was distributing 150,000 food rations daily (one-third of which went to whites), and by 1870 it had established 4,000 schools. Blacks eagerly took advantage of these schools because gaining an education was almost as important to them as gaining land. Thanks to the Freedmen's Bureau, the Southern black literacy rate rose to 30 percent by 1880. On the other hand, agents were often criticized by both blacks and whites. Some agents were racists who had little faith in the freedmen's ability to adjust to the new order and treated blacks condescendingly. The freedmen resented being treated like children, and Southern whites resented the agents for attempting to educate blacks and for taking their side in labor disputes. Freedmen's Bureau agents often found themselves in a dangerous situation because they rarely pleased anyone, and sometimes lived in isolated areas with little protection.

others struck me with a stick, and told me they was a going to kill me and every other negro who told them that they did not belong to any one; but one of them who knew me told the others to "Let Henry alone, for he is a hard-working nigger, and a good nigger and I will fight for him." They left me, and I then went on to Shreveport. I seen over twelve colored men and women beat, shot, and hung between there and Shreveport.

Sunday I went back home. . . . On the 18th of September, I and eleven men and boys left that place . . . and started for Shreveport. . . . I had my two hundred dollar horse along; my brother was riding him, and all of our things was packed on him. Out come about forty or fifty armed men (white) into the public road and shot at us and taken my horse; said they were going to kill every nigger they found leaving their masters, and taking all of our clothes and bed-clothing and our money. . . . In October and November and December I was searched for pistols and robbed of $250 in goods and money by a large crowd of white men . . . and the law would do nothing about it. . . . The same crowd of white men broke up five churches (colored). . . . [W]hen any of us colored people would leave the white people, they would take everything we had . . . they would take all the money that we made on their places when we went to leave . . . and they killed many hundreds of my race when they were running away to get freedom.

*After these violent Reconstruction experiences, Henry Adams served three years in the U.S. Army. He then organized plantation laborers in Louisiana, Arkansas, and Texas and worked with other black veterans to investigate the plight of Southern freedmen.*

"Select Committee to Investigate the Causes Which Have Led to the Emigration of Negroes from the Southern States to the Northern States," Serial Set Nos. 1899–1919, 46th Congress, 2nd Session. Washington, D.C.: U.S. Government Publication, pp. 190–192.

Eventually, the Freedmen's Bureau was caught up in a political dispute between President Andrew Johnson and the Radicals. Johnson vetoed a Freedmen's Bureau bill to renew the agency in February 1866, but Congress successfully passed another in July. Johnson vetoed that bill as well, but Congress was able to override it. Nevertheless, the work proved too much, and the agency slowly faded away until it closed its offices in 1872.

## JOHNSON'S RECONSTRUCTION

**May 29, 1865: Johnson announces his Reconstruction plan**
**May 1, 1866: Memphis Riot**
**June 30, 1866: New Orleans Riot**

When Johnson was sworn into office after Lincoln's assassination, the Radicals had every reason to believe he would support their vision of Reconstruction. Less than a week into his presidency, Johnson reinforced this notion when he declared, "It is not promulgating anything that I have not heretofore said, to say that traitors must be made odious, that treason must be made odious, that traitors must be punished and impoverished. They must not only be punished, but their social power must be destroyed." His words could easily have come from Charles Sumner or Thaddeus Stevens, but Johnson's actions did not match his rhetoric.

## The Resurgent South

Unveiling his Reconstruction policy on May 29, 1865, Johnson announced he would appoint provisional governors for the Southern states and pardon all former Rebels under the rank of colonel who owned less than $20,000 in property. Numerous "excepted" classes of Southerners, including high-ranking Rebels and those with more than $20,000 in property, would be disenfranchised, although they could apply individually to the president for pardons. To be readmitted to the Union, the Southern states had to repeal their secession ordinances, repudiate the Confederate debt, and ratify the Thirteenth Amendment. At first, it seemed Johnson's plan was unusually harsh because it disenfranchised so many leading Southerners, but the Radicals were outraged when they found out a year later he had granted 7,000 individual requests for pardons. Johnson did so because he was a Democrat in a Republican-dominated government and needed political allies. By pardoning all low-ranking Rebels and freely dispensing pardons to prominent ones, he ensured the Democrats would control the Southern states and send Democratic congressmen to Washington.

The Radicals quickly criticized Johnson's plan. It did not provide for black voting rights, and it would actually increase Southern representation in Congress because the Thirteenth Amendment would end the Three-fifths Compromise and count all freedmen for representation purposes. The Democrats might take control of Congress and the White House and repeal Republican wartime measures. Adding to the Radicals' anger was the fact that the Johnson administration failed to prosecute Jefferson Davis, Robert E. Lee, or any other prominent Confederate. Lee was allowed to go home, but Davis was held prisoner under harsh conditions in Fort Monroe, Virginia, for two years, then released on bond in May 1867. The Radicals thought Johnson's leniency was odd considering his previous threats against the Rebels, but he actually had practical reasons for not pursuing treason charges. General Grant opposed such action against Lee because he believed it would violate the surrender terms that promised not to punish the Confederates as long as they obeyed the law. Also, few in the federal government looked forward to a trial that would give Davis and other Rebels a public forum to defend their actions. It was simply easier to let them go and hope they faded away.

Seizing the moment, most former Confederates cooperated with Johnson. State conventions carried out his demands, and elections were held to choose new slates of "loyal" politicians. When Congress reconvened in December 1865, one Georgian declared, "It looked as though Richmond had moved to Washington." The Southern delegations included four former Rebel generals, five colonels, and several former members of the Confederate government, including Vice President Alexander Stephens. A Republican newspaper predicted ominously, "What can be hatched from such an egg but another rebellion?" The Republican Congress refused to seat the Southerners over Johnson's protests, but most Northerners joined the Radicals in condemning the new state governments and blaming Johnson for the secessionists' return to power. To oppose the president's lenient policy, Congress formed the Joint Committee on Reconstruction to devise more appropriate rules to readmit the Southern states.

## The Black Codes

One of the Southerners' greatest problems was a labor shortage caused by the war's casualties and many freedmen leaving home to seek better opportunities elsewhere or to search for relatives. To restart the plantations it was imperative that the freedmen continued to work in the fields and remain subservient. To do this the Southern states passed Black Codes. These laws prevented freedmen from voting, serving on juries, and sometimes from even owning or leasing land. Blacks were required to sign one-year labor contracts, and they were forbidden under penalty of imprisonment to leave the plantation until the contract expired. Black Codes in some states required freedmen to work only as field hands or house servants, and they could be fined for "insulting" a white. Denied land, mobility, and the vote, freedmen were effectively placed back under the control of their former masters.

The Black Codes infuriated Northerners. Not only were the former secessionists back in power, they had successfully instituted an almost slavelike labor system to benefit the plantation owners. Many Northerners who had never really cared about black suffrage now saw it as necessary to keep the former Rebels from growing in strength. A Chicago newspaper wrote, "As for Negro suffrage, the mass of Union men in the Northwest do not care a great deal. What scares them is the idea that the rebels are all to be let back . . . and made a power in the government again."

## The Fourteenth Amendment

Relations between Johnson and the Radicals deteriorated further in early 1866 when Congress passed the Civil Rights Act and a bill to renew the Freedmen's Bureau. The Civil Rights Act provided blacks with some protection against the Black Codes by granting them equality under the law, but Johnson vetoed both bills because the Southern states were not represented in Congress, and he claimed the bills violated states' rights. The vetoes demonstrated just how out of touch Johnson had become with the Northern people. When Congress overrode both vetoes, one observer called him "the dead dog of the White House."

The Civil Rights Act was a victory for the Radicals, but they feared the Democrats might someday repeal the measure. To make equal protection for freedmen permanent, Thaddeus Stevens and the Joint Committee on Reconstruction sponsored the Fourteenth Amendment in April 1866. This amendment defined a U.S. citizen for the first time as someone who was born in the United States or who was naturalized, and it declared that a U.S. citizen was also a citizen of the state in which he resided. All citizens enjoyed Bill of Rights protections and equal protection under state and federal laws, and no state could deprive a citizen of life, liberty, or property without due process of law. Any former congressman or federal official who had supported the rebellion was prohibited from holding state or federal office unless two-thirds of Congress voted to pardon him, and the Southern states had to repudiate the Confederate debt to be readmitted to Congress. The amendment did not address black suffrage because that was a state's right, but it did declare that a state's congressional delegation and electoral vote would be reduced proportionately if it denied blacks the right to vote. If ratified, the Fourteenth Amendment would override the Dred Scott decision by granting both federal and state citizenship to African Americans and prevent states from discriminating against citizens. The Republicans also made sure the amendment would strengthen their party no matter what the Southerners did. If Southerners enfranchised blacks, the freedmen would probably always vote Republican; if they denied blacks the vote, their congressional delegations and electoral votes would be reduced proportionately.

The Fourteenth Amendment passed Congress, but Johnson urged the Southern states to refuse ratification so the required approval by three-fourths of the states could not be achieved. Johnson also went on a national speaking tour known as the "Swing Around the Circle" to build support for his reconstruction policies before the critical 1866 congressional elections. Northern voters were already angry at him for pardoning former Rebels and allowing the Southern Democrats to return to power, and the Swing Around the Circle only made things worse. More voters turned away from Johnson and to the Radicals when he frequently lost his temper and cursed and threatened his opponents when hecklers provoked him. In the fall election, the Republican Party won every Northern gubernatorial race, majorities in every Northern legislature, a three-to-one majority in both houses of Congress, and made gains in three Border States. Northern voters had clearly given the Radicals a mandate, and there was little Johnson could do to prevent them from seizing control of Reconstruction.

## Southern Violence

Johnson's poor performance on his Swing Around the Circle was not the only reason Northern voters turned to the Radicals. There was increasing Southern violence against freedmen that Northerners thought might be a prelude to a new war, and they were determined to prevent that from happening. The

Southerners actually had no intentions of fighting again, but they were committed to maintaining some semblance of the old order and frequently used violence to keep the freedmen subdued.

Across the South there were hundreds of attacks on freedmen and frequent mob violence. On May 1, 1866, a seemingly insignificant collision between black and white carriages in Memphis, Tennessee, led to a bloody three-day riot. When the police arrested the black driver, a large crowd gathered, and white mobs (including policemen and firemen) attacked and burned a shanty town, three churches, fifty homes, eight schools, and killed forty-six blacks. Another riot erupted in New Orleans on June 30 when freedmen and white Republicans held a rally in support of a new state constitution to grant black voting rights. As the demonstrators marched down the street, gunshots rang out, and a mob (which again included city policemen) chased the demonstrators into a building, where more were killed. As many as 200 freedmen were killed or wounded in what military governor Philip Sheridan called "an absolute massacre."

## Carpetbaggers and Scalawags

In this campaign of violence, the former Rebels not only targeted freedmen but also whites they branded carpetbaggers and scalawags. Carpetbaggers were Northern whites who lived in the South during Reconstruction. Many were former Union soldiers who saw an opportunity to make money rebuilding the devastated country, while others worked for the Freedmen's Bureau or were involved in politics, teaching, or missionary work. Their famous nickname was a reference to their carpetbags, a type of cheap luggage they carried that was made from scraps of carpet. Later during Reconstruction, more than half of the Southern governors and nearly half of the congressmen were carpetbaggers. Scalawags were native white Southerners who joined the Republican Party. Most had opposed secession, but some were former Rebels who simply believed it was in the South's best interest to cooperate with the North. Two of the most famous scalawags were former Confederate General James Longstreet and the "Gray Ghost," John S. Mosby.

Southern whites hated carpetbaggers and scalawags and considered them opportunists who were taking advantage of the turmoil to enrich themselves through corruption. Some, in fact, were corrupt. Louisiana's carpetbag governor Henry Clay Warmoth once claimed, "I don't pretend to be honest. . . . I only pretend to be as honest as anybody in politics. . . ." He was accused of various corrupt activities and an investigative committee later estimated he accumulated about $1 million during his four-year term—on an $8,000-a-year salary. In 1871, Louisiana's legislature spent more than $1 million (more than ten times the amount spent by any previous legislature) on such personal items as travel expenses, cigars, food, and an open bar in the capitol's basement.

It is not fair to single out Southern Republicans for corruption when the notorious Democratic Tammany Hall ran New York City at the same time. Much of the increased spending by Southern legislatures, in fact, was necessary. New state constitutions mandated the education of black children, which required

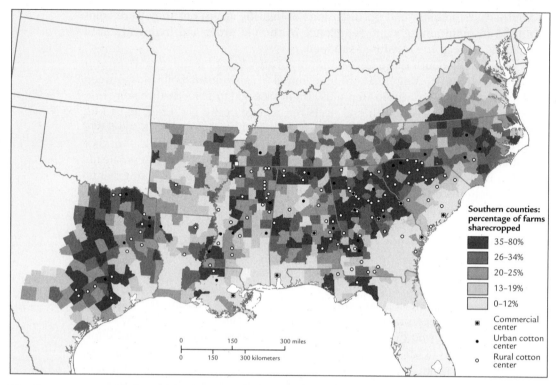

**The Sharecropping and Crop-Lien Systems, 1880.** With slavery dead and no money to pay wages to freedmen, Southern farmers turned to the sharecropping and crop-lien systems to get their fields back into production following the Civil War. This map shows by counties the percentage of 1880 farms that were involved in these systems. The highest rates are found in those areas where slavery was strongest before the war.

doubling the education budget, and there were towns, railroads, and levees to rebuild. Some carpetbaggers and scalawags were corrupt racists who were only interested in making money, and they pushed for black voting rights because they knew the freedmen would always support the Republican Party. Others were dedicated reformers who believed in equality and risked their lives to educate and enfranchise the freedmen because it was the right thing to do. Carpetbaggers and scalawags were simply a cross section of America, and it is difficult to make generalizations about them.

## Sharecropping and Crop Liens

The land distribution experiments begun during the Civil War gave freedmen hope of obtaining their own farms. However, President Johnson opposed confiscation policies, and he eventually restored all property to the white

## Table 5     *Per Capita Agricultural Income in Seven Cotton States*

The Civil War and Reconstruction dramatically affected the income of all Southern farmers. As this table shows, the income of black and white farmers in seven Southern states changed in almost reversed ratios between 1857 and 1879. Black income rose almost 46 percent, while white income fell almost 35 percent.

|         | 1857    | 1879    |
|---------|---------|---------|
| Black   | $28.95  | $42.22  |
| White   | 124.79  | 80.57   |
| Average | 74.28   | 60.13   |

owners. More freedmen then had to return to working on the plantations, but they found the labor shortage gave them considerable bargaining power. If landowners tried to use slavelike punishment or treated them unfairly, freedmen reported them to the Freedmen's Bureau, initiated a strike or slowdown, or simply left. In the first few years after the war, black income increased while white income declined because planters had to either pay better wages or face a labor crisis. This shift in economic power helped fuel some of the white-on-black violence in 1866. Unfortunately, cotton prices quickly declined after the war because there was less demand when the military downsized and competition from India, Brazil, and Egypt increased. Planters suffered a cash shortage and found it difficult to purchase the needed supplies to plant a crop, let alone pay the freedmen a wage. As a result, new methods had to be devised to keep the land in cultivation, provide a living for freedmen and poor whites, and earn landowners a profit.

Sharecropping and the crop lien system were the two most popular farming methods adopted. In both cases, freedmen sometimes took the lead in convincing planters to try them because both methods allowed blacks some independence. In sharecropping, landowners divided their property into small plots and signed a contract with individuals to work each plot. The typical contract required the planter to provide a house for the sharecropper and the necessary seeds, tools, and draft animals to produce a crop. The sharecropper was allowed to work the land as if it were his own (although the landowner decided what crop to grow), and the planter paid him a percentage of the harvest. Sharecropping provided planters with workers without expending much cash, and it gave freedmen and poor whites a way to make a living. Initially, freedmen liked the system because it gave them a stake in the land and allowed them to benefit directly from their labor. They also enjoyed the independence of not being under the landowner's constant supervision and not having to work in a large slavelike labor gang.

Sharecropping had its advantages, but it also created a cycle of debt. Sharecroppers did not receive any money until they sold their share of the crop, but they still had to buy food, clothing, and other essentials throughout the year. Most large planters had plantation stores and sold these items to their workers on credit at often exorbitant prices and high interest rates. At harvest time, sharecroppers had to pay their store debt first, but if the harvest was poor they might not have enough money to pay it off entirely. Nonetheless, sharecroppers had to buy on credit the supplies needed for the coming year, and most sank so deeply in debt they could never pay off their bills. When state laws were passed requiring sharecroppers to stay on the plantation until the bills were paid, they became little more than serfs tied to the land.

The crop lien system was caused by the chronic cash shortage, the declining value of land, and the fact that there were not enough banks to serve the agricultural industry. To raise a crop and pay their workers, planters were forced to borrow money, but their land had dropped so much in value that they could not use it as collateral for the necessary loans. To fill the need, private merchants began advancing supplies and money to planters in return for liens. A lien served as collateral and was usually taken out on the upcoming harvest, but it could be placed on such things as personal property or land. If the planter did not pay his debt, the merchant could take legal action and seize whatever he had a lien on. Landowners, laborers, and sharecroppers used the crop lien system to obtain loans, credit, or supplies. Unfortunately, low prices and poor harvests often prevented them from paying their debts, and the merchants either foreclosed on the lien or negotiated a new loan so the farmer could get through the next year's harvest.

The sharecropping and crop lien systems plunged everyone into debt. Sharecroppers were indebted to the landowners, and the landowners were indebted to the merchants or banks. Ultimately, white land ownership declined as more planters faced foreclosure when they failed to pay their loans or taxes. White Southern property owners dropped from 80 percent at the beginning of the Civil War to 67 percent by the end of Reconstruction. While the freedmen embraced sharecropping at first, they soon became dissatisfied because they still had no land of their own or any control over what they planted, and they continued to be dependent on their former masters and tied to the same plantations on which they had been slaves.

## CONGRESSIONAL RECONSTRUCTION

**March 2, 1867: Congress passes the Military Reconstruction Act**
**May 16, 1868: U.S. Senate acquits Johnson in his impeachment trial**
**December 25, 1868: Johnson pardons all but the highest-ranking former Rebels**
**April 13, 1873: Colfax Riot**
**September 14, 1874: Battle of Liberty Place**

The freedmen's dream of owning land was dashed fairly quickly after the Civil War ended, but not so their aspirations to secure the right to vote. In a January 1867 speech, Thaddeus Stevens declared, "I am for Negro suffrage in every rebel state. If it be just, it should not be denied; if it be necessary, it should be adopted; if it be a punishment to traitors, they deserve it." After Southern violence increased in 1866, more moderate Northerners began to support black suffrage as a way to help the freedmen protect themselves against the former Rebels, but it was the freedmen who often took the lead in the fight. African Americans lobbied congressmen and wrote letters to the president. Typical of such letters was the one in which a Mississippi freedman asked Johnson, "We stood by the government when it wanted help. . . . [Now] will it stand by us?" Some freedmen even shed blood in the suffrage struggle. In New Orleans hundreds of black veterans were attacked and many were murdered by a white mob when they demonstrated for voting rights in 1866. Once the Radicals gained control of Congress in the 1866 election, they moved quickly to make the freedmen's dream of voting a reality.

## The Military Reconstruction Act

In March 1867, Congress passed the Military Reconstruction Act to take Reconstruction away from President Johnson. Except for Tennessee (which had been readmitted to Congress after ratifying the Fourteenth Amendment), the South was divided into five military districts, each with a military governor appointed by the president. With the freedmen participating, the states would write new constitutions to enfranchise black men, disenfranchise the former Rebels singled out in the Fourteenth Amendment, and ratify the Fourteenth Amendment. When a majority of voters ratified a state's constitution and Congress approved it, the state would be readmitted to the Union.

It soon became a battle of wills between the antagonists. Preferring the status quo of Johnson's reconstruction over black suffrage, the Southerners refused to hold the required constitutional conventions. To force the issue, Congress passed a supplement to the Military Reconstruction Act that authorized the army to begin registering voters and start the convention proceedings. In retaliation, the Southerners refused to vote in the ratification process because the law required ratification by a majority of registered voters. The Radicals then passed another supplement changing the ratification requirement to a majority of votes cast.

The resultant constitutions made sweeping changes in the South. Not only were voting rights extended to black men, Bills of Rights were adopted for the first time, free public education was mandated for both races in integrated schools, and public conveyances and facilities were fully integrated. By September 1867, there were 735,000 black voters in the Southern states and 635,000 whites (about one-third of whom were Republicans). After the state constitutions were ratified, the Republicans took control of the Southern states, with black voters composing a majority in South Carolina, Mississippi, Louisiana, Alabama, and Florida. Sixteen African Americans eventually served

# BIOGRAPHY

## Pinckney Benton Stewart Pinchback:
## America's First Black Governor

**P. B. S. Pinchback**

P. B. S. Pinchback (1837–1921) was the son of a white planter and a woman of color who was his father's mistress. Despite his mixed blood, Pinchback was recognized as the planter's free son and lived comfortably on his Mississippi plantation. He and his brother were even sent to school in Ohio, but they had to return home when their father fell ill. After the father's death, the brother became mentally ill, and Pinchback found himself head of the family at age twelve. His white relatives quickly disinherited them, and Pinchback and his mother and siblings fled to Ohio to avoid being enslaved.

After marrying Nina Hawthorne, Pinchback traveled to New Orleans in 1862 to join the Union army. Because of his light skin, he actually was allowed to enlist in a white regiment but soon left it to raise a company for the Louisiana Native Guards. Pinchback served as the company's captain, but, like all black officers, he was harassed by white soldiers and the army's examining board. When Pinchback's situation worsened, he wrote Major General Nathaniel P. Banks, "I find nearly all the officers inimical to me, and I can foresee nothing but dissatisfaction and discontent which will make my position very disagreeable indeed." After being passed over for promotion twice, Pinchback resigned his commission in 1863. However, his patriotism remained strong, and Banks allowed him to organize a company of cavalry. Pinchback used his own money to raise and equip the horsemen, but the army refused to let him serve with the unit because he was black.

During Reconstruction, Pinchback moved to Alabama, where he spoke out against the violent night riders who targeted African Americans. He called for blacks to become

in Congress, two in the Senate, six as lieutenant governors, and Louisiana's P. B. S. Pinchback became America's first black governor. Scores of other African Americans were elected to city and local positions.

Under the Military Reconstruction Act, the army supervised voter enrollment and had the power to arrest and try civilians. While the Radicals and most Northerners saw this as necessary, the legislation clearly violated previous Supreme Court rulings. In 1866, the Court ruled in *Ex parte* Milligan that military tribunals, even in wartime, could not be used to try civilians if the civil courts were open. The South's civilian governments and courts were functioning in 1867, although not to the Radicals' liking. Fortunately for the latter, the Supreme Court simply chose to stay out of Reconstruction for the most part. Under the Military Reconstruction Act all of the Southern states were reconstructed and readmitted to the Union by 1870.

politically active, and he worked tirelessly to extend voting rights to African Americans. During the Civil War, Pinchback once told a crowd that black soldiers "did not ask for social equality, and did not expect it, but they demanded political rights—they wanted to become men."

Returning to New Orleans, Pinchback became active in Republican politics and continued to push for equality. He once declared, "I am groping about through this American forest of prejudice and proscription, determined to find some form of civilization where all men will be accepted for what they are worth." Many whites hated Pinchback, and one tried unsuccessfully to assassinate him on a New Orleans street. Nonetheless, he went on to serve as a delegate to Louisiana's 1868 constitutional convention (where he wrote the state's first civil rights article) and ran for the state senate. After narrowly losing the election, Pinchback convinced the Republican-controlled senate to seat him after accusing his opponent of voter fraud.

When Lieutenant Governor Oscar J. Dunn (another black man) died in office, Pinchback was elected to the position. Soon afterward, in 1872, Governor Henry Clay Warmouth was impeached and suspended from office, and Pinchback served as Louisiana's governor for thirty-five days. He was America's first black governor and the only black governor during Reconstruction. The following year, Pinchback became Louisiana's first black to be elected to the U.S. Senate, but opponents charged him with voting fraud and succeeded in getting the white candidate seated instead. Pinchback went on to serve on the State Board of Education and as a delegate to the 1879 constitutional convention. There, he succeeded in establishing Louisiana's Southern University, a college for black students, and he later served on the University's Board of Trustees, as a U.S. marshal in New York City, and as a Washington lawyer.

Congressional Reconstruction placed the Southern states in the hands of the Republican Party, but there was a nagging problem. The black vote had been granted by state constitutions, and there always was a danger the states might amend them in the future to disenfranchise freedmen again. To prevent that from happening, the Republicans banded together in 1869 to pass the Fifteenth Amendment. This amendment prohibited states from denying anyone the right to vote because of race, color, or previous condition of servitude. It was a triumph for the Republicans because it protected Southern blacks and strengthened the Republican Party by expanding voting rights to African Americans living in the North. Susan B. Anthony and other women's rights leaders opposed the measure because it did not extend voting rights to women, but the amendment was ratified the following year.

**The Ku Klux Klan.** The Ku Klux Klan used violence and intimidation in its fight against the freedmen and white Republicans. The elaborate costumes were designed both to hide the Klansmen's identities and to spread fear among their enemies.

# The Night Riders

Realizing they could not defeat the Republicans at the polls, the Southerners began turning more to violence as a way to assert their influence. In 1866, Confederate veterans in Tennessee organized the Ku Klux Klan, and it spread rapidly across the South. However, the Klan never had much influence in Catholic strongholds such as South Louisiana because it opposed the Catholic Church as well as the Republican Party. In those regions, the Knights of the White Camellia became more popular because it shared the Klan's goal of home rule but not its anti-Catholic bias. These organizations became the military arm of the Southern Democrats, and their activities increased after the freedmen won the right to vote. Terror was the main tactic used to frighten Republicans away from the polls. Members usually operated at night dressed in elaborate masks and robes pretending to be the ghosts of dead Confederates, and they sometimes even put costumes on their horses. Their methods of intimidation included burning of homes and barns, beatings, and murder. Any Republican—freedman, carpetbagger, or scalawag—who was politically active, engaged in teaching blacks, or was seen as a threat was likely to be visited by the night riders.

The Republicans formed the Union League to counter the night riders, but it was never a match for the Klan and Knights. In the 1868 election alone, more than 1,000 Republicans were murdered across the South, and precinct returns showed that the violence was successful in driving Republicans away from the polls. One Georgia county that recorded 1,222 Republican votes in the April 1868 gubernatorial election had just 1 vote in the November presidential contest.

# Impeachment

Included in the Military Reconstruction Act legislation were two measures aimed at weakening Johnson's executive power. The Command of the Army Act required him to issue all army orders through General-in-Chief Grant, who could not be replaced or relieved without congressional approval. The Tenure of Office Act stated that the president could not dismiss any federal official who had been confirmed by the Senate without Senate approval. The main purpose of the Tenure of Office Act was to protect Secretary of War Edwin Stanton, who kept the Radicals informed of White House plans. The act was constitutionally questionable, but the Supreme Court followed its policy of not becoming too involved in Reconstruction and did not rule against it until 1926.

In February 1868, Johnson forced a showdown with the Radicals by dismissing Stanton, and the House retaliated by voting to impeach the president for eleven "high crimes and misdemeanors." Eight of the charges related to Stanton's removal, and the others involved violating the Command of the Army Act, failing to cooperate with Congress, and opposing Congress with "disgrace, ridicule, hatred, contempt, and reproach." If Johnson was convicted, the law at the time dictated the presidency would fall to Radical president pro tempore of the Senate Benjamin Wade because there was no vice president.

During the trial, Johnson's attorneys argued that no crime had been committed because the acts in question were unconstitutional. Furthermore, convicting a president for politically opposing Congress would violate the doctrines of checks and balances and separation of powers. Prosecutors Benjamin F. Butler and Thaddeus Stevens countered by claiming no criminal act was necessary to convict the president because impeachment was a political process that could be used for political purposes. When the vote was taken on May 16, 1868, the result was 35 to 19 for conviction—one shy of the 36 needed to convict. Seven moderate Republicans had voted with the Democrats because they feared setting such a precedent for removing a president.

## Grant's Reconstruction

Although Johnson escaped conviction, he lost all political support. In the 1868 election, the Republicans nominated Ulysses S. Grant and the Democrats chose New York governor Horatio Seymour. Grant had never been interested in politics or shown any support for the Radicals. He was simply a professional soldier who carried out orders and enforced the government's policies. Nonetheless, the Republicans nominated Grant because the Radicals believed he would support their Reconstruction policies, and the moderates believed he could win. The Republicans' campaign was largely based on "waving the bloody shirt," or blaming the Civil War on the Democrats. This tactic derived its colorful name when Benjamin F. Butler once waved a torn, bloodstained shirt in Congress and claimed it came from a flogged carpetbagger. By advising Northerners to "vote as you shot," the Republicans easily won the election. Four years later, they reversed their strategy and secured Grant's reelection by using the campaign slogan "Let Us Have Peace!" and calling for national reconciliation.

Lame-duck President Andrew Johnson took a parting shot at the Republicans on Christmas Day by issuing a blanket pardon to many former Confederates. This increased the number of white Southern voters and made the opposing factions more evenly matched. As a result, the violence only increased as the Klan and other white organizations stepped up their attacks to drive more Republicans away from the polls. The Republicans fought back with the Ku Klux Klan Acts of 1870 and 1871. This legislation greatly increased the government's ability to protect the freedmen by allowing federal district attorneys to prosecute cases involving conspiracies that denied blacks political rights or the right to serve on juries. The Ku Klux Klan acts also prohibited voter discrimination based on race and authorized the president to suspend habeas corpus and use the army to enforce civil rights and arrest suspected Klan members. Over the next several years, Grant frequently exercised these executive powers. In October 1871, he declared a state of emergency in nine South Carolina counties, suspended habeas corpus, and sent the army in to arrest hundreds of suspects. Scores of other military expeditions were also launched across the South, and federal grand juries indicted more than 3,000 people for violating civil rights (about 600 were convicted). These aggressive tactics were effective, and the Ku Klux Klan waned in power and largely disappeared.

## White Leagues and Red Shirts

When the Klan was routed, the Southerners quickly created new organizations to carry on the fight. In Louisiana, the White League spread across the state and became a potent military force, so-called Rifle Clubs sprang up in Mississippi and other states, and the Red Shirts were active in South Carolina. All were dedicated to driving out the hated Republicans by any means necessary.

Few places were as volatile as Louisiana, where black and white communities lived in fear that the other was preparing to launch an all-out race war. In April 1873, a large number of freedmen seized control of Colfax and hundreds of whites assembled to confront them. On Easter Sunday, a massacre ensued after the freedmen murdered two whites who approached the courthouse under a flag of truce. In what proved to be the single bloodiest Reconstruction incident, approximately 100 freedmen were killed, many of whom were executed after being captured. The following year, another clash occurred in New Orleans. On September 14, 1874, several thousand White League members converged on the city to drive out the carpetbagger government. Former Confederate General James Longstreet led 500 policemen to disperse the crowd, but the White League responded with gunfire. A bloody street fight known as the Battle of Liberty Place raged for hours, and approximately 130 men were killed or wounded, but the outnumbered and outgunned police were finally defeated. The Republican governor was forced to flee and a Democrat was installed, but President Grant quickly dispatched warships to the city and had the army intervene. This show of military power forced the White League to withdraw, and the Republican Governor resumed his office. Similar clashes erupted in other Southern states, and Grant used the army in Arkansas to install the Republican candidate there after a disputed gubernatorial election. Such incidents made it apparent to everyone that the Southern Republicans remained in power only because the U.S. Army protected them.

# THE END OF RECONSTRUCTION

### March 2, 1877: Democrats and Republicans agree to the Compromise of 1877

By the mid-1870s, the Northerners' wartime passion had cooled, and they began to tire of Reconstruction after years of violence, corruption, and political turmoil. In addition, the mounting scandals in Congress and Grant's administration, the western frontier movement, Indian wars, and national economic and political issues were diverting attention away from Dixie. Now that it was obvious the Southerners had no intentions of starting another war, Northern voters began turning away from the Radicals, and in 1874 the Democrats won back control of the House. The voters' desertion of the Radicals was partly due to the Northerners' own racist beliefs. They felt they had done their part in uplifting Southern blacks by destroying slavery and extending the right to vote. As one Illinois newspaper put it, "[T]he negro is now a voter and a citizen. Let him hereafter take his chances in the battle of life." Many people even sympathized with the Southern whites because they knew they would never tolerate black equality or political activity in their states. A growing number of Northerners had simply had enough. At great sacrifice, they had defeated the rebellion, emancipated the slaves, and provided freedmen the means with which to protect themselves and to prosper. Their failure to do either convinced many Northerners that the freedmen were unworthy of further help.

Various Supreme Court rulings also weakened Reconstruction. In 1870 and 1871 the Court declared that the Fourteenth and Fifteenth Amendments only applied to oppressive actions taken by states against citizens, not actions taken by individuals. Federal authorities could intervene if a *state* denied someone due process or prevented them from voting because of race, but it was the state's responsibility to prosecute if *individuals* did so. Because individuals usually carried out such acts, this ruling greatly weakened the federal government's ability to protect the freedmen. In 1873, the Supreme Court made a similar ruling in the Slaughterhouse Cases when it declared that the Fourteenth and Fifteenth Amendments did not give the federal government the right to intervene in state matters. The court ruled that these amendments were intended to protect the freedmen's *national* citizenship rights, such as voting in federal elections; they were not intended to restrict a state's police powers. In the Slaughterhouse Cases, the Court for the first time recognized that Americans held both national and state citizenship. Constitutional amendments protected national citizenship rights, but each state still had the responsibility to enforce state civil rights.

Southern Republicans suffered another blow in May 1872 when Congress restored the political rights of all but 300 of the most prominent former Rebels and significantly increased the Democratic vote. Only the presence of the army prevented the Southern white leaders, now known as "Redeemers," from regaining control in states dominated by the Republicans.

## The Compromise of 1877

In the election of 1876, the Republicans nominated Civil War veteran Rutherford B. Hayes, and the Democrats nominated Samuel Tilden, a popular New York politician who had broken up the Tweed Ring. By that time, Reconstruction was on its last legs. All of the Southern states had been readmitted to Congress, but the army continued to occupy Louisiana and South Carolina to defend their Republican governments. Reconstruction was only one of many issues. Most voters were more concerned about cleaning up government corruption, the struggling economy, and civil service and monetary reform. When the ballots were tallied, Tilden had 184 electoral votes to Hayes's 165. A candidate needed 185 to win. The critical twenty electoral votes of Louisiana, South Carolina, and Florida were disputed because the opposing parties submitted separate returns to Congress.

Forced to settle the election, Congress created a 15-man commission in January 1877 to investigate the returns of the three disputed states. Seven commissioners were to be Democrats, seven Republicans, and one independent. At the last moment, however, independent David Davis resigned his senate seat to accept a Supreme Court appointment and was replaced by a Republican. Fearing defeat, the Democrats threatened a filibuster to prevent official returns from being counted in Congress. If the filibuster succeeded, there would be no one to inaugurate in March, and politicians shuddered to think what might occur. However, in secretive backroom meetings, the Southern Democrats decided to compromise as a way to restore home rule. Just two days before inauguration, an unofficial agreement that became known as the Compromise of 1877 was made in which the Democrats agreed to let Hayes have the twenty disputed votes and win the election. In return, the Republicans agreed to withdraw the last federal troops from Louisiana and South Carolina, effectively ending Reconstruction. There were also vague Republican promises to appoint a Democrat to the cabinet and provide funds to rebuild the South's economy. President Hayes kept his part of the bargain by withdrawing the army from Louisiana and South Carolina and appointing David Key, a Democrat and former Confederate, as postmaster general. Not all Northerners agreed with the compromise, and some referred to Hayes as "Rutherfraud," but most accepted the agreement as a way to finally end Reconstruction. In doing so, they essentially sacrificed the freedmen to the Redeemers as the price to pay for reunification.

## Reconstruction's Legacy

In some ways Reconstruction left more hatred and divisiveness than the war itself. It began with great promise of making sweeping social and political changes but ended in bitter disappointment for the freedmen. In 1876, blacks accounted for about half the Southern vote. Twenty-five years later they had been virtually removed from politics after the Redeemers adopted literacy tests and poll taxes to disenfranchise blacks by the hundreds of thousands. In 1865, the freedmen had high hopes of receiving their own land, but by 1877 most were tied to the plantations as sharecroppers. W. E. B. DuBois summed up Reconstruction by declaring, "The slave went free; stood a brief moment in the sun; then went back again toward slavery." No one in America was satisfied with the way Reconstruction had played out. African Americans resented their betrayal after supporting the Union so loyally during the Civil War, Northern whites resented the former Rebels' return to power, and Southern whites resented the political domination and social upheaval brought on by the Radicals.

Many historians see Reconstruction as a failed revolution. Americans had a unique opportunity to make fundamental political and social changes to bring to fruition the ideals of the Declaration of Independence. But attempts to destroy Southern aristocratic influence and provide freedmen with the means to be self-sufficient failed. The Republicans share some of the blame for this failure because most believed that if blacks were given the right to vote they could control their own destinies. They underestimated the difficulty of forming a biracial Republican Party in the South and were not able—or willing—to pay the price necessary to counter Southern white violence. Northern whites allowed the Redeemers to regain control because they believed in white supremacy and had no real desire to see African Americans become equal. In the back of many Northerners' minds was the realization that every political and social gain made by blacks in the South would eventually extend to blacks in the North.

But should Reconstruction be considered a failure? Is it fair to judge the participants based on what we think they *should* have done rather than what they *intended* to do and what was possible? Reconstruction's problems might have been too large to be addressed successfully at that time. It has been suggested Congress should have uplifted and protected the freedmen better, but the goal of most Northerners was to reunite the Union and prevent a future war, not achieve social revolution. The majority of Northerners firmly believed in the sanctity of property, state, and individual rights, white supremacy, and limited government. They probably would not have supported the radical changes necessary to make Reconstruction successful. Others say the North should have kept troops in the South longer to keep the peace, but that would not have been politically possible. Maintaining a large standing army was not an American tradition, and Northerners would have opposed occupying American soil militarily after it became apparent that the Southerners were not going to start another war. It has also been suggested that the federal government should have instituted a massive aid program like the New Deal or Marshall Plan to uplift all Southerners. But such large-scale federal aid was unprecedented, and it is doubtful Johnson and Grant could have convinced the Northern people to fund something so massive. The New Deal was only possible in the 1930s because *all* Americans were desperate and they had already seen large federal programs at work during World War I and under President Herbert Hoover. During Reconstruction, there was no such desperation or history.

Rather than being an abject failure, Reconstruction actually did enjoy some limited success. The nation was reunited, slavery was abolished, federal and state citizenship were extended to blacks, many black families were reunited, black men gained the right to vote (thousands kept that right even after Reconstruction ended), and more blacks, became property owners and were educated. Per capita income for Southern blacks rose 46 percent between 1857 and 1879, while white per capita income declined 35 percent (even so, black income never rose to more than half that of whites), and black land ownership rose from virtually zero in 1861 to about 20 percent by 1877. Reconstruction might best be seen as the nation taking two steps forward and one step back. Although certainly disappointing, it was a beginning that allowed dramatic social and political changes to occur later.

## FOR FURTHER READING

Lincoln's Proclamation of Amnesty and Reconstruction
Wade-Davis Bill
Thirteenth Amendment
Fourteenth Amendment

## CHAPTER 26

# The Long Shadow of War

Remembering the Civil War

The Civil War's Military Legacy

The Never-Ending War

The Birth of a Nation

---

One quiet summer day long ago, thousands of battle-tested men converged on the sleepy town of Gettysburg. The weather was hot and humid, making any outdoor activity uncomfortable, but southern Pennsylvania buzzed with activity. Rather than preparing to repel Rebel invaders, however, the people were rolling out the red carpet. It was July 1913, and 53,000 scarred and grizzled Civil War veterans were coming to Gettysburg to commemorate the battle's fiftieth anniversary in what became known as the "Peace Jubilee."

By the early twentieth century, the North and South had come to a comfortable understanding about the Civil War. Every soldier had fought bravely, and the war was just the result of a political dispute gone awry, with the North fighting to preserve the Union and the South fighting to defend its constitutional rights. Among the Confederate veterans at the Gettysburg reunion was Virginia's Governor William Hodges Mann, who explained, "We are not here to discuss the genesis of the war, but men who have tried each other in the storm and smoke of battle are here to discuss the great fight. We came here, I say, not to discuss what caused the war of 1861–65, but to talk over the events of the battle as man to man." The nation was fascinated by the event, and photographs appeared in many newspapers and magazines depicting old blue and gray veterans shaking hands over the famous stone wall where Pickett's Charge was stopped.

President Woodrow Wilson, the first Southern-born president since the Civil War, addressed the large crowd. "We have found one another again as brothers and comrades in arms," he beamed, "enemies no longer, generous friends rather, our battles long past, the quarrel forgotten—except that we shall not forget the splendid valor, the manly devotion of the men then arrayed against one another, now grasping hands and smiling into each other's eyes."

**The Peace Jubilee.** When President Woodrow Wilson (wearing glasses) spoke at the Peace Jubilee, the veterans' reunion for the fiftieth anniversary of Gettysburg, it was seen as a symbolic gesture confirming that the nation had finally healed its wounds. Wilson is flanked by veterans carrying the U.S. and Confederate flags. African American veterans were not invited to attend.

The reunion was a huge success, but bitter emotions still boiled in the hearts of some veterans. Not all were as eager to forgive and forget as those who met at Gettysburg in 1913. Four years later, 8,000 veterans descended on Vicksburg, Mississippi, for a four-day reunion just months after the United States entered World War I. Patriotic fervor was high, and the army actually helped organize and transport the old men. Bands played "Dixie," and there were the obligatory photographs of handshakes and Civil War veterans saluting Doughboys heading to France. But a local newspaper also reported some veterans "refought the war" and loudly argued about who had the best commanders. One Yankee even refused to ride in a truck with Southerners. He paid a quarter to take a taxi and declared defiantly, "I don't care if it costs $500. I won't trust myself with those Johnny Rebs." Emotions continued to run high until a huge free-for-all, dubbed the "walking stick war," erupted at the encampment after the veterans began arguing about the battle. One witness claimed the old soldiers, some of whom were missing arms and legs, bit, clawed, and bashed each other in a furious Second Battle of Vicksburg.

Despite the violence at Vicksburg, veterans' reunions such as Gettysburg's were hailed across the nation as the final symbolic acts that reunited the two sections. But there was something missing at the gatherings that few visitors probably even noticed. Like the Grand Review forty-eight years earlier, there is no evidence that any black veterans attended or were even invited. The only African Americans present at Gettysburg were those laboring under the hot sun erecting tents and preparing the grounds, and at Vicksburg black musicians stood on the sideline to play "Dixie" to the cheering crowd. Jim Crow had won out. Not only had African Americans been segregated across the nation, they had even been written out of the Civil War.

# REMEMBERING THE CIVIL WAR

In the years immediately following the Civil War, the North and South remained bitter toward one another, and few people wanted to dwell on the conflict. By the time Reconstruction began winding down in the mid-1870s, passions had cooled, and Americans began to reflect on the war and seek ways to honor those who had sacrificed so much. Veterans created organizations to promote and preserve their stories, and the resultant books and articles (and later movies) renewed interest in the conflict. The nation began a reconciliation process that focused more on honoring the soldiers' bravery than remembering the war's causes. When issues such as slavery and equality faded from the nation's collective memory, African Americans were left out of the history books, and the Civil War came to be seen as purely a white man's struggle.

## Veterans' Organizations

Union soldiers were the first to create a veterans' organization when some officers met in Philadelphia in April 1865 to create the Military Order of the Loyal Legion of the United States (MOLLUS). Lee's surrender at Appomattox meant the war was almost over, but these officers wanted to make sure the peace would last. In creating MOLLUS, they pledged their support to the federal government and promised to come to its aid in the future if it proved necessary. Membership was open to all Union officers who had served honorably, along with their descendants. MOLLUS spread across the North, but when it became apparent the peace would last, the organization began stressing social activities and concentrating on such veterans' issues as providing relief to war widows and orphans and compiling personal reminiscences and unit histories.

In 1866, other Union veterans organized the much larger Grand Army of the Republic (GAR). The GAR was also a social organization that aided disabled veterans and the families of the deceased, politicked for veterans' pensions, and promoted patriotism. With the participation of African Americans, who were segregated in their own chapters, the GAR became the largest veterans' organization in the country and claimed 428,000 members by 1890. Because it constituted such a large voting bloc, it also became a potent political force, and there was a running joke that GAR stood for "Generally, All Republicans."

One of the GAR's main activities was lobbying Congress for veterans' pensions. During the war, the federal government gave pensions to disabled soldiers and the widows and orphans of soldiers who died, with the amount being based on the soldier's military rank. But the GAR wanted pensions for all veterans and successfully pressured Congress to pass the Dependent Pension Act in 1890. This bill greatly expanded the pension system to include all disabled veterans (even old age was eventually accepted as a disability) who had served honorably and their widows. The number of pensioners mushroomed to almost 1 million, and by 1911 the federal government had spent $4 billion on the program—more than the cost of fighting the war.

**Decoration Day.** Both the North and South adopted Decoration Days after the Civil War to honor their respective dead. Such ceremonies led to the modern Memorial Day, but their focus on white casualties pushed black American soldiers to the back of the nation's collective memory. Ironically, it was black soldiers who held the first Decoration Day in 1865.

# DID YOU KNOW?

## Memorial Day

Today's Memorial Day is a visible reminder of Civil War veterans' organizations. On May 1, 1865, black Union soldiers and white abolitionists in Charleston, South Carolina, held a "Decoration Day" ceremony to honor the war dead at a local cemetery. The following year, Southern women led a similar movement to lay flowers on the graves of Confederate dead. This ceremony quickly became a Southern tradition, but there was no set date on which it was performed.

Southerners were rather late in forming a veterans' organization because they were overwhelmed dealing with Reconstruction and rebuilding their shattered lives. Not until 1889 did the former Rebels create the United Confederate Veterans (UCV). Like its Union counterparts, the UCV sponsored social activities, supported disabled veterans and widows, raised money for monuments, and promoted the Southern view of the war. Although the UCV had 160,000 members, it never matched the GAR in influence. However, they did successfully lobby the Southern states in the late nineteenth century to provide pensions to veterans who suffered service-related disabilities and their widows and dependents, but the amount was usually lower than the federal pensions.

Such ceremonies gained strength in 1868 when GAR commander John A. Logan encouraged his members to conduct memorials at cemeteries and to put flowers on the graves of the Union dead. Members responded enthusiastically, and on May 30, 1868, memorials were held at 183 cemeteries in 27 states. In 1873, New York became the first state to make May 30 a legal holiday, and every other Northern state soon followed suit. Both the North and South eventually adopted the name Memorial Day and used it as an opportunity to promote the memory of their Civil War

**United Confederate Veterans.** As passions cooled in the late nineteenth century, both sides formed veterans' organizations for social, political, and philanthropic reasons. In the South, the United Confederate Veterans held reunions and promoted the Lost Cause doctrine. These Confederate veterans were members of Virginia's R. E. Lee Camp No. 1.

soldiers. National reconciliation was hastened when the GAR and UCV began holding joint Memorial Day ceremonies to honor the bravery and sacrifice on both sides. After World War I, however, the Civil War faded from memory on Memorial Day as Americans began honoring all of the nation's war dead. In 1971, Congress changed the date of Memorial Day from May 30 to the last Monday in May so federal employees could enjoy a three-day weekend.

## The War in Words

One of the main goals of the veterans' organizations was to compile a record of their armies' battlefield exploits. The journals the *National Tribune* and the *Confederate Veteran* were published by the GAR and the UCV, respectively, and the UCV also sponsored the 12-volume *Confederate Military History*. The journals included soldiers' reminiscences, personality sketches, unit and battle histories, and humorous anecdotes, while the multivolume work was a history of the military activity within each Southern state. The Military Order of the Loyal Legion of the United States also compiled a huge amount of similar material that is known as the MOLLUS Papers. Although naturally biased, these materials collected by Civil War veterans are a treasure trove for historians.

In the postwar period, Southerners often took the lead in writing about the conflict, disproving the oft-quoted claim that the victors write the history. During Reconstruction, Southerners were particularly concerned that Northern domination would prevent their accounts of the war from being remembered. Determined to preserve this history, the former Rebels began publishing magazines and journals to counter what they claimed were Yankee lies about the Confederacy. *The Land We Love* (1866), the *Southern Historical Society Papers* (1876), and the *Southern Bivouac* (1882) stressed Confederate honor, recounted brave deeds, and depicted slaves as loyal, devoted servants who were quite happy with the peculiar institution.

The *Southern Historical Society Papers* was the most important of these publications. The Southern Historical Society was organized in 1869 to present the "true history" of the war because the federal government was denying Southerners access to captured Confederate documents. When the government announced its intention to publish all of the war's military records, Southerners were concerned that the project would venerate the Union cause and condemn the Confederacy. To ensure its point of view was presented, the Southern Historical Society began publishing the *Southern Historical Society Papers* in 1876. Included were articles by former Confederate soldiers, previously unpublished Confederate military and government reports, memoirs, diaries, correspondence, and other valuable material.

In 1881, the War Department published the first of 128 volumes of Civil War records. Entitled *War of the Rebellion: A Compilation of the Official Records of the Union and Confederate Armies,* it contained virtually all of the wartime campaign and battle reports, telegrams, orders, official correspondence, and prisoner of war records in the government's possession. Three years later, the 31-volume *Official Records of the Union and Confederate Navies in the War of the Rebellion* was published to cover the naval aspect of the war. Because many Confederate documents had been destroyed or were in private hands, the army and navy *Official Records* included far more Union documents than Confederate. Nonetheless, today they are the most important source of Civil War primary material.

By the 1880s, remembering the Civil War had become big business. Reconstruction was over and enough time had passed to cool bitter feelings. Veterans' reunions became commonplace, and more prominent generals and ordinary soldiers began publishing their memoirs. In 1884–1887, *Century Magazine* capitalized on this renewed interest by publishing a series of war-related articles. The magazine contacted many famous veterans to write the articles for pay, an offer that they eagerly accepted because they wanted to record their views for posterity. The soldiers avoided discussing controversial subjects such as causes of the war, politics, slavery, and African Americans because *Century* wanted to attract readers from both sides. Instead, they stressed personalities, strategy and tactics, and battlefield exploits in which every soldier was a hero. The handsomely illustrated articles were a huge success, and they were later compiled into four volumes entitled *Battles and Leaders of the Civil War*. What the general public did not see were the fierce fights that raged behind the scenes between authors who used the forum to defend their record and attack their rivals. The editors mediated the fights as best they could, but one declared, "[T]he general reader never knew the violence of it."

While white veterans published scores of works on the war, little was written about the African American experience. Only a handful of such books made it to the press, partly because many black veterans were illiterate and partly because white Americans had effectively marginalized both the role of slavery in causing the war and the contributions African Americans had made to the Union victory. There simply was no interest or market for such books. Among the few that were published was William Wells Brown's *The Negro in the American Rebellion* (1867), George Washington Williams's *A History of the Negro Troops in the War of the Rebellion, 1861–1865* (1888), and Joseph T. Wilson's *The Black Phalanx* (1892). Williams and Wilson were black veterans of the Civil War, with Wilson having served in both the Louisiana Native Guards and the 54th Massachusetts. Williams (1849–1891) wrote the best of the postwar books on African Americans in the Civil War. After fighting with Mexican forces to overthrow Maximilian, he reenlisted in the U.S. army and was wounded while serving on the frontier. Williams then became the first African American to graduate from the Newton Theological Seminary and the first black elected to the Ohio legislature. His book *A History of the Negro Troops in the War of the Rebellion* was the first such study that was well researched and written fairly objectively. It remained the best treatment of black Civil War soldiers until Dudley Taylor Cornish published *The Sable Arm* in 1956.

## The War in Movies

The Civil War remained a popular topic even after movies began to compete with the written word. David W. Griffith's *The Birth of a Nation* (1915) was one of the first Civil War movies. With its epic battle scenes, creative camera angles, subplots, and character development, the silent film was the first modern movie, but it is also one of the most controversial. Griffith based the movie on the novel *The Clansman,* and both book and movie depicted African Americans as drunken and violent rapists who threatened peaceful Southern whites during Reconstruction until the Ku Klux Klan regained control of the region. The commercial success of *The Birth of a Nation* ensured that other filmmakers would use the Civil War as a story line. From *Gone With the Wind* (1939) to *Cold Mountain* (2003), Hollywood producers have mined the rich history of the war with great effect.

Some Civil War movies used dramatic license to portray historical events. *The Horse Soldiers* (1959) was based on Colonel Benjamin Grierson's cavalry raid during the Vicksburg Campaign, *The Great Locomotive Chase* (1956) told the story of James J. Andrews's 1862 raid into Georgia, *Glory* (1989) depicted the saga of the 54th Massachusetts, and *Gettysburg* (1993) and *Gods and Generals* (2003) examined major battles and leaders in the eastern theater.

*The Birth of a Nation.* Although they lost the Civil War, Southerners seemed to have won the peace by the early twentieth century. In 1915, D. W. Griffith's *The Birth of a Nation* portrayed the Ku Klux Klan as liberators who saved the South from the evil freedmen and carpetbaggers.

Some of these movies, such as *Glory* and *Gettysburg*, made an effort to be historically accurate. Other Civil War films, however, never let historical accuracy get in the way of a good story.

Many Civil War movies also made commentary on the day's social issues. *The Birth of a Nation* was produced during the height of Jim Crow and reflected the William A. Dunning school of thought on Reconstruction. Dunning popularized the image of carpetbaggers and scalawags being corrupt and power hungry and the freedmen being unable to control their baser instincts. *Gone With the Wind* depicted a stereotypical view of the antebellum South where slaves were loyal and eager to defend their masters. It also carried a Depression-era message of hope. Heroine Scarlett O'Hara lost everything in the war but managed to rebuild her shattered life, and the movie even ended on a somewhat hopeful note by hinting that she might someday win back her husband, Rhett Butler. Later movies that carried a contemporary message include *Major Dundee* (1965) and *The Undefeated* (1969), which were released during the Civil Rights Movement and stressed social harmony. In both films, Yankees and Rebels fought together against a common enemy. In the former, a Union officer releases Confederate prisoners so they can help him fight Indians; and, in the latter, Union and Confederate veterans join forces in post-Civil War Mexico and confront the French army. *Major Dundee* even included some African American soldiers among the cast.

## The Lost Cause

Some of the movies produced during the first half of the twentieth century helped to reinforce a view of the Civil War that became known as the Lost Cause doctrine. The term was first used in Edward A. Pollard's book *The Lost Cause,* an 1866 history of secession and the Confederacy. With the notable exception of Native Americans, Southern whites are the only Americans to have been defeated in war and had their homeland occupied by the enemy. The Civil War traumatized the Southern people because it destroyed virtually everything they held dear. In the antebellum South, honor, bravery, and military ability were revered, yet Confederate soldiers had been unable to defend their women, homeland, or way of life. As Southerners became more enlightened, they were also burdened with the fact that the Confederacy had fought a war to perpetuate slavery. The Lost Cause doctrine enabled Southerners to emerge from the war with their honor intact and come to terms with their support of slavery and defeat by claiming they were morally, spiritually, and militarily superior to the North.

The Lost Cause doctrine hailed secession as a constitutional duty and portrayed the Confederacy as protecting the Founding Fathers' dream of self-government. Lost Cause advocates claimed the antebellum period was an idyllic time when the Southern people lived in harmony with their slaves. They believed the South was forced into war to protect its constitutional rights, and that all Confederates were brave soldiers who fought in a Christian manner. The North was seen as a tyrannical invader that waged war in a brutal and evil manner and only won because of its overwhelming superiority in industry and manpower. Because Southerners were Christians who fought for a just cause, Lost Cause advocates saw no dishonor in being forced to capitulate by superior numbers.

The United Daughters of the Confederacy (UDC), formed in 1894, was one of the main proponents of the Lost Cause doctrine. It aggressively molded Southern opinions by distributing educational material explaining the Confederate side of the war, launching campaigns to name schools for Confederate heroes, writing editorials and articles for newspapers, and dedicating memorials and monuments across the South. The UDC was so successful that most Southern whites soon forgot the role slavery had played in starting the war.

Religion also played an important role in the Lost Cause doctrine. Southern whites viewed Confederate leaders such as Davis, Lee, and Jackson as Christian heroes and the Yankees as little more than murderers. Southern children learned this lesson at an early age. When a priest noticed his young niece staring at a crucifix, he asked if she knew who crucified Jesus. "Oh yes," she replied, "I know, the Yankees." Even though most Southerners came to accept slavery as an evil institution, the Lost Cause doctrine absolved them of that sin because their soldiers' suffering and death paid any moral debt they owed God and the nation. And because virtually every family had a Confederate ancestor, everyone had a "saint" who was martyred to pay the price for slavery's sin. This religious aspect of the Lost Cause was effective because Southerners shared a Protestant heritage that had long defended slavery and the Confederacy.

Many Southerners even came to view the Civil War as a Christian blessing. While brutal and devastating, the war was a necessary trial the South had to endure to reach its full potential. At the 1875 dedication of Stonewall Jackson's statue in Richmond, Virginia, one minister reflected this attitude when he declared, "Defeat is the discipline which trains the truly heroic soul to further and better endeavors." Southerners such as this minister believed God used the war to test the South in a Job-like manner to see if the people were worthy of greater blessings. The Confederates held fast to their faith, even in defeat,

# BIOGRAPHY

## Jubal Anderson Early: Lee's Bad Old Man

**Jubal Anderson Early**

A native of Virginia, Jubal Early (1816–1894) graduated from West Point in 1837 and served in the Seminole Wars before resigning his commission to study law. Afterward, he was elected to one term in the Virginia legislature and served in the Mexican War. Early also was a delegate to the state secession convention, where he voted against secession. He later recalled, "The adoption of that ordinance wrung from me bitter tears of grief, but I at once recognized my duty to abide by the decision of my native State, and to defend her soil against invasion." Despite his vote, Early became committed to the Confederacy and once said of the Yankees, "I not only wish them all dead but I wish them all in Hell."

Appointed colonel of the 24th Virginia, Early quickly rose through the ranks to become a major general and division commander under Stonewall Jackson. He fought well in most of the Army of Northern Virginia's battles and was severely wounded in the shoulder at the Battle of Williamsburg. During the Wilderness Campaign, Early was placed in command of the II Corps when Richard S. Ewell became ill and he later was promoted to lieutenant general. In June 1864, he drove the enemy out of the Shenandoah Valley and made a raid on Washington, but his reputation was tarnished when his cavalry burned Chambersburg, Pennsylvania, and Philip Sheridan defeated him in a series of battles. Robert E. Lee admired Early's fighting spirit, but public outcry over the Valley defeats forced him to relieve Early late in the war. Nonetheless, Lee wrote of Early,

and God rewarded them by allowing the devastated South to rise again in a Christ-like manner, free from the sin of slavery and transformed into an even greater, more virtuous, New South.

Robert E. Lee planted the seeds of the Lost Cause when he told his soldiers at Appomattox they had been defeated because of "overwhelming numbers and resources." After the war, Lee planned to write a history of his army and asked Jubal A. Early for information since most of Lee's records had been lost. Lee never wrote his history, but Early took up the mantle after the general's death. As president of the Southern Historical Society, he helped publish a voluminous amount of material defending the Confederacy and portraying Lee and Jackson as the epitome of Christian warriors. In Early's opinion, Lee and Jackson did no wrong, so other generals must have lost the war. A favorite target was Confederate-turned-Republican James Longstreet, who was blamed for the Gettysburg defeat. Although Early sometimes played loose with the facts, he was so successful in promoting the Lost Cause that many Northerners came to accept Lee and Jackson as national heroes. One Chicago high school even adopted the "Rebel" mascot while Union veterans still lived there.

"He exhibited during his whole service high intelligence, sagacity, bravery and untiring devotion to the cause in which he had enlisted."

Known to his men as "Old Jube" or "Old Jubilee," Early was just over six feet tall, but stooping caused by arthritis made him look shorter and older than he was. One soldier claimed "he looked more like an animated scarecrow than the commanding general of any army." Described as a "queer fish," the general was well liked by his men, nonetheless, and they came to admire his bravery and aggressiveness in battle. One officer remembered, "I have seen him at times and places that tried men's souls, and he was always in the thickest of the battle." Early liked to drink and curse, disdained pretentiousness, and was cynical and outspoken. He was described as having a "snarling, raspy disposition," and one soldier claimed his "wit was quick, his satire biting, his expressions vigorous, and he was interestingly lurid and picturesque." Lee fondly called Early "my bad old man."

After the war, Early briefly lived in self-imposed exile in Mexico and Canada, but he finally returned to Virginia and became president of the Southern Historical Society. More than anyone, he promoted the hero worship of Lee and popularized the Lost Cause doctrine. In an 1872 address to commemorate Lee's birthday, Early asked the audience, "Shall I compare General Lee to his successful antagonist [Grant]? As well compare the great pyramid which rears its majestic proportions in the valley of the Nile, to a pigmy perched on Mount Atlas." Early took to task anyone who remotely criticized Lee, prompting one Confederate veteran to write, "Long as 'the old hero' lived, no man ever took up his pen to write a line about the great conflict without the fear of Jubal Early before his eyes." He was the epitome of the unreconstructed Rebel.

## Reconciliation

Since the opposing sides in the Civil War developed such hatred for one another, it is surprising how quickly Americans healed their bitter wounds. Several things made this possible. Once Northerners realized the South was not going to fight again, it was much easier for them to modify harsh Reconstruction policies. Both sections also firmly believed in the republican system, which made it easier for Southerners to return to the fold. Reconciliation was greatly aided by the fact that most white Americans agreed on fundamental racial issues, and they focused their attention on shared battlefield experiences and honorable service rather than the evils of slavery. The Spanish-American War completed this reconciliation process. In that conflict, Southern men flocked to the old flag once again to fight side by side with their Northern brethren. Two former Confederate generals, Joseph Wheeler and Fitzhugh Lee, even became generals in the new war. The Spanish-American War was a defining moment in healing the old wounds and invigorating Americans with a new sense of *national* pride.

The good feelings created by the Spanish-American War finally allowed the federal government to carry out a policy that had first been suggested by President Grover Cleveland in 1887. Cleveland proposed returning captured battle flags to the Southern states as a reconciliation gesture, but the GAR bitterly opposed the move and blocked the plan (the fact that Cleveland hired a substitute during the war did not help his case). Northerners were more receptive to returning the flags after the Spanish-American War, and former Union General James Wilson even sent an open letter of support to *Confederate Veteran*. "[A]s for the flags," he wrote, "send them back. The men who fought under them are as loyal to the stars and stripes now as if they had never thought of any other standard. They know as well as we do that their flags represent nothing today, but are dear to them because of associations connected with painful memories." Congress agreed, and the captured flags were returned to their respective states in 1905–1906.

Passions had cooled so much by 1899 that North Carolina senator Marion Butler proposed the federal government grant Confederate veterans pensions. He pointed out that Southern congressmen had always voted for Union pensions, and now it was time to cover Southern veterans as well. An incredulous Iowa senator asked Butler why the federal government should pay pensions to men who had rebelled against that very government. Butler replied, "The grave of every Southern soldier is as great a tribute to American valor as the grave of every Northern soldier made in defense of the constitutional rights of his State as he understood them. . . ." The Iowa senator was not the only one outraged by Butler's proposal. Even some Confederate veterans condemned the senator for "debauching the manhood of the South." Accepting Yankee dollars, they argued, would dishonor the Confederate veteran and the cause for which he had fought. Butler's proposal failed, but in 1958 Congress finally did pension the last two surviving Confederate veterans and about 1,000 widows. At that time, Louisiana's Senator Russell Long proudly declared, "The War Between the States [has] at last been concluded."

## The White Civil War

Northern and Southern whites came to ignore the role slavery and African Americans had played in the Civil War because they wanted to pave the way for reconciliation. African Americans did not agree. Black Union veterans had compiled an impressive record of brave and honorable service, and they expected future generations to remember them. One pointed out that black soldiers had "washed the blood scars of slavery out of the American flag, and painted freedom there; they snatched the black lies out of every false star upon its folds and set in their stead the diadem of liberty. . . . They tore the Dred Scott decision from the statutes and wrote there, 'All men are equal before God.'" Thousands of African American veterans joined the GAR and became active in postwar celebrations, but they were almost always segregated. While some white GAR members welcomed and cooperated with their black comrades, most increasingly ignored their role in the war. White Union veterans had much more in common with the former Rebels, with whom they held joint reunions and came to respect each other's wartime records.

Black veterans were frustrated at their inability to gain the recognition and respect they deserved. Frederick Douglass and others tried to keep the nation's attention focused on the fact that the Civil War was not just a war to save the Union; it also was a struggle that pitted freedom against slavery, a peaceful democratic majority against a violent rebellious minority, and equality against racism. Douglass was particularly disappointed that Decoration Day ceremonies simply honored the soldiers' bravery and ignored such wartime issues as slavery and equality. In one address, he reminded the audience, "There was a right side and a wrong side in the late war that no sentiment ought to cause us to forget." Douglass urged the people to use such ceremonies to stress the "moral character of the war," but his plea fell on deaf ears. On one occasion he lamented, "As the war for the Union recedes into the past and the negro is no longer needed to assault forts and stop rebel bullets, he is in some sense of less importance. Peace with the old master class has been war for the negro. As the one has risen the other has fallen."

After Reconstruction, the black veterans in the South essentially became enemy aliens in their own homeland. As the last of them passed away, the role of black Union soldiers was quickly forgotten because the threat of violence prevented African Americans from creating organizations to rival the United Daughters of the Confederacy or the Sons of Confederate Veterans. Even during the centennial celebration in 1961–1965, virtually all events commemorated major battles and ignored the slavery issue or the contributions made by black soldiers. Adding insult to injury, some African American delegates to centennial celebrations were refused rooms in the hotels where events were held. Jim Crow triumphed, and the memory of black Union soldiers was pushed to the dark recesses of the nation's consciousness.

## THE CIVIL WAR'S MILITARY LEGACY

The Civil War continues to fascinate military historians for a variety of reasons. One of the largest wars of the nineteenth century, it occurred on the cusp of modernity and introduced many technological innovations. Some consider the Civil War to be the first modern war, while others believe it was the last Napoleonic-type conflict because tactics did not significantly change and the technological innovations were not widely adopted afterward. The Union's seemingly thin margin of victory, despite its military superiority, also intrigues historians, and they continue to speculate about whether the Confederacy could have won the war.

### The First Modern War?

Based on the number of military firsts, the Civil War in many ways does qualify as the first modern war. It was the first time a submarine successfully sank a warship, and it saw the first widespread use of steam-powered ironclad warships, rotating gun turrets, rifles, rifled cannons, repeating weapons, railroads, telegraphs, airships, wire entanglements, land mines, and telescopic sights. On the other hand, Civil War armies continued to maneuver and fight largely in the same manner as they had done since the Revolutionary War, generally exchanged fire at the same distances as in the Revolution (despite the use of rifles), and couriers still had to ride across the battlefield to deliver handwritten orders to officers. If the Civil War was the first modern war, one would expect America's military to have permanently adopted more modern ideas and technology in the postwar years, but that did not occur. While the army did begin to use metallic cartridges, it continued to fire them in single-shot rifles until nearly the twentieth century. The Indians who defeated George Custer at the Little Big Horn were, in fact, better armed with modern repeating weapons than Custer's cavalrymen. The military also made no attempt to modernize its organizational structure despite the tremendous problems it had faced in coordinating armies and logistics during the Civil War.

The military's failure to modernize in the postwar period can largely be attributed to the fact that Civil War officers were notoriously conservative, and they remained in important positions for decades. If the system was good enough to defeat the Rebels, high-ranking officers such as Grant, Sherman, and Sheridan saw no need to make radical changes. It was not until they died or retired that more progressive younger officers such as Emory Upton could begin creating a modern military. Only after the Spanish-American War was the position of general-in-chief abolished and a modern chief of staff appointed; the National Guard was fully integrated into the army using federal money and weapons; training was standardized; and the Army Staff College and War College were created to train officers in advanced military science. Because of this lack of progress in modernizing the military, the Civil War is best considered to have been a transitional war that linked the old and new rather than the first truly modern war.

## Could the South Have Won?

In considering whether the South could have won the Civil War, historians use a concept known as contingency. During the war, one action taken by individuals led to a particular outcome, but if a different action had been taken it would have led to a different outcome. Whether the South could have won the war is, of course, an unanswerable question, but pondering that question leads to some interesting "what if" scenarios. While there have been an almost infinite number of contingencies proposed to bring about a Confederate victory, the following are some of the more widely considered.

It has become popular in modern times to attribute the Confederate defeat to Robert E. Lee's aggressiveness. If he had adopted a more defensive strategy and conserved his strength, or even carried out guerrilla warfare after Appomattox, Lee could have held the North at bay until it tired of the conflict and quit. But was this really possible considering the expectations of the Confederate people? Southerners were convinced they were superior soldiers and expected their armies to defeat the enemy on the battlefield. Politically, Lee could not have adopted a purely defensive strategy because the people would not have stood for it. Most Southerners expected the Yankees to be defeated as quickly as possible, and they never would have tolerated their armies remaining inactive for long periods of time. Guerrilla warfare also was not an option. Events in Missouri, Tennessee, and other areas where guerrillas operated clearly showed how such brutal warfare devastated entire regions and broke down morale. There simply would not have been enough popular support to sustain such a strategy for long.

Some people argue that the Confederates could have won if they had held Atlanta, Mobile, and the Shenandoah Valley beyond the 1864 election. Northern voters, dispirited by the stalemate, would have elected George B. McClellan president, and he might have bowed to the Democratic Party's peace faction and opened negotiations with the Confederates. But this speculation is not supported by historical fact. McClellan received the Democratic nomination two days *before* Sherman's armies occupied Atlanta, and in his acceptance letter he clearly rejected the peace plank. His promise to prosecute the war until the Rebels were defeated actually garnered him many votes because some Northerners believed he could win the war more quickly than Lincoln. There seems little doubt that McClellan would have continued to fight if he had become president, and the Union still would have eventually won. Another consideration that is sometimes overlooked is that a defeated Lincoln would have had four months left in office to achieve victory. Undoubtedly, he would have done everything in his power to end the war before inauguration day by launching winter campaigns on all fronts. As it turned out, Grant forced Lee to surrender just over one month after the inauguration—without taking such drastic measures. If a defeated Lincoln had adopted such an aggressive policy, the Union armies probably would have forced an Appomattox-like surrender before McClellan even took office.

Confederate defeat has also been blamed on King Cotton diplomacy. If the Confederates had sent as much cotton as possible to Europe before the blockade became effective instead of hoarding it to create a shortage, they could have established lines of credit to purchase ample war material for years. This argument is true, but it misses the point. While the Confederates did suffer severe shortages by mid-war, they never lost a battle because of a lack of guns, ammunition, uniforms, or medicine. They *did* lose battles because of a lack of men and a broken-down railway system that made it difficult to move troops and materials to critical points. The increasingly effective blockade would have prevented the importation of railroad iron and other supplies no matter how much credit the Confederates accumulated overseas.

Another diplomatic "what if" concerns European intervention. In the fall of 1862, Great Britain and France were on the verge of extending diplomatic recognition to the Confederacy and offering to mediate a peace, but they backed away when the Union won the Battle of Antietam. In this scenario, if Lee had won, then Great Britain and France would have recognized the Confederacy and mediated a peace to secure Southern independence. In reality, however, there is little likelihood the Europeans would have become involved in the war. They had already extended belligerent status to the Confederacy, which allowed it to purchase supplies and use European ports. Diplomatic recognition would have enhanced the Southerners' prestige, but it would not have materially affected their ability to wage war. And if the British had offered to mediate a peace, Lincoln certainly would have rebuffed them. Then what? It is not likely the British would have rushed to the Confederates' aid by breaking the blockade and provoking a war with the United States. By late 1862, emancipation had become a Union war goal, and the abolitionist British people would never have supported their government becoming militarily involved to defend slavery. British officials also had not forgotten that American privateers devastated the nation's merchant fleet in the War of 1812. There also was no economic incentive for Great Britain to become a Confederate ally because the cotton shortage created by the blockade was soon alleviated by cotton from Egypt and India. More important, the trade Great Britain conducted with the United States far outweighed the significance of Southern cotton.

Some historians have blamed the Confederate defeat on the region's strict adherence to states' rights and its failure to develop a strong sense of nationalism. If the Southern people had been more successful in forming a national identity, Davis could have nationalized the railroads and industry, and the governors would have cooperated more with Richmond. A powerful central government and stronger sense of national identity would also have helped sustain morale when the war began to go badly and have kept the people fighting. Instead, the Southerners' belief in states' rights kept the governors at odds with the central government and weakened the military effort, and the breakdown in civilian morale caused more soldiers to desert, weakened the army, and led to battlefield defeats.

Rather than blaming the Confederates' defeat on a lack of nationalism, one should marvel at the fact that they maintained their government as long as they did. Southerners created a viable nation from scratch, including a functioning constitutional government and a formidable military machine that included 80 percent of eligible white males. The Southern people quickly developed a sense of nationalism in the first year of the war because they believed they had to form a separate nation to avoid Northern domination. The string of victories in Virginia in 1861–1862 only increased this national pride. Even when the war began to go badly and the enemy occupied large sections of the Confederacy, most Southern whites became even more determined to fight because they knew their homes would be the next to feel the invaders' wrath if they did not.

Slavery and racial views also played an important role in Confederate nationalism. When the Emancipation Proclamation was issued, Southern whites' resolve strengthened because they realized that if they lost the war, the very cornerstone of their society would be destroyed. The sight of black soldiers deep in the Confederacy's heartland outraged and disheartened Southern whites, but in the war's last year those same Southerners were willing to contemplate enlisting the slaves to fight on their side. Confederate emancipation would have been unthinkable earlier in the conflict, but by 1865 many Southerners supported recruiting slaves as a way to strengthen the army and win European recognition. To achieve independence, they were willing to sacrifice the very thing they went to war to protect.

Blaming the Confederates' defeat on a lack of resolve and national identity comes down to this question: Did a lack of nationalism break down morale and lead to battlefield defeats, or did battlefield defeats break down morale, weaken nationalism, and convince the people the war was lost? There was, indeed, conflict between Davis and some governors over national policy, but no governor ever tried to negotiate a peace with the Yankees. There also was friction between the upper and lower class, and many people vehemently opposed some government policies, but most Southern whites were united in the common cause of winning independence. Morale did eventually weaken, but not until very late in the war. Even in the spring of 1864, Southerners were confident that Robert E. Lee would defeat Grant and somehow save the nation. It was not until late that year—when battlefield defeats became commonplace, casualties mounted, food and supply shortages became chronic, and the countryside was ravaged by Jayhawkers, deserters, and enemy armies—that morale crumbled. But such feelings were a *result* of military defeats not the *cause* of those defeats.

## Counterfactual History

In debating the South's chances of winning the war, it has become popular to indulge in counterfactual history. In this mental contingency exercise, a battle or other historical event is changed to show how it could have affected the war's outcome. If Grant had been defeated at Shiloh, for example, he would have been permanently removed from command. Without Grant, there would have been no Sherman or Sheridan, and without them the Union would have lost the war. If Lincoln had been assassinated earlier in the war, Hannibal Hamlin might have been persuaded to negotiate a peace. Or if Stonewall Jackson had survived Chancellorsville and fought at Gettysburg, he would have pushed on to capture Cemetery Hill on the first day. Lee would have won the battle, and the Confederates would have captured Harrisburg or Baltimore and forced Lincoln to the negotiating table.

Counterfactual history is just another term for fiction. Although it is entertaining, it has no place in serious historical study because it is impossible to predict what might have happened if historical events had produced different outcomes. In fact, one could argue just as persuasively that nothing would have changed even if these scenarios had actually occurred. If Grant, Sherman, and Sheridan were removed from the battlefield, other Union generals such as Thomas, Hancock, and McPherson would have risen to the top and perhaps won the war. And no one knows what additional talent was hidden among other officers because they never got the chance to command an army. While Lincoln's steady hand certainly was an asset to the North, he was not the only determined Union politician. Even if he had been assassinated at mid-war, the Republicans still would have controlled Congress and would have probably impeached Hamlin if he had tried to negotiate with the Rebels. As long as there were leaders like Stanton, Chase, Sumner, and Stevens, the North would have continued fighting, with or without Lincoln. As for Stonewall, it is interesting that no one ever mentions the possibility that the Jackson at Gettysburg might have been the Jackson of the Seven Days. Exhausted after the long march, he might have curled up in a fence corner and taken a nap on the afternoon of July 1. Or Jackson might have taken one look at the thousands of enemy troops and dozens of cannons on Cemetery Hill and agreed with Ewell that it was too strong to attack. At Fredericksburg, in fact, Jackson did change his mind about counterattacking the enemy after examining their strong defensive position.

Most historians today believe the South could have won the Civil War, and there are notable examples in history where a weaker people defeated a stronger one. The American Revolution and the Vietnam War immediately come to mind, but the Americans and North Vietnamese had the military backing of the superpowers France and the Soviet Union, respectively. The Confederacy had no such backing, and a credible argument can be made that its defeat was almost inevitable. In virtually all cases where a weaker people have prevailed, they had a greater determination to win and were willing to fight for years and suffer horrendous casualties to wear down the enemy. What many fail to recognize is that Northerners viewed the war as almost a religious struggle, and they were just as committed to winning as the Southerners. Some saw it as a war to free the slaves, while others fought to ensure the survival of their republican form of government. America was the world's last great hope for democracy, and if the South destroyed the Union by force, that light of liberty might have been extinguished forever. Lincoln once said the North must prove "that popular government is not an absurdity. We must settle this question now, whether in a free government the minority have the right to break up the government whenever they choose. If we fail it will go far to prove the incapability of the people to govern themselves." The South may have been fighting to preserve a way of life and to protect its constitutional rights, but so was the North. If the Southern people kept fighting even after the devastating defeats at Gettysburg, Vicksburg, and Chattanooga, why should we not believe the North would have kept fighting even if the Confederates had won Gettysburg, Vicksburg, and Chattanooga?

The fact is that both sides were equally dedicated to their cause. Commitment and morale being the same, the stronger side prevailed.

## THE NEVER-ENDING WAR

Just how deeply the Civil War continues to affect our nation can be seen in the many controversies it still invokes. In some ways, Americans were better reconciled 100 years ago when the North and South were more interested in honoring their soldiers than reflecting on the war's divisive issues. Now, more people are pondering what the war was actually about. It is deeply troubling to consider how one section of the nation could read the Bible and be convinced that enslaving another race was ordained by God while the other section read the same Bible and believed slavery was a sin. Today, we are both puzzled and fascinated at how an enlightened people who shared a common history, culture, language, and religious beliefs, and who revered the Constitution and agreed on the basic principles of republican government, could slaughter one another so mercilessly. It has been said if the United States was an individual the Civil War was the great traumatic event of its adolescence. The war left America scarred both physically and emotionally, and nearly 150 years later we are still trying to make sense of it and come to terms with its bitter legacy.

### What's in a Name?

Today, Americans cannot even agree on what to call the Civil War. Over the years, the conflict has been referred to as the War of the Rebellion, the War Between the States, the War of Northern Aggression, the War for Southern Independence, and the Civil War. One historian actually counted 126 different names that have been used. The federal government adopted War of the Rebellion when it published the *Official Records,* but former Confederates became sensitive to the term "rebel" and began to prefer the War Between the States because it was more benign and did not imply any blame for the conflict.

Technically, the war was a rebellion because the South was trying to form its own nation, not take over the federal government as in a civil war. However, Civil War has always been the term most commonly used by both sides. Lincoln referred to it as a civil war in his Gettysburg Address, and the term was used by Confederate leaders such as Jefferson Davis, Robert E. Lee, P. G. T. Beauregard, John B. Gordon, and Nathan Bedford Forrest. Even the United Confederate Veterans adopted "civil war" because they thought War of the Rebellion reflected poorly on the Southern soldier. To use the word "rebellion" implied that the South did not have the right to secede and form its own government. The former Rebels even issued a statement calling for the war to be referred to as "the civil war between the States," but the term was later shortened to "the war between the States." During the war's centennial celebration, official government publications used both Civil War and War Between the States so as not to offend anyone.

## Honoring the Confederacy

How to honor the Confederacy and its soldiers is one of the greatest Civil War controversies today. Many Americans consider the Confederates to have been evil because they fought a war to maintain slavery. African Americans, in particular, have taken the lead in trying to keep the slavery issue in the forefront of Civil War studies, and they argue that neither the Confederacy nor its soldiers should be honored with memorials and monuments. Some Southern whites, however, strongly disagree. They stress that few Southerners owned slaves and argue that the war was not just about slavery; it also was about states' rights, self-determination, and self-defense. While admitting slavery was cruel and inhuman, these Southerners point out slavery was legally protected by the Constitution, and it is not fair to vilify Confederates for defending slavery while ignoring the fact that midwestern Yankees were just as racist and wanted to prevent all blacks from living in their states.

This clash has become more intense in recent years as the National Association for the Advancement of Colored People (NAACP) and others have urged the removal of all Confederate symbols from public display. Bitter fights have erupted within communities over the display of Rebel flags, the location of Confederate monuments, or the naming of public schools and other facilities after Confederate heroes. In 1993, the people of New Orleans engaged in a highly publicized debate over the Liberty Place Monument, a memorial erected in 1891 to honor the White League members who were killed in the 1874 Battle of Liberty Place. African Americans wanted it removed from Canal Street because it was a racist insult. White citizens agreed it was racist but argued that historical objects should not be removed simply because we no longer believe in what they stand for. As a compromise, the monument was moved to a more remote location and a new inscription was added honoring all who fought at Liberty Place, but no one was satisfied. In 2003, Vanderbilt University removed the word "Confederate" from its Confederate Memorial Hall (which was constructed by UDC donations), and the University of the South took down a collection of state flags in its chapel because some of them incorporated the Confederate battle flag, replacing them with banners of the Episcopal dioceses that own the school. School mascots have also come under fire. In 2003, the University of Mississippi abandoned its mascot, "Colonel Rebel." Even Richmond's Museum of the Confederacy, one of the nation's largest Civil War museums, announced in 2007 plans to drop "Confederacy" from its name.

**Symbol of the Confederacy.** In 1962, teenage students in Birmingham, Alabama, waved the Confederate flag and sang "Dixie" to protest the integration of West End High School.

## The Confederate Battle Flag

No other Civil War symbol evokes as much controversy as the Confederate battle flag, but this phenomenon only became a major issue when the Ku Klux Klan and other extremists began displaying the flag in the mid-twentieth century. There is no evidence that the original Klan carried the battle flag during Reconstruction, and the second Klan organized in the 1920s favored the U.S. flag. During World War II, many American soldiers viewed the Confederate battle flag as a symbol of military prowess, and it was the first flag the Marines raised over Okinawa's Shuri Castle when they captured that stronghold. Later, soldiers fighting in Korea and Vietnam also decorated their bunkers and armored personnel carriers with the flag. After World War II, the Rebel banner was commonly displayed at football games, at Kappa Alpha's "Old South" balls, and by people wanting to publicize their Southern roots.

It was not until 1948 that the flag began to be linked to racism. That year the States Rights Democratic Party, commonly called the Dixiecrats, split from the Democratic Party in opposition to civil rights issues and began using the flag as its symbol. As the Civil Rights Movement strengthened in the 1950s, more white Southerners began displaying the flag as a political statement to oppose integration, and the Ku Klux Klan and American Nazi Party adopted it as well.

Not long after World War II, the editor of the *Richmond Afro-America* recognized the flag's new symbolism and summed up most African Americans' view of the controversy. "The Confederate flag stands for slavery and human degradation," he wrote. "The Confederate flag stands for rebellion and treachery. The Confederate flag stands for bloodshed and segregation. The Confederate flag stands for oppression and disfranchisement. The Confederate flag stands for white supremacy and everything in which democracy and Christianity are opposed. These are no laughing matters. AWAKE AMERICA!"

During the turbulent post–World War II years, many white Southerners opposed using the flag for political purposes and tried to restrict its display to proper memorial settings. Even the UDC protested the flag's "misuse" when the Dixiecrats adopted it as a symbol and Georgia incorporated it into the state flag. Virginius Dabney, the Pulitzer-Prize-winning editor of the Richmond *Times-Dispatch,* wrote during the war's centennial celebration, "The Confederate flag is being used in Alabama in a manner which represents a gross perversion of things it stood for a century ago. . . . [T]rue Southerners object strenuously to having the flag under which their forefathers fought and died dragged into today's interracial controversies, where it is almost invariably made to seem synonymous with 'bigotry' or 'racism.'"

Despite these protests, the Confederate battle flag remained linked to racism and oppression. A defining moment in the flag's history occurred in 1962 when the South Carolina legislature raised it over the Columbia statehouse as a defiant gesture against federally mandated integration. South Carolina became a focal point in 2000 for those who opposed the flag. The NAACP waged a year-long campaign to remove the flag and even called for an economic boycott against the state until the flag was taken down. South Carolina lost millions in revenue when more than 200 conventions canceled their plans to meet there. On January 17, 2000, 50,000 people gathered in Columbia on Martin Luther King Day to protest the flag on the capitol building. The flag debate even became an issue in that year's presidential election. Democratic candidates called for the flag's removal while the Republicans generally avoided taking a stand on the grounds that the decision belonged to the people of South Carolina. The controversy was finally settled when the legislature decided in May to remove the flag and place it at a nearby Confederate monument.

The South Carolina episode was just one of many controversies involving the Confederate battle flag. Afterward, pressure was put on Mississippi to change the design of its state flag, which had included the Confederate flag since 1894. The issue was put to a statewide referendum in 2001, and 65 percent of the voters chose to keep the flag unchanged. That same year Georgia did redesign its flag, which had incorporated the Rebel flag in 1956. The new flag included miniature former state flags, including the one with the battle flag, but it was so controversial that another flag was adopted in 2003 without the Confederate emblem.

The fight over the flag has also been waged on university campuses. For many years, students at Louisiana State University waved Rebel flags in the school's purple and gold colors at football games. In 2005, Chancellor Sean O'Keefe banned the sale of Confederate flags on campus so as not to offend anyone. Although he did not forbid their use, O'Keefe encouraged students not to wave the flag at football games. Not surprisingly, his actions provoked a storm of controversy, with some students and alumni supporting his actions, but most bitterly opposing the attack on tradition. One student wrote in the university newspaper that waving the Confederate flag was tantamount to "celebrating German cultural and intellectual achievements by parading around with swastikas." In contrast, another student pointed out that LSU's mascot name, "Fighting Tigers," was a reference to the Civil War's Louisiana Tigers and claimed it was appropriate to wave Confederate flags because they were part of the school's history.

Today, the Confederate battle flag controversy cuts across sectional and racial lines, and there seems to be no middle ground on which the two sides can meet. The flag is a symbol that will always be associated with rebellion, slavery, and oppression. Virtually all African Americans and a large percentage of white Americans oppose displaying it and argue it is time to retire the banner from public view as a way finally to lay slavery to rest and help heal the painful wounds it left behind. Most Americans who have Confederate ancestors vigorously oppose the Klan and Nazis using the flag as a symbol for their racist views. They point out that its adoption by those hate groups should not be confused with racially tolerant Americans who want to display the flag to honor their ancestors. To them, the flag is a military symbol of a South that put up a heroic struggle against overwhelming odds. People are so polarized on the subject there may be no solution on how to honor ancestors who served in the Confederate army without insulting those whose ancestors fought against them.

# THE BIRTH OF A NATION

While dying of throat cancer in 1885, Ulysses S. Grant reflected on the Civil War. Although the physical destruction had been repaired and reconciliation was well under way, bitter feelings still lingered over the war and Reconstruction. Grant, however, was optimistic about the nation's future and mused, "We must conclude that wars are not always evils unmixed with some good." Most historians would agree and consider today's America to be a product of the Civil War. Noted diarist George Templeton Strong put it well when he wrote at war's end, "The people has [sic] (I think) just been bringing forth a new American republic—an amazingly large baby—after a terribly protracted and severe labor, without chloroform."

## A New Beginning

The most obvious long-term effect of the Civil War and Reconstruction was the settling of two of the nation's most divisive issues. The Northern victory nullified the right of secession and it would never again be seriously considered. The war also destroyed slavery, and the Reconstruction amendments were a step forward in fulfilling the Declaration of Independence promise that all men were created equal. African Americans won both national and state citizenship, and everyone's civil rights were strengthened. The freedmen had a long road to travel in the struggle for equality, but the Civil War and Reconstruction were the first steps down that road. The social changes wrought by Reconstruction also opened the way for women and Native Americans to obtain more of their rights.

The Civil War changed the very way in which Americans viewed their country. With secession no longer an option, we began to see ourselves as a unified nation rather than a confederation of sovereign states. This process was hastened by rapidly growing federal power. Before the conflict, people identified more with their state because the federal government rarely intruded in their lives. Except for the postal service, most Americans never saw the government at work. During the Civil War and Reconstruction, however, the federal government became omnipresent. In addition to involuntary conscription and the presence of thousands of soldiers, the government began to affect people in ways never seen before. Everyone was touched by the income tax and various types of banking, currency, education, railroad, and homestead legislation. For the first time, the federal and state governments also began to provide large-scale direct relief to those affected by the war through such programs as the U.S. Sanitary Commission and Freedmen's Bureau, disability pensions, and provision of prostheses to amputees. The war also changed the political relationship between the states and the national government because various wartime measures and constitutional amendments made the federal government supreme over the states. The Thirteenth, Fourteenth, and Fifteenth Amendments and various types of civil rights legislation increased the federal government's authority to intrude on what previously had been the states' domain. The Fourteenth Amendment, in fact, was the first to expand federal power rather than to limit it, and it allowed the government to enforce the Bill of Rights for the first time. The amendments also increased the power and importance of the federal court system because the courts were left to interpret the amendments. This trend continues today, with the federal government now largely controlling such things as voting rights that previously were purely state matters.

## The Dark Legacy

Unfortunately, not all of the war's legacies were positive. The Civil War may have destroyed slavery, but African Americans soon sank into debt peonage with the adoption of the sharecropping and crop lien systems. Not only did blacks become tied to the land once again, they lost their hard-won political and social rights. With the failure of Reconstruction, Southern whites regained control of their states and used literacy tests, poll taxes, and intimidation to disenfranchise black voters. Louisiana officials were so successful that they eliminated 90 percent of the black vote in just six years. The Southerners then moved against blacks with Jim Crow laws that completely segregated them in society. Such action kept African Americans subjugated for more than sixty years. Through it all, Northerners as a whole acquiesced in the process and took no steps to protect African American rights.

Lynching was one of the darkest legacies of the Civil War and Reconstruction. Throughout the 1880s and 1890s, illegal executions of African Americans and other violent attacks became widespread across the South because the failure of Reconstruction left the freedmen defenseless. In fact, there were more lynchings than legal executions. Louisiana led the nation in lynchings between 1877 and 1890 with 285 (all but 53 of the victims were black). The purpose of lynchings and other violence was to intimidate African Americans from participating in politics or certain areas of employment and to punish them for perceived wrongs. Black men were often accused of raping white women, but there usually was little evidence to support the charge. More often, some small incident such as petty theft, drunkenness, or insult sparked the attack. Between 1889 and 1918 there were 2,522 lynchings in America involving hangings, burnings, and stabbings, but few of the lynchers were ever punished.

Ida Wells was one African American who fought back against the lynchings. Born a Mississippi slave, she became educated and championed women's rights and racial equality. While living in Memphis, Tennessee, Wells worked as a teacher and fought segregation, but she lost her job when she published a newspaper article criticizing the school board for not funding black schools properly. In the 1880s, Wells began to concentrate on exposing lynchings. When three of her close friends were murdered for competing with white businessmen (they were falsely accused of crimes), she condemned the killings in an 1892 article that was published in the Memphis *Free Speech*, a newspaper she co-owned. An infuriated white mob destroyed the press and threatened to lynch Wells. Forced to flee to the North, she remained in exile for the next forty years. Wells eventually settled in Chicago and married Ferdinand L. Barnett, a lawyer and publisher of the city's first black newspaper, the *Conservator*. She became a popular speaker and writer, helped found the NAACP, and published *Southern Horrors: Lynch Law and Mob Rule in New Orleans* and her autobiography, *Crusade for Justice*.

## Some Things Remain the Same

While much has been made of the Civil War's lasting impact, it should be pointed out that some things remained the same. Economically, it is somewhat surprising the war did not bring about any great changes in terms of new industries, technologies, or a shift in direction. Americans were already in the Industrial Revolution when the war began, so they generally continued

# EYEWITNESS

## Ida B. Wells-Barnett

*In 1899, Ida B. Wells-Barnett (1862–1931) helped send a Chicago detective to Georgia to investigate the lynching of nine African Americans. Prominent Atlanta newspapers had openly encouraged the murders and afterward reported on them in gruesome detail. When her investigation was completed, Wells-Barnett published her findings in a pamphlet that included the following introduction.*

CONSIDER THE FACTS

During six weeks of the months of March and April just past, twelve colored men were lynched in Georgia, the reign of outlawry culminating in the torture and hanging of the colored preacher, Elijah Strickland, and the burning alive of Samuel Wilkes, alias Hose, Sunday, April 23, 1899.

The real purpose of these savage demonstrations is to teach the Negro that in the South he has no rights that the laws will enforce. Samuel Hose was burned to teach the Negroes that no matter what a white man does to them, they must not resist. Hose, a servant, had killed Cranford, his employer. An example must be made.

Ordinary punishment was deemed inadequate. This Negro must be burned alive. To make the burning a certainty the charge of outrage [rape] was invented, and added to the charge of murder. The daily press offered reward for the capture of Hose and then openly incited the people to burn him as soon as caught. The mob carried out the plan in every savage detail. Of the twelve men lynched during that reign of unspeakable barbarism, only one was even charged with an assault upon a woman. Yet Southern apologists justify their savagery on the ground that Negroes are lynched only because of their crimes against women. The Southern press champions burning men alive, and says, "Consider the facts." The colored people join issue and also say, "Consider the fact." The colored people of Chicago employed a detective to go to Georgia, and his report in this pamphlet gives the facts. We give here the details of the lynching as they were reported in the Southern papers; then follows the report of the true facts as to the cause of the lynchings, as learned by the investigation. We submit all to the sober judgment of the Nation, confident that, in this cause, as well as all others, "Truth is might and will prevail."

*The pamphlet went on to describe all of the murders in great detail. Particularly gruesome were the newspaper accounts of the burning of Samuel Hose. The Atlanta* Constitution *reported that 2,000 people watched Hose be tied to a tree, mutilated with knives, and then burned alive. Afterward, his bones were taken away as souvenirs.*

Ida B. Wells-Barnett, "Lynch Law in Georgia" (Chicago: Chicago Colored Citizens, 1899).

what they had been doing, although on a greater scale. Some historians even argue the war hurt the economy. The terrible death toll (and the loss of future Americans that would have been fathered) slowed the nation's growth, and abolition caused the Southern states' contribution to the nation's wealth to drop from 30 percent in 1860 to just 12 percent in 1870. Postwar labor problems and a lack of capital also contributed to the decline in cotton production during Reconstruction; Southern planters did not reach their antebellum levels again until the 1870s.

The two-party system remained intact after Reconstruction, and there were no fundamental changes in politics. The Northern victory ensured that the Republicans remained strong in the North, and the failure of Reconstruction ensured that the Democrats controlled the South, which had been the case before the war. The greatest political change was the Southerners' loss of power within the federal government. No Southerner was elected president for fifty years after the war, only one was chosen Speaker of the House, none became president pro tempore of the Senate, and only five became Supreme Court justices. The Republicans were able to capitalize on the war and win votes by passing veterans' pensions and waving the bloody shirt. However, such tactics did not prevent the Democrats from having tremendous influence. Once the Redeemers regained power in the South and the African American vote was restricted, the two parties were almost evenly matched. In the four presidential elections between 1876 and 1888, the difference in popular votes was never more than 1 percent. The Democrats even regained control of the House before Reconstruction ended, and they returned to the White House in 1884. The Democrats also controlled the House more often than the Republicans over the next twenty years, although the Republicans controlled the Senate.

## The Long Shadow of War

In his 1861 inaugural address, Abraham Lincoln reminded the nation that all Americans were bound together by the "mystic cords of memory." Those words still ring true today, particularly in regard to the Civil War. No other event looms so large in our collective memory or has had such an effect on us physically and psychologically. The Civil War and Reconstruction settled the critical issues of secession, slavery, and citizenship, but they also left deep wounds that are still raw and angry and painful to the touch.

One reason the Civil War resonates so strongly with us today is because it is a recent event in our memory. The last Union veteran died in 1956 and the last Confederate in 1959. Incredibly, the last widow of a Union veteran died in 2003 and the last widow of a Confederate veteran in 2004. The war may have ended nearly 150 years ago, but many Americans today are only one generation removed from Appomattox, and family history is judged in terms of generations, not years. During their lifetime, today's middle-aged Americans will personally know relatives spanning four centuries. As youngsters, they frequently visited with family members who were born in the nineteenth century (and who personally knew Civil War veterans), and before they pass on they will have known relatives who will live into the twenty-second century. A family's collective memory is strong, and in that memory the guns have not been long silent. In our imagination, the ashes of Civil War campfires are still warm, and Rebel Yells and Yankee huzzahs still echo in the hills.

## FOR FURTHER READING

Ida B. Wells-Barnett, "Lynch Law in Georgia"

# Bibliography

This bibliography is divided into eight categories and contains many worthy studies. With so many Civil War books available, however, choosing what to include was a daunting task. Because it is virtually impossible to keep up with all of the new books being published each month, entries in this bibliography, with a few exceptions, are limited to those that were reviewed in the journal *Civil War History* through 2007. For some older works, reprinted editions are cited here. For a comprehensive Civil War bibliography, readers should consult *The American Civil War* Web site, at www.mhhe.com/jones1e.

## General Studies and Reference Sources

Beringer, Richard E., Herman Hattaway, Archer Jones, and William N. Still, Jr. *Why the South Lost the Civil War.* Athens: University of Georgia Press, 1986.

Commager, Henry Steele, ed. *The Blue and the Gray: The Story of the Civil War as Told by Participants.* 2 vols. Indianapolis: Bobbs-Merrill, 1950.

Cunningham, Sumner Archibald, and Edith D. Pope, eds. *Confederate Veteran.* 40 vols. Nashville, TN: S. A. Cunningham, 1893–1932.

Davis, William C. *LOOK AWAY! A History of the Confederate States of America.* New York: Free Press, 2002.

Donald, David H., ed. *Why the North Won the Civil War.* Baton Rouge: Louisiana State University Press, 1960.

Early, Jubal A., et al., eds. *The Southern Historical Society Papers.* 52 vols. Wilmington, NC, and Dayton, OH: Broadfoot and Morningside, 1990–1992.

Eicher, David J., comp. *The Civil War in Books: An Analytical Bibliography.* Foreword by Gary W. Gallagher. Champaign: University of Illinois Press, 1996.

Evans, Clement A., ed. *Confederate Military History: A Library of Confederate States History.* 19 vols. Wilmington, NC: Broadfoot, 1987–1989.

Foote, Shelby. *The Civil War: A Narrative.* 3 vols. New York: Vintage, 1986.

Gallagher, Gary W. *The Confederate War.* Cambridge, MA: Harvard University Press, 1997.

Gienapp, William E. *The Civil War and Reconstruction: A Documentary Collection.* New York: W. W. Norton, 2001.

Griffith, Paddy. *Battle Tactics of the Civil War.* New Haven, CT: Yale University Press, 1989.

Hattaway, Herman. *Shades of Blue and Gray: An Introductory Military History of the Civil War.* Columbia: University of Missouri Press, 1997.

Hattaway, Herman, and Archer Jones. *How the North Won: A Military History of the Civil War.* Urbana: University of Illinois Press, 1983.

Johnson, Robert Underwood, and Clarence Clough Buel, eds. *Battles and Leaders of the Civil War.* 8 vols. Harrisonburg, PA: Archive Society, 1991.

McPherson, James M. *Battle Cry of Freedom: The Civil War Era.* New York: Oxford University Press, 1988.

Military Order of the Loyal Legion of the United States. *Papers of the Military Order of the Loyal Legion of the United States, 1887–1915.* Wilmington, NC: Broadfoot, 1991–1996.

Miller, Francis Trevelyan, ed. *The Photographic History of the Civil War.* 5 vols. Secaucus, NJ: Blue and Grey, 1987.

Moore, Frank, ed. *The Rebellion Record: A Diary of American Events, with Documents, Narratives, Illustrative Incidents, Poetry, etc.* 11 vols. New York: G. P. Putnam's Sons, 1861–1868.

Nevins, Allan. *Ordeal of the Union.* 8 vols. New York: Charles Scribner's Sons, 1947–1971.

Nevins, Allan, James I. Robertson, Jr., and Bell I. Wiley, eds. *Civil War Books: A Critical Bibliography.* 2 vols. Baton Rouge: Louisiana State University Press, 1967–1969.

Randall, James G., and David H. Donald. *The Civil War and Reconstruction.* 2nd ed. Boston: D. C. Heath, 1969.

Roland, Charles P. *An American Iliad: The Story of the Civil War.* Lexington: University Press of Kentucky, 1991.

Stampp, Kenneth M. *And the War Came: The North and the Secession Crisis, 1860–1861.* Baton Rouge: Louisiana State University Press, 1970.

U.S. War Department. *Official Records of the Union and Confederate Navies in the War of the Rebellion.* 30 vols. Washington, DC: U.S. Government, 1895–1921.

———. *The War of the Rebellion: A Compilation of the Official Records of the Union and Confederate Armies.* 128 vols. Washington, DC: U.S. Government Printing Office, 1880–1901.

## Military Studies

Ballard, Michael B. *Vicksburg: The Campaign That Opened the Mississippi.* Chapel Hill: University of North Carolina Press, 2004.

Bennett, Michael J. *Union Jacks: Yankee Sailors in the Civil War.* Chapel Hill: University of North Carolina Press, 2004.

Castel, Albert. *Decision in the West: The Atlanta Campaign of 1864.* Lawrence: University Press of Kansas, 1992.

Catton, Bruce. *The Army of the Potomac.* 3 vols. *Mr. Lincoln's Army, Glory Road,* and *A Stillness at Appomattox.* Garden City, NY: Doubleday, 1951–1953.

Coddington, Edwin B. *The Gettysburg Campaign: A Study in Command.* New York: Scribner's, 1984.

Connelly, Thomas Lawrence. *Army of the Heartland: The Army of Tennessee, 1861–1862.* Baton Rouge: Louisiana State University Press, 1967.

———. *Autumn of Glory: The Army of Tennessee, 1862–1865.* Baton Rouge: Louisiana State University Press, 1971.

Current, Richard Nelson. *Lincoln's Loyalists: Union Soldiers from the Confederacy.* Boston: Northeastern University Press, 1992.

Engle, Stephen D. *Struggle for the Heartland: The Campaigns from Fort Henry to Corinth.* Lincoln: University of Nebraska Press, 2001.

Fellman, Michael. *Inside War: The Guerrilla Conflict in Missouri During the American Civil War.* New York: Oxford University Press, 1989.

Freeman, Douglas Southall. *Lee's Lieutenants: A Study in Command.* 3 vols. New York: Charles Scribner's Sons, 1942–1944.

Geary, James W. *We Need More Men: The Union Draft in the Civil War.* DeKalb: Northern Illinois University Press, 1991.

Glatthaar, Joseph T. *The March to the Sea and Beyond: Sherman's Troops in the Savannah and Carolinas Campaigns.* New York: New York University Press, 1985.

Gosnell, H. Allen. *Guns on the Western Waters: The Story of the River Gunboats in the Civil War.* Baton Rouge: Louisiana State University Press, 1993.

Grimsley, Mark. *The Hard Hand of War: Union Military Policy Toward Southern Civilians, 1861–1865.* New York: Cambridge University Press, 1995.

Hennessy, John J. *Return to Bull Run: The Campaign and Battle of Second Manassas.* New York: Simon and Schuster, 1993.

Hess, Earl J. *Banners to the Breeze: The Kentucky Campaign, Corinth, and Stone's River.* Lincoln: University of Nebraska Press, 2000.

Hewitt, Lawrence L. *Port Hudson: Confederate Bastion on the Mississippi.* Baton Rouge: Louisiana State University Press, 1987.

Joiner, Gary Dillard. *Through the Howling Wilderness: The 1864 Red River Campaign and Union Failure in the West.* Knoxville: University of Tennessee Press, 2006.

Jones, Terry L. *Lee's Tigers: The Louisiana Infantry in the Army of Northern Virginia.* Baton Rouge: Louisiana State University Press, 1987.

Linderman, Gerald F. *Embattled Courage: The Experience of Combat in the American Civil War.* New York: Free Press, 1987.

Luraghi, Raimondo. *A History of the Confederate Navy.* Translated by Paolo E. Coletta. Annapolis, MD: Naval Institute Press, 1996.

Marvel, William. *Andersonville: The Last Depot.* Chapel Hill: University of North Carolina Press, 1994.

———. *Lee's Last Retreat: The Flight to Appomattox.* Chapel Hill: University of North Carolina Press, 2002.

McPherson, James M. *Crossroads of Freedom: Antietam, the Battle that Changed the Course of the Civil War.* New York: Oxford University Press, 2002.

———. *For Cause and Comrades: Why Men Fought in the Civil War.* New York: Oxford University Press, 1997.

Nolan, Alan. *The Iron Brigade: A Military History.* Introduction by Gary W. Gallagher. Bloomington: Indiana University Press, 1994.

Reardon, Carol. *Pickett's Charge in History and Memory.* Chapel Hill: University of North Carolina Press, 1997.

Rhea, Gordon C. *The Battle of the Wilderness, May 5–6, 1864.* Baton Rouge: Louisiana State University Press, 1994.

———. *The Battles for Spotsylvania Court House and the Road to Yellow Tavern, May 7–12, 1864.* Baton Rouge: Louisiana State University Press, 1997.

Robertson, James I., Jr. *The Stonewall Brigade.* Baton Rouge: Louisiana State University Press, 1987.

Robinson, Charles M., III. *Shark of the Confederacy: The Story of the CSS Alabama.* Annapolis, MD: Naval Institute Press, 1995.

Sanders, Charles W., Jr. *While in the Hands of the Enemy: Military Prisons of the Civil War.* Baton Rouge: Louisiana State University Press, 2005.

Sears, Stephen W. *To the Gates of Richmond: The Peninsula Campaign.* New York: Ticknor and Fields, 1992.

Sutherland, Daniel E. *Fredericksburg and Chancellorsville: The Dare Mark Campaign.* Great Campaigns of the Civil War, edited by Anne J. Bailey and Brooks D. Simpson. Lincoln: University of Nebraska Press, 1998.

Sword, Wiley. *Embrace an Angry Wind: The Confederacy's Last Hurrah—Spring Hill, Franklin, and Nashville.* New York: HarperCollins, 1992.

———. *Shiloh: Bloody April.* Dayton, OH: Morningside, 1993.

Tanner, Robert G. *Stonewall in the Valley: Thomas J. "Stonewall" Jackson's Shenandoah Valley Campaign, Spring 1862.* Garden City, NY: Doubleday, 1976.

Trudeau, Noah Andre. *The Last Citadel: Petersburg, Virginia, June 1864–April 1865.* Boston: Little, Brown, 1991.

Walker, Peter F. *Vicksburg: A People at War.* Wilmington, NC: Broadfoot, 1987.

Wert, Jeffry D. *From Winchester to Cedar Creek: The Shenandoah Campaign of 1864.* Carlisle, PA: South Mountain Press, 1987.

———. *Mosby's Rangers.* New York: Simon and Schuster, 1990.

Wiley, Bell Irvin. *The Life of Billy Yank: The Common Soldier of the Union.* Baton Rouge: Louisiana State University Press, 1993.

———. *The Life of Johnny Reb: The Common Soldier of the Confederacy.* Baton Rouge: Louisiana State University Press, 1993.

Wise, Stephen R. *Lifeline of the Confederacy: Blockade Running During the Civil War.* Columbia: University of South Carolina Press, 1988.

Woodworth, Steven E. *Six Armies in Tennessee: The Chickamauga and Chattanooga Campaigns.* Lincoln: University of Nebraska Press, 1998.

## Biographies and Personal Narratives

Alcott, Louisa May. *Hospital Sketches.* Boston: James Redpath, 1863.

Alexander, Edward Porter. *Fighting for the Confederacy: The Personal Recollections of General Edward Porter Alexander.* Edited by Gary Gallagher. Chapel Hill: University of North Carolina Press, 1989.

Ambrose, Stephen E. *Halleck: Lincoln's Chief of Staff.* Baton Rouge: Louisiana State University Press, 1993.

Andrews, Eliza Frances. *The War–Time Journal of a Georgia Girl, 1864–1865.* New York: D. Appleton, 1908.

Basler, Roy P., ed. *The Collected Works of Abraham Lincoln,* 8 vols. New Brunswick, NJ: Rutgers University Press, 1953.

Billings, John D. *Hardtack and Coffee: Or, The Unwritten Story of Army Life.* Edited by Richard Harwell. Chicago: Lakeside Press, 1960.

Casler, John O. *Four Years in the Stonewall Brigade.* Notes by James I. Robertson, Jr. Dayton, OH: Morningside, 1982.

Castel, Albert. *William Clarke Quantrill: His Life and Times.* New York: Frederick Fell, 1962.

Chamberlain, Joshua Lawrence. *The Passing of the Armies: An Account of the Final Campaign of the Army of the Potomac, Based on Personal Reminiscences of the Fifth Army Corps.* Foreword by John J. Pullen. Dayton, OH: Morningside, 1986.

Chase, Salmon P. *Inside Lincoln's Cabinet: The Civil War Diaries of Salmon P. Chase.* Edited by David H. Donald. New York: Longmans, Green, 1954.

Chesnut, Mary. *Mary Chesnut's Civil War.* Edited by C. Vann Woodward. New Haven, CT: Yale University Press, 1981.

Connelly, Thomas Lawrence. *The Marble Man: Robert E. Lee and His Image in American Society.* Baton Rouge: Louisiana State University Press, 1991.

Coulter, E. Merton. *William G. Brownlow: Fighting Parson of the Southern Highlands.* Introduction by James W. Patton. Knoxville: University of Tennessee Press, 1971.

Crist, Lynda Laswell, Kenneth H. Williams, and Peggy L. Dillard, eds. *The Papers of Jefferson Davis.* Volume 10, *October 1863–August 1864.* Baton Rouge: Louisiana State University Press, 1999.

Davis, Jefferson. *The Papers of Jefferson Davis.* Edited by Haskell M. Monroe, James T. McIntosh, Lynda Lasswell Crist, Mary Seaton Dix, and Kenneth H. Williams. 12 vols. Baton Rouge: Louisiana State University Press, 1971–.

———. *The Rise and Fall of the Confederate Government.* 2 vols. Introduction by James M. McPherson. New York: Da Capo Press, 1990.

Davis, William C. *Jefferson Davis: The Man and His Hour.* New York: HarperCollins, 1991.

Dawes, Rufus R. *Service with the Sixth Wisconsin Volunteers.* Introduction by Gregory Coco. Dayton, OH: Morningside, 1984.

Dew, Charles B. *Apostles of Disunion: Southern Secession Commissioners and the Causes of the Civil War.* Charlottesville: University of Virginia Press, 2001.

Donald, David. *Charles Sumner and the Rights of Man.* New York: Alfred A. Knopf, 1970.

———. *Lincoln.* New York: Simon and Schuster, 1995.

Douglas, Henry Kyd. *I Rode with Stonewall.* Chapel Hill: University of North Carolina Press, 1987.

Early, Jubal A. *Jubal Early's Memoirs: Autobiographical Sketch and Narrative of the War Between the States.* Introduction by Craig L. Symonds. Baltimore: Nautical and Aviation Publishing, 1989.

Freeman, Douglas Southall. *R. E. Lee: A Biography.* 4 vols. New York: Charles Scribner's Sons, 1934–1935.

Fremantle, Arthur J. L. *The Fremantle Diary: Being the Journal of Lieutenant Colonel James Arthur Lyon Fremantle, Coldstream Guards, on His Three Months in the Southern States.* Edited by Walter Lord. Boston: Little, Brown, 1954.

Gienapp, William E., ed. *This Fiery Trial: The Speeches and Writings of Abraham Lincoln.* Oxford: Oxford University Press, 2002.

Goodwin, Doris Kearns. *Team of Rivals: The Political Genius of Abraham Lincoln.* New York: Simon and Schuster, 2005.

Gordon, John B. *Reminiscences of the Civil War.* Introduction by Ralph Lowell Eckert. Baton Rouge: Louisiana State University Press, 1993.

Grant, Ulysses S. *Personal Memoirs of U. S. Grant.* 2 vols. Introduction by William S. McFeely. New York: Da Capo Press, 1982.

———. *The Papers of Ulysses S. Grant.* Edited by John Y. Simon, David L. Wilson, J. Thomas Murphy, et al. 20 vols. Carbondale: Southern Illinois University Press, 1967–1995.

Hallock, Judith Lee. *Braxton Bragg and Confederate Defeat.* Vol. 2. Tuscaloosa: University of Alabama Press, 1991.

Hay, John. *Inside Lincoln's White House: The Complete Civil War Diary of John Hay.* Edited by Michael Burlingame, with John R. Turner Ettlinger. Carbondale: Southern Illinois University Press, 1997.

Haynes, Captain Dennis E. *A Thrilling Narrative: The Memoir of a Southern Unionist.* Edited by Arthur W. Bergeron, Jr. Fayetteville: University of Arkansas Press, 2006.

Holmes, Oliver Wendell, Jr. *Touched with Fire: Civil War Letters and Diary of Oliver Wendell Holmes, Jr., 1861–1864.* Edited by Mark DeWolfe Howe. New York: Da Capo Press, 1969.

Hood, John Bell. *Advance and Retreat: Personal Experiences in the United States and Confederate States Armies.* Introduction by Richard M. McMurry. New York: Da Capo Press, 1993.

Howard, Oliver Otis. *Autobiography of Oliver Otis Howard.* 2 vols. Salem, NH: Ayer, n.d.

Jacobs, Harriet A. *Incidents in the Life of a Slave Girl: Written by Herself.* West Berlin, NJ: Townsend Press, 2004.

Johnston, Joseph E. *Narrative of Military Operations, Directed, During the Late War Between the States, by Joseph E. Johnston, General, C.S.A.* Introduction by Frank E. Vandiver. Millwood, NY: Kraus Reprints, 1990.

Jones, John B. *A Rebel War Clerk's Diary at the Confederate State Capital.* Baton Rouge: Louisiana State University Press, 1993.

Jones, Terry L., ed. *Campbell Brown's Civil War: With Ewell and the Army of Northern Virginia.* Baton Rouge: Louisiana State University Press, 2001.

Klement, Frank L. *The Limits of Dissent: Clement L. Vallandigham and the Civil War.* Bronx, NY: Fordham University Press, 1998.

Lincoln, Abraham. *The Collected Works of Abraham Lincoln.* Edited by Roy P. Basler. 11 vols. New Brunswick, NJ: Rutgers University Press, 1953–1955.

Longstreet, James. *From Manassas to Appomattox: Memoirs of the Civil War in America.* Introduction by Jeffry D. Wert. New York: Da Capo Press, 1992.

Marszalek, John F. *Sherman: A Soldier's Passion for Order.* New York: Free Press, 1993.

McClellan, George B. *The Civil War Papers of George B. McClellan: Selected Correspondence, 1860–1865.* Edited by Stephen W. Sears. New York: Da Capo Press, 1992.

McClellan, H. B. *I Rode with Jeb Stuart.* Edited by Burke Davis. New York: Da Capo Press, 1994.

McFeely, William S. *Grant: A Biography.* New York: W. W. Norton, 1981.

McKinney, Gordon B. *Zeb Vance: North Carolina's Civil War Governor and Gilded Age Political Leader.* Chapel Hill: University of North Carolina Press, 2004.

McMurry, Richard M. *John Bell Hood and the War for Southern Independence.* Lincoln: University of Nebraska Press, 1992.

McWhiney, Grady. *Braxton Bragg and Confederate Defeat, Vol. 1: Field Command.* Tuscaloosa: University Press of Alabama, 1991.

Meade, Robert Douthat. *Judah P. Benjamin: Confederate Statesman.* New York: Arno Press, 1975.

Morris, Roy, Jr. *Sheridan: The Life and Wars of General Phil Sheridan.* New York: Crown, 1992.

Neely, Mark E., Jr. *The Fate of Liberty: Abraham Lincoln and Civil Liberties.* New York: Oxford University Press, 1991.

Niven, John. *Salmon P. Chase: A Biography.* New York: Oxford University Press, 1995.

Oates, Stephen B. *To Purge This Land with Blood: A Biography of John Brown.* New York: Harper and Row, 1970.

Parks, Joseph H. *Joseph E. Brown of Georgia.* Baton Rouge: Louisiana State University Press, 1977.

Pfanz, Donald C. *Richard S. Ewell: A Soldier's Life.* Chapel Hill: University of North Carolina Press, 1998.

Pinkerton, Allan. *The Spy of the Rebellion.* Introduction by Patrick Bass. Lincoln: University of Nebraska Press, 1989.

Porter, David Dixon. *Incidents and Anecdotes of the Civil War.* New York: D. Appleton, 1885.

Porter, Horace. *Campaigning with Grant.* Edited by Wayne C. Temple. Bloomington: Indiana University Press, 1961.

Rhodes, Elisha Hunt. *All for the Union: The Civil War Diary and Letters of Elisha Hunt Rhodes.* Edited by Robert Hunt Rhodes. New York: Orion Books, 1991.

Robertson, James I., Jr. *Stonewall Jackson: The Man, the Soldier, the Legend.* New York: Macmillan, 1997.

Russell, William Howard. *My Diary North and South.* 2 vols. London: Bradbury and Evans, 1863.

Schott, Thomas E. *Alexander H. Stephens of Georgia: A Biography.* Baton Rouge: Louisiana State University Press, 1988.

Schurz, Carl. *The Reminiscences of Carl Schurz.* 3 vols. New York: McClure, 1907–1908.

Sears, Stephen W. *George B. McClellan: The Young Napoleon.* New York: Ticknor and Fields, 1988.

Semmes, Raphael. *Memoirs of Service Afloat, During the War between the States.* Edited by Philip Van Doren Stern. Bloomington: Indiana University Press, 1962.

Seymour, William J. *The Civil War Memoirs of Capt. William J. Seymour: Reminiscences of a Louisiana Tiger.* Edited by Terry L. Jones. Baton Rouge: Louisiana State University Press, 1991.

Sheridan, Philip H. *Personal Memoirs of P. H. Sheridan.* 2 vols. Introduction by Jeffry D. Wert. New York: Da Capo Press, 1992.

Sherman, William Tecumseh. *Memoirs of General W. T. Sherman: Written by Himself.* 2 vols. Introduction by B. H. Liddell. Bloomington: Indiana University Press, 1957.

Simpson, Brooks D. *Ulysses S. Grant: Triumph Over Adversity, 1822–1865.* New York: Houghton Mifflin, 2000.

Skoch, George, and Mark W. Perkins, eds. *Lone Star Confederate: A Gallant and Good Soldier of the Fifth Texas Infantry.* College Station: Texas A&M University Press, 2003.

Stephens, Alexander H. *A Constitutional View of the Late War Between the States: Its Causes, Character, and Results.* 2 vols. Harrisonburg, VA: Sprinkle Publications, 1994.

Stiles, Robert. *Four Years Under Marse Robert.* Introduction by Robert K. Krick. Dayton, OH: Morningside, 1988.

Stone, Sarah Katherine Holmes. *Brokenburn: The Journal of Kate Stone, 1861–1868.* Edited by John Q. Anderson. Baton Rouge: Louisiana State University Press, 1972.

Symonds, Craig L. *Joseph E. Johnston: A Civil War Biography.* New York: W. W. Norton, 1992.

———. *Stonewall of the West: Patrick Cleburne and the Civil War.* Lawrence: University Press of Kansas, 1997.

Taylor, John M. *William Henry Seward: Lincoln's Right Hand.* New York: HarperCollins, 1991.

Taylor, Richard. *Destruction and Reconstruction: Personal Experiences in the Late War.* Introduction by T. Michael Parrish. New York: Da Capo Press, 1995.

Thomas, Benjamin P., and Harold M. Hyman. *Stanton: The Life and Times of Lincoln's Secretary of War.* New York: Alfred A. Knopf, 1962.

Thomas, Emory M. *Bold Dragoon: The Life of J. E. B. Stuart.* New York: Harper and Row, 1986.

———. *Robert E. Lee: A Biography.* New York: W. W. Norton, 1995.

Thomas, John L. *The Liberator: William Lloyd Garrison.* Boston: Little, Brown, 1963.

Trefousse, Hans L. *Andrew Johnson: A Biography.* New York: W. W. Norton, 1989.

———. *Thaddeus Stevens: Nineteenth-Century Egalitarian.* Chapel Hill: University of North Carolina Press, 1997.

Tunnard, William H. *A Southern Record: The History of the Third Regiment, Louisiana Infantry.* Introduction by William L. Shea. Fayetteville: University of Arkansas Press, 1997.

Van Deusen, Glyndon G. *Horace Greeley: Nineteenth-Century Crusader.* Philadelphia: University of Pennsylvania Press, 1953.

Vandiver, Frank E. *Ploughshares into Swords: Josiah Gorgas and Confederate Ordnance.* College Station: Texas A&M University Press, 1994.

Varon, Elizabeth. *Southern Lady, Yankee Spy: The True Story of Elizabeth Van Lew, A Union Agent in the Heart of the Confederacy.* New York: Oxford University Press, 2003.

Watkins, Sam. *"Co. Aytch," Maury Grays, First Tennessee Regiment; or, a Side Show of the Big Show.* New York: Simon and Schuster, 1997.

Welles, Gideon. *The Diary of Gideon Welles.* 3 vols. Edited by Howard K. Beale. New York: W. W. Norton, 1960.

Wert, Jeffry D. *Custer: The Controversial Life of George Armstrong Custer.* New York: Simon and Schuster, 1996.

———. *General James Longstreet, the Confederacy's Most Controversial Soldier: A Biography.* New York: Simon and Schuster, 1993.

White, Laura A. *Robert Barnwell Rhett: Father of Secession.* New York: Century, 1931.

Williams, T. Harry. *Lincoln and His Generals.* New York: Alfred A. Knopf, 1952.

Wills, Brian Steel. *A Battle from the Start: The Life of Nathan Bedford Forrest.* New York: HarperCollins, 1992.

## Political, Economic, and Diplomatic Studies

Blackett, R. J. M. *Divided Hearts: Britain and the American Civil War.* Baton Rouge: Louisiana State University Press, 2000.

Case, Lynn M., and Warren F. Spencer. *The United States and France: Civil War Diplomacy.* Philadelphia: University of Pennsylvania Press, 1970.

Clark, John E., Jr. *Railroads in the Civil War: The Impact of Management on Victory and Defeat.* Baton Rouge: Louisiana State University Press, 2001.

Davis, William C. *"A Government of Our Own": The Making of the Confederacy.* New York: Free Press, 1994.

DeRosa, Marshall L. *The Confederate Constitution of 1861: An Inquiry into American Constitutionalism.* Columbia: University of Missouri Press, 1991.

Faust, Drew Gilpin. *The Creation of Confederate Nationalism: Ideology and Identity in the Civil War South.* Baton Rouge: Louisiana State University Press, 1988.

Hubbard, Charles M. *The Burden of Confederate Diplomacy.* Knoxville: University of Tennessee Press, 1998.

Klement, Frank L. *Dark Lanterns: Secret Political Societies, Conspiracies, and Treason Trials in the Civil War.* Baton Rouge: Louisiana State University Press, 1984.

———. *Lincoln's Critics: The Copperheads of the North.* Shippensburg, PA: White Mane, 1999.

Neely, Mark E., Jr. *Southern Rights: Political Prisoners and the Myth of Confederate Constitutionalism.* Charlottesville: University Press of Virginia, 1999.

Oberholtzer, Ellis Paxson. *Jay Cooke: Financier of the Civil War*. 2 vols. New York: Augustus M. Kelly, 1968.

Owsley, Frank Lawrence. *King Cotton Diplomacy: Foreign Relations and the Confederate States of America*. Edited by Harriet Chappell Owsley. Chicago: University of Chicago Press, 1959.

———. *State Rights in the Confederacy*. New York: Peter Smith, 1961.

Randall, James G. *Constitutional Problems Under Lincoln*. Urbana: University of Illinois Press, 1996.

Richardson, Heather Cox. *The Greatest Nation of the Earth: Republican Economic Policies During the Civil War*. Cambridge, MA: Harvard University Press, 1997.

Sibley, Joel H. *A Respectable Minority: The Democratic Party in the Civil War Era, 1860–1868*. New York: W. W. Norton, 1977.

Tap, Bruce. *Over Lincoln's Shoulder: The Committee on the Conduct of the War*. Lawrence: University Press of Kansas, 1998.

Thomas, Emory M. *The Confederacy as a Revolutionary Experience*. Columbia: University of South Carolina Press, 1987.

U.S. Congress. *Congressional Record*. Washington, DC: U.S. Government Printing Office, 1873–1877.

U.S. Congress. *Joint Committee on the Conduct of the War. Report*. Washington, DC: U.S. Government Printing Office, 1863.

U.S. Congress. *The Congressional Globe*. Washington, DC: Congressional Globe, 1834–1873.

U.S. State Department. *Foreign Relations of the United States: Diplomatic Papers*. Washington, DC: U.S. Government Printing Office, 1861–1876.

Wilson, Harold S. *Confederate Industry: Manufacturers and Quartermasters in the Civil War*. Jackson: University Press of Mississippi, 2002.

## African American, Women's, and Ethnic Studies

Abel, Annie Heloise. *The American Indian in the Civil War*. 3 vols. Introductions by Theda Perdue and Michael D. Green. Lincoln: University of Nebraska Press, 1993.

Attie, Jeanie. *Patriotic Toil: Northern Women and the American Civil War*. Ithaca, NY: Cornell University Press, 1998.

Berlin, Ira, et al. *Free at Last: A Documentary History of Slavery, Freedom, and the Civil War*. New York: New Press, 1992.

Blanton, DeAnne, and Lauren M. Cook. *They Fought Like Demons: Women Soldiers in the American Civil War*. Baton Rouge: Louisiana State University Press, 2002.

Bordwich, Fergus M. *Bound for Canaan: The Underground Railroad and the War for the Soul of America*. New York: Amistad, 2005.

Burton, William L. *Melting Pot Soldiers: The Union's Ethnic Regiments*. Ames: Iowa State University Press, 1988.

Campbell, Edward D. C., Jr., and Kym S. Rice, eds. *A Woman's War: Southern Women, Civil War and the Confederate Legacy*. Richmond: Museum of the Confederacy and Charlottesville: University Press of Virginia, 1997.

Chesnut, Mary. *Mary Chesnut's Civil War*. Edited by C. Vann Woodward. New Haven, CT: Yale University Press, 1981.

Clark, Kathleen Ann. *Defining Moments: African American Commemoration and Political Culture in the South, 1863–1913*. Chapel Hill: University of North Carolina Press, 2005.

Clinton, Catherine, and Nina Silber, eds. *Divided Houses: Gender and the Civil War.* New York: Oxford University Press, 1992.

Cornish, Dudley Taylor. *The Sable Arm: Negro Troops in the Union Army, 1861–1865.* Foreword by Herman Hattaway. Lawrence: University Press of Kansas, 1987.

Cumming, Kate. *Kate: The Journal of a Confederate Nurse.* Edited by Richard Barksdale Harwell. Baton Rouge: Louisiana State University Press, 1959.

Daniels, Nathan W. *Thank God My Regiment an African One: The Civil War Diary of Colonel Nathan W. Daniels.* Edited by C. P. Weaver. Baton Rouge: Louisiana State University Press, 1998.

Dawson, Sarah Morgan. *Sarah Morgan: The Civil War Diary of a Southern Woman.* Edited by Charles East. New York: Touchstone, 1992.

Durden, Robert F. *The Gray and the Black: The Confederate Debate on Emancipation.* Baton Rouge: Louisiana State University Press, 1972.

Edwards, Laura F. *Scarlet Doesn't Live Here Anymore: Southern Women in the Civil War Era.* Urbana: University of Illinois Press, 2000.

Emilio, Luis F. *A Brave Black Regiment: The History of the Fifty-fourth Regiment of Massachusetts Volunteer Infantry, 1863–1865.* Introduction by Gregory J. W. Urwin. New York: Da Capo Press, 1995.

Faust, Drew Gilpin. *Mothers of Invention: Women of the Slaveholding South in the American Civil War.* Chapel Hill: University of North Carolina Press, 1996.

Giesberg, Judith Ann. *Civil War Sisterhood: The U.S. Sanitary Commission and Women's Politics in Transition.* Boston: Northeastern University Press, 2000.

Glatthaar, Joseph T. *Forged in Battle: The Civil War Alliance of Black Soldiers and White Officers.* New York: Free Press, 1990.

Gooding, James Henry. *On the Altar of Freedom: A Black Soldier's Civil War Letters from the Front.* Edited by Virginia M. Adams. Amherst: University of Massachusetts Press, 1991.

Higginson, Thomas Wentworth. *Army Life in a Black Regiment.* Introduction by Howard Mumford Jones. East Lansing: Michigan State University Press, 1960.

Humez, Jean M. *Harriet Tubman: The Life and the Life Stories.* Madison: University of Wisconsin Press, 2003.

Leonard, Elizabeth D. *All the Daring of a Soldier: Women of the Civil War Armies.* New York: W. W. Norton, 1999.

Litwack, Leon F. *Been in the Storm So Long: The Aftermath of Slavery.* New York: Alfred A. Knopf, 1979.

Livermore, Mary A. *My Story of the War: The Civil War Memoirs of the Famous Nurse, Relief Organizer, and Suffragette.* Introduction by Nina Silber. New York: Da Capo Press, 1995.

Lonn, Ella. *Foreigners in the Confederacy.* New York: Peter Smith, n.d.

———. *Foreigners in the Union Army and Navy.* New York: Greenwood Press, 1979.

Massey, Mary Elizabeth. *Women in the Civil War.* Introduction by Jean V. Berlin. Lincoln: University of Nebraska Press, 1994.

McFeely, William S. *Frederick Douglass.* New York: W. W. Norton, 1991.

Oates, Stephen B. *A Woman of Valor: Clara Barton and the Civil War.* New York: Free Press, 1994.

Pember, Phoebe Yates. *A Southern Woman's Story: Life in Confederate Richmond.* Edited by Bell I. Wiley. Jackson, TN: McCowat-Mercer Press, 1959.

Ramold, Steven J. *Slaves, Sailors, Citizens: African Americans in the Union Navy.* DeKalb: Northern Illinois University Press, 2002.

Rose, Willie Lee. *Rehearsal for Reconstruction: The Port Royal Experiment.* New York: Oxford University Press, 1976.

Rosen, Robert N. *The Jewish Confederates.* Columbia: University of South Carolina Press, 2000.

Shaffer, Donald R. *After the Glory: The Struggles of Black Civil War Veterans.* Lawrence: University Press of Kansas, 2004.

Silber, Nina. *Daughters of the Union: Northern Women Fight the Civil War.* Cambridge: Harvard University Press, 2005.

Solomon, Clara. *The Civil War Diary of Clara Solomon: Growing Up in New Orleans, 1861–1862.* Baton Rouge: Louisiana State University Press, 1995.

Stone, Sarah Katherine Holmes. *Brokenburn: The Journal of Kate Stone, 1861–1868.* Edited by John Q. Anderson. Baton Rouge: Louisiana State University Press, 1972.

Wells-Barnett, Ida B. *Crusade for Justice: The Autobiography of Ida B. Wells.* Edited by Alfreda M. Duster. Chicago: University of Chicago Press, 1970.

Williams, George Washington. *A History of the Negro Troops in the War of the Rebellion, 1861–1865.* New York: Harper and Brothers, 1888.

Wilson, Joseph T. *The Black Phalanx: A History of the Negro Soldiers of the United States in the Wars of 1775–1812, 1861–'65.* Hartford: American Publishing, 1892.

## Miscellaneous Topics

Ash, Stephen V. *When the Yankees Came: Conflict and Chaos in the Occupied South, 1861–1865.* Chapel Hill: University of North Carolina Press, 1995.

Bernstein, Iver. *The New York City Draft Riots: Their Significance for American Society and Politics in the Age of the Civil War.* New York: Oxford University Press, 1990.

Blair, William A. *Cities of the Dead: Contesting the Memory of the Civil War in the South, 1865–1914.* Chapel Hill: University of North Carolina Press, 2004.

Blight, David W. *Race and Reunion: The Civil War in American Memory.* Cambridge, MA: Belknap Press of Harvard University Press, 2001.

Blum, Edward J. *Reforging the White Republic: Race, Religion, and American Nationalism, 1865–1898.* Baton Rouge: Louisiana State University Press, 2005.

Bollet, Alfred Jay. *Civil War Medicine: Challenges and Triumphs.* Tucson: Galen Press, 2002.

Brinsfield, John W., William C. Davis, Benedict Maryniak, and James I. Robertson, eds. *Faith in the Fight: Civil War Chaplains.* Mechanicsburg, PA: Stackpole Books, 2003.

Bulloch, James D. *The Secret Service of the Confederate States in Europe; Or, How the Confederate Cruisers Were Equipped.* 2 vols. Introduction by Philip Van Doren Stern. New York: Burt Franklin, 1972.

Cashin, Joan E., ed. *The War Was You and Me: Civilians in the American Civil War.* Princeton, NJ: Princeton University Press, 2003.

Clinton, Catherine, ed. *Southern Families at War: Loyalty and Conflict in the Civil War.* New York: Oxford University Press, 2000.

Connelly, Thomas L., and Barbara L. Bellows. *God and General Longstreet: The Lost Cause and the Southern Mind.* Baton Rouge: Louisiana State University Press, 1982.

Coski, John M. *The Confederate Battle Flag: America's Most Embattled Emblem.* Cambridge: Harvard University Press, 2005.

Cullen, Jim. *The Civil War in Popular Culture: A Reusable Past.* Herndon, VA: Smithsonian Institution Press, 1995.

Davis, William C. *The Lost Cause: Myths and Realities of the Confederacy.* Lawrence: University Press of Kansas, 1996.

Dawsey, Cyrus B., and James Dawsey, eds. *The Confederados: Old South Immigrants in Brazil.* Foreword by Michael Coniff. Tuscaloosa: University of Alabama Press, 1995.

Dean, Eric T. *Shook Over Hell: Post-Traumatic Stress, Vietnam, and the Civil War.* Cambridge, MA: Harvard University Press, 1997.

Fahs, Alice. *The Imagined Civil War: Popular Literature of the North & South, 1861–1865.* Chapel Hill: University of North Carolina Press, 2001.

Fahs, Alice, and Joan Waugh, eds. *The Memory of the Civil War in American Culture.* Chapel Hill: University of North Carolina Press, 2004.

Feis, William B. *Grant's Secret Service: The Intelligence War from Belmont to Appomattox.* Lincoln: University of Nebraska Press, 2002.

Foster, Gaines M. *Ghosts of the Confederacy: Defeat, the Lost Cause, and the Emergence of the New South, 1865 to 1913.* New York: Oxford University Press, 1987.

Freehling, William W. *The South vs. the South: How Anti-Confederate Southerners Shaped the Course of the Civil War.* New York: Oxford University Press, 2001.

Gallagher, Gary W., and Alan T. Nolan, eds. *The Myth of the Lost Cause and Civil War History.* Bloomington: Indiana University Press, 2000.

Gallman, J. Matthew. *The North Fights the Civil War: The Home Front.* Chicago: Ivan R. Dee, 1994.

Goldfield, David. *Still Fighting the Civil War: The American South and Southern History.* Baton Rouge: Louisiana State University Press, 2002.

Grant, Susan-Mary, and Peter J. Parish, eds. *Legacy of Disunion: The Enduring Legacy of the American Civil War.* Baton Rouge: Louisiana State University Press, 2003.

Hanchett, William. *The Lincoln Murder Conspiracies.* Urbana: University of Illinois Press, 1983.

Harwell, Richard B. *Confederate Music.* Chapel Hill: University of North Carolina Press, 1950.

Holzer, Harold, and Mark E. Neely, Jr. *Mine Eyes Have Seen the Glory: The Civil War in Art.* New York: Orion Books, 1993.

Horowitz, Tony. *Confederates in the Attic: Dispatches from the Unfinished Civil War.* New York: Pantheon Books, 1998.

Jimerson, Randall C. *The Private Civil War: Popular Thought During the Sectional Conflict.* Baton Rouge: Louisiana State University Press, 1988.

Jones, J. William. *Christ in the Camp; Or, Religion in Lee's Army.* Harrisonburg, VA: Sprinkle Publications, 1986.

Letterman, Jonathan. *Medical Recollections of the Army of the Potomac.* New York: D. Appleton, 1866.

Lively, Robert A. *Fiction Fights the Civil War: An Unfinished Chapter in the Literary History of the American People.* Chapel Hill: University of North Carolina Press, 1957.

Lowry, Thomas P. *The Story the Soldiers Wouldn't Tell: Sex in the Civil War.* Mechanicsburg, PA: Stackpole Books, 1994.

Marius, Richard, ed. *The Columbia Book of Civil War Poetry.* New York: Columbia University Press, 1994.

Marten, James, ed. *The Children's Civil War.* Chapel Hill: University of North Carolina Press, 1998.

Martinez, J. Michael, William D. Richardson, and Ron McNinch-Su, eds. *Confederate Symbols in the Contemporary South.* Gainesville: University Press of Florida, 2000.

Massey, Mary Elizabeth. *Ersatz in the Confederacy: Shortages and Substitutions on the Southern Home Front.* Introduction by Barbara L. Bellows. Columbia: University of South Carolina Press, 1993.

McCann, William, ed. *Ambrose Bierce's Civil War.* Washington: Regnery Gateway, 1956.

Miller, Randall M., Harry S. Stout, and Charles Reagan Wilson, eds. *Religion and the American Civil War.* New York: Oxford University Press, 1998.

Mitchell, Reid. *The Vacant Chair: The Northern Soldier Leaves Home.* New York: Oxford University Press, 1993.

Pressly, Thomas J. *Americans Interpret Their Civil War.* New York: Collier, 1962.

Rose, Ann C. *Victorian America and the Civil War.* New York: Cambridge University Press, 1992.

Rutkow, Ira M. *Bleeding Blue and Gray: Civil War Surgery and the Evolution of American Medicine.* New York: Random House, 2005.

Shackel, Paul A. *Memory in Black and White: Race, Commemoration, and the Post-Bellum Landscape.* Walnut Creek, CA: AltaMira Press, 2003.

Shattuck, Gardiner H., Jr. *A Shield and a Hiding Place: The Religious Life of the Civil War Armies.* Macon, GA: Mercer University Press, 1987.

Starr, Louis M. *Bohemian Brigade: Civil War Newsmen in Action.* Introduction by James Boylan. Madison: University of Wisconsin Press, 1987.

Tidwell, William A. *April '65: Confederate Covert Action in the American Civil War.* Kent, OH: Kent State University Press, 1995.

Tidwell, William A., James O. Hall, and David Winfred Gaddy. *Come Retribution: The Confederate Secret Service and the Assassination of Lincoln.* Jackson: University Press of Mississippi, 1988.

U.S. Surgeon General's Office. *The Medical and Surgical History of the Civil War.* 15 vols. Wilmington, NC: Broadfoot, 1990–1992.

Wilson, Edmund. *Patriotic Gore: Studies in the Literature of the American Civil War.* New York: W. W. Norton, 1994.

# Reconstruction

Baggett, James Alex. *The Scalawags: Southern Dissenters in the Civil War and Reconstruction.* Baton Rouge: Louisiana State University Press, 2003.

Cimbala, Paul A., and Randall Miller, eds. *The Freedmen's Bureau and Reconstruction.* New York: Fordham University Press, 1999.

Craven, Avery. *Reconstruction: The Ending of the Civil War.* New York: Holt, Rinehart and Winston, 1969.

Current, Richard N. *Those Terrible Carpetbaggers.* New York: Oxford University Press, 1988.

Du Bois, W. E. B. *Black Reconstruction in America.* With an Introduction by David Levering Lewis. New York: Atheneum, 1992.

Dunning, William A. *Reconstruction, Political and Economic, 1865–1877.* New York: Harper & Brothers, 1907.

Foner, Eric. *Reconstruction: America's Unfinished Revolution, 1863–1877.* New York: Harper & Row, 1988.

Gillette, William C. *Retreat from Reconstruction, 1869–1879.* Baton Rouge: Louisiana State University Press, 1979.

Hyman, Harold M. *A More Perfect Union: The Impact of the Civil War and Reconstruction on the Constitution.* Boston: Houghton Mifflin, 1973.

————. *The Radical Republicans and Reconstruction, 1861–1870.* Indianapolis: Bobbs-Merrill, 1967.

Litwack, Leon. *Been in the Storm So Long: The Aftermath of Slavery.* New York: Knopf, 1979.

Perman, Michael. *Emancipation and Reconstruction, 1862–1879.* Arlington Heights, IL: Harlan Davidson, 2003.

Rable, George C. *But There Was No Peace: The Role of Violence in the Politics of Reconstruction.* Athens: University of Georgia Press, 1984.

Richardson, Heather Cox. *The Death of Reconstruction: Race, Labor, and Politics in the Post–Civil War North, 1865–1901.* Cambridge: Harvard University Press, 2001.

Rose, Willie Lee. *Rehearsal for Reconstruction: The Port Royal Experiment.* Indianapolis: Bobbs-Merrill, 1964.

Stampp, Kenneth M. *The Era of Reconstruction, 1865–1877.* New York: Knopf, 1965.

Sterling, Dorothy, ed. *The Trouble They Seen: The Story of Reconstruction in the Words of African Americans.* New York: Da Capo Press, 1994.

Trefousse, Hans L. *The Radical Republicans: Lincoln's Vanguard for Racial Justice.* Baton Rouge: Louisiana State University Press, 1969.

## Journals, Magazines, and the Internet

*Abraham Lincoln Quarterly*, Springfield, IL

American Civil War home page at the University of Tennessee: http://sunsite.utk.edu/civil-war

*America's Civil War,* Leesburg, VA

"Been Here So Long": Selections from the WPA American Slave Narratives: http://newdeal.feri.org/asn/index.htm

*Civil War History*, Kent, OH

*Civil War News*, Tunbridge, VT

*Civil War Times*, Leesburg, VA

"Civil War Women: Online Archival Collections": http://scriptorium.lib.duke.edu/collections/civil-war-women.html

Cornell University's online edition of *The War of the Rebellion: A Compilation of the Official Records of the Union and Confederate Armies:* http://cdl.library.cornell.edu/moa/browse.monographs/waro.html

*Journal of American History*, Bloomington, IN

*Journal of Negro History*, Washington, DC

*Journal of Southern History*, Baton Rouge, LA

*North & South,* Auberry, CA

Thomas, William G., and Alice E. Carter. *The Civil War on the Web: A Guide to the Very Best Sites.* Wilmington, DE.: Scholarly Resources, 2001.

United States Civil War Center at Louisiana State University: www.cwc.lsu.edu

University of Virginia online archives: http://etext.lib.virginia.edu/subjects/American-Civil-War.html

"The United States Navy in the Civil War: Western Rivers and Gulf of Mexico": www.brownwaternavy.org

# Credits

## Chapter 1

**p. 7:** National Archives and Records Administration (Public)/Historicus, Inc.; **p. 8:** © Bettmann/Corbis; **p. 9:** Smith College Museum of Art; **p. 22:** *(left)* Library of Congress/Historicus, Inc., *(middle)* Library of Congress/Historicus, Inc., *(right)* Library of Congress Prints and Photographs Division [LC-DIG-cwpbh-02605]; **p. 26:** Library of Congress/Historicus, Inc.

## Chapter 2

**p. 31:** Library of Congress, Prints and Photographs Division [POS - TH - 1923 .U53, no. 1 (recto)]; **p. 32:** Library of Congress, Prints and Photographs Division [LC-USZ62-11212]; **p. 36:** Library of Congress Prints & Photographs Division [LC-USZ62-14827]; **p. 38:** © North Wind/North Wind Picture Archives; **p. 44:** Library of Congress, Prints and Photographs Division [LC-USP6-2415-A]; **p. 47:** The Granger Collection; **p. 52:** Library of Congress/Historicus, Inc.

## Chapter 3

**p. 60:** © Royalty-Free/Corbis; **p. 62:** Library of Congress Prints & Photographs Division [LC-DIG-cwpb-05515]; **p. 74:** Rhode Island Historical Society

## Chapter 4

**p. 82:** Cook Collection, Valentine Museum; **p. 90:** Library of Congress Prints & Photographs Division [LC-DIG-cwpb-06437]; **p. 92:** Library of Congress Prints & Photographs Division [LC-DIG-cwpb-01402]; **p. 96:** Library of Congress Prints & Photographs Division [LC-B813-3713]; **p. 98:** Library of Congress Prints & Photographs Division [LC-DIG-cwpb-04762]; **p. 102:** Massachusetts Commandery Military Order of the Loyal Legion of the United States and the U.S. Army Military History Institute; **p. 105:** © Medford Historical Society Collection/Corbis

## Chapter 5

**p. 116:** Library of Congress/Historicus, Inc.; **p. 123:** Library of Congress Prints & Photographs Division [LC-USZC4-1910]; **p. 127:** Source: *Battles and Leaders of the Civil War* (1888) by Robert Underwood Johnson. Public Domain; **p. 132:** Library of Congress Prints & Photographs Division [LC-B813-1406]; **p. 134:** State Historical Society of Missouri

## Chapter 6

**p. 140:** © Royalty-Free/Corbis; **p. 148:** © Corbis; **p. 154:** © Medford Historical Society Collection/Corbis

## Chapter 7

**p. 164:** Library of Congress Prints & Photographs Division [LC-USZC4-7984]; **p. 169:** Library of Congress Prints & Photographs Division [LC-B811-553]; **p. 170:** Library of Congress Prints & Photographs Division [LC-USZC4-7984]; **p. 175:** © Royalty-Free/Corbis

## Chapter 8

p. 187: National Archives and Records Administration [111-B-129]; p. 191: National Archives and Records Administration [165-C-630]; p. 193: Reproduced with permission of Punch Ltd., www.punch.co.uk; p. 198: © Royalty-Free/Corbis

## Chapter 9

p. 213: © Royalty-Free/Corbis; p. 218: © Bettmann/Corbis; p. 219: Library of Congress Prints & Photographs Division [LC-DIG-ppmsca-18444]; p. 222: © Louie Psihoyos/Corbis; p. 223: *(left & right)* © Corbis; p. 227: © Corbis; p. 232: © Royalty-Free/Corbis

## Chapter 10

p. 238: Library of Congress Prints & Photographs Division [LC-USZ62-21907]; p. 240: The Granger Collection; p. 242: National Archives and Records Administration [111-B-2458]; p. 251: Reproduced with permission of Punch Ltd., www.punch.co.uk

## Chapter 11

p. 260: National Archives and Records Administration [111-B-4270]; p. 265: Library of Congress Prints & Photographs Division [LC-DIG-ppmsca-08275]; p. 267: *(top and bottom)* The Granger Collection; p. 273: © Medford Historical Society Collection/Corbis; p. 276: Library of Congress Prints & Photographs Division [LC-DIG-cwpb-02092]

## Chapter 12

p. 282: © Bettmann/Corbis; p. 294: Library of Congress Prints & Photographs Division [LC-DIG-cwpbh-04845]; p. 299: The Granger Collection; p. 300: Library of Congress Prints & Photographs Division [LC-USA7-16837]; p. 304: © Corbis

## Chapter 13

p. 314: Library of Congress Prints & Photographs Division [LC-DIG-cwpbh-04224]; p. 325: Library of Congress Prints & Photographs Division [LC-USZ62-89582]; p. 329: Library of Congress Prints & Photographs Division [LC-DIG-cwpbh-01511]

## Chapter 14

p. 342: Library of Congress Prints & Photographs Division [LC-DIG-cwpb-05008]; p. 347: © Royalty-Free/Corbis; p. 350: Library of Congress Prints & Photographs Division [LC-DIG-cwpb-06085]; p. 356: © Corbis

## Chapter 15

p. 362: © Bettmann/Corbis; p. 367: © Bettmann/Corbis; p. 371: Library of Congress Prints & Photographs Division [LC-USZ62-90939]; p. 376: Library of Congress Prints & Photographs Division [LC-USZC4-7948]; p. 382: © Medford Historical Society Collection/Corbis

## Chapter 16

p. 390: National Archives and Records Administration [111-B-4791]; p. 396: Library of Congress Prints & Photographs Division [LC-DIG-cwpb-07196]; p. 402: Chattanooga-Hamilton County Bicentennial Library; p. 404: © Corbis; p. 406: © Cook Collection, Valentine Museum History Center

## Chapter 17

p. 415: Library of Congress Prints & Photographs Division [LC-USZC4-7983]; p. 417: © Corbis; p. 422: The Granger Collection; p. 423: © Library of Congress Prints & Photographs Division [LC-B818-T01-10045]; p. 430: Library of Congress Prints & Photographs Division [LC-B8184-10573]; p. 435: © Corbis

## Chapter 18

p. 442: The Granger Collection; p. 445: Library of Congress Prints & Photographs Division [LC-DIG-cwpb-01063]; p. 447: National Archives and Records Administration [79-T-2265]; p. 459: Library of Congress Prints & Photographs Division [LC-USZC4-7976]

## Chapter 19

p. 472: Indiana Historical Society, P0388, Neg. C8924; **p. 475:** © Corbis; **p. 476:** Library of Congress Prints & Photographs Division; **p. 478:** Library of Congress Prints & Photographs Division [LC-B8171-7753]

## Chapter 20

p. 489: Library of Congress Prints and Photographs Division [LC-DIG-cwpbh-03501]; **p. 491:** Library of Congress Prints & Photographs Division [LC-DIG-ppmsca-10794]; **p. 493:** © Royalty-Free/Corbis; **p. 496:** © Royalty-Free/Corbis; **p. 501:** Kansas State Historical Society; **p. 502:** State Historical Society of Missouri; **p. 508:** The Granger Collection

## Chapter 21

p. 524: © Corbis; **p. 526:** © Corbis; **p. 527:** Library of Congress Prints & Photographs Division [LC-DIG-cwpb-01182]; **p. 538:** Minnesota Historical Society Loc# E425.11 r40 Neg# 24013

## Chapter 22

p. 547: © Corbis; **p. 550:** Library of Congress Prints & Photographs Division [LOC-DIG-cwpb-00995]; **p. 552:** © Corbis; **p. 556:** © Royalty-Free/Corbis; **p. 558:** © Corbis; **p. 564:** Library of Congress Prints & Photographs Division [LC-DIG-cwpb-02237]

## Chapter 23

p. 578: Library of Congress Prints & Photographs Division [LC-DIG-cwpbh-03074]; **p. 580:** © Corbis; **p. 587:** © Royalty-Free/Corbis; **p. 590:** Library of Congress Prints & Photographs Division [LC-DIG-cwpb-03391]

## Chapter 24

p. 600: © Royalty-Free/Corbis; **p. 613:** Library of Congress Prints & Photographs Division [LC-DIG-cwpb-02553]; **p. 617:** Library of Congress/Historicus, Inc.; **p. 621:** Library of Congress Prints & Photographs Division [LC-DIG-cwpb-04229]; **p. 622:** © Royalty-Free/Corbis

## Chapter 25

p. 627: © Corbis; **p. 630:** Library of Congress/Historicus, Inc.; **p. 635:** Library of Congress Prints & Photographs Division [LC-DIG-nclc-00520]; **p. 646:** Library of Congress Prints & Photographs Division [LC-DIG-cwpbh-03857]; **p. 648:** Rutherford B. Hayes Presidential Center

## Chapter 26

p. 656: RG25: Records of Special Commissions. Courtesy of Pennsylvania Historical and Museum Commission. Pennsylvania State Archives; **p. 658:** © Bettmann/Corbis; **p. 659:** © The Museum of the Confederacy, Richmond, Virginia; **p. 662:** Library of Congress Prints & Photographs Division [LC-USZC4-2427]; **p. 664:** Library of Congress Prints & Photographs Division [LC-DIG-cwpb-07033]; **p. 675:** © Bettmann/Corbis

# Index

*Page numbers in italics refer to illustrations*